OBJECTIVITY, SCIENCE AND SOCIETY

OBJECTIVITY, SCIENCE AND SOCIETY

INTERPRETING NATURE AND SOCIETY IN THE AGE OF THE CRISIS OF SCIENCE

Paul A. Komesaroff

ROUTLEDGE & KEGAN PAUL

LONDON AND NEW YORK

First published in 1986
by Routledge & Kegan Paul plc
11 New Fetter Lane, London EC4P 4EE

Published in the USA by Routledge & Kegan Paul Inc.
in association with Methuen Inc.
29 West 35th Street, New York, NY 10001

Set in 10 on 11pt Monophoto Times
and printed in Great Britain
by Butler & Tanner Ltd, Frome and London

Library of Congress Cataloging in Publication Data

Komesaroff, Paul A.
    Objectivity, science, and society.
    Bibliography: p.
    Includes index.
    1. Science——Philosophy.   2. Science—— Social aspects.
3. Objectivity.   I. Title.
Q175.K65 1986   306'.45   85-25739

British Library CIP Data also available

ISBN 0-7102-0381 0

Contents

Part IV
The diversity within modern science

Part V
Introduction to the sociology of objectivity

Part VI
Conclusions

Preface

This is an essay in the philosophy and sociology of natural science. It begins with the assumption that science today faces many problems regarding its social meaning, its technical applications and its internal content. The contemporary theories of science, furthermore, seem not altogether adequate to meet the challenges confronting them. This does not mean that there are insufficient resources available within modern thought to identify or to interpret the great issues at stake. On the contrary, deep insights have been won by both modern philosophy and modern social theory; the problem is rather that the two great bodies of thought, represented by natural science and contemporary philosophy, have so far failed to make proper contact. Both science and philosophy have been assumed to follow their own characteristic mode of discourse, according to their own special, internal imperatives. Hence the profound discoveries of each have been withheld from the other – to the detriment of both. One of the tasks facing modern science is to redress this circumstance; to apply the innovations won by the human sciences to outstanding dilemmas both within and regarding the sciences of nature, and conversely, to realize within contemporary philosophy and social theory the rich treasures of insight of modern science.

Two main areas of interest will occupy our attention in this essay. On the one hand we will be concerned with the content of science, with its assertions and its implications. On the other, we shall be considering the dependence of this content on social variables – that is, on contingencies specific to a given social and historical configuration. In order to reveal the deep connection between these two groups of problems we shall adopt as a central issue for our investigation the question of objectivism and we shall place particular emphasis on the philosophical theory referred to as phenomenology. Objectivism is, in brief, the attitude which correlates theoretical propositions with matter of fact; that is, it takes the relations between empirical variables expressed in theoretical propositions to be self-subsistent. Hence it denies in principle any contribution to the production of truth from either a conscious subject or the theoretical apparatus itself. Objectivism has a long and varied history; it can be traced, in one form or another, for example, in philosophical doctrines as diverse as Scholastic realism, utilitarianism and modern positivism. However it is not the history of the concept that interests us but rather the role that it plays in the theory of nature. It is probably not an exaggeration to say that objectivism has been the dominant philosophical attitude in the natural sciences since the time of Isaac Newton; but whether this is true or not, in the present period it is certainly the perspective most widely accepted. This remains the case despite the fact that in social theory and philosophy much effort has been expended in developing rigorous and cogent refutations of the objectivist position. It is our contention that, accordingly, the problem of objectivism is a possible site at which a fruitful intersection between the major components of modern thought may be apprehended. In fact we shall attempt to show that such an application of social theory to science yields profound consequences.

Phenomenology is the philosophy developed by Edmund Husserl and his followers and today widely applied in social theory and elsewhere. In this essay phenomenology will be taken as a major theoretical instrument for introducing or exposing new problems. The features of the phenomenological perspective will of course be developed in some detail later. However it is necessary to state plainly at the very outset the spirit in which it is being employed. We are making use of phenomenology largely as a matter of convenience, since it contains many features appropriate for our purposes. It is, for instance, an extremely rigorous, internally consistent body of thought; it has been applied at some length to reflections on science; it has been utilized extensively and effectively within social theory; and it embraces a powerful critique of what it regards as the objectivist illusion. Extensive use will be made of both phenomenological methods and the results obtained by phenomenological philosophers – especially Husserl himself, whose reflections on science will be examined at length. This does not mean however, that the essay itself is committed to phenomenology. On the contrary, as will become apparent, we maintain that the phenomenological programme contains severe deficiencies. The utility of its insights is not for our purposes thereby compromised; hence it is possible to say that we commit ourselves to no more than the fecundity of its deliberations.

One final point on terminology will be mentioned here. In this essay the word 'science' will be used to refer to the natural sciences – that is, to the theory of nature – in general. Hence the term will apply to the study of natural phenomena in all societies, and so will contain no connotations regarding ontology, epistemology or the use, for example, of mathematics or particular varieties of logic. On the other hand the expression will thereby deliberately exclude the so-called 'social' or 'human' sciences; if it is intended that these be denoted then they will be referred to as such explicitly.

Acknowledgments

I gratefully acknowledge the help and advice given by Dr Johann P. Arnason in the preparation of this essay.

The publisher and I would like to thank the following:

Faber and Faber for permission to quote from Goethe's *Faust*, translated by Louis MacNeice, 1948;

Martinus Nijhoff, Publishers, for permission to quote from Edmund Husserl, *Formal and Transcendental Logic*, translated by Doron Cairns, 1969;

Martinus Nijhoff, Publishers, and Northwestern University Press for permission to quote from Edmund Husserl, *The Crisis of European Sciences and Transcendental Phenomenology*, translated by D. Carr, 1970.

I
The sociology of science: Issues and hypotheses, orientations and disorientations

1

Antecedents: Science and society; objectivism; some philosophical issues

To say that the sciences of nature have profoundly influenced modern society is a triviality. To say that many of these effects have been harmful ones is a commonplace. Yet the forms of mediation between society and science remain obscure.

Certainly, we are very familiar with the all-pervasiveness of the cultural impact of science. The 'disenchantment of the world', for example – a process closely linked to the rise of scientific modes of thought and once recognized as a poignant and controversial symbol of the consequences of modernity – is today widely accepted, with resignation.[1] The formerly predominant heavenly phenomena have been extirpated; in their place remain merely the mundane and the spiritless. No more is it possible to aspire to a life characterized by a simple, organic harmony with nature: instead we find ourselves thrust inexorably into the midst of a profane totality relentlessly denuded of all meaning and all spiritual purpose. The change is accepted with resignation. However consciousness of what was lost has been retained. We are still moved by the lament of the ageing Faust, reflecting on his years of laborious scholarship:

> Infinite Nature, where can I tap thy veins?
> Where are thy breasts, those well-springs of all life
> On which hang heaven and earth,
> Towards which my dry breast strains?
> They well up, they give drink but I feel drought and dearth.[2]

Science, which promised so much, appears to many to have conspired against us – and then, in the spoils of victory, to have moved also to cut off the possibilities for escape.[3] Certainly, the reverence for the given that in one respect had been so fraught with hope, and indeed so fecund, in another seems to have undermined the very impulses that had given rise to it. The tragic paradox is that the price of the new insights was the enervation of that realm within which classically reflection had taken place on the possibilities for a world that would transcend the given – a world in which the inequities and painful disharmonies of everyday life would be overcome. Today, we must live with the consequences of this ambivalent circumstance and endure the jejune, intractable society that remains, in which the social forms are branded with the all-pervasive stigmata of manipulation and domination and where much of what passes as protest and opposition does little more than affirm and beautify the state of unfreedom.[4]

We recognize readily the process of decay even within science itself. Intellectual values once proclaimed to embody what was noble and precious have been defiled by the imperatives of 'dirty science', of 'reckless' science, of 'bureaucratic' science, of 'entrepreneurial' science and so on.[5] Where technical progress had previously offered the promise of transcending the limitations imposed on society by our impotence before the natural world, today when we think of these things we try to suppress scepticism and scorn. Where once the sciences were a source of optimism and hope, today, when their results are displayed for all to see, they are capable of evoking only disillusion and despair.

This is not the first time, of course, it has been claimed that science is in crisis. Indeed, at almost every point in its history – and certainly, with increasing frequency since the beginning of this century – there have been people who have argued that a crisis of science exists.[6] But however that may be, today it is certainly easier than ever to justify such an assertion. The modern inventory of problems can all too readily be drawn up: the design and fabrication of ever more sophisticated devices for war and mass destruction; pollution and the ruination of the natural environment; the degradation and disruption of work; the trivialization of culture associated with the conceptual aridness of the intellectual forms themselves – these are all problems directly linked with science and from which science cannot evade culpability.

What is original about the contemporary crisis of science is just this comprehensive character. Today, the malaise affects all the dimensions of science. There is a crisis in the *meaning of science*: we can no longer rely upon the social matrix within which its validations had formerly been established. There is a crisis in the *practice of science*, since questions are now raised about the scien-

4

tific community, its ethos and motivations and the directions of the current public science policies. And there is a crisis *within science itself*: thrown into question are the specific truth claims of science and even the more extensive criteria of validity formerly assumed to be inviolable. This *all-pervasiveness* of the crisis of science is what is new: what is *not* new is the implicit assumption behind the notion of crisis itself – the assumption that science is subject to change, that things had once been different. This is an important point that is often overlooked. The commonplace conviction that science is subject to crisis necessarily entails at once the hypothesis that, in all three dimensions, science is invested with a precarious temporality – precarious, because within it the structures of meaning and the communicative contexts of knowledge can never be certain or reliably and exhaustively fixed.

A science is a system of truths and meanings about the world, transmitted through the mediation of a formal theoretical structure. What is at issue today is the reliability of these truths and the adequacy of these meanings, judged against the experiences and requirements of social life. This, precisely, defines the task facing the modern theory of science. If such a theory is to contribute to the discovery of solutions to the weighty problems of the times then it must provide us with an instrument for identifying both the boundaries of science and the relationship between science's theoretical forms and the forms of social life. It must be able to help us to identify the meaning not only of science but also of nature itself. It must supply us with the means to assess the truth of science's specific claims – at least in respect of those that are philosophically based. It must enable us to unfold the process within which the interchange between science and society occurs. And it must also allow us to decide whether within this interchange limitations are imposed on either or both of the components. The theory of science is not secondary to science; it must not be parasitic upon it. Instead, it must open up possibilities, provide new approaches and perspectives with which science can work. It must relentlessly criticize the given. It must provide a source of fresh directions, of intellectual ferment.

* * * * * *

It would be an understatement to say that in the current context the extant theory of science fails to fulfil these tasks. One of the most important symptoms of the present crisis of science is the gulf that has opened up between philosophy and the practice of science.

5

Historically, of course, the situation was quite different. Until at least the inception of its modern phase the theory of nature was plainly philosophical in character and committed itself openly in respect of problems that asserted themselves at the level of practical life. It is only relatively recently that the practitioners of science deliberately disclaimed competence regarding these broader issues. The result has certainly been an enhancement of the precision with which science deals with its presently existing object domain – but also, simultaneously, there has followed an abrogation of the interchange – formerly taken for granted – between reflection on the phenomena of nature and social and philosophical thought. Subsequent to the breach science and social theory have developed substantially in isolation from each other. The profound insights of the theory of nature are now largely withheld from social life – except insofar as they are able to command technical mediations in the latter; while conversely, developments in the other areas of modern thought have failed to penetrate science, which, accordingly, now operates within a philosophical ambient that is elsewhere largely obsolete.

As this essay progresses, we shall attempt to define in detail this theoretical structure to which science adheres. We shall characterize it under the rubric of 'objectivism' and provide arguments which in fact contradict its main claims. As will become clear, it is our contention that a significant proportion of the pathology of modern science can be accounted for by the continued ascendency of the objectivist problematic. This will be discussed at length below; at the present stage we would like to emphasize more particularly that in these circumstances a problem of major proportions is just how we should go about reconstructing a social theory of science – that is, how, in the current context, a theory such as the one we are seeking could be possible at all. One of the principal tasks of the modern reflection on science will be to re-establish the link between knowledge of nature and knowledge of society. For this it will be necessary to follow to their roots both science and social theory, with a view to discovering a common source. This will require detailed and meticulous work; furthermore, it will necessitate an investigation that encompasses simultaneously sociology, philosophy and science. This is itself a substantial point. The main interest of this essay is scientific knowledge: thus its concern must be as much with facts as with the philosophical and sociological issues of meaning. Accordingly, the path to a social theory of science will not be a direct one; on the contrary, this endeavour will have to pass through a detour of considerable theoretical complexity.[7]

At this point it is appropriate to make some remarks regarding the methodological issues that are raised in the course of this enterprise; however these remarks will be kept brief since we prefer to postpone a fuller discussion for a later stage. There is a problem contained inherently in the investigation we are proposing, due to the fact that one of the principal issues to which this investigation must direct itself concerns the epistemological consequences of the adoption of a given theoretical standpoint. Now in such circumstances it is impossible to approach the study on the basis of a rigorously delimited methodological system which has been derived extrinsically, anterior to the analysis to which it is to be applied; for clearly to do so would be to compromise the investigation before it had even begun. Indeed, some method of proceeding must be found which would enable us to examine a variety of perspectives without committing ourselves to any particular one, but in such a way that we would be capable of applying to them all a consistent theory of truth.

To satisfy these requirements there is not, of course, any all-encompassing perspective available to us under which could be subsumed, ontologically or epistemologically, all other conceivable viewpoints; that is to say, it would be pointless to set out in search of a theoretical standpoint which, in the logical sense, would occupy first place. On the other hand however – it is worth stating immediately – there is not within the proposal we are advancing any internal contradiction which would at the outset exclude such an investigation as a matter of principle. We mention this point because the question of such a difficulty is raised by the sheer complexity of the proposed project, which would, for example, have not only to account in detail for itself but also to provide the means for its own interpretation. We shall discuss this issue at greater length later; here we merely make the simple observation that the everyday fact that it is possible to talk meaningfully about contending perspectives and, in addition, about the epistemological variation associated with them, shows that a study like the present one is, at the least, feasible. Indeed, simply from our use of language we are familiar with a theoretical medium which satisfies the conditions mentioned; that is, which is at once universally applicable and self-reflective. As we said, these matters will be discussed at length later; we refer to them here specifically to affirm that our proposed investigation is not compromised in advance either by the expanse of the project or by a priori logical imperatives.

The study we are proposing then, is neither impossibly broad nor self-contradictory. However, if it intends to avoid committing

7

itself to any particular philosophical standpoint or methodological schema, how will its unity be guaranteed? Surely, without the existence of a definite theoretical framework in relation to which its specific propositions can be located the entire enterprise will be under constant threat of disintegration. We emphasize that this is a dilemma which faces the present study (and ones like it) only because for us the major issues include the variety of the perspectives available to science and their individual coherence; it is not a difficulty that emerges invariably in relation to other issues, or even in the study of science in general. This is a special case, that is to say, and special means must be invoked to deal with it.

It is also appropriate to point out here that the problem at stake is not that which has so long perplexed thinkers in the Western tradition of providing a theory of truth free from presuppositions. This problem, of course, has been an immensely fecund one in the history of philosophy and many of its fruits are certainly relevant for our study. In fact, an important part of this essay will comprise a detailed examination of some aspects of the theory of science proposed by Edmund Husserl, a thinker whose entire work was motivated by the search for a philosophy that could provide reliable, certain knowledge, free of presuppositions. However here the issue is not presuppositionlessness. For even a presuppositionless philosophy, if such an entity were in fact to exist, would have to commit itself to certain protocols of procedure and method which in the present context would themselves be subject to scrutiny. Thus the mere use of mathematics in science, not to mention its associated forms of reasoning, raises the question of whether theoretical prejudices are thereby imported into the scientific project; this is a question, incidentally, which we shall consider at length later.[8] Or to take another example, more extensively studied: of all thinkers, Hegel is perhaps the one who sought most relentlessly after a philosophy free of presuppositions; indeed, his greatest works, the *Phenomenology of Mind* and the *Logic*, are directed explicitly to this quest. However, as is apparent in retrospect, his very commitment to certain truth and to an architectonic of knowledge imposed substantial obligations on the resulting theoretical project, thereby significantly distorting its results. Hegel's 'system' of knowledge is firmly embedded in the Western tradition of thought which views concepts and ideas just as it regards things – as objects subject to manipulation and capable of being applied where needed to achieve predetermined results. The 'System of Science' is a profoundly technological enterprise. It proposes a world of ideas that is rational and reliable, in which concepts are drawn into the system like instruments into an instrumental complex. 'Subject and object tend to merge as they do in a thoroughgoing technological system. Hegel's system of impersonal truth comes about so long as the individual does nothing, but merely identifies himself with the process in its entirety.'[9] In a word, Hegel's being is instrumental being; the very intention to develop a comprehensive, presuppositionless system of thought betrays the profound biases of the milieu within which it was formulated.[10]

This essay then, does not aim to establish a theory free of presuppositions. It aims merely to examine a variety of perspectives without adopting the viewpoint of any particular one. In this endeavour it is clearly impossible to begin with a set of precepts regarding either the nature of science or the methodological strategy that should be employed to study it. Accordingly, in what follows, the unity of the discussion will be derived not in this way but rather by the common focus of our arguments on a number of fundamental, abiding questions concerning science. In other words, we shall rely for the unity of this study on its orientation with respect to an array of problems, issues and themes which we shall take as our guide. In consequence, our arguments will cohere primarily in relation not to sense but to reference[11] – a circumstance, of course, in many ways familiar from the great proliferation of approaches in science itself.

Here we have, however, another problem. The questions and issues which we shall be taking as our guide must be identified. But as in the previous case the process of identifying them cannot be subject to a preassigned theoretical or methodological perspective. Thus once again an alternative strategy must be adopted: our array of problems will have to be assembled from a preliminary study of the existing theories in the sociology and philosophy of science. In this preliminary investigation it will be necessary to gather together problems and themes, ideas and hypotheses, that are relevant to the underlying concerns with which we have embarked on this project. We shall aim to identify broad constellations of issues, each of which bears in some way on the relationship between society and science or on the meaning of scientific knowledge. By these means, mindful of the limitations of the proposed procedure, we shall attempt to compose a research programme to which our subsequent deliberations can be directed; that is, we shall attempt to delineate a series of intersecting tasks which may help elucidate the matters in which we are interested.[12]

Within this research programme, as we have said, we shall have to be able to scrutinize the disparate perspectives that are applied in science. In particular, we must be able to utilize each of these to interrogate the others, thus exposing the respective strengths and weaknesses of all of them. Furthermore, we must be in a position to identify common ideas between perspectives, or at least problems that are theorized similarly therein. Finally, given any particular issue it must be possible for us to choose that standpoint within which this issue might most effectively be understood. The research programme, then, can only be derived at the end of a lengthy process of analysis and investigation; once formulated, however, it will be subject to scrutiny in relation to several exacting criteria.

No more will be said at this stage regarding methodological issues. It will be better to delay further discussion until later in the essay. Nonetheless, it is important to realize that these early problems are not merely incidental. Much of our study will be taken up with a consideration of detailed questions of meaning and a pursuit of underlying presuppositions and assumptions; thus it is especially important that sufficient care is taken in the original constitution of the inquiry. In addition, what distinguishes the present project from other studies of science is precisely its specific subject matter. Accordingly, one of our main objectives is to provide a satisfactory account of the object domain to which, we contend, attention should be applied. The achievement of this objective would be a substantial result in itself, for it may conceivably make possible further developments. Here once again we can draw on an analogy from science itself. In the formation of a new theory it is often the case that the most important, yet most difficult, work is taken up with the original identification of a field of problems for investigation – that is, with the first recognition of an object domain;[13] subsequently, the results may follow with somewhat diminished difficulty. We are not, of course, claiming to be founding a new theory here; nevertheless an identical principle holds.

Stated briefly then, the perspective of this essay is as follows. Given the fundamental fact that today society and science are rigorously interdependent, a critical imperative has developed to determine the structure of the relationship between them. In addition, the contemporary crisis of science raises the questions of the meaning and validity of scientific theories; hence these issues must be considered in detail also. The study that would emerge in this way would certainly serve strictly intellectual interests; however, more importantly, it would also contribute to and reflect upon the task of social reconstruction. For if, for example, as is often claimed, science – by various mediations – exerts a particular efficacy at the level of politics then the question of the elimination of domination cannot be asked in the absence of an interrogation of the scientific structures. Against this background a number of specific problems will be addressed. The social character of science will be at issue – in all its senses, but especially in relation to the role of social forces in shaping scientific systems. Further, the actual meaning-content of science will be examined and the question – obvious, though perplexing – of its standing with respect to philosophical argument will be considered. Finally, the relationship between this meaning-content, appropriately characterized, and the formal structures will be scrutinized.

These and other questions will be addressed in the course of this essay. At its conclusion, this study, through some elementary adumbrations and methodological orientations, will, we hope, have contributed in a small way to two important tasks: the clarification of the conditions for a social theory of science and the provision of some indications for a formulation of science in accordance with a rigorously justifiable philosophical perspective.

Dialectic of Enlightenment: objectivism and the tragedy of science

One of the most potent cultural critiques of science emerged in the writings of the early Frankfurt School. Here, directly or indirectly, were raised many of the fundamental issues with which a social theory of science must be concerned. Accordingly, these writings are of the greatest interest for us, seeking as we are to delineate problems and hypotheses on the basis of which a rigorous theory of scientific knowledge could be constructed.

The arguments we are about to discuss were formulated from the rather idiosyncratic perspective to which the name 'critical theory' was given. Now it must be stated at once that no attempt will be made here to provide a detailed account of the great expanse covered by the complex and subtle perspective of critical theory. For we are interested only in the results of its analyses which bear specifically on science and scientific knowledge. What is more, these can be appropriated without difficulty in the absence of an extended discussion of the entire corpus. It will be enough for our purposes simply to remark that in its original sense 'critical theory' was the name given by Max Horkheimer in the 1920s and 1930s to his particular formulation of Marxism; it was later taken up, occasionally with substantial modifications, by a number of important philosophers and social critics, amongst whom may be included Theodor Adorno, Herbert Marcuse, Friedrich Pollock, Leo Lowenthal

11

and, more recently, Jürgen Habermas.[14] All these thinkers accepted that in some sense knowledge must be regarded as historically conditioned; however they insisted that an independent moment of criticism was nevertheless a possibility. Their main intellectual antecedents were to be found in the great works of the German philosophical tradition – in this regard, of greatest importance being those of Kant, Hegel and Marx. The objective of the movement was to formulate a number of critiques of contemporary forms of social practice in such a way as to expose their inner logic and their – frequently destructive – human implications. There was to be no concerted attempt to describe an alternative; the most that could be said was that, from a philosophical point of view, such an alternative would have to be based on foundations that were both materialistic and non-objectivist.

A substantial part of the efforts of the critical theorists was devoted towards an examination of the problem of science. Here, the main thrust of their critique was an attempt to trace the consequences for society of the rapid expansion of the mathematical sciences. In the course of this endeavour they achieved a number of incisive and cogent insights into both the philosophical content of science and its social efficacy. To be sure, no member of the Frankfurt School ever undertook a detailed investigation of the structure of science – a fact which, undeniably, limited this aspect of their theory. Nevertheless many of their conclusions remain both suggestive and compelling, and this is enough to justify a continuing interest in their work.[15]

In what follows, one particular pivotal work of critical theory will be discussed – *Dialectic of Enlightenment*, by Horkheimer and Adorno. This book, first published in 1947, is a famous attack on science and its pernicious influences in which the cultural consequences of the contemporary view of nature receive a poignant, sometimes dazzling, exposition. It is now well-recognized that it contains some severe shortcomings; nevertheless we shall argue that it includes also an aspect that has been inadequately appreciated: it embraces the germ from which a comprehensive and rigorous social theory of science could be developed. It is from this perspective specifically, and subject to the general circumscription enunciated above, that we shall formulate some of the arguments and conclusions proposed by the two authors.

* * * * * *

What is in question for Horkheimer and Adorno is nothing less than Enlightenment itself – the process of the extension of reason that was explicitly recognized and promoted in eighteenth century Europe but which on the one hand can be traced back to its roots in important tendencies in the Renaissance, and on the other continues substantially to characterize contemporary Western thought. In its original conceptions the goals of Enlightenment unequivocally contained progressive elements. For all its versions (of which there were many) had, quite explicitly embraced the objective of 'liberating men from fear and establishing their sovereignty'. In the result however these noble objectives had been vitiated. 'The fully enlightened world radiates disaster triumphant'.[16] The growth of science and the development of technology, the abolition of superstition and the extirpation of myth, the irrefragable commitment to reason and logic – all these tendencies had promised to deliver man from his self-imposed immaturity. But in the process of its realization Enlightenment had turned upon itself. What had been intended as liberating forces emerged in fact as new, more potent instruments of slavery; the drive to oppose all domination issued instead in a domination of an all-pervasive, more virulent kind.

In this drama, according to Horkheimer and Adorno, one of the chief culprits is the natural sciences. Of course, it could not be claimed that science alone was responsible for the tragedy of Enlightenment. For after all, comparable results could be recognized in the barbarism of Nazi Germany, which was distinguished substantially by its liquidation of the inroads of scientific thought into social organization (an accomplishment which, to be sure, coexisted paradoxically with the full realization of that thought).[17] The problem is to be found not merely in the factual results of science but in its underlying conceptual forms and, in particular, in its philosophical presuppositions. Accordingly, the critical study of social phenomena must seek out these forms and these presuppositions, and it must explicate their potency within the existing social configuration. This having been said, however, it must be admitted that for *Dialectic of Enlightenment* science occupied a special place, since it revealed a fundamental ontological fact about the world. Unlike for Marx, for whom the roots of the contemporary forms of domination were to be traced back to the intersubjective forms and, especially, to the social relations of production, for Horkheimer and Adorno these roots were to be found at a still more fundamental level: in the invariant relationship in which all societies stand to nature; what is more, it was argued, this relationship was perfected, propagated and adequately represented by mathematical science. In this sense, science was indeed deserving of a major share of the blame.

To return specifically to the account given by Horkheimer and Adorno, science has produced a greatly enhanced technical power over nature. However '(d)omination of nature involves domination of man. Each subject not only has to take part in the subjugation of external nature, human and non-human, but in order to do so must subjugate nature in himself. Domination becomes "internalized" for domination's sake.'[18] The modes of understanding nature and of modifying it technically are continuous with the forms of political control. This continuity, furthermore, derives not principally from the technological applications, as is usually supposed, but conceptually, from the philosophical core of Enlightenment. For the substitution of 'objective' knowledge for superstition and myth is achieved by the progressive formalization of thought, the replacement of concepts by formulae. But formulae are in principle exempt from the dialectical mediations of subject and object. Hence '(t)he reduction of thought to mathematical apparatus conceals the sanction of the world as its own yardstick. What appears to be the triumph of subjective rationality, the subjection of all reality to logical formation, is paid for by the obedient subjection of reason to what is directly given. What is abandoned is the whole claim and approach of knowledge: to comprehend the given as such. . . .'[19]

Clearly, in these arguments there is adopted a specific view of science and of the conceptual forms with which it is associated. More precisely, the theory of nature is assumed to be inherently and inexorably 'objectivist' – that is, subjective and intersubjective contributions to conceptual constitution are excluded from it, along with any cultural variability to which the meaning or truth of the theoretical forms might be supposed to be subject. Indeed, according to Horkheimer and Adorno, it is only on the basis of such a presupposition that science could aspire to the ideal of a *mathesis universalis* – a deductive theory encompassing the whole of reality, to which all phenomena appear as apprehensible exclusively through calculation and logic.[20] For the Frankfurt School precisely herein lay the most conspicuous and abiding characteristics of contemporary science. In science was realized the *telos* to which Enlightenment had always tended: it was total, exact, deductive and objectivist. As mentioned above the actual structure of the special sciences receives no detailed attention in *Dialectic of Enlightenment*; thus, beyond formulations of the kind presented, no further attempt is made to justify this view. Nevertheless, at least in the case of classical mechanics, that in objectivism lies its philosophical content cannot be disputed. And indeed, nor has it been – either amongst the early protagonists of science or amongst its contemporary interpreters.

Natural science embodies a generalization to all conceptual thought of the ideals of Enlightenment. *Dialectic of Enlightenment* takes as its central theme an examination of the consequences of this generalization, insofar as they affect the social forms. Its conclusion is that the success of the theory of nature has conveyed major social liabilities. In fact, it finds that no aspect of social life is now left unaffected by the totalizing power of instrumental reason unleashed by the sciences. Today, 'whatever does not conform to the rule of computation and utility is suspect';[21] and whatever cannot be reduced to numbers – and ultimately to the one – becomes illusion.[22] In the mathematical symbol existence is appropriated and perpetuated by knowledge as a schema.[23] Thus denied a place in the flux of social life phenomena are subject to processes that are only formal. In the absorption of factuality into mathematical formalism history gives way to mere repetition: the new appears as 'the predetermined, which is accordingly the old'.[24]

As for nature itself: in the era of formalized reason it is stripped of all intrinsic value or meaning.[25] Of course this is no longer surprising, given the foregoing and the familiar observation that at its crucial turning points Western civilization made the subjugation of nature – rather than its understanding or spiritual meaning – the absolute purpose of both external and internal life.[26] What might be surprising is just the completeness with which the transition from domination of nature to domination of man was made. In the conceptual realm domination is embodied in the universality of ideas as developed by discursive logic,[27] and hierarchy and coercion in the deductive form.[28] Translated into the social realm these ideas help constitute the hierarchy, coercion and domination that characterize modern social life. Thus the evolution of the machine culminates in the machinery of domination. Society and the advance of technical reason – which had always been interwoven – 'converge in the total schematization of men'.[29] The individual is reduced to 'the nodal point of the conventional responses and modes of operation expected of him',[30] while intersubjectivity loses its expansive, communicative function and, under the force of the new, totalizing logic, regresses into monologue.[31] This process is intensified further in capitalist society, where the formalization of reason comes together with mechanisation and production for profit. Now, '(d)omination survives as an end in itself, in the form of economic power'.[32] Every activity of the worker is regulated: when he eats, drinks, sleeps – even his enjoyment, his love and his hatred.[33] 'The more complicated and precise the social, economic and scientific apparatus with whose service the production system has long harmonized the body, the more impoverished the experiences it can offer.'[34] Everything and everybody is organized, classified and labelled. 'The pigeon-hole into which a man is shoved circumscribes his fate.'[35]

Thus the enlightened world is a truly disenchanted one which has, furthermore, succumbed tragically to the process of rationalization of which Weber had spoken with such foreboding.[36] For Horkheimer and Adorno, it is true, these tendencies were not, as they were for Weber, the product of an irreversible, endogenous social logic;[37] rather they were the unintended consequences of a project of reason which nevertheless maintains some true liberating potential. What is more important than this, however, at least for our purposes, is just the relationship that *Dialectic of Enlightenment* revealed between society and science. By following the achievements of science to their outcomes in society and culture – that is, by hunting the scent of science through the social forms – it discerned a deep concinnity between the two. At its core mathematical science embraces substantial philosophical contents, through the mediation of which it acquires an efficacy in social life. It is a paradox of modern times that the meaning with which objectivist science is thereby associated, and of which modern society also partakes, is no more than the renunciation of all claim to meaning.[38]

One more step, already foreshadowed in this paradox, completes the tragedy of Enlightenment. Under the advancing sway of the latter not only the political form but also thought and language themselves succumb. That this might be so is certainly not difficult to see, for the distance is short between Bacon's identification of knowledge with power and Hobbes's injunction to replace the 'false coins' of language with the more precise, neutral counters of science. In the world of the latter, objective reality is reproduced by words, reduced to signs from which all aesthetic nuances of connotation and allusion have been removed. The language, therefore, within which knowledge of nature is formulated is a debased one; it is a system of empty signs, susceptible to manipulation, in which any aspiration to transcend the given has been disclaimed.[39] The generalization of this language reproduces the process we have observed above: once again, the forms of the theory of nature are inscribed within the social ones with malign consequences. Mathematical procedure becomes the 'ritual of thinking'; hence thinking

16

itself becomes an 'automatic, self-activating process – an imperson-
ation of the machine that it produces itself so that the machine can
replace it'.[40] Science's abhorrence of specific representation trans-
lates in language as the exchange of representation for the fungible:
'universal interchangeability'.[41] Everything, even the human individual, 'is converted into the repeatable, replaceable process, into
a mere example of the conceptual models of the system ... The
conceptual apparatus determines the senses, even before perception
occurs; a priori the citizen sees the world as the matter from which
he himself manufactures it.'[42] It is not just that the triumph of
Enlightenment presaged the ultimate desuetude of ideas. The linguistic medium within which ideas had been formulated was itself
corrupted. 'There is no longer any available form of linguistic
expression which has not tended toward accommodation to dominant currents of thought.'[43]

Let us recapitulate the argument so far. According to *Dialectic
of Enlightenment*, science is by no means just a formal system of
signs conveniently organized for the arrangement of natural phenomena. On the contrary, it must be regarded as a particular philosophical disposition which finds an effective realization in the formal apparatus; furthermore it is this formal system that is
dependent on the philosophical content for its semantic criteria. In
addition, the entire theory is of significance not only for the study
of nature. Indeed a close inspection of the contemporary social
phenomena reveals the all-pervasiveness of its conceptual ambient.
The traces of science can be recognized throughout social life: in
work, in art, in culture, in language and so on. However, for this
very reason the reflection on science, which would make possible
the identification and scrutiny of the philosophical positions assumed by science, is compromised. The potential critical dimension
within which the meaning of the theory is to be constructed is
infiltrated by the conceptual forms of the latter and thus, in advance, rendered harmonious with it. An independent such dimension ceases to exist. The theory of nature is caught in a circle;[44]
science circumscribes its own meaning.

* * * * * *

The self-affirming character of science revealed in this analysis was
to become a major theme for critical theory in general. Here already, however, it is traced back to the objectivism underlying the
philosophical content of the natural sciences. Indeed, *Dialectic of
Enlightenment* even provides a general refutation of objectivism, at
least in respect of the kinds of phenomena with which it is con-

17

cerned. Objectivism, it will be recalled, resides in the arbitrary diremption of thought from its products. Under its rubric thought objectifies itself to become an automatic, self-activating process[45] – thus from the beginning losing its power of self-reflection.[46] In the specific case of science, as we have seen, when the theory can no longer be conscious of itself it remains as no more than a tool.[47] In fact this result holds in general. The intellectual procedures acquire the appearance of objective necessity,[48] independent of all subjectivity and culture; thought itself becomes like a thing, an instrument to be applied where needed.[49] One consequence of this is evident at once. Under such circumstances the world as it is can be the only criterion by which the world may be judged.[50] Thus the critical moment of thought disappears; reason is subjected only to what is directly given by reason itself.[51] But this means that truth also must undergo a similar reduction; in this case it remains only as the truth of a gigantic analytic judgement. Thought becomes mere tautology.[52]

A second negative consequence depends upon the conception of truth adopted by critical theory itself. For the latter, truth is indissociable from the intersubjective forms, although it is not identical with them.[53] For objectivism, however, the world can be known only as the outcome of a series of mechanical operations;[54] thus theory can in this case do no more than merely apprehend, classify, calculate and so on.[55] Other tasks of cognition are now inaccessible. The relation of general to particular[56] for example, is suppressed, as is also – especially – the relation of thought itself to the social totality. Indeed, this last deficiency is clear from the very definition of objectivism. But then truth also, thus reduced to scientific systematization, must have an independent existence – an existence, that is, independent of the intersubjective variables. Truth can appear only as an adventitious occurrence in the world. Here the circle of objectivism turns into a self-contradiction: objectivism, which is a philosophical accomplishment of social beings, produces as an outcome the systematic denial of all such accomplishments.

As we noted, these arguments against objectivism are general ones – that is to say, they apply in respect of all the kinds of phenomena with which critical theory deals. In particular, in the work under consideration both social processes and the knowledge of nature are at stake; thus the refutation of objectivism applies to the social as well as to the natural sciences. Of course, domains of objects may well exist in relation to which objectivism is both legitimate and appropriate; one could argue, for example, that such a domain is to be found within some fields of pure mathematics.

In that case, obviously, the critique presented above would not apply and instead objectivism would be properly regarded as a coherent philosophical problematic from which justifiable validity claims could be derived. We add this remark in order to emphasize that it is not suggested here that objectivism as such is self-contradictory; rather, what is claimed is merely that when extended to certain classes of objects it no longer retains its truth.

It is one of the consequences of the arguments of *Dialectic of Enlightenment* (repeated, in fact, in many of the other works of the authors involved) that such a class of objects is the domain theorized by the natural sciences. This is a somewhat surprising result, for it implies that critical theory should be obliged to confront some of the deepest conceptions of classical physics. Of course it is a fact that no such step was ever taken by either Horkheimer or Adorno. Both of them resiled from an acceptance of the conclusion that the objectivist approach to nature had actually been refuted; instead, they were content to argue merely that this approach had been rendered problematic. It had been shown that objectivism was rooted in the imperative to domination; and it had been shown that the price of the domination of nature was the alienation from that which is dominated. However there was never any suggestion that a cogent alternative to objectivism in the theory of nature – or even, for that matter, a rigorous critique of the limits of objectivism – could be conceptualized.

Critical theory sought to apply its philosophical insights not only to cultural phenomena but also to nature itself. Notwithstanding this, the fundamental epistemological questions were never raised; the discourse of science remained intact. To be sure, from the new vantage point, 'truth' was to be understood more broadly, implying that the truth of science was in some sense to be demoted. But regarding the validity of the actual truth-claims of science: this was never challenged.[57] Indeed, the critique of science undertaken by *Dialectic of Enlightenment* proceeds very little beyond the results already described. We shall argue presently that the inability of critical theory to continue to develop its critique of science was not purely accidental; rather it is an outcome of both the form of its argument and its presuppositions. Like the society it was examining therefore, we shall conclude, critical theory limits itself by its own internal imperatives. This circumstance in itself, however, is an instructive one for us; for like the profound results we have already examined, it contributes powerfully to the clarification of the issues which must be addressed by the theory of science. To this end, therefore, and also for the sake of obtaining some methodological

19

guidance for our endeavour, we now proceed to describe briefly a number of deficiencies in the argument put forward by Horkheimer and Adorno.

From the point of view of a potential social theory of science the most obvious shortcoming of the argument of *Dialectic of Enlightenment* is the absence in it of any serious analysis of the nature of science itself. A fundamental claim of the work is that scientific theory is associated with certain social and philosophical consequences. However no account whatever is attempted of the passage from the discursive structures to either the epistemological or political forms. Instead, a caricatured conception of science is adopted in which the philosophical content is exhausted by the mathematical techniques that are employed. Thus: '(n)ature, before and after the quantum theory, is that which is to be comprehended mathematically.... In the anticipatory identification of the wholly conceived and mathematized world with truth, Enlightenment ... confounds thought and mathematics.'[58] Now a twofold conclusion follows from this assumption. On the one hand, the objectivistic disposition of science is therefore bound immanently to the use of mathematical technique. On the other, alternative theories of nature which escape the falsehood of objectivism are excluded in principle – at least if they aspire to incorporate mathematics, the truth of which is nevertheless not itself contested. In relation to the former point, the least that can be said is that it is not self-evident. It is well-known that scientific thought involves rather more than the mere manipulation of symbols and at any rate the objects to which the mathematical terms refer are not inevitably the objectivistically conceived objects of classical physics. In relation to the latter point, the very example mentioned in the quotation above shows that this is not obvious either: that a sustained controversy involving both physicists and philosophers was possible on fundamental issues concerning the implications of quantum mechanics suggests that not all the philosophical options were securely sealed by the time of Galileo.[59]

If then the conception of science with which Horkheimer and Adorno operate is inadequate, what is a more adequate account? If science does issue in philosophical outcomes, how is this transition effected? If objectivism as such can be refuted – or at least, subjected to a fundamental questioning – what would be required for the construction of a non-objectivistic theory of nature? These are open problems that emerge from *Dialectic of Enlightenment* and which must be resolved by any more comprehensive social theory of science. That they remain open for the work under consideration, however, is in itself an important fact. For it is not due to a mere failure of nerve on the part of the authors. Rather, it is a necessary consequence of the theoretical project they were trying to realize. This project, furthermore, arose in relation to a series of basic presuppositions with which critical theory began.

Let us examine this in more detail. As we have seen, one of the irreducible starting points of *Dialectic of Enlightenment* was the assumption of the existence, at a basic ontological level, of an 'inescapable compulsion to social domination of nature' in which all other social effects, including culture and labour, are grounded.[60] 'Men have always had to choose,' they argued, 'between their subjection to nature or the subjection of nature to the self.' However, even though with the development of science and the extension of the bourgeois economy 'the dark horizon of myth is illumined by the sun of calculating reason', at the same time 'beneath (its) cold rays the seeds of the new barbarism grow to fruition. Under the pressure of domination human labour has always led away from myth – but under domination always returns to the jurisdiction of myth.'[61] If this is the case, the critique of Enlightenment must from the very outset place itself outside this dialectic; it can proceed only by means of a special kind of theory which would circumvent the separation of subject and object characteristic of traditional theory.[62] Now in the latter both the genesis of particular objective facts and the practical application of the conceptual systems within which facts are formulated are taken to be external to the theoretical thinking itself.[63] Furthermore, the subject of theory is taken to be either the isolated individual or the sum total of individuals. Critical theory, however, must oppose itself strictly to this conception. It must instead take for its subject 'a definite individual in his real relation to other individuals and groups, in his conflict with a particular class, and, finally, in the resultant web of relationships with the social totality and with nature.'[64] In consequence, critical theory puts itself outside 'the idealist belief that any theory is independent of men and even has a growth of its own'.[65]

Once such a perspective is established, however, critical theory must return to its motivating impulses. The critique of Enlightenment was provoked by the recognition that the rationalization and disenchantment of the world, associated with science, were already well advanced. As has been mentioned several times, the validity of science in its own domain was not to be called into question but only the malign consequences of its generalization to social phenomena.[66] Accordingly critical theory must incorporate a special category within which a relationship can be established between man and nature. Of course, this category already exists: it was predetermined in what we identified as one of the basic presuppositions of the theory. The mediation between subject and nature occurs exactly in the category of domination. The bearing of society towards nature is established in the 'inescapable compulsion' of the former to dominate the latter. It is technical practice – that is, instrumental action – that predominantly characterizes the relationship between the two. This fact is primary even with respect to social phenomena, for social domination, both over men and over instincts, derives from it; while in any case it constitutes an unsurpassable limit that must be respected in social practice generally.

Now to argue thus is not to claim that forms of action beyond instrumental action are either inconceivable or impossible. On the contrary, one of the basic objectives of critical theory was to show precisely that such alternatives still exist. However, the pre-Enlightenment categories which once simultaneously coexisted with, and stood in defiance of, the technical utilization of nature are no longer available. Both mimesis,[67] which purported to act out a communicative dialogue with nature, and anthropomorphism,[68] which attempted to naturalize the subjective, were, with the coming of Enlightenment, rendered progressively more marginal. For Enlightenment cannot tolerate any view of nature as a subject; hence it denies the possibility of any form of communication with it. And of course, there is no question of a return to the pre-Enlightenment state; in any case, it is a fact that today 'social freedom is inseparable from enlightened thought'.[69] In the present world, therefore, the alternatives are very limited. Even social exchange, which may once have appeared to contain the germ of a form in opposition to domination, can now be seen to be contaminated with the scientific principles of equivalence and calculability.[70] *Dialectic of Enlightenment*, and indeed critical theory in general, in these rather bleak circumstances offer us only one last possibility: the dialectical method of their investigation itself, where transcendence is preserved in its last refuge, the spontaneity of the concept.[71]

This is the perspective adopted by the work under consideration. It is also the outlook developed by Adorno at much greater length in his last work, *Negative Dialectics*. The later Horkheimer adopted a different perspective, repudiating many of his earlier conceptions.[72] What was never repudiated by either author, however, was the underlying view of the relationship between man and nature which we have been discussing – the view that comprehends this relationship as inexorably of domination, oriented exclusively to-

22

wards technical and instrumental goals. The negative dialectic that opposes the debasement of Enlightenment does not extend to the interaction with the natural world.

There are many problems that follow from these conceptions that cannot be considered in the present context. There are difficulties, for example, with the possibilities for political practice emerging from such a theory. There are difficulties with the theoretical analysis of different kinds of social structure that can be formulated on the basis of it. There are difficulties with the problem of the unfolding of an individual identity within a social context and with many other issues.[73] Here we merely advert to the existence of these problems and point out a further consequence that is destructive for the possibilities of a theory of nature formulated from a qualitatively different, non-objectivist perspective. In particular, the assumption a priori that nature stands to society inexorably in a relation of domination excludes in principle the possibility of theorizing this relationship as mediated through the intersubjective forms. For Marx, it will be argued later, it was precisely this that was the case: the theory of nature was imbedded in the immanence of social life. For critical theory, however, technical practice and the drive to subjugate nature alone, independently of changing social circumstances, provided the ambience within which science was inscribed.[74] This does not mean that critical theory adopted a view of the relationship between subject and object that was identical to the classical Cartesian one. On the contrary, opposition to this conception represented one of its main epistemological thrusts.[75] Within it, the subject was conceived only as existing in a necessary relation to something non-identical with it. Nevertheless at the same time the latter was itself subsumed under the category of nature, which appeared only under the signs of opposition, subjugation and control. Thus the anti-objectivism of critical theory was efficacious in the case of social and cultural phenomena; however, in respect of the theory of nature the possibility of any application of its insights was repudiated in advance. It was necessary to revise social theory but the validity of science had to be accepted unchallenged.[76] A social theory of science, therefore, could do no more than assess the effects in the cultural realm of a theory of nature in relation to which it was otherwise helpless.

In its attempt 'to escape the trance-like captivity of bourgeois immanence'[77] critical theory had sought to establish a sphere which a non-objectivist theory could inhabit – even if, in the face of Enlightenment, the security of such a theory could never be *guar-*

anteed. It was unable to conceive however that the existing form of science could itself be open to scrutiny. Thus the solution chosen was rather to throw a *cordon sanitaire* around nature (at least, as the latter was classically conceived) and to set about reviving the subject-object dialectic in the space that was left – the realm that now included only certain legitimate social phenomena. That a scientific theory could be fashioned which captured in its theoretical terms any aspect of intersubjective life was denied in advance. *Dialectic of Enlightenment* then, affected its escape from the contamination of the dark power of Enlightenment, but with consequences that were not inconsiderable. For this achievement was won only at the expense of handing over to the positivists the entire study of nature.

* * * * * *

To conclude this brief discussion of *Dialectic of Enlightenment* let us attempt to collect some of our results.

The question which we are considering is that of how a social theory of science could be possible at all. We are seeking, therefore, first of all to formulate the problems which such a theory would properly address. In this regard, despite its limitations, the work of the early Frankfurt School provides some helpful and suggestive indications.

That the conceptual forms with which science is associated penetrate social life and preponderate there is the substantive outcome of *Dialectic of Enlightenment*. The historical process of the enhancement of the mastery over nature, and the abolition of superstition, which was originally conceived as a programme for universal emancipation, had produced instead a generalization and intensification of domination. The philosophical locus of this intercession of science in society is objectivism: the radical disjunction of subject and object within which what is other than subjectivity appears in theory as irreducibly independent from it. Objectivity understood as objectivism and introjected into social life led to the reification of cultural phenomena which thus could assume the role of tools of social and political control. Furthermore, insofar as it comes to dominate both objects and the medium of theory itself, objectivism limits the possibilities for an effective reflection into its own origins. An additional, major achievement of *Dialectic of Enlightenment* was its provision of a general refutation of objectivism.

These insights could only have been won by means of a social critique. Nevertheless in critical theory itself the critique is not pushed to its limits. While it is shown that a continuity exists between the specific modes of discourse of science and the historical forms of domination no analysis is undertaken of how this transformation occurs. No detailed study is made of the structure of science, in order to locate the site of the philosophical contents. No attempt is made to characterize science beyond the recognition of its obvious use of mathematical techniques. Indeed the theory itself in its elementary conceptions prohibits the development of a view of science that goes beyond the simplistic and caricatured conventional views.

The problems, however, will be as helpful as the insights for the task of identifying the scope and possibilities of a social theory of science. For we now have a range of problems – both epistemological and social – against which other, more detailed existing theories can be measured. It is to these theories – to the sociology of science in general – that we therefore must turn.

A note on science and metaphysics

Before proceeding with this discussion however, in view of the arguments we have just examined and also those to follow, it is appropriate to add one further, brief note for the purposes of clarification. We have questioned the self-evidence of the identity that is usually assumed between science and objectivism and indeed between science and its philosophical content. But if no identity can be claimed, nevertheless some relationship between the terms undoubtedly exists. What can be said about this relationship without compromising the social and philosophical investigation of science?

The answer to this question lies in an observation that is today frequently taken to be obvious; however, obvious or not, it is certainly non-trivial. This is the observation that both objectivism and mathematical science share a common root in a metaphysics in which the subject appears as a privileged entity and in particular, as the specific locus in relation to which the concepts of knowledge and truth are defined. This result is non-trivial for the following two reasons. First, if science and objectivism share the same metaphysics of the subject then their coincidence is possible but not inevitable. For within a single metaphysics a variety of epistemologies is available; thus objectivism is one epistemology open to science but not the only one. Secondly, if mathematical science is necessarily inscribed within a given metaphysics then in spite of this epistemological openness certain philosophical limits nevertheless have to be recognized. For example, not all epistemologies are thereby available to science and in addition a philosophical perspective that places itself outside the dominant Western tradition will in general prove to be incommensurable with mathematical science as a whole;[78] other theories of nature, of course, may be formulated but they will be of a qualitatively different kind.

The recognition of the central position of the category of the subject in any metaphysics associated with science is of course attributable to the two principal figures in the early philosophical reflections of science: Descartes and Kant. In fact precisely this insight forms the subject of the famous Cartesian formula in the fourth *Discourse on Method*,[79] while at the beginning of the *Critique of Pure Reason* Kant refers to his own specific innovation as the realization in philosophy of a 'Copernican Revolution'[80] – that is, a fundamental reinterpretation of human knowledge as no longer outside man, external to him, but rather as in him as a human accomplishment and an ultimate goal. Clearly it is not possible in this essay to give a complete account of the metaphysics of Kant and Descartes, and none will be attempted. Instead, in brief arguments, a sketch will be presented of the role of the subject in mathematical science as it appears (not necessarily explicitly) from Descartes's philosophy.

In particular, we would like to oppose the common view of Descartes's philosophy that, in opposition to the erstwhile petrified forms of Aristotelian philosophy, seeking absolute certainty, and a presuppositionless foundation for all knowledge he merely subjected all common experience to rigorous doubt.[81] Through doubting, so this account goes, Descartes systematically revealed the one thing that could be certain: the knowing subjectivity. All knowledge could be traced back to an autonomous, thinking subject. Henceforth, all philosophy was subject to this insight. Not just all subsequent philosophy, but also all that which had gone before had now to be interpreted as a production of the ego. Philosophy and epistemology were henceforth coincident.

In spite of the recognition that it accords to the place of the subject in Descartes's thought and its appreciation of the importance of epistemology for modern philosophy, this view is profoundly mistaken – and in the error itself lie important consequences. In fact, this interpretation even contradicts Descartes's own self-proclaimed objectives. For he started quite explicitly from the presupposition of a world already formed according to the precepts of mathematical science. His very early work – for example, his *Rules for the Direction of Mind* – thus began with an injunction to pursue 'what we can clearly and insightfully intuit, or deduce with steps of certainty, for in no other way is knowledge arrived at'.[82] There are, he perceived 'two ways by which we arrive at the knowledge of things, viz., either by experience or by deduction.' The former however is 'often fallacious' because it is 'imperfectly understood'. Indeed, in certitude 'arithmetic and geometry far surpass all the other known disciplines.... They alone treat of an object so pure and simple as to admit of nothing that experience can render uncertain; they entirely consist in a sequence of consequences which are rationally deduced.'[83] In his somewhat later work, the *Discourse on Method*, he declared his conviction that thinking should proceed according to a rigorously elaborated method.[84] And in the *Meditations*, where he seeks arguments to demonstrate beyond any doubt the existence and character of the familiar objects of experience, the universally theoretical character of the world and its accessibility to the thinking subject are simply taken for granted.

Without precluding the discussions to follow we can observe here that in advance of his deliberations Descartes had thus already accepted a number of principles that were fundamental for any mathematical science. For example, implicit in the application of Euclidean space to the experienced world is the notion that the universe within which all experience takes place must be an infinite one. Koyré has shown that the idea of the infinite universe is a crucial presupposition for modern science[85] and that furthermore the conception of the infinite is an important one in Descartes's thought – so important, in fact, that 'Cartesianism may be considered as being wholly based upon that idea'.[86] In Descartes's philosophy the infinity of the world seems to be established beyond doubt and beyond dispute – although in spite of this, somewhat curiously, Descartes himself never asserts it.[87] More important for our present purposes however than this acceptance of the infinitude of the universe is its theoretical antecedents. In particular, Descartes's thought assumed that natural knowledge now could be susceptible to no foundation outside of itself; it could be subject, that is, to no supernatural realm. Instead, all the criteria for knowledge had to be sought in the procedures of the thinking cogito. No new facts of course were adduced by Descartes – indeed he openly sought to achieve no more than to justify old ones. Nevertheless the context within which they were apprehended was quite new. For now things were determined not according to qualities that

27

flowed from their immanent being, from which they could not be dissociated. Rather, the criteria of thought now preceded all such determinations; experientially autonomous in this regard from things, the subject was now in a position to grasp the regularities observed by things.

For Aristotle, even though the *logos* certainly regulated the determination of the categories, nevertheless it was the nature of the thing, its essence, wherein the impulse to all movement lay. Thus the study of physical nature involved the classification of the various kinds of motion and an interpretation of their relationships to the *physis*.[88] For modern science, however, nature and the knowledge of it are regarded quite differently. Nature is no longer an inner principle from which the forms of motion of a body flowed. Rather nature becomes the infinite multiplicity of the changing positions and motions of the bodies themselves. It is now no more than the sum of effects of nature, as they show themselves. That they can indeed show themselves however depends on a further, fundamental hypothesis: there must exist also a single consciousness before whom all phenomena can be unified into a unique realm of commensurable entities. If nature is to be regarded as the space-time context of motion rather than as its innermost essence, if things are to be determined according to principles of method which strictly pre-exist them, then natural knowledge is possible only on the presupposition of the existence of a subject before whom all phenomena are presented and all theory is held accountable.

Descartes's starting point then, was exactly the starting point for modern science. His assumptions, and those on which the contemporary study of nature substantially depend, are coincident. His task was not to suspend all presuppositions about the world but to introspect into a new set of such suppositions. At the birth of modern philosophy thought undertakes a self-reflection into the newly acquired, proto-scientific perspective.

Much of what has been said above concerning Descartes applies equally to Kant. However, in spite of the incomparably richer and deeper thought of the latter, we are restricting our discussion here to the earlier philosopher. This is because it was with Descartes that the first explicit recognition of the metaphysics of the subject occurs. He was the first to appreciate the implications of the new mode of thought. Implicit in the perspective that he had explicitly adopted for his philosophy is the assumption that what can be asserted in thinking always necessarily involves an 'I think'. 'I think, I am': the two claims always come together. The highest

28

certainty to which I can aspire is the certainty of my own thinking; the certainty of my knowledge of objects comes from my own existence as the certainty of my positing.[89]

Earlier, in the fourth *Discourse*, Descartes had given the same insight the famous form 'I think, therefore I am'.[90] As Kant pointed out, however – and as has been widely recognized since – this proposition could not contain a genuine inference.[91] Indeed it is evident from Descartes's arguments in both the earlier and the later works that such was never intended. Rather, he was undertaking a reflection on the act of positing itself, from which he discovered that implicit within it is the proposition 'I think'. The ego now becomes an entity distinguished from all others: it is the subject, which 'underlies' all knowledge. No longer just an object amongst objects, it is recognized as a specific subject, in relation to which all other things are now determined. Indeed, things themselves now become objects precisely insofar as they are defined in relation to, but as something different from, subjectivity. Thus subjectivity assumes a central position in the new metaphysics. It is no longer merely one region amongst many; it is precisely that region to which all metaphysical claims can be traced.

The being of things can be determined only in relation to subjectivity and reason. This was the essential perception of which it was the task of Enlightenment to propagate. It had fallen to Descartes to articulate the fundamental premise. It fell to Kant and to later philosophers to draw out in detail its consequences – and its limitations. Science and Enlightenment share a common root: indeed this is now apparent from the most elementary claim of modern science to be 'objective' knowledge.

Dialectic of Enlightenment had sought (amongst other things) to expose the social consequences of the growth of science. However, seeing that the current form of the theory of nature was objectivist, it made the mistake of identifying all science with objectivism. But it is clear that objectivism – the radical suppression of all subjective effects within the object – is not implicit in the mere identification of subjectivity and its centrality. Indeed, critical theory itself operates also with this very category, which it invokes explicitly for its overcoming of objectivism.

Certainly, science and positivism – or objectivism, which is the attribute of the latter to which we are referring, in order to distinguish it from the theory of nature in general – share a common root. Nevertheless, they are not identical. Both are inscribed within the metaphysics of the subject – a fact which renders them commensurable both with each other and with more directly social phenomena – but this does not imply that they are indistinguishable. Indeed not only objectivism but also every *critique* of objectivism falls within this metaphysics. The particular epistemology to which science can subscribe remains open. It may be positivism, or it may not be: this issue remains to be decided.

The contemporary sociology of science: A source of problems and possibilities

The general problem in which this essay is interested is that of the relationship between society and contemporary science. In order to approach this problem we are seeking to demarcate the theoretical space within which the appropriate questions can be asked and their solutions identified. So far, we have observed that it is a widely held perception that science today is in crisis, although the exact diagnosis of this crisis varies widely. In addition, we have considered briefly some themes from a major modern study of the interpretation of science and society; here, we were able to appreciate that the theoretical vehicle by means of which science exerts at least some of its malign social effects is the objectivism that characterizes its classical form; furthermore, we saw that, in respect of the application of objectivism to the interpretation of natural as well as social phenomena, cogent arguments can be found asserting that such an application is not only inappropriate but may actually be false. Having obtained these results, the task that now confronts us embraces on the one hand, the identification of the possible mechanisms by which science and society influence each other and on the other, a more detailed assessment of both the structure of science and the practice of scientists. For this endeavour the natural direction in which to turn is towards the sociology of science and to some branches of the modern philosophy of science. In these areas the most sustained efforts have occurred in recent years to theorize the society-science relationship. What is more, within them, for this purpose, there has been fashioned a wide variety of perspectives and approaches – and in the present preliminary process of demarcation and clarification this is exactly what we are seeking. Accordingly, in what follows, a brief survey will be undertaken of some themes in the sociology and philosophy of science, with a view to obtaining methodological guidance for our own project, as well as identifying specific insights, fruitful hypotheses and unresolved problems.

It is necessary to emphasize at the outset that the discussion on which we are about to embark will not pretend to supply either a summary or a critique of the field; nor will it presume to propose a more 'correct' theory in the place of the existing ones. In fact, it is apparent that there are available many approaches to the study of science which are perfectly valid in relation to the particular range of questions they address. Our object is not specifically to scrutinize these; rather, as we have said, it is to do something quite different: it is to demarcate a space, to gather the problems and issues for a research project that has not hitherto been sharply distinguished. The procedure will be to discuss in turn some aspects of the works of particular authors whom we consider to have contributed in ways potentially fruitful for this study. To this end, in the present chapter several writers are discussed whose work can be said to fall strictly within the sociology of science, while in the sequel some consideration is given to a number of the broader philosophical issues which will arise in the course of the discussion.

Robert Merton and the origin of the sociology of science

In a discussion of the contemporary sociology of science the work of Robert Merton is undoubtedly an obvious place to start. For ever since the publication in 1938 of his first book he has been the thinker against whom (at least until relatively recent times) later theorists invariably have measured their work. Furthermore, his writings on science encompass diverse fields: the social influences at work in the development of science; the system of norms observed by scientists; social policy and the direction of science; the use of empirical techniques in investigations into the nature of science and so on. They concern the broadest questions about the modes of interplay between society and science and the influence of patterns and rates of social interaction on the latter's development.[1] This is not to say of course that Merton's efforts are beyond reproach: on the contrary, almost every aspect of his arguments and methods has been subjected to the most strenuous criticism. Nevertheless, in the sociology of science he remains a central figure who cannot be ignored. Here we shall advert in particular to two fundamental aspects of his work: the study of the social forces contributing to the rise of science in the first place, and the more specific investigations into the social structure of science as it is practised today. In the case of the former, as Merton himself has explained,[2] the original impulse to study this area derived from the work of one of the major founders of sociology: Max Weber.

In precisely the same essay in which he grimly acknowledged that '(t)he fate of our times is characterized by rationalization and intellectualization and, above all, by the "disenchantment of the world"',[3] Weber had set out an implicit programme for the sociological study of science. All scientific work, he argues,

> presupposes that the rules of logic and method are valid; these
> are the general foundations of our orientation in the world;
> and, at least for our special question, these presuppositions are
> the least problematic aspect of science. Science further
> presupposes that what is yielded by scientific work is important
> in the sense that it is 'worth being known'. In this, obviously,
> are contained all our problems. For this presupposition cannot
> be proved by scientific means. It can only be interpreted with
> reference to its ultimate meaning, which we must reject or
> accept according to our ultimate position towards life.[4]

This means that science is a cultural value; hence belief in scientific truth is not derived from nature but is rather a product of definite cultures.[5] The place and meaning of science in our culture are therefore appropriate subjects for sociology and philosophy. They can answer the questions inaccessible to science. 'Natural science gives us an answer to the question of what we must do if we wish to master life technically. It leaves quite aside, or assumes for its purposes, whether we should and do wish to master life technically and whether it ultimately makes sense to do so.'[6] In addition, philosophy and sociology can provide some account of the cultural environment within which scientific values were first asserted. In a passage clearly reminiscent of his earlier work, *The Protestant Ethic and the Spirit of Capitalism*, Weber adumbrated the direction such an account might take.

> If you recall Swammerdam's statement, 'Here I bring you the
> proof of God's providence in the anatomy of a louse', you will
> see what the scientific worker, influenced (indirectly) by
> Protestantism and Puritanism, conceived to be his task: to
> show the path to God. People no longer found this path
> among the philosophers, with their concepts and deduction....

God is hidden, His ways are not our ways, His thoughts are not our thoughts. In the exact sciences, however, where one could physically grasp His works, one hoped to come upon the traces of what He planned for the world. ...[7]

It was exactly to the realization of a theory such as the one suggested in this brief passage that a substantial portion of Merton's *Science, Technology and Society in Seventeenth Century England* was directed. This having been said, however, it must be added immediately that in the later author there was none of his predecessor's sober apprehension regarding the advance of science. Today, Weber noted pensively, when science is identified with culture,

> all 'culture' appears as man's emancipation from the organically prescribed cycle of natural life. For this very reason culture's every step forward seems condemned to lead to an ever more devastating senseless-ness. The advancement of cultural values, however, seems to become a senseless hustle in the service of worthless, moreover self-contradictory and mutually antagonistic ends. The advancement of cultural values appears the more meaningless the more it is made a holy task, a 'calling'.[8]

In fact, far from echoing these sentiments, Merton's view is, if anything, quite the opposite.

* * * * * *

Taking this general argument of *The Protestant Ethic* as its explicit point of departure,[9] *Science, Technology and Society* set out to examine the relations between Puritanism and science. Puritanism was a religious movement incorporating powerful motivations and dominant cultural values; thus it could be expected to have important consequences for the new science. However, as Merton noted at the outset, it was unlikely that any simple relationship would be found to pertain between them. Rather what had to be studied were 'the complex modes of interaction between a religious ethic and science ... as they occurred in the course of actual social development.'[10]

To this end, Merton, rather as Weber had done, first identified some salient characteristics of the so-called 'Protestant ethic'. A devotion to the glorification of God 'as the end and all of existence'[11] and, specifically, the utilitarian interpretations given to this precept,[12] an emphasis on diligence and industry in one's calling,[13] an exaltation of reason as a unique and characteristic quality of man and a powerful weapon against idolatry[14] – all these, among others, were important features of the Puritan spirit that would prove to be of importance for the development of science. In fact, '(u)naided by forces which had already gripped man's will, science could claim only a bare modicum of attention and loyalty. But in partnership with a powerful social movement which induced an intense devotion to the active exercise of designated functions, science was launched in full career.'[15]

From the point of view of the ethos of Puritanism, science was interpreted as an activity directed towards the manifestation of the glory of God and the enhancement of the good of Man.[16] Further sanctification of science derived from science's contribution to the extension of man's domination over nature. For according to Puritanism 'anything which tends "to question the lives of mortals", to facilitate their material well-being, is good in the sight of God';[17] in fact this principle was even stated in its most general form: '(k)nowledge is to be valued according to its usefulness'.[18] In addition, a scientific life was an industrious life in which the individual could apply himself with diligence and devotion to a never-ending task. Thus the patterns of behaviour embodied in science were also congenial to Puritan tastes.[19]

As the full import of the Puritan ethic manifested itself in society this close harmony between Puritanism and the aims and activities associated with the sciences thrust the latter into the focus of social interest.[20] Many turned to the study of nature, among them nobles and wealthy commoners. Particularly in these cases, direct economic benefits were a negligible consideration, for science afforded them 'the opportunity to devote their energies to an honoured task'. In fact, such a devotion had now become an obligation as the new scale of values execrated unrelieved idleness and comfort.[21] Under the impact of the great influx of new workers and its enhanced social position the young science began to flourish.

Merton, in the elaboration of this argument, was careful to discount any suggestion that a direct causal relation between Puritanism and science might be involved. He was not claiming, he emphasized, that specific discoveries could be directly attributed to the sanction of science by religion. On the contrary, '(s)pecific discoveries and inventions belong to the internal history of science and are largely independent of factors other than the purely scientific'.[22] Nor was it implied that – to use the functionalist terminology – religion was the 'independent variable' while science was the 'dependent' one. Rather, religious conceptions were 'definitely integrated with sentiments basic to the contemporary science and philosophy: there was throughout a reciprocal interaction'.[23] What was important was just that the social values inherent in the Puritan ethic were such 'as to lead to an approbation of science because of a basically utilitarian orientation, couched in religious terms and furthered by religious authority'.[24] What is more, the changing class structure of the times reinforced these Puritan sentiments favouring science; for many Puritans came from the rising bourgeois class whose hatred of the existing class structure appeared to coincide exactly with science's implicit commitment to progress and change.[25] Finally, it cannot be claimed that Puritanism was indispensable for the acceptance of science; indeed in its absence 'other functionally equivalent ideological movements' could have served just as well to provide the emerging science 'with widely acknowledged claims to legitimacy'.[26] The most that can be claimed is that at a particular time and place 'religion and economy coalesced to provide arguments for the "utility" of science'.[27]

We have dealt at some length here with the early, Weberian aspect of Merton's sociology of science because of its suggestiveness regarding the relationship between society and modern science in general. Merton shows that the truth of science cannot be regarded as self-evident, and that indeed nor is science neutral with respect to the social and cultural institutions. On the contrary, belief in science is itself shown to be a cultural fact with extensive cultural implications. Thus on the one hand, different societies may adopt widely varying theories of nature, while on the other, science as we know it may assume a value only in specific types of society. In fact Merton even goes so far as to claim that this idea constitutes 'the principle assumption underlying the entire book. The substantial and persistent development of science occurs only in societies of a certain kind, which provide both cultural and material conditions for that development'.[28]

But exactly what is this science which has experienced in Western societies such vigorous acceptance and extensive development? Most philosophical studies today emphasize its conceptual structure and the particular choice of objects on which its methodological apparatus operates. In Merton's theory, however, these aspects of science are specifically excluded from its social mediation. The sociological study of the development of science takes into account only the practice of science and the behaviour of scientists. What is important about Puritanism is that it sanctifies the study of nature. Nothing can be said about the actual content of science or its discursive structure: these are assumed to be exempt from the social processes. To be sure, Merton suggests in some brief passing references to Whitehead that the *object domain* of science is in fact, like belief in the truth of science, an accomplishment of culture.[29] However, the obvious implication of this argument – that not just the acceptance of scientific knowledge but also that very knowledge itself is a social variable – was never even entertained. Indeed, once established and widely accepted science was said to acquire a 'functional autonomy'[30] with respect to the social structure. It became a value in its own right and was no longer called upon to justify itself by arguments bearing on the social and cultural milieu.[31] Even if once science had been to some extent dependent on the form of society, that was so no longer – at least, except in special circumstances (to which we shall refer later) in which the ethical consensus obtaining among scientists was contradicted by the social and political conditions. 'Once the initial problems (had) become evident'[32] scientific research proceeded largely independently of social forces; now, scientists formed an independent community pursuing an antonomous investigation of nature.[33]

Many of the claims of the preceding paragraph have been disputed by the later philosophy of science, to which Merton of course did not have access – although he was certainly aware of (and in fact made explicit reference to) the general question, which had long been an issue, of the social variability of scientific knowledge.[34] We shall return to these issues repeatedly. For the moment we merely observe that today it is once again becoming accepted that the truth of contemporary science is not necessarily self-evident, and indeed that it might not be appropriate to identify science's specific assertions with either the intellectual standards to which it claims adherence or the rigorous, analytical truth of its mathematical techniques. Merton writes: 'It is the character of an intellectual discipline that its evolving rules of evidence are adopted before they are used in asserting a particular inquiry.... (T)he margin of autonomy in the culture and institution of science means that the intellectual criteria, as distinct from the social ones, for judging the validity and worth of that work transcend extraneous group allegiances.'[35] However, it is possible that such intellectual criteria, that is, criteria that are strictly independent of all social influences, simply do not exist. If this were the case then all validity-claims of any kind would have to pass through some social mediation. This would not by any means require that truth in general were no longer possible, but merely that all truth was immanently social in character and, accordingly, stood in relation to specifically social objects. Regarding science in particular, it could

37

then occur that the theory of nature obtaining in a given society might be true according to objective standards but nevertheless convey immanently a content subject to social and historical contingencies.

But these are problems to be taken up in more detail later; here we are still searching for issues and hypotheses. Thus, instead of pursuing the discussion of Merton's theory we shall turn to a brief consideration of some studies which treat similar or related issues from rather different perspectives. Only a small number of such studies will be cited and the discussion of them will be short, for, as we have indicated, our purpose is principally to establish the existence of issues and theoretical perspectives absent from Merton's work. Subsequently, we shall return once more to Merton himself to consider – again briefly – the other major aspect of his work: the sociological study of the scientific community.

Edgar Zilsel: capitalism and the birth of modern physics

In the first place, we mention the work of Edgar Zilsel, a member (albeit a rather peripheral one) of the Frankfurt School while it was based in New York. Zilsel is of interest because he treats apparently the same issue that Merton deals with – the question of the sociological roots of science – from a point of view heavily influenced by Marxism. Accordingly, whereas Merton emphasized the significance of Puritanism in the development of science, for Zilsel it was the economic and historical circumstances that were decisive. More important however than a mere variation in emphasis between the two authors is a fundamental difference in their approaches to the problem and in their assessments of what has to be proved. For Merton the social roots of science must be sought in the cultural context that induces people to study science, for 'the very existence of science and scientists presupposes that they occupy some positive level in the social scale of values which is the final arbiter of the prestige attached to various pursuits'.[36] His conclusion was, as we have seen, that the 'persistent development of physical science occurs only in societies of definite order, subject to a peculiar complex of tacit presuppositions and institutional constraints'.[37] For Zilsel, by contrast, what was of interest was rather the social forces at work in the actual formation of scientific knowledge.[38] Indeed, he assumed that phenomena occurring at the level of economic and cultural life find an expression in the theoretical constructions developed to understand that context. Thus, in the case of science, the advent of the new theory can be explained with the help of studies of both science itself and the economic configuration: within the theoretical structures we can expect to find traces of the contemporaneous social and economic transformations. Zilsel therefore proposes a social theory of the structure of science and to this extent makes good a deficiency we observed in Merton. That his social theory is at best rudimentary and his conception of science mistaken in some important respects does not concern us here: what is notable is the project he succeeded in formulating.

Zilsel's argument, in brief, was as follows. Science had brought forth in a unity three types of intellectual activity formerly unconnected: those of university scholars, humanists and artisans.[39] The first two were rationally trained – although their methods differed fundamentally from the methods of science – and furthermore they despised practical activities such as manual labour and experimentation. The last were the pioneers of causal thinking and appreciated by force of necessity the value of both co-operative endeavour and practical investigation – even though in general they lacked rigorous intellectual training. Now the development of capitalism was accompanied by cultural effects and also technical requirements: on the one hand magical thinking, the belief in authority, etc., were weakened; on the other, new and more efficient machines were needed for the expanding economy. Science was born when these two processes coincided and the social prejudice against manual labour was overcome; for under these conditions the experimental method could be adopted by rationally trained scholars. The scholastic method of disputation was now replaced by scientific method and the humanistic ideal of individual glory gave way to beliefs in progress, the control of nature and scientific co-operation.

In a sense Zilsel's work complemented the perspective of *Dialectic of Enlightenment* with which it was contemporaneous. It provided a theory of the social origins of the process of the universalization of reason which concerned Horkheimer and Adorno. On the other hand, however, precisely in its search for origins and in its devotion to causal explanations, it offended the other work's deepest impulses. In fact Zilsel himself – not without some justification – was regarded by the other members of the Frankfurt School as a positivist[40] and his work was given little attention. Nevertheless, his theories are of interest, both for the contrast they present to the theories that are more familiar today in the sociology of science and for their attempts to realize a sociological exposition of the structure of science.

Alexandre Kojève: culture and the origins of science

In connection with the foregoing discussion it may be appropriate to mention a brief essay by Alexandre Kojève that appeared in 1964. This essay, on 'The Christian origins of modern science',[41] has not been especially influential and – it must be admitted – has even been accused in the subsequent literature of containing serious errors.[42] Nevertheless, its approach incorporates both philosophical and sociological perspectives in such a manner that it might be said to stand halfway between Merton and Zilsel, and for this reason it is of interest to us. Indeed, for our purposes even the controversial aspects are suggestive of problems requiring attention. Accordingly, it is in this spirit that the essay in question will be approached.

Kojève's argument is in fact quite a simple one. He is interested in the question of why modern science was born specifically in sixteenth century Western society. His answer will be that these societies were dominated by a particular version of Christian theology which was capable of supplying the necessary impulse for the development of science. First however he attempts to show that pagan cultures were inimical to the fundamental idea of a mathematized nature. In particular, in non-Christian theologies men stand in a relationship to God that can be surpassed neither in life nor death. Unlike in Christianity it is not enough for them simply to die in order to rupture the veil separating heaven from earth. In fact the *theos* of paganism 'surpassed irremediably the Beyond to which the pagan wants eventually to pass after his death'.[43] For this reason, the realm of the Beyond must be rendered in unfamiliar terms. For Plato, for example, it is conceived as the ideal, 'utopian *cosmos*', while for Aristotle it is in the *ouranos* – the planetary heaven and 'etherial space': in either case the non-terrestrial region has no precise position in space, even though it remains strictly spatial in character. 'Because the theory ... of the Platonic *cosmos* or the Aristotelian *ouranos* is the summit beyond which the pagan can pass neither in life nor death, this very *cosmos* and *ouranos* also establish the extreme limit of the possible manifestations or incarnations of their God'.[44] The consequences for Greek science are obvious. On the one hand the transcendent world inhabited by God is 'a well ordered ensemble of rigorous relationships, fixed forever between eternal and precise numbers'.[45] On the other hand the profane world could never be characterized by such relations for, far from being a single ordered and denumerable unity, this region contains only temporal, unstable and fluctuating qualities.

If mathematical laws are to exist, then they cannot apply to the world of the senses: they must be restricted to that pure realm from which all matter is excluded.

Only in Christianity does the possibility arise of penetrating the veil. For in the uniquely Christian doctrine of the Incarnation the human body can be at the same time the body of God. Earth and heaven form an immanent unity. But if – as even the Greeks knew – the movements of the heavenly bodies correctly reflect the eternal relations between mathematical entities, then for the Christian no obstacle remains to a similar study of worldly phenomena. Indeed, the Incarnation implies nothing less than the all-pervasive presence of God in the temporal world inhabited by men; hence the perfection that must be presupposed in mathematical formulations lies always ready to hand in everyday experience. If Christianity then was a crucial factor in the advent of modern science, 'it is the Christian dogma of the Incarnation which bears exclusive responsibility'.[46]

Now this conclusion is undoubtedly too strong. It cannot be assumed a priori that other influences – social, religious or philosophical – did not also contribute. At any rate, the dogma of Incarnation itself is susceptible to many different interpretations, and it is an historical fact that prior to the twelfth century a world-denying fideism and self-effacement had prevailed and not the worldliness of seventeenth century Puritanism. Thus Kojève's account begs an important question: it remains to be explained why in a particular social and historical context a specific theological perspective was adopted in preference to all other available ones.

This is not an insubstantial criticism, and indeed nor is it the only one that can be made. Nevertheless what we would like specifically to draw attention to is rather the character of the argument itself. Kojève maintains that the rise of science was subject to the influence of religion and philosophy. This much is accepted also by Merton and Zilsel: for the former, Puritanism provided a justification for individuals to turn to the study of nature; for the latter, a variety of intellectual trends congealed with the practical circumstances to establish the characteristic form of scientific investigation. However, what distinguishes Kojève's argument is that in it the philosophical perspectives are assumed actually to penetrate the content of science itself. A theory of nature proposes immanently a philosophy regarding the form or the substance of its object. Furthermore, that philosophy is susceptible – at least from subsequent perspectives – to scrutiny and possible contestation.

That modern science might depend on an ontology that can be

41

traced to social and historical contingencies is not a small claim. However, in the essay in question it is neither articulated directly nor developed further. In fact in the argument itself there are many deficiencies. In addition to the problem that we have mentioned of accounting for the acceptance of a particular interpretation of Christian doctrine at a particular time, for example, it is clear that Kojève fails to appreciate the difference between science and technology – a distinction carefully made by Merton and which has become commonplace in the ensuing literature. Further, it may be observed that the qualitative perfection of nature does not self-evidently entail as a consequence quantitative precision;[47] rather, that such an inference was in fact made historically is a substantial problem. Finally – and more importantly for our own investigations – the converse of this last point can also be contested: it is not at all obvious that the acceptance of a mathematized nature compels the scientist to adopt any particular ontology. On the contrary, from historical experience it can be shown that mathematical science is not associated with a unique interpretation of the nature of the world.[48] This point will be taken up in detail later, where it will be shown – in relation to contemporary physics – that the ontological implications of a mathematized nature are indeed ambiguous.

Boris Hessen: the philosophical content of classical mechanics

From Kojève and Zilsel we turn to another Marxist writer, Boris Hessen – a Russian who, by virtue of the single paper by which he is known in the West, exercised considerable influence amongst left-wing scientists in England during the 1930s and 40s. Hessen also considers the early history of modern science. However, he does not concentrate on the problem of its origins but on the philosophical and social content of its early formulations. Specifically, he examines the context within which Newton's *Principia* was constructed. At a time when the feudal economy was disintegrating and the accumulation of merchant capital intensifying, technical problems were raised for which immediate solutions were demanded. In communications, transport, war and industry generally, the development of the young capitalist economy was frustrated by practical difficulties that had not previously been encountered. These difficulties, taken together, formed a coherent complex of problems dealing with every aspect of applied mechanics and it soon became apparent that what was necessary was

not an empirical resolution of isolated problems but the provision
of a comprehensive, 'stable theoretical basis for the solution by
general methods of all the aggregate of physical problems, set ...
by the new technique'.[49] This precisely was the historical task the
accomplishment of which fell to Newton.

'Science flourished,' according to Hessen, 'step by step with the
development and flourishing of the bourgeoisie. In order to develop
its industry the bourgeoisie needed science, which would investigate
the qualities of material bodies and the forms of manifestation of
the forces of nature.'

> Hitherto science had been the humble servant of the church, it
> was not allowed to pass beyond the bounds established by the
> church. The bourgeoisie had need of science and science arose
> together with the bourgeoisie despite the church. Thus the
> bourgeoisie came into conflict with the feudal church ...[50]

Thus far, Hessen's analysis is interesting but unremarkable. It
provides an account from an economic perspective of the formation
of social conditions congenial for the development of science. Also
(it might be worth observing) in spite of first appearances, none of
its major contentions are inconsistent with the other theories described previously. Hessen's real contribution derives from his
analysis not of the social conditions to which the *Principia* was a
response but of its philosophical content. There was, he maintained, concealed within the interstices of the technical discourse a
definite social and philosophical perspective. The main tendency of
his argument is conveyed in the following quotations:

> The importance of the *Principia* is not confined only to
> technical matters. Its very name indicates it forms a system, a
> conception of the universe....[51]

> On English soil mechanistic determinism came to be generally
> accepted, although it was found interwoven with religious
> dogma ... This peculiar combination ... is found also in
> Newton. The universal acceptance of the principle of
> mechanical causation as the sole and basic principle of the
> scientific investigation of nature is due to the mighty
> development of mechanics. Newton's *Principia* is a grandiose
> application of this principle to our planetary system....[52]

> Newton's matter is inert in the full sense of the meaning of the
> word. An outside impulse is always necessary to bring it into
> movement or to alter or end this movement. Further, as

Newton accepts the existence of an absolute, immovable space, to him inertia is possible only as absolute inertia and thus the existence of absolutely immovable matter ... is physically possible.

It is clear that such a conception of the modality of movement must inevitably lead to the introduction of an extrinsic motive force, and with Newton this role is filled by God.[53]

In sum, Hessen maintains, Newton adopts the philosophical viewpoint of a 'theological idealism'.[54]

We shall not repeat in more detail Hessen's elaboration of Newton's philosophy; not shall we consider his attempted refutation – from his own point of view of dialectical materialism – of almost all the above propositions. What is of principal interest to us here is rather the mere existence of the argument at all. Like Kojève, Hessen maintains that science may well embrace a philosophical perspective. However, his arguments are directed not to science in general but to classical mechanics only and the philosophical content is found not in the presuppositions but in the technical details themselves. Further, the philosophy underlying the scientific reasoning is shown to stand in a definite relation to the social conditions, and this relation is given as an explanation for its widespread acceptance at that time. Hessen does not contest the appropriateness of mathematics to physics nor does he locate Newton's philosophy in the methodological apparatus of the *Principia*. Rather, mathematics is assumed to be compatible with a variety of philosophical viewpoints. Consequently, the philosophical critiques are possible within mathematical science and they are subject to the criteria of truth applied generally in theoretical discourse and not exclusively to empirical criteria. Finally, it is thus conceivable that the outcome of such a critique might be simply that the scientific doctrine or theory is mistaken so that an alternative must be sought; in fact this is precisely Hessen's conclusion in relation to Newton's formulation of classical mechanics.

These conclusions are indeed challenging ones and raise fundamental questions which we shall have to take up. There are substantial difficulties too, of course, and these will have to be considered also. The actual arguments about classical mechanics are imprecisely formulated and on occasions lack conviction. The alleged philosophy contained within Newton's work is inadequately specified. Broader conclusions are lacking: the role of the scientists' prejudices in relation to his entire theory is not considered and indeed no guidance is provided for the identification of such prejudices in other theories. No rigorous analysis of the theoretical structure of science is undertaken which might indicate which of its components can be properly regarded as socially variable. And there is no discussion of truth in general, and of its place in the formal system – in fact, such a discussion is actually confounded by what appears to be a perfunctory characterization of classical mechanics as ideology. These are outstanding problems that, from the foregoing discussions, present themselves for examination. Attempts will be made in due course to take them up in some detail.

Paul Forman: quantum mechanics and the Weimar Republic

One further study will be mentioned before we return to Merton. Having a quite different focus from those referred to above, this study nevertheless also deals with an important period of flux and transformation in science. It is a relatively recent essay by Paul Forman about the atmosphere of mounting crisis in Weimar Germany and its impact on German physicists and mathematicians. We mention it here because of its intrinsic interest, because it raises once more the issue of the 'crisis of science' – to which we have already adverted and which has become important once again in recent years – and because we shall consider in some detail later the work of Edmund Husserl, including in particular, his book *The Crisis of European Science and Transcendental Phenomenology*.

Forman undertakes a close study of the intellectual environment of Germany during the years 1918 to 1927. He finds that it was marked by a generalized perception of a 'crisis of learning'.[55] The dominant philosophy was 'a neo-romantic, existentialist "philosophy of life", revelling in crises and characterized by antagonism toward analytical rationality generally and toward the exact sciences and their technical applications particularly.'[56] Reason was rejected as an epistemological instrument because it was considered inseparable from positivism; it was replaced by a glorification of 'life', intuition, 'unmediated and unanalyzed experience, with the immediate apprehension of values, and not the dissection of a causal nexus, as the proper object of scholarly or scientific activity.'[57] This atmosphere was epitomized by Spengler's *Decline of the West*,[58] the 'most fundamental proposition' of which was 'the opposition of the destiny-idea and the causality-principle'.[59] The general tone of the times was widely recognized and commented upon – not the least of all by the German physicists of the period.[60] In fact it was not long before the question of causality was raised in relation to science itself, although in these debates 'causality' was usually employed ambiguously.[61] Nevertheless the notion that nature could not be described adequately in causal terms gained popularity with extraordinary speed. For the scientists concerned the realization often appeared like a religious revelation, with physicist after physicist appearing in public lectures to declare his new-found faith.[62] These 'conversions' were made primarily on philosophical or ethical grounds; it was only later that they were given a formulation in physics itself – and then, due to the widespread acausal sentiment, they achieved instant assent.[63] Later still, when the quantum theories of Schrödinger, Heisenberg and others were formulated, acausal physics appeared to have been completely vindicated.

The conclusion then is that the apparent paradox of the flourishing of physics in a time of extreme hostility to it is really not at all surprising. For in fact the scientists exactly mirrored the intellectual milieu and adopted the popular conceptions either because they wanted to regain favourable public attitudes towards science,[64] or simply because they were following the fashion.[65] Thus the program of dispensing with causality in physics achieved a substantial following in Germany *before* it was justified by the advent of a mathematical theory which appeared, at least on the face of it, actually to realize an acausal physics. Hence, in brief: 'in the genesis of the acausal persuasion ... substantive problems in atomic physics played only a secondary role; ... the most important factor was the social-intellectual pressure exerted upon the physicists as members of the German academic community.'[66]

Now this argument is obviously an historical rather than a philosophical one. In fact Forman deliberately avoids an extended discussion of the relationship between quantum mechanics and the causality principle – a matter that is still controversial. Nevertheless it is undeniably suggestive; and after all, the remarkable florescence of physics during the period in question can hardly escape attention. Further, some of the ideas referred to previously in relation to the early development of science strike immediate resonances in the later context. Because these are quite clear they will not be repeated. Instead, we shall just draw attention to two or three of the most important implications.

First is the presupposition of Forman's entire argument: that it is possible to ascribe to quantum mechanics a philosophical disposition that departs substantially from that of its predecessors. This view is of course by no means uncommon; indeed it was held by most of the protagonists in the drama he describes. Nevertheless, it is anything but unimportant, as also is the particular philosophy at stake. For as we shall see later the rejection of causality was in fact associated with a challenge of the most fundamental kind to objectivistic physics. Further, this implication is related to a second point, which is in fact the article's major conclusion. Extrinsic forces may impinge upon physics, and even direct its immediate development. The exact character of this influence is not altogether clear. However in the case in question the social mediation is exerted by way of the generalized 'intellectual milieu', rather than, for example, more directly by the economic circumstances. Thirdly, this last point can be expressed in more formal terms. It is proposed that the cultural environment within which physicists work supplies them with both problems and possibilities. Subsequently, these may be projected into the immediate theoretical field of physics itself where they can be interpreted as potential meanings for a formal theory. Ultimately, such a theory may in fact be devised, which would thus realize in the formal realm new meanings which had arisen first of all in social life. The character of the new theory of course remains open; nevertheless, it is conceivable that if the philosophical innovations are sufficiently substantial then the formal characteristics of the erstwhile theory will be fundamentally transformed. It is a familiar fact that advances in science may well convey important consequences for society; the claim of the argument under consideration is that the converse of this proposition also holds: that a 'reverse continuity' may also obtain between society and science. Or to put the same contention differently, using a language which we shall later employ extensively: the pragmatic relations of science may contribute to the shaping of its semantic context, while in turn, changes in the latter dimension may be efficacious for the syntactical forms. Thus this argument claims that the pragmatic, semantic and syntactical components of science are interrelated and that variations in one may ultimately be reflected in the organization of the others. In fact even more than this is claimed in respect of quantum theory: it is asserted that a 'crisis' in the pragmatic dimension of science – such as undoubtedly existed in Weimar Germany – was propagated, by means still obscure, through its semantic and syntactical realms.

These results clearly raise questions of the highest importance, which will certainly be considered later. Here we end this discussion for the present by mentioning as a last point merely one obvious difficulty. This difficulty involves the question of truth in physics and in philosophy. At least on the surface, it appears that the two disciplines deal with quite different conceptions of truth and, in particular, in assessing a given proposition employ divergent criteria of validity. It appears that science depends upon technical and practical criteria, for example, whereas philosophy incorporates variously social, cultural and logical standards. But a consequence of the above argument is that in some sense physics is susceptible to philosophy, so that a conception of the latter may appear also, perhaps in a modified form, in the former. If this were the case, then the two conceptions of truth would have to be reconciled and furthermore internal criteria of consistency, coherence, and so on would have to be transformable from one to the other. Yet how this may occur is certainly not self-evident. In other circumstances the philosophical contentions may be, in relation even to their own standards, confused, inconsistent or even wrong. Indeed many of Spengler's arguments are regarded today as somewhat unconvincing. In this case, it must be asked, is an application to science prohibited in principle? Or – more perplexing still – if such an application does occur, how can it be understood?

Practical considerations in science and scientific knowledge

The purpose of our study of the sociology of science is to discover ideas, hypotheses and problems surrounding the relationship between science and society. Thus far, in a cursory glance, we have mentioned in particular the work of five authors: Merton, Zilsel, Kojève, Hessen and Forman. The choice may appear curious, since the studies vary considerably in quality and significance and furthermore are from disparate points of view. Nevertheless, some convergent themes and persistent problems have already emerged; indeed, even if they agree on nothing else, all the authors accept that a deep relation exists between a society and the theory of nature predominant within it and that further, this relation has many facets. One particular aspect has become prominent today and appears repeatedly in discussions about science. This is the problem of the social determination of scientific truth. It was once the common view that the truth of science was independent of the social variables. However, even from the brief discussion so far it can be seen that this contention is questionable. In fact today once again the view is gaining acceptance that science immanently incorporates social phenomena, as is argued in different ways in several recent studies.[67] This is an issue we would like to analyse in more detail in the present essay. However, it requires that some further preliminaries be established. For if the social forms penetrate to the farthest reaches of scientific theory then they must, to some extent at least, be conveyed already in the thinking and behaviour of scientists. Thus a theory of the social determinations of scientific knowledge must take into account the actual practice of the producers of science. In the remainder of this discussion of the sociology of science, it is to this question that we shall therefore direct ourselves.

As before, a convenient starting point is the sociology of Robert Merton. Here, however we consider not that aspect of his theory dealing with the origins of modern science, but rather his study of the social structure of the scientific community. This investigation constitutes perhaps the main part of Merton's work. Certainly it was the part of his sociology of science that he himself favoured.[68] Adumbrated in his early work, where the distinction is made between personal and social influences on scientific research,[69] it was nevertheless not until subsequent papers that the theory was developed in full. Then the appropriate focus of the sociologist in respect of the study of science – which had originally in *Science, Technology and Society* been set very broadly – was narrowed to include only science's social institutions. Now science was studied with regard to the characteristic patterns of activity of scientists, their competitive co-operation, the rewards for which they strived, the norms that guided their behaviour and so on. In particular, the goal of scientific investigation was also specified from this perspective. Science was studied precisely to extend certified knowledge. 'The technical methods employed toward this end provide the relevant definition of knowledge: empirically confirmed and logically consistent statements of regularities (which are, in effect, predictions). The institutional imperatives (mores) derive from the goal and the methods. The entire structure of technical and moral norms implements the final objective.'[70]

With this formulation the sociological study of science is identified with the study of the behaviour of scientists and the determination of their social institutions. In the argument about the Puritan influence on science the exact relationship between society and science had remained unclear. We were told that Puritanism had sanctified the study of nature and that, furthermore, science could flourish only in certain societies; but more precise details remained untheorized. From the new perspective, a comprehensive theory of the social mediation of science was at last accessible, and both personal motives and institutional imperatives could be incorporated together. Additionally, an explanation could be provided for the impact of political change on the conduct and productivity of scientific research.

An assumption of course underlying this project is that it is indeed possible to identify for science a definite social structure. This Merton set out to justify by examining in detail some specific cultural aspects of science. For example, he asked about the attractions that science may offer its practitioners. 'These attractions are essentially twofold: generally prized opportunities of engaging in socially approved patterns of association with one's fellows and the consequent creation of cultural products which are esteemed by the group.'[71] The approbation of the latter, he claimed further, is distributed to scientists in the form of characteristic rewards for the performance of roles. These rewards are largely honorific and are meted out in accordance with accomplishment. 'When the institution operates effectively,' therefore, 'the augmenting of knowledge and the augmenting of personal fame go hand in hand; the institutional goal and the personal reward are tied together.'[72] From time to time, however, the institution gets out of control and the two objectives come into conflict. The culture of science 'can lead scientists to develop an extreme concern with recognition which is in turn the validation by peers of the worth of their work. Contentiousness, self-assertive claims, secretiveness lest one be forestalled, ... the occasional theft of ideas, ... the fabrication of data' – all these and others have occurred in the history of science. In the situation of stress 'all manner of adaptive behaviours are called into play, some of these being far beyond the mores of science.'[73]

The elaboration of these 'mores', in fact, forms a substantial project in its own right – and also probably the most controversial aspect of Merton's theory. In a famous paper published in 1942 he proposed that science was associated with an ethos incorporating four principal norms: universalism, communism, disinterestedness and organized scepticism.[74] These norms were said to regulate the behaviour of scientists and so to direct the course of research. They were claimed to possess a methodologic rationale; nevertheless they were 'binding, not only because they are procedurally efficient but because they are believed right and good. They are moral as well as technical prescriptions.'[75]

A detailed discussion of Merton's description of the ethos of science will not be given here; it will suffice for us merely to mention that in the ensuing debate both additional norms were suggested[76] and the existence of those asserted previously was questioned.[77] But however this debate might be resolved, it is important to recognize that the paradigm itself allowed Merton to elucidate several aspects of the society-science interaction. For instance, the value of organized scepticism may be converted, in the cultural domain, into iconoclasm: simply by its imperative to subject them to scrutiny, science may seem to challenge the validity of existing institutions.[78] More importantly, the social presuppositions of the practice of science can be specified. Science – it now appears – can flourish only where its abiding institutions are compatible with those of the existing cultural and political order. A political ethic may come into conflict with the scientific one and in these circumstances the pursuit of science may be curtailed, modified or even prevented altogether.[79] The harmony of Puritanism with science can also be understood in these terms; not only did the two come together in their utility for the developing economic order but also, crucially, as a condition of the possibility of their coexistence, their ethical systems coincided. In more recent times – for example in Nazi Germany – the harmony of science with the political order was replaced by an antagonism; in these circumstances its very existence became uncertain. In fact, modern opposition to science can be characterized more generally. 'In part, the anti-science movement derives from the conflict between the ethos of science and of other social institutions.... Conflict arises when the social effects of applying scientific knowledge are deemed undesirable, ... when the expansion of political or religious or economic authority limits the autonomy of the scientist, when anti-intellectualism questions the value and integrity of science and when non-scientific criteria of eligibility for scientific research are introduced.'[80]

These results, together with many others proposed by Merton, are suggestive and have certainly proved productive of further insights. Nevertheless, the whole discussion is marked by the most elementary and obvious deficiencies. The entire argument, for example, omits any reference to the substantive content of science, so that the possibility of an immanent social mediation within science is excluded a priori. The conception of science to which Merton holds is a rather caricatured one, in which science is distinguished by its demands for 'logical consistency' and 'adequate and reliable' empirical evidence.[81] In fact, his view comes close to the 'standard view of scientific knowledge' as it is summarized by Michael Mulkay:

From the perspective of the standard view, the natural world is to be regarded as real and objective. Its characteristics cannot be determined by the preferences or intentions of its observers. These characteristics can, however, be more or less faithfully

51

represented. Science is that intellectual enterprise concerned with providing an accurate account of the objects, processes and relationships occurring in the world of natural phenomena ... (The) basic empirical regularities can be expressed as universal and permanent laws of nature, which tell us what is always and everywhere the case. Unbiased, detached observation furnishes the evidence on which these laws are built. This accepted scientific knowledge, because it has satisfied ... impersonal, technical criteria of adequacy is independent of those subjective factors ... which might otherwise distort scientists' perception of the external world.[82]

Today, of course, many aspects of this 'standard view' are contested. Indeed, we have already seen that this holds particularly in relation to its central philosophical impulse – the acceptance of the perspective of objectivism. In the theory of science this issue has been debated widely in relation to a more limited question: the possibility of a dependence of observation on theory. However, even in regard to this restricted problem Merton's conception excludes so much as a serious consideration of its results, within the sociological reflection on science. This is not an insignificant consequence – especially if it in fact turns out to be true either that science embraces immanently a philosophical outlook or that in some other way the truth of its propositions depends on variables that are not exclusively empirical. Indeed, even Merton's own discussion of the ethos of science would come into question under such circumstances, for its conclusions claim to be derived from observation.

At the same time however, it must be recognized that the absence of a proper discussion of science itself is not merely a chance omission of Merton's work. Rather, it emerges from a deliberate strategy to delimit the sociological study of science by bracketing all such questions. Thus Merton writes at the beginning of his essay on 'The Normative Structure of Science':

Science is a deceptively inclusive word which refers to a variety of distinct though interrelated items. It is commonly used to denote (1) a set of characteristic methods by means of which knowledge is certified; (2) a stack of accumulated knowledge stemming from the application of those methods; (3) a set of cultural values and mores governing the activities termed scientific; or (4) any combination of the foregoing. We are here concerned in a preliminary fashion with the cultural structure of science, that is, with one limited aspect of science as an institution. Thus, we shall consider, not the methods of science, but the mores with which they are hedged about. To be sure, methodological canons are often both technical expedients and moral compulsives, but it is solely the latter which is our concern here. This is an essay in the sociology of science, not an excursion in methodology. Similarly we shall not deal with the substantive findings of sciences (hypotheses, uniformities, laws), except as these are pertinent to standardized social sentiments towards science. This is not an adventure in polymathy.[83]

Now the efficacy of such an approach is clear, for it makes possible precisely the kind of result to which we have adverted above. Nevertheless it is not altogether obvious that polymathy is the issue. Merton seeks to mark out the legitimate territory for a social theory of science – as he was also to attempt to do, more systematically, in the slightly later essay on the sociology of knowledge.[84] But it is not merely that alternative forms of explanation are possible – that, for example, the Hopi rain dance can be interpreted either as a vehicle for social cohesion or as an example of a particular series of images of knowledge which can themselves be functionally related to the socio-cultural milieu.[85] Rather, it may be that scientific knowledge itself, its conceptions and its methodological apparatus, are from the beginning deeply implicated in the social processes. That such a possibility cannot be excluded in advance emerges out of the discussions above, from *Dialectic of Enlightenment* to quantum theory and Weimar Germany. If this possibility indeed proves to be true then science and the practice of scientists cannot be conceived independently of each other – even for the purposes of an abstractive idealization preceding analysis. Under such circumstances the theory of nature itself would have to take into account the social variables, while conversely, in sociology, the institutional forms – of which Merton provides such a cogent description – would have to be considered in relation to the specific conceptual content of that theory.

For Merton the social intersection of science occurs through its pragmatic dimension – but through a pragmatics conceived strictly independently of truth, meaning and syntax. Thus any consideration of the correspondence between either science and philosophy or the formal structure of science and the social forms is excluded from his sociology in advance. Further, by presupposing the nature of science and, in particular, of scientific truth he limits his possible descriptions of the activities of scientists to purely formal terms. Here we mention only one consequence of this – the most critical.

53

While communication between scientists in the scientific community obviously cannot be ignored, it will from different perspectives nevertheless be interpreted in different ways. In one view communication appears in general as the very process within which the advent of meaning occurs. For functionalism however the meaning of science is extrinsic to it and so cannot be formed along with the theory itself, as would be the case if communication and meaning were coterminous. Thus communication can fulfill only the formal function of the transmission of information and an analysis of it will accordingly consist of no more than a description of the procedures associated with scientific publication: with criteria of choice of manuscripts applied by editors and referees[86] and their patterns of evaluation,[87] with status differences between manuscripts,[88] with institutionalization of the referee system[89] and so on.

The radical British scientists

Merton's theory contains an undeniable core of truth, attained nevertheless at the price of foreclosing fundamental questions bearing on the complex relationship between science and society. This is true equally of his account of the social influences in the development of science and his description of the practice of science. Previously, some divergent perspectives on the former problem were described; shortly the same will be done in relation to the latter. First however it is not inappropriate to observe in passing that if Merton accepted without argument the validity of objectivist science then he was nevertheless not the only one to do so. Indeed, this so-called 'standard view' of science and its presumed consequences for social policy have been widely adopted by even the most radical commentators. For example, this was precisely the case for a group of writers in many ways as different from Merton as they could possibly be. The British radical scientists of the 1930s and 1940s – who included such illustrious names as Haldane, Bernal, Needham, Hogben, Blackett and others besides – had become conscious of the misapplication of the results of science in the interests of destruction, class oppression and war. Through their 'Association of Scientific Workers' (which had, incidentally, existed from 1918, when it had been established with an explicitly socialist platform under the name of the 'National Union of Scientific Workers'),[90] they agitated for the introduction of a social policy that would regulate scientific research and ensure its redirection for more human ends. To be sure, many of them recognized an interdependence between science and the broader social configuration. As Bernal wrote in his important book *The Social Function of Science*: '(t)he relationships between science and society depend fundamentally on the principles of organization of society itself. Up till now in discussing science in all countries there have been the same basic social assumptions, those of capitalism.... Inside this structure autonomous traditions of religion, literature and science have grown up, but they are in the last instance dependent on their fitting in with the general scheme. They must effectively pay their way.... (Science's) main line of development has been determined by the needs, not of the great mass of the population, but of those producing for profit....'[91] However, for this very reason they conceived of the solution exclusively in terms of effective political measures. Thus Bernal wrote a little later, '(o)nly if the system is changed and production is made for public use instead of for private profit can ... the applications of science increase rapidly without the complications of unemployment and economic instability.'[92]

Science here is understood as external to society and scientific truth as a historical invariant. The political consequences of science are considered to derive entirely from phenomena extrinsic to its content. Thus science and social change are assumed to be related only by way of variations in government policy and the distribution of power. Because of their exemplary integrity and courage the British radical scientists of the thirties remain a source of optimism and strength for those, even today, still struggling for a more humane redirection of science.[93] Yet in their social writings, exactly like the more detached observers in sociology, these scientists resiled from any close scrutiny of the present content of science itself. Curiously, for sociologist and scientist alike objectivist science was accepted without question.

* * * * * *

There is much that is of interest in the contemporary sociology of science. In fact, this field now commands a vast and rapidly expanding literature on almost every aspect of scientific practice – in relation to all of which, furthermore, it is able to apply novel and pregnant insights. Nevertheless, we shall not devote a more extensive consideration to this subject here, for the present discussion was intended to achieve no more than the demarcation of a field of problems and the identification of some potentially fruitful hypotheses and concepts. At this point what is necessary is rather to pursue some of the issues that have been raised, but left unresolved, by the sociology of science – issues that are nevertheless of considerable importance for the development of a social theory of scientific knowledge; in particular, we refer to those problems which bear on the inner character of science itself and on its possible dependence on – or at least, its interrelationship with – the actual practice of science. These problems, of course, take us beyond what is conventionally regarded as the sociology of science; this is in spite of the fact (which we would like to emphasize) that their concerns do not deviate from those at the heart of social theory.

The philosophy of
science and social theory:
The contemporary debates

The major tendencies in what is commonly referred to as the sociology of science have ignored the structure and the content of science. In their deliberations on the theory of nature these theories have concentrated largely on the impact that has been exerted by the latter on society – or, at least, on the relationship between the two, insofar as this relationship can be described independently of the specific commitments of science itself. However as we have seen, evidence enough exists to justify at least a serious consideration of the additional hypo.hesis that the social phenomena actually infiltrate the theoretical forms; if this hypothesis proves to be true then the relationship between science and society may be more profound and more complex than was hitherto assumed. To be sure, along with many other insights, there is present in the work of Robert Merton a recognition that an adequate social theory of science must provide an account of the actual practice of scientists, although here only one aspect of such an account is provided. Left unconsidered are two moments of at least equal significance, the study of each of which would constitute a substantial research project in its own right: on the one hand, the phenomena with which the scientist deals and the operations that he performs in the process of judging, and on the other, the determinations imposed by the behaviour of the practitioners on the theoretical outcomes. Of these two projects the former would seek to trace the source of the results of science – including especially its meaning and its characteristic forms of truth – in the immanent context within which the scientist, considered as a conscious individual, is embedded; thus it would require an analysis of the modes of presentation of rational phenomena as well as of the structure of science. The development of such a theory – which thereby commences, it might be immediately observed, from a radically antiobjectivist perspective – has in fact constituted a major pre-occupation of phenomenology (that is, the body of thought deriving from the writings of Edmund Husserl) and will be discussed in some detail later. The latter project, by contrast, can be neither so readily delineated in its tasks nor so clearly illustrated with a perspicuous example from the existing theory. Nevertheless, both the need for such a project and the development of substantial results appropriate to it do emerge with growing force – albeit uneven recognition – in the contemporary philosophy of science. The basic problem to which this body of theory would devote itself would be that of the relationship between the structure of science and the cultural variables operative within either the scientific community or society as a whole; thus it is clear that the issues at stake would be of great importance for this essay. Accordingly, the present chapter will be devoted towards an examination of the extant philosophy of science, with a view to identifying themes and preliminary hypotheses that might help to make good the lacunae in the present theory.

Karl Popper: an early convergence between social theory and the philosophy of science

The unassailable pioneer of the contemporary convergence between social theory and the philosophy of science was Karl Popper. His theory of science, first proposed in *The Logic of Scientific Discovery*, published in 1934, and further elaborated in a number of essays, later to be collected and published as *Conjectures and Refutations*, established the basic perspective in relation to which much of the contemporary philosophy of science is situated.[1] To be sure, subsequent philosophers have subjected almost every detail of his work to strenuous criticism and it may be fairly said that some of his ideas have now been superseded. But the very attention that he has attracted and the fact that many of the later ideas emerged from a close scrutiny of his work only emphasizes his prominence.

The central idea of Popper's theory is the notion of falsification. This idea was introduced in order to deal with a number of problems with which Popper had been concerned – most conspicuously, the problems of induction[2] and what he called the 'problem of demarcation' – the identification of 'a suitable distinguishing mark'[3] of empirical science. The theory that had formerly commanded the most widespread support was that propounded by Carnap, Neurath and the remainder of the so-called 'Vienna Circle' of philosophers. Following Wittgenstein, these thinkers had adopted as the principle of scientificity of a theory the criterion of verifiability. Philosophical or metaphysical propositions, they claimed, were really only pseudo-propositions.[4] All genuine propositions, by contrast – such as those of the natural sciences[5] – were truth functions of the elementary propositions that described atomic facts – that is, facts which can in principle be ascertained by observation. 'In other words, meaningful propositions were fully reducible to elementary or atomic propositions which were simple statements describing possible states of affairs, and which could in principle be established or rejected by observation.'[6] In accordance with these ideas, Carnap had set out to develop the formal basis for a universal language of science in which every legitimate proposition of science would appear as a well-formed formula and from which all metaphysical statements would be automatically excluded. Such a language was intended to accomplish two things: on the one hand it would definitely banish from science not only metaphysics but also all subjective experiences – which were, incidentally, thus rendered at the same level; and on the other, it would convert all scientific statements, including those of psychology and the social sciences, into intersubjectively testable sentences of the thing-language.[7] This last point was of fundamental importance, for it embodied the claim that the basic predicates of the language of unified science are physical predicates which are both meaningful and testable.

Popper's objection to Carnap's programme was not merely that it had been decisively compromised at an early stage by the appearance of the famous results of Gödel.[8] He claimed further that in fact the entire project had been misconceived from the beginning. Popper, as we mentioned, was concerned with the problem of demarcating science. To this end, he examined the criterion of demarcation applied by the 'Vienna Circle' philosophers. Finding that this criterion was in fact identical to Wittgenstein's verifiability criterion, he was also able to recognize a fundamental mistake. For as he put it '(n)o scientific theory can ever be deduced from observation statements, or be described as a truth-function of observation statements.'[9] The argument he advanced in support of this proposition was as simple as it was convincing. The possible applications of a theory can never be exhausted experimentally. Thus, no matter how many positive decisions are obtained in the testing process, the possibility of a subsequent negative result can never be ruled out in principle. Therefore, the most that could be claimed for a scientific theory is that it has been 'corroborated' by past experience but not confirmed by it.

Although this conclusion was a simple one, its consequences were profound. In the first place, it implied that 'no such thing as induction' existed. But then also 'inference to theories, from singular statements which are "verified by experience" (whatever that may mean), is logically inadmissible. Theories are, therefore, *never* empirically verifiable. If we wish to avoid the positivist's mistake of eliminating ... the theoretical systems of natural science, then we must choose a criterion which allows us to admit to the domain of empirical science even statements which cannot be verified.'[10] In Popper's view, such a criterion is to be found not in the principle of *verifiability* but in that of *falsifiability* – the assertion that a theoretical system may be said to be scientific if it can in principle be not confirmed but *refuted* by experience.[11]

According to Popper, this is in fact exactly how science proceeds. 'A serious empirical test always consists of the attempt to find a refutation, a counter-example.'[12] The scientist begins with a theory that can be regarded as no more than a hypothesis or conjecture. He then seeks rigorously to refute that hypothesis through empirical experience. To the extent that no such refutation can be established it is provisionally accepted by the scientific community. Of course the absence of a disproof is not the only thing we demand of a theory; we require also – and more importantly – that it describe and explain the widest possible range of phenomena – that is, the theory must correspond in some way with the facts. But if the development of science is characterized by the constant process of the arising and passing away of theories, none can be said to apprehend the truth completely. Consequently, according to Popper, in speaking about scientific systems we can refer not to truth itself but only to 'degrees of verisimilitude'.[13] A greater verisimilitude is possessed by that theory which more closely approximates the truth – that is, which contains a larger 'truth content' and a smaller 'falsity-content'[14] – than its opponent. The development of science proceeds by the production of theories possessing a monotonically increasing verisimilitude. In short, it is not the accumulation of observations which occurs, but rather 'the repeated overthrow of scientific theories and their replacement by better or more satisfactory ones'.[15]

Popper's work claims to provide an adequate criterion by means of which the scientificity of a theory could be identified and – for the first time – a theory of scientific discovery itself. In fact, as we have just seen, for him the two occur together. Thus the distinguishing character of science emerges only in relation to the actual practice of scientists – or, put differently, to the 'social dimension' of science, where this last expression is understood to mean the behaviour exhibited by individual members of the scientific community. Now to argue thus is not by any means to imply that the theoretical aspect of science is thereby diminished. However it does suggest that the theory and the facts cannot be understood independently of each other. In fact, this is the central contention of the critique of the notion of induction that emerges from Popper's account of falsification. Previously, he had argued that induction was impossible because no verification of an hypothesis can occur on the basis of experience, but only its potential falsification. But if that were the case, then in scientific procedures facts could be apprehended only with the help of pre-existing theories. This is exactly what he now claims.

> Without waiting, passively, for repetitions to impress or impose regularities upon us, we actively try to impose regularities upon the world. We try to discover similarities in it, and to interpret it in terms of laws invented by us. Without waiting for premises we jump to conclusions. These may have to be discarded later, should observation show they are wrong. . . .
> (T)he belief that we can start with pure observation alone, without anything in the nature of a theory, is absurd. It needs a chosen object, a definite task, an interest, a point of view, a problem. . . .[16]

Science starts with problems and not with observations;[17] on the contrary, observations themselves presuppose a theory. The observations may certainly be shown subsequently to contradict the original hypotheses that give rise to them – or more precisely, the 'basic statements' associated with the observation may contradict the statement of the theory.[18] However, even in this case a new theory is required in order for us to be able to recognize where the old theory was deficient.[19] Facts and theories cannot be dissociated and, in science, both must be conceived in relation to the conduct of enquiry.

Briefly then, according to Popper, the scientificity of a theory depends upon the place occupied by the statements of that theory in the behavioural system described by the community of scientists; in particular, if the relationship of statements to the formalized experience of the testing procedure is one of conjecture and refutation, then scientificity is guaranteed. Even prior to this however, what might be called 'social' phenomena enter into the construction of a science, for the facts themselves exist only for observers and *then* only in relation to theories – that is, only in relation to a pre-existing intersubjective apparatus. Merton, of course, had also recognized that what scientists did was important for the social consequences of science. Popper for his part accepts this view and adds the much stronger converse that exactly what scientists do, broadly speaking, is what constitutes science in the first place. On the other hand, however, Merton – as we saw – assumed that the content of science was irrelevant to the sociological phenomena associated with it – a claim with which Popper vigorously disagrees. Certainly, it is clear enough from what we have already said that Popper conceives of the activity of the scientist in more than a merely technical sense; elsewhere he is quick to assert additionally the existence of ethical imperatives of wide application emerging from what he considers to be the inherently anti-totalitarian procedure of science.[20]

These last matters however refer to separate issues which will not be pursued here. What is important for the subsequent discussion is just the central major point that has been stressed above: in Popper's work, once again, is adumbrated an intersection between social theory and the study of science and furthermore, in this case the intersection is discovered in that dimension within which science is actually practised. Presently some reference will be made to the critique of Popper's ideas that has been developed within social theory, with a view to developing an assessment of this aspect of his work. Before doing this, however, it will be useful to turn to a brief consideration of the other component of the critical rationalist theory of science – its study of science's actual structure.

Thomas Kuhn: the unity of science and the enigma of change

The most important current critic of Popper is Thomas Kuhn. His book, *The Structure of Scientific Revolutions*, first published in 1962, has been widely read and discussed, its influence being felt in the humanities and social sciences as well as in the philosophy of science itself. Although the actual references to Popper in this book are few – indeed Kuhn himself claims to have read none of the latter's work prior to writing it[21] – the book has been interpreted frequently as a direct attack on the so-called 'Popperian methodology'. Certainly, in several respects Kuhn's arguments are in fundamental disagreement with Popper's claims, but it should be realized that at the same time there are many equally fundamental convergences. Kuhn, in a later article, even lists some of the concerns he shares with Popper.

> Both of us reject the view that science progresses by accretion; both emphasize instead the revolutionary process by which an older theory is rejected and replaced by an incompatible new one; and both deeply underscore the role played in this process by the older theory's occasional failure to meet challenges posed by logic, experiment, or observation. Finally, Sir Karl and I are united in opposition to a number of classical positivism's most characteristic theses. We both emphasize, for example, the intimate and inevitable entanglement of scientific observation with scientific theory; we are correspondingly sceptical of efforts to produce any neutral observation language; and we both insist that a scientist may properly aim to invent theories that *explain* observed phenomena and that do so in terms of real objects, whatever the latter phrase may mean.[22]

We shall return shortly to the similarities between the arguments of Popper and Kuhn. Regarding their differences, the dominant issue at stake is the actual process by which science progresses. For Popper, science is in a state of permanent revolution fuelled by unrelenting criticism. By contrast, for Kuhn, revolution is an exceptional circumstance – indeed an extra-scientific one – while criticism is specifically excluded in the normal course of scientific work, only becoming important as the science enters a period of 'crisis'. For the most part, Kuhn argued, scientists within a given discipline work at 'normal science',[23] which is characterized by the broad acceptance by the scientific community of stable fundamental principles designating the forms of problems to be solved, the kinds of available solutions, the methods to be applied in examining them and so on. During these periods of normal science – which, incidentally, account for by far the greatest part of the history of science – the questions at issue therefore do not concern the elementary constitutive precepts of the science, as had been assumed by Popper. Rather, they are of the form of 'puzzles' – mere technical problems generated, and thus theoretically circumscribed, by these precepts.[24] Hence Kuhn rejected Popper's contention that science progresses according to the procedure of conjecture followed by refutation. In fact, he argued, within the life of a given paradigm – as he called the series of principles organizing a discipline at a particular time – evidence always abounds to refute the current theories, but this evidence is either accommodated into the existing framework by elaborate explanations or else it is simply dismissed as an 'aberration'.[25] Regarding specific instances of falsification, Kuhn doubted that they even existed at all.[26]

For the most part then, according to Kuhn, science consists of long periods during which its practitioners work at the exacting and tedious task of solving puzzles. Here, change is gradual and cumulative, as 'the accepted beliefs of the scientific community are fleshed out, articulated and extended'.[27] However, from time to time the history of science is punctuated by short periods of sharper, more dramatic change. Under the impact of mounting technical problems, social pressures and even philosophical innovations the old paradigm starts to lose its credibility and the entire discipline it commands enters into a crisis. The exact details of the changes that now occur are unclear; indeed, it may be that in principle no detailed account of them can be given. Nevertheless the outcome is clearly apprehensible: the old paradigm is given up altogether and replaced by another (usually pre-existing) one. Thus the most basic conceptual commitments of the science are fundamentally transformed; a 'scientific revolution' has taken place. For the scientists themselves the change is also fundamental – they experience an alteration of their world-view in a manner similar to a 'gestalt switch',[28] which is often also a source of considerable personal excitement. Once the modifications in the paradigm have been accepted however, the excitement subsides and the work of resolving the multitude of technical problems generated by the new theories is resumed; 'normal science', that is to say, begins again.

Paul Feyerabend: incommensurability and the goals of science

There are certainly problems with Kuhn's theory as he has elaborated it. The notion of 'paradigm', for example, is now the subject of a substantial literature and the actual processes involved in 'crisis' and 'revolution' remain controversial. Nevertheless it can be said that the theory in its general outline has gained widespread acceptance – a fact that can be judged from the circumstance that its basic hypotheses are accepted by even its most vigorous critics. A case in point is that of Paul Feyerabend, who takes issue with Kuhn's account of 'normal science' – and indeed also, equally trenchantly, with that of Popper. At the same time, however, he achieves a significant development of some of the central ideas of Kuhn's theory. For example, he elaborates in detail the essentially Kuhnian idea of 'incommensurability', according to which 'the content classes of certain theories' can be incomparable 'in the sense that none of the usual logical relations (inclusion, exclusion, overlap) can be said to hold between them'.[29] In the Popperian schema it had been assumed that competing theories could always be compared with respect to their content and, indeed, arranged linearly in accordance with increasing verisimilitude. Further, Popper had argued, scientific investigation always starts with a problem and proceeds by solving it. If, however, science progresses through a series of revolutionary 'ruptures' in the accepted theoretical contexts, such a procedure could not be possible; for then different theories could address different problems from different perspectives and with different methodological tools. In fact, as Feyerabend demonstrates, 'frameworks of thought' exist which are incommensurable;[30] consequently, 'the views of scientists, and especially their views on basic matters, are often as different from each other as are the ideologies that underlie different cultures.' 'Even worse,' Feyerabend goes on,

> there exist scientific theories which are mutually incommensurable though they apparently deal 'with the same subject matter'. Not all competing theories have this property and those which have the property have it only as long as they are interpreted in a special way, for example, without reference to an 'independent observation language'. The illusion that we are dealing with the same subject matter arises in these cases as a result of an unconscious confusion of two different types of interpretation. Using an 'instrumentalistic' interpretation of the theories which sees in them no more than instruments for the classification of certain 'facts' one gets the impression that there is some common subject matter. Using a 'realistic' interpretation that tries to understand the theory in its own terms such a subject matter seems to disappear although there is the definite feeling (unconscious instrumentalism) that it must exist.[31]

A scientific theory then, in Feyerabend's view, is not just a mere series of conjectures about the world. Rather, it is embedded in a comprehensive theoretical framework which designates in advance certain crucial possibilities open to natural phenomena. In this sense, the context within which a science is inscribed functions something like a language. Feyerabend quotes Benjamin Lee Whorff: 'the background linguistic system (in other words, the grammar) of each language is not merely a reproducing system of voicing ideas, but rather is itself a shaper of ideas, the programme and guide for the individual's mental activity, for his analysis of impressions, for his synthesis of his mental stock in trade.'[32] Similarly, he himself argues that the formal aspects of a theory may convey ontological consequences[33] and that indeed '(w)ithin the sciences incommensurability is closely connected with meaning'.[34] Against Popper's claim then that science proceeds by proposing a problem and then solving it, Feyerabend rejoins that it may also occur that problems are not *solved* but rather *dissolved* in the formulations of a new theory. For in the latter the properties of things and processes that had constituted fundamental categories for its predecessor may simply appear no longer to exist.[35] Thus ontological change and conceptual change occur together. 'The discovery that certain entities do not exist may prompt the scientist to re-describe the events, processes, observations which were thought to be manifestations of them and which were therefore described in terms assuming their existence.'[36] At times, the consequences of this transformation may be extensive – for example, when the elements of the erstwhile ontology had been thought to have been present in every process in a certain domain. 'In *this* case, *every* description inside the domain must be changed and must be replaced by a different statement (or by no statement at all). Classical physics is a case in point.' The conceptual system of relativity theory, for instance, 'does not just *deny* the existence of classical states of affairs, it does not even permit us to *formulate statements* expressing such states of affairs. ... Other examples are the quantum theory vs. classical mechanics, the impetus theory vs. Newton's mechanics, materialism vs. mind-body dualism, and so on.'[37]

Many of Feyerabend's other conclusions follow largely from these results. Several of these are of great importance for the contemporary philosophy of science. However, in spite of their intrinsic interest, for reasons of space and immediate relevance in the present context, they will not be elaborated in detail here. Instead, it will suffice for our purposes merely to mention a few of the most conspicuous conclusions. For example, Feyerabend developed Kuhn's insight that a precondition for the rejection of a given theory is the existence of competing theories – which is also thereby a precondition for progress in science. Now this result is clearly in direct contradiction to Popper's contentions; indeed it seeks to translate the entire focus of inquiry from the putative logic of investigation to exogenous theoretical and even social circumstances. On the other hand, however, Feyerabend at the same time proposes a theory of perception that could be regarded as decidedly Popperian, for it emphasizes particularly the 'theory-ladenness' of observation.[38] To be sure, Feyerabend places greater stress on this aspect than did his predecessors, claiming even that observation has a historical character and that it may depend on hidden assumptions, theories otherwise regarded as obsolete, unconscious expectations, and so on.[39] We shall return to this point presently; we mention it here only in order to be able to repeat another of his substantive conclusions. If a theory is susceptible to criticism then new observations must be available – themselves deeply theoretical. But equally possible is the opposite alternative: a more adequate theory may be rejected for the simple reason that the appropriate forms of observation are not yet accessible.

It is exactly at this point that one of the major differences between Feyerabend and Kuhn emerges. The point at issue is nothing less than the nature of normal science. For Feyerabend, the aim of science is discovery and change. Given the conclusions described above, he maintains that this aim could be effectively promoted only if within society a broad diversity of opinions and heterogeneity of perspectives were encouraged – that is, only if a proliferation of theories was not only tolerated but actively fostered, including those theories currently regarded as false.[40] The gravamen of his objection to Kuhn's account is thus clear:

> Whenever I read Kuhn, I am troubled by the following question: are we here presented with methodological prescriptions which tell the scientist how to proceed; or are we given a description, void of any evaluative element, of those activities which are generally called 'scientific'? Kuhn's writings, it seems to me, do not lead to a straightforward answer. They are ambiguous in the sense that they are compatible with, and lend support to, both interpretations. Now this ambiguity ... is not at all a side issue. It has had quite a definite effect on Kuhn's readers ... The recipe, according to these people, is to restrict criticism, to reduce the number of comprehensive theories to one, and to create a normal science that has this one theory as its paradigm. Students must be prevented from speculating along different lines and the more restless colleagues must be made to conform and 'to do serious work'. *Is this what Kuhn wants to achieve?*[41]

It is interesting to observe that a very similar complaint is also articulated by Popper earlier in the same book. ' "Normal" science,' writes Popper, 'in Kuhn's sense, exists ...'

That it is a phenomenon which I dislike (because I regard it as a danger to science) while he apparently does not dislike it (because he regards it as 'normal') is another question; admittedly a very important one. In my view, the 'normal' scientist, as Kuhn describes him, is a person one might be sorry for ... The 'normal' scientist, in my view, has been taught badly ...

I believe, however, that Kuhn is mistaken when he suggests that what he calls 'normal' science is normal.[42]

* * * * * *

These brief considerations illustrate a few of the major issues in the controversy involving Popper, Kuhn, Feyerabend and others which constitutes one of the central features of the recent philosophy of science. As we said, the debate in question is of great interest; however, to follow it further would take us beyond the main concerns of the present argument. Accordingly, it will not be elaborated in greater detail. We refer to it here to show the kind of discussion currently being conducted in this field and to display the nature of the disagreements that still occur following what we have referred to as an overall acceptance of Kuhn's theory; in addition, it raises a number of more general questions that we shall have to take up later. For example, there is the question of the actual character of normal science – obviously a major substantive issue. But also, and perhaps more importantly, there is the question of just what an account of science should seek to achieve. Should such an account, as Kuhn claims, merely provide a description of the present practice of science? Or should it be essentially prescriptive, seeking to promote some putative 'aims of science', as is the case for Popper and Feyerabend? Should the theory of science attempt to intervene in the process of the development of science? Or would it merely, by recapitulating the features of 'industrialized science',[43] be thereby providing the latter with an imprimatur it otherwise lacks – thus intervening by subterfuge in any case? This is not a small issue, as we shall see when we come to examine the question of the objectivism of modern science, at which point we shall encounter directly the great and pregnant problem of whether it is part of the job of the theory of science to provide suggestions for philosophical new departures within science.

A third – and final – question that is raised implicitly by this debate is also fundamental. Kuhn himself, in formulations that could apply not only to the theory of nature but at the same time equally to its metatheory, argues that social and psychological variables enter into the construction of a paradigm. Now Popper and Feyerabend, at the least, announce openly their own personal political perspectives and seek quite consciously to incorporate these perspectives into their theories. Furthermore, the accounts of what might at first be assumed to be an unambiguous, common object – that is, science – differ markedly and fundamentally from author to author. The question arises: to what extent do historical, social and other extrinsic factors determine the *metatheory* of science, with respect either to the issues of which it treats or to the methods it applies? Now, to raise this issue is not to be merely querulous. For the development of a theory of the social determinants and commitments of science immediately provokes the problem of the reflexivity of the metacontext. In addition, as we shall see, this question is involved in the problem of the relationship between theory and facts – also a major issue for the critique of objectivism. We recall that this matter was a central one for the argument of *Dialectic of Enlightenment*. Although in the latter work, to be sure, the problem was expressed in slightly different terms, it nevertheless remained essentially the same: what is the relationship between the theory of nature and the modes according to which it is interpreted? Or equally: what is the relationship between science and its socially produced meaning? Regarding Popper and Kuhn, this question is certainly not an innocent one, as Habermas has argued. In an analysis which will be considered below, the last author rediscovered the verdict which the earlier work had made in relation to science in general: science contaminates the theoretical forms of society and, accordingly, to a substantial degree circumscribes its own meaning.[44] From this problem therefore, as from the previous one – the problem of the aims of a theory of science – we can conclude that the ways in which science and its interpretations affect each other must be clarified in any adequate social theory of science.

Implications of the debate

Many important differences separate the perspectives of the three authors to whom we have been referring. Nevertheless it appears that a number of major conclusions bearing on the problem of a social theory of science emerges from the debate. These conclusions command general assent among the protagonists, although they are formulated by them in sharply differing ways. We mention in particular three especially important ones.

In the first place, a major innovation of the new philosophy of science derives from Kuhn's introduction of the notion of a *paradigm*. There is, it must be admitted, much confusion regarding the actual meaning of this term, around which a considerable literature has in fact accumulated.[45] It has been claimed, for example, that in *The Structure of Scientific Revolutions* the word 'paradigm' is used in no fewer than twenty-one different senses (although of course not all of them inconsistent);[46] these uses are said to encompass metaphysical, sociological and instrumental descriptions of scientific work.[47] However, in spite of such problems, the general idea underlying the concept in question remains clear and compelling: from the history of science it is apparent that scientific theories can be clarified according to broad unifying principles. The relation thus defined on the set of all scientific theories may not be an equivalence relation, but nevertheless a series of classes can be described which define an abiding structural unity and within which individual theories cohere. Progress and change can occur both within and between classes. The major scientific innovations however have usually involved the elaboration of a new class altogether. Now the existence of such a relation or series of relations defining unified classes for scientific theories is generally accepted today – thanks at least in part to Kuhn's pioneering work – even though the particular ways in which these relations are conceived vary widely. In addition to Kuhn's different senses referred to above, for example, is the more strictly epistemological usage of Feyerabend and Lakatos's conception of a research programme (from which, in fact, Feyerabend, with the help of the notion of incommensurability, developed his own conception). Even Popper in his later writings has adopted a related idea. Although earlier he had written that we do not 'need any definite frame of reference for our criticism',[48] in his contribution to *Criticism and the Growth of Knowledge*, where he attempts to refute a notion he attributes (not necessarily with accuracy) to Kuhn, that ' "normally" we have one dominant theory – a "paradigm" – in each scientific domain',[49] he adopts a rather different view. For there, he speaks with ease about 'different frameworks',[50] 'competing frameworks', and so on, within which contending theories occur. Here, it seems, the existence of 'paradigms' – that is of 'mode(s) of explanation ... considered so satisfactory by some scientists that they demand (their) general acceptance'[51] – is taken for granted; what is assumed to be at issue is instead merely the possibility of 'rational discussion between frameworks'.[52]

In fact, a close examination of Popper's writings reveals that, at least from time to time, in relatively early works he employed related concepts. To mention just one example, he occasionally made reference to the notion of an 'horizon of expectations', a concept he explained as follows:

> at any instant of our pre-scientific or scientific development we are living in the centre of what I usually call a 'horizon of expectations'. By this I mean the sum total of our expectations, whether these are subconscious or conscious, or perhaps even explicitly stated in some language. Animals and babies have also their various and different horizons of expectations, though no doubt on a lower level of consciousness than, say, a scientist, whose horizon of expectations consists to a considerable extent of linguistically formulated theories or hypotheses.... Yet in all these cases the horizon of expectations plays the part of a frame of reference: only their setting in this frame confers meaning or significance on our experiences, actions and observations.[53]

A second conclusion appeared in a developed form already in Popper's work. This is the conclusion that in empirical science in general, facts can be apprehended only in relation to theories. In Kuhn's version, of course, the latter were replaced by more extensive entities, paradigms; within these, facts were said to be organized into broad, coherent unities. Later, the idea was further refined by Feyerabend, who stressed particularly the theoretically and historically contingent nature of observation – and indeed, even of perception. In more recent works still, many other authors have contributed to the discussion, helping to elucidate a number of the considerable perplexities raised in it.[54] Many problems remain, of course, in relation to the particular issues at stake here; for example, the actual details of the relationship between fact and theory even now awaits a satisfactory elaboration. Nevertheless, it can fairly be said that broad agreement has been reached that it must be accepted that in some sense empirical statements are 'theory-laden'.[55]

Finally, there is an outcome of Kuhn's work which, while closely related to the two preceding ones, even more than the previous two conclusions carried the clearest possible consequences for social theory. As was argued above, implicit in Popper's account of science was the contention that the nature of science was established at least partially in the regular patterns of behaviour exhibited by scientists – that is, that a fundamental interaction of science with society occurred in what we have referred to above as 'the pragmatic dimension of science'. With Kuhn however, this stress in the philosophy of science on the social aspect of the latter for the first time became explicit. Certainly the motivation for this emphasis is not difficult to find in the remainder of Kuhn's theory. An essential and elementary aspect of a paradigm – regardless of the sense in which it is intended – is that it commands acceptance among scientists. Thus, if a conception of paradigm is to be possible at all then we must be able to appeal to some conception of a community of scientists within which communication and, perhaps, consensus, might be realized. In fact, Kuhn argues:

> the term 'paradigm' enters in close proximity, both physical and logical, to the phrase 'scientific community'.... A paradigm is what the members of a scientific community, and they alone, share. Conversely, it is their possession of a common paradigm that constitutes a scientific community of a group of otherwise disparate men.... If the term 'paradigm' is to be successfully explicated, scientific communities must first be recognized as having an independent existence.[56]

Within scientific communities, thus characterized, professional communication occurs relatively unproblematically and professional judgement can be relatively unanimous.[57] Hence, 'a scientific community functions as a producer and validator of sound knowledge.'[58]

Now at first sight this approach appears somewhat similar to those much earlier sociological works which also stressed the importance of consensus and communication within science.[59] However, in relation to these works, Kuhn's perspective is indeed new and different since, for the first time, it demonstrates a fundamental interdependence between the technical matter of science and the social field. On the one hand, he argues, 'the emergence of the paradigm affects the structure of the group that practises in the field'.[60] On the other, 'one of the things that a scientific community acquires with a paradigm is a criterion for choosing problems that, while the paradigm is taken for granted, can be assumed to have solutions.' In fact, such problems, and only such problems, will normally be admitted as scientific; thus a paradigm can 'even, insulate the community from those socially important problems that are not reducible to the puzzle form, because they cannot be stated in terms of the conceptual and instrumental tools the paradigm supplies'.[61] These insights have been widely recognized as important landmarks in the development of a sociological theory of science by sociologists disaffected with the superficiality of the conception of science employed in much extant work. As one writer has justly put it:

> (t)he profound influence that Thomas Kuhn's work has begun to exert upon sociologists stems from the insights it offers into research as a social process. Put in sociological terms, Kuhn's thesis is that technical, esoteric models of procedure and interpretation are maintained within particular disciplines and provide the basis for both the practice and evaluation of research. The open rational mind is not the ideal instrument for recognizing a scientific truth, as empiricist philosophers and sociologists would have it, rather an elaborately prepared conceptual and procedural frame of reference is essential. By pointing to the paradigmatic assumptions of scientists, and the way they define cohesive groups of researchers, Kuhn offers a sociological approach to the research process.[62]

This having been said however, it must also be observed that, taken from the perspective of social theory, Kuhn's account contains many deficiencies. Despite the emphasis on communication and 'rules' for example (eminently 'social' variables), no attempt is made there to provide a coherent analysis of these or similar entities. Indeed, the analysis of the scientific community itself in Kuhn's work is no more than rudimentary – although to be sure, in several passages of *The Structure of Scientific Revolutions* some intimation is made of a value system not unlike that proposed by Merton.[63]

Problems also arise in relation to the account that Kuhn gives of the history of science. Regarding this issue, it is his view that early in the development of a new field 'social needs and values are a major determinant of the problems on which its practitioners concentrate';[64] later however – he maintains – when a science has achieved maturity this situation is altered and the relationship to society is severed. At this stage, the scientists constitute a special subculture 'effectively insulated from the cultural milieu'; the problems on which the practitioners work no longer bear reference to the wider society but only to internal imperatives of the discipline itself. In fact, '(t)o an extent unparalleled in other fields, the developments of an individual technical speciality can be understood without going beyond the literature of that speciality and a few of its near neighbours.'[65]

Elsewhere, Kuhn has written that '(w)hatever scientific progress may be, we must account for it by examining the nature of the scientific group, discovering what it values, what it tolerates, and what it disdains.'[66] Now, this statement certainly stands in an apparent conflict with the quotation in the previous sentence. However for our present purposes what is of greater interest is rather the *continuity* between the two assertions. There is a constant assumption underlying Kuhn's entire argument here: the assumption that it is possible in the first place to conceive of science and society as essentially independent entities, the relationship between which can subsequently be raised for consideration. The point involved here is not a minor one. Indeed, the presupposition to which we are referring pervades all of Kuhn's writings; its effect is to beg the vital question of the interchange between society and science. Thus it makes little difference that, following the recognition of the theory-dependence of observation and of the fact that scientific theories are themselves subject to unifying regularities, an attempt is made to effect some degree of rapprochement between the two. For in Kuhn's argument the reconciliation of the two terms can be conceived only as the outcome of the operation of extrinsic contingencies. According to his view scientific endeavour is *not* to be understood as immanently a social activity in which (like in every other theoretical endeavour) men struggle together to establish the meaning of the world. If such a perspective as this last one had in fact been adopted it would have become necessary to develop in detail an explication of the intersubjectively-generated meaning structures in relation to which the actual scientific productions could be said to acquire their intelligibility; hence from this viewpoint the content of science would have been taken to be more than merely technical; further, the paradigms of the latter would then appear similarly to be inherently social, rather than mere haphazard collections of phenomena coexisting in some putative 'cultural milieu'. Such a view would evidently have significant advantages; nevertheless, neither it nor any similar approach was ever developed in Kuhn's work. For him, if an interchange occurs between society and science its locus is not community or sociality as such; rather, such an interchange is to be understood by means of no more than the empirical characteristics of the contemporaneous scientific community.

We shall return presently to the major issue involved here, which is raised again forcefully in Habermas's critique of Popper. For the moment, we quickly conclude the present part of the discussion by mentioning with great brevity a number of additional consequences of the viewpoint adopted by Kuhn. In the first place, it is evident that a major issue raised by Kuhn's account of science concerns the motor of revolutionary change and the meaning of this change for individual scientists. However, despite having raised the issue,

Kuhn's theory cannot supply a satisfactory answer. For it can provide no convincing explanation of why an accepted paradigm is given up and another adopted in its place. A crisis, Kuhn argues, is largely precipitated by internal difficulties accumulating within a paradigm and the most common claim in favour of the new perspective is that it resolves some of these outstanding difficulties. But as he further points out, while such a claim can certainly at times be upheld it is rarely sufficient, and, what is more, it cannot always legitimately be made.[67] Rather, he maintains instead, '(i)ndividual scientists embrace a new paradigm for all sorts of reasons and usually for several at once'.[68] These reasons may depend upon idiosyncrasies of autobiography and personality;[69] they may depend on the individual's sense of 'the appropriate or the aesthetic',[70] they may depend on 'the wish' of a man trained as a puzzle-solver 'to preserve as many as possible of the prior puzzle-solutions obtained by his group',[71] and so on. In other words, from this perspective, the explanation for change ultimately falls to psychology – that is to say, it is held that an account of the origins of and the processes involved in the periodic massive shifts in theoretical perspective must be sought in the psychologies of individual scientists belonging to the scientific community. In fact, as we have mentioned previously, Kuhn himself frequently repeats his own description of the experience of a scientist undergoing such a change as a 'gestalt switch'.[72]

Rather than embark on a detailed critique of these claims, we shall simply quote a passage from Lakatos, who reviewed the consequences of this aspect of Kuhn's theory. In Kuhn's view, according to Lakatos,

there can be no logic but only a psychology of discovery. For instance, in Kuhn's conception, anomalies, inconsistencies *always* abound in science, but in 'normal' periods the dominant paradigm secures a pattern of growth which is eventually overthrown by a 'crisis'. There is no particular rational cause for the appearance of a Kuhnian 'crisis'. 'Crisis' is a psychological concept; it is a contagious panic. Then a new 'paradigm' emerges, incommensurable with its predecessor. There are no rational standards for their comparison. Each paradigm contains its own standards. The crisis sweeps away not only the old theories and rules but also the standards which made us respect them. The new paradigm brings a totally new rationality. There are no super-paradigmatic standards. The change is a bandwagon effect. Thus in Kuhn's view scientific revolution is irrational, a matter for mob psychology.[73]

This matter will not be pursued further here.[74] It is certainly true that there exists a vast distance between the objective, reliable logic of scientific discovery proposed by Popper and the haphazard series of subjective accidents invoked by Kuhn in his theory of scientific change. Furthermore, the distance is similar which separates Popper's claims discussed above that science develops in the direction of increasing truth-content and Kuhn's belief that no objective truth exists at all. But which of these two views is correct? This is a deep question, with extensive and profound implications, to which no definitive answer can presently be given. Here we suggest merely that one possibility which deserves consideration is that in fact no decision on this question *can* be made exclusively within the history of science. This view is made plausible by the circumstance that the matters involved are not factual ones in the trivial sense: they embrace social meanings, understood most broadly, including, in particular, changing perceptions of the relation between society and the natural world – and even of the nature of truth. However, much argument remains to be adduced in relation to this hypothesis; if it does prove able to be sustained successfully then we may conclude that a resolution of the dilemma we have mentioned will have to await a clarification of the philosophical content of science – or, equivalently, the development of an authentic social theory of scientific knowledge.

Habermas and the positivism dispute

In our efforts so far to gather issues, problems and hypotheses for an investigation of the relationship between natural science and social phenomena we have encountered three broad regions of concern. First, in our consideration of *Dialectic of Enlightenment* we examined its very radical claims that science commits itself to a definite philosophical content – to objectivism, in the case of modern Western science – by means of which it penetrates the social forms and consequently may even influence in advance the categories that are applied to interpret it. Second, a number of studies in the sociology of science suggested that the global phenomena of society – economy, culture, religion, etc. – may be implicated in the processes of scientific development and change. Third, in the discussion of Karl Popper and the contemporary philosophy of science, the hypothesis was encountered that the nature of science is indissolubly linked to its practice of inquiry so that what had hitherto been considered narrowly social in character was now seen to enter immanently into the structure of science itself. Regarding Popper in particular, we observed that there is to this theory a social moment and a structural moment, and we proceeded to examine the latter. As was observed, many profound and suggestive results have emerged from the studies of Kuhn, Feyerabend and others, who have also applied themselves to develop and to criticize the perspective established by Popper. However, another outcome of this discussion that has also become apparent cannot escape comment: that even the most technical debates about the structure of science cannot avoid reverting to references to the 'scientific community' and to the 'behaviour' of scientists.

At this point, an obvious question to ask concerns the consistency of the three groups of hypotheses. In relation to Kuhn's theory there seems – at least at first sight – to be no obvious difficulty. One version of the concept of paradigm identifies the latter with a given epistemological perspective. If this usage were adopted then, without loss of consistency, Kuhn's argument could be extended to encompass an epistemological variation with respect to social phenomena; in addition, it would be postulated that there exists a particular paradigm marked by objectivism. Regarding Popper, he of course rejects Kuhn's relativism in favour of his own unitary schema, thus excluding any such epistemological variability; nevertheless, even for him a fundamental concordance obtains between liberal capitalist society and critical rationalism. In consequence, we can say that, in terms of the existing theories, it appears that great problems are presented neither by the historical transformations exhibited by science nor by the possibility that these may be dependent upon social and cultural contingencies.

On the other hand, however, real difficulties do arise when the actual details of the social mediation within science are sought. Indeed, in the authors we have considered no systematic consideration of this question is even attempted; consequently, their discussions fail to advance beyond broad generalizations concerning the scientific community. In Popper's work in fact this 'social dimension' never becomes more than merely implicit,[75] whereas Kuhn provides nothing more substantial than broad generalizations regarding psychology in order to explain social phenomena. Now there can be no doubt that the discovery of the 'theory-ladenness' of facts is a major insight in the philosophical understanding of science – and it would seem to provide a potentially powerful weapon for both the further development of the critique of objectivism that had been initiated by Horkheimer and Adorno and the analysis of the social contribution to scientific knowledge. However, neither such a critique nor such an analysis has emerged within any of the philosophical schools we have discussed – a circumstance which, in view of the powerful developments that have occurred, would seem to be quite remarkable. Accordingly, the questions arise of the reasons for this deficiency and of whether it derives from fundamental sources.

In this context we would like to refer to some objections to Popper's philosophy that have been raised by Jürgen Habermas in a famous exchange that has become known as the 'positivist dispute in sociology.'[76] In this debate, it is Habermas's major contention that, despite the results we have quoted, and despite also Popper's vigorous claims to the contrary, the work of the latter is deeply objectivistic. Before proceeding to explicate Habermas's argument, we add the simple observation that if this view is in fact correct then there are substantial implications to be drawn for our own study. In particular, a task worthy of considerable sustained work has been identified: the task of characterizing the specific philosophical content of science and of elucidating the relationship involving this content, the structure of science and its social determinations.

We turn now to a brief exposition of Habermas's point of view, insofar as it touches the concerns of this essay. The actual target of Habermas's attacks in the debate in question, it must be admitted at once, is not specifically objectivism, but rather an inherent positivism that he claims to detect in Popper's position. Notwithstanding this it is necessary to recognize that the meaning of the word 'positivism' is not carefully defined by Habermas in any of his contributions – as indeed is the case for all the other protagonists. Nevertheless from Habermas's other work his own meaning is clear. In *Knowledge and Human Interests* for example, he stated that '(p)ositivism stands and falls with the principle of scientism, that is, that the meaning of knowledge is defined by what the sciences do and can thus be adequately explicated through the methodological analysis of scientific procedures.'[77] Now such a notion is not useful for the present discussion, for which both the meanings and the structure of science are in fact principal problems. Further, objection will be taken later to Habermas's own conception of science as inscribed irrevocably within a cognitive interest in technical control. Consequently, in what follows no attempt will be made to reproduce faithfully his actual reasoning. Instead, his arguments will be reconstructed in relation to the particular problems that have emerged hitherto in the discussion of Popper's philosophy and additionally, in the brief consideration of Kuhn's work. Indeed it seems to us – and as we shall try to show – that Habermas's writings provide an incisive critique of the major strengths and weaknesses of the theories proposed by both authors.

To come directly to the central issue with which Habermas deals: a fundamental problem for Popper is that presented by 'basic' (or 'protocol') statements. These are the sentences which report observational data and thus define the locus of the contact between experience and theory. For Carnap the protocol statements had been the vehicles for the representation of experience: they referred to the 'given', to the 'sense-date', thus describing 'the contents of immediate experience, or the phenomena; and thus the simplest knowable facts'.[78]

They were to be deployed, of course, in the proposed endeavour of verifying a theory. Popper however, as we know, rejected the idea of verification. Accordingly, for the tests sanctioned by his theory what was required was no more or less than a series of elementary reports about empirical states of affairs. Hence the basic statements chosen by him were just 'singular existential statements';[79] that is, 'statements asserting that an observable event is occurring in a certain region of space and time',[80] and the testing of a theory now consisted in a process of determining the agreement or disagreement of the theory or its consequences with one or a number of basic statements. Now all this seems clear enough. However, it is at this point that major difficulties arise. For how precisely are the basic statements chosen? Popper's answer is simple: they are accepted 'as the result of a decision or agreement; and to that extent they are conventions. The decisions are reached in accordance with a procedure governed by rules.'[81] What is involved here, therefore, is not a justification in the logical sense: scientific enquiry depends ultimately on intersubjective agreements established through communication within the scientific community. 'If some day it should no longer be possible for scientific observers to reach agreement about basic statements, this would amount to a failure of language as a means of universal communication.... In this new Babel, the soaring edifice of science would soon lie in ruins.'[82]

Thus the problem is just that of the nature and role within Popper's theory of the scientific community. Habermas seizes upon this issue as symptomatic of a crucial weakness. For 'it involuntarily confirms', he argues, 'that the empirical validity of basic statements, and thus the plausibility of theories, is by no means decided in a scientifically elucidated context.... But, rather, scientists discuss whether to accept a basic statement' or whether to apply an hypothesis to a given state of affairs.[83] Research is an institution composed of people who act together and communicate with one another.[84] The decisions to accept or reject basic statements are not made arbitrarily; rather, as Popper himself says, they are made in accordance with rules, which cannot be derived logically. Habermas's point is that nor are these rules merely conventional: they are derived discursively in relation not merely to the adventitious value-system of the scientific community but also to implicitly pre-understood goals arising at the most fundamental level of social life.[85] The same argument, applies not just to the basic problem as stated. For the process of falsification itself requires criteria of validity and to justify these criteria we must adduce arguments. '(B)ut where ... are we to look for these if not in the very dimension – not of the origin but of the formation of knowledge – which has been ruled out? Otherwise, the standards of falsification remain arbitrary.'[86] For critical rationalism, in other words, criteria rooted in the conditions of possibility of intersubjective life are lacking and hence even the 'faith in reason' on which it ultimately depends can be traced back to nothing better than an 'arbitrary decision.'[87]

Habermas explicitly directs his arguments exclusively against Popper. However they apply equally to Kuhn. Of course, the problem in *The Structure of Scientific Revolutions* concerns not the adoption of basic statements but of paradigms. In fact, as we have already seen, for Kuhn, observations are substantially determined by these paradigms, within which the problems to be considered are articulated[88] and these paradigms are adopted through the establishment of a tacit consensus within the scientific community. To be sure, Kuhn emphasizes the role of communication in the development of this consensus,[89] and he identifies constant standards in relation to which decisions are made.[90] But he fails to pursue the origins of these standards beyond the community of scientists. If he had, he would have discovered that in some sense an understanding of the meaning of science must pre-exist its practice. For example, the 'demand for controlled observation as the basis for decisions concerning the empirical plausibility of law-like hypotheses' – a demand accepted by both Popper and Kuhn – 'already presupposes a pre-understanding of certain social norms'.[91] More than this, through the definition of the preconditions for testing, the possible meaning of the empirical validity of statements is established in advance.[92] For indeed, 'the meaning of the research process as a whole must be understood before I can know to what the empirical validity of basic statements is related, just as the judge must always have grasped the meaning of judicature as such. The *quaestio facti* must be determined with reference to a *quaestio juris* understood in its immanent claims.'[93]

Thus for Habermas the research process cannot be understood independently of the social totality.[94] Rather its embeddedness in a context that can only be described hermeneutically must be recognized.[95] The 'judicial' circle of which Popper speaks[96] – and which is certainly not foreign to Kuhn – is in fact a hermeneutic circle. Its resolution is to be found not in an arbitrary agreement, but in the conditions of discourse itself. Habermas expresses this in a fundamental statement of his position:

> (W)e can conceive of criticism – which cannot be defined
> because the standards of rationality can only be explained
> within criticism itself – as a process which, in a domination-free
> discussion, includes a progressive resolution of disagreement.
> Such a discussion is guided by the idea of a general and
> unconstrained consensus amongst those who participate in it.
> Here, 'agreement' should not reduce the idea of truth to
> observable behaviour. Rather, the categories, with whose help
> agreement can be achieved in each case, are themselves
> dependent upon the process which we interpret as a process for
> achieving consensus.... I presuppose (rational discussion) as a
> fact since we always find ourselves in a communication which is
> intended to lead to agreement.... At the same time, however,
> this empirical fact possesses a distinctive feature: namely, a
> transcendental precondition ...[97]

Although both Popper and Kuhn, therefore, made important insights into the interrelationship between facts and theories neither pursued these results to the limits. Instead, both chose to pass over the question of the manifold origins of scientific theories in social practice in favour of descriptions of methodological conventions, the values of the scientific community and even psychological phenomena.[98] However all of these in fact arise primordially in intersubjective life and have historical, cultural and traditional components. The failure to recognize this is the source of the abiding objectivism which Habermas exposes in the positions of both Kuhn and Popper. For both authors it is still assumed that in some way scientific theory represents facts[99] – a claim that is made explicitly in Popper's correspondence theory of truth,[100] but also, more subtly, in Kuhn's argument that both theory and fact are constructed according to a gestalt associated with a given paradigm.[101] What is required for the sublation of objectivism however is not the acceptance within the metacontext of a reciprocal dependence of theory and world but an incorporation of this dependence immanently within the theory itself. Neither Popper nor Kuhn achieve this and nor could they; for according to Habermas such a perspective is apprehensible only to a theory that proceeds *dialectically*. Indeed, a qualitatively different relationship between fact and theory is one of the distinguishing marks of dialectics and hence (we may add) one of the main themes upon which Habermas himself dwells. Within the dialectical purview alone - according to this argument - is the possibility demonstrated of constructing a theory that does not hypostatize the relationship between concept and object. For here, theories are constituted in relation to objects and goals, which themselves came into being through particular structures of experience and action; and the whole is conveyed in the process of elucidating the rich complexity of the social whole.[102]

These are very general formulations, of course. However, no attempt will be made here to endow them with a more precise content. What is at this point most important for us is merely the point that Habermas himself wishes to make: that the objectivism of the contemporary philosophy and sociology of science is not inevitable but that on the contrary, a serious programme exists to circumvent it. The very existence of this programme, furthermore, suffices to expose substantial deficiencies in the extant theories - their objectivism, their suppression of the question of origins and the inadequacy of their concept of community. This last problem has not been emphasized in the discussion above; nevertheless, it underlies it continuously as a principal theme. Popper, despite his occasional reference to the importance of communication, works strenuously to minimize the dependence of the content of scientific theories on social variables; this is hardly surprising given his aim of developing a general logic of scientific discovery. Kuhn, for his part, also places some stress on sociological factors;[103] however, as has been repeatedly emphasized, 'sociological' in his view is understood only in the narrow sense - indeed for him the alleged autonomy of the scientific community with respect to the larger society is one of science's characteristic marks.[104] From the viewpoint of Habermas the problem with both these approaches lies in their common, deficient concept of social action. In accordance with the objectivist disposition, which prejudges the relationship between theory and experience, they comprehend social action only as 'behaviour' - that is, as the trajectory described by individual scientists under determinable conditions. This is, of course, a conception particularly appropriate to modes of procedure assumed for the sciences, in which only one type of experience is tolerated – that being itself defined therein. In these modes of procedure, '(o)nly the controlled observation of physical behaviour, which is set up in an isolated field under reproducible conditions by subjects inter-changeable at will, seems to permit intersubjectively valid judge-ments of perception.... Empirical sciences in the strict sense insist that all discussable statements should be checked, at least indi-rectly, by means of this very narrowly channelled experience.'[105]

Dialectics opposes directly this conception of experience. Instead, it proceeds hermeneutically: it regards the comprehension of mean-ing, 'to which the analytical-empirical theories attach a merely heu-ristic value, (as) constitutive.'[106] Dialectics assembles its categories 'from the situational consciousness of acting individuals them-selves; in the objective spirit of a social lifeworld, that meaning is articulated which sociological interpretation takes up through identification and critique.'[107] Hence for dialectics the prior ex-perience of society as totality 'shapes the outline of the theory in which it articulates itself and through whose constructions it is checked anew against experiences.'[108]

With these arguments Habermas is able to claim that the histor-ical situation in which science emerged was 'by no means external to the structure of empirical science'. Up until the seventeenth century, he goes on,[109]

the roles of theory and of the reproduction of material life had been strictly divided socially; the monopolization of the acquisition of knowledge by the leisure classes had remained unchallenged. It is only within the framework of modern bourgeois society, which legitimizes the acquisition of property through labour, that science can receive impulses from the experimental realm of manual crafts and research can gradually be integrated into the labour process. The mechanics of Galileo and his contemporaries dissects nature with reference to a form of technical domination which had just been developed within the framework of the new modes of manufacture....[110]

Habermas's arguments against Popper's position – of which no more than the most rudimentary of outlines has been presented here – are detailed and thorough. However, those of his conclusions which are relevant for the future development of a social theory of natural science are both clear and compelling. The scientific com-munity, he maintains, cannot be conceived in isolation from the remainder of society. Nor, furthermore, can the content of science itself be isolated as a mere technique from which reference to social action has been eliminated. Instead, he claims that the research process itself must be understood in terms of its embeddedness in the intersubjective context and thus as an aspect of social action. In fact, the social action associated with empirical science conveys an immanent and irreducible reference to social labour.[111] But this also means that the research process, being carried out by human subjects, 'belongs to the objective context which itself constitutes the object of cognition, by virtue of cognitive acts.'[112] This objective context, that is, can become an object of study. However, he concludes – and this is his important methodological point – '(t)he dimension in which this combination of the research process with the social life-process is formed belongs neither to the sphere of facts nor to that of theories.... Rather, in the comprehensive communicative context of scientific criticism one moment links itself to another.... As a result, neither the sociology of knowledge nor a pure methodology are sufficiently appropriate at this level of reflection. Their combination ... is more appropriate.'[113]

Habermas's critique of positivism, therefore, which began as a rather limited attack on the philosophical position of critical rationalism, at its conclusion issues in substantially more extensive implications. In fact, implicitly, this critique contains a proposal for a comprehensive theory of science which from a non-objectivist perspective would seek to apprehend the content of its object in terms of the historically conditioned practice of scientists. Now it must be admitted at once that the elaboration of such a theory would represent a major task, owing to the fact that no more than a few preliminary – albeit important – steps are presently available. Nevertheless, it is equally clear that this endeavour would be of great significance for the present essay, since some of the central themes with which it would be concerned intersect with those of the project we are in the process of assembling. Accordingly, where appropriate, in what follows, Habermas's work will be consulted as an important source of guidance. Unfortunately however, Habermas himself has never undertaken the development of the project which we are maintaining can be found adumbrated in his arguments against positivism. Indeed, just the contrary is the case: by the adoption of what seems to be an unnecessarily restrictive concept of science he has actually foreclosed many of the positions suggested in the discussion above. In particular, by the designation of science in his work as inscribed within the technical knowledge-constitutive interest the possibilities for the development of a radically anti-objectivist theory of nature are unwittingly compromised. For this reason, in our description of Habermas's arguments we have found it necessary in the preceding - and we shall continue to find it necessary in what follows - to impose a deliberate bias towards the preservation of open questions regarding the theory of nature itself; thereby it is hoped that a level of generality can be retained similar to that which might have existed prior to the assignment to science of a place, such as the one we have just described, within the interest structure of knowledge and action.

Having said this however we would like to emphasize immediately that we are not thereby denying the great utility of the notion of a structure of interests underlying knowledge and action. What is more, we stress that Habermas himself has demonstrated no detailed concern with the actual contents of the natural sciences; consequently, his proposals here may not contain the same degree of rigour as do those he advances in respect of other matters - and hence an examination of science might not impose a serious burden on the remainder of his theory. Nevertheless, regarding the question of the interpretation of science as essentially instrumental in character, this is a point on which the present essay cannot compromise: no investigation which hopes to elucidate the social dimension of scientific knowledge can commence with such a limiting presupposition about the nature of the science itself. It is not necessary at this stage actually to refute Habermas's view (although this is the conclusion at which, in due course, we shall arrive); what is crucial is merely to avoid assuming in advance the results of the analyses to follow. Accordingly, for the moment we shall endeavour strenuously to keep open the relevant questions. The issue at stake here is of such importance (and indeed, the view that Habermas assumes such a common one), that it is appropriate here, before completing this introductory discussion of the sociology of science, to offer some further remarks regarding it. Hence in what follows, by way of a slight digression from the development of our themes, we shall make some additional comments on the subject of science and interests.[114]

Science and interests

Regarding Habermas's position on the nature of science, it will be argued in what follows that this position neither has been effectively proved nor is self-evident. Indeed, in spite of the fecundity of Habermas's approach, we shall suggest, it even produces consequences which militate against the unqualified acceptance of his own formulations.

At the basis of Habermas's project is a search for the roots of knowledge in human life.[115] The 'specific viewpoints from which ... we apprehend reality,' he maintains, have their 'basis in the natural history of the human species.'[116] They are tied to 'imperatives of the socio-cultural form of life.'[117] These 'general orientations' towards the world, delimiting spheres of knowledge and action, are what are called by Habermas – adopting a term from Kant – 'interests'. Interests can be revealed through argumentation and social analysis; or, more precisely, they can be demonstrated (that is, rather than deduced) in the process of an analysis of the fundamental categories obtaining in various modes of theoretical reflection, of testing procedures and other forms of activity, and so on. Hence their existence is an empirical one, yet they function as conditions of possibility for certain types of knowledge and action: they have a 'quasi-transcendental'[118] status. To qualify their ontological status thus, however, is not to compromise their fundamentality: the basis of human interests for Habermas is to lie unequivocally in 'the natural history of the human species.'[119]

The interest with which we are most concerned here is the one that guides the natural sciences. The identification of this interest requires that an answer be found to the question as to just what scientific statements disclose about reality – or, equivalently, the question regarding to what specific kinds of action the meaning of these statements bears special reference. Habermas's answer is that the natural 'empirico-analytic' sciences yield information that is characterized by its technical utility – understood, of course, in a transcendental and not a realist sense. He maintains that this conclusion can be discovered from a study of the origins, the structure and the applications of scientific statements.[120] With regard to the last two, furthermore, he believes that scientific theories are hypothetico-deductive systems of statements susceptible to some kind of comparison with empirical experience.[121] Both testability therefore and predictional accuracy are inherent characteristics of science; hence they belong to the constitutive features of our knowledge of nature and cannot be accidental outcomes of it. In addition, he replies to the implicit query of *Dialectic of Enlightenment* and *One-Dimensional Man:* whereas different *attitudes* to nature are possible (in the sense of personal proclivities), there can be only one form of *cognition*[122] – that emerging from the determinations of the technical interest of knowledge.

86

It need hardly be added that Habermas's own position is a profoundly anti-objectivist one: both the contents of knowledge and the states of affairs against which they are measured are, within his theory, determined according to the deepest imperatives of social life. However, at the same time – somewhat curiously – as is already apparent, he takes over without modification the objectivistic account of the theory of nature. Thus, while condemning this theory vehemently as 'positivist', he resiles from challenging the veracity of its actual validity claims; in fact, as has been previously observed, he even *identifies* positivism with science, adding that for the former objectivism is an irreducible characteristic.[123]

Now it seems to us that this perplexity is not merely adventitious, but that rather it is indicative of an important weakness in Habermas's conception. To see this, it is first of all important to recognize that nowhere does he attempt rigorously to justify his description of science through references to the actual contents of the sciences. Instead, he appeals to the contemporary experience of nature and the present dominant form of its theoretical reflection. Thus he argues that the scientific object domains are only extensions of everyday procedures[124] and that statements about things and happenings in general cannot avoid an implicit reference to 'technologies and strategies'.[125] Indeed, the categories of the natural sciences themselves – such as 'bodies in motion', 'matter', energy and so on – are said to embrace a priori a commitment to the enhancement of technical control over nature.[126] Science and the development of technology are assumed to be indissociable. Regarding the possibility of an alternative science, therefore, in his reply to Marcuse Habermas insists that such a project would of necessity be coterminous with the development of a 'new technology'; however, he asserts, this is impossible since technology is implicated in the behavioural system of instrument action, which has its primary roots in the human organism itself.[127] In fact, '(t)he idea of a New Science will not stand up to logical scrutiny any more than that of a New Technology, if indeed science is to retain the meaning of modern science inherently oriented to possible technical control. For this function, as for scientific and technical progress in general, there is no more "humane" substitute.'[128]

Against this position however, it can be argued simply that it is not self-evident that the objective of any theory of nature – or even of its metatheory – either is or should be to preserve the goals and standards of industrialized science. What is more, by adopting such an assumption, Habermas makes himself susceptible to the same argument (to which we have adverted) that was advanced by Popper and Feyerabend against Kuhn: the argument that here confusion exists regarding the putative descriptive and prescriptive parts of the analysis. The apparent objective of Habermas's theory was to explicate the structure of science generally; in practice, he has taken an empirical fact – the present form of science – and elevated it into a principle which is said to hold for all science. Such an inference, of course, is inadmissible. However of greater importance are the results presupposed by this procedure – that societies stand in one, and only one, relation to nature, and that the conceptual structure of science is – even in principle – invariant with respect to historical and cultural forms. In our view, for which we shall argue at length in later chapters, both of these assumptions are mistaken; this is the case in spite of the fact that they are deeply implanted within Habermas's theory.

Further, it can be added that, regarding the special sciences, this conception issues in an important conclusion – carefully and deliberately drawn by Habermas himself – which seems, in the light of present experience, to be highly questionable. Not only does the interpretation of science as essentially technical and instrumental exclude the possibility of an alternative practical orientation to nature; it also dismisses the possibility of any differential meaning-content within science. More precisely, the meanings of statements, unlike procedures of argumentation and validity claims, can only be understood in relation simultaneously to conscious and intersubjective processes. Now the discursive procedures of science may be invariant, and its validity claims may correspond to forms designated a priori by the interest structure; however its meanings must refer to subjectively apprehended and intersubjectively realized rules. What then are the rules guiding the meanings of the sciences? Habermas's answer is immediate and unambiguous:

> Theories comprise hypothetico-deductive connections of propositions, which permit the deduction of lawlike hypotheses with empirical content. The latter can be interpreted as statements about the covariance of observable events; given a set of initial conditions, they make predictions possible. Empirical-analytic knowledge is thus possible predictive knowledge. However, *the meaning of such predictions, that is their technical exploitability, is established only by the rules according to which we apply theories to reality.*[129]

Meaning in science then is attached only to 'applications' – which here of course can refer only to either experimentation or technological employment; hence the 'rules' involved are less forms of social conduct than mere formulae. It would be not just a quibble to ask whether these usages of 'meaning' and 'rules', at first sight very similar to those appearing in other parts of Habermas's work dealing with communication and emancipation, are in fact even consistent with them. However here it is more important to observe that for him in science all cognition, including that associated with 'observation and perception, is subordinated to technical control: (i)n reality basic statements are not simple representations of the facts in themselves, but express the success or failure of our operations.'[130]

That the proper goal of any theory of nature is the enhancement of technical control over nature is by no means obvious. That the meaning of such theories is exhausted by the scope of their applications seems to contradict both contemporary experience and the historical facts. Indeed it appears that in making such claims Habermas ignores a distinction to which reference was made at the very outset of this essay. Science, it was pointed out there, is embedded in a particular metaphysics which may be associated with a positivistic theory of knowledge; however, not only positivism is consistent with science, but in fact the latter admits of a rather considerable potential epistemological variation. To this result we add here that it is simply not the case that understanding of the nature-culture relationship has invariably been guided by an interest in maximizing technical power. In fact the domination of nature – which undeniably has ancient roots – became a central feature of science only under rather limited social and historical conditions.[131] Against Popper, Habermas had argued that although the descriptive content of science cannot be disputed, this content 'is only valid with reference to prognoses for feedback-regulated actions in predictable situations. All the answers which the empirical sciences can supply are relative to the methodical significance of the questions they raise and nothing more.'[132] In his theory of the interests of knowledge, he made what is here apparently a description of the existing sciences into a general principle governing all knowledge of nature. However it is a familiar fact of everyday life that other bearings towards nature exist than those of a purely purposive-rational kind and that other outcomes are sought from the study of nature than purely technical ones. The experience of sexuality, the appreciation of beauty in general, our irreducible corporeal involvement in the world, are enough to show this.[133] Cosmologies, explanations of unusual natural phenomena and so on may unify social life and help to elucidate the relationship between nature and culture – a fundamental constituent of social life, invariably replete with both technical accomplishments and practical significations.[134] And lest these arguments may seem tendentious, it can be pointed out also that many of the debates in twentieth century physics have concerned issues unrelated to technical control but crucially related to understanding.[135]

Habermas's conception of the relationship between society and nature is not just an incidental addendum to his theory; in fact extensive implications follow from it which he has accepted at length. To mention just one example, he has argued that labour also can be effectively characterized as instrumental action – a view that has been convincingly criticized.[136] At this point, however, we are concerned only with the theory of nature. In this regard, we have argued that in his emphasis on the pragmatic dimension of science Habermas goes too far: he forecloses all those other questions bearing on its syntax and its semantics; he fails to appreciate the wide range of meanings with which nature can be endowed in social life; and he is unable even to formulate other problems bearing on syntax, such as the one that has already been encountered (and is almost certainly not trivial) concerning the possibility of an epistemological compulsion inhabiting the formal structures of a theory.

The attempt to identify knowledge of nature, therefore, with knowledge derived under the rubric of the extension of technical control, seems misguided. To hypostatize science as a correlate of instrumental action is also to prescind the development of a non-objectivist theory of nature. These claims, it must be emphasized, do not diminish the many fundamental insights achieved in Habermas's work; indeed we shall draw on these at length later. Nevertheless, it is not an insignificant result that a major theory which has achieved considerable success in extirpating positivism from the social sciences should resile from an application of its own results in respect of the natural sciences. That this is a consequence of Habermas's theory is of great interest. However, this is not of course the first time we have encountered this conclusion. For here we find – somewhat unexpectedly – a close parallel between *Knowledge and Human Interests* and *Dialectic of Enlightenment*. Like the earlier work, that of Habermas sought explicitly to oppose the malign consequences of the development of the sciences. Like the earlier work it succeeded powerfully in this regard, while simultaneously opening up fruitful new regions for social reflection. However, also like the earlier book, it fails to transmit its own conclusions into the theory of science itself: at the end, Habermas and Adorno together, having rescued it for an instant, return the theory of nature to objectivism.

In closing these brief remarks on the concept of interest we would like, for the purpose of avoiding misunderstanding, to re-emphasize the form of the conclusion we have just reached. It is our view that Habermas's arguments in respect of his hypothesis that science can be subsumed under the knowledge-constitutive interest of purposive-rational action cannot be sustained. For the purpose of showing this we have examined in detail some of the main contentions he puts forward in support of this hypothesis. We are not claiming here, however, that Habermas's position is a false one; that is, we are not at this stage explicitly denying his assertions. We remark on this point here because it must be recognized that the question of interest cannot be judged conclusively until the analysis of science itself is complete. To assume in advance a hypothesis regarding this issue would be to impose prior limits on the conduct of this analysis; in consequence it could not escape the suspicion that it comprised no more than an elaboration of the theoretical status quo. It will in fact later be claimed that Habermas's hypothesis is actually false and can be refuted. For the present, however, the question is left open.

* * * * * *

The new philosophy of science initiated by Popper, Kuhn and others, together with Habermas's critique of the sociological positions implicitly entailed therein, have opened up new horizons for the social theory of science. The appreciation of the fact that the practice of science plays a constitutive role in scientific discourse for the first time exposes the structure of science itself to sociological study. The demonstration that science progresses through a series of transformations of theoretical unities which may be mutually incommensurable provides insights which may eventually facilitate the specification of its content from a philosophical point of view. The interpretation of the research process as an integral component of social life, rather than as an exceptional activity dissociated from society at large, suggests the possibility of identifying within science itself traces of the dominant cultural and economic themes. And the recognition that all observation is to some extent theoretically determined throws into doubt the previously unquestioned assumption of objectivism as the single epistemological standard for all science.

These conclusions mark great advances in the understanding of science and, especially, of its role in the understanding of social life. But they also, as we have seen, comprise an equal number of profound and perplexing questions. What is more, as Habermas demonstrated, these insights have failed to eliminate objectivism as a force in the sociology of science; and, indeed, as we have found, paradoxically, from Habermas's own work, not even the most advanced thinkers have recognized the need for an effective critique of objectivism within science itself.

The emphasis on the pragmatic component of science, to be sure, elucidates hitherto obscured aspects of the place of science in the social totality, and, in addition, of the reciprocal influences between them. At the same time it suffers from considerable deficiencies. However, even these deficiencies can be illuminating. In what follows, therefore, it will be necessary to acknowledge both the strengths of this approach and its weaknesses.

Retrospect and prospect

The review of a number of aspects of the contemporary philosophy and sociology of science having been completed, an attempt can now be made to formulate the major issues to which the ensuing investigation must be directed.

As we stated at the outset, the entire project, of which the present study is only a preliminary part, is guided, quite explicitly, by a definite social purpose. Consequently, from the beginning we take for granted certain propositions which we make no attempt to hide. For example, we assume that modern science has an influence on the social processes and indeed, may well affect them profoundly; what is more, we accept that these effects are not all benign. Actually, rather more than this is assumed: we commence in fact from the point of view that contemporary society displays in its most minute recesses the stigmata of the acquisitions of, and the innovations wrought by, science, and that as a result, through some process yet to be elucidated, political life has been attenuated and intellectual life in general debilitated. On the other hand, we are prepared to begin this essay by accepting that it is at least a possibility that the development and content of science may – again, through the mediation of processes not yet properly understood – be subject to determinations imposed by the social phenomena; and consistent with this we are willing to entertain the rather radical hypothesis that the present form of science is not self-evidently the only possible one.

Thus we commence with a number of deliberate assumptions

regarding both the context within which reflection on science must take place today and the kinds of possibilities it may properly consider; of these, the most important is the elementary premise of the whole discussion – the assumption that science and society are intricately intertwined. This starting point however is not too broad for the endeavour in which we are engaged; it will not occlude discussion or foreclose results. On the contrary, it will facilitate the investigation by permitting all the problems and issues that we have identified to be oriented in relation to it. What is more, it will enable us to keep open a question with potentially important social consequences which has emerged forcefully – albeit only tacitly – in the foregoing: the question of whether the reconstruction of modern society, commanded by economic, cultural and political exigencies, would require as a condition of its possibility the reconstruction of science.

The present essay is intended to provide preliminary orientations for a larger project. This project would pursue in greater detail the study, suggested by these formulations, of the contents of science in the light of their manifold social constituents. The review above of current themes in the philosophy and sociology of science was conducted in order to enable an object domain for such a study to be demarcated and possible methodological perspectives and hypotheses to be identified. A wide variety of approaches to a number of aspects of the subject has been considered, in varying degrees of detail; in spite of the differences between their particular points of view – and, indeed, in spite of their often disparate subject-matter – a number of converging themes emerged. A general consensus seemed to exist, for instance, that social variables were of considerable importance for the original formation of modern science, even though in the actual accounts of the locus of this intersection the emphases were placed rather differently. Thus it was shown how a cultural context which allowed – and at times actually encouraged – individuals to turn to this study of science was of importance, and how also were other aspects of the social and economic configuration. It was shown that extrinsic forces might impinge on existing sciences subsequently directing not only their focuses of inquiry, but even possibly also their syntactical development. It was suggested that a given science might be said to embrace a philosophical perspective – or, at least, that such a locution might not be entirely without meaning. Furthermore, the possibility was raised that these problems could be considered in detail in relation to specific social circumstances; on the other hand, regarding the scientific theories themselves, it was concluded that they occur only

93

as structural unities of meaning or method and that it is possible that two theories could be so different that they were even incommensurable. In this last case, it was observed that the problem arises of the unity of science, but that resources for the overcoming of this difficulty were available within the sociology of science. In particular, it emerged that the unity of science was preserved less by the method or content of science than by its social dimension – that is, by the interchanges which comprise the community of scientists – which was also, incidentally, the point of immediate contact between science and society at large. Accordingly, it became apparent that the study of the scientific community was not merely the peripheral matter it first seemed, although, to be sure, it was clear that to achieve its goals this study needed to be radicalized. A number of works, in fact, identified the community as the site at which the important structural features of science were determined, though it must be admitted that others sought to minimize this constituent role.

Underlying all these conclusions was the constant, abiding question concerning the philosophical content of the present form of science. Here we referred to a number of classical studies in which this content – or at least a major component of it – was found to be characterized by a deep-seated objectivism. This result was important for two additional reasons. On the one hand, objectivism has been widely studied in relation to its social role in the ideology of positivism; hence much material is available on the subject of its possible consequences within society as a whole. On the other, insofar as it entails restrictive precepts concerning the relationship between theory and the world, objectivism also pervades the context within which reflection on science takes place. This is an important problem confronting the interpretation of science today, for it implies that even the most perceptive commentators have accepted unwittingly the latter's major philosophical imperatives. It is possible only to speculate about the consequences of this circumstance; however at the least, it is plausible that the insights available to the theory of science have thereby been systematically limited.

This last point, of course, raises substantial methodological problems for any study of science, to which some remarks must be directed here. Many studies – notably, in critical theory (which has already been mentioned), phenomenology and structuralism – have been devoted to the criticism of objectivism and to the task of fashioning perspectives from which objectivism can be specifically excluded. In some of these a major effort has been applied to construct a special theoretical apparatus that would accommodate the anti-objectivist perspective. The details of the most important of these approaches will be considered later; in particular, close attention will be paid to some of the major arguments of Husserl's phenomenology that bear on this question. Furthermore, as will become apparent, many of the substantial consequences of these studies will be accepted. For its own part, however, this essay makes no claim to methodological innovation. Instead, it seeks to achieve no more than the classification of some fundamental problems and the formulation of a number of elementary hypotheses in relation to them. To this end, it will proceed on the assumption that a variety of traditions and methodological strategies can be drawn upon without compromising the unity of the project as a whole. That such an approach might be possible is given some additional credence by the sheer diversity of disciplines which must be taken into consideration in the development of a social theory of science; in the present essay alone, for example, many of the discussions traverse philosophy, social theory and physics. Furthermore, the existence of a series of specific problems which define the constant focus of enquiry itself provides a unifying principle – a principle, that is, extrinsic to the particular methodological apparatus or theoretical perspective that might be applied to solve them.

To attempt to proceed in this way is not to make the ingenuous claim that our own approach is free of prejudices. Indeed, against this, on the one hand, we have already suggested as a major issue the question of the existence of philosophical imperatives residing within even a formal apparatus; and, on the other, the possibility of incommensurable theories has been referred to at length. Obviously this essay would not be exempt from any of the consequences of these results. Nevertheless, the procedure of admitting alternative perspectives may facilitate the identification of the biases imposed by any particular one of them. In addition, as we shall argue later, even incommensurable theories can elucidate different facets of a problem, thereby deepening the appreciation of its implications and its nuances. However, regardless of these arguments, it is not our intention to attempt to supply a complete, all-embracing theory of science; indeed, it is one of our major contentions that such an objective would be fundamentally misguided. Rather, we shall be satisfied in this essay if our deliberations do no more than open for investigation a number of possibilities not hitherto properly recognized.

Accordingly, in what follows there will be no adoption a priori of any particular standpoint. Indeed, the constellations of problems that have emerged from the foregoing discussion will be taken as the principal foci in relation to which contending perspectives will be allowed to interrogate each other. Thus a number of theoretical viewpoints will be examined for their contributions regarding the issues we have identified. Subsequently, discrepancies between the various sets of results will be scrutinized in order either to verify or to augment the results so obtained. Where no immediate reconciliation is possible an attempt will be made at least to identify the site and type of inconsistency involved. This procedure will be applied – sometimes directly, sometimes implicitly – to several important philosophical perspectives and in relation to the questions regarding both the content and the social meaning of science. In this way, it is hoped, different aspects of common questions will be elucidated and a variety of possibilities for the future course of analysis will be suggested.

* * * * * *

The possibility of a social theory of science rests on a dual circumstance: that science makes claims about the world that are interpreted within philosophy and social theory while, conversely, the insights of philosophy transform the facts with which science works. However, merely to formulate the relationship between science and social theory in this way, as a reciprocal interaction, is to degrade it to the level of the specious. For in fact the two can be compared at all only because they share in advance a common reference to the world on the one hand and to the social field of meanings and significations on the other. That an empirical justification of a theory presupposes an extra-scientific context of interpretation is true and indeed important, as also is the statement that philosophy must take into account the validity of a given scientific hypothesis. However, more fundamental than these propositions – and assumed in both of them – is the fact that a scientific theory can transmit a non-negligible content regarding a domain which cannot be characterized independently of social phenomena. Put differently: science speaks about, and exerts an influence on, the world – but a world that is already irreducibly social; thus both the production and content of scientific theories cannot be dissociated from the social processes. These are consequences of the foregoing discussion which in themselves issue in substantive results. Science intervenes in society not just technically but also at the level of meaning. It is the job of the social theory of science to scrutinize and to interrogate this meaning.

But science of course operates as a formal system with its own rigorous internal constitution. How are social meanings transmitted by such a system? Indeed, what is the relationship between a formal system and philosophical outcomes in general? Can the former impose limitations on the latter, or enforce certain commitments? Further, what is the effect of social and historical change on a contemporaneous theory of nature? Can major transformations within science be interpreted in relation to social contingencies? And, in any case, just what does science tell us about the world? What does, say, modern physics tell us that is not present in classical physics? Finally, if science can make a claim about the world at the level of the social field of meanings, then what is the role of philosophical justification in respect of its technical propositions?

These are great questions, and no pretence is maintained here to answer them definitively. Nevertheless, an attempt will be made at least to provide a schema within which they can be organized and some possibly fruitful directions of investigation identified. To this end, a preliminary step can be taken at once by observing that we have throughout our discussion so far been dealing with three broad, though interrelated, series of problems. These are the *technical problems*, involving formal questions concerning the structure of the specific sciences; these will, later in this book, be expanded to include the substantive issues with which these sciences deal. There are the *problems of meaning* – philosophical questions bearing on the significative content of science. And there are the *cultural questions* concerning the application of science in society and the production of scientific propositions within the scientific community. Expressed in the terms derived from the theory of language of which we have from time to time made use, these three series of problems correspond roughly, in turn, to the syntactical, the semantic and the pragmatic levels of science;[137] that is, the first deals with imperatives arising from the formal structure of a theory or discipline, the second with issues of meaning, objectivity and so on and the third with the actual conditions of use of theoretical formulations, communication and community.

It must be stated at once that it is obvious that the three levels thus identified are closely interwoven, and so their mutual distinction can be of heuristic value only. Nevertheless, we believe that, for our purposes, the analogy with language is highly suggestive, and is capable of providing fruitful indications for the investigation to follow. This will prove especially true in relation to the problem of objectivism which, after all, in one formulation amounts to a denial of the contribution of linguistic phenomena to natural scien-

97

tific knowledge. Furthermore, as an immediate result, it can help to clarify the concept of a 'crisis of science', to which various meanings have been attached and with a reference to which we began this essay. The quasi-linguistic schema helps us to see that this crisis is in fact likewise tripartite, expressing itself as it does simultaneously at the levels of form, meaning and culture. In addition, as we saw, these different events are also interdependent. The technical aporia may be expressive of philosophical dilemmas which, in turn, may expose real meaning deficits at the level of social life. Conversely, as was suggested in a study examined earlier, a series of cultural perplexities may coalesce in a single philosophical doctrine, thereby precipitating a major revision of a current scientific theory. Or to express this point as we did once before: a crisis originating in the pragmatic dimension of science may propagate through its structure, producing effects also at the semantic and syntactical levels.

Let us return once again to objectivism, which is a key problem for the present study. Arguments have been quoted above which claim to provide a refutation of its main tenets, at least in respect of social and natural phenomena. Now many theories of science have assumed that knowledge of nature is always of necessity objectivistic. However, if a refutation of objectivism in general terms can be provided, then this assumption clearly runs into major problems. Regarding this issue specifically, we have considered an important series of arguments which seek to demonstrate an inexorable technical interest implicit within all knowledge of the natural world. Here, we found not that such an interest does not exist, but that science's circumscription within it had not been conclusively demonstrated. In the light of this result, together with that of the critique of objectivism, we maintained that it was inappropriate for the study of science to foreclose its own options by assuming in advance the philosophical disposition of its object; that is to say, when we study science, we must not presuppose as necessary any one theoretical perspective within it.

Here we are back at the very heart of the matter. It cannot be denied that the present form of science *is* objectivist. Physics, chemistry, medicine, biology all conceive of themselves - and propagate themselves conceptually - as objectivistic disciplines. However, if objectivism is wrong, then what must this mean for the truth content of their actual propositions? It must be admitted that the answer to this question, so baldly stated, remains unresolved. Nevertheless, sufficient indications do exist to suggest a larger project that would be an extension of the present one. This project would involve nothing less than the reconstruction of science about the anti-objectivist axis; accordingly, it would represent a task with potentially far-reaching consequences within both society and the theory of nature. To be sure, even the articulation of such a possibility is unpopular today, for historical reasons that are not altogether impossible to understand.[138] Such reasons, however, should not be allowed to obstruct the further development of our understanding. Thus we shall argue vigorously below that adumbrations of a non-objectivist science already exist – albeit in an implicit form – within several branches of contemporary science; further, we shall propose that problems within others call stridently for similar developments there also.

These then are the results of our discussions of the social theory of science. In the course of these discussions we have examined many problems and observed the intricate interweaving of society and scientific knowledge. Now we are able to state the aims of this essay. Put very simply, our ultimate objective is twofold. On the one hand, we intend to consider the general problem of the social determinants of scientific knowledge – the problem, that is, of how a social theory of science might at all be possible. On the other, we shall seek to prepare the ground for the formulation of a possible non-objectivistic theory of nature. In this context, the importance of our defence above of an approach that admits of a variety of perspectives can perhaps be better appreciated. This essay seeks to contribute – in a preliminary way – to a major social task that has become excruciatingly necessary. This task is itself twofold: on the one hand, it is to apply, systematically and for the first time, the substantive philosophical apparatus to the scientific domain, where problems once conceived as purely formal are now recognized as embracing from the outset complex social and cultural contents; and, on the other hand, no less than this, it is to discover the profound consequences for our understanding of both the social and the natural worlds of the great innovations that have been accomplished by the contemporary sciences of nature.

In Part I of this book we have brought together the combined resources of the sociology and the philosophy of science in order to formulate an array of questions and hypotheses regarding the theory of nature. To this end, we have made reference to a number of key debates that have characterized the recent history of those disciplines; we have found many of the arguments proposed by the protagonists in these debates to be both suggestive and fecund, not only in their substantive affirmations but even in their absences. Subsequently, we have proceeded to delineate some elements of a research programme which appeared to emerge naturally out of these discussions. We can now say what the immediate course of this study should be. In the first place, we shall attempt to pursue further both the critique of objectivism and the analysis of the structure of science. To this end, a close analysis will be undertaken of the conception of science developed by the phenomenological philosopher Edmund Husserl. Following this, we shall consider in some detail the question of the relationship between a scientific theory and a social formation. Subsequently, attention will be turned to an unexpected application of the implicit consequence of Husserl's work to the interpretation of the theories of quantum mechanics and relativity; here we shall see demonstrated the impossibility of limiting the reflection on science to either a strictly sociological or a strictly philosophical endeavour. Lastly, more general philosophical problems will be considered concerning the question of a possible sociology of objectivity.

First however, Edmund Husserl.

II
Husserl: Insights and dilemmas

Husserl's *Formal and Transcendental Logic:* The phenomenological account of the structure of science

It was not only amongst sociologists and cultural critics that objectivistic science provoked unease. The permeation of positivistic tendencies throughout philosophical thought also became an issue for thinkers concerned with the foundations of knowledge. For despite the apparent successes of the sciences they seemed nevertheless unable to justify the certainty they claimed for themselves in respect of either specific insights or methods. In fact it was from a philosopher preoccupied with exactly these issues that one of the most powerful critiques of objectivism emerged. This philosopher was of course Edmund Husserl; his philosophy, of which the undermining of modern positivism was an abiding theme, was phenomenology. The self-appointed task of phenomenology was the establishment of firm foundations on which certain knowledge would be possible. The guarantor of this certainty was to be found in consciousness, at the end of a rigorous process of introspection and questioning. Husserl's object was to develop a series of procedures that could be applied methodically to realize this process and so make widely available to a variety of sciences the possibility of a clarification of the status of their particular assertions and an elucidation of their ultimate human origins. Thus the *subject* was irreducibly at the centre of the phenomenological project and that to which all truth could be traced; indeed the criterion for existence itself now incorporated a demand for the possibility of an evidential presentation of phenomena to consciousness.[1]

This basic assumption by phenomenology of a starting point in subjectivity is at once its most characteristic feature and the source of the great potency of its attack on objectivism; it is also the source of many of its major dilemmas. Wherever intersubjectivity or culture or society or history are involved, phenomenology, as a theory of the isolated monadic subject, finds itself confronting profound difficulties. Some of these problems can be overcome – even if only at the expense of the self-evidence and apodicticity the attainment of which formed its original impulse. However other problems retain the perplexity to the last; in these cases, if a plausible formulation is achieved it is through the incorporation of concepts strictly exogenous to Husserl's system. As we shall see, this double circumstance is as true of the theory of science emerging from the phenomenological project as it is of any of the latter's other major themes; and what is more, this theory was pursued with a particular rigour and a relentlessness that only intensified as Husserl's corpus approached its conclusion. Accordingly, at its limits, the phenomenological critique of science is both powerful and perplexing: it demonstrates not only the strengths but also the underlying tensions of the theoretical perspective constructed by phenomenology. The same applies specifically to the refutation of objectivism it incorporates; indeed, we shall attempt to argue that there emerges from the endeavour not one such refutation but *two* – both of them convincing but only one of them properly phenomenological. If this is true, then it may not be inaccurate to speak of Husserl's philosophy as concealing a deep ambiguity which reveals itself in his epistemology and in his accounts of objectivity and history. Moreover – and this will be one of the major claims of the argument of ensuing chapters – neither of the alternatives is either wholly false or wholly true; and what is more, *both* are realized elaborately within contemporary science.

Husserl's two tasks

If there is indeed an ambiguity with Husserl's thought such as the one claimed then it is apparent from the very beginning in the problems which Husserl saw himself as addressing. His philosophy was quite consciously directed towards the accomplishment of a two-fold task: on the one hand, to achieve for philosophy what had already been achieved for the positive sciences – that is, to provide it with an unassailable basis of certainty and rigorous technique; and on the other, to oppose the generalization of science to all branches of knowledge, an incipient process which had already provoked a 'Crisis of Humanity'. With respect to the former, the 'crisis' was in the aims of philosophy. To the prestigious positive sciences was opposed philosophy, which seemed to lack any reliable theoretical method and thus appeared to represent the world only as a result of arbitrary imaginative speculation. 'No reasonable person will doubt the objective truth or the objectively grounded probability of the wonderful theories of mathematics and the natural sciences,'[2] he exclaimed. 'Science is a title standing for absolute, timeless values. Every such value, once discovered, belongs thereafter to the treasure trove of all succeeding humanity and obviously determines likewise the material content of culture (and) wisdom ...'.[3] Yet in relation to philosophy: 'no philosophy actually in existence is a rigorous science'.[4] Consequently, 'the spiritual need of our time has become unbearable'.[5] This need has its source in science and only science can overcome it.

> If the sceptical criticism of naturalists and historicists dissolves genuine objective validity in all fields of obligation into nonsense, if unclear and disagreeing, even though naturally developed, reflective concepts and consequently equivocal and erroneous problems impede the understanding of actuality and the possibility of a rational attitude toward it ... then there is only one remedy for these and all similar evils: a scientific critique and in addition a radical science, rising from below, based on sure foundations, and progressing according to the most rigorous methods – the philosophical science for which we speak here.[6]

To be sure, in spite of his respect for science and this insistence that its standards of clarity and rigour be applied also to philosophy it has to be stressed that Husserl always recognized the existence of a multiplicity of divergent object domains of enquiry. It was never one of his claims that philosophy as rigorous science would replace any of the genuine sciences already in existence. The realm of knowledge had to be understood as a system of theoretical structures, each having its own object, methods and problems standing in relation to each other in 'a certain logical harmony'.[7] Indeed the failure to recognize this was precisely what precipitated the second 'crisis': a crisis in the aims of *science*. For as a result of the very success of natural science its objectivistic ideal has been generalized and subsequently promoted in the fields of culture, history and philosophy. In consequence, science had been left without a foundation and at the same time the special character of the other disciplines had been undermined. This meant that the task was now *to extricate* philosophy from science:

It is high time that people got over being dazzled, particularly in philosophy and logic, by the ideal and regulative ideas and methods of the 'exact' sciences – as though the In-itself of such sciences were actually an absolute norm for objective being and for truth. Actually, they do not see the wood for the trees. Because of a splendid cognitive performance, though with only a very restricted teleological sense, they overlook the infinitudes of life and its cognition, the infinitudes of relative and, only in its relativity, rational being with its relative truths. But to rush ahead and philosophize from on high about such matters is fundamentally wrong; it creates a wrong sceptical relativism and a no less wrong logical absolutism, mutual bugbears that knock each other down and come to life again like the figures in a Punch and Judy show.[8]

But the second crisis was in fact qualitatively different from the first. It was by no means a comic matter that now confronted us. Nor was it simply a problem of reconstructing the specificity that had been occluded of the object domains. The problem facing humanity was of a new and urgent kind; it involved no less than the question of its very survival. The issues no longer concerned matters of degree. And the responsibility of philosophy was total. For science, which once seemed so promising, had no more to offer. 'The true struggles of our time,' Husserl claimed, 'are struggles between humanity which has already collapsed and humanity which still has roots but is struggling to keep them or find new ones.'[9] In our vital need 'science has nothing to say to us. (For) (i)t excludes in principle precisely the questions which man, given over in our unhappy times to the most portentous upheavals, finds the most burning; questions of the meaning or meaninglessness of the whole of human existence.'[10] It is the task of philosophy to keep alive the possibilities of reason and truth; insofar as it falls to them alone to accomplish this task, philosophers are thus 'functionaries of mankind'.[11]

This sombre perception by Husserl of a crisis of potentially tragic dimensions in the foundations of knowledge and learning was of course not his perception alone. Indeed, between 1890 and 1933 a deepening sense of impending catastrophe gripped German intellectual life. War, inflation, the growth of science and the dawn of the machine age provoked at times an excitement, but more often a profound pessimism that all that had been of value in culture and learning was coming to an end. In addition to Husserl, the debate was joined by Max Weber, Karl Mannheim, Ernst von

Aster, Oswald Spengler, Karl Jaspers, Wolfgang Kohler, Max Scheler, Heinrich Rickert and many others.[12] Accordingly, the intellectual and cultural climate of intensifying despair within which Husserl's works were produced must certainly be taken into account in any attempt to understand his philosophy in its entirety; for only thus can the problems to which he addressed himself be elucidated and the true originality of the answers he proposed be appreciated. Nevertheless, apart from the brief acknowledgment in these introductory comments, this issue will not be taken up here. For our principal interest in Husserl's theory of science is rather in its formal structure and in the technical possibilities it exhausts; and our purpose is primarily to evaluate the extent to which this theory admits of an application to the contemporary problems we have been discussing. In this context, the historical and social circumstances are certainly relevant, but only to the extent that they raise for the first time within phenomenology the questions of history and the historicity of science.

The tasks then to which the phenomenological project was addressed were both complementary and directly opposed. On the one hand a method had to be provided for philosophy that would secure firm foundations for it. On the other, philosophy itself had to be mobilized in a critique of the idea of science that was threatening philosophy's own foundations. Thus phenomenology as rigorous science has to be distinguished from phenomenology as philosophy of science. Nevertheless there is indeed a constant notion of *science* operating here. Science is, in brief, that which directs itself towards the 'knowledge of what actually is' in order 'to understand it in its ultimate sense'.[13] It produces 'absolute, timeless values'[14] which, once discovered, belong thereafter 'to the treasure trove of all succeeding humanity'.[15] In addition, these objectively valid results must be available to a whole research community of individuals working within the science.[16]

These characteristics define the *telos* of any science; we can also say something about its structure. Most importantly, a science must have 'a systematic coherence in the theoretical sense', that is, it must both be itself a unity and provide for the grounded validation of knowledge in a systematic way.[17] Without a regular form there would be no science[18] and nor would there be a science if the validating arguments conformed to no laws.[19] Finally, all sciences, while proceeding methodically in the pursuit of truth 'employ more or less artificial aids in order to bring to knowledge truths or probabilities that would otherwise remain hidden, and in order to use the obvious or the already established as a lever for achieving what is remote and only mediately attainable.'[20]

Method

Different sciences are distinguished from each other by their specific object domains and their methods. We shall turn shortly to the case of natural science; first however it is necessary to make some reference to the fundamental characteristics of the method of phenomenology itself – which is the 'science' by means of which the structure of natural science is to be determined. We emphasize that we are not concerned here to provide an explication of phenomenology but rather to examine the way it deals with certain problems; thus no attempt will be made at a comprehensive formulation. Indeed it would be disingenuous to suggest that any such formulation were possible at all. For the details are certainly not unambiguously available from any of Husserl's works, many of which in fact claimed – in their entirety – to provide a description of the phenomenological method; and at any rate the techniques changed substantially over the years – this fact itself being a controversial issue. What we can do therefore is no more than merely advert briefly to some of the key methodological concepts frequently applied in phenomenology, in order both to emphasize that phenomenology as a 'science' in its own right does indeed have a distinctive method and, thereby, to distinguish it from the object to which it is applied, that is, natural science.

* * * * * *

We have said that the objective of phenomenology is to secure certain founded knowledge about the world by means alone of an introspective interrogation of consciousness. This programme is based on the elementary hypothesis that all knowledge comes from, and remains within, experience; indeed, that the world itself is precisely the totality of objects that can be known through experience. Furthermore, it is claimed that this knowledge can be acquired through orderly theoretical thought on the basis of direct, present experience.[21] Another hypothesis however is presupposed here also: the hypothesis that the class of experiences of which we are speaking displays a single common property – that of 'intending, of referring to what is objective, in a presentative or other analogous fashion'.[22] This second hypothesis becomes Husserl's principle of intentionality. For him it marks a characteristic feature of consciousness and is that which justifies him in describing the whole stream of experience as at once a stream of consciousness and unity of one consciousness;[23] he later states this principle in the famous aphorism 'consciousness is consciousness *of*'.[24] As for the actual method of phenomenology, it is based on a further principle – the 'principle of all principles': 'every primordial dator Intuition is a source of authority for knowledge, that whatever presents itself in "intuition" in primordial form (as it were in its bodily reality), is simply to be accepted as it gives itself out to be, though only within the limits in which it then presents itself.'[25]

From these simple ideas much of phenomenology follows. By taking the phenomena just as they give themselves, that is, in intending, perceiving, imagining, remembering, and so on,[26] their deep essential structures can be determined. These structures, or 'essences', are just what emerge as invariant across the flux of conscious life and they constitute the end-point of phenomenological reflection. Several techniques are available to facilitate the process of their identification; we mention two of these in particular. The dator presentation of a given series of phenomena can be deliberately transformed in a methodical way in order to establish a number of alternative 'profiles'; these profiles will be found to appear within a 'horizon', which defines the limits within which the phenomena retain their characteristic identity. Furthermore, out of the process of so-called free variation an invariant appears, 'the indissolubly identical in the different and ever-again different, the essence common to all, the universal essence by which all "imaginable" variants of the example, and all variants of any such variant, are restricted. This invariant is the ontic essential form (a priori form), the *eidos*, corresponding to the example'.[27] This first technique is called the 'eidetic reduction'.[28] The second technique to which we refer is the 'phenomenological reduction' – actually a complex of procedures described variously (and not always consistently) throughout Husserl's work. In one common classification three separate such reductions are identified:

1 The phenomenological reduction in the strict sense, which involves regarding phenomena as they are, exclusively in relation to the intentional subject, that is, from the perspective from which the question of their actual being is suspended;

2 The socio-historical reduction to the lifeworld, the world of our immediate experience; this reduction marks one of the specific innovations of Husserl's last work;

3 The transcendental reduction, which leads from the lifeworld and

the phenomenal worldly subject to absolute, transcendental subjectivity and in which consists the ultimate presuppositions of both.

The phenomenological reductions will be discussed in more detail below, where they will be explicated in the context of Husserl's theory of science. Here, to conclude this brief introductory sketch of phenomenological method, we would like merely to emphasize once more some of its most conspicuous features. Phenomenology is intended as a pure descriptive science which studies the whole field of pure transcendental consciousness in the light of pure intuition.[29] In its method it seeks to follow the nature of the things to be investigated and not our prejudices and preconceptions of them.[30] Thus, through the study of consciousness alone, it hopes to be able to provide a foundation for objectivity. Its claims to presuppositionlessness and certainty are made possible by the restriction of its deliberations to acts of reflection alone: to the modes of immanent apprehension of essences on the one hand, and to the modes of immanent experience on the other.[31] Consequently, it sets itself a standard against which its claims to rigorous 'scientificity' can be judged: '(t)o claim nothing that we cannot make essentially transparent to ourselves by reference to consciousness and on purely immanental lines.'[32]

With this standard in mind – which certainly appears to depart somewhat from the precepts of physics, chemistry and biology – we turn to the theory of science provided by phenomenology.

The phenomenological theory of science

Two basic points guide the whole of Husserl's analysis of natural science. In the first place, there was, built into phenomenology at its very core, an automatic critique of objectivism. Only that could be claimed, it said, which could be made essentially transparent to us by reference to consciousness. Thus any assertion or set of assertions which claimed privileged access to a world postulated outside the realm of conscious acts automatically came under suspicion. We have already quoted Husserl's belief that objectivistic natural science today has nothing to say to us. He maintains that the same is true for modern psychology, for which he in fact reserves his most strenuous critique; indeed, in the case of the latter he also attacks repeatedly both its methods and its conception of its own objects. The very last sentences of the text of the *Crisis* are intended to be directed at all the positive sciences. 'To call physicalism philosophy is only to pass off an equivocation as a realization of the perplexities concerning our knowledge in which we have found ourselves since Hume. Nature can be thought of as a definite manifold, and we can take this idea as a basis hypothetically. But insofar as the world is a world of knowledge, a world of consciousness, a world with human beings, such an idea is absurd for it to unsurpassable degree.'[33]

Secondly, however, in respect of physics and the other positive natural sciences, Husserl at the same time never for a moment doubted the truth content of their specific validity claims. Immediately before his assertion of the spiritual emptiness of science in the *Crisis*, he is careful to add that his comments concern 'not the scientific character of the sciences but rather what they, or what science in general, (have) meant and could mean for human existence'.[34] For the crisis 'does not encroach upon the theoretical and practical success of the special sciences'.[35] Elsewhere, discussing the crisis in the humanities, he deliberately contrasts their condition with 'the greatness of the natural sciences'.[36] And rather earlier, in *Ideen III*, in the same vein, he says:

> the advances of science have not enriched us in treasures of insights. The world is not in the least more intelligible through them; it has only become more useful for us. Treasures of knowledge may be in the sciences, indeed they must be in them, since we cannot doubt that the claim to validity of their statements is a good one, even though within limits still to be defined. But these treasures of knowledge we do not have; we must first win them. For knowledge is insight, is truth drawn from intuition and thereby completely understood ... The point is to lead the sciences back to their origin, which demands insight and rigorous validity, and to transform them into systems of intuitive knowledge through work which clarifies, makes distinct and grounds ultimately ...[37]

It can be readily seen that, as radical as were Husserl's assertions regarding the meaning of science, this radicalness was nevertheless abruptly prescinded by the adoption of a rather conventional view of its sense. Science's truth was unassailable insofar as its claim fell within the territory marked out by the knowledge-constitutive interest of instrumental action. Philosophy could only take issue with it when it tried to assert itself beyond that realm. The validity of science's specific claims was thus in principle inaccessible to philosophical thought. Adorno has argued that Husserl's desire to attain an ultimate, indubitable source-point of all knowledge and meaning – a desire which certainly betrays his affinity to the natural sciences

– itself incorporated important presuppositions. 'This desire ... to get hold of the Absolute and, in the last analysis, to deduce with an absolute stringency everything from one absolute point, is an idealist desire.... Once attempting to build up a philosophy of the Absolute, he is thrown back to the same principle of the Ego, the spontaneity of which he has rejected ... (T)he ultimate notions to which his philosophy resorts are idealistic ones.'[38] It can be argued with equal force that the acceptance a priori of one particular view of *science* compromised *that* part of his analysis similarly. This often becomes clear when the question of the actual content of science arises. Thus, for example, in *Formal and Transcendental Logic* he asserts that '(n)atural science ... *must* rely on external experience, only because external experience is precisely that mode of having something itself which pertains to natural objects, and therefore without it there would be absolutely nothing conceivable to which believing about Nature ... might adjust itself.'[39] But this is clearly a specious argument once the assumption about science has been removed; and indeed in that case the task would remain of discovering the 'mode of having something' posited by any given theory of nature.

To be sure, Husserl himself is always very precise about the objectives of this theory of science – and they never include the penetration of the scientific disciplines themselves. What he does in fact hope to achieve on the other hand follows naturally from the two points just mentioned, that is, from the implicit critique of objectivism and the abiding faith in science. Husserl hopes to demarcate the boundaries of science: to characterize the object domains to which it applies and the kinds of problems to which it may legitimately devote itself – to provide for it, that is, a critique in the Kantian sense. In addition, he hopes to clarify the foundations of science, to discover its origins in human conscious activity and thus, by making available to it for the first time certain truth, render it truly rigorous. Finally, through securing the meaning of *science* Husserl hopes to rescue the faith in 'absolute' reason, through which the *world* has its meaning: 'the faith in the meaning of history, of humanity, the faith in man's freedom, that is his capacity to secure rational meaning for his individual and common human existence.'[40]

In what follows we shall describe in some detail the two main strategies that Husserl employed in his attempt to realize these aims. These strategies correspond roughly to the first two phenomenological reductions mentioned previously, the third being common to both of them. That which we shall describe first seeks to classify the various ontologies associated with the sciences, their corresponding forms of evidence and thus their intentional structures and modes of truth. After that we shall discuss the socio-historical reduction to the lifeworld elaborated in the *Crisis* and the associated themes of Galileo's mathematization of nature and of history and intersubjectivity. In each case we shall argue that inherent problems arise within the phenomenological account itself – fundamental tensions of which Husserl was aware but could not resolve. And in each case we shall argue that the anti-objectivistic critique of phenomenology produced like a shadow another critique – radically different from it – and another conception of science.

The strategy of *Formal and Transcendental Logic*

Let us consider the sciences of nature. At the outset we can say no more about them than that their objects in some way embrace natural phenomena and that they are, in fact, 'scientific' – that is, that they display a systematic unity in form and method. There are many questions therefore to answer: How are the different sciences to be classified? How are their principles of unity to be identified? What distinguishes two sciences from each other? Do all appeal to similar forms of evidence? Do they depend on identical concepts of truth? And so on. Clearly, satisfactory and exhaustive solutions to these problems will not be provided by mere haphazard reflection. What is needed is a systematic theory of theories that will enable us to determine the possible forms that a science may take and the aspects in which it may be differentiated from others. It is exactly the construction of such a theory that is one of Husserl's major intentions in his logical works, and especially in *Formal and Transcendental Logic*. To do so he utilizes some of the distinctions of traditional logic – which, after all, was intended as a theory of science from the very beginning[41] – and insights from contemporary mathematics – both of which he interprets, of course, from the phenomenological perspective.

Before proceeding to examine the theory of logic proposed by Husserl, however, it is necessary to make a few preliminary observations. Every science involves the making of judgements about a delimited set of objects. (Here and in what follows, apart from where an exception is explicitly made, the term 'judgement' will be used not in the technical sense of the *Logical Investigations* but, in the more general usage employed in the work under consideration, as anything that can be asserted or posited, whether or not predicatively formed.[42]) Furthermore, it is the objects that are of primary interest (and so of course the knowledge of them thereby derived) rather than the judgements themselves. Nevertheless, a distinction can always be made between that which is asserted by a judgement and the condition of its being presented in evidence as a fact. Indeed, it is on the possibility of such a distinction that the potential for verification of any science rests. It can even be said that this is one of the characterizing marks of a science and the one which determines its peculiar mode of procedure of 'zigzagging', as Husserl puts it, between the 'givenness of something' and an 'idea of an evidence' that is to be tested.[43] Thus it is not surprising to discover that Husserl takes this difference between the process of judging and a set of objects about which such judgements presume to speak as fundamental in the development of his theory of science. As simple as this decision may seem however, it carries with it some immediate, important consequences for the organization of the problems with which a theory of scientific theories is to deal. In particular, two broad foci have now been separated: *judgements* – the subject of traditional logic – and *objects as given* – the subject of Husserl's own phenomenology. What will thus henceforth be at issue will be the possible forms of and interconnections between judgements, the possible forms of objects and their interconnections and of course the relationship between the two realms. More precisely, the theory of logic is now confronted with a threefold task: to elucidate the primitive concepts belonging to the correlative categories of significance and the object, to distinguish laws applying to each category and thus to provide the elements of a 'theory of theories' – which will at this level also be a theory of the forms of 'any possible object whatever'.[44]

As we have said, traditional logic provided classifications for judgements but excluded from its consideration any reference to the realm of objects. It is Husserl's specific innovation to have expanded the scope of logic to include this region also.[45] In deference to Aristotle the study of judgements is called 'apophantics'; in the theory to be developed it is formal apophantics that is at issue because the judgements are to be considered only formally, as empty and unfulfilled – that is, with the question bracketed of their possible adequation to things. The study of objects as given is called 'formal ontology'; it too is formal because its interest is in the structures of such objects rather than in their particular modes of givenness in evidence, which is the object of a 'material' ontology. Formal ontology had already been distinguished as early as

Ideas, where it is described as 'the eidetic science of objects in general', it 'conceals in itself the forms of all possible ontologies' and thereby prescribes to the material ontologies 'a formal constitution common to all of them'.[46] But it is not until *Formal and Transcendental Logic* that its relationship with and distinction from apophantics is elevated to a central theme. Indeed, for clarity and because it is so important, it might be emphasized that it is precisely with the themes of each domain,[47] rather than with specific techniques associated with each of them, that we are concerned. Formal ontology is the theory of logic considered from the point of view of the object of any possible judgement, dislocated from any particular one; it deals with the most general categories of the object (objects, sets, numbers, facts, equality, identity, relation and so on).[48] Formal apophantics is logical theory from the point of view of the judgement as meant – its concern is primarily with categories of signification (judgement, predicate, proposition, syllogism and so on).[49]

In his analysis of apophantics Husserl distinguishes three 'levels' of logic, corresponding to the kinds of evidence to which they would refer for substantiation. The first level is that previously defined in the fourth *Logical Investigation* (although incompletely developed there) as the theory of pure forms of signification or the grammar of pure logic.[50] In *Formal and Transcendental Logic* it is referred to 'as the pure morphology of judgement' or the theory of its pure forms. It treats the 'mere possibility of judgements as judgements, without enquiry whether they are true or false, or even whether, merely as judgements, they are compatible or contradictory'.[51] This is certainly a rudimentary stratum and the evidence associated with it may be 'vague and confused' – or even contradictory.[52] Nevertheless it is not vacuous, for it is on this level that we are able to clarify some formal aspects concerning the universal structures of judgement, the operations by which they may be combined, and so on. Furthermore it is only after such clarification has been effected that we can ascend to the second level, that of 'consequence logic' also called the 'logic of non-contradiction'.[53] Here we are dealing with judgements that are consistent with each other – that is, we exclude those that would involve an analytic contradiction when the laws of the first level were applied. This logic of course represents a very considerable field and treats problems of great importance, such as analytic consequence, consistency and inconsistency, the compatibility of judgements and so on.[54] Its determinations specify the possible forms of true judgements, although it itself prescinds from raising questions of truth and falsity. Since its task is to make judgements distinct insofar as they are regarded merely as judgements and independently from the act of performing them, we may say that the evidence corresponding to this level is *distinct* evidence. It is only on the third level that the question of the facts that make up the subject-matter of the judgement can be considered. Thus here there is a new form of evidence that applies: the *clear* evidence, according to which is given, 'with full clarity', 'the affairs themselves ... the predicatively formed affair-complex itself at which one aims in the judging'.[55] It is only now, at last, that we are dealing with a 'logic of truth', where questions can be asked concerning the adequation of judgements to the affairs themselves.[56] Now the judgements can be thought of as capable of verification and thus 'not as mere judgements, but as judgements pervaded by a dominant cognitional striving, as meanings that have to become fulfilled, that are not objects by themselves, like the data arising from mere distinctness but passages to the "truths" themselves that are to be attained.'[57] Hence in this matter the theoretical focusing on mere judgements is exchanged for a focusing instead on cognition.[58]

With the logic of truth then we have already reached science, for as we have noted it is exactly the 'interest in cognizing' – in knowledge – that is science's distinguishing characteristic.[59] However the movement has been too fast, for we are not yet at the point where we can consider a theory of possible theories. We have so far dealt only with single judgements and facts as meant, whereas science deals with unified systems of judgements and with facts as given. A description of both of these presupposes a logic of the forms of objects – that is, a formal ontology.

Objects can be given to us in two ways, according to Husserl. They can be present in immediate experience; here we are dealing with so called substrate objects.[60] Or else they can be produced predicatively in judgements; these latter are called 'categorial objects' and are the kind with which we are concerned in *Formal and Transcendental Logic*. It should be noted that substrate objects are not absolutely prepredicative, as is often supposed; for example they can have an identity only insofar as it is constituted in an act of judgement.[61] However this point will be more relevant in a later context. Formal ontology is the study of categorial objects, which are the only objects available to us as cognitive-judging subjects[62] and thus as scientists. Indeed '(t)ruly existing Nature, truly existing sociality or culture, and the like – these have absolutely no sense other than that of being certain categorial objectivities, to press on toward which by scientific method, generating them by following that method, is the whole aim of science.'[63]

116

The study of categorial objectivities was conceived by Husserl explicitly on the basis of the example of formal mathematics. For he saw that

> the theory of sets and the theory of cardinal numbers relate to the empty universe, any object whatever or anything whatever, with a formal universality that, on principle, leaves out of consideration every material determination of objects. . . . Going on from there, one recognizes that . . . the other formal mathematical disciplines are formal in the sense of having as fundamental concepts certain derivative formations of anything – whatever. This gives rise to the idea of an all-embracing science, a formal mathematics in the fully comprehensive sense, whose all-inclusive province is rigidly delimited as the sphere of the highest form-concept, any object whatever . . . with all the derivative formations generable (and therefore conceivable) a priori in this field – formations that always go on yielding new formations as products generated in a constructing that is always reiterable. . . . (I)t is natural to view this whole mathematics as an ontology (an a priori theory of objects), though a formal one, relating to the pure modes of anything – whatever. In so doing, one would also acquire the guiding idea for determining the separate provinces of this ontology – this mathematics of all objectivities as such – by a priori structural considerations.[64]

Husserl's emphasis on mathematics in these formulations raises a problem which he himself acknowledges but does not seem to resolve satisfactorily. Here – and indeed from his very earliest deliberations on these questions in the *Prolegomena* – an implicit bias is imposed in favour of one particular kind of science, namely nomological science. But certainly other, non-deductive sciences exist – for example, history, sociology, phenomenology. What would the proposed theory have to say about them? Husserl's answer seems to be: nothing. For their principle of unity is different: whereas the unifying sense of a nomological science can be determined analytically, the others only 'hang together by virtue of their objects'; thus we can become cognizant of their principles of unity only by going beyond the analytico-logical form. It is only in the deductive sciences, he argues, that the object domains can be definitely understood as mathematical manifolds.[65] This seems clear enough, until it is recalled that formal ontology is defined simultaneously as the theory of all possible forms of objects and as formal mathematics. How general then are the results? Husserl himself is undecided, saying that in fact about the name 'science' in general no more can be asserted than the following: 'It means a certain universe of propositions that arose somehow from theoretical effort and have a systematic order wherein a certain universe of objects becomes determined.'[66] Thus although analytics may be considered a first step in the development of a general theory of science the 'open problem' nevertheless remains of just what 'can still be aspired to a priori under the name of such a theory.[67] It seems to us that, until the notion of *mathesis universalis* is assumed, many of his arguments are nevertheless general ones; for it is only beyond that point that technical mathematical concepts apply and so presuppose certain strict conditions on the categorial objects. This is the viewpoint that we shall adopt: that the generality within Husserl's theory must be sought, as measured in relation to its own consciously formulated *telos* – the realization of a 'science of (all) possible categorial forms in which substrate objectivities can truly exist'.[68]

But let us return to consider more carefully the sets of objects with which sciences deal. As Husserl puts it in the *Prolegomena*, '(t)he object correlate of the concept of a possible theory, definite only in respect of form, is the concept of a possible field of knowledge over which a theory of this form will preside.'[69] This field is determined exhaustively by the fact that it falls under a theory of such a form which also prescribes the kinds of relationships that are possible between individual objects. The objects remain indefinite as regards their matter; only their possible forms, and those of their interrelationships, are determined.[70] Thus the sets of objects are endowed with a unity which in some sense pre-exists the particular procedures that are employed in the actual practice of the science. This applies to sciences at all levels. Thus '(l)ogic relates, not to what is given only in active evidence, but to abiding formations that have been primally instituted in active evidence ...; it relates to them as objectivities which are henceforth at hand, with which ... one can operate in thinking, and which ... one can further shape categorially into more and more new formations.'[71] Similarly for any other science: the scientist's aim is to cognize his province determiningly and this province is itself determined by its form of categorial objectivity (or correlatively in the realm of apophantics by such objectivity as supposed).[72]

This apparently simple point in fact raises many questions, as we shall see. For example, a problem with which Husserl will be especially concerned, and which will become central for us, is just that of whence such categories of objects derive. Some effort is still required before Husserl's own answer can be explained. Neverthe-less, inherent in the very concept of a categorial objectivity are some profound insights regarding science in general which are in-deed relevant here. In *Experience and Judgement* Husserl distin-guishes the achievement of knowledge from the 'merely receptive activities'[73] of apprehension, explication, contemplation and so on. For the very fact that the object of knowledge appears as an abid-ing unity in objective time, capable of apprehension even when the original intuition is over, shows that a special activity must be involved which makes possible such a continuous presentification or renewed self-giving. Furthermore, this special activity cannot be one that is merely attached to the pregiven and receptively appre-hended objectivities; rather, 'in predicative knowledge and its de-posit in the predicative judgement new kinds of objectivities are constituted which can then themselves be apprehended again and made thematic as logical structures'. These objectivities – which arise from the *kategorein*, the act of declarative judgement – are of course exactly the categorial objectivities of which we have been speaking. Thus 'the work of cognition, this higher stage of activity, must ... be characterized as a creative spontaneity, itself already productive of objects'. Only in this way can cognition be deposited so that it can really become an abiding possession apprehensible identically not only by me but also at the same time by others.

Thus the objects of science are actively produced in theoretical work. Indeed, where a definite theoretical unity is involved we can be more explicit still and regard the judgement-objects exactly as syntactical formations; for in this case the categorial concepts are just the syntactical forms by means of which the object is appre-hended.[74] These results are general ones. The mere concept of nature in science, which we tend to take for granted and to identify with something pregiven before all thinking, is in fact itself a highly refined product of theory; its 'existence', its 'properties', its 'predi-catively formed affair-complexes' and the like are acquired 'only from our judging, and (it) has them only for possible judgers'.[75] Indeed objects in general can now be regarded precisely as *effects* of syntactical formations,[76] as outcomes of the theoretical appar-atus.

An immediate consequence of this result does not escape Hus-serl.[77] He observes that the theoretical constitutive process can be reactivated at any time by me or by anyone else. Hence the cate-gorial products associated with them are in principle available to the entire community of judgers. Any syntactical form can be re-peated, in the sense of being re-constituted by any judger. Thus the 'nature for me' with which we started becomes at once a 'nature for all of us'.

The considerations in which we have been engaged are of a general kind, applying to the object domains of all sciences. We turn briefly now to the question – in fact treated by Husserl at some length – of the conditions which these domains must fulfil in order for the science to be a deductive one. This is obviously a crucial issue for the understanding of modern physics and will be taken up again, although from a quite different perspective, in the discussion of Galileo's mathematization of nature in the *Crisis*. In *Formal and Transcendental Logic* the problem is stated directly: 'Any science whatever is a multiplicity of truths – not haphazardly thrown together, but combined and relating in any case to a unitary province. When does the whole that comprises the infinite multiplicity of propositions making up a science have a systematic unity-form that can be constructed a priori, on the basis of a finite number of pure axiom-forms, by means of logical-categorial concepts?'[78] In fact, the answer can be obtained from the foregoing considerations merely by a reformulation of the question: 'When is the group of axiom-forms that defines a theory-form definite and the province-form, correlatively, a "mathematical" or "definite" multiplicity'?'[79] For precisely when this condition is fulfilled the form of the whole is that of a deductive science. The solution, as we said, is now present in the question. A science is deductive only when both its judgements and its objects can be subsumed under a universal unifying abstraction. Only then, in *mathesis universalis*, can formal structures be articulated prior to their roles as either facts as given or facts as supposed.[80] Only then do we have a realm of universal construction, of pure operational formations, which can be governed a priori. Thus Husserl can conclude: 'Precisely this is the answer to the question of when a science or a scientifically closed group of propositions has, according to purely analytic (mathematical) principles a unitary, mathematically constructable, system-structure.'[81]

If we restrict our gaze to those sciences – that is, the nomological ones – occurring under the rubric of *mathesis universalis* we in fact have available to us the possibility of a rigorous theory of theories. For according to Husserl, under such circumstances the object domain of a science, considered purely formally, can be understood in terms of the mathematical concept of 'multiplicity' (elsewhere called 'manifold').[82] Thus the theory of multiplicities could be applied to the task of developing a comprehensive theory of deductive sciences. In this case the power of the formal viewpoint, within which pure mathematics and philosophical logic come together, would become apparent, for deep structural kinships could be identified between theories, the similarity of which was formerly concealed by the differences in their actual contents. Indeed, at the highest level to which this approach could be taken – a theory of the possible forms of multiplicities in general – we would even be able to talk about the accomplishment of the 'all embracing task' articulated by Husserl: the development of the 'highest theory' which would comprise 'all possible forms of theories ... as mathematical particularizations'.[83]

These suggestions – of which the details remain to be provided – are interesting ones. However more important for our purposes is the convergence which they imply between the two dimensions which we so carefully separated at the outset. In fact it is now clear that we have been operating from the beginning with a logic, the duality of which was only apparent. Ultimately the theory of judgement as meant and the theory of objects as given emerge as indistinguishable. Originally the distinction between them had been defined as the difference between focusing on the objects and focusing on judgements. However, we are interested in them only insofar as they can help us to understand the structure of science. And all science occurs within the horizon of an interest in knowledge, so that only those judgements are of interest to the scientist which admit ultimately of an adequation to the affairs themselves.[84] All the objectivities which appear in formal ontology show themselves to be in fact systems of judgements generated in the process of judgement; they are syntactical formations, themselves subject to further syntactical operations. Conversely, the study of judgement which once seemed self-contained must embrace also the theory of object forms, for when we judge, we are always necessarily directed through the judgement to the object.[85] Thus formal ontology and formal apophantics occur together simultaneously and inseparably: the two realms are correlated and homogeneous and display an inner unity.[86] In advance of the demonstration of this unity their separation had been 'merely provisional, resting only on a difference of point of view and not of domain'.[87] This difference in theme was not, and is not, inconsequential. On it, for example, as we have seen, depends science's entire 'zigzag' procedure of verification. But so also – finally – does the differentiation between many theories and in particular, between two types of theories that we have been discussing – science and logic; for they are differentiated precisely by the fact that in science the immediate theme is the object and the judgement the intermediate theme, whereas in logic the judgement is immediate, while the object is only mediate.[88]

Thus far Husserl has elaborated a theory of the structure of science from an explicitly anti-objectivist viewpoint. Starting from the assumption that 'objects exist for us, and are what they are for us, exclusively as the objects of which we are at any time conscious'[89] he has examined the relationship between the systems of possible judgements and the systems of possible object forms for a given science. His conclusion is that, within the horizon of an interest in knowledge – which circumscribes theoretical science – the two cannot be separated. Moreover, the formal region of objects is a systematic unity, the elements of which are theoretical products of syntactical operations either within that region or within the larger domain of all possible judgements. This latter entity also has a systematic form and thus is subject to certain requirements regarding its own inner structure. The object region and the theoretical problematic are interdependent because the objects form within the system of judgements and thereby reciprocally endow it with form. When the whole structure can be subsumed under a universal formalization, a *mathesis universalis*, then the conditions exist for a possible deductive science; in this case it is conceivable that a more elaborate theory of scientific theories would be possible.

Now it is obvious that something is missing from this account. For it is not enough to know that the meaning of a scientific theory is indissociable from the relationships between the objects that occur within it. The scientist is interested not only in the formal structure; he is interested also – indeed principally – in the things themselves. He is interested not merely in judgements as supposed; his interest is in judgements adequate to the facts. A theory of science must have continuous with its theory of forms a theory of truth. There is nothing unexpected about this, of course; it arises quite naturally from science's concern with knowing. Yet what it means is that a whole new logic must be provided to fill in the formal structures that have so far been thought of only as cores – to 'let fullness flow back into these cores, which have been kept emptily universal'.[90]

According to Husserl the achievement of this goal would mean the discovery of a 'material a priori that has universal significance for the theory of science'.[91] He is not very specific about the nature of this a priori but nevertheless it is clear that at least two things are involved. In the first place, it must incorporate a material ontology to complement the formal one. We can see the need for such an ontology by considering briefly the question of the conditions under which a science can be a deductive one. As Husserl points out[92] this question in fact has two parts. There is the problem of the conditions for the conceptual constructions to be exact. This question has already been answered: a *mathesis universalis* is a necessary precondition. And there is the problem of the character of the domain that would conform to such structures. This question is plainly an ontological one. This argument can in fact be stated generally: if we are to be able to apprehend the principles of unity of scientific theories then we must have an ontology of the things themselves, as they are partitioned appropriately into regions. Secondly, what is required is a theory of the subjective origins of science. The material logic must supply a theory of the constitution in conscious life of experience and of the objects of experience. It must be able to demonstrate once and for all the foundational structures on which all phenomena rest.

* * * * * *

We are at last talking directly about knowledge – and knowledge of course refers implicitly to truth. From the discussion so far it is clear that at least two types of truth are at stake for Husserl. There is the logical truth that is generated within a given system of judgements. Here a truth signifies 'a correct critically verified judgement – verified by means of an adequation to the corresponding categorial objectivities "themselves", as given in the evidential having of them themselves: given originaliter, that is, in the generating activity exercised on the basis of the experienced substrates "themselves"'.[93] And in addition we have the truth associated with the substrate itself – that is, with the givenness in evidence of the actually, or truly, existent.[94] Put somewhat differently, '(O)n the one side, we have the question of constitution of forms (of judgement) and their laws and, on the other, that of the subjective conditions of the attainment of self-evidence'.[95] It might be observed that in the sixth *Logical Investigation* another typology of truth was presented;[96] however the one under discussion is the more useful in the present context. For science is concerned with cognitive truth and systematic theories and thus it proceeds precisely by a process of conscious adequation of judgements to categorial objects that are themselves given in evidence; that is, it proceeds by a process of adjustment of 'originally correct judgements ... to the truly and actually existent itself, ideally embracing and ... exhausting all the true being of the province'.[97]

We note in advance of our argument that it is not altogether

123

obvious that the two types of truth are in fact compatible – for as defined, one refers to a matter that concerns an individual consciousness alone while the other refers to a discursive event. This issue in one sense is central; however in another it lies at the very periphery of phenomenology, for it raises the question of the linguistic structure within which in general meanings are developed and communicated – and indeed conscious identities are formed. It was to deal with these and related topics that the theory of structural linguistics was fashioned; and the approach of the latter was of course quite different from that of phenomenology. Nevertheless, here we are operating strictly within the phenomenological problematic and accordingly, strictly phenomenological means must be employed to overcome the problem. As we shall see, Husserl was himself acutely aware of the problem and attempted at length to overcome it. His proposed solution, which we shall presently describe in detail, sought to overcome the divergence between the two forms of truth by the identification of specific, divergent forms of evidence, which were to come together in their common acquisition of self-evidence for a single consciousness.

Before considering these matters in more detail however, it is necessary to elaborate somewhat on Husserl's conceptions of truth and evidence in general. Science is a striving towards cognition and as such is directed towards truth. In this context truth is coterminous with knowledge which, as knowledge of the truth, is just the striving to obtain truth as such. For Husserl the experience of truth towards which knowledge tends presupposes a lower experience and embraces it. For the fact as known requires in advance the fact as intended which can be brought to fulfilled verification in the self-givenness of the substrate objectivities. Thus a conception of knowledge is employed, which Husserl 'defines' as follows:

> knowledge is the consciousness of the 'agreement' between an empty anticipatory belief, in particular a predicative belief (empty or not genuinely intuitive), and the corresponding experience which gives at first hand the object of this belief – the object judged in the predication – as the experience of its self-evident givenness – an agreement in which the anticipatory belief comes to synthetic coincidence with the belief from experience and is fulfilled in it.[98]

We have knowledge about the world when a hypothesis we might make about it – or about particular objects in the world or the relationships between such objects – is shown on the basis of worldly experience to have a full and rich content. We must therefore be able in advance of knowledge to formulate hypotheses which are capable of fulfilment. But this means that the things about which we are making the judgements must already be present in mind either in an empty way or as intuitively self-given. Thus every activity of thought presupposes pre-given objects. However more than this still can be said: clearly, it is not sufficient that objects be merely 'pregiven'; they must actually be given in such a way that knowledge about them is possible – that is, they must present themselves 'self-evidently', as they are.[99] If knowledge in the phenomenological sense is to be possible, then, there must be a concept of evidence to support it. This evidence thus appears as a universal primal phenomenon of intentional life. It is a 'quite pre-eminent mode of consciousness' which, specifically, consists in 'the self-appearance, the self-exhibiting, the self-giving, of an affair, an affair-complex (or state of affairs), a universality, a value or other objectivity, in the final mode: "itself there", "immediately intuited", "given originaliter"'.[100] It is the original consciousness of presence in which the things themselves appear – though prior to any adequation of judgements about them. It is related immanently both to experience and to truth. For experience (in the ordinary sense) is a particular evidence, while conversely all evidence 'is experience in a maximally broad, and yet essentially unitary, sense';[101] indeed, as a subregion of the wider concept of experience, it might even be said that 'evidence is ... nothing but the experience of truth'.[102] Finally, it is worth repeating that, insofar as all knowledge of the empirical world depends upon it, evidence – either as actuality or as possibility – points to an essential fundamental trait of all intentional life. 'Any consciousness, without exception, either is itself already characterized as evidence (that is, as giving its object originaliter) or else has an essential tendency towards conversion into givings of its object originaliter'.[103]

Thus knowledge – and simultaneously, truth – presuppose an evidential pre-giving to consciousness of the objects of knowledge. But as we have seen, science involves at least two types of knowledge. Not surprisingly then, we find also two corresponding types of evidence. There is the evidence in which affair-complexes are presented to consciousness as truly existing instances of the objective forms. And there is that in which the correctness of the judicial meaning is presented – correct that is, by virtue of its fitting the evidence in the first sense.[104] These two types of evidence – logical evidence and factual evidence – refer to two different levels of inquiry[105] of which only one – formal apophantics – was available to traditional logicians. However, even in this well-studied case, the outstanding problems are considerable. In particular, there is a conspicuous ambiguity adhering to judgements. On the one hand truth and falsity signify predicates of judgements but according to the phenomenological view can clearly not be predicates included in the essences of the latter;[106] for there, judgements refer to acts of meaning formation which occur in advance of any process of adequation by evidence. On the other hand, however, for every logician all judgements are indeed always 'decided in themselves' and truth and falsity are habitually attributed to their essences.[107] This apparent contradiction, which undoubtedly refers to a tension between the individual intuiting consciousness and intersubjective processes of meaning constitution, is resolved by Husserl by an appeal to the inherent character of cognitive thought. The decisions respecting truth and falsity, he says, derive from 'a "method", a course of cognitive thinking ... existing in itself and intrinsically pursuable, which leads immediately or mediately to an adequation, a making evident of either the truth or the falsity of any judgement.' 'All this,' he admits, certainly

> imputes an astonishing a priori to every subject of possible judging and therefore to every actual or conceivable human being – astonishing: for how can we know a *priori* that courses of thinking with certain final results 'exist in themselves'; paths that can be, but never have been trod; actions of thinking that have unknown subjective forms and that can be, though they never have been carried out? ... But after all, we do have de facto cognition; ... that there are indeed truths in themselves, which one can seek ..., is surely one of life's unquestioned truisms ...[108]

When we turn to a study of that which above was called 'factual' evidence we are considering once more the problem of the unity of a science. As we know, the principle of unity of a given science – even a nomological science – is deposited in its characteristic object province, which stands in a close correspondence with the system of judgements out of which its objective forms are constituted. Now it is clear also that an objectivity, insofar as it establishes a particular kind of bearing of consciousness towards the world, is expressive of a specific form of intentionality:

> (A)ny straightforwardly constituted objectivity (for example: an Object belonging to Nature) points back, according to its essential sort (for example: physical thing *in specie*) to a

correlative essential form of manifold, actual and possible intentionality ... which is constitutive for that objectivity.[109]

But it is also true that evidence, which presents the world to consciousness, and intentionality are closely related. Indeed, it follows from the brief characterization of evidence given above that evidence is a universal mode of intentionality which pervades the whole life of consciousness. Thus we may conclude that the unity of a science can be found from an analysis of the evidential modes that can be identified within it. In fact, this is exactly Husserl's conclusion and the insight on which a substantial part of his programme is based. For now it is apparent that objectivity and evidence are perfectly correlated, that '(t)o every fundamental species of objectivities – as intentional unities maintainable throughout an intentional synthesis and, ultimately, as unities belonging to a possible "experience" – a fundamental species of "experience", of evidence, corresponds, and likewise a fundamental species of intentionality indicated evidential style.'[110] Thus the task that confronts us is clear: the 'great task ... of exploring all these modes of the evidence in which the objectivity intended to shows itself.'[111] This task is one of constructing an ontology – or rather, a series of ontologies – but it goes well beyond formal ontology. For '(f)ormal ontology, conceived as analytics, relates with empty universality to any possible world whatever'; however the ontology in the construction of which we shall now be engaged – ontology, that is, in the sense of 'ontology of realities' – will explicate this idea in respect of 'the structural forms essentially necessary to a world'.[112]

It is worth noting briefly that these ideas had in fact been more or less clear to Husserl since *Ideas*, where he first articulated the notion of a regional ontology. There, he observed that '(e)very theoretical science binds an ideally limited whole of being together by relating it to a domain of knowledge which on its side is related to a higher genus. We first reach a radical unity through reverting to the highest genus of all, to the relevant region and to the regional components of the genus.... To each region there corresponds a regional ontology with a series of self-limited regional sciences.'[113] Later, he pointed out that '(t)o every region and category of would-be objects corresponds phenomenologically not only a basic kind of meaning or position, but also a basic kind of primordial dator consciousness of such meaning, and, pertaining to it, a basic type of primordial self-evidence.'[114] Finally, in the closing pages of the book substantial possible consequences for the theory of science were claimed. '(R)egions of inquiry open up which treat of all genuine matters of principle in all the material sciences'; the 'basic concepts and fundamental forms of knowledge' find, 'indeed must find, (their) systematic unfolding in corresponding regional ontologies'.[115] Nevertheless it was not until *Formal and Transcendental Logic* that the logical problems involved could be treated in detail and the theory therefore fully elaborated. Indeed, it was not until this text was attained that the great problems inherent in the whole endeavour could become prominent.

Two conclusions: facts in context

We shall shortly consider the emergence of these problems. However first it is necessary to secure two important conclusions that follow from the results so far achieved. Husserl has shown that there exist different modes of objectivity which are constituted in intentional life as syntheses of manifold experiences.[116] Furthermore the domains of objects correspond exactly with provinces of meaning. Science deals exclusively with artifacts of this kind - with things, states-of-affairs and truths which are the outcome of both formal and subjective operations[117] and which cohere in unities structured systematically. Thus for phenomenology objects or existents are not considered as they exist in themselves as isolated entities, but only as they come together within a living horizon of human experience. Things are now complex bundles of intentional implications, and truth, no longer falsely absolutized, is truth within an horizon - 'the living truth from the living source, which is our absolute life'.[118] The horizon is thus a kind of totality, within which the intentional subject-object unities of experience are articulated. It is a totality the outline of which the phenomenologist must strive to explicate if he is to 'make understandable to himself how, within the immanency of conscious life and in thus and so determined modes of consciousness belonging to this incessant flux, anything like fixed and abiding objective unities can become intended and, in particular, how this marvellous work of "constituting" ideal objects is done in the case of each category of objects.'[119]

The second conclusion - which is perhaps an obvious one - relates to the conception of objectivity thus established and its implications for science itself. Here also are two points to be made. In the first place, it is now clear how profoundly anti-objectivist is the theory of science developed by phenomenology. This is so even at times in spite of itself. For if the objects, concepts and categories of science are all constructs of intentional life then, regardless of the attractiveness of a notion of some putative 'external experience' to which they might refer, even within the very work of science they will be able to be theorized adequately only if this subjective dimension is taken into account. This is the case precisely because science directs itself towards objects and so is not purely a formal matter. Thus the anti-objectivist results of phenomenology cannot be restrained within the meta-theoretical context but, in fact, must impinge on science's actual procedures. What this may mean for science of course remains undetermined and at any rate Husserl, himself 'dazzled' by its apparent successes, fails to draw this conclusion.

On the other hand however, this very formulation of the problem of objectivity raises considerable difficulties. Husserl has resiled from developing further a second conception of objectivity, to which we have previously drawn attention,[120] within which objectivity emerges as an effect of the determinate theoretical apparatus of a given system of discourse. We note that this, incipient, alternative conception is also an anti-objectivistic one, for in it the categories of objectivity cannot be conceived independently of the intersubjective field. Furthermore, here, for this very reason, the disparate truth claims associated with the alternative theoretical systems can be reconciled, for they can be subsumed under the common processes of meaning constitution inhering in the linguistic structures. Nevertheless this conception is not fully developed and the problem of the proliferation of the forms of truth in fact becomes a rather substantial one. For in the phenomenological view objectivity is bound to evidence, as we have seen, which is in turn a precondition for knowledge about objects. Husserl adds: '(t)o every object "that truly is" there intrinsically corresponds (in the a priori of the unconditioned generality of the essence) the idea of a possible consciousness in which the object itself can be grasped in a primordial and also perfectly adequate way. Conversely, when this possibility is guaranteed, the object is *eo ipso* "that which truly is"'.[121] This could perhaps be expressed slightly differently, though in more familiar terms, as the thesis that the conditions of the possibility of experience in general are also the conditions of the possibility of the objects of experience – although of course Husserl here makes no explicit reference to Kant. Such an interpretation of the 'highest principle of all synthetic judgements' from the perspective of modern phenomenology is certainly striking, but the difficulties it presents within a structurally differentiated field of categorial objectivities are at the same time immediately clear. In particular, if evidences are similarly differentiated, then so also in a radical way must be the forms of truth. This would mean that no single conception of truth were possible, but only a multiplicity of relative ones. But this is exactly the point of view that Husserl has, from the very outset, vehemently opposed. In the *Prolegomena* he derided the 'relativist' hypothesis as 'absurd', claiming emphatically instead that '(w)hat is true is absolutely, intrinsically true: truth is one and the same, whether men or non-men, angels or gods apprehend and judge it'.[122] And this belief was maintained unbroken to the very end, where, in 'The Origin of Geometry', the logical structures are said to display a 'supertemporal' validity.[123] It now becomes a major task for phenomenology to re-establish the integrity of truth and to provide for it a single, unitary ground.

It may be observed in passing that this problem of the identity of truth, does not appear within objectivism. For there, truth can, quite simply, be assumed a priori.

Just as the realities beonging to the world are what they are, in and of themselves, so also they are substrates for truths that are valid in themselves.... In the cognizing subjects there are corresponding possibilities of cognition, of seizing upon these truths themselves in subjective evidence-processes, in absolute evidences as seizings upon of the absolute truths themselves, the very ones that are valid in themselves. All of that is claimed a priori. The truths that hold for what exists in itself – for what exists absolutely, and not for what exists relatively or subjectively ... are absolute truths.[124]

The error in this view is now of course very familiar to us and can be stated in a single sentence. The conception of evidence as absolutely apodictic, as the property of a single mental event torn from the concrete context of the subjective processes, occludes precisely the fact that not only the idea of the absolutely existing object but even the idea of the absolute truths in themselves pertaining to such an object are mental constructs, constituted in the flow of intentional life.[125]

Phenomenology however seeks not an arbitrary, ultimate hypothesis but a firm foundation for knowledge. It seeks not a series of gratuitous claims in relation to which the validity of logical judgements is assumed but a systematically developed discipline which will secure once and for all the ground on which logic is based and thence the unity not only of truth but also of all the sciences. This discipline must have the further special quality of providing the grounds for its own justification and hence in this sense will be a 'transcendental' logic; thus will be completed the last step in the development of a truly radical, presuppositionless theory of science. We already have the material before us out of which Husserl will begin the construction of this ultimate science. In addition, of course, we already know the origin from which this science will claim all sense flows: for Husserl the only thing that is prior to all phenomena is the ego.

Constitution, origins and subjectivity

It is in the ego that all sense is constituted. Indeed nothing exists for me other than by performance of my own consciousness.[126] It can even be said that the world is constituted by me if by that we mean that it is only by virtue of my effective intentionality that the world comes truly to exist for me. For certainly 'whatever I encounter as an existing object is something that ... has received its whole being sense for me from my effective intentionality'.[127] Thus my constituting subjectivity pre-exists all else that is conceivable: all existent objects, all judgements and all knowledge. 'I, the "transcendental ego", am the ego who "precedes" everything wordly.'[128] The subjective a priori is prior to 'the world, the being of everything, individually and collectively, for me, the thinking subject'[129] and the being of God. 'Even God is for me what he is, in consequence of my own productivity of consciousness.'[130] Subjectivity is the absolute origin to which all phenomena can be traced.

Consequently, it is the task of logic to go back systematically from the ideal formations to the consciousness that constitutes them phenomenologically[131] and to define their places within the structures of intentional life. To accomplish this task, clearly, much remains to be done and great problems remain to be overcome. In particular, there is the most obvious problem: the simple fact – which nevertheless appears within phenomenology as far from simple – that the world which I experience is also the world for others, an intersubjective world within which communication about a wide variety of phenomena occurs. Before considering how Husserl executes this final phase of his argument however we shall pause briefly to comment, for the sake of what follows later, on the question of 'origins' involved therein.

It is important to recognize that the origins which Husserl seeks are not *chronological* origins. The objectives of this project are stated on the very first page of *Experience and Judgment* which, after all, is explicitly devoted to an elaboration of a 'genealogy of logic':

> In this clarification of origin, which has as a theme neither a
> problem of the 'history of logic' in the usual sense, nor one of
> genetic psychology, the essence of the structure whose origin is
> sought is to be elucidated. Our task is thus a clarification of the
> essence of the predicative judgement by means of an
> exploration of its origin.[132]

The origins that are sought are not historical, nor psychological,
nor even logical: what is sought is the primordial origin of all of
these. Phenomenology seeks to dismantle everything which already
exists in the sedimentations of the world of experience and to interrogate these sedimentations relative to the subjective sources out
of which they have developed. It seeks to elucidate the subjectivity
whose questions of sense have made the world which is pregiven to
us what it is.[133] This elucidation is to be effected by means of a
twofold regression, which we shall consider: a regression to the
original world experience of all individuals and a regression to the
subjective operations from which even the lifeworld is said to arise.
Thus the search for origins to which phenomenology is devoted is
for primordial, pre-predicative origins in which consist the conditions of possibility for all other experience.

> We ... understand ourselves, not as subjectivity which finds
> itself in a world ready-made ... but as a subjectivity bearing
> within itself, and achieving, all of the possible operations to
> which this world owes its becoming. In other words, we
> understand ourselves in this revelation of intentional
> implications, in the interrogation of the origin of the
> sedimentation of sense from intentional operations, as
> transcendental subjectivity, where, by 'transcendental', nothing
> more is to be understood than the theme, originally
> inaugurated by Descartes, of a regressive inquiry concerning
> the ultimate source of all cognitive formations, of a reflection
> by the knowing subject on himself and on his cognitive
> life ...[134]

The question of 'origins' is a problematic one and, as we shall
see, has been subjected justly to rigorous criticism. Nevertheless,
regardless of the shortcomings in relation to its own aims, stated
above, of the particular approach it does adopt, phenomenology
intends 'origins' in a special sense and thus by and large exempts
itself from these criticisms.[135]

The completion of the transcendental grounding of logic must
overcome two problems. It must reconcile within an individual ego

the multiplicity of truths appearing to it. And it must reconcile within the human community the truths appearing to a multiplicity of egos. It is not surprising that within Husserl's theory both tasks occur together. The principle of unity, as we have said, is the ego. Thus what must be accomplished is, on the one hand, the tracing back to it of the grounding of any objectivity and on the other, the discovery within any one ego of the structures that must be common to all. Regarding the former, we have seen how any object – real or irreal – is built up in a synthesis of manifold experiences. To every type of objectivity corresponds a form of evidence. But an evidence is only a giving immanently to consciousness of an object itself. The unity of a particular object accrues from the intersection in consciousness of a multiplicity of original experiences of its presence, an event made possible by the inherently intentional character of experience. The 'transcendence' of an object is certainly constituted in the immanent sphere. However, more important than this is the ideality thus associated with objectivity in general, which is consequently 'the universal ideality of all intentional unities over against the multiplicities constituting them'.[136] It is precisely in these terms that evidence and hence objectivity must be understood. Evidential givings on the one hand must be characterized as the constitutive processes whereby objectivity arises; on the other hand however, at the same time, evidence 'quite universally, is indeed nothing other than the mode of consciousness ... that offers its intentional objectivity in the mode belonging to the original "it itself"'.[137] Previously, we saw another argument for the same result from the opposite direction. Objectivities are constituted in judgements but obviously not merely adventitiously; thus they must in some sense already be present as entities intended to within the original production. The site of these intentional depositions is once again the original evidence within which the primal constitutive processes leading to the ideal objectivities occur. In summary then, the disparate evidential modes associated with the regional ontologies come together (that is, they are 'grounded') in a more original evidence that represents the general structures which all must incorporate. It is at this higher level of generality that the invariant structures of experience will be found that ultimately will be common to all individuals.

This may seem like an easy result. However, a higher level of generality is not a higher level of abstraction. On the contrary, generality represents a more specific and immediate form of experience from which the more elaborate constructions can in fact be derived. Thus an extensive task remains for phenomenology: the identification of the most elementary constituents of experience and the characterization of the hierarchy of evidences corresponding to the various levels of the latter. This task belongs to other aspects of Husserl's work and we only mention it here. In relation to judgements we are led back to ultimate substrates, ultimate predicates, ultimate universalities, ultimate relations.[138] In relation to truth we are led back to truths that are linked directly to their matters and material spheres, or to individual objects.[139] Regarding experience in general the primal modes include the prepredicative ones of direct perception of objects, memory, imagination, internal time-consciousness, and so on. Finally, it is on this basis that the hierarchy of evidences is built up: from pure and simple experiential judgements we proceed to non-evident judgements and thence to formal and materially filled universalities.

In this way the various strata of subjectivity are elucidated. However it is not enough simply to display them as invariant structures of subjectivity alone. They must simultaneously present themselves as necessary conditions for any possible subjectivity – that is, for intersubjectivity also. Thus not just predicative truth but world experience in general must be demonstrated to be in its very nature not merely my private acquisition but in fact a communal accomplishment.[140] Only under these conditions could there be established a single identical world within which individuals could reach agreement regarding knowledge and the objects of knowledge. We shall not pursue at this point Husserl's complex argumentation regarding intersubjectivity. Nor shall we consider the substantial difficulties associated with this theory – except to observe that it is indeed remarkable that so elementary a fact as intersubjective communication is apparently so intractable within phenomenology. To follow these questions here would delay the present argument, which is more concerned with the theory of the structure of science that emerges from phenomenology – and at any rate it will be more relevant in the context of the following chapter. Here it is sufficient merely to advert to Husserl's conclusions in order to sketch the character of the final ground for knowledge to which phenomenology recurs. That the world is there for us according to Husserl does not alter the fact that in the first place it is there for me.[141] Indeed it is exactly in my ego that is constituted the open plurality of other egos.[142] More precisely, transcendental intersubjectivity is derived from, and thus remains relative to, my transcendental ego: in fact it represents just that part of transcendental subjectivity that is not primordially and indissolubly my own. Nevertheless as we shall see, the advent of intersubjectivity in practice occurs at a lower level, for its actual possibility is derived in the first place from an apperceptive transfer, as a result of analogy, of the sense of my bodily organism to that of the other. In fact it emerges that the other as other is given in a manner unlike that of ordinary objects, for he can only ever be appresented: he can only ever be thought of as analogous to that which pertains to me. Along with this appresentation of the other's ego, by a similar process of analogy, are appresented everything that belongs to him: his primordial world, thus his fully concrete ego[143] and, finally, that nature which he has constituted for himself.[144]

This then is the ultimate origin in which phenomenology culminates. In transcendental subjectivity and in transcendental intersubjectivity – which is derived from it – are to be found the sources of knowledge and experience. The science of transcendental subjectivity provides the original grounding of all the sciences and thus 'gives them unity, as branches of a constituted production from the one transcendental subjectivity'.[145] It 'gives a legitimate sense, and indeed the only conceivable one, to the ideal of grounding cognition with an absolute freedom from presuppositions'.[146] This means of course that transcendental subjectivity, 'as constituting within itself the being-sense of the world, precedes the being of the world and accordingly bears wholly within itself the world's reality, as an idea constituted actually and potentially within this same transcendental subjectivity'.[147] Thus transcendental subjectivity precedes the world in which the sciences arise. Furthermore, it 'alone ... exists "in itself and for itself"'.[148] It alone finds, as constituted within itself, 'all "objective" being and all "objective" truth, all truth legitimated in the world'.[149] This being however and this truth are quite contrary to the absolute existence and the absolute truth of objectivism. For here both are ultimately relative to transcendental subjectivity.[150] This is perhaps a surprising result: that within transcendental logic all truth is in fact relative. However 'relativity' here is of course intended in a special sense. Certainly, every truth about reality, 'whether it be the everyday truth of practical life or the truth of even the most highly developed sciences conceivable, remains involved in relativities by virtue of its essence'. But this relativity of truth and evidence cannot be separated from 'the infinitely distant, ideal absolute truth beyond all relativity'; for each has its special legitimacy and each demands the other.[151] Nevertheless the relativity remains a radical one:

> The trader in the market has his market-truth. In the
> relationship in which it stands, is his truth not a good one, and

the best that a trader can use? Is it a pseudo-truth, merely
because the scientist, involved in a different relativity and
judging with other aims and other ideas looks for other truths
– with which a great many more things can be done, but not
the one thing that has to be done in a market?[152]

Transcendental logic provides an absolute, ultimate, grounding
of all truth. However this truth is not an arbitrarily absolutized
one. It is a multifaceted truth displaying infinite and various perspectives yet united in its essential character as human truth, as
appearing within the horizons of human knowledge. Transcendental logic, thus conceived, emerges from the self-examination of that
knowledge, in the 'constant spirit of self-responsibility'. It alone
provides 'continuously anew the living truth from the living source,
which is our absolute life.'[153]

An anti-objectivist theory of science

Within Husserl's theory of science, or at least that aspect of it
represented in his logical works, there appear – either explicitly or
implicitly – many themes that will be of considerable importance
for what follows. Especially, Husserl's investigations move on two
levels: as a philosophical reflection on the meaning of science in its
contemporary form, and as a critique of the presuppositions on
which actual scientific theorising proceeds. It will be argued that
such a duality is a property of any adequate theory of science. At
the same time however it has been stressed – and this also will be
important for the following argument – that these investigations
occur strictly within a cohesive theoretical programme which specifies in advance the character of its own theoretical objects, the
criteria of truth against which its own arguments will be judged,
and so on. The phenomenological theory of science can only be
understood in this sense: as elucidating major perplexities from its
own distinctive perspective while at the same time, precisely
because of that perspective, raising considerable new problems of
its own.

What makes Husserl especially interesting for the purposes of
this essay is the original intuition on which his entire philosophy is
based. His theory is from the start a radically anti-objectivist one;
indeed, we have argued that Husserl himself did not realize to what
extent. But if the objectivity associated with any entity is a theoretical construct of which the provenance in conscious life can be

demonstrated then science itself – which after all, presents itself precisely as the theory of objectivities – must be made to recognize this fact. What is more, it must be made to recognize also an elementary consequence that then follows: that science therefore deals not purely with formal constructions but also with meanings, and that these meanings are inherently susceptible to scrutiny from varying cultural and philosophical perspectives.

This last point – however obvious it may appear in retrospect – is also a major insight of Husserl's work. In his theory of categorial objectivities he was able to show a direct correlation between the object province of a science and the theoretical system within which questions concerning its meaning and truth arise. Thus facts cannot be considered as innocent or unproblematically perspicuous. They are theory-laden from the start and implicated into systems of meaning which themselves are closely correlated with the formal techniques. A given science can be characterized adequately only when both dimensions are taken into account: this means only when both its formal apparatus and its philosophical content – or, in the language of phenomenology, its specific intentional structure – are displayed.

The very advances that phenomenology produced in these respects, however, also threatened to undermine it. The distinction between judgements and the process of judging – which permitted an attractive characterization of the verificational procedures of science – unfortunately at the same time produced a bifurcation in the conceptions of objectivity and also truth itself. And when the great variety of distinct objective domains became apparent the bifurcation in the forms of truth turned into a multiplicity. Phenomenology, which had set out to establish a single, unambiguous foundation for all knowledge suddenly found itself facing instead a proliferation of knowledge types, each equally valid in relation to its own special province. The source of the problem of course lay at its very heart, with its fundamental assumption of consciousness as the irreducible origin of all phenomena and its consequent fundamental commitment to truth as presence. Indeed, the identification, via evidence, of objectivity and truth obviated the possibility of separating the two and locating the latter within the intersubjectively available discursive apparatus. This possibility was in fact suggested – although admittedly only in an incipient form – by Husserl's own analysis. If developed it would have provided an alternative anti-objectivist theory and furthermore one in which intersubjectivity would no longer have been a problem. However the solution that Husserl required had to be one that was faithful to the fundamental principles of phenomenology. Thus he had no option but to execute instead at this point another reduction – this time from the phenomenological ego (with which he had previously been working) to the transcendental ego. In the latter, it was claimed, were to be found the ultimate, invariant, trans-subjective structures underlying all evidence, objectivity and truth. In this final phase – beyond which no further reduction was possible – unity would at last be established and, through its radical relativity to transcendental subjectivity, certain truth guaranteed. At its culmination, phenomenology was to become a transcendental logic under which all other theory would be subsumed.

It may be remarked that this solution is not altogether a satisfying one. Indeed, setting aside the problem of intersubjectivity, the doctrine of the transcendental ego is perhaps the most controversial of Husserl's work. Certainly it is not difficult to construct objections to it. For example, there is the difficulty raised in a much-quoted work by Jean Cavaillès regarding the supposed ability of transcendental logic to provide its own justification. What is needed by Husserl is a logic to give norms not only for the constitution of the constituted being but also for the constitution of the constituting being. But, Cavaillès asks, '(d)o the successive enlargements of ontologies corresponding to successive stages of phenomenological investigation come to the unique domain of an absolute formal ontology which absorbs and totally realises the prior investigations?'[154] His own answer is a negative one:

(I)f the absolute and ultimate science also requires a doctrine which governs it ... it cannot include this as part of itself. Perhaps we abuse the singularity of the absolute by withholding from it the coincidence between constituting moment and constituted moment. Besides, there is not really a coincidence but an insertion of the first in the second, since the norms of the constituting constitution are only one portion among the constituted constitutions. Now it seems that such an identification of planes is especially difficult to admit for phenomenology, where the motive of research and the foundation of objectivities are precisely the relation to a creative subjectivity. If this subjectivity is in its turn subject to norms, a new transcendental investigation would be needed in order to relate its norms to a higher subjectivity, since no content but rather consciousness alone has the authority to posit itself in itself. If transcendental logic really founds logic, there is no absolute logic (that is, governing the absolute subjective activity). If there is an absolute logic, it can draw its authority only from itself, and then it is not transcendental.[155]

Another objection is formulated by Suzanne Bachelard, who believes that Husserl was in practice unable to maintain his conception of an absolute transcendental subjectivity.[156] According to her, he was in fact unconsciously oriented towards 'a dialectic of reason and the structural form'. From his own statements, she argues, it is suggested that one should speak not of an interchange between subjectivity and its objective products but rather of an actual *duality* between subjectivity and the structural forms in which it manifests itself. These forms could then themselves be considered precisely as objectivity over against the constituting subjectivity, from which they are irrevocably separated 'by ... structural necessity'. Bachelard believes that such a theory in which subjectivity and its formal structure are disjoined and thence considered at different levels, would overcome objections like those of Cavaillès quoted above. For thereby, she maintains, it would be possible to explain 'how a formal ontology taken in the broad sense can be an ontology which applies also to the constituting subjectivity'. Thus phenomenology could overcome its unconscious 'embarrass(ment) by untenable absolutes'.[157]

We mention, before closing this chapter, just one additional objection to the doctrine of transcendental subjectivity, since it is related to the two preceding ones and not irrelevant to what will follow. This is the objection of Roman Ingarden to Husserl's transcendental idealism, which, he claims, has a built-in absurdity. Here, for the sake of brevity, we shall merely state Ingarden's conclusion and make only the most limited reference to his actual arguments.[158]

For Ingarden, the problem arises because pure consciousness in phenomenology seems to be excluded from every relation with the world. Thus the question must be asked of how then it can constitute the latter as a unity. Now the conscious acts of the philosophizing subject can in general, as we have seen, be related to the world in two ways: through acts of judgement with respect to the world or directly to the presentification of objects as, for example, in perception. However, as Husserl states explicitly on a number of occasions, a unity of a whole necessarily presupposes a community of essences amongst the parts, and certainly the essences of consciousness and of material things are of different kinds. Thus:

> pure consciousness becomes not only excluded from the world
> (this was asserted already by the phenomenological reduction)

139

but, besides, also excluded from every essential relation to the world, and it cannot create with it a uniform whole. It becomes some kind of a special factor outside the world and opposed to it, and it becomes unintelligible that it can, nevertheless, remain in some relations with it and, moreover, how it can, as the consciousness of certain living beings, remain inside its limits in causal relations with the processes taking place in the world.[159]

The principal difficulties of Cartesian dualism are thus revived. Only two alternatives remain: 'either one has to give up any essential unity between pure consciousness and the real world ... or at last understand the relation between the real world somehow quite otherwise and give up the two factors' which could, by virtue of their cognate essences, remain in a real relation. The latter alternative of course, is the one Husserl must take; it is precisely the final step to transcendental subjectivity. However what is thereby sacrificed is the entire realm of material nature. For now 'the material things given in perception and thought in the cognitive acts superstructured over perception (belong not) to an autonomous sphere of being; they are only something that exists in its essence "for" the conscious subject performing the perceptive acts.'[160] Thus phenomenology culminates in an absurdity: the refusal to accept the manifold structure of reality as it is in itself leads to a total failure of its philosophy to apprehend anything about the real world at all.

* * * * * *

Clearly, cogent objections can be gathered against the final act of phenomenology. However in respect of the theory of science, transcendental subjectivity does not represent the only outstanding problem. In fact many other problems exist also. In particular, as Husserl himself points out in the conclusion to *Formal and Transcendental Logic*, the task remains to be completed of elucidating the formative processes according to which exact natural science came into being.[161] This task of course is exactly that to which Husserl directs himself in the *Crisis*. For our purposes this issue is of pre-eminent importance since it involves explicitly an intersection between the phenomenological deliberations and social theory. Hence it approaches directly the principal issues with which this essay is concerned: the philosophical content of science and its potential social and historical contingency. At the same time it compels phenomenology to consider in detail the question of the possibility within it of a genuine theory of history – thus applying pressure at one of the points at which phenomenology is most vulnerable. Accordingly, it is appropriate, on this note of puzzlement and controversy, to turn to a consideration of Husserl's last great work.

Husserl's *Crisis of European Sciences*: Science and the social world

It is not difficult to see the problem presented to phenomenology by the question of history. The emphasis on consciousness and presence as the sources of all truth and knowledge would seem to exclude in principle the historical variability of phenomena. To be sure, Husserl speaks constantly of 'origins', but as we have seen he is careful to avoid any impression that it is history that is at stake – as is apparent from the scrupulous disclaimer on the very first page of *Ideas*. It has already been observed that to reconcile with phenomenology the mere fact of intersubjective communication the most complex argumentation was required while, to ensure the possibility of objective truth for science, the elaborate construction of the transcendental ego became necessary. In Husserl's account of the structure of science which we have been explicating time is not even a variable that is considered; indeed the conception of science that emerges appears to exclude temporality from its innermost structure.

In fact, the problems of history and of the history of science are closely related. A given science coheres as a structured unity, itself incorporating an articulated system of structures. Thus the question of the history of science involves the possibility of an account of the historical sequence of the discursive formations within which scientific knowledge is localized. Similarly, intersubjective phenomena appear within structured totalities which define the cultural forms, the principles of organization of a society and its patterns of social integration. History is just the study of the temporal variability of these structures. It cannot be doubted that such a variability exists in relation to historical phenomena in general. In the case of science however it is certainly not obvious that the theoretical structures are subject to anything like a similar dynamic. On the contrary, it is often considered that the present form of the theory of nature is distinguished from all others precisely by some quality that marks off it alone as true for all time.

To Husserl however it gradually became apparent that the truth of science if not actually contingent was at least limited. On the one hand the analyses of *Formal and Transcendental Logic* showed clearly that science incorporates a definite meaning-structure from which the formal procedures are indissociable. On the other hand the intellectual upheaval in Germany and the cataclysmic political events evoked the image of a crisis of culture that threatened to fracture the precious, fragile structures of modern life. In this context it was clear that the meanings produced by science were insufficient to meet the challenge of the times. Thus the crisis of modern society was at once a crisis of science.

This perception is the explicit premise on which the entire text of *The Crisis of European Sciences and Transcendental Phenomenology* is based. Indeed this work - by far the most moving and evocative of Husserl's writings - conveys often the author's great sense of foreboding in respect of the prospects facing humanity. However for the phenomenology to which Husserl had devoted his life the very conception of a 'crisis of science' raises profound questions. In particular, it suggests immediately the historical contingency of science and demands an account of the course traced in the process of its evolution.[1] But if such an account could be given then the scientific structure must be able to be located in relation to a matrix of other variables and, specifically, amongst these must be included that of time. The phenomenological investigations of temporal phenomena established so far, however, could distinguish only objective time - which excluded any human contribution - and inner time-consciousness which with its analyses of retentions, protentions and recollections in turn could apprehend only the presentation to consciousness of a given event within the absolute flux of temporality.[2] But, clearly, neither of these alternatives was adequate for a description of the series of transformations which characterized the birth of a science. A whole new conception was necessary which would be capable of embracing the historical forms in such a way as to admit of their potential variability.

The new conception, of course, was that of the lifeworld. Here, in the arcane residuum of all theoretical and practical life, was to be found deposited the 'ultimate meaning-fundament of natural

143

science',[3] the only real, actually-given world[4] from which all theories are constructed. This concept – perhaps the major theoretical innovation of the *Crisis* – accordingly stands at the centre of the phenomenological account of history and hence also of science. It introduces a new reduction in Husserl's work, this time to the social and cultural reality within which historical phenomena congeal, and thus permits a description of science from a new perspective.

The theory of science propounded in the *Crisis* is developed in the form of a description of the 'mathematization of nature' – the event – usually attributed to Galileo – which marked the birth of exact physics. It is to an examination of this theory that we now pass.

Galileo's mathematization of nature

Mathematical science and the conception of nature accompanying it are today almost universally taken for granted. Nevertheless neither is by any means obvious. Indeed, the rather recent emergence of science and the proliferation of theories of nature preceding it attest to the facts that the modern understanding of nature is not only socially and historically contingent but in fact represents an elaborate and complex theoretical accomplishment. How then did mathematical science appear? How can its advent in a particular culture and at a particular time be understood? To answer these questions we must return to the birthplace of modern physics, seventeenth century Italy, and retrace the arguments which must have preoccupied its principal originator, Galileo Galilei.

To be sure, Galileo's great discovery required not just an appropriate cultural milieu but also substantial philosophical antecedents. In particular, it required the highly developed geometry that he inherited from a long tradition originating with the ancient Greeks. It may perhaps seem surprising to speak of geometry as a philosophical inheritance but in fact it is not difficult to see that, like science itself, it embodies a considerable theoretical achievement. Thus, also like science, it must have an origin which is accessible to us. According to Husserl the origin of geometry is to be located in a practice of idealization and construction.

So familiar to us is 'the shift between a priori theory and empirical inquiry in everyday life that we usually tend not to separate the space and the spatial shapes geometry talks about from the space and spatial shapes of experiental actuality, as if they were one and the same'.[5] In reality however in the intuitively given

144

surrounding world that we actually experience we do not encounter geometrically ideal bodies. Rather, we find things with many different and variable properties, subject either to continuity or to change. Nor even with the most precise instruments can perfect straight lines or circles be constructed. And what is more, those properties that I do apprehend can never be perfectly communicated, for they are irrevocably dependent on the particular perspective from which I am perceiving the object and on a multitude of subjective effects. It is only when my empirical praxis with things in the world is replaced by an idealizing praxis that the possibility of a pure geometry arises. Then, on the basis of intramundane experience the forms of bodies can be idealized and perfected until the 'limit-shapes' are reached[6] with which the abstract theory deals. By virtue of the methodical character of this process its products are intersubjectively available, that is, objective.[7] By virtue of the exactness that is thereby achieved the ideal shapes can be determined 'in absolute identity' and recognized 'as substrates of absolutely identical and methodically, universally determinable qualities'.[8] Using them, more and more shapes can be constructed which, because of the universality of the method employed, are also intersubjectively and univocally determined. In this way the possibility emerges of producing 'constructively and univocally, through an a priori, all-encompassing systematic method, all possibly conceivable ideal shapes'.[9] Thus, taking the simpler shapes as elementary, there results directly a rigorously deductive, axiomatic geometric theory.

A second source required by Galileo is related to geometry and probably anterior to it. The complete determination of ideal shapes probably required in advance a methodology, which exists in all cultures, of surveying and of measuring in general; certainly this is suggested by the very etymology of the word 'geometry'. The art of measuring, of course, does not supply a deductive or axiomatic theoretical system but it does provide – and indeed this is its main purpose – the possibility of an objective determination of certain properties of experienceable bodies. For once again, since the processes of measurement can be infinitely repeated their results are in principle available to all individuals.

It is not difficult to see the relevance for the yet to be developed science of a methodology for arriving at objective determinations of any object in general and of a model of rigorous deductive theory. However something more is needed to bring them together – a motivating idea which would incite Galileo's fundamental conception. This idea, in fact, emerged from a basic theme of the

Renaissance – and in particular from its return to the ideals of ancient philosophy. Now, the possibility was raised once more of philosophy as *episteme* achieving an objective science of the world.[10] An interest in knowledge[11] and in maximizing cognitive power[12] was the purpose of the 'bold generalizations' and the 'exuberant hypotheses' that so readily 'found a receptive audience'.[13] Galileo himself worked within the imperatives of this theoretical interest and thereby was induced to recapitulate in the much expanded domain the ancient transition from surveying to geometry. The empirical praxis of his predecessors thus gave way to a 'theoretical praxis';[14] 'nature' was converted into a mathematical manifold.[15]

This account – so hastily presented – of the birth of modern science delineates the presumptive sources of the latter and suggests the special role of the cultural context within which Galileo worked in combining both technical and theoretical acquisitions. It is, however, clearly deficient, for it omits precisely the major innovation for which Galileo was responsible: the actual process of the conversion of the field of natural phenomena into a region accessible to mathematics. Furthermore, to encompass this achievement a substantial new body of theory must be developed. For we wish to explain the formation of the new system of categorial objectivities as abstractions from the world of actual experience. Thus we must be able to have recourse to a conception of a non-mathematical, pre-theoretical stratum of life within which would be found worldly experiences more fundamental than those with which science deals. In addition, this world must be intelligible to us and – even though pre-theoretical – accessible to theory; and it must remain so, no matter how extensive the transformations in the philosophical and scientific domains it underlies.

The region thus adumbrated – to which Husserl gives the name lifeworld (*Lebenswelt*) – is one simultaneously of extreme simplicity and extreme complexity. It is made a theme for inquiry through the execution of the *epoché* of objective science, that is, a suspension of 'all theoretical interests, all aims and activities belonging to us as objective scientists or even simply as ordinary people desirous of this kind of knowledge'.[16] It will emerge later that the pregivenness of the life-world can become 'a universal subject of investigation in its own right', only after the execution of a second, more radical reduction[17] which is apparently in most respects indistinguishable from the transcendental reduction. In the present discussion however we are oriented towards what exists in the lifeworld and not to the lifeworld itself as the universal horizon;[18] thus this latter reduction will not concern us here. The lifeworld that is revealed after the *epoché* of the natural attitude is 'the spatiotemporal world of things as we experience them in our pre- and extrascientific life and as we know them to be experienceable beyond what is actually experienced'.[19] It is true that Husserl gives several characterizations of the lifeworld which are not necessarily identical. Nevertheless the general propensity of his argument is clear. The lifeworld is 'the original ground of all theoretical and practical life – the immediately intuited world'[20] within which occurs 'truly immediate intuition and originally intuitive thinking'.[21] It is 'the pregiven world',[22] the one that is 'actually given through perception';[23] its 'open, endless horizons' are the horizons 'of things unknown'.[24] In it are to be found all bodily shapes, for after all, 'it is in this world that we ourselves live, in accord with our bodily (*lieblich*), personal way of being'.[25] On the other hand however – and this is precisely why the lifeworld is of such interest – here no geometrical idealities are to be found and no mathematical abstractions; here, in the world prior to geometry, there is no geometrical space and no mathematical time.[26]

The fundamental, great problem which faced Galileo is thus clear. His task was to undertake the construction of the domain of objectivities of the new science – that is, it was to fashion from the premathematical plenum of properties a range of entities susceptible to theorizing in a rigorous, deductive way. The idealization of the world prescribes to each of the things of factual world experience an ideal, 'the ideal of a knowledge of it which is thinkable *idealiter*, can be perfected *in infinitum*, and can come to absolute perfection in the traversing of the conceived infinity'.[27] The formulation of the new science presupposed precisely the construction of such a realm of idealities susceptible to knowledge. From the objects of prescientific experience there had to be fashioned a class of entities to which logical and mathematical operations could apply[28] and which furthermore were hypothetically substructured in advance[29] in respect of the forms of possible correlations between them.

Galileo recognized that only a world of objects which is idealized mathematically and thus from which sensible, purely subjective qualities have been removed by abstraction can become attainable for our objective knowledge. The transition from merely subjective, contingent phenomena however, to intersubjectively available, infinitely repeatable ones required more than just the construction of a realm of idealities. For if things remained accessible to us only singly, imperfectly and accidentally then objective knowledge would still be impossible. Instead, objects must be rendered accessible to us systematically through the application of a rational coherent method.[30] Thus Galileo reasoned to himself as follows:

> Wherever such methodology is developed, there we have also overcome the relativity of subjective interpretations which is, after all, essential to the empirically intuited world. For in this manner we attain an identical, non-relative truth of which everyone who can understand and use this method can convince himself. Here, then, we recognize something that truly is – though only in the form of a constantly increasing approximation, beginning with what is empirically given, to the geometrical ideal shape which functions as a guiding pole.[31]

In fact, exact objectivity is itself a major accomplishment which 'presupposes a method of systematic and determined idealization creating a world of ideals which can be produced determinately and constructed systematically *in infinitum.*'[32]

The new science then of which Galileo was the principal originator required in advance both a real praxis of measurement and an ideal praxis of geometry, united under the interest in the unlimited extension of cognitive knowledge which characterized the Renaissance and its aftermath. In addition, it required the inspired construction out of the immediately intuited experiences of the lifeworld of a region of idealities to which the formal operations could apply. Finally, in order to yield objective knowledge the productions of science had to be of such a kind that they could be generated repeatedly, methodically and systematically from its theoretical structures. Mathematical science thus required a philosophical disposition, a syntactical system and a region of categorial objectivities already filled with contents irreducibly present in the lifeworld.

The mathematization of the plena and the structures of the lifeworld

Husserl provides a sketch of the link in this argument that remains to be completed: the description of the actual process of the mathematization of the sensible plena. Only a sketch is possible because a fully developed science of the lifeworld is not yet available; nevertheless the impression cannot be avoided that the account he adumbrates would not be altogether satisfying. That any theory can be offered at all follows from the inescapable fact that the lifeworld has, in all its relative features, a general structure.[33] This general structure to which is bound everything that exists relatively is not itself relative. Thus it can be examined by us in its generality and its features made accessible to all. Furthermore,

> as lifeworld the world has, even prior to science, the "same" structures that the objective sciences presuppose in their substruction of a world which exists 'in itself' and is determined through 'truths in themselves' . . .; these are the same structures that they presuppose as a priori structures and systematically unfold in a priori sciences, sciences of the *logos*, the universal methodical norms by which any knowledge of the world existing 'in itself, objectively' must be bound.[34]

In particular, pre-scientifically the world is already a spatio-temporal world. To be sure,

> in regard to this spatiotemporality there is no question of ideal mathematical points, of 'pure' straight lines or planes, no question at all of mathematically infinitesimal continuity or of the 'exactness' belonging to the sense of the geometrical a priori. The bodies familiar to us in the lifeworld are actual bodies, but not bodies in the sense of physics. The same thing is true of causality and of spatiotemporal infinity. These categorial features of the lifeworld have the same names but are not concerned, so to speak, with the theoretical idealizations and the hypothetical substructions of the geometrician and the physicist.[35]

The regularities observed by the phenomena of the lifeworld are available to us through intuition. Sensible bodies – and in particular the properties of bodies that are referred to in Aristotle as special and common sensible qualities – are experienced in the mode of 'belonging together';[36] that is, bodies and the relationships between them are directly intuited as unities in everyday experience. Furthermore these 'things' of the intuited surrounding world 'have, so to speak, their "habits" – they behave similarly under typically similar circumstances'.[37] Taken together, these habits constitute for the empirically intuited surrounding world 'an empirical over-all style'[38] which is invariant in relation to free variations induced in perception, imagination, memory and so on. In this way it becomes apparent that 'universally, things and their occurrences do not arbitrarily appear and run their course but are bound a priori by this style, by the invariant form of the intuitable world. In other words, through a universal causal regulation, all that is together in the world has a universal immediate or mediate way of belonging together. . . .'[39] We now have a world as a whole, displaying a universal causal style; hence it becomes possible to make hypotheses, inductions and predictions about unknowns of the present, past or future.

As for mathematics itself, we have already seen how, under an idealizing praxis evolved from the art of measurement, common sensible qualities were represented in limit-shapes within the deductive system of pure geometry. Now that the correlative structure of the lifeworld is apparent we can also see conversely how geometry can be applied in practical circumstances to the world. Thus only the special sensibles – tone, colour, warmth, etc. – remain. Now these cannot be directly mathematized as, for example, can form. However the causal style revealed above was a universal one: that is, like spatio-temporal localization it applies to all changes affecting all bodies.[40] Thus we must assume that the special sensible qualities that can be experienced 'are closely related in a quite peculiar and regulated way with the shapes that belong essentially to them.'[41] More specifically, what we experience in pre-scientific life as colours, tones and so on belonging to the things themselves and experienced causally in relation to those things must be taken as an index of previously mathematized qualities.[42] This insight, or more correctly, this hypothesis, which is certainly indispensable for any truly universal science of nature is another of Galileo's major innovations. According to it anything that manifests itself as real must now be considered either as directly mathematizable or else as having a mathematical index in events belonging to the realm of directly mathematizable entities. We have finally reached the point where we can say that 'the whole of infinite nature ... (has become) the object of a peculiarly applied mathematics'.[43]

Advantages

This formulation of the birth of modern science carries with it certain major advantages. It elucidates the structure of science presented in *Formal and Transcendental Logic*, showing the complexity and interdependence of its various components, and even their cultural and historical provenance. It reveals that science is in fact 'a human spiritual accomplishment which presupposes as its point of departure, both historically and for each new student the intuitive surrounding world of life, pregiven as existing for all in common'.[44] This surrounding world and indeed more radically, the lifeworld, furthermore, are left unchanged by the elaborate constructions of science;[45] in fact they are even accessible to an appropriate theoretical investigation. Within the accomplishment of science, objectivity in particular emerges as a considerable cognitive accomplishment in its own right,[46] effecting the crucial passage from merely subjective, contingent phenomena to universally available intersubjective ones through the application of a rigorous, systematic and coherent method.[47]

At the same time – perhaps even as a consequence of these insights – the crisis of science and Galileo's fateful error now become intelligible. Science is a major accomplishment of humanity, grounded in its common lifeworld and accompanying self-evidences; thanks to this rootedness, 'objective science has a constant reference of meaning to the world in which we always live'.[48] Nevertheless for Galileo himself and for the ensuing generations of scientists this fact precisely was occluded. Instead, idealized nature – the mathematically substructed world of idealities – was surreptitiously substituted for prescientifically intuited nature.[49] This substitution is exactly what is referred to when we speak of a crisis of science.

At the birth of modern science the lifeworld was fitted with a 'garb of ideas' consisting of the so-called objective scientific truths.[50] These ideas represented the lifeworld, as a sign represents its signified. Subsequently however the 'surreptitious substitution' occurred and the symbols themselves were taken for the reality. The mere method of science was mistaken for the being itself of nature.[51]

Neither Galileo nor his successors reflected closely on the process of theorizing in physics, nor, in particular, did they reflect on the antecedents of the mathematization of nature. They did not inquire back to the roots of scientific truth,[52] which in consequence remained opaque for them. To be sure, the geometry that Galileo inherited was similarly afflicted: its underlying, originating activity had not been in question since antiquity[53] and so it also could be said to have been in crisis. Nevertheless this crisis became a general one – a 'crisis of humanity' – only with the advent of modern science. For then reality itself was redefined to make the being of objects within it identical to scientific modes of being. In other words, scientific meaning was made absolute and consequently the distinction between the mathematical world and the world as it really exists and is experienced was lost. The contribution of human subjectivity to the production of scientific knowledge was suppressed and nature was transformed into a self-enclosed world of bodies.[54] The process by means of which this circumstance was established was, of course – as is immediately evident from the description just given – also exactly that of the advent of objectivism. Accordingly the latter event was conjoined with the birth of science, although it subsequently acquired its own formulations in the Cartesian doctrine of the dualism between body and spirit, in modern psychologism and elsewhere.

Galileo then was at once a 'discovering and concealing genius':[55] the products of his insight were simultaneously enriching and limiting. Indeed herein lies the great, tragic paradox of modern times. The interest in an ever-expanding, objective knowledge of the world, in *episteme*, which had been a theme for culture since the very earliest times, had given rise to mathematical science. However, once established, science had acquired a life of its own. Becoming a mere *techne*, an elaborate and powerful machine to be operated by highly skilled technicians, it imposed a suzerainty over all other knowledge. And thus, in consequence, the original, precious interest in true knowledge was first subverted and then lost altogether.[56]

From these sombre deliberations the task facing modern man can be discerned. True to the spirit of the times it is an 'infinite task'.[57] Science must be rediscovered as a human project and praxis. Its meaning and validity must be traced back to their primordial roots in the lifeworld. We must come to recognize the contingency and partiality of science and that its hypothesis of a mathematized nature is in fact but one hypothesis amongst the many practical hypotheses and projects which make up the lives of human beings in their lifeworld.[58] Our task, in short is

> to make vital again, in its concealed historical meaning, the
> sedimented conceptual system which, as taken for granted,
> serves as the ground of (our) private and non-historical work.
> It is to carry forward, through (our) own self-reflection, the
> self-reflection of our forebears and thus not only to re-awaken
> the chain of thinkers, the social interrelation of their thinking,
> the community of their thought, and transform it into a living
> present for us but, on the basis of the total unity thus made
> present, to carry out a responsible critique, ... which has its
> ground in these historical, personal projects, partial fulfilments
> and exchange of criticism rather than in what is privately taken
> for granted by the present philosopher.[59]

We must return to the proper naivety of life, 'but in a reflection which rises above this naivety'.[60] For this is the only possible way to overcome the philosophical naivety to which objectivist science has succumbed.

152

Problems

Husserl's formulation, as we said, carried with it substantial advantages – and even some poignancy. Nevertheless, considerable difficulties remain. In the first place, as previously, problems emerge in relation to Husserl's unchallengeable faith in the achievements of mathematical science in respect of its proper field of application, which of course has now been shown to be limited. His belief that the crisis of science 'does not encroach upon the theoretical and practical successes of the special sciences'[61] has already been mentioned. In fact he at no stage resiled from this conviction. Although objectivism as a philosophical position could be completely refuted it nevertheless remained the proper starting point for physics; accordingly, while for philosophy it had to be abolished, for science it required only a 'grounding'. Husserl's implicit confidence in mathematical science and his great admiration for its achievements are everywhere apparent.[62] It is clear, for example, that for him the only theory of nature capable of aspiring to true knowledge is a mathematical theory. But what is more, the very mathematical character of this theory exhausts its philosophical content. Indeed the issue concerning Galilean science is just the mathematization of nature it incorporates and not any other specific claim with which it can be associated. However it is one thing to affirm that, regardless of whether its true sense is understood, science sustains a continuous validity;[63] it is entirely another to maintain that 'nothing is changed' by the innovations in modern physics since they leave its mathematical character intact.[64] For Husserl, 'what is essential in principle' is that 'nature ... is in itself mathematical; it is given in formulae, and it can be interpreted only in terms of the formulae'.[65] Thus the objects with which science deals cannot be understood as specific philosophical constructions, as seemed to emerge from *Formal and Transcendental Logic*. Rather, they are the constructions of mathematical method, which also teaches us how to deal with them operatively and systematically.[66] If a philosophical critique of science is possible, then it can be only a critique of the process of mathematization, for after that, science's independence from philosophy is irrefragable.

It will be argued below that all of Husserl's assertions referred to in the preceding paragraph are false. Here, we shall continue by referring to another series of problems raised by his theory. These problems were mentioned briefly in our discussion of *Formal and Transcendental Logic*, where Husserl himself observed that from his account emerged two distinct conceptions of truth. In the *Crisis* the problem associated with this duality becomes explicit. Indeed it is perhaps a property of any theory that proposes the existence of a realm of knowledge prior to all discourse that it must accommodate two different kinds of truth. Thus Husserl distinguishes pre-scientific knowledge from scientific knowledge[67] and, associated with these, 'two sorts of truth'.[68] With the former are to be found 'everyday practical situational truths'; with the latter scientific truths – leading back, to be sure, in their grounding, to the situational truths, 'but in such a way that scientific method does not suffer thereby in respect to its own meaning, since it wants to use and must use precisely these truths'.[69] The difference between the two is absolutely irreducible. In fact '(t)he idea of objective truth is *predetermined in its whole meaning* by the contrast with the idea of the truth in pre- and extra-scientific life. This latter truth has its ultimate and deepest source of verification in experience which is "pure" '.[70] These words must be understood only 'as pre-scientific life understands them; ... one must not inject into them from current objective science any psychophysical, psychological interpretation'.[71] For at stake are actually two, quite different meanings: 'with the most compelling self-evidence, the true, the only real meaning' of the theories that evolve from the lifeworld, 'as opposed to the meaning of being a *method*, which has its own comprehensibility in operating with the formulae and their practical application, technique'.[72]

Two truths and two objectivities

Between lifeworld and scientific theory, then, there are two types of truth. As previously, the truth associated with the lifeworld has its origins in consciousness and subjectivity.[73] Indeed, the lifeworld is itself 'a realm of original self-evidences'.[74] And that which is given in self-evidence is 'in perception, experienced as "the thing itself", in immediate presence, or, in memory, remembered as the thing itself; and every other manner of intuition is a presentification of the thing itself'.[75] Here, 'what is primary in itself is subjectivity', which 'pre-gives the being of the world'.[76] The thematic direction is towards the act of judging and towards those who make the judgements. On the other hand, we have the truth associated with systems of discourse. Here, the thematic focus is quite different: it is towards 'a systematic universe of "logical laws", the theoretical totality of the truths destined to function as norms for all judgements which shall be capable of being objectively true.'[77] This region is not a pre-theoretical one. On the contrary, the constructions within it are precisely the products of theory. They are 'logical constructs, ... logical wholes and logical parts made up of ultimate logical elements. To speak with Bolzano, they are "representations in themselves", "propositions in themselves", inferences and proofs "in themselves", ideal unities of signification whose logical ideality is determined by their *telos*, "truth in itself"'.[78] The propositions in this realm are not to be judged according to criteria of presence and self-evidence, for they are of a different kind. They are constructions of method, of intersubjectively available rules and thus it is in purely discursive terms that their validity must be evaluated. 'The propositions, the theories, the whole edifice of doctrine in the objective sciences are structures attained through certain activities of scientists bound together in their collaborative work – or, to speak more exactly, attained through a continued building-up of activities, the later of which always presuppose the results of the earlier.'[79] The truth of these propositions is 'objective and logical';[80] it is derived from scientific method[81] which appropriates and operates with such propositions.

Along with these two concepts of truth and meaning, as might be expected, there are two corresponding conceptions of objectivity. On the one hand there is the view with which we are familiar, according to which the world which constantly exists for us through the flowing alteration of manners of givenness is recognized as a universal mental acquisition, 'the construct of a universal, ultimately functioning subjectivity'.[82] It is on this subjectivity that all objectivity depends; for the former is always presupposed in the latter.[83] Subjectivity objectifies, or exteriorizes, itself as an element of the world; subsequently 'all objective consideration of the world' is in fact 'consideration of the "exterior" and grasps only "externals", objective entities. The radical consideration of the world is the systematic and purely internal consideration of the subjectivity which "expresses" (or "externalizes") itself in the exterior.'[84] In brief, objectivity is just the externalization of subjectivity: 'knowing subjectivity (is) the primal locus of all objective formations of sense and ontic validities.'[85] The products of subjectivity are common ones because, as before, they derive from forms that are essential to any subjectivity – that is, from transcendental intersubjectivity.[86] On the other hand, there is the objectivity that derives from method. This is the objectivity on which geometry depends and which Galileo appropriated for his science from the art of measuring. Indeed, it was only with the acquisition of a systematic method that shapes – or later, scientific propositions – could become intersubjectively determinable and communicable in their determinations.[87] Husserl says explicitly: the sciences 'have their own "objectivity" ... i.e., a necessary validity to be appropriated purely methodically, which we and everyone can verify precisely through this method.'[88] Or, in another formulation, he claims that the full accomplishment of science is in fact designated by its method of determined idealization and of a systematic operative construction of ideal objects which makes it possible to master the totality. The world of these objects is 'objective insofar as the knowledge it affords, the ideals formed of it, are absolutely identical for anyone who practises the method, no matter how much his empirically intuitive representation may differ from what serves others in their intuition-based idealization.'[89]

It must be stressed that we are not here pretending to reproduce faithfully Husserl's argument. On the contrary, the disparate concepts that we have been describing are nowhere specified in detail by him; rather they have had to be extracted painfully from the interstices of his text. Of course, as in his earlier works, he recognizes the existence of the problem and actually formulates it on several occasions.[90] Furthermore a number of arguments are offered to reconcile the dichotomy, some of which we shall consider presently. As might be expected, his own discourse in these arguments is phenomenological and thus he seeks to subsume the discrepant 'logical' or 'systematic' perspective under the rubrics of consciousness and evidence, and transcendental subjectivity. The conclusion that he will reach is in fact the only one available to him, given the imperatives of his own problematic: subjectivity is primary and all logical conceptions are ultimately founded upon it. Against this problem we shall propose that the two conceptions, while interdependent, nevertheless enjoy a relative autonomy and therefore must be considered as existing on the same level. Each has its own integrity and furthermore, in its critique of science, each is anti-objectivist. This view will be defended later. However our present argument is not yet completed: we have yet to consider Husserl's own attempts to overcome the difficulty – attempts in which, as we shall see, he is forced into radical modifications of his programme.

Husserl's attempt at a solution

Phenomenology starts from the premise that what is primary is not being in the world but rather subjectivity, 'understood as that which naively pregives the being of the world and then rationalizes or ... objectifies it.'[91] Thus it is natural that all objective science shall be able to be traced back to a single ground – that of anonymous subjectivity in which is contained all that is taken for granted or presupposed by thinking and other activities of life with all its ends and accomplishments.[92] On this deeply concealed subjective ground objective science rests; its elucidation will for the first time reveal the true ontic meaning of the latter – as a transcendental-subjective meaning.[93] Logical truth then, like the truths of perception, must be able to be grounded in the lifeworld – that is, it must have its own characteristic form of evidence directly apprehensible to consciousness on the basis of which its 'truth' could be established. Thus Husserl claims that besides the giving of the thing itself in immediate presence – which is, for example, the evidence associated with perception – there is an 'objective-logical'[94] or 'formal-logical'[95] self-evidence corresponding to mathematical and natural scientific insight; from it 'the path leads back to the primal self-evidence in which the lifeworld is ever pregiven.'[96] All verification must be able to be traced back to immediate presence, since this is the locus of all intersubjective experience; in particular, any substruction of thought, insofar as it makes a claim to truth, 'can have actual truth only by being related back to such self-evidence'.[97]

To be sure, Husserl does claim that the truth of objective science is but one hypothesis 'among the many practical hypotheses and projects which make up the life of human beings in this life-world'.[98] And he does state that 'when we are thrown into an alien social sphere, that of the Negroes in the Congo, Chinese peasants, etc., we discover that their truths ... are by no means the same as ours.'[99] Indeed, he repeats some of the formulations from the earlier works which we have previously discussed: anything stands in correlation with its own manners of givenness,[100] so that there is a correspondence between forms of objectivity, of intentionality and of evidence; and furthermore to each mode of objectivity corresponds a specific mode of validity.[101] Since the form of objectivity associated with science is certainly different from that of the lifeworld[102] and since their characteristic modes of evidence are quite different also, Husserl seems to be tending towards a radical relativism like that which produced substantial difficulties in *Formal and Transcendental Logic*. However (despite frequent statements to the contrary, to which we have adverted at length), Husserl states clearly at the outset that the 'formula-meaning' which unavoidably accompanies the technical development and practice of method is in fact a 'superficialization of meaning'.[103] Thus the

arithmetization of geometry 'leads back almost automatically ...
to the emptying of its meaning'.[104] Mathematics and geometry
have been reduced to a mere technique[105] and indeed if science
also is like a machine[106] then it must be true to say that scientists,
like mathematicians, are no more than highly brilliant technicians.[107] But for such 'a mere art of achieving, through a calculating technique according to technical rules' the genuine sense of
truth can be attained 'only by concretely intuitive thinking actually
directed at the subject matter itself'.[108] It is only the 'original
thinking' that can genuinely give meaning, that is, the primordial
evidence experienced in the lifeworld. 'No objective science ... explains or ever can explain anything in a serious sense. To deduce
is not to explain.... The only true way to explain is to make
transcendentally understandable.'[109]

Objective science then is grounded in the lifeworld which is the
ultimate source of its truth. It bears 'a constant reference of meaning to the world in which we always live'.[110] The foundation of its
knowledge lies in the self-evidence of the lifeworld, which is pregiven to the scientific worker or the working community.[111] To the
extent that science produces true results, these are validities for the
lifeworld also[112] and so can be brought to the appropriate mode
of self-evidence. 'The concrete lifeworld ... is the grounding soil of
the "scientifically true" world and at the same time encompasses it
in its own universal concreteness.'[113]

If there seem to be two sides to our account of Husserl that is
because both are to be found in the text. The argument just
presented is the proper, consistent, phenomenological one. But
even as Husserl states it he becomes aware of the problems. Immediately after the passage just quoted, he goes on to say:

> We are posing questions whose clarifying answers are by no
> means obvious. The contrast and the inseparable union we
> have been exploring draws us into a reflection which entangles
> us in more and more troublesome difficulties. The paradoxical
> interrelationships of the 'objectively true world' and 'lifeworld'
> make enigmatic the manner of being of both. The idea of a
> true world in any sense, and within it our own being, becomes
> an enigma in respect of the sense of this being. ...[114]

Later as previously he will restate his conclusion in terms of the
originary source of transcendental subjectivity (the exact relationship of which to the lifeworld, incidentally, is never made precisely
clear). Thus, after formulating the problem once again he goes on
to reply:

158

The answer, of course, is as follows: it is precisely the result of inquiry within the *epoché* ... that the natural, objective world-life is only a particular mode of the transcendental life which forever constitutes the world, but in such a way that transcendental subjectivity, while living on in this mode, has not become conscious of the constituting horizons and never can become aware of them.[115]

Nevertheless it is clear from both contemporaneous and subsequent texts that Husserl himself was not altogether satisfied with this 'solution' – and at any rate, it remains subject to the objections to the notion of the transcendental ego to which we previously referred. Furthermore, it is difficult to accept the mere *juxtaposition* of the two sides of the dilemma to which he sometimes resorts, as when he says that 'exact objectivity is the accomplishment of method, practised by men generally in the world of experience ... – practised not as a commercial praxis, as a technique of shaping and reshaping things pregiven in experience, but as a praxis in which those imperfectly determining thing-representations make up the material'; or, alternatively, when he says that '(o)bjectification is a matter of method, founded upon pre-scientific data of experience'.[116]

In fact, there are indications that Husserl at times inclined towards the belief that what was called for was a more fundamental revision and that, in particular, the conception of the lifeworld as it had been formulated needed to be reassessed. For example, it is not difficult to see that if the lifeworld is to be the true repository for all objectivity – that is, for both theoretical objectivity and that of immediate experience – then it must incorporate more than just the abstract structures of transcendental intersubjectivity: it must contain also the means by which objective truths are formulated and communicated. Thus Husserl observes that 'what is pre-scientifically given' is just 'what can be named, asserted, described in common language ... as it can be expressed in the language of our linguistic community.' For 'the lifeworld' he goes on, 'the "world of us all" – is identical with the world that can be commonly talked about. Every new apperception leads essentially, through apperceptive transference, to a new typification of the surrounding world and in social intercourse to a naming which immediately flows into the common language. Thus the world is always such that it can be empirically, generally (intersubjectively) explicated and, at the same time, linguistically explicated.'[117]

Now this is certainly a substantial change from the original description of the lifeworld as 'the only real world, the one that is actually given through perception' and as 'the immediately intuited world ... the original ground of all theoretical and practical life'.[118] It is a major change from the first, motivating conception of a pre-theoretical world that was to be *the ground* for all theoretical idealizations. To be sure, adumbrations of this modified position are to be found even in *Experience and Judgement*, where Husserl states that the lifeworld 'is already pre-given to us as impregnated by the precipitate of logical operations. The world is never given to us as other than the world in which we or others, whose store of experience we take over by communication, education and tradition, have already been logically active in judgement and cognition.'[119] However, if language is to be incorporated into the lifeworld then great problems are posed for the entire theory to the construction of which the *Crisis* is devoted. For in the first place language itself operates according to systematic 'logical' modes. Its statements are generated by the application of intersubjectively available rules to a systematically structured unity. Furthermore, the determination of the truth-value of an utterance depends at least in part on the possibility of reconstructing the methodical formative processes that constitute it and in part also on the social and cultural context within which it occurs. These matters will be discussed in more detail later; here we only mention the consequence for the lifeworld theory: the problem of reconciling the 'logical' and the 'phenomenological' modes of truth remains. In fact this problem has now been displaced into the interior of the lifeworld itself, the very identity of which concept is thereby put at risk.

According to phenomenology it is from consciousness and presence that all knowledge derives. Thus theory must have a foundation in some primordial realm of purely intuited givenness, a realm which precedes all theoretical constructions and to which all evidences can be reduced. Indeed, such an invariant underlying stratum is also demanded by the task of providing a phenomenological theory of the origins of modern science which would at once elucidate the accomplishment of Galileo and demonstrate the true unity of the sciences. However, as the phenomenological approach is pursued it becomes apparent that, at least from its own perspective, there are in fact two kinds of truth, two types of meaning and two forms of objectivity: on the one hand there is the properly phenomenological truth, associated directly with self-evidence and immediate presence; on the other, there is a 'structural' notion of truth, in which knowledge emerges as a specific effect of a given system of discourse. Phenomenology of course must be able to reconcile the two – and that means that the latter must be subsumed under the rubric of the former. But this in turn means that the system of rules according to which consensus is established in respect of the productions of any coherent theoretical system must also belong to the lifeworld; specifically, the lifeworld must encompass language and the structures of intersubjective communication. But although this innovation is necessary it nevertheless only compounds the problem. For now two things happen. In the first place, the dichotomy between phenomenological and 'logical' truth remains, although now it occurs within the lifeworld rather than between lifeworld and the categorial realm. And secondly, the lifeworld itself can no longer be absolutely precategorial, as it was first postulated to be.

Indeed, in addition to the passages already cited, Husserl frequently concedes these discrepant properties of the lifeworld. Thus he refers to certain of its 'categorical features',[120] he claims that the theoretical results of science are incorporated into the composition of the lifeworld;[121] and he even suggests that the sciences themselves belong to it.[122] In 'The Origin of Geometry' Husserl considers at length for the first time the problems associated with the introduction of language into the lifeworld. He recognizes that the existence of stable intersubjective meanings requires the lifeworld to be structured in a determinate way. Accordingly, he invents the concept of 'sedimentation', which is intended to refer to a structural unity encompassing the past achievements of numerous subjects, but which is yet directly intuitable; that is, it is a generalization of the idea of 'logical self-evidence'.[123] More precisely, 'sedimentation' refers to the transformation of a cognitive accomplishment into a unity which is not only constant in time but also accessible intersubjectively. It is a store of knowledge that is 'freely available, preservable and communicable'.[124] Husserl argues that all objectivity presupposes the 'sedimentation' of meaning into the realm of the lifeworld.[125] Thus for example, regarding geometry, its objectivity consists in 'a transformation of the original mode of being of the meaning structure within the geometric sphere of self-evidence'.[126] Similarly, propositions, cultural structures, the whole pre-given deductive science, the total system of propositions in the unity of their validities,[127] become apprehensible as objective entities only when transformed into sediments which can be brought to self-evidence.[128] Even traditions are sedimented, along with the other less temporally-dependent structures of meaning. All these sedimentations, furthermore, as manifold and complex as they might be, according to Husserl's conception, belong to the directly intuitable substrate of experience and hence are incorporated into the lifeworld, where they constitute 'working materials' for new achievements.[129]

We shall not consider at length here the concept of sedimentation; nor shall we attempt to evaluate whether it could seriously render logical unities susceptible to the truth of the lifeworld. Later, in another context, we shall have occasion to refer once again to this notion and to the place that it occupies within Husserl's philosophy.[130] However for our present purposes these issues are not of particular importance. What is important here is just that if the concept does succeed then the concept of the lifeworld itself must in consequence be fundamentally modified. For the latter would then be subject both to history and to culture. In fact, it is precisely this possibility that Husserl declares to be the case. He proclaims that the lifeworld must now be regarded as the 'one cultural world', corresponding to 'one human civilization'.[131]

In sum then, the lifeworld is transformed into a cultural world. Thus it cannot be 'pregiven for all', as was first intended. Furthermore, precisely to the extent that it incorporates cultural sedimentations it will be subject to new discoveries and innovations in science itself. What is more, in consequence of this, nor will it be true that as Husserl claimed previously, the lifeworld is left unchanged by science.[132] Finally, as also observed earlier, at least one other principal attribute of the lifeworld can no longer be sustained – its pre-theoretical character. Like Husserl's conceptions of truth, meaning and objectivity, the lifeworld concept oscillates between the individual and the community, between self-evidence and the accomplishments of discourse, between presence and theory. Ultimately however it succumbs to the very tensions it was supposed to overcome.

Intersubjectivity

It is perhaps appropriate here to add a note on the question of intersubjectivity in Husserl's phenomenology. We have observed previously that for a philosophy starting with consciousness and its effects as the source of all knowledge it comes as no surprise that intersubjectivity and communication between subjects presents a problem. In fact Husserl expends considerable time and effort in trying to prove precisely the possibility of the recognition by my ego of other egos and further, of communication between them.

Regardless of the success or failure of these endeavours this circumstance cannot be regarded as less than remarkable – that the most familiar, elementary experience of everyday life presents for phenomenology a perplexity of the greatest proportions.

It is however not only with regard to the explicit question of the existence of the other that the problems arise. Indeed many of the tensions and paradoxes in phenomenology with which we have been confronted can be traced back to this source. Thus the problem of the two kinds of knowledge in *Formal and Transcendental Logic* and the *Crisis* is in fact that of the reconciliation of phenomena presented intuitively in my primordial sphere with those presented irreducibly in discourse. The mechanisms employed by Husserl to deal with this dilemma varied with time and context. As early as *Logical Investigations*, for example, he found himself faced with the question of the intelligibility of judgements. Since knowledge was necessarily based on intuitions and the direct presentation of evidence to consciousness, a special, non-sensible form of intuition had to be distinguished which would allow such a presentation of the discursive forms. Consequently, he proposed the existence of a 'categorial intuition', according to which syntactical relations became available perspicuously to an isolated, monadic ego.[133] But syntactical relations are no more than the forms of the linguistic mode of intersubjective communication – which is itself thereby not merely circumvented but even rendered problematical; for if language itself is contracted to the sphere of my primordial givenness then no structure remains which immanently incorporates a multiplicity of egos and so could guarantee a priori communication between them. The problems facing the doctrine of categorial intuition are in fact quite considerable. Here no further detailed comment is appropriate. However, we may mention that in spite of the difficulties no supporting arguments are offered by Husserl to establish its integrity as a concept, or indeed to explain why it should be taken in any but a merely metaphorical sense.

Elsewhere other solutions are proposed to deal with essentially the same problem. In the logical works (and also, to a lesser extent, in the *Crisis*) for example, as we have seen, special modes of evidence were proposed for the rule-governed productions of discourse in order to permit their direct presentation in evidence. However the problem was thereby only compounded. For then objectivity and truth were reduced to the same level at exactly the same time as the discovery was made of the proliferation of the modes of the former. This dilemma could be overcome only at the expense of a construction of the utmost complexity. Later, in 'The

Origin of Geometry' and also, adumbrated, in the *Crisis*, another alternative was attempted. The logical and linguistic structures were said to compose 'sediments' directly apprehensible to consciousness. However this solution was also afflicted with problems. In particular, the lifeworld and thus subjectivity in general were now susceptible to the historically variable outcomes of social praxis. In other words, subjectivity was subordinate to the structures of intersubjectivity – exactly the situation Husserl wanted to avoid.

It may not be too much of an exaggeration to say that in substantial part phenomenology can be understood as a dialogue between the point of view that attributes primacy to the individual consciousness and that which attributes primacy to communication and discourse instead – recounted, of course, from the perspective of the former. Indeed it often appears that it is a result of phenomenology itself that many dilemmas would be avoided by the choice of a more appropriate starting point in intersubjectivity and the structures of sociality. To be sure, phenomenology does have its own special efficacy and is productive of the most substantial and penetrating insights – many of which we have encountered and considered at length, and some to which we shall refer later in relation to the specific details of science. But nevertheless the problems remain: how can an ego constrained within its own sphere of immanence understand the possibility of the existence of an other? How is another ego given to me within phenomenological experience as a subject? And in particular, how can I communicate with him?[134]

These problems preoccupied Husserl over many years and he returned to them again and again. It was only with the fifth of his *Cartesian Meditations* that the elements of a definitive solution were offered.[135] We shall not consider in detail the argument of this theory, as important as it is with regard to Husserl's work as a whole. However it will be useful just to indicate briefly two of the points at which problems related to those we have been discussing intrude also into this aspect of his philosophy.

For phenomenology every sense that any existent whatever has or can have for me is a sense in and arising from my intentional life.[136] Thus the explication of the specific experience associated with the Other must begin with a systematic account of the overt and implicit intentionality in which the being of others for me 'becomes "made" and explicated in respect of its rightful content – that is, its fulfilment content.'[137] To this end it is necessary to distinguish in advance the peculiar 'ownness' associated with a given ego.[138] This sphere of ownness is attained by the execution of a special reduction within the transcendental sphere; it includes, among other things, objects and nature, though not yet as objective entities.[139] In particular, within this primordial nature one body is uniquely singled out. It is my own animate organism, the only object that I truly 'rule and govern'[140] and in relation to which the kinaesthesias pertaining to my organs 'flow in the mode "I am doing", and are subject to my "I can"'.[141] Under the force of this reduction that which I experience I experience as mine alone. I have a nature, a body and so on that are, to be sure, 'transcendent' in a weak sense[142] but which nevertheless are constituted merely as a 'multiplicity of objects of pure experience, this experience being purely my own life'.[143]

But it is certainly true that I do experience others – and not just as merely inanimate objects but actually as subjects. Furthermore it is obvious that the other ego cannot be given to me originally in my own experience, for otherwise it would merely be a moment of my own essence.[144] Thus there must exist a mode of my consciousness corresponding to my awareness of an Other.[145] Hence the problem is to understand how the ego forms within itself intentionalities of this transcending kind – and how therefore other subjects are in fact presented to me. Husserl's answer, in brief, is that I constitute the ego of the Other on the basis of an analogizing apperception that construes his being as of the same kind as my own. For the apprehension of an alter ego presupposes an understanding of the sense of 'ego' – which of course in phenomenology is available in the form of my own ego.[146] If another man enters my perceptual sphere his body is presented as primordial. To the extent that I attribute to him the sense of another subject then, it must be because I effect to him an analogizing transfer from my own animate organism. '(O)nly a similarity connecting, within my primordial sphere, that body over there with my body can serve as the motivational basis for the "analogizing" apprehension of that body as another organism'.[147] The body that I perceive must therefore, by virtue of this similarity, enter into a phenomenal 'pairing' with mine.[148] Furthermore, this identification will be continuously confirmed by the flow of experiences that follow, which reproduce what I recognize as familiar modes of behaviour.[149] On this basis of analogy all that goes with an ego is constituted for the Other. '(W)ith the other ego, there is appresented, in an analogizing modification, everything that belongs to his concretion: first *his* primordial world, and then his fully concrete ego. In other words, another monad becomes constituted appresentatively in mine.'[150]

Here, in what is perhaps the central argument of the fifth *Carte-*

sian Meditation, there is apparent a major error. Husserl assumes that I can make a transfer on the basis of my experience of my own living body to that of another perceived body. In reality however my subjective experiences are quite dissimilar from my experiences of the external world – so dissimilar in fact as to render it extremely unlikely that the appearance of another human body could be generalized on the basis of perception alone to display an identical mode of being to that of my own. Further, if this is true – that is, if I do not experience my lived body in the same way as I experience objects in the perceptual world – then it follows also that the mere lawful regularity of the movements of the perceived body will not be sufficient to distinguish it from other phenomena of nature. In fact here phenomenology actually presupposes the discursive approach to which it is opposed. For if Husserl's assumptions and mode of reasoning are accepted then the Other can be experienced neither immediately nor apperceptively. Rather, it can appear only through the mediation of a symbolic system within which a sequence of phenomena interpreted as representations acquire meaning. It is only within such a pre-existing system of discourse, associated immanently with symbolic praxis and incorporating a system of rules which are a priori intersubjectively available that a perceived body can be rendered intelligible as a living body. Under such circumstances the body that I 'rule and govern' is understood as a body that observes and recognizes rules which obtain in the intersubjective field. The perceived body then is seen to describe behaviour that is not necessarily similar to that of my own; indeed it can be quite original. Nevertheless, insofar as it is construed as a series of 'gestures', 'expressions', and so on this behaviour can be attributed a meaning that is fully in harmony with the meanings of my own actions. It can be seen that Husserl's account presupposes the existence of such a system of discourse within which the phenomenological data are already embedded.

A second weakness in the argument is one which Husserl himself recognizes yet fails to overcome; its consequence is identical to that of the problem just described. The requirement of communication and objectively existing nature demands that phenomena appear to me identically as they appear to others. Thus to the recognition of the subjectivity of the Other must be added a conviction that his perspective is equivalent to mine, that there has occurred an 'objectivating equalization'[151] of my existence with that of the Other. In Husserl's argument the basis of this equalization is to be found in the spatial modes of appearance of all bodies. In my primordial sphere my own animate body is experienced as uniquely 'here' while that of the Other appears with the mode of givenness 'there'.[152] Further, by virtue of my kinaesthesias the orientation 'there' can be freely varied, and in addition, by moving from place to place, I can occupy any spatial locus, thereby converting any 'there' into a 'here'. Within this context the ego of another is recognized not only as an ego but also, because of its discrepant spatial location, as an 'Other'.[153] But now the Other appears similarly as a subjectivity appresented by an animate body susceptible to free variations in its position in space. Thus not only is the ego's governing in his own body – the body over there – appresented, but also

> his governing in the Nature to which the body over there
> belongs, identically the Nature that is my primordial Nature. It
> is the same Nature, but in the mode of appearance: 'as if I
> were standing over there, where the Other's body is'. The body
> is the same, given to me as the body there, and to him as the
> body here, the central body. . . . '(M)y' whole Nature is the
> same as the Other's . . .[154]

The mistake here is exactly analogous to that in the previous argument. My experience of the spatial location 'here' – from which my entire perspective on the world is built up – is qualitatively different from that of the location 'there'. What is more, to the extent that I recognize the equivalence of all possible spatial perspectives, that equivalence is constituted in me as the universal centre of all experience. But however that may be, the reciprocity required for communication is altogether different from a mere exchangeability of position. What is required in discourse is rather a symbolic exchangeability of perspectives – which embraces theoretical possibilities and the equal capacity of the other to mobilize the elements of the representational apparatus in systematic and reproducible ways. If this is true then as in the previous case the methodically generated intersubjective discourse does not follow as a consequence of the phenomenological data but is rather presupposed in it. Further, the interchangeability of world perspectives is not now an outcome of the perceptual experience either: rather, within the context of a determinate system of representation, the latter acquires the character of a metaphor for the former.

With these brief comments we shall leave Husserl's discussion of the problem of intersubjectivity. Our aim here was not to analyse his arguments in detail but rather merely to advert to two junctures at which the problematic of discourse asserts itself within that of phenomenology. We have in fact claimed that the theory propounded by Husserl presupposes assertions that occur properly within the perspective he is opposing. Once more, at its apex, phenomenology culminates in a dilemma.[155]

Concluding words on Husserl

With these remarks we shall bring to a close our present discussion of Husserl's theory of science. The results that we have obtained will be utilized at length in succeeding chapters. Furthermore, there will be many occasions on which it will be appropriate to refer again directly to Husserl's works. Now in respect of the foregoing it will be clear that the attitude to phenomenology being adopted by this essay is hardly an uncritical one. Nevertheless we maintain our commitment that this body of thought embraces a wealth of insights into the structure and meaning of science – insights that are of incalculable value for the project of formulating a social theory of scientific knowledge. Husserl's philosophy is certainly not without its problems; indeed, in certain cases the truth-value of some of its fundamental claims is in doubt. However both in the issues it raises and in the answers it proposes it opens up vast and potentially fruitful possibilities; even where it is deficient its fecundity is undiminished.

The justification of these last statements, of course, will have to wait for the discussion to come. Here, we shall conclude the second part of this essay merely by mentioning briefly once again some of the salient aspects of the argument so far; this will serve the purpose of clarity as well as that of facilitating future references.

In our examination of Husserl's theory we have concentrated on two broad fields of interest that are of central importance for a social theory of science. We have emphasized on the one hand the problem of the nature of science and on the other the questions of history and of the relation in which scientific knowledge might stand to society. Regarding the former set of issues, we found that phenomenology produces an account of science that rests on a perspective that deliberately and rigorously eschews objectivism. Furthermore, concerning the actual structure of science, we discovered from phenomenology that the theoretical apparatus it employs is heterogeneous in composition: on the one hand, the realm of objectivities depends upon a construct of the system of judgements from which it at the same time retains some degree of autonomy; on the other hand, conversely, the realm of meanings of a science corresponds to – but cannot be identified with – its object domain. In general, from Husserl's account it emerges that science is a human accomplishment, the meaning and truth of which are derived anterior to the formal procedures. This result is, as we shall see, a profoundly anti-objectivist one, which strikes resonances deep within science itself. The fact that Husserl in his writings failed to recognize some of the radical implications of his own discoveries does not limit the force of these conclusions.

Regarding phenomenology and history, we have spoken only of the history of science – and then only indirectly, as Husserl himself does. Indeed, often when Husserl refers explicitly to history he is really talking of no more than the historical succession of philosophies and philosophical ideas. It would even perhaps not be going too far to say that a coherently developed theory of history is absent from Husserl's work – and in fact it is arguable that no such theory is even possible. If a truly phenomenological theory of history could be developed it would be an 'internal' history, in which an articulation was effected of a phenomenological theory of intersubjectivity with the theory of internal time-consciousness. The historical present would then be just the intersubjective mode of the present as it is given to consciousness with its intersubjective retentions and protentions. Husserl of course never attempts to develop such a theory – and indeed does not even advert to its possibility. Nevertheless in relation to science some more specific conclusions can be inferred. In particular, since science occurs necessarily in the form of a systematic unity its changes can be either of an 'evolutionary' or, more radically, of a 'structural' kind. In the former, gradual changes may occur within a given theoretical unity: in the latter, there occurs transformations between unities. This indeed is the core assertion of the lifeworld theory in relation to this problem: the history of science can only be understood as the historicity of discursive unities, radically disjunct yet nevertheless displaying broad structural continuities. As for the source of the dynamic of science, however, Husserl's theory gives no indication as to where this might lie. To be sure, since truth and evidence in phenomenology occur together, the sciences can be differentiated according to their evidential modes; furthermore, analysis can reveal philosophical and cultural moments within its formative processes. However, phenomenology abstains from a penetration into the content of science, while at the same time failing to provide an account of the variation of philosophical ideas and forms of evidence in relation to cultural variables; thus the most obvious possibilities are eliminated a priori. In actuality, the site of the historicity of science remains an open problem for Husserl's phenomenology – a fact perhaps not unrelated to his implicit faith in the unvarying truth of the specific sciences.

Phenomenology produces a rigorous and conclusive attack on objectivism. Exactly as its own theory unfolds, however, it gives rise to another, quite different critique. This circumstance is not purely adventitious; in fact it is symptomatic of an underlying, abiding dualism within phenomenology itself. The theory of consciousness brings forth a second theory from which consciousness is in principle excluded. In every aspect of Husserl's theory of science the dualism is apparent. There are two meanings of science: science is either the creation of Galileo's consciousness or it is a systematic outcome of the appropriated conceptual systems. There are two kinds of objectivity of science: objectivity is an externalization of consciousness, or it is an effect of the methodological apparatus of a given theoretical structure. There are two, contending, aspects of the lifeworld theory: it is the realm of original self-evidence, or else it is the repository for the intersubjective structures of language and method in respect of the productions of which evidence becomes a question. And, inclusive of all of these, there are two forms of truth: as presence and as intersubjectively verifiable discursive truth. In fact, out of the interstices of phenomenology emerges a second epistemology different from it – or rather, complementary to it – in almost every detail except for one, shared commitment against objectivism.

At its inception phenomenology had sought a presuppositionless theory that would establish the truth of science. At its conclusion it shows that science embraces a conceptual content of its own and so must be understood not as the discovery of a pre-existing truth but as an accomplishment. For itself, phenomenology also sought certain truth, but through its own mechanisms erupts into a bifurcation. Phenomenology is true, perhaps. But then science cannot be taken as phenomenology wanted to take it. Now science must be understood not as one truth amongst many but as one philosophical claim amongst many, subject to a rich diversity of theoretical, practical and cultural influences.

III
Objectivist science and capitalism: The possibility of non-objectivist science

Objectivity and capitalism: The theory of fetishism

This book has two main themes: the sociology of science and the conceptual content of science itself. As we have suggested above, discussions of science have hitherto gravitated generally to one pole or to the other. The sociologists of science, for example, have largely remained aloof from science's actual discoveries, as momentous as they have been, whilst at the same time, those concerned with the content of science – whether physicists or philosophers – have usually abstained from a consideration of social themes. Nevertheless as we have argued, there is definitely a case for an examination of the socially contingent aspects of the conceptual forms of science. Indeed, the need for such an examination is implicit in the mere question of the possibility of a philosophy of science. For this question already suggests the hypothesis that the familiar modes of the presentation of nature necessarily presuppose an epistemological commitment; and insofar as epistemology is the outcome of processes of social discourse and subject to historical variation we are compelled to ask whether the same may apply also to science.

Regarding the content of a social theory of science, however, this of course cannot be anticipated. The most that can be said in advance is that such a theory may well entail an intersection of social theory not merely with the philosophy of science but also with the study of nature itself. For one of the major problems of which sociology provides a most convincing account – the problem of objectivism – is, as we shall see, also a central issue for science itself. Accordingly, as we have already argued in detail, it is natural to apply to the latter the results of the former. A social theory of science, therefore, may well, either directly or indirectly, raise the question of a non-objectivist theory of nature.

At this stage, however, little more can be said. The few attempts we have discussed which seek to explain the relationship between the social forms and the conceptual structures of science have, for one reason or another, proved unsatisfactory. Thus *Dialectic of Enlightenment* was one of the most outstanding and rigorous of these attempts; it sought directly to explicate the social connection of scientific knowledge. However its programme was fatally compromised by its parodoxical commitment to – or, at least, its paradoxical inability to criticize effectively – the validity of the prevailing objectivist conception of nature – a circumstance which, incidentally, had demanded the development of a special delicacy in the fashioning of its arguments. Similarly, to mention just one other example, Husserl, especially in his last work, had focused explicitly on the mutual interchange between the process of social constitution and natural science. His project also failed, however, due to a number of difficulties in his account – amongst which were the deficiency of his concept of history and the inadequacy of his theory of intersubjectivity; thus he too was prevented from formulating an adequate characterization of the specific effectivity of the material structures of society in the processes of categorial evolution. Consequently, for a further clarification of the issues at stake and an identification of the possibilities which might be examined, it is natural to turn elsewhere – to a theory which, while not directly addressing the problem of science, nevertheless effected a profound reflection on the intersection between philosophy and social theory; that is, it is natural to turn to a consideration of the theoretical tradition initiated by the writings of Karl Marx.

The aspect of Marx's own work which will be of greatest interest to us in what follows is that embraced by his theory of the 'fetishism of commodities'. As we shall argue, the implicit central problem of this theory is the question of the characteristic forms of the presentation of things in capitalist society. Of course, the 'things' with which Marx was concerned specifically were social and cultural objects. However we shall claim that similar considerations might be able to be applied more generally, to include the study of nature as well.[1] Indeed, once again, there is a link between sociology and science, which is here established through the abiding and apparently ubiquitous problem of objectivism. To be precise, the fetishism of commodities, we shall see, is just the objectivistic presentation of these commodities within the conceptual configuration associated with a capitalist social formation; Marx's aim is to elab-

174

orate these capitalist forms of objectivity and to describe their emergence within the context of the contemporaneous relations of production. We shall claim that the resulting theory contains indications for an explication of the social and historical determinants of classical science and in addition, proposes a number of rather suggestive hypotheses regarding the structure of science in general.

In what follows we shall describe briefly the theory of the fetishism of commodities as it appears from the vantage point of the study of natural science. In this account we shall be able to make use of many of our previous results – in particular, those emerging from our discussion of phenomenology. At the outset it will be necessary to refer, again briefly, to the two outstanding current approaches to the fetishism of commodities. Subsequently, we shall suggest the outlines of a more general theory and proceed to mention some of its possible areas of application. Illustrations of the direct relevance of considerations of this kind for the understanding of contemporary science, and suggestions regarding the further development of the understanding of the specific problem of the social determinants of objectivity, will be offered at a later stage.

The two approaches

The basic idea of Marx's theory of the fetishism of commodities is that in the commodity economy the social relations of production inevitably acquire the form of things and cannot be expressed except by means of things. In consequence, actual relationships between individuals are concealed or obscured, and interchanges based on human qualities tend to be replaced by the quantitative exchange of commodities. Conversely, the things themselves, which had acquired their specific characteristics substantially from cultural sources, are conceived as entities subsisting in radical independence from the social relations of production. Hence the resulting confusion is a multiple one, afflicting at once the understanding of the domains of society and of nature, of subjectivity and of objectivity.[2]

Marx developed his ideas on the subject in question in a variety of texts over many years; these texts include in particular, the *1844 Manuscripts*, the *German Ideology*, the *Grundrisse* and *Capital*. In view of the profound developments displayed by Marx's thought over the compass of these works, it is not surprising that his theory of the fetishism of commodities is susceptible to varying interpre-

175

tations. In fact, there are two main interpretations of this theory, each of which places particular emphasis on one of its important features. The *theory of reification* emphasizes the question of subjectivity; the *structuralist interpretation* emphasizes the questions of system, structure and representation. As we shall see, both these perspectives have considerable insights to offer. However neither in its present form can be considered to be satisfactory.

* * * * * *

Of those theories that can be said to adopt the general approach of the theory of reification, the most rigorous and evocative certainly remains the critique elaborated in the early 1920s by Georg Lukács. In his celebrated (and at times, reviled) work, *History and Class Consciousness*, he sought with strikingly radical formulations to address the question of how far commodity exchange, together with its structural consequences, is able to influence the total outer and inner life of a society.[3] Now it is necessary to state immediately that it is not our objective to discuss at great length here Lukács's theory – or for that matter, the contending structuralist one. In fact, we shall not even attempt to provide a comprehensive outline of the main aspects of the theory of reification which bear on our present concerns. Instead, we intend merely, by way of a few abbreviated comments, to advert to the decisive importance of this body of thought for the development of the modern views of the problem of fetishism – and indeed to the rich resources which it contains for the understanding of the relationship between scientific knowledge and society.

According to Lukács, one of the central features of Marx's theory is its demonstration that in capitalist society 'a man's own activity, his own labour becomes something objective and independent of him, something that controls him by virtue of an autonomy alien to man'.

There is both an objective and a subjective side to this phenomenon. Objectively a world of objects and relations between things springs into being (the world of commodities and their movements on the market). The laws governing these objects are indeed gradually discovered by man, but even so they confront him as invisible forces that generate their own power ... Subjectively ... a man's activity becomes estranged from himself, it turns into a commodity which, subject to the non-human objectivity of the natural laws of society, must go

176

its own way independently of man just like any consumer article. . . . [4]

In even this brief quotation some important features of Lukács's thought can be recognized. In particular, it is clear that Lukács, who is referring here specifically to Marx's concept of fetishism, interprets the latter to incorporate much of the Marxist notions of alienation and reification. In fact, the concept of fetishism which thus emerges constitutes an effective vehicle for fusing these last two entities – a tendency which itself forms one of the major underlying themes of *History and Class Consciousness*. Within Marx's own work it was only during his later period that the conceptions of reification and alienation were rigorously differentiated; then, the latter came to refer to the antagonistic character of the historical process of socialization, while the former adverted to the antagonistic character of the intensifying social domination of nature which had progressively disjoined labour from social interaction. [5] Earlier, in the *1844 Manuscripts*, the two sets of ideas had been identified. It is certainly interesting that Lukács, who had no access to these writings, recreated an important aspect of the thought of the young Marx. [6] Of course, this accomplishment carried both positive and negative implications, just as it had in Marx's original theory. We shall mention some of the problems with this approach below; substantially, they derive from the absence of certain fundamental theoretical distinctions and the substitution instead of a variety of Utopian inclinations adopted in satisfaction of the prevailing spirit of pre-revolutionary optimism. At the same time however, Lukács's approach endowed his work with a profound radicalism: it enabled him to raise, in a challenging and provocative way, the deepest questions regarding man, society and nature. He was able to show from his theory that reification is essentially a phenomenon of the capitalist mode of production – that is, that the present antagonistic relationship between nature and culture is itself an historical product. This is a conclusion of particular interest for the theory of science. It is also especially desirable from the Marxist viewpoint, for it provides the possibility of establishing a normative basis for the theory without compromising the antiontological elements contained within the project inherited from Hegelianism. Autonomy, which in Kant had been posited as an elementary ethical goal, for Lukács was transformed into the essential *telos* of subjectivity. [7] Further, this *telos* was to be realized by the proletariat, not as the site of an arbitrary collection of subjective impressions but as the weapon of history, [8] whose mission unfolds alongside the historical transformations in the forms of objectivity.[9] In addition, of particular importance for our present purposes is the implication which follows from this last insight: the implication that it is possible to develop a general, radical critique of objectivity, in which the objective forms can be characterized as social phenomena and in which, specifically, objectivism would emerge as a phenomenon of capitalist society.

Of course, it would be a misinterpretation of Lukács (ironically, one of which he himself is guilty in his 1967 preface to the work in question[10]) to assume that he is claiming merely that reification is located in the material life activities of a society. To be sure, he makes many comments suggesting a close relationship between, for example, social class and scientific method[11] or the scientific attitude to nature and capitalism.[12] Nevertheless, one of his major results is that 'value is not only the "reified-mediator" of use-value in capitalism due to which even the most elementary needs remain regularly unsatisfiable ... but that it also penetrates the content of use-value itself and becomes its precondition ... since it socially transforms the human needs in a direction dictated by the requirements of the capitalist economy.'[13] Accordingly, capitalism 'determines not only the conditions of the application of machinery, but also the direction of its very technological development'.[14] In fact, it is possible to claim even more than this. Nature itself is a social category,[15] in the sense that, both practically and theoretically, its forms cannot be dissociated from the social relations of production.[16]

Lukács himself is quite aware of the profound radicalism of this last assertion. In his studies both of capitalism and of pre-capitalist societies[17] he shows that the forms of nature – and in particular, of the knowledge of natural phenomena – are subject to determinations originating in social life. Thus we see that 'nature's form, its content, its range and its objectivity, are all socially conditioned'.[18] The very concept of objectivity, which obviously underlies the contemporaneous theoretical apprehension of nature, unfolds out of the social processes.[19] Indeed, at times Lukács goes even further than this, to suggest that different social structures might be associated with different sets of categories and different systems of truth[20] – although it must be conceded that the last idea is incompletely developed.

These insights, and others, enable Lukács to restate the problem of commodity fetishism in a particularly elegant and suggestive way. In brief, it emerges from his work that fetishism can be interpreted as a problem of the formation and preponderance of distorted conceptions of objectivity in relation to certain variable social and historical conditions.[21] What is more, regarding capitalism in particular, it becomes clear that the distorted objectivity in question is none other than objectivism.[22] Thus, in accordance with this idea, the hypothesis is put forward that there exists an internal, structural congruity between the social formation – that is, capitalism – and the objective form – that is, objectivism.[23] This conception, at first sight possibly rather inconsequential, in fact constitutes one of the most powerful, evocative, and indeed profoundly radical, claims advanced in the entire work under discussion. Lukács argues that '(t)he economic system ... does in fact show marked similarities with the objective structure of that Nature which is the object of study of physics and the other natural sciences.'[24] Elaborating this point in detail, he formulates the similarities referred to in terms strikingly reminiscent of our earlier characterizations of objectivism.

> (The economic system) is concerned with relations that are completely unconnected with man's humanity and indeed with any anthropomorphisms – be they religious, ethical, aesthetic or anything else. Man appears in it only as an abstract number, as something which can be reduced to number or to numerical relations. Its concern, as Engels put it, is with laws that are only understood, not controlled, with a situation in which – to quote Engels again – the producers have lost control of the conditions of life of their own society. As a result of the objectification, the reification of society, their economic relations have achieved complete autonomy, they lead an independent life, forming a closed, self-validating system.[25]

In numerous other passages he adds to these arresting insights, unfolding in brilliant descriptions the inner logic of familiar phenomena – of quantification and contemplation, of bureaucracy and rationalization.[26]

At this juncture it is appropriate to emphasize two important points regarding the arguments of *History and Class Consciousness*. In the first place, it must be recognized that, in spite of the fact that we have presented Lukács's view in a relatively direct and unambiguous way, this work is in reality both fragmentary and contradictory. It does not develop exhaustively and systematically a single theoretical perspective. Rather, it is a collection of loosely connected essays on a variety of broadly related themes – a circumstance which at once constitutes a deficiency and, insofar as it

179

makes possible evocative speculative hypotheses, a considerable strength. This point is particularly relevant when it comes to evaluating the arguments referred to above. Secondly, it is necessary to appreciate that Lukács makes a deliberate distinction between the forms of objectivity prevailing in capitalist and non-capitalist societies. Indeed, this is a subject which at times creates substantial difficulties for the interpretation of his text. It is contended that the encounter between nature and man in the pre-capitalist world differed in fundamental ways from that which became familiar under capitalism: it was somehow more direct and immediate, not yet subject to the complex and uncompromising determinations of the capitalist totalization of the social forms.[27] In earlier societies a creative dialogue was established with nature which became sedimented in cultural works; remnants of this dialogue are still recognizable in the enduring productions of art, religion and philosophy.[28] With the coming of capitalism the categories of nature became for the first time fully subordinated to the process of socialization.[29] The indissoluble unity which had hitherto characterized the relationship between society and nature was fractured; in its place was substituted a dialectical totality within which mutually interdependent forms of nature, culture and economy would interact.[30] In both cases 'nature is a social category', in the deep sense that the different social formations theorize nature according to 'completely different systems of categories';[31] indeed, for this reason it is also possible to say – for science as much as for economics – that 'different laws are seen to obtain in different social milieus and the validity of any given type of law is tied to quite definite social presuppositions.'[32] Nature is a social category – this is one of Lukács's fundamental claims. However while affirming this it is important not to omit the underlying distinction which he stressed between the actual forms of social mediation of nature within the capitalist and pre-capitalist configurations.

The theory of reification provides many interesting and innovative suggestions for the development of a social theory of science. However it must be admitted that beyond this its usefulness for such a purpose is strictly limited. For Lukács's formulation of the problem depended too heavily on the account of rationality given by Max Weber. In his conception, as in that of the latter, he took as the primary issue the extension of the process of rationalization, as demonstrated in the permeation throughout social life of the intellectual forms of calculation and mathematization which also characterized modern natural science.[33] To be sure, as we indicated

180

previously, Weber's interpretation of calculating reason as constitutive of a cultural a priori of modern science is itself of great
interest;[34] what is more, it is clear that, insofar as he retains a faith
in the possibility of non-reified relations between nature and man,
Lukács does in fact propose a development beyond Weber.[35] Nevertheless, by accepting the problem of rationalization as the central
issue Lukács imposes a curious limitation on his own thought. From
his deliberations he concludes that the forms both of truth and of
objectivity are cultural variables; yet he never proceeds to consider
the full implications of this for the theory of nature. He never
accepts that, therefore, the epistemological precepts of science must
be open to scrutiny – and even, potentially, susceptible to refutation. He never raises the question of the actual validity – that is,
the truth-content – of the intellectual forms he is criticizing. He is
never prepared to entertain the suggestion that not only is the
contemporary conception of science associated with a multitude of
malign social consequences but that some of its deepest commitments may even be mistaken.

It cannot of course be said that Lukács is unaware of the great
complexity of the transition between nature and epistemology, as
our remarks above show. However his failure to pursue relentlessly
the consequences of his own insights prevented him from exposing
the deep ambiguity within the currently accepted conceptions.
Thus, in spite of the fact that he himself provides the necessary
instruments, he prescinds from embarking on a refutation of the
philosophical contentions of Newtonian mechanics.[36] In spite of
his recognition of the historical variability of the forms of truth
and scientific laws he is prepared to concede the enduring validity
of the propositions of conventional science.[37] And in spite of his
efforts to characterize independently the society-nature relationship
in pre-capitalist societies he still maintains that the capitalist stage
represents a qualitatively higher level, in which 'by the process of
civilization' the 'umbilical cord' between the two is at last cut.[38] In
the final analysis, positive science escapes from the critical gaze of
the theory of reification with some of its social effects condemned
but its theoretical structure altogether unscathed. Indeed, in this
particular respect it may be said that the young Lukács was somewhat more 'orthodox' than was appreciated at the time (though it
should be added at once that here also he is in the company of the
young Marx!).

There is another respect in which Lukács's work fails to provide
us with the necessary requirements for a social theory of science. It
does not pursue in detail another set of issues with which such a

theory would be concerned: those issues relating to the means by which science acquires its social efficacy. This is a problem to which Lukács does in fact refer but which he leaves undeveloped. It is the problem of elaborating the substructure of a second transition: the transition between epistemology and domination. As we have already seen, in a later work by Horkheimer and Adorno – who were certainly familiar with *History and Class Consciousness* – rigorous emphasis was placed on exactly this question. Regarding Lukács himself however, in spite of the fact that in numerous passages he demonstrates his awareness of its importance[39] he nevertheless provides no indications for a solution.

In summary, therefore, for the theory of science Lukács's work contains many pregnant suggestions. As we shall see, many of these can today be substantiated and developed. Nevertheless in his writings they remain *only* suggestions, and he does not proceed to develop a coherent theory of scientific knowledge. For after all, the elaboration of the social theory of science would be concerned substantially with just the two transitions to which we have referred above – that is, the transitions between nature and epistemology and between epistemology and domination – and which Lukács fails to consider adequately.

Of course the legacy of *History and Class Consciousness* is a very broad one and covers many other aspects of Marxist thought. If it were possible to review this legacy in a few words one would perhaps say that Lukács raised deep questions, to which answers were not readily available. It is in this respect that he is owed a prodigious debt from the theory of science.

Before leaving the problematic of reification it is perhaps worth noting in passing that within its general compass is contained also a second approach, which is quite popular. This approach is rather less rigorous than the theory propounded by Lukács; indeed it is not an exaggeration to say that it contains a naive objectivist bias. Its basic conception appears to be no less than the acceptance literally and at face value of Marx's diagnosis that 'a definite social relation between men assumes, in their eyes the fantastic form of a relation between things',[40] things which 'rule the producers instead of being ruled by them'.[41] We refer to this view here for the purpose only of making two points: that the postulated conversion of inanimate objects into political powers is not completely perspicuous; and that the very concept of a 'relation between things' presupposes a specific process of social constitution formed through and articulated in language. These two problems were in fact specifically recognized by Marx and a substantial – and perhaps even the most interesting – part of his theory was devoted towards answering them.[42]

* * * * * *

The other major interpretation of Marx's theory of fetishism is the structuralist one. This approach, which originated largely with Louis Althusser, emphasizes not subjectivity and human relationships, not the 'inner and outer life of a society', but *structures* and the relationships between them. The various aspects of capitalist society can be understood only at the end of a detailed analysis of its internal structure and their mutual effects. This applies in particular to fetishism, that is, to the 'ideological effects directly implied by the economic structure'.[43] Thus Althusser can write that *Capital* 'measures a distance and an internal dislocation in the real, inscribing in its *structure*, a distance and a dislocation such as to make their own effects themselves illegible, and the illusion of an immediate reading of them the ultimate apex of their effects: *fetishism*.'[44] Further, he continues later,

> Despite the massive 'obviousness' of the economic 'given' in the capitalist mode of production, and precisely because of the 'massive' character of this fetishized 'obviousness', the only way to the essence of the economic is to construct its concept, i.e., to reveal the site occupied in the structure of the whole by the region of the economic, therefore to reveal the articulation of this region with other regions (legal-political and ideological superstructure), and the degree of presence (or effectivity) of the other regions in the economic region itself...[45]

The structuralist perspective, then, attempts to circumvent the problems of the theory of reification by disengaging the concept of fetishism from the subjective moment on the one hand and from the forms of domination on the other. Thus, for Rancière (the author of a major study from this perspective), fetishism represents 'not an anthropological process but the specific dislocation according to which the structure of the capitalist mode of production presents itself in the field of *Wirklichkeit*, of *Altagsleben*, and offers itself to the consciousness and action of the agents of production, the supports of capitalist relations of production.'[46]

Now it is evident at once that in terms of the Althusserian discourse to which it claims allegiance this last formulation is defective, ignoring as it does the epistemological conditions for the elaboration and critique of a theoretical ideology. Nevertheless it expresses clearly the overall purpose of this perspective on the theory of fetishism: the displacement of the appearance-essence interpretation in favour of a more general study of the epistemological effects of a social formation. However at the same time it betrays a similar weakness to the previous view (that is, the view of the theory of reification), which similarly excludes it from an application to the theory of science. The subjective and cultural aspects of the process of social constitution clearly cannot be theorized from such a perspective. This is the case not merely for reasons of disdain for the notion of subjectivity, but because at its most primitive level the theory insists on a relationship between science and ideology that is characterized by rupture and not articulation. Thus in its urgency to protect its own scientistic programme this interpretation systematically ignores major problems which the reification theory had at least glimpsed. The ultimate effect however is not dissimilar: structuralism, like its predecessor, conceals from its own vision the contingency of the nature-epistemology relation, hence foreclosing the possibility of developing a non-objectivist theory of science. This does not mean that no critique of objectivism could be forthcoming from the structuralist perspective, as we shall see later. Nevertheless, such is in fact the case for the theory propounded by Althusser and for this reason he may with real justification be regarded as a positivist.[47]

It is of course necessary, when discussing the structuralist perspective on the problem of fetishism, to make mention of the fact that the views of many of the authors involved have changed considerably over the years. This is of no particular consequence for the present argument, since our intention here is primarily to outline the main – and the most suggestive – contending positions. It is interesting nevertheless that in the more recent writings of Balibar – to choose one fairly representative example – a self-criticism has been offered which takes account of the dislocation between science and ideology to which we have just adverted. Indeed, this fact is especially interesting because the new conception involves explicitly the dismissal of the notion of fetishism altogether. According to this view, the theory of fetishism articulated in Balibar's earlier work must be rejected because it was 'totally idealist;[48] this was the case because it presupposed, albeit inadvertently, a conception of the subject. It necessarily makes the misrecognition inherent in ideology dependent upon 'the place occupied by the individual *as a subject* in the structure of exchange';[49] furthermore it makes the commodity itself 'the origin or subject of its own misrecognition'.[50] Thus, according to Balibar, the theory of fetishism was a theory of the genesis of the subject as an alienated subject.[51] Accordingly, it prevented the 'scientific explication of particular ideological effects implied by commodity circulation', as well as making it appear - falsely - that the '"transparency" of the social relations is an automatic effect ... of the suppression of the "commodity categories", that is to say of the commodity.'[52]

As we have said, the transformations in Balibar's views - and along with him, those of many other members of the structuralist school - are of no consequence for our present argument. However as we shall see later his identification within structuralism of a place occupied by a concept of the subject is in fact substantially correct. What he failed to realize was that the existence of such a concept within a given problematic does not necessarily reduce that problematic to idealism. On the contrary, the possibility of defining the role of the subject is a precondition for the development of any theory of objectivity and hence of science. It appears to us therefore that the strictly post-structuralist problematic proposed by Balibar - assuming it were feasible - could have little or nothing to offer to the theory of science.

Some of these issues will be taken up in more detail in a later chapter. At this stage, however, it may be worth emphasizing the obvious fact that the arguments we are offering can hardly be intended to provide decisive refutations of either perspective under review. Such refutations in fact are not at all our purpose; rather, our objective here is merely, by means of selective, incomplete and extremely rudimentary arguments, to indicate both some strengths and some weaknesses of these views for the study of science. In general, the debate over their respective merits and demerits remains far from being settled. Indeed, it is not easy even to specify just what kinds of arguments may be decisive. For example - as Rancière himself has pointed out in his later writings - it may occur that in certain circumstances political arguments tend to predominate over purely theoretical ones. This point is of particular relevance to the general problem of the theory of alienation: although the *theoretical* status of this concept is extremely controversial, it would, as Lefebvre has argued, constitute 'supreme pedantry' to deny it the status of a concept altogether; in fact, it has a status which is not *epistemological* but *social*, for it has provoked a 'prodigious ferment, an inexhaustible fecundity', in the understanding of practical conditions among workers, women, youths and colonized peoples.[53] Notwithstanding this general argument, the study of science itself remains primarily a theoretical enterprise, and indeed the critique of objectivism is antecedent to that of alienation. Accordingly, although the ultimate partiality of its categories must be recognized, the principal criteria of this analysis will remain theoretical ones.

In spite of these comments it is possible to draw some elementary conclusions from the preceding discussion. The specific focuses of the two major theoretical outlooks dealing with the problem of fetishism differ substantially – from the early Frankfurt School preoccupation with the transformation into conditions of domination of an epistemological framework identified with the study of nature, to the structuralist diagnosis of the formation of non-scientific theoretical systems in the context of a 'structure in dominance'. Both provide substantial insights into the meaning of the economic structure of capitalism and of the respective roles of theory and ideology. At the same time however, from the point of view of the theory of science, both display important deficiencies. In particular, the two share a common presupposition in their faith in the inviolability of the presently constituted form of science; hence both prescind from a critique of the objectivism of natural science. In the light of these facts, and having regard to the conclusions we have established in previous chapters, it seems that a case exists for a reconsideration of the Marxian theory of fetishism which would place particular emphasis on the problem of science. This endeavour would take as its point of departure a twofold investigation: an analysis of the a priori identifications according to which the existing theories seek to resolve fundamental problems not otherwise apprehensible within them – in particular, of course, the identification of the world of nature with positive science; and secondly, an exploration of the historically contingent features of the process of fetishism and hence of the possibilities of a more generally applicable theory.

It may be worth adding here in passing that these two tasks are by no means gratuitous. On the contrary they have been rendered very pressing by a number of contemporaneous social impulses. For example, there is the culturally presented questioning of science that formed one of the starting points of this essay. This questioning emerged once science had become a social force – as a consequence of which the need arose for the development of a theory of nature that would encompass the manifold of its own complex origins and effects. In addition, there has occurred in the late capitalist societies a general diversification of social phenomena which has made impossible any exhaustive characterization of either the social processes or the forms of their knowledge in terms of the commodity form alone; that is, developments have occurred which have challenged the predominance of the labour process in the present-day capitalist dialectic. It is suggestive to ask whether the proliferation of epistemological perspectives in the theory of nature may be related to this process of cultural diversification.

Subsequently – to continue the outline of the project for a review of the notion of fetishism – a general theory would be sought which would consider the problem of the presentation of objects in a specific cultural environment. This theory would of necessity incorporate a critique of objectivism in relation not just to social objects but also to natural ones. Further, while encompassing the moment of intersubjective constitution of a scientific body of thought, the theory must also be capable of providing an appreciation of some of the specific features of science, such as for example its contemporary diversification, mentioned above, and its characteristic historical variability. What is sought, in short, is a theory of the specific processes according to which in capitalist societies natural phenomena are endowed precisely with distinct styles of 'naturalness'; that is, what is sought is a theory of just what is 'natural' about nature.

Some further preliminary results from phenomenology

In the development of a rigorous theory of the process of the social constitution of nature many of the results of our previous discussions will be of use. The insights achieved within the sociology of science are valuable resources for the present task, as also are those of the two major extant theories of fetishism. But of particular value will be some of the results of our analysis of Husserl's philosophy. It must be stressed at once however that such an application of phenomenological concepts to the interpretation of Marxism does not imply that the latter can be subsumed under the problematic of phenomenology. On the contrary, it is our view that this is not at all the case. Rather it appears to us that Marxism contains a multitude of truths which are apprehensible, in differing degrees, from a variety of perspectives; that is, it is our view that this theory is susceptible to a number of interpretations, each of which may be considered to contain some degree of validity. For example, we are claiming that it may be the case that – in principle, at least – both the phenomenological and the structuralist interpretations of Marxism may be able to be accepted as valid – with each providing a different perspective on it. Except to the extent that Marxism might contain contradictory formulations, therefore, all these interpretations would be consistent; however they need by no means be identical, or even wholly commensurable. This unusual circumstance is attributable to the peculiar status of Marxism in general: it is not a single theory which can be given a unique, unambiguous formulation; rather, it is a constellation of theories which come together in their common focus on a number of issues of pressing social and political importance. Or to put the matter metaphorically, Marxism is a *language*, within which in varying ways attempts are made to resolve certain classes of problems.[54]

In the present context it is convenient to adopt as our point of departure the phenomenological perspective. Our analysis of Husserl's philosophy established that any lifeworld theory – that is, any theory which seeks to apprehend the unity of a system of discourse in terms of the constitutive unity of a lifeworld – must have a theory of the formation and articulation of meaning structures in continuity with it. Furthermore, exactly as such a theory obviates the need for an a priori commitment to positive science so it at once demands the development of a radical anti-Cartesianism; for in order to avoid the Scylla of idealism and the Charybdis of naive realism a new theory of intersubjectivity is required which accounts first of all for *the possibility of the concept* of the Other. But then the totality in relation to which meaning is fashioned is at once social, and endowed with cultural and theoretical accomplishments.

Now from this result the analysis may move in either of two directions. It may proceed directly to trace the existing material processes of social constitution and hence to examine the dialectic of the labour process or – equivalently – of 'praxis'. This route would necessarily issue in a characterization of the process of the development of meaning as a dialectic of essence and appearance. Or else it may proceed via a detour into the implications of the anti-Cartesian turn. This approach would retain the focus on the general conditions of our knowledge *of nature* and ultimately must lead back to the other; accordingly, it is the one most suitable for the study of science.

Let us, therefore, for the moment assume – without prejudicing the ensuing argument – the existence of a lifeworld in which is embodied the texture of the social and natural worlds. Then, to continue the Husserlian terminology, this lifeworld constitutes for us an *horizon*. That is, as both subjective and encompassing the whole of reality it at once guarantees the scope of human space and designates its limits; it provides the perspective according to which the world acquires its human features and, in particular, objects acquire their orientation and mutual interrelations.[55]

Furthermore, as Merleau-Ponty has shown, the horizon is more than a physical limit, a purely optical phenomenon; it is connected with man's shape, his upright posture, his field of vision and his power to perceive the order and structure of the world around him as fixed within its inherent restriction.[56]

Now there are two important consequences of these ideas which we shall utilize. The first is Merleau-Ponty's generalization of Husserl's theory of intersubjectivity, according to which the human body is able to see and to touch visible things because 'being of their family, itself visible and tangible, it uses its own being as a means to participate in theirs ... because the body belongs to the order of the things as the world is universal flesh'; that is, because 'they have an internal equivalent in me; they arouse in me a carnal formula of their presence'.[57] And the second, which depends on this commensurability between bodily perception and conceptual organization and which represents the substantive outcome of the entire lifeworld theory, is the nature of the process of symbolization, in which we recapture in the intersubjective field our corporeal existence and apply it communicatively.

On the basis of these ideas several applications to specific areas of science already suggest themselves. They will not however be pursued here; some applications to psychology have been elaborated by Merleau-Ponty and others; further possibilities will be referred to later in this essay. At this point we shall instead recapitulate briefly the three major results that will be employed in the sequel. These results have been derived from phenomenological arguments; they are however consistent with Marxian theory, as we shall see. First of all, it follows from the above considerations that nature must be conceptualized as part of an interchange in which the social and natural worlds reciprocally inter-present themselves. Secondly, to the extent that the lifeworld incorporates theoretical and cultural effects it can no longer be considered as the primordial domain of pre-scientific experience; and indeed, to the achievements of science must therefore be attributed a fundamental validity and integrity. Finally, the characterization of science now reveals itself as a problem of the social constitution of objects, of a determination of specific modes of intentionality of a society.

It is to a consideration of this last problem that we now turn.

The fetishism of commodities: 1

On the basis of these results the fetishism problem can now be restated: can there be developed, independently of any presupposed table of categories or forms of intuition, a general theory of the presentation of objects in a concrete, social context? Or more specifically: can the forms of capitalism be characterized from a consistently and radically anti-objectivist perspective? This latter question is a special case of the former; an answer to one would facilitate an answer to the other. Now it should be clear that the problems thus formulated are generalized versions of problems addressed directly by Marx. Alternatively, they may be considered to constitute radical restatements of the questions to which the reification theory was directed – restatements, that is, which avoid the objectivist presuppositions that compromised Lukács's arguments. Accordingly, since the problems are generalized cases of the problems considered by the original theory it will be necessary, in the search for solutions, to utilize a more general formulation of the main terms. In fact, as will become apparent towards the end of the present chapter, the process of generalization will have to extend even further than this. We have said that it is necessary to ask the question regarding the possibility of a general theory of the *presentation* of objects in a social field. This formulation was meant to convey the implication that the *constitution* of natural objects is also at stake; however we have avoided this expression as much as possible because it would tend, inescapably, to bear the unintended connotation that the analysis on which we are to embark were inscribed within the phenomenological framework. Nonetheless, processes of constitution are indeed involved and for Marxism these are necessarily linked to social labour. As we shall see, the development of the theory of fetishism will require the generalization of this fundamental concept.

To this end then, and for the purposes of the present chapter only, let us call 'specific fetishism' the specific form of objectivity which is the predominant one characterizing both animate and inanimate objects in a given society. In phenomenological terms this would be the specific form of intentionality accepted as 'natural' in a particular cultural context. Thus fetishism refers to kinds of objectivity; however not *every* kind is admitted. Rather, the term is restricted to those species of objectivity which are universalized within social formations – that is, which occlude the contingency of their own theoretical forms. In other words, what is central for the new concept is the relationship between objectivity and society on the one hand and the actual or potential self-consciousness of this relationship on the other: there are only specific fetishisms of particular societies and these fetishisms are necessarily opaque. Employing this terminology, the issue at stake can be stated simply: it is just the development of a general critique of fetishism – that is, the characterization of the specific fetishism of a society in terms of its particular structures of social constitution and interaction; beyond this, there is the still broader task of the construction of a general social theory of objectivity, which would entail the elucidation of the social and historical variables implicit in the emergence of the various objective forms.

It must be admitted at once that this proposed usage departs significantly from the conception traditionally associated with Marx's use of the word 'fetishism'. His theory was intended to connote a special kind of mystification associated with the capitalist forms; we have sacrificed this connotation in order to develop a hypothesis dealing with a more general phenomenon, in relation to which Marx's description refers to the specifically capitalist form. In so doing however it is not the case that we have given up the critical acumen of the concept of fetishism; on the contrary, by freeing it from any commitment to preconceived ideas about nature we have refined and sharpened it. Fetishism, as we said, is always to be understood in relation to particular social configurations; it specifies the predominant contemporary form (or forms) of natural phenomena. The error implicitly incorporated into any variety of fetishism is the systematic denial of its social and historical contingency. It is the critical purpose of a general theory of fetishism to reconstruct the path linking society and nature – that is, to expose to view the abiding, inner connections between objectivity and philosophy and between objectivity and the social forms.

In our new usage, of course, we can still speak of a 'fetishism of commodities'. By definition however, the expression now refers to *a particular mode of the presentation of reality as it is refracted in the capitalist categories*. The specific feature of fetishism, furthermore, is no longer the systematic reduction of social facts to postulated 'natural' ones but a particular fetishized logic that is also applied to nature. Indeed, as we shall argue, just what emerges from Marx's works is the discovery of this 'logic of capital', according to which commodities *qua* forms penetrate the medium of intersubjectivity and there subsequently preponderate with their own structures.

In the detailed description of this process several problems arise; these are partly due to an indisputable objectivist bias in Marx's own account, and partly to the need to maintain the irreducible distinction – discovered by Kant – between the ontic reality and its theoretical reflection. In particular, there is the problem of the continuity between Marx's 'fetishism of commodities' and the notion of fetishism suggested here – formulated as it is within a radically anti-Cartesian, non-objectist perspective. It is obviously desirable, if we are to be able to have access to the remainder of the insights of Marxism, to have shown that our present interpretation, far from being inconsistent with the concepts of the latter, is actually implicit within them. Accordingly it is to this issue, rather than to the general exposition of Marx's theory of value, that the following comments will be directed.

The fetishism of commodities: 2. Marx's theory

In capitalist society, which is of course based on the production of commodities, individuals are, according to Marx, related to each other through the relations of production but not as members of society, not as particular persons who participate in the process of production; rather they are related only as the owners of certain definite things, as the 'social representatives' of the various factors of production. The capitalist is merely 'capital personified'; the landlord is the personification of land;[58] the worker of abstract labour. Relations between individuals in capitalist society are dependent on the apparent relations between things. In particular, 'the social character of men's labour appears to them as an objective character stamped upon the product of that labour; because the relation of the producers to the sum total of their own labour is presented to them as a social relation existing not between themselves, but between the products of their labour.'[59]

Now these formulations are certainly very evocative and, in reference to the familiar capitalist reality, carry an undeniable ring of truth. However as we have already pointed out, in this approach there are major problems which demand solutions. For example, the above quotations suggest a conception of 'things' that identifies them with the objects of natural science; that is, they suggest an objectivist conception of objectivity. At the same time, there is postulated a relationship between things that excludes the determinations of either the social structure or the theoretical apparatus. But these issues are exactly the ones that are at stake in the analysis of the fetishism problem. Marx in fact was not oblivious to this dilemma; in order to solve it he found it necessary to call upon his laborious examinations into the nature of labour, profit and capital.

In these examinations it was shown that, under capitalist production, bonds between individuals were established through the movement of things. However these things must therefore be understood as possessing a social form. If 'the social qualities of labour' are to be endowed with 'material characteristics', then so also must objects embrace 'social characteristics'.[60] Thus the commodity economy moves simultaneously in two directions: towards, on the one hand, the 'personification of things' and on the other, towards 'the conversion of production relations into entities'.[61] But even this is not in itself sufficient. It is necessary to recognize that in fact the capitalist reality finds its expression in, and only in, the peculiar configuration of material forms which results. Equivalently, the economic categories

> express different production relations among people and the social functions which correspond to them, or the social-economic forms of things. These functions or forms have a social character because they are inherent, not in things as such, but in things which are parts of a definite social environment, namely things through which people enter into certain production relations with each other.[62]

Seen from this perspective, therefore, things can no longer be regarded as independent of social and economic influences; but nor are they mere 'material receptacles of homogeneous human labour'.[63] This explains the confusion regarding the formulations quoted earlier. Once the nature of the objects to which Marx is referring and their relationship to the capitalist reality are clarified there is no need for ambiguity. Thus Marx can write, on the one hand, that capital 'is not a thing, but rather a definite social production relation, belonging to a definite historical formation of society, which is manifested in a thing and lends this thing a specific social character.'[64] On the other, he can claim that capital 'more and more acquires a material form, is transformed more and more from a relationship into a thing, *but a thing which embodies, which has absorbed, the social relationship ... It is the form of its reality*, or rather its real form of existence.'[65] Whereas it seemed earlier that Marx was himself adopting te objectivist conception of objects it is now apparent that he is in fact arguing that this conception precisely is an outcome of the capitalist process. The thinglike quality of commodities – understood in the objectivist sense – to which Marx referred at length both in his early writings and in *Capital*, volume I, emerges as just *the form of capitalist reality*. Both the theory of the fetishism of commodities and the entire theory of value, with its dual characterization of labour, are directed towards achieving a detailed exposition of the unfolding of this form of the reality associated with capitalism.

No general discussion of the specific features of Marx's labour theory of value will be undertaken here; instead we shall state only its substantive outcome in relation to our interpretation of the fetishism question. This is, specifically, that it is only through the equalization of all concrete forms of labour, effected as an equalization of all the products of labour as values, that the social connection can be realized between the working activities of individual commodity producers.

> (W)hen we bring the products of our labour into relation with each other as values, it is not because we see in these articles its material receptacles of homogeneous human labour. Quite the contrary: whenever, by an exchange, we equate as values our different products, by that very act, we also equate, as human labour, the different kinds of labour expended upon them. We are not aware of this, nevertheless we do it.[66]

The process of exchange therefore governs simultaneously social and economic, and material processes. But it also, once again, imposes its form on both. Value in reality is an expression of an underlying structure of social relationships.[67] Under capitalism it is transformed, so that it appears rather as a natural, innate property of things. Through the equalization of the many forms of concrete labour 'the social character of activity, as well as the social form of the product, and the share of individuals in production' are rendered 'alien and objective, confronting the individual, not as their relation to one another, but as their subordination to relations which subsist independently of them and which arise out of collisions between mutually indifferent individuals'.[68] Marx is arguing, therefore, that exchange based on abstract labour is in fact a determinate social relation.[69] This is an important result in itself, of course; however we would like to stress particularly the additional point that seems to emerge from Marx's discussion: that it is precisely these processes of abstraction and exchange which provide the characteristic coordinates of the natural and social worlds of the capitalist configuration. This is to say, it is through these processes that, for individuals living within capitalist society, the material and conceptual organization of the world is effected. Of course, the resulting social and theoretical forms, while they may accurately apprehend the capitalist reality, are not thereby rendered free of perplexity; for it is, after all, 'an enchanted, perverted, topsy-turvy world in which Monsieur le Capital and Madame la Terre do their ghost walking as social characters and at the same time directly as things.'[70]

For the sake of avoiding misunderstanding, and because we are relying so heavily on his actual works, we would like to add clearly here that the interpretation of Marx's theory which we are advancing is not the usual one. As will be apparent from the conclusions we have just drawn, of particular importance for our purposes are the roles of culture and, especially, of the realm of the symbolic in the formation of natural objects. Now it is clear that Marx's writings lack a full and explicit treatment of these dimensions – and indeed it may be true that, as is sometimes claimed, they actually contain countervailing themes which would tend to undermine the very possibility of such an account. It is our contention, however, that there exists within the corpus of his work, and in particular, within his treatment of the problem of fetishism, deep and pregnant suggestions that may contribute to the development of the kind of theory that is required. Of course, Marx's own arguments are articulated specifically in relation to the issues of productive labour and capital and hence these must be discussed; but such an emphasis does not imply that absolute priority is thereby being conferred on either labour or the productive process. Some further remarks will be directed to this issue below.

The phenomenon we have been discussing under the dual rubric of the objectification of social relations and the equalization of the forms of labour, is the fetishism of commodities. It should be clear from this account that it is not Marx's contention that what is at stake here is the mere false appearance of an essence. Rather, he shows that fetishism is just the objectivist mode by which bourgeois society manifests itself; that is, it is the *specific form* of capitalist reality. Similarly, to expose its inner structure it is not sufficient merely to attempt to trace it back to the 'peculiar social character of commodity-producing labour'.[71] Instead it must be understood as emerging from the latter as its *necessary* form.[72] In addition, it can be seen at once that it is incorrect to construe the fetishism of commodities as an ideology. For, on the contrary, by providing a categorial framework within which social characters and natural objects are identified it must be thought of rather as the *provenance* of ideological thought, the site on which ideologies are constructed. In this interpretation, in brief, the theory of the fetishism of commodities is nothing less than a dynamics of the modes of givenness of capitalist reality.

195

A fundamental problem: reality and form

This account solves many of the problems to which we adverted at the outset of the present discussion. In particular, it overcomes the principal objections to the main perspectives on alienation which were mentioned. For it lays the basis for a theory of knowledge and of social phenomena which is not compromised by the prejudice of objectivism. However from the point of view of the theory of science it still suffers from a serious deficiency. It tends to suppress the problematic transition between reality and form that is central to the discussion of natural science. For any theory which seeks to display science as dependent in some degree on social and historical variables must be able to offer some indications regarding the actual nature of this relationship. That is to say, it must be able to supply at least some rudimentary suggestions as to how in a given social configuration a specific object domain of science comes into being. However the theory of fetishism as we have presented it so far provides no such indications: indeed it even seems to resist the very formulation of the question. To be sure, the problem at stake is an extremely complex one and satisfactory solutions to it are presently lacking. Nevertheless the question must be raised and, once again, it is appropriate to examine Marx's theory for resources which may be of use in the search for an answer.

Of course it is the case that Marx himself recognized some aspects of the problem and in fact introduced it explicitly in the context of the fetishism of commodities. Thus he spoke of the dual process (to which we have already referred) of the 'materialization of the social features of production and the personification of the material foundations of production'.[73] Now both these aspects are certainly of great importance; however in the present context it is the former that is of particular relevance. For it identifies specifically the problem of 'the conversion of social relations into things, the direct coalescence of the material production relations with their historical and social determination'.[74] As we said, this problem is one of extreme complexity and has in fact occupied many thinkers since Marx's time. Marx's own answer must be taken to comprise his entire theory of the dialectical process of production and reproduction. It is inappropriate, of course, to commence an examination here of this aspect of Marx's work; however it is possible to cite just a few simple results which indicate the direction in which his analysis moves.[75] In particular, it is clear from Marx's account that social forms emerge only as a result of a long social and historical process. At the levels of subjectivity and inter-

196

subjectivity sedimentations are laid down of production relations of a similar type. As a mode of production develops or is extended its associated relations of production become generalized, as also do the sedimentations establishing constant regions within the structures of intersubjectivity. In the capitalist process, of special importance here is the development of money, since this introduces a symbolic relation between objects which can be infinitely reproduced in the communicative domain.[76]

We shall not proceed further with these remarks. Instead we shall use them, rudimentary as they are, along with our previous comments, to make some observations specifically regarding the theory of fetishism. In the first place, they help us to see some important convergences as well as differences between Marxism and phenomenology. As we saw, Husserl derives as a necessary trans-social condition for the appearance of objects a concept of history as the intersubjective form of the present – that is, as a dynamic structure located at once in the intentional forms of consciousness and in the intersubjective community. Now Marx's results are apparently consistent with this conception, if not actually inclusive of it. On the other hand, however, Marx's analyses develop further in a characteristic and unique direction: they explore the boundary surface – that, incidentally, Marx himself had discovered – along which this history encounters the specific countours of a living society. As a result – and this is the second and major point – he made possible the development of a theory which could expose the objectivist form of objectivity characteristic of capitalist society as just that conferred by the fundamental symbolic structure which provides this society's general co-ordinates for social interaction. This structure is – like Husserl's lifeworld – at once pre-categorial and a cultural accomplishment, for it designates the form of sociality presupposed in all social intercourse. For Marx himself of course, to the extent to which he considered the question directly, this specific form of sociality, the principal of reciprocity characteristic of capitalistic society, was ultimately associated with commodity exchange:

> The reciprocal and all-sided dependence of individuals who are indifferent to one another form their social connection. This social bond is expressed in *exchange value*, by means of which alone each individual's own activity or his product becomes an activity and a product for him; he must produce a generalized product – exchange value or ... money.[77]

In this way, by inserting the material conditions into the matrix of the symbolic exchanges of a society, it can be said that the Marxist theory establishes the basis on which a materialism can be dialectical.[78] But at the same time, and more importantly for our present purposes, this theory displays the countervailing inner logic of value that we have been discussing. In this logic abstract labour, a presupposition of the exchange process, operates also as a social rule; thereby it converts the 'reciprocal dependence' and 'mutual interaction' established by the market into 'alien and objective' forces.[79] The properties which distinguish the processes of exchange in the commodity economy – their formal character, their reduction of varying qualities to commensurable quantities and especially, their apparent independence of social and historical determinations – are therefore seen to penetrate and to overwhelm the normal conduct of intersubjective exchange. Thus the Marxian theory arrives at one further characterization of the fetishism of commodities: it can be understood as a particular kind of distortion introduced into the symbolic field – a distortion that can perhaps best be described as a disjunction of the code from the actual processes of interaction it both constitutes and mediates.

The fetishism of the signifier

At this juncture we would like to point out that these considerations do not completely solve the problem in relation to which we introduced them – the problem, that is, of the formation of the object domain of science within the cultural context of capitalism; this is a matter to which we shall return at length in a later chapter. However the above conclusions do indeed provide important insights into the process of fetishism. In particular, they emphasize that in fetishism it is not the *object* that is endowed with special power but rather the *processes of signification* by means of which the object is represented. Previously we expressed this point by saying that fetishism was to be recognized in objectivist notions of objectivity. Here we can express the same thing by claiming that the fetishism of commodities is a fetishism of the *signifier*, and that therefore the manipulation that it entails is not a manipulation of forces but a manipulation of signs.[80]

Some indications for a rigorously developed theory of fetishism from this perspective – which is, of course, that of semiotics – have been provided by the French philosopher Jean Baudrillard. Now Baudrillard has over a number of years developed a thorough and uncompromising critique of Marx's theory of labour. Writing in what he regards as both a post-phenomenological and a post-structuralist tradition, he has sought to show that Marx's own thought failed to escape from the categories of political economy in radical opposition to which it had originally been offered.[81] According to Baudrillard, the fundamental flaw of the Marxist project is its continuous adherence to what he calls 'productivism' – the logical priority of use-value over exchange-value and the reduction of all social and cultural effects to the material forms of production. Marx's thinking, he argued, was unable to pass beyond the traditional Western assumptions about man, precisely because he failed to subject this underlying assumption to radical analysis.[82] Thus he was unable to penetrate the real dynamic of culture and social life, which lies, in fact, not in production but in symbolic exchange.

In Baudrillard's view then, Marx 'changed nothing basic'.[83] 'Radical in its *logical* analysis of capital, Marxist theory nonetheless maintains an *anthropological* consensus with the options of Western rationalism in its definitive form acquired in eighteenth century bourgeois thought.'[84] In consequence, failing to conceive of a mode of social wealth other than that founded on labour and production, 'Marxism no longer furnishes in the long run a real alternative to capitalism. Assuming the generic schema of production and needs involves an incredible simplification of social exchange by the law of value.'[85] This inability to appreciate the true complexity of the symbolic domain is what ultimately compromises the radicalism of Marxism. The real rupture – that of greatest importance for both understanding and changing society – occurs not between abstract and concrete labour but 'between symbolic exchange and work (production, economics)'.[86]

Far from designating the realm beyond political economy which it claimed to reveal, according to Baudrillard, 'use-value is in fact only the horizon of exchange-value';[87] it is produced by the play of exchange-value.[88] What is required now, he argues, is precisely a theory of the latter – a theory which would once again take seriously the hypothesis of the autonomy of the structures of consciousness and which would revive the appreciation of the role of the symbolic and the imaginary in human culture. 'The exchange of signifieds has always hidden the "labour" of the signifier,' he declares; 'let us liberate the signifier and the textual production of meaning!'[89]

Attempting to apply this injunction to the theory of fetishism, Baudrillard asserts that the latter is not 'the sanctification of a certain object or value'; it is the sanctification 'of the system as such, of the commodity as system'. It is thus 'contemporaneous with the generalization of exchange value and is propagated with it'.[90] As further sectors of society are systematized, he argues, the extent of fetishism is increased and at the same time, identically, further domains of social phenomena are reduced to commutable sign values. In consequence, the fetishism of commodities can be described as:

> the fetishization of a product emptied of its concrete substance of labour and subjected to another type of labour, a labour of signification, that is, of coded abstraction (the production of differences and of sign values). It is an active, collective process of production and reproduction of a code, a system, invested with all the diverted, unbound desire separated out from the process of real labour and transferred onto precisely that which denies the process of real labour.[91]

For Baudrillard, therefore, fetishism is firmly attached to the sign object. However, that object is 'eviscerated of its substance and history, and reduced to the state of marking a difference, epitomizing a whole system of differences'.[92]

Hence once again – although here it is formulated somewhat differently – fetishism is presented as the 'mode of givenness' of capitalist society. What is new is just that element which we found to be demanded by our previous analysis but which was lacking from the phenomenological perspective: the systematic, symbolic character of the fetishistic intervention into the semiotic structures.

It is not our intention to pursue any further here a discussion of Baudrillard's theory. This is despite the great interest of both his interpretation of Marx and the alternative he proposes, which involves an original adaptation of some themes of the work of Lacan and Castoriadis. It is however appropriate, before we pass on to a formulation of the main hypotheses of this chapter, to make a remark about the relationship between his view and the results of our own investigations into the problem of fetishism in modern society.

*   *   *   *   *   *

In the pages above we have emphasized Marx's own writings and, in particular, his theory of labour. Notwithstanding this, our original formulation of the questions we were considering certainly exceeded those to which Marx explicitly directed himself; what is more, our conclusions regarding the relationship between fetishism and distorted processes of symbolization also go beyond the usual interpretations of his theory. Now we admit that in so doing we are biasing our account, both of *Capital* and of Marx's other works, towards the perspective that is to be found in the *Grundrisse*, where rather less emphasis is placed on the derivation from material sources of the principal categories.[93] It is our view that if Marx had proceeded to develop these ideas rigorously he would have been led to a detailed consideration of culture and of the realm of the symbolic. However he did not. Accordingly, our interpretation is open to the objection that we are attempting to extract from the interstices of Marx's corpus a problematic that is belied by his own dominant themes. We concede this possibility; however we add that from the beginning our interest here was not primarily with the textual debates – as important as they may be – but with particular problems regarding the theory of science. And in this respect we have succeeded in drawing out of Marx's works some important and fruitful results for our project.

In conclusion then, to sum up these last points: from a reading of the very writings Baudrillard criticizes we have come to a number of conclusions not altogether dissimilar from his own; or at least, from a reading of these writings we derived some adumbrations not inconsistent with the formulations he has made. However we have decided to prescind from a discussion of the fidelity of our conclusions to the Marxist corpus as a whole. In later chapters many of the results of the present one will be developed; in particular, we shall suggest that the views we are here presenting can be taken to comprise a kind of 'psychoanalysis of society' – presumably an endeavour that would, in principal, be appreciated by Baudrillard. Nonetheless, we shall go on to find that the theory even thus regarded is unable to supply an adequate base for a social theory of science; for this, we shall conclude, something more is required.

Review and general hypothesis

Let us quickly review some of our results. The Marxian theory of fetishism can be regarded in a number of different ways. These various approaches while not identical are nevertheless coterminous. They come together in a central constant focus: the problem of characterizing the dynamic interchange between economy and society – that is, between the material structures according to which production is organized and the corresponding forms of intersubjectivity. Accordingly, fetishism can be understood as *the form of capitalist reality*, as the structure of meaning that emerges from the social and conceptual organization associated with the commodity economy. Alternatively, it can be regarded as characterizing the modes of givenness of phenomena in a specific material and categorial environment. Finally, fetishism can be considered to consist in a particular organization of the system of signs by means of which, in capitalist social formations, the overall configurations of sense and meaning are constructed.

In all these interpretations what is at stake, in one way or another, is the actual process of symbol formation and its sedimentation in political and social structures; as they emerge from the Marxian theory commodities are already formed and hence already susceptible to participation in human interchange. This is where the aspect of fetishism emerges which is of most direct use for the theory of science: as a determinate structure of objects which immanently embraces the intersubjective and communicative processes it represents the specific socio-historical form of the subject-object relation. The critique of the fetishism of commodities is concerned not with *things* and society but with the constitution of *thinghood* in relation to social processes; it shows that objectivity is formed, or crystallizes, from the social relations that characterize a given social formation. Thus fetishism itself is the *particular form* of objectivity characteristic of capitalist society. As we have emphasized repeatedly, of course, the dominant form of objectivity within capitalism is objectivism; this is a result which follows implicitly from Marx's works and has been elaborated in detail in subsequent writings: objects, both natural and social, tend to appear under the objectivist rubric. Accordingly, we might add, it would not be at all surprising if the content of the theory of nature formulated from the capitalist perspective displayed features deriving from this predisposition towards objectivism.

At the same time, the theory of fetishism, as a theory of objectivity, engages a second problem: it is also an account of the apparent naturalness of the forms of a given society, of how they appear as necessarily natural and unproblematic, as valid and true. For insofar as the patterns of objectivity of a society – and hence its modes of givenness of objects in general – are developed conjointly with the characteristic categorial formations of that society, the criteria according to which these patterns might be scrutinized become progressively less rigorous. The issue here concerns the emergence of specific domains of objects with respect to constant regions within the field of intersubjectivity. While, as we have pointed out, it is not yet possible to give an exhaustive characterization of this problem, it can nevertheless be seen that, at the least, it must be understood to encompass at once objectivity and epistemology, *and* society. Once further preliminaries have been established we will be able to take up these matters again, at greater length.[94]

Marx's theory of the fetishism of commodities, like his work in general, can be viewed from a variety of perspectives. In this discussion we commenced by adopting the terminology of phenomenology. Now this strategy was not intended to entail (and did not entail) an hypothesis that a comprehensive account of Marxism could be given by situating it within the problematic of phenomenology. Rather, all that was claimed was that at least some aspects of Marx's work were susceptible to phenomenological interpretations. In fact, we identified what could be regarded as both convergences and divergences between the thoughts of Marx and Husserl.[95] We also saw – although again only briefly – that at least one other interpretation of Marx's theory of fetishism was possible; the particular alternative interpretation that we mentioned was the semiotic, or structuralist, one. Certainly it is clear, even from our brief formulations, that in many respects this latter perspective approaches substantially the same issues and arrives at substantially the same conclusions as the phenomenological one. Nonetheless, it is also apparent that important differences between the two exist and that particular insights might be accessible to one that are denied to the other. Furthermore, we might add in passing, in the development of our account of fetishism, exactly as in our discussion of Husserl's philosophy, the structuralist view emerged at the *periphery* of the phenomenological perspective and in relation to the problem of sedimentation and the need to characterize systematic unities of thought. We mention this result here not because it is central to the present analysis but first of all because of its interest and secondly because, like the previous point, it will in fact acquire rather greater importance in succeeding chapters.

* * * * * *

These, then, are the general results of our discussion regarding the Marxian theory of the fetishism of commodities in capitalist society, as this theory emerges both from Marx's own writings and from those of some of his principal commentators. Our particular interest, of course, in introducing this theory was not to be able to make use of its insights into the workings of capitalism; rather our interest was primarily in its possible implications for the theory of science. Accordingly, before embarking on our consideration of Marx's arguments we explicitly posed the problem of fetishism in the most general possible way. In the discussion which ensued, we sought strenuously to circumvent the objectivist presuppositions which had appeared to contaminate earlier discussions of fetishism; with this in view, we referred not just to the fetishism of commodities but to a broader concept, the 'specific fetishism' of a society, which was intended to encompass the particular form of objectivity which predominated within the latter. In this usage the fetishism of commodities was to appear as a special case – as the specific fetishism of capitalist society, or, more precisely, having regard to the results of our own discussion, as the specific fetishism of the social formation historically associated with capitalism. As a result of the adoption of this terminology we were faced immediately with the problem of describing the relationship between Marx's own concept and our more general one. What we discovered was that, in respect of some of their most important aspects, a continuity existed between the two; in the case of others, it was apparent that there existed at least a substantial consistency. Thus we were able to draw – fruitfully and at length – on the arguments offered by the Marxian theories. Indeed, we concluded that a useful way to regard these theories was that they attempted with some – although certainly not complete – success to provide an account of the particular form of objectivity which emerges most naturally in the capitalist context.[96] Implicitly, it followed that this last endeavour might best be understood as just one part of a yet to be formulated more extensive theory: that is, as part of a general theory of the relationship between a social configuration and its specific fetishism.

Now taking these results into account, it will be seen that the conclusions extracted from the Marxian tradition enable us to formulate some hypotheses concerning both the content of science and its dependence on social phenomena. From these conclusions – and indeed from other results mentioned earlier – it has become apparent that capitalism (or, as we said, the social formation associated with it) conveys a peculiar disposition towards objectivist modes of thought and that these are applied not only in philosophy and social theory but also in the interpretation of natural phenomena. Thus it is possible to state that the theory of nature as it is presently constituted is only *one specific social form* of our interaction with the natural world in the capitalist epoch. We would like to propose this idea as a general hypothesis. The social and the natural worlds are engaged in a complex process of reciprocal interpretation. Nature is a realm of objective entities mapped out in relation to historically defined regions of intersubjective invariance. Conversely, social phenomena are always subject to the circumscriptions imposed by natural contingencies. At any particular time the contemporary form of nature can be given a theoretical formulation; this formulation, which will constitute the core of the science of the day, must therefore be faithful to the extant conceptions of objectivity. Employing our usage above, this hypothesis can be expressed in a single thesis, which, we claim, emerges naturally from the Marxian theory. This thesis states simply that *it is in the specific fetishism of a society that the deep structure of its science resides.*

We shall not at this point attempt any further justification of this thesis. We believe that it arises naturally as a generalization of the most potent insights of the Marxian theory of the fetishism of commodities. Furthermore, we believe that a strong – if so far only circumstantial – case for its validity can be provided. At this stage however we intend its main function to lie in its suggestiveness for the discussion which follows, in which it will therefore be adopted provisionally as a working hypothesis. It proposes a profound relationship between the theory of nature and society, which actually encompasses the content of science itself. However it is at least as valuable for what it does not say – for the problems that it poses instead. To illustrate this point we shall mention just four of the most obvious of these problems, all of which will demand detailed attention in subsequent chapters.

In the first place, the thesis suggests implicitly that theories of nature that are *not* objectivist are in fact possible. However, quite simply, it provides no further indication of their character. Accordingly, it remains a major outstanding task to demonstrate the possibility, or even the existence, of such theories. Secondly – more generally – our thesis embraces the claim that a scientific theory indeed has a 'deep structure' – that is, that it contains a theoretical core which determines its characteristic modes of representation of the natural world, its epistemological criteria, its object domain and so on. However, once again, the nature of such structures is left open. Thirdly, the concept of 'specific fetishism' not only involves the claim that a variety of object domains and problematics – unspecified – are in principle possible for science; it also suggests that they can be characterized as alternative modes of the subject-object relation. But the role of the subject, and indeed the nature of objectivity itself, are currently controversial issues, the outcomes of which cannot be anticipated. Finally, the expression, 'the specific fetishism of a society', may suggest that a possible causal relationship between social formations and the object domains of science is being proposed – a claim that would seem generally to be at variance with the Marxist project out of which the hypothesis emerged.

These issues and their implications will be taken up later. Regarding the last problem, however, it is worth pointing out immediately that by the mode of theorizing itself such a relation is strictly excluded. The technique applied, in both Marx's arguments and our own, is not a causal one: rather, these arguments proceed by rendering the social and cultural phenomena at the same level of symbolization so that they are commensurable. Thus the question of causality does not arise; it might better be said, in the language of another discourse, that what Marx is engaged in is a 'psychoanalysis' of society. Nevertheless this in itself presents a problem, for the theoretical status of such an endeavour itself demands elaboration. And, at any rate, there remains the outstanding question raised by the existence of several contemporaneous forms of science.

Relativity theory and philosophy

Every scientific theory is the bearer of an immanent and irreducible philosophical content. This content, like philosophical ideas in general, is open to scrutiny in theoretical discourse. What is more, the elaboration of its meaning, and hence of the meaning of the theory itself, cannot be complete in the absence of accounts of both the social and historical condition for its emergence and the style of its accommodation into the existing bodies of thought. These conclusions have so far been applied to classical physics alone. We have argued for example that this theory is committed philosophically to objectivism. However on close examination the objectivistic problematic cannot be sustained: at least in relation to the phenomena with which theories of nature are concerned, arguments are available which must exclude this perspective. On the other hand, it has also been found that objectivism stands in a natural relationship to the forms of life of capitalist society. Thus it is not completely inappropriate to speak of a deep, inner bond between classical physics and capitalism – although such a locution provides no indications regarding the precise origins or future course of this relationship.[1]

An evident, immediate perplexity is evoked by these results. If objectivism is wrong then what does this mean for contemporary science? How variable in fact is the philosophical content of science? Is it possible – we dare to ask – to conceive of a non-objectivist theory of nature that would not mean the total relinquishment of the great insights that have hitherto been won? Answers to these questions will require a clarification of the relationship, in the contemporary context, between science and philosophy. For if such a clarification is achieved then the main philosophical issues confronting modern science could perhaps be identified, together with the principal problems concerning the relationship between the various theories. Subsequently, the further issue – that of the role of social variables in the development of theories of nature – could be addressed, or at least properly formulated. In this way some progress could be made towards, on the one hand, an appreciation of the meaning of science in the modern world and on the other, the establishment of a satisfactory social theory of scientific knowledge.

On this question of a sociology of science, however, it must be stated at once that the problems involved are very complex, even in comparison with the strictly philosophical issues. This indeed should be clear from the discussions of the previous chapters. Of all the questions confronting the theory of science, those bearing on the latter's relationship to society are perhaps the least accessible. This may be because these questions are of a different order of complexity, incorporating not only the dilemmas of science itself but the problems of its metadiscourse and of social theory as well. Whatever the reasons however, the consequence is that the results of this aspect of the study will be neither immediate nor unequivocal. The most that can be hoped at this stage is the achievement of some fruitful and suggestive insights, together with the precise demarcation of the problems with which a mature theory might deal.

To come to the objectives of the present chapter, in what follows we shall attempt to initiate the investigation of modern science from the perspective indicated above. Specifically, we shall concentrate on the theory of relativity, the philosophical meaning of which we shall try broadly to characterize. Relativity theory has been chosen for this discussion both for historical reasons – it represents the first major breach with the classical ideas – and because its own internal conceptual content is unambiguous; later, the discussion will be extended to include also quantum mechanics. The point of view for which we argue in this chapter is at once simple and perhaps a little surprising. Relativity theory, properly understood, it will be maintained, not only provides a profound critique of classical physics but also proposes a comprehensive non-objectivistic alternative to it. Furthermore – and possibly more surprising still – the critique of objectivism implicit in this theory is in all important respects identical to that articulated at length by Husserl. More still can be said: in brief, we shall claim that relativity theory represents essentially the realization in the theory of nature of the whole phenomenological perspective.

208

This is not an essay in physics nor even first of all in the philosophy of physics. Accordingly, our account of relativity theory will be quite non-technical and non-mathematical. This, admittedly, will have the dual effect of making the discussion both more straightforward and more difficult – the difficulties following from the fact that certain detailed technical formulations will have to be omitted, while at the same time more will have to be assumed on the part of the reader. These problems however will not be decisive if the main purposes of this chapter, which are essentially very simple, can be fulfilled. The aims of the discussion which follows will be satisfied if we are able to illustrate effectively by specific examples from science itself the main, general conclusions of the previous chapter; if we are able to provide a plausible case for the hypothesis that some at least of the most important dilemmas of science arise from perplexities well-established in the philosophical tradition; and if we can succeed in showing that a non-objectivist theory of nature is rather more than a mere idle speculation.

Kant

Before entering directly into our consideration of the theory of relativity it will be useful to make some remarks regarding the critical philosophy of Immanuel Kant; for such remarks may help to motivate the ensuing discussion by clarifying the philosophical context Einstein was addressing. Indeed, as is often observed, Einstein's own philosophy was in many ways quite close to Kant's – a perception which was shared by Einstein himself, even though his few explicit references to the philosopher were more usually for the contrary purpose of stating the difference between them.[2] Of course, this is not to suggest that the two philosophical perspectives were essentially the same; that is certainly not the case, as we shall later see. What is more, it does not follow that Einstein's stated philosophical beliefs may be taken to represent faithfully the philosophical outcome of the theory of relativity. Once again, as will become apparent later, this is in fact not the case. At times, Einstein's personal views may illuminate profoundly the meta-theoretical dilemmas; at other times however they appear to diverge sharply from the compelling consequences of his own thought. This was especially true in Einstein's celebrated debate with Neils Bohr over the quantum theory, to which we shall have occasion to refer in a later chapter.[3] In that debate, as we shall see, it appears that Einstein's position was not that of relativity theory at all but rather – perhaps surprisingly – of classical physics.

The most important reason for introducing the theory of relativity by means of Kant's philosophy however is indirect. It is to rectify a mistake that is often made: the mistake of seeing in Einstein's work the gratuitous product of isolated genius. Einstein's insights are not diminished by the recognition that they are embedded firmly within a continuing philosophical tradition and that they were influenced decisively by specific philosophical antecedents. In fact, relativity theory represents a response to certain, apparently insoluble, problems of classical physics. These problems were not – as is popularly supposed, in spite of Einstein's own testimony – empirical ones;[4] they were irreducible, theoretical difficulties in the Newtonian perspective. Furthermore, Einstein was certainly not the first to notice them; they had been recognized previously by a number of scientists and philosophers. In particular, many of them had been elaborated in full, years earlier, by Immanuel Kant.

One of Kant's greatest insights was that any theory of nature embraces an epistemology. His own personal project of course involved in particular the elucidation of the epistemology associated with Newtonian physics: specifically, he sought to establish the theoretical conditions to which the world must be subject if Newtonian science were to be possible.[5] There can be no doubt that this a priori acceptance of the presuppositions of classical mechanics substantially compromised his endeavours; and there is certainly more than a little truth in the allegation that his assertions often appear as mere 'philosophical circumlocutions'[6] of these presuppositions. Nevertheless, many of his conclusions are general ones and remain valid today. In spite of his prejudices Kant succeeded in driving his own philosophical deliberations beyond the limits of classical scientific thought. In so doing he revealed precisely that his thought was limited and that it in fact depended on certain irreducible assumptions. These assumptions, furthermore, concerned issues with which the classical philosophy was powerless to deal: issues concerning the mutual relationships between truth and theory and between objectivity and man himself.

Kant's reflection on some of the core conceptions of classical science revealed, in brief, that precisely those regions claimed to be the most withdrawn from subjective determinations were in fact profoundly dependent upon them. Every scientific object, measurement, inference has corresponding to it a particular subjective index. All the phenomena with which science deals incorporate theoretical presuppositions of some kind – axioms, principles, hypotheses, established results or some other entity. What is supposed to be free of theory is in fact inexorably intertwined with it. The reality with which the scientist deals is not the world as it is immediately presented in intuition; it is the world as it is mediated by the categorial determinations which also enable its elements to be drawn together into a system.

This of course was the most elementary result of Kant's philosophy; it was, furthermore one which he had subsequently to reconcile with the existence of objects as such – that is, with the existence of 'objective' entities, the properties of which were not contingent upon individual consciousnesses. The details of his solution to this latter problem – which is contained essentially in his doctrine of the transcendental unity of apperception – we shall not attempt to elaborate here. It will suffice merely to note that for him the unity that defines the object 'can be nothing else than the formal unity of consciousness in the synthesis of the manifold of presentations'.[7] The objectivity of the object, that is, is grasped not by the fabrication of a transcendent unity from empirical data but from the attainment of a synthetic unity encompassing a totality of measurements and observations given in experience. Put differently, what distinguishes the object is not a specific collection of empirical data associated with it, but a constancy that appears at a deeper level – an invariance regarding the process of determination invoked by the object across the manifold of sensuous presentations.[8] The objects of science for Kant were certainly objects 'in the phenomenal world'; however it must be understood at once that this expression implies no suggestion that objects are tied to an arbitrary or contingent subjectivity. On the contrary, it is ideal, invariant forms that underlie the constitution of the phenomenal reality in the first place; they, precisely, embody the underlying themes in which both experience and factuality are grounded.[9]

Science therefore does not deal with objects that are given in themselves, fixed once and for all. Rather, its concern is with entities which are formed, through the mediation of concepts and categories.[10] Different sciences deal with different domains of objects; hence we may regard each as exploring the world from a unique conceptual perspective.[11] Within a particular science, on the other hand, the theoretical standpoint that fixes the objects is constant. However another perspective is allowed to vary instead: that associated with the intuitive – i.e. spatio-temporal – presentation of individual objects. The lines of invariance here of course designate not sciences but the objects themselves and, specifically, the laws governing the relations between them.

These brief formulations are not intended as a faithful introduction to Kant's philosophy. They are, rather, a somewhat tendentious rendition of only a few of its important themes. The mode of expression, furthermore, has been deliberately chosen to suggest parallels with Einstein's thought. For there, also, the focus is explicitly turned to the constitution of scientific concepts. There also the subjective index of objectivity is stressed, with the true identity of the latter being found once again in the underlying manners of the determination of physical quantities. There too it is made explicit that the concern of knowledge is with the phenomenal world alone. And there, as previously, the insight is made that the definitive scientific laws can be secured by a variation in the spatio-temporal perspective.

The parallels between Kant's philosophy and Einstein's theory of relativity can be multiplied without difficulty.[12] That in itself is perhaps not surprising. What is surprising is rather that in all those respects listed above in which relativity theory resembles Kant's Idealism the latter departs significantly from classical physics; it is in this sense that the relationship between the two thinkers is most profound. For both Kant and Einstein truth was distinguished from that which merely appeared. In opposition to the tradition, both stressed that what was presented to consciousness on the basis of mere appearances was necessarily contingent upon the perspective of the subject. Kant's theory argued against the conception of the object as a kind of copy or pictorial representation of reality. Instead it took objects to be entities of a rather higher order; they were 'concept(s), with reference to which presentations have synthetic unity'.[13] Thus truth is gained not from specific empirical data nor even from their association; rather it emerges from the reciprocal co-ordination of data from all possible theoretical perspectives. Einstein's theory adopted these results almost exactly, even if it interpreted their implicit imperatives somewhat differently: the rules of understanding underlying the theoretical laws of experience, for example, were here replaced by mathematical formulations of the laws of nature, while the theoretical perspectives took the form of hypothetical spatio-temporal viewpoints.

At this point two obvious objections to any attempt to unify Kant's philosophy with Einstein's theory suggest themselves. There is the fact, already acknowledged, that Kant from the beginning was profoundly committed to the validity of Newtonian science. And there is the conspicuous absence from his thought of any reflection on the possible contingency of Euclidean geometry. Now it seems to us that these objections must in general be upheld. What is more, it is apparent that they are not the only, nor even the most telling, such objections available. From the viewpoint of later theory Kant's philosophy is deficient in many respects: in its very conception of the thing-in-itself;[14] in its incomplete reflection, from its own perspective, on the constitutive character of subjectivity and its consequent untheorized presupposition of the surrounding world of everyday facts and cultural products;[15] in its dogmatic assertion of the invariance and completeness of the table of categories,[16] and so on.[17] Kant's philosophy cannot be identified with the philosophical standpoint of the theory of relativity. However, as is often the case with a great thinker like Kant, even the most obvious objections on careful examination are less straightforward than they first appear. This is especially so regarding Kant's dependence on Newtonian physics and Euclidean geometry. A full discussion of these matters is not appropriate here, despite their great interest and importance. Accordingly, we shall close this section with no more than a few brief remarks to indicate this complexity.

Regarding Kant's conception of space and time, it is true that there is no suggestion that he was ever aware of the possible contingency of Euclidean geometry.[18] However at the same time it is important not to underestimate the depth of his thought here. In fact, his conclusions cannot be identified with those of classical physics. For him, space and time were no longer absolute. Indeed, they were not even 'things' any more; they were the 'forms of intuition' and thus their role was to contribute to the structure of experience rather than to supply it with content. Hence space and time were not conceived independently of empirical objects; instead, they were understood to be indivisible from the specific character of the being of the latter. 'Empirical intuition,' he argued, 'is not a composite of appearances and space. ... The one is not the correlate of the other in a synthesis; they are connected in one and the same empirical intuition as matter and form of the intuition.'[19] Similarly, time is not 'something which exists in itself, or which inheres in things as an objective determination. ...'[20] Nor can we say that 'all things are in time, because in this concept of things in general we are abstracting every mode of their intuition and therefore from that condition under which alone objects can be represented as being in time.'[21] Time, like space, is a constituent of experience; considered separately, empirical objects and the forms of intuition have no meaning.

213

As is well known, Einstein's theory once again comes close to these conclusions. The special theory incorporates a substantial meditation on the spatio-temporal determinations of phenomena. While preserving the Euclidean framework it nevertheless reveals the close connection between the being of objects, insofar as it is of importance for science, and their spatio-temporal presentation. It is only with the general theory, however, that the radicalness of this insight is truly realized. There, matter and geometry are explicitly unified, with the space-time metric providing a complete account of the distribution of matter. The form of this metric however is imposed by the requirement of general covariance – that is, the requirement that the general laws of nature be expressed by equations which hold good for all systems of co-ordinates – and necessitates a redefinition of space and time. For example, the definition of length must now take into account the variation in the length of a measuring rod, having regard to the Lorentz contraction elucidated in the previous theory; similarly, time must be defined in such a way that the rate of a clock depends on where the clock may be. Consequently, in the general theory 'space and time cannot be defined in such a way that differences of the spatial co-ordinates can be directly measured by the unit measuring rod, or differences in time co-ordinate by the standard clock.'[22] The general covariance of the laws of nature implies that no co-ordinate system is to be preferred over any other. Taken together, therefore, the two results, in Einstein's own words '(take) away from space and time the last remnant of physical objectivity.'[23]

Regarding Kant's unquestioned assumption of the validity of Newtonian mechanics and, in particular, of its inherent objectivism, both more and less needs to be said. This assumption represents in Kant's philosophy one of its great outstanding dilemmas. To be sure, in his deliberations on the problems emerging in relation to this question Kant extended the Newtonian perspective to its limits, revealing the latter's own hidden presuppositions. But his refusal to give up his commitment to this perspective itself provided an insurmountable inner boundary for his thought. The results of his reflections are accordingly somewhat ambiguous; however this fact only goes to emphasize further the great, penetrating power of his insights. The 'highest principle of all synthetic judgements' was intended to supply a firm foundation for Newtonian physics; what it achieves is rather its undermining. Kant asserts that 'the conditions of the possibility of experience in general are likewise the conditions of the possibility of the objects of experience.'[24] Now, the conditions of our experience are the categories and the pure forms of intuition. Further, through experience we come to know objects. This can be possible, according to Kant, only if the conditions of the existence of these objects are also the conditions of our experience. Thus objects are sensations, but sensations given size and duration and intensity, and related conceptually. For they can *be* only as they can *be experienced*; only with experience can both subjects and objects exist. There is no thinker independently of the experience of things. And there are no things except as they are experienced and thought by a subject.[25]

Kant's reflections, which had been intended to provide a justification for objectivistic science, in fact conclude with the suggestion of its partiality; at the limit of the classical perspective Kant discovered the inextricable intertwining of man and nature, and of man and man. The implications for natural science of these results however were pursued neither by Kant nor by subsequent philosophers. Instead, they were left as problems, haunting the Newtonian tradition. It was only with the advent of modern science that the fundamental nature of these problems became evident and ways to resolve them were at last devised; as it happened, the cost of this resolution was the abandonment of the entire classical system.

Relativity

One of the most startling features of both the special and the general theories of relativity is their great conceptual simplicity. This especially true of the earlier theory, which derived its results entirely from two elementary hypotheses. These hypotheses were the 'principle of special relativity', which stated that 'the laws of physics are the same in all inertial systems', and the 'principle of the constancy of the speed of light', which stated that 'the speed of light in free space has the same value in all inertial systems'. With these assumptions, both of them intuitively evident in the light of elementary considerations, Einstein succeeded in drawing the most far-reaching conclusions. The hypothesis of the ether was dispensed with; the Lorentz transformation equations were derived; the invariance of Maxwell's equations between inertial systems was assured; a new account of the addition of relative velocities was provided; the aberration of light waves from stars to the motion of the earth was explained; a transverse Doppler effect was predicted (and subsequently confirmed); and later, one of the greatest results, the equivalence of mass and energy, was deduced through the application of equally simple arguments.

215

Einstein, of course, carried out his calculations and formulated his conclusions in mathematical terms. However it is important to recognize that his great innovations were not primarily mathematical ones. On the contrary, the profound insights for which he was responsible were first of all in the field of philosophy; in this regard he was a true successor to Galileo. Einstein's great accomplishment was to have succeeded in applying to the mathematical study of nature a perspective which was valid in itself and departed fundamentally from the classical viewpoint. Now some of the new features of Einstein's perspective have been referred to above. The admission that the objects of experience incorporate a subjective aspect was a major innovation. Einstein formalized this result in his requirement that physical quantities be defined in operational terms. This in turn had the effect of restricting the study of nature in principle to the description of phenomena. Or equivalently, it restricted the objects of physics to purely phenomenal objects in the world.

The conclusions of the theory, as might be expected, are in harmony with its presuppositions. Thus the destruction of the ether, which was to have provided an absolute frame of reference, was consistent with the tendency of the theory (in fact already realized) to confer epistemological primacy on the subject. And the consequences of the Lorentz transformations in respect of the structure of space and time were similarly consistent with the assumptions, implicit in Einstein's mode of theorizing, regarding the physical presentation of the objects under investigation. These consequences were discussed previously. Although available from the earlier theory they were not to be given a full formulation by Einstein until the publication of the general theory of relativity in 1916. It was apparent from the dilation of time and the contraction of length that the classical conception of measurement had to be revised. However in the special theory Einstein had still adhered to the assumption of a Euclidean geometry and thus to a form of space-time that was independent of subjective determinations. It was only with the adoption of the 'principle of general covariance', as we have already commented, that 'the last remnant of physical objectivity' was removed from space and time and they were transformed into structures that were inseparable from both empirical and theoretical contingencies.

The new perspective adopted by Einstein, as we have said, for the first time granted epistemological primacy to the subject. It must be understood however that this subject cannot be thought of as an individual consciousness. Rather, it is a *theoretical* subject and accordingly, the part that it plays in the mathematical constructions is a purely formal one. The purpose of the theory is to determine the forms of presentation of phenomena to such a subject and to explicate their transformations across various subjective loci. Both truth and objectivity are now referred through an established - although possibly hypothetical - subjectivity; indeed the latter may even be considered as a nodal point at which objective and theoretical forms coalesce. Hence in the strict context of relativity theory the subject is that entity which traces the line of intersection between the conceptual and the empirical realms. In such an account there is no danger of a sacrifice of the ideals of science to a doctrine of arbitrary and contingent subjectivity. There is no suggestion that the origin of relativity is 'the privacy of the world of sense perception.'[26] Rather, the claim is merely that Einstein's theory studies the ideal forms and conditions of knowledge, where the latter is understood in the phenomenological sense of the presentation of phenomena to a consciousness. These forms and conditions are found to be ordered and regular; indeed, it is even shown that they provide the ground for what are taken to be the regularities of objective facts.

This last point is not without significance. From all that has been said so far it is evident that the objects with which relativity theory deals are constituted objects. Furthermore, their objectivity is not a property endowed from without and merely apprehended by the observer. In fact, it is now known that such an objectivity was an illusion, for even the forms of space and time cannot be freed from theoretical influences. The new theory shows that objectivity is itself a work of theory; it is the outcome of a multitude of empirical determinations that have been shown to correspond mutually and to be co-ordinated with each other according to definite rules.[27] Just as in the apprehension of a visual object acts of perception, from numerous perspectives, and apperception are brought together to constitute the thing in question, so also in the conceptions of relativity theory a variety of perspectives is obtained by considering a number of hypothetical observers; what is invariant across these frames of reference is taken to be constitutive of objectivity. The object is gained not from a claimed movement from empirical observations to absolute fact but by the unification of the experiences associated with the object into a complete whole. It is one of the great achievements of relativity theory that it was able to recognize this process and to draw out its deepest implications for science.

Exactly the same argument applies to a possible objection to this approach to the theory of nature – that by disposing of the old ideas of objectivity and absolute properties it destroys the notion of science altogether. While we do not wish to enter into a discussion about the accurate definition of science it is possible to say that such an objection is mistaken. For at the least, between the varying approaches to science one thing is constant: the commitment to the discovery of general laws. Accordingly, if it is considered appropriate, this commitment itself may be taken as establishing science's identity. Now this is a small point; however it illustrates a somewhat larger fact. Knowledge is possible from different theoretical points of view; nevertheless every true proposition carries an implicit reference to a particular philosophical standpoint. Just as in relativity theory every measurement or observation can have meaning only within a specified frame of reference so also philosophical truths are possible only within comprehensive theoretical frameworks. Relativity theory emphasizes this fact in a manner that is perhaps not without some irony. For it demonstrates that truth cannot be equated with mere appearances but must be appreciated as an accomplishment of theory and experience. However, if this is so then alternative theoretical perspectives may well produce alternative sets of truthful propositions concerning nature; if in turn this were the case then it would follow that the approach of relativity – which after all came into being criticizing the false claims to absolute truth of classical physics – would itself be only partial. This is an important issue, to which we shall return.

Einstein's theory differs from classical mechanics in the place that it gives to the subject and in the objects with which it deals. These differences can be formulated as a single new departure for the theory of nature devised by Einstein: unlike classical physics, relativity theory is non-objectivist. The entities with which the new theory deals are not understood as radically independent of all traces of subjectivity. On the contrary, they are just congellations of intentional relations between consciousness and the world. It is precisely in relation to a possible consciousness that objects now exist in their substantiality. And similarly, the knowledge of objects now appears in an inexorable, irreducible interdependence with the conditions of consciousness. We come to know objects, and the relationships between them, only insofar as these objects can be displayed as present to us; to this extent relativistic physics stands in continuity with the philosophical tradition. What is new is the implicit postulate of the theory that the knowledge thus acquired can be truly grounded only as its subjective, ideal conditions are brought to self-consciousness; what marks the theory off for greatness is its documentation of how these results can be applied, deliberately and methodically, for the production of new insights.

It is not difficult to see that this critique of objectivism which emerges from relativity theory is in all respects similar to that elaborated at length in the phenomenology of Edmund Husserl. In the context of our earlier remarks it is perhaps worth adding that it also displays an evident harmony with some of the principal themes of Kant's philosophy. This is no accident of course: both phenomenology and, as we have shown, relativity theory are firmly entrenched in the tradition of thought that Kant inaugurated. Nevertheless by now it should be clear that in spite of the important similarities between the critical philosophy and relativity theory there are major, unavoidable differences between them. We claim that these differences are in fact fundamental ones, so that relativity theory cannot be accommodated within Kantianism. In the previous discussion some of the divergences between the two bodies of thought were stated explicitly, while others have emerged from it subsequently, by implication. Accordingly, to support our present claim it will not be necessary to list them comprehensively. Instead we shall restrict ourselves merely to restating as a conclusion that relativitiy theory rejects two of the essential presuppositions of Kant's philosophy. These presuppositions were identified by Hegel, whose *Logic* can be regarded substantially as a dialogue with the First Critique; here, we adopt the formulation of them proposed by Habermas.[28]

The first presupposition has been discussed briefly already: it is Kant's adoption of a normative concept of science.[29] By relying systematically on the example of Newtonian mechanics Kant had imported into his theory a model of the organization of our cognitive faculty strictly appropriate to classical science. Hence his philosophical system had unavoidably incorporated the imperatives of this perspective both in the organization and in the construction of its concepts. Einstein's rejection of this assumption is self-evident, for herein precisely lay his greatest innovation.

The other basic presupposition of Kant not shared by relativity theory is closely related to the former one; it is his assumption of a normative concept of the subject.[30] Coterminous with the adoption of classical physics as a model for all knowledge was the acceptance of its specific subject – a complete and fixed ego which at once both precedes and supersedes the analysis. Kant, as is well-known, claimed that his goal was to establish a tribunal which would be capable of adjudicating all disputes of reason.[31] It is

219

clear however that such a tribunal could refer to one judge alone – the 'I think' accompanying all my representations. Hence, even if it were true that the transcendental unity of apperception can only be comprehended in the actual course of the investigation as arising from the ideas of original apperception,[32] it must nevertheless be conceded still that, as Habermas puts it, 'the identity of the ego must already have been taken account of at its beginning on the basis of the undoubted transcendental experience of self-reflection.'[33] Now the theory of relativity is not of course formulated as a comprehensive philosophy. Hence it is impossible to appeal to specific texts to show how it departs from this presupposition. Nevertheless our previous discussion of the subject in that theory is sufficient to show that it is in fact profoundly different: on the one hand, the subject is understood as a unifying principle for a series of intentional directions towards the world; on the other, the categories which it applies in this process of unification are themselves subject to empirical limitations.[34]

In making these comments regarding the differences separating relativity theory from Kant's philosophy we note also that on the subject of the two presuppositions mentioned Husserl also departed deliberately from Kant. In fact the considerations that we have completed so far enable us to make a rather stronger claim regarding the relationship between Einstein's theory and phenomenology. We have seen that both theories are implanted within the Western metaphysical tradition; that both attribute epistemological priority to the subject; that both conceive of objects and of the subject/object relationship in the same way; and that both embrace the same critique of objectivism. Hence we draw the conclusion that we set out to establish in the present discussion: the theory of relativity is conceptually similar to phenomenology and so may be considered to embody the realization of that perspective in the domain of the theory of nature.

Relativity, phenomenology and society

That relativity theory conceptually is embedded in the problematic of phenomenology is not a small result. The consequences will be discussed as we proceed, in this chapter and in later chapters. It is worth making a note immediately however that this conclusion may enable us to clarify with some precision the differences between Newtonian and relativistic physics and hence to resolve an outstanding problem in the theory of science. Further, the conclusion may prove to be of more than merely philosophical interest, for the reason that an understanding of the conceptual foundations of science may facilitate its further development. For the moment, it is clear that the results we have established, together with further results regarding quantum mechanics for which we shall argue later, are not widely appreciated amongst physicists. On the contrary, the latter mostly continue to work within the philosophical framework of objectivism, even though the inappropriateness of this perspective can readily be demonstrated. In this circumstance it is perhaps not implausible to suggest that the anachronistic philosophical apparatus may well have concealed possible insights.

But if our results are not widely appreciated amongst scientists even less so are they understood by philosophers. Indeed there have even been several attempts to analyze modern physics from the phenomenological point of view which have failed to recognize the deep concinnity of Einstein's and Husserl's theories. Some of these accounts, to be sure, have been of some help for the present discussion – for example, studies by A. Gurewitsch,[35] O. Becker,[36] H. Weyl,[37] S. Bachelard,[38] J. Kocklemans[39] – however usually more for their suggestiveness than for their explicit formulations. Commonly, theories start – as did Husserl himself – from the assumption that science is necessarily objectivist, due to metaphysical exigencies bearing on our place in the world. On the basis of this hypothesis – which we hope to have shown is mistaken – it is understood that the task of philosophy is to reconcile the true, phenomenological attitude with the 'natural' attitude of objectivistic science, and thereby to reveal that even the latter is a human accomplishment. But due to the original error this task is an impossible one. For phenomenology and objectivism are mutually contradictory and cannot be reconciled. What is more, the failure both to admit that, philosophically, classical physics was in error and to recognize the true character of the difference of the new science occluded precisely what was at issue in the search for cultural roots. If all science is necessarily objectivist then social and historical changes can have no bearing on it; consequently the cultural sources that the *epoché* was supposed to reveal must be invariant in all cultures. Thus phenomenology could have nothing to say regarding the most important 'cultural' issues associated with science: the extraordinary variation and change displayed in the history of science and the constantly fluctuating – and uncertain – relationship between science and society. On the other hand, if the view of this essay is adopted then both questions can at least be addressed. For then the problem is much more straightforward:

it is to understand, against a background comprising social and cultural variables and their associated structures of meaning, the changing perspective applied in the theory of nature.

These remarks indicate the 'sociological' relevance of our discussion of modern science. As we have said, these themes will be taken up directly at a later stage. For the present, however, we shall conclude our consideration of relativity theory by making some reference to several aspects of general relativity which are of importance in this context.

General relativity

So far in our discussion we have devoted most – but not all – of our attention to special relativity. This does not imply that our conclusions are less applicable to the general theory. On the contrary, they are more so. For as Einstein himself realized it was only with the general theory of relativity that his philosophical vision was brought to fruition; or in our terms, only there were the phenomenological descriptions made complete. It is not difficult to see that the earlier theory retained traces of the Newtonian problematic. The most obvious of these has been adverted to already. The assumption of a flat space as in special relativity is essentially an objectivist assumption: it takes the physical world as describable in terms of a framework conceived independently of both the laws of motion of the phenomena themselves and of the perceiving or theorizing subject. That this proposed 'objectivity' of space-time should be intolerable for phenomenology seems clear enough; what is perhaps surprising is that this fact was never recognized by Husserl, even though it fell within his own particular sphere of mathematical competence.[40]

However this may be, the immediate, motivating considerations for the general theory, like those for the special theory, are extremely simple. To enable the generalization of the earlier results to include gravitational fields, Einstein added to his elementary postulates the so-called 'principle of equivalence',[41] which stated (possibly for the first time in an explicit form) that inertial and gravitational mass are equivalent. Taking this principle together with the results of the special theory – and in particular with that concerning the equivalence of mass and energy – it is not difficult to see how it leads to the conclusion that, viewed from the perspective of Minkowski (that is, 'flat') space, light rays will not propagate in a rectilinear fashion through a gravitational field;

rather, like matter in general, they will there describe paths which are curved.[42] However it is precisely the trajectories of light rays that constitute the phenomenal field. Hence in the vicinity of a massive body the classical descriptions of motion will be distorted and the familiar physical laws will not be able to be upheld. What is needed therefore in these regions is a description of space within which the curved light paths play an analogous role to the straight lines in Euclidean space: that is, in which these curved paths describe the most 'natural' trajectories of particles released under specified force field conditions. At the same time, in the new geometry thereby constructed, more general conditions must be able to be stated regarding the physical laws which are to remain invariant with respect to transformations between reference frames.

The solutions to these problems Einstein developed in his general theory of relativity. Here, the usual mode of description of physical quantities was replaced by tensor formulations, which retain their form under continuous linear transformations between co-ordinate systems. This enabled a simple expression to be given to the principle of general relativity. Further, the tensors were to be defined on a Riemannian space, the metric of which was to be allowed to vary. The problem was now the discovery of the coefficients of this metric (that is, the discovery of the principal tensor) under specified conditions. Einstein was able to show that general conditions for the local validity of special relativity could be formulated simply as the requirement that a particular tensor (the Riemann-Christoffel tensor) should vanish. Similarly, he provided arguments regarding the general form of space for a matter-free gravitational field. This also was a tensor equation; it amounted to the requirement that another specified tensor (the Ricci tensor) should vanish. The solution to this latter set of equations (known as the field equations) would specify the equations of motion of a free particle released into a gravitational field; if, for example, this solution were required to be time-independent, radially symmetric and asymptotic to the Lorentz metric at large distances, then it would specify the motion of the particle in the familiar Newtonian situation of a gravitational field surrounding a point mass.

The mathematics associated with these considerations admittedly becomes somewhat complex in a technical sense. Nevertheless, the underlying ideas remain lucid and straightforward. In particular, it is clear how this later theory continues the task established in the earlier one of providing a general description of the modes of presentation of phenomena under certain familiar conditions (for example, conditions of relative motion or of a gravitational field).

Once again, since, by hypothesis, phenomena can be described only from the point of view of a putative subject, a major problem became the guaranteeing of the identities of these phenomena. And here also, as previously, this problem was solved by a detailed examination of the outcome of transformations between reference systems; as in the special theory, objectivities were established as the invariant structures emerging from a process of perspectival variation (which may be regarded as a rather formal kind of 'eidetic' variation). Regarding space, Einstein shifted the focus of analysis from the conventional consideration of what space is to that of how phenomena appear within it.[43] From his elementary reflections he recognized that the appearance of mass under the rubric of either gravitation or inertia is essentially a matter of perspective; the two are unified only at the level of the concept of a general law. The description of the physical world, therefore, cannot involve deliberations regarding space in itself, matter in itself or force in itself: the three cannot be separated for scientific examination. At bottom they form a unity which has been obscured only because the different contexts (that is, the different theoretical perspectives) in which each appears were never clarified.

This conclusion, of course, is an extraordinary one from the point of view of classical physics, and its radical implications have been widely recognized. The inference that can be drawn from it was stated by Hermann Weyl:

> (t)he world is a $(3+1)$-dimensional manifold; all physical field-phenomena are expressions of the metrics of the world.
> (Whereas the old view was that the four-dimensional metrical continuum is the scene of physical phenomena; the physical essentialities themselves are, however, things that exist 'in' this world, and we must accept them in type and number in the form in which experience gives us cognition of them: nothing further is to be 'comprehended' of them).... Descartes's dream of a purely geometrical physics seems to be attaining fulfilment in a manner of which he could certainly have had no presentiment ...[44]

Various attempts have been made to continue the development of this programme and to provide descriptions of other phenomena – including charge – in geometrical terms. These attempts have in fact been able to achieve considerable success, especially in the work of their best known exponent (and in fact, the originator of this modern approach), John Archibald Wheeler. Despite their extreme interest, however, we shall not follow up these developments further here, except to make two important observations.[45] In the first place, the new theory attributes an enhanced role to mathematical derivations, especially regarding the multiplicity of consistent, non-Euclidean geometrical systems. In this circumstance it may appear that the role of experience in relation to the theory is modified; it might be maintained, for example, that experience no longer grounds the theory but only selects from among the several possibilities that it offers. That this is not in fact the case should be evident from our previous considerations. Even if experience cannot suggest the particular form a metric might take this does not mean that it is irrelevant to the derivation of the latter. On the contrary, what we have seen is that experience still retains a founding role for the new theory but that its intervention occurs at an earlier stage. The part of the enterprise that is motivated by experience is not the final deduction but rather the search for a geometrical description of matter in the first place. The mathematical conclusions and the subsequent empirical selection between alternatives are quite consistent with this state of affairs. The second observation we would like to make concerns the distinction in Kant between epistemology and ontology. It would seem that the unification of matter and space contradicts this distinction, making the forms of knowledge – in particular, the categories and the forms of space and time – dependent upon the structure of matter itself. Once again however, this is an illusion. Einstein himself was acutely aware that the presentation of empirical facts presupposed a theoretical viewpoint which specified what kinds of propositions would be accepted as being true. 'It is the theory,' he once said, 'which decides what we can observe.'[46] And the distinction between the forms of knowledge and the forms of matter is preserved at every level of his thought. We are familiar with this distinction as it operates in the underlying phenomenological problematic. At the level of the mathematical formulations it can still be seen, though here it is represented in the difference between the metric (which specifies the forms of knowledge) and the various other tensors, such as the Riemann tensor, the Ricci tensor, the matter tensors etc. (which specify the form and distribution of matter). If anything, Einstein's theory actually supports Kant's view, for it emphasizes the relationship that the latter had discovered and stated so emphatically: the objects of a science and its forms of knowledge are irreducibly distinct, yet reciprocally interrelated. This was one of the insights implicit in the 'highest principle of all synthetic judgements' – that the specification of the object domain of a science was sufficient to specify its epistemological forms as well, so that, given certain other agreed conditions, it was capable of providing a description of the science as a whole.

Review and general hypotheses

In our discussion of relativity theory we have emphasized its relationship with the phenomenological standpoint. The two are coincident in the matters of metaphysical assumptions, ontology, conceptions of truth and critiques of objectivism. Phenomenology was devised as a general philosophical outlook; relativity theory is its realization in the domain of the theory of nature. To make these claims however and to arrive at these conclusions is not to suggest that the content of relativity theory is exhausted by this characterization. On the contrary it is undeniable that relativity theory has produced, largely through its application of mathematical techniques, many startling new results which could not have been anticipated from philosophical considerations alone. Furthermore it should be clear that in order to draw the conclusions that we have it has been necessary to extend somewhat the intentions of phenomenology; unlike its major proponents we have sought to project it as a formal structure of thought, the main elements of which can be precisely determined. The meaning of the term phenomenology as we have been using it in this chapter may therefore be uncongenial to some. Nevertheless we claim that the philosophical system that it describes is consistent with that elaborated by Husserl. What is more, the usage that we have adopted makes possible certain new insights into the conceptual content of contemporary science.

For example, in addition to the specific conclusions that have already been referred to some general ones can be stated. It is now clear that the material consequences of a theory cannot be dissociated from the conceptual apparatus that was applied to produce it. Every scientific theory represents an attempt to realize a particular philosophical disposition. This 'disposition' embraces at once a specification of both the questions to be confronted by the theory and the legitimate forms of their answers; in addition, it encompasses the criteria by which the theory's objective focus and the truth or falsity of its propositions are to be recognized. All these conditions must logically have preceded the actual derivations by which the theory is known. As this philosophical perspective varies then so also does the manifest content of the theory; a new outlook may provide new insights, or else it may be no longer capable of producing old ones. In the field of knowledge, therefore, a theoretical perspective functions somewhat like a light source in an otherwise darkened visual field: under its illumination certain objects or features of objects are rendered visible, while others are obscured or transformed. This relativity of content does not of course threaten to compromise the notion of truth itself; on the contrary, a comprehensive truth emerges only out of the manifold of distinct but consistent schemata of reality established in the processes of perception and apperception.

It is a consequence of these results that the meaning of a scientific theory, including its specific conclusions, is certainly not fully determined by its use of mathematics.[47] It is possible in principle, to be sure, that the form of mathematical analysis may impose some limitations on the range of meanings available; indeed it will be argued later that there is at least some relationship between the two. However within the overall project of mathematical science great divergences of concept and meaning still occur, and these can be understood only in terms of the broad, varying philosophical perspectives that are involved. The identity of modern science cannot be summed up in its mathematical character; rather, science is a deeply philosophical enterprise and the process of the development and change of its concepts has by no means yet been concluded.

The Galilean and the Newtonian conception of a world in which space, time and motion could be described as absolute entities represented for the study of nature a new philosophical departure. In the years between Galileo's time and the present day this conception, and many of those associated with it, have been vigorously contested. Newton's theory of time was contradicted by Bergson's lived time, for example; the mechanical interactions of the Newtonian cosmos were opposed by the implicit field theory of the Hegelian totality; and Kant, Leibniz, Kierkegaard, Nietzsche, Husserl, Horkheimer and Adorno, Einstein and many others have offered arguments in attempts to refute important tenets of what they considered to be the Newtonian world-view. It may be that these opposing views, and even Newton's epistemology, are, within appropriately circumscribed fields of application, equally legitimate; at the least, the criteria for discriminating between them must be sought elsewhere than within the conceptual structures themselves: in culture, in society, in the associated practical preoccupations, and so on. Of all the views listed however, for the study of nature Einstein's theory of relativity has, in the modern period, demonstrated a special fecundity. But it is more than mere fecundity that draws our attention to it: relativity theory, by casting a

227

reflection on all the erstwhile conceptions of nature, reveals to us some abiding truths regarding natural science in general.

It is at this point that we come to see a profound harmony between Einstein's work and those aspects of the Marxian tradition with which we were concerned in the previous chapter. The principal foci of interest of these two thinkers were of course quite different; and we certainly would not claim that Marx's philosophy can be comprehensively characterized as 'phenomenological'. But there are deep parallels, and these are due to more than the fact alone that both thinkers were responsible for great conceptual revolutions. In particular, both relativity theory and Marxism initiated a deep reflection on their respective philosophical traditions. Both issued in an examination from within of the modes of presentation of objects in the existing theory. Thus, since a conception of nature is the outcome of an ontology, both led to a detailed scrutiny of the extant views of the physical world. The conclusions of relativity theory and Marxism, moreover (at least, regarding the interpretation of the latter being proposed in this essay) were substantially the same. Both produced the same discovery that the 'objectivity' of the classical theories was in fact contingent – although at the same time their apparent 'naturalness' was quite intelligible. Rather, objectivity, they both recognized, was a theoretical construction. It depended on a multiplicity of influences: on philosophy, on tradition, on culture, on economy and society.

The theory of relativity culminates in an account which bears a strong resemblance to what we have referred to formerly as a 'general theory of fetishism'. Relativity theory is a dynamics of appearance articulated within the conceptual medium of a specific philosophical system. It presents a theory of the modes of givenness of reality as they are refracted through a particular set of epistemological categories. That the categories specifically favoured by relativity theory were essentially those of phenomenology is not in this context of importance. What is important is just that Einstein's theory, like Marxism, contains an irreducible self-reflective moment which elucidates the inner character of all theorizing about nature. In their most general sense both theories illuminate the trajectory described by knowledge in a given categorial environment. Similarly, both exhibit the genuine content of the theories they are supplanting. As bourgeois ideology contains a real moment of truth in which it exposes 'the heart of a heartless world'[48] so also Newtonian physics is not mere phantasm. Its truth however is limited – and not just because its own philosophical approach is open to question. Like its counterpart in bourgeois society classical mechanics comprises an inherent distortion. For within it the only available form of the presentation of its objects necessarily occludes the fact of the contingency of their implicit categorial perspective – and in particular, of the inexorable interdependence between experience and theory.

It is worth pointing out at this juncture that, in consequence of these results, although the qualitative discrepancies between classical and relativistic physics are often quite small the two theories could in fact hardly be more different. Just as Marx had done, Einstein broke with the erstwhile objectivistic programme of his discipline and developed in its place a more dynamic and fertile theory of phenomena as they occur within definite theoretical – and hence implicitly social – conjunctures. But here precisely for both Marx and Einstein arise truly great problems. For both thinkers the world is structured at once by words and molecules.[49] However the characterization of the structures of systems of thought – both objectivist and non-objectivist – is still an open question. And on the other hand it remains to be determined how the alternative systems of truth – which after all, develop out of the symbolically mediated life-processes of a society – have their advent in real complexes of meaning. These are problems unresolved by either Marx or Einstein. The path from history to knowledge is still an obscure, indistinct one.

IV
The diversity within modern science

Phenomenology and structuralism

This chapter will be a short one, for it has only a simple task to perform. From our previous investigations, and in particular, from our examination of Husserl's philosophy, we have identified a bifurcation in the critique of objectivism – a bifurcation which appeared to reflect deep theoretical divisions. It is now time to invest this hypothesis with a rigorous content.

In Chapters 4 and 5 we concluded that Husserl's account of science issues in two conceptions of meaning, and indeed, two conceptions of truth. Our original formulation of this opposition emphasized on the one hand the fundamental phenomenological orientation, in which meaning and truth both derived from – or were recognized only in relation to – an individual conscious subjectivity; and on the other, that orientation which took as primary the linguistic variables and the constitutive structures of theoretical systems. In our further studies we have adumbrated a parallel problem within science itself: an apparent ambiguity appeared to emerge, either in science itself or in its interpretations, between the semiotic problem associated with the theory of nature and the question of its meaning for individual and social subjects. What is necessary at this point is to elucidate in detail the nature of this alleged ambiguity and to specify more precisely Husserl's two epistemologies. As will be seen, it will be an outcome of this chapter that the 'ambiguity' is well-founded. Indeed, we shall argue that its very existence strikes deep resonances both within the interpretations of science and within contemporary science itself, while raising fundamental questions about the possible character of any adequate social theory of science.

In respect of the non-phenomenological moment of Husserl's theory we shall continue to employ our previous usage and we shall refer to it as 'structuralism'. Consistent with our formulations above this term will also refer to the linguistic theory of Ferdinand de Saussure. We shall not at this stage attempt to support this identification; indeed, we shall not even attempt to specify the place of other so-called 'structuralist' theories in relation to the concepts we are seeking to describe. Instead (hopefully) we shall merely allow the appropriateness of this designation to emerge as we proceed. The objective of this chapter can now be stated precisely: it is to examine and to explicate the relationship between phenomenology and structuralism and to assess the relevance of each of these for the theory of science.

The problem of the relationship between the two theories in question has in fact been the subject of many previous, extensive examinations. For example, it is an important theme of major studies by, amongst others, Merleau-Ponty, Ricoeur, Derrida and Habermas. In Husserl's own work the problem is usually allowed to pass unformulated. Nevertheless, at times a rudimentary explicit consideration is offered. We have already referred to some of these occasions – specifically, in the concepts of the lifeworld, of history, of objectivity and in the accounts of the inauguration of modern science. In the last of these is to be found the most explicit consideration of the problem of structure; for here, with his concept of 'sedimentation', Husserl demonstrates a keen awareness of the issues at stake.[1] For this reason the notion of sedimentation is an appropriate place for our present discussion to start.

While considering the originary foundation of geometry Husserl encounters the problem of how the ideal primal accomplishment of the 'first geometer' can acquire an objective validity. In the detailed answer that he proposes, writing is given a pivotal role. For writing alone fixes the immanently apprehensible meanings into stable, communicable and objective unities, as required for a systematic science. However – and this is the main point that Husserl makes – the introduction of writing into science is not merely an extraneous addition. Rather it carries with it major theoretical consequences. Indeed 'the writing-down' actually 'effects a transformation of the original mode of being of the meaning-structure, (e.g.) within the geometrical sphere of self-evidence, of the geometrical structure which is put into words. It becomes sedimented, so to speak'.[2] Within this transformed 'mode of being', coherent and unified meanings are produced, but they are of a quite different character from the immanent, subjective ones. In particular, they are distinguished by what Husserl calls their 'passivity'. 'Written signs', he argues,

> are, when considered from a purely corporeal point of view, straight-forwardly, sensibly experienceable; and it is always possible that they be intersubjectively experienceable in common. But as linguistic signs they awaken, as do linguistic sounds, their familiar significations. The awakening is something passive; the awakened signification is thus given passively, similarly to the way in which any other activity which has sunk into obscurity, once associatively awakened, emerges at first *passively* as a more or less clear memory.[3]

Passivity is the form of meaning appearing within the transformed mode of being of written expression: '(p)assivity in general is the realm of things that are bound together and melt into one another associatively, where all meaning that arises is put together passively.'[4]

The realm of writing, of sedimented meanings and of passive significations is nothing less than the structural, or semiotic, moment of theory as it appears from the phenomenological viewpoint. Of course, Husserl attempts to maintain the continuous priority of the logic of presence over the contending perspective that he has uncovered, but this does not prevent him from recognizing their difference. Thus he distinguishes carefully the two forms of meaning: 'sedimented (logical)[5] sentence meaning' and that derived from the self-evidence apprehended by consciousness, to which he refers as the 'actual meaning, (the) truth-meaning'.[6] Out of sentences with sedimented signification, logical operations can produce only sentences of the same character.[7] This is true in general with regard to language, which has its own 'peculiar "logical" activity' associated with it, 'as well as to the ideal cognitive structures that arise ... within it'; for to any sentence structures emerging within passive understanding 'there belongs essentially a peculiar sort of activity'.[8] More specifically, this is exactly how science proceeds.[9] There, sedimented productions give rise, through the application of the formal apparatus, to ever new and deepening insights which are nevertheless invariably of the same kind. Indeed, with these observations even history can be given a new formulation. Thus Husserl writes: '(w)e can also say now that history is from the start nothing other than the vital movement of the coexistence and the interweaving of original formations and sedimentations of meaning. Anything that is shown to be an historical fact, either in the present through experience or by a historian as a fact in the past, necessarily has its *inner structure of meaning ...*'[10]

We shall not pursue this argument further here. Our aim has been to show merely that there is within Husserl's work a rudimentary recognition of the problem of structure and to indicate its possible implications for phenomenology. Of course, these insights do not reduce his conviction concerning the priority of presence and self-evidence. On the contrary, this priority is a presupposition on which his thought proceeds, a fact that he sometimes acknowledges – as, for example, when he asserts that the fact that 'all new acquisitions express an actual geometrical truth (i.e., in opposition to a sedimented one, as above) is certain a priori under the presupposition that the foundations of the deductive structure have truly been produced and objectified in original self-evidence ...'.[11] Further, it is, consequently, a constant claim of Husserl that the 'structural' meanings are always capable of 'reactivation' – that is, they can always be converted into the properly phenomenological mode.[12] For 'without the actually developed capacity for reactivating the original activities contained within its fundamental concepts,' it seems to him, 'geometry would be a tradition empty of meaning.'[13] But even here he appears occasionally to waver when he reflects upon the differences between phenomenological signification and passivity, which seem to follow alternative internal logics. 'Thus,' he observes, frequently 'a meaning arises which is apparently possible as a unity – i.e., can apparently be made self-evidence through a possible reactivation – whereas the attempt at actual reactivation can reactivate only the individual members of the combination, while the intention to unify them into a whole, instead of being fulfilled, comes to nothing; that is, the ontic validity is destroyed through the original consciousness of nullity.'[14]

As we have repeatedly seen, the relationship of structuralism to phenomenology constitutes a major internal problem for Husserl's philosophy – and indeed for science in general. Husserl's own explicit formulations in relation to this issue however – some of which we have just presented – remain only rudimentary. To be sure, they raise substantial issues: about the alleged transformation in the mode of being, for example, and about the possibility of an underlying continuity between the two forms; about the problem of reconciling the objectivity identified in *Experience and Judgement* and *Formal and Transcendental Logic* with the new, structural objectivity of the 'Origin of Geometry'; about the question of whether and how the phenomenological 'presupposition' can in fact be sustained, and so on. However, these questions although raised implicitly are not systematically dealt with in Husserl's phenomenology. Indeed, it may well be that they cannot be satisfactorily elaborated within his problematic; in the discussion above for example one cannot escape the impression that Husserl may be attempting to resolve incommensurable theoretical perspectives. For a decision on this problem to be possible a more detailed consideration must be undertaken of the relationship between the phenomenological and the structuralist viewpoints.

Ricoeur and Merleau-Ponty

One outstanding attempt to understand this relationship, and which we shall take as our guide, is that emanating from the works of Paul Ricoeur.[15] Now Ricoeur took as his point of departure not Husserl's philosophy of language but rather that of Merleau-Ponty, who refers explicitly both to Husserl and to Saussure. According to Ricoeur, Merleau-Ponty, like Husserl, failed to consider language seriously as an autonomous system in its own right. The 'return to the speaking subject,' he argues, 'which Merleau-Ponty foresaw and began, following the later Husserl, is conceived in such a way that it rushes past the objective science of signs and moves too quickly to speech.'[16] In the *Phenomenology of Perception* Merleau-Ponty had likened language to gesture. As in the expressiveness of sexuality, a style of behaviour, a rhythmic relationship between things, was said to be embodied in the material characteristics of language itself. The words were not to be understood as signs, in the sense of an encoded representation of an independently subsisting thought; in their sonority, their rhythm, their physiognomy, they were said actually to accomplish the thought.[17] Later, in *Signs*, invoking Husserl's concept of sedimentation, he elaborated this view into a whole theory of truth.[18] There he wrote: '(t)ruth is another name for sedimentation, which is itself the presence of all presents in our own. That is to say that even and especially for the ultimate philosophical subject, there is no objectivity which accounts for our super-objective relationship to all times, no light that shines more brightly than the living present's light.'[19] Thus Merleau-Ponty, like Husserl, subordinates, a priori, structure to presence. Truth for him is less an accomplishment within a linguistic system than the recovery to self-evidence of meanings, the advent of which occurs at the level of conscious life.

In consequence, argues Ricoeur, Merleau-Ponty's philosophy is one-sided and partial, for it occludes a crucial problem that must be taken into account in any theory of language: the problem of the structure of the semiotic system.

In his attempt to identify the roots of this error Ricoeur engages in some more technical consideration of Merleau-Ponty's argument. At its basis, he says, is a misinterpretation of one of Saussure's fundamental conceptions. In particular, from the beginning Merleau-Ponty places in opposition the phenomenological attitude and the objective attitude.[20] Saussure had distinguished between *langue* and *parole*. This distinction is interpreted as the opposition of structure and subject by Merleau-Ponty, who then proceeds to resolve the two in favour of the latter.[21] Similarly, Saussure distinguishes within *langue* between synchrony and diachrony, whereas Merleau-Ponty understands this as the opposition between subject and object.[22] Ricoeur comments: '(h)aving thus associated synchrony with the speaking subject and diachrony with the objective aspect of science, phenomenology proposes to incorporate the objective in the subjective point of view, and thus to show that the synchrony of the spoken word includes the diachrony of language.'[23] He adds: 'Merleau-Ponty thinks that he is in agreement with Saussure when he attributes to him the distinction between "a synchronic linguistics of speech and a diachronic linguistics of language". This is obviously an error.'[24]

In opposition to what he considers to be Merleau-Ponty's attempt to accommodate language into phenomenology by diminishing the special structural properties of the former, Ricoeur proposes a detailed study of both. If a true dialogue between phenomenology and structuralism is to occur, he considers, the differences between them as well as their intersections must be clarified. To this end it is useful to emphasize a few basic oppositions that occur between them.

The first of these oppositions has already been alluded to: it concerns the objects with which each philosophy deals. Phenomenology of course deals primarily with meanings as they are apprehended by conscious subjects. Thus in respect of the problem of language the latter is regarded as the form of mediation between subject and world. Structuralism however directly opposes this postulate. It treats not the intentional aimings of a subject but rather the objective significations of a semiological system. It is not necessary to dwell on this point, which is very familiar. Thus we will be satisfied merely with a statement by Ricoeur of the position concerning the treatment of language.

The ultimate presupposition of any structural linguistics is that language is an *object*, like other objects, that is, like the subject-matter of the other sciences, where, also, the 'thing' is resolved into a relationship, a system of internal dependencies. For phenomenology, however, language is not an object but a mediation, that is to say, it is that by which and through which we move towards reality (whatever it may be). For phenomenology, language consists in saying something about something: it thereby escapes towards what it says; it goes beyond itself and dissolves in its intentional movement of reference.[25]

A second opposition is closely related to the first. For the phenomenologist the linguistic units are meaningful signs with manifesting, meaning and referring functions. By mobilizing these functions they are able to express the lived experience of a speaker. The knowledge embodied in language thus always bears a necessary, immanent reference to a subject. For the structuralist, on the other hand, signs do not enjoy the possibility of independent signification. Rather, they subsist only as elements of a system, from the differences between which meaning is generated. They are adopted conventionally and acquire significative power subsequently, exclusively in relation to other signs. For structuralism therefore knowledge is formulated independently of any commitment to a speaking subject.

Thirdly - and finally - we shall mention again the role of synchrony and diachrony in the two philosophies. For semiotics, diachrony is subordinated to synchrony, that is, 'the comprehension of system states precedes that of changes, which are conceived only as the crossing from one system state to another.'[26] Further, as mentioned above, both occur with language (i.e. *langue*) as opposed to speech; indeed in structuralism speech itself does not even appear as a unique object of scientific study.[27] For phenomenology, of course, the situation is quite different. There, speech is primary - and that in which the order must be revealed. Language in general appears through the prism of expression and communication; this holds for its structural features as well as for the changes it exhibits. Thus Merleau-Ponty writes: '(w)hatever the hazards and confusions in the path of the French language ... it is still a fact that we speak and carry on dialogue, that the historical chaos of language is caught up in our determination to express ourselves and to understand those who are members of our linguistic community.'[28] If a distinction between diachrony and synchrony can be sustained in phenomenology, then, it must be, as mentioned above, between, respectively, a 'linguistics of *language*, which gives the impression, in the extreme, that language is a series of chaotic events,' and a 'linguistics of *speech*, which would reveal in it at each moment an order, a system, a totality without which communication and the linguistic community would be impossible.'[29] Here then the two systems do not so much oppose each other as display contrary purposes: systematic explication of structures in the one case, and the interpretation of communicative meaning in the other.

These three oppositions between phenomenology and structuralism demonstrate the deep-seated differences between the two perspectives. Indeed, this was exactly our purpose in introducing them. We did not seek to use them to assert the priority of one or the other view but rather to show (or at least, to suggest) that each conveys its own legitimate insights.[30] This is in fact one of Ricoeur's major conclusions. After examining carefully the claims of both structuralism and phenomenology he ends by recognizing both, while asserting the possibility of a 'convergence'. 'A renewed phenomenology of meaning,' he writes,

> cannot be content with repeating descriptions of speech which do not acknowledge the theoretical status of linguistics and the primacy of structure over process which serves as an axiom for linguistics. Nor can it be content to juxtapose what it would call the *openness* of language to the lived world of experience to the *closed* state of the universe of signs in structural linguistics: it is through and by means of a linguistics of language that a phenomenology of speech is possible today.[31]

Thus, he goes on, one does not have to choose between a philosophy of the sign and a philosophy of representation: 'the first articulates the sign at the level of potential systems available for the performance of discourse; the second is contemporaneous with the accomplishment of the discourse.'[32] The two approaches are complementary and convergent,[33] examining within language two different object domains. On the one hand is the semiological order, the field of signs from which the subject is absent. This must be studied objectively, according to appropriate techniques. On the other hand is the field of phenomenology. The 'semiological order does not constitute the whole of language. One must still pass from language to discourse: it is only on this level that one can speak of signification.'[34] This then is the conclusion: 'the possibility of designating the real by means of signs ... is complete only when it is thought in terms of the double principle of difference and reference, thus in terms of an "unconscious" category and an "egological" category.'[35]

The relationship between phenomenology and structuralism

We now proceed to formulate the relationship – that is, the similarities and the differences – between phenomenology and structuralism.

Phenomenology and structuralism represent independently legitimate programmes. To be sure, their fields of problems have a non-empty intersection. Nevertheless it is clear that within them distinct ideal objects are formed – and subsequently theorized – in characteristically different ways. Where they diverge the divergences appear to be irreducible. Occasionally conflicts occur regarding common issues; more often however, and of fundamental significance, is the fact that they frequently address contrary – and incommensurable – fields of problems. On some foundational questions, such as the locus of knowledge and the role of the subject, the differences between them are total.

In order to understand the inner tension that we have identified in Husserl's philosophy, as well as similar tensions in the theory of science and even in science itself, it is necessary to clarify the status of this opposition between structuralism and phenomenology. To attempt to do this we shall make use of a concept which we have already employed on a number of occasions. This is the concept of 'problematic' – a notion originally conceived by Gaston Bachelard[36] and expanded and developed by Louis Althusser, to whose account we shall refer. The concept is employed by Althusser as a tool aiding the classification and specification of different theoretical projects. It is nowhere in his work given a precise formulation; nevertheless its major features become clear from his two books *For Marx* and *Reading Capital*. There, a problematic is described as that in which the identity of a body of thought lies. It is not the specific propositions of a theory that characterize it but rather its structure, its systematically interrelated set of concepts which unifies all its elements.[37] Within such a unity the determination of a content becomes possible and hence also a meaning. The problematic of a theory therefore can be said to form 'the objective internal reference system of its particular themes' designating not just the types of available answers but equally the systems of questions and forms of problems which command appropriately structured solutions.[38]

This last point is fundamental; it means that a problematic, as the underlying structure of a theory, specifies the overall topography of the theoretical field. It determines the objects that are recognized by the theory in question and the particular issues to which it might direct itself.

> This introduces us to a fact peculiar to the very existence of science: it can only pose problems on the terrain and within the horizon of a definite theoretical structure, its problematic, which constitutes its absolute and definite condition of possibility, and hence the absolute determination of the forms in which all problems must be posed, at any given moment in the science.
> This opens the way to an understanding of the determination of the visible as visible, and conjointly, the invisible as invisible, and of the organic link binding the invisible to the visible. Any object or problem situated on the terrain and within the horizon, i.e., in the definite structured field of the theoretical problematic of a given theoretical discipline, is visible.[39]

At the same time as revealing certain problems it must also of course prevent others from being raised.

> The same connexion that defines the visible also defines the invisible as its shadowy obverse. It is the field of the problematic that defines and structures the invisible as the defined excluded, excluded from the field of visibility and defined as excluded by the existence and peculiar structure of the field of the problematic.[40]

In what follows the specificity of the concept of problematic will be assumed. In addition, we shall assume its applicability to each of phenomenology and structuralism. That these two conceptual strategies in fact represent theoretical entities as distinct as problematics is certainly plausible from our previous investigations. For we have seen repeatedly that they differ, absolutely and irreconcilably, on the most fundamental of issues. However the actual proof that each constitutes a problematic in its own right can only be established by delineating the respective structures; hence the achievement of such a proof must be delayed for a few pages. This then is the task with which we are now presented: the elaboration of the similarities and differences, and thereby the structures, of the problematics of structuralism and phenomenology. .

Before turning to this directly, however, there is one more point that is worth mentioning. The status of the concept of problematic is itself not altogether perspicuous. For on the one hand, implicit in the existence of this concept is the claim that any systematic thinking falls within some particular problematic and that, in principle, the range of problematics partitions the entire field of human knowledge. However on the other hand, the concept of problematic itself, and the theoretical activity according to which it is specified, obviously cannot belong to any problematic at all. Therefore, there must exist concepts, and operations upon them, which lie beyond the expanse of the concept of problematic. It is not appropriate at this point to examine in detail this problem, which really raises the question of the status of our investigation in general. However it is certainly an interesting and important problem, which has obvious affinities to some classical logical dilemmas. Accordingly, we shall make some further remarks relevant to it at a later stage. Here, for the sake of enabling the argument to proceed, we merely point out that systematic thought is certainly possible outside all problematics; however such thought can occur only on the condition that it avoids any commitment in respect of those structural features which determine problematics. Furthermore, there does exist at least one self-reflective theoretical medium capable of encompassing all conceptual perspectives. In fact this medium is very familiar: it is language itself.

* * * * * *

We now proceed directly to attempt to specify the divergent structuralist and phenomenological problematics. Many of the substantial differences between these two problematics have in fact already been described. In the first place, of crucial importance, as we have repeatedly seen, is the concept of the *subject* in each and the theoretical role played by this concept. For phenomenology, the subject is central – whether manifesting itself through a transcendental ego or through more complex structures of intersubjectivity. This is the case whether in the particular version of phenomenology it is the absolute upsurge of subjectivity that is fundamental or rather the event of articulation, whether meaning is constituted or instituted. For structuralism on the other hand, all epistemological definitions derive from the denial of a central subjective focus. This is so, usually explicitly, for every structuralist thinker; it is expressed in the description of language as a system of signs, in the priority within cultural formations of unconscious categories of thought,[41] in the designation of history as 'a process without a subject'[42] and so on.[43]

Following these different conceptions of the subject, and closely associated with them, are the characteristic forms of the *objects* that present themselves for investigation within each problematic. As was mentioned, a problematic prescribes the theoretical environment within which certain kinds of questions can be asked and certain kinds of answers formulated. Accordingly, it also prescribes the locally specific conception of *truth*. In the phenomenological perspective, where the subject is central, truth is derived from presence – either directly, or indirectly by way of its mediation through the intersubjective forms. Here therefore there always exists an implicit epistemological centre or origin in relation to which all objects can in principle be located. Thus the object domain of phenomenological knowledge consists of entities knowable to a subject in the mode of presence and intentionally related to it. For structuralism on the other hand, it is precisely the denial of the existence of such a centre that prevails. Instead, the object field is structured as a system of differences, and individual objects are considered as knowable only in and through the ensemble of their relations and states.[44] This is how the object domain of structuralism is characterized. Further, it can be seen that there truth no longer appears as a presence to a consciousness. Rather the role of the subject in this regard is systematically denied, and truth is read from the epistemological space as the interpretation of a 'text'. This circumstance explains why the structure of the theory itself assumes such an importance within structuralism.

The concepts of *change* and *transformation* accessible to the two problematics also diverge. In particular, we refer to the phenomenon of a theoretical 'crisis' exhibited by a theory inscribed within a given problematic. Such a crisis is invariably indicative of substantial and – at least temporarily – irresoluble problems encountered by that theory; it may presage radical change either within or between problematics. Structuralism and phenomenology incorporate rather different conceptions of crisis – a fact which also helps to distinguish between them. For the former, not surprisingly, a crisis appears as a disturbance in the arrangement of structures. In the extreme case it leads to a decisive rupture in the epistemological manifold, associated with fundamental transformations of the theoretical structures themselves and of the relations between them. For phenomenology, insofar as a conception of crisis is articulated at all, it is quite different. There, a crisis of a theory occurs as a radical questioning of the categories according to which the world is presented within it. Under such conditions it may eventuate that these categories, which had formerly been assumed to be invariant, are exposed as contingent. In this circumstance, from the emerging perspective an assessment of the old one is developed which can be represented under the general rubric of a 'critique of fetishism'. We have already analyzed in some detail an example of such a critique when we discussed how Marxist theory, interpreted from a phenomenological viewpoint, might regard the erstwhile objectivist problematic.

While speaking once more of objectivism a further, fundamental point might be added. Many other divergences between the two perspectives in question have previously been mentioned. However there is a major issue on which they are united and which must be emphasized. Both offer, either explicitly or implicitly, an effective *critique of objectivism*. Husserl's critique of objectivism has already been closely examined. Indeed, as we have stressed, his recognition that such a critique was urgently needed was one of the crucial motivations of the *Crisis*. On the other hand however, the claim in respect of structuralism may seem somewhat surprising. For after all, one of the most frequent accusations against structuralist thinkers is that their work displays positivist tendencies. Such criticism has been levelled particularly against Althusser and his followers, Lévi-Strauss, Piaget and others.[45] Nevertheless we claim that a critique of objectivism is in fact a key component of the structuralist project. Thus to the extent that, for example, Althusser's work can indeed justly be criticized as positivist, such positivism derives from sources extraneous to the structuralist purpose – and, it may be added in passing, exogenous also to Marxism. Some further remarks are necessary to clarify these contentions.

Objectivism claims, at its root, that the objectivity of knowledge demands its radical independence from all social, communicative and subjective variables. One of the most effective series of critiques of objectivism emerged from critical theory; there, either the argument proceeded directly from the Hegelian category of totality or else, more broadly, it attempted to identify irreducible subjective or intersubjective preconditions for all knowledge. Another potent critique – that of phenomenology – also adopted the point of view of the subject – although of course, considered as a transcendental ego rather than as an immanently social entity. The implicit refutation of objectivism which emerges from the structuralist perspective argues rather differently. Here, the general strategy of critique involves the incorporation into the theory, as an important focus, the structural preconditions for truth itself. Structuralism develops the insight that 'truth' is only ever *formulated*, arguing that therefore it can never be dissociated from its own idiosyncratic mechanisms of production. These mechanisms include, in particular, the processes of the emergence of theoretical constructions from the characteristic semiotic systems of opposition and difference, in accordance with certain relationships and uniformities that themselves are susceptible to theory. From this point of view it can even be said that truth itself is exactly the 'ensemble of ordered procedures for the production, regulation, distribution, circulation, and functioning of statements.'[46] The really important conclusion for our purposes, however, is just that 'truth-effects' are produced within discourses. Now these discourses form within the conceptual environments of particular social formations. Hence it follows that the implication of truth in the world, and indeed its subjection to the mutual effects of culture and power, cannot be avoided. This is a major, anti-objectivist contention. It emerges forcefully and emphatically from the work of all the major structuralist thinkers. The argument as we have presented it (albeit in extremely abbreviated form) can be seen immediately to be consistent with the claims especially of Lévi-Strauss, Barthes and Foucault.[47] It is unusual of course for these thinkers to apply themselves explicitly to a consideration of the question of objectivism; indeed the comment that Merleau-Ponty made about Saussure – that he does not always realize to what extent his own findings remove us from positivism[48] – is true generally in relation to the structuralist philosophers. For they have shown that each society has its own regime of truth. In every social formation are to be found characteristic types of discourse that are promoted and caused to function as true. Further, and more precisely, the mechanisms and instances vary which enable one to distinguish true from false statements, as also do the techniques and procedures which are valorized for obtaining truth, and so on.[49]

An outcome of the structuralist problematic then, is that absolutely objective knowledge in the primitive sense of objectivism is not only impossible but that indeed a reflection on the conditions of knowledge must be incorporated into the very structure of knowledge itself. Meaning and its linguistic, semiotic and historical context are intertwined; together they establish the comprehensive system of references within which articulations can be formed, endowed with value[50] and interpreted.

We now summarize in a table what we have been saying about the differences between structuralism and phenomenology. These two perspectives constitute legitimate and distinct theoretical programmes. Unified in their opposition to objectivism, they neverthe-less diverge in their ontologies (that is, in the general form of their object domains), their epistemologies, their conceptions of theoret-ical change and the details of their critiques of objectivism. These results may be expressed in the form of the table below:

Problematic:	Phenomenology	Structuralism
Ontology:	Focuses on subject-object intentional re-lations	Focuses on relations and states of systems of elements
Epistemology:	Truth dependent on the presentation of evidence to a subject	Truth 'decentered', emerging instead from systems of differences and coalescing in texts
Crisis theory:	Critique of fetishism	Theory of epistemo-logical rupture
Objectivism critique:	Stresses the centrality of the subjective pro-cesses in knowledge	Stresses the structural determinants of dis-course

* * * * * *

We have now largely fulfilled the intentions of this chapter. How-ever a few comments must be made regarding the discussion in which we have just engaged. In the first place, we would like to emphasize that we are not claiming here to be providing a fully conclusive and exhaustive specification of the problematics of pheno-menology and structuralism. That would require an investigation well beyond the scope of this essay – an investigation which, amongst other things, would have to clarify precisely in what the proper accomplishment of such an endeavour might lie. The absence of such a comprehensive account however does not affect our present argument, since for our purposes here rough outlines of the problematics are sufficient. Additionally, the perhaps ob-vious point should be mentioned that under the rubrics 'pheno-menology' and 'structuralism' we are characterizing pure theoreti-cal structures; it does not follow that there is any direct correspondence with the works of particular authors. Of course, we know that it occurred that the problematic of *phenomenology* was developed rigorously and relentlessly in the philosophy of

Husserl; however it is a fact that regarding *structuralism* no single comparable corpus of writings exists. To be sure, there are many authors who have worked broadly within the structuralist tradition; we have mentioned, for example, Saussure, Althusser, Lévi-Strauss and Piaget. But even if a thinker identifies himself as working within a particular conceptual domain we cannot conclude that all of his works – or indeed, even all of any single work – lie properly within that problematic. This problem becomes especially acute when we come to writers who deal quite deliberately with a variety of problematics. Thus some of the philosophers who have commented most powerfully and evocatively on the problems of structuralism and phenomenology have strictly been outsiders to both; these include writers who have exercised a considerable influence on our own account: Ricoeur, Merleau-Ponty, Foucault, Derrida, Kristéva and so on. There can be no doubt that these are complicating factors; nevertheless they do not imply that except in rare cases the identification of concepts like phenomenology or structuralism is of no value. On the contrary, it is one of the intentions of this essay to show that such an identification can indeed produce results of extreme value.

We have repeatedly referred to Althusser and Lévi-Strauss. These authors in particular illustrate the peculiar problem associated with structuralist thought which we mentioned above. Structuralism itself, as we have explained, is inherently an anti-objectivist philosophy; this is shown by many writers – especially those dealing directly with semiotics. However both Lévi-Strauss and Althusser combine in their works both anti-objectivist and very positively objectivist themes. Regarding Althusser, some relevant comments were made in Chapter 6 which need not be repeated; it is only necessary to add that in all his major works – both before and after the self-criticism in which he declared that he had earlier been guilty of 'theoreticism'[51] – both tendencies can be found to co-exist side by side.[52] In the case of Lévi-Strauss a similar situation occurs; positivist and non-positivist themes are developed simultaneously. This is especially so in his earlier works where, as has been widely noted, the positivism is sometimes quite blatant.[53] It still coexists, of course, with the great discoveries that are the perduring legacy of Lévi-Strauss's thought. His recognition of the role of the symbolic in the shaping of social phenomena, his appreciation of the cultural as a distinct order of reality subject to its own characteristic inner structure, his explication of a wide range of phenomena – myths, totemism, kinship systems, to name but three of the most important – as meaningful unities, hitherto unacknowledged – all these are great achievements that have profoundly altered our understanding in these areas. However at the same time as Lévi-Strauss is introducing these innovations he is also – curiously – undermining his own radicalism. For along with the forceful anti-objectivist tendency of his work he proposes an equally forceful positivism.

In an essay written in 1960 Lévi-Strauss asserts that anthropology is a semiology: it studies 'the life of signs at the heart of social life'.[54] The difficulty seems to be that at times Lévi-Strauss takes his own formulation too literally. In his studies of particular phenomena, it has often been claimed,[55] he becomes excessively formal. At these times, it is only processes of signification and transformation that remain important for him. Symbols are replaced by signs, meanings by codes;[56] sense in general becomes identified with the logical relationships established within systems of differential signs. Whether he is discussing different cuisines or the categories of language, the names of animals or kinship structures, the semiotic system is granted complete autonomy; within it the combinatory syntax takes over from meaning. The signs 'at the heart of social life' are thus depicted as having lives exclusively of their own. Lévi-Strauss himself is here in fact very clear about his own intentions. The objective, he says quite explicitly, is to set up 'constitutive units (which, for this purpose, have to be defined unequivocally, that is, by contrasting them in pairs) so as to be able by means of them to elaborate a system which plays the part of a synthesizing operator between ideas and facts, thereby turning the latter into signs.'[57] In this endeavour, 'the recovery of meaning is secondary and derivative compared with the essential work, which consists of taking apart the mechanisms of an objectified thought.'[58]

It is unnecessary at this juncture to elaborate a critique of this position, on which the phenomenological opponents of structuralism have dwelt at length.[59] We wish merely to point out the existence within Lévi-Strauss's work of this scientistic emphasis on formalism, and to observe that it is a tendency consistent with the 'super-rationalist' project which he evidently set for himself at an early age.[60] Furthermore, we would like to mention that this approach conveys substantial consequences for his theory, which indeed he has both recognized and developed. For example, it follows from the extreme formalism of this position that communication in general should be similarly reducible; and this is exactly what Lévi-Strauss implies when he calls for the application of information theory to the study of communicative processes and indeed even to language in general.[61] In accordance with this view the mind itself consequently appears as no more than an elaborate computer;[62] and from this conclusion it is a small step to the affirmation that cultural phenomena can be effectively explained in physical terms. Thus Lévi-Strauss declares that within our grasp now is 'the reintegration of culture in nature and finally of life within the whole of its physico-chemical conditions' – and he goes on to add: '(t)he opposition between nature and culture to which I attached much importance at one time ... now seems to be of primarily methodological importance.'[63]

It is obvious at once that this past position represents for Lévi-Strauss a substantial reversal – indeed, a falsification – of the entire structuralist project. For it tends to contradict one of the original premises on which his work had quite explicitly been based: that the realm of culture constitutes a distinct order of reality. It undermines the specificity of the symbolic dimension and renders it susceptible to the forms of thought of natural science. In consequence of these developments structuralism is left with neither a purpose nor a method. In fact the structuralist discourse itself is placed in doubt, for it could under such circumstances be little more than an effect of the operation of the unconscious mind; this would be the case whether or not the extreme hypothesis of biological reductionism were upheld.[64]

We have devoted space to these rather simplified arguments regarding Lévi-Strauss not because his work is unusual for the existence of such problems, but because it is typical. A powerful outcome of the structuralist movement has been the construction of a compelling and conclusive attack on objectivism. However it is undeniable that in many versions of structuralism this tendency has been accompanied by a paradoxical *capitulation* to objectivism. Indeed, the phenomenon is so well-marked that it is even suggestive of the existence within the structuralist problematic of an inner bifurcation analogous to that which we uncovered in regard to phenomenology.[65] However, to the extent that this last hypothesis appears to contain validity, it is based on a misconception. One of the original impulses of the structuralist movement was the recognition of the need to redefine the role of the subject in modern thought. This was a profoundly progressive development, which came about at first in response to a number of specific outstanding tasks and which bore immediate fruit in the form of substantial new theoretical insights. The difficulty appears to be that, frequently, confusion emerges regarding the precise character of this redefinition. Often it is assumed that what is at issue is the metaphysics of the subject – that is, the very existence of this concept

- rather than its epistemological role. However, as we have seen, metaphysics and epistemology can vary independently; furthermore, any science claiming to be objective of necessity presupposes the possibility of *some* concept of the subject. Now it is conceivable, as we mentioned once before, that a coherent theory could be constructed on the hypothesis of a reversal of the metaphysics of the subject: some preliminary indications for such a theory have in fact been provided by Jacques Derrida (and perhaps Michel Foucault[66]). However this theory would certainly differ in fundamental respects from those with which we are familiar; in particular, it would exclude in principle the possibility of an objective science of nature. Without an underlying reversal of this kind, and with a continuing insistence on the need for a theory of nature in the conventional sense – and especially, with an insistence on the application of the methods and concepts of the natural sciences as they are presently constituted – the attempt to deny the existence of the subject produces quite another outcome. It simply reproduces, in a slightly modified theoretical context, all the features of objectivism. To put this more precisely, the epistemological denial of the subject within a continuing metaphysics of the subject issues directly in a return to objectivism; this is the mistake that has occurred commonly amongst structuralist authors.

It is not the case, therefore, that the positivism to be found so often in structuralist texts emerges naturally or necessarily from the problematic of structuralism itself. Rather, it marks merely a frequent error based on an elementary confusion. Such a confusion is made possible by the crucial concern of this perspective with the problem of the subject. It is added to by the historical fact that the original development of the approach was motivated primarily by particular practical tasks and not, as with phenomenology, by a specific injunction to overcome objectivism. There is no explanation for the positivist error to be found within the inner structure of structuralist theory. Furthermore – and this point is of no less importance than the other conclusions – the commission of this error has no bearing on the underlying, enduring insights made available to us by the structuralist movement.

Phenomenology, structuralism and science

We have now specified in some detail the two theoretical viewpoints which we discovered to have emerged implicitly from the critique of objectivism developed in Husserl's works. To close this chapter, and to bring the discussion back once more to the theory of nature itself, we shall make a few additional remarks regarding the relationship between the phenomenological and structuralist problematics.

We would like to emphasize in particular that in spite of the substantial differences separating them these two problematics cannot adequately be conceived independently from each other. This is a result that was elaborated especially by Ricoeur and to which we referred above. We shall not labour the point here but merely remark that it is perhaps not surprising, when viewed from the perspective of language itself, within which both approaches are embedded. From this perspective it is not difficult to appreciate that there is indeed a relationship of mutual interdependence between the generation of meaning by a subject, or even its evolution within a definite intersubjective context, and the construction of formulations capable of assuming a value in a discursive context.[67]

It is necessary to identify the source of this logical dependence. In fact, the answer to this problem has already been provided in our discussion, at the very outset of this essay, of Descartes and the roots of objectivism; in addition, we have adverted to it several more times above. In our earlier arguments we showed that objectivism and science in general shared a common metaphysics, within which occurred, characteristically, the category of the subject. Such a metaphysics, it was argued, is a precondition for any theory of nature that seeks to incorporate some conception of objective, or intersubjectively valid, knowledge. Its existence, while providing an underlying, continuous unity for all science, is nevertheless consistent with a wide range of epistemologies. One such epistemology which is possible within this metaphysics is objectivism. We now claim that so also are the anti-objectivist epistemologies associated with phenomenology and structuralism.

It has been seen that the two problematics diverge fundamentally at the levels, at least, of ontology and epistemology. Throughout, moreover, it has been clear that the principal issue of contention between them concerns the role of the subject in knowledge. It is here exactly, with this very issue, that the irrefragible, abiding unity that encompasses both is to be found. For in spite of their divergences the two perspectives occur in a strict, precisely delimitable relationship to each other. In particular, they are defined mutually and antithetically about the single axis of the subject. Thus, while, as we have argued, the presence of the subject as epistemological origin is the distinguishing feature of the conceptual topography of phenomenology, so also is the palpable absence of the subject in its rival. The 'metaphysics of presence' is more precisely a metaphysics of presence/absence. By providing the theoretical other of phenomenology, structuralism opens up a new epistemology while simultaneously inscribing itself within a continuing metaphysics. If, therefore, the limitations of either phenomenology or structuralism are sought they will not be found in, for example, the incomplete execution of particular projects or in particular deficiencies regarding empirical phenomena. Rather, such limitations will be found to reside in the more fundamental – though perhaps somewhat paradoxical – fact that each perspective comes into existence as the actualization of a more general project already present as an absence within the unbroken tradition of a perduring metaphysics. While phenomenology and structuralism, therefore, are linked at the most basic possible level they nevertheless simultaneously display an inescapable and irreducible antagonism.

Our entire discussion about the relationship between phenomenology and structuralism arose in the first place out of a consideration of Husserl's philosophy, which appeared to issue in a bifurcation in its epistemology and its critique of objectivism (and, it might be added, subsequently emerged again – albeit in a somewhat modified form – in our discussion of Marx's theory of the fetishism of commodities). However the examination of the actual questions at stake evoked resonances also of other problems relating to science which had arisen both in this and in more general contexts. The phenomenology-structuralism debate has relevance, for example, for the problem of the formal structure of science and its bearing on the philosophical content of the latter, for the problem of the meaning of science and its dependence on social variables, and so on. Further, it is of consequence for some additional issues we have been considering such as the status of objectivism and the possibility in general of non-objectivist epistemologies. In fact, this whole discussion is of profound importance for the theory of nature.

Specifically in relation to the question of epistemology and metaphysics in science, we have arrived at several conclusions in both our earlier discussions and in the one just completed. We have found that among the crucial preconditions for the inauguration of modern science was the formation and recognition of the category of the subject, in relation to which the mathematized – or at least, formalized – objective contents could be determined. We have seen also that at the same time this very innovation provided the preconditions for an epistemological strategy that was to compromise the philosophical self-understanding of science and even perhaps to limit its actual development. This is an extraordinary irony in the story of science.

Nevertheless non-objectivist philosophical possibilities exist. In fact, we have examined two of them. More precisely, we should say that these are *anti*-objectivist epistemologies, for insofar as they also are inscribed within the metaphysics of science they must address the question of the subject and so take a stand on the issue of objectivism. We mention this because it is undoubtedly possible to conceive of a metaphysics that circumvents the classical Western one of presence and absence. Any epistemology within such a metaphysics would then necessarily be non-objectivist; however since under these circumstances the category of the subject would be excluded altogether, such an epistemology could have no relevance for a theory of nature in any familiar sense.

At any rate, we have considered two anti-objectivist epistemologies. Here the question cannot be escaped: how do these bear on the internal content of science itself? This is a very radical question, to which the answer is appropriately radical. The dual critique of objectivism discovered by Husserl, which we have characterized as the opposition between phenomenology and structuralism, has its correlates in the theory of nature. In modern science itself is realized – albeit of course in a rudimentary and as yet insufficiently explicated form – the double critique of objectivism first identified in philosophy. Specifically, the problematic of phenomenology is realized in the theory of relativity, while that of structuralism is realized in quantum mechanics. Arguments have, of course, already been presented in support of the former contention. We are now ready to justify the latter.

The theory of nature was once thought to be necessarily and inexorably objectivist. The contemporary experience has refuted this assumption and revived science's ancient commitment to the consideration of questions of meaning that are vital also at the level of social life. This is no small claim – and nor are its potential consequences small. If, as we have argued, objectivism is in fact mistaken then a non-objectivist theory of nature must be possible. If much of contemporary science is predicated on objectivistic presuppositions then many of its claims must be wrong – either in fact or in their philosophical interpretation. If more than one non-objectivist epistemology is realized in modern science then it is probable that at least some of the contemporary scientific perplexities are at root philosophical in nature rather than purely formal.

These questions will be considered later. For the moment, we must complete our argument regarding the anti-objectivism of modern science. In particular, we must now discuss the philosophical claims implicit in the theory of quantum mechanics.

9

Quantum mechanics and philosophy

Quantum mechanics, perhaps even more than relativity theory, provoked a profound reflection on the fundamental assumptions of science. Questions about knowledge, causality, the very nature of reality, were raised in a new and challenging way. The greatest scientists of the century participated in a debate that threw into doubt many of the most cherished conceptions of physics. This debate, it may be added, by and large remains unresolved: many of the issues hotly debated in the 1920s and 1930s are just as perplexing today.

It will be argued below that it is possible to formulate what is new and different in quantum mechanics. In particular, it will be claimed that this theory is the outcome of the application to the study of nature of a coherent philosophical perspective. Furthermore, this perspective will be seen to differ in fundamental respects from those of both classical mechanics and relativity theory; in fact these differences will prove to be so severe that many of the questions raised from one perspective will not be able to be decided from the others. Nevertheless, it will be possible to define adequately the various positions and to formulate properly the problem of their mutual relationships.

These results will, it is hoped, help substantiate the views being proposed in this essay regarding the structure of science in general and the nature of modern science in particular. Further, it is suggested that they may prove useful for the eventual clarification of some of the outstanding dilemmas of contemporary physics.

Preliminary comments

Before entering directly into our discussion of quantum mechanics some preliminary points must be made. In the first place, it is necessary to emphasize that this is strictly not an essay either in the philosophy of relativity theory or in that of quantum mechanics. Rather our principal concern is with the implications for science of some themes of contemporary philosophy and social theory. Hence it would in fact be inappropriate to attempt to present a detailed account of the philosophical problems confronting modern physics. Accordingly, no such presentation will be attempted and a discussion of any substantive outcomes of our proposals will be deferred to a later work. This approach will not impose a decisive limitation on the present argument, for indeed, to fulfill our purposes here it will be sufficient merely to render plausible some major contentions and to indicate their most important future lines of development. If this last objective can be accomplished it will be enough to allow us to continue to pursue our main purpose: the clarification of the large-scale philosophical structure of the theory of nature and its interdependence with the major themes of contemporary society.

The second point we would like to make here concerns just what it is that should be taken to constitute quantum mechanics in these discussions. Clearly, this theory is more than the formalism itself, since a naked formalism is necessarily devoid of meaning or practical intent. But at the same time it is inappropriate to adopt the rather common approach of identifying the theory with a formalism to which has been appended 'rules of correspondence' defining a link between the mathematical entities and an independent but isomorphic 'reality'.[1] For after all, by the very process of its formulation such a characterization would involve the gratuitous assumption of a particular ontology (in fact, an objectivistic one) in advance of the supposedly clarificatory, philosophical reflection.

To avoid presupposing our conclusions and to facilitate other aspects of the investigation we have chosen the following alternative: in this discussion 'quantum mechanics' will be taken to embrace *both* the formalism and the rules whereby the empirical institution of the theory is effected. Now it must be stated at once that the divergence between this approach and the model-theoretic one just referred to is greater than may first appear. To use the language employed earlier: whereas the latter specifies at the outset a syntax and a semantics for quantum theory the approach being adopted here is prepared to make a commitment only to syntax

257

and pragmatics. The syntax – that is, the formalism – is of course uncontroversial; furthermore (unlike for relativity theory) it was the first aspect of the theory to be properly elucidated. On the other hand, no precise formulation of the pragmatic dimension is possible, for it deliberately makes no claims in respect of either the non-theoretical world or the question of meaning. As for the rules it embraces, these are not, as previously, mathematical functions defined on the event space circumscribed by the formalism; rather, they are conventions accepted by scientists and articulated in and through the natural language.

There are several simple advantages to this approach of regarding quantum theory as a special kind of discourse. For instance, it is faithful to the actual historical development of the theory – that is, to its emergence prior to a philosophical interpretation; hence it does not foreclose divergent theoretical perspectives. It enables the early debates about quantum mechanics to be understood, refraining from reducing them to apparent mere sophistry, as do the more formal approaches. It acknowledges the special generative power of the formalism itself and preserves the perplexities associated with measurement in quantum theory. Finally, by emphasizing the actual process of the institution of a theory in such a way as to highlight the connection of the latter with language, it emphasizes the constitutive contribution of social phenomena to the development of scientific theory.

In this context it is appropriate to make a few remarks about the question of the 'interpretation' of quantum mechanics. As is well known, interpretations of all kinds are now available to explain the theory: the Copenhagen interpretation, realistic interpretations, hidden variables interpretations, many-world interpretations – even dialectical materialist and Buddhist interpretations; hence, it may be thought that the addition of yet another would serve little purpose. But what *is* an interpretation of a scientific theory and what is such an interpretation intended to achieve? Jammer has identified four different senses in which the word is used. First, there is the formal model-theoretic approach referred to above. Second is a 'unifying principle' operating on the model, establishing within it 'an internal coherence' and thereby endowing it with 'explanatory and predictive power'.[2] Third, an interpretation may provide a 'picture' for the theory – that is, a system of propositions with a logical structure similar or isomorphic to the model but an epistemological structure that may be quite different.[3] (According to Jammer, a common error associated with this kind of interpretation has been the mistaken identification of the picture with the theory itself.) Finally, Jammer notes an additional procedure according to which, under the influence of the proposed interpretation, the formalism is modified to obtain the desired harmony between the two.

It is the specific intention of this essay to conform to *none* of these usages. For it seems to us that the most interesting and productive debates about quantum mechanics have concerned not which 'rules of correspondence', 'unifying principle', 'picture' etc. might be the most appropriate, but rather, the questions of the very possibility of such rules in the first place, and of the possible epistemological exigencies adhering to the formalism itself. In other words, anterior to the formal interpretative problems referred to above, what is really required is a crucial meta-reflection on the process of interpretation itself. Here, the search would not be to subsume the equations under a single principle but – to put it simply – to understand just what it is that the theory as a whole tells us about the world. After all, the interpretation of a theory begins with the fundamental question of the conceptual organization of reality – that is, with the conceptions of being consistent with the theory and the notion of truth to which the latter is committed; and the clarification of these issues is essentially a philosophical and an historical task. Accordingly, a satisfactory interpretation of quantum mechanics could be accomplished only by examining the intellectual context within which the advent of the new theory took place and by identifying its specific new departures in the light of both current knowledge and the views of the protagonists of the day. It is precisely in this sense that the present essay would like to raise once more the question of the interpretation of quantum mechanics.

Principal hypothesis

The main hypothesis in support of which we intend to argue has already been made plain. We seek, in brief, to establish the embeddedness of quantum mechanics in the structuralist problematic. To this end it must be shown in particular that the metaphysics, ontology and epistemology of this theory are coincident with those of structuralism and that its object domain is of a structuralist kind.

In the discussion that follows much use will be made of the writings of Neils Bohr regarding the philosophical aspects of quantum mechanics; in fact, we shall develop our argument as an elaboration of his philosophy. We believe that the main points which we shall be proposing are consistent with Bohr's thinking and, indeed, that they were recognized, either explicitly or implicitly, by him. Nevertheless no attempt will be made here to achieve a full presentation of his philosophy.

Bohr is certainly an appropriate figure to discuss in this context because he was one of the first to appreciate the true radicalness of the implications of the quantum theory. To be sure, this very radicalness sometimes made his suggestions puzzling or opaque, and as is the case with many pioneering thinkers, his writings often lacked the rigour that would be demanded of a fully developed system. In spite of this, however, his ideas are always richly suggestive and their study cannot fail to prove rewarding.

To be sure, other figures could have been chosen for this endeavour. The most obvious of these would, of course, have been Werner Heisenberg – himself the developer of a profound interpretation of quantum theory. However we have chosen to discuss Bohr rather than Heisenberg in this essay because his emphasis on the linguistic and epistemological aspects of the new theory is of greater relevance to our purpose than is Heisenberg's emphasis on the place of the theory in the philosophical tradition. In addition, Bohr was the originator of the concept of complementarity, which is of great significance in the present context; in this regard Heisenberg explicitly acknowledged the older man as his mentor.

The scene for the development of quantum mechanics

As we shall see, one of the central ideas of Bohr's philosophy was precisely this notion of complementarity, in relation to the origin of which we shall here say a few words. The motivation for the concept derived explicitly from what had come to be recognized as a situation of extraordinary perplexity regarding the experimental evidence on the nature of light.[4] For many years it had been accepted that light is composed of waves. This wave theory had been the outcome of one of the classic debates in the history of physics two hundred years earlier. Then, Newton on the one side had argued that light was corpuscular in composition while on the other, Hooke, Huygens and others had asserted its wave character. At the beginning of the twentieth century it was a commonplace result that light consisted of waves; certain well-known and easily demonstrated results were thought to prove this – not to mention the great success of Maxwell's equations. Around this time however new results began to appear which the wave theory could not explain. The photoelectric effect, the problem of the specific heat of solids and the problem of black body radiation all suggested strongly that one of the central claims of the corpuscular theory – that light is made up of discrete packets of energy, or 'quanta' – could no longer be discounted. In fact, a general formulation of this result was already available in Planck's hypothesis – stated in 1900 – that energy is discretely distributed. It soon became clear that *both* descriptions of light were accurate: the electromagnetic description which employed Maxwell's theory and the quantum description which utilized Planck's hypothesis. These two interpretations however were found not to apply simultaneously; rather a given experiment would demonstrate either wave or particle characteristics.

But this was not all. A few years after the hypothesis of the exclusive validity of the wave theory of light had been discredited, exactly the same was shown in reverse for another, equally fundamental theory. The corpuscular theory of matter had been accepted as unquestioningly as the wave theory of light; that the properties of particles such as electrons could be fully described in terms of the motions of discrete moving bodies seemed absolutely evident. However in 1928, experiments by Davisson and Germer, Kikuchi, Thompson, Rupp and others showed that streams of electrons could be diffracted and were capable of interference exactly as if they were waves. That is, just as electromagnetic waves had been found to exhibit corpuscular behaviour so also had streams of particles been shown to exhibit wave behaviour. In addition, as before, the wave or particle manifestation of a beam of electrons was found to depend on the nature of the specific experimental investigation.

These results produced an absolutely extraordinary situation in physics. Two classical sets of concepts, previously considered mutually exclusive or even directly contradictory, had been shown to apply with equal validity to common and basic domains of investigation. It was substantially to resolve this apparent paradox that the two forms of the quantum theory (later shown to be equivalent) were devised.

At this juncture it should be added that even with the successful formulation of the basic formalism of quantum mechanics – later amply confirmed by experiment – the conceptual dilemmas remained unresolved. Several attempts to develop interpretations consistent with classical notions were made. Schrödinger, for example, argued for the view that the new theory could be understood in terms of the wave picture alone. He showed how most of the effects associated with the 'particle' view could be understood in wave terms: the Compton effect, the Franck-Hertz experiment, etc. However the conceptual cost of this interpretation was very high. It meant giving up the by now established notion of 'quantum jumps' – that is, of discontinuities in the energy state of an electron[5] – and it meant giving up the fundamental concept of energy itself in the microphysical domain.[6] Both of these concepts were to be replaced by the oscillatory effects of atoms. These difficulties, along with technical problems such as the impossibility of resolving the question of the hydrogen atom from this point of view,[7] meant that the wave interpretation was not widely accepted after 1927 – although Schrödinger personally remained committed to it throughout his life.

Other interpretations of a classical nature were also offered, of course. In particular, hydrodynamic interpretations were attempted by, for example, Madelung, Isakson and others, and efforts were made to provide an interpretation of the wave function as a probability density applying to a purely classical system of particles.[8] None of these attempts proved successful, either; accordingly, they will not be discussed further here.

By 1926 most physicists were becoming convinced that the experimental data the quantum theory was attempting to explain in fact suggested crucial deficiencies in the classical models. This view was dramatically confirmed the following year with the discovery by Heisenberg of his now famous uncertainty relations. Heisenberg, in an elementary argument from the formalism of quantum mechanics, showed the impossibility of a simultaneous arbitrarily precise determination of the position and momentum of a particle – a result which was later proved by a variety of methods and extended to include also the precise determination of energy at a given moment. Now this notion of uncertainty was completely foreign to classical physics. For many, it suggested that there was now no alternative to a complete revision of the classical ideas and the provision of an entirely new set of concepts.

Neils Bohr, who had been puzzling over the problems presented by quantum mechanics for many years, had already embarked upon such a project. He argued that both the wave and particle descriptions of phenomena should be accepted but that the internal constitution of the phenomena themselves should be reviewed. Before elaborating in detail this hypothesis, however, Bohr spent some time trying to clarify the relationship of the new theory to classical physics.

Neils Bohr: The correspondence principle

This relationship between quantum mechanics and classical theory Bohr formulated in a single proposition he was to call the 'correspondence principle'. At first appearance, the ideas involved in this concept were quite straightforward. However, as Bohr himself quickly realized, the implications were, in fact, far-reaching. In particular – and most importantly – the development of the correspondence theory led directly to the rather more radical hypothesis of complementarity.

The starting point for Bohr's ideas was, naturally enough, the apparently contradictory experimental conclusions referred to above. For the development of a coherent theory of subatomic phenomena it seemed that two facts in particular were unchallengeable. In the first place there could be no doubt about the validity of Planck's discovery of the so-called quantum of action, which imposed upon individual atomic processes an element of discontinuity quite foreign to the fundamental principles of classical physics – according to which all actions may vary in a continuous manner.[9] Secondly it seemed indisputable that nevertheless the quantum theory must be regarded 'in every respect as a generalization of the classical physical theories'.[10] Now these facts had an immediate consequence. It was clear to Bohr that 'it would be a misconception to believe that the difficulties of the atomic theory may be evaded by eventually replacing the concepts of classical physics by new conceptual forms'.[11] This apparently simple proposition in fact meant two very important things. In the first place Bohr contradicted those who still adhered to the classical view of physics. What was at stake in quantum theory was *the entire conceptual structure of science*; what is more, it was becoming apparent that the latter would have to be altered in fundamental ways. For example, as we shall see, Bohr was later to argue that the classical notions of causality and of the relationship of the theory to reality must be given up. The mere *substitution* of one set of terms for the classical ones, which would, accordingly, leave the epistemological structure of physics unchanged, would be insufficient to solve the quantum dilemmas. On the other hand however, Bohr also opposed those who were convinced that the classical concepts could no longer be considered to contain any validity whatsoever. On the contrary, he argued, the classical concepts were still applicable in the macroscopic domain – and indeed were indispensable there for the understanding of everyday phenomena.

The correspondence principle was an attempt to formulate this

263

simultaneous continuity and discontinuity between classical and quantum physics. Bohr achieved this by postulating an 'analogy' between the terms of the classical expressions and those of the quantum ones.[12] He claimed, that is, that the relationship between the two theories was not restricted to the obvious asymptotic co-incidence. That this was the case could be seen for example by comparing the quantal description of line spectra with the classical description of the periodic motion of the electron: there, it appeared that there existed a correspondence between the Fourier coefficients in the classical theory and the quantum transitions.[13] Now both these theories produced the correct results, even though the mechanisms postulated were quite different; this applied to the determination of the intensities of the emitted light as well as to the frequencies. Bohr reasoned that this circumstance could not be coincidental: the correspondence between the quantities determined by the two methods 'must have a deeper significance'.[14] Indeed, Bohr went so far as to suggest that the correspondence was of the status of a 'general law';[15] for this law – the correspondence principle – he proposed the following formulation: 'the possibility of every transition process connected with emission of radiation is conditioned by the presence of a corresponding harmonic component in the motion of the atom'.[16]

> Not only do the frequencies of the corresponding harmonic
> components agree asymptotically with the values obtained from
> the frequency condition in the limit where the energies of the
> stationary states converge, but also the amplitudes of the
> mechanical oscillatory components give in the limit an
> asymptotic measure for the probabilities of the transition
> processes on which the intensities of the observable spectral
> lines depend.[17]

From these considerations Bohr drew the following general conclusion:

> The correspondence principle expresses the tendency to utilize
> in the systematic development of the quantum theory every
> feature of the classical theories in a rational transcription
> appropriate to the fundamental contrast between the postulates
> and the classical theories.[18]

In our interpretation of Bohr's philosophy we are placing particular emphasis on his early formulation of the correspondence principle for several reasons. First of all, this principle occupied a central position in his initial attempts to interpret the emerging quantum theory. Thus it is a convenient place to start, from an historical point of view. Secondly, the development of these ideas led directly to Bohr's mature philosophy of complementarity. From them it is possible to identify the problems with which Bohr had become concerned and to the resolution of which his later writings were specifically directed. Finally, and most importantly, the correspondence principle reveals in a particularly clear way the new departures on which Bohr embarked in his thinking; it shows how his perspective diverges from that of the philosophical tradition and thus facilitates the elucidation of the distinguishing features of his mature thought.

Bohr emphasized that our access to the physical world was always mediated by macroscopic phenomena. Events in the subatomic domain could only be detected by interpretation of events manifesting themselves at the level of the experimental apparatus. In our attempts to understand the world what is available to us is no more than that which can be directly apprehended by us through our senses or such extensions of our sensory perception as we are able to devise.[19] Now this does not mean that the experimental conditions merely magnify the phenomena under investigation or translate them into familiar terms. On the contrary, insofar as these conditions are necessary components of any physical description they must be regarded as constituting in fact 'the only basis for the definition of the concepts by which phenomena are described'.[20] What we can know about the subatomic world is determined by the compass of experimental arrangements that can be constructed to obtain information about it. Both in principle and in practice the forms of our intervention in this world shape in their fundamental details our subsequent insights into its workings. Hence the familiar macroscopic world - the domain, that is, of classical scientific thought - cannot be discounted by the quantum theory.

From these hypotheses Bohr proceeded in two directions. On the one hand he stressed emphatically his belief in the continuing validity, in their proper domain, of the classical concepts. This may seem somewhat surprising in the face of the great radicalism of the remainder of Bohr's thought. Nevertheless he insisted that 'only with the help of classical ideas is it possible to ascribe an unambiguous meaning to the results of observation'.[21] Indeed, it could even be said that '(i)t lies in the nature of physical observation ... that all experience must ultimately be expressed in terms of classical concepts ...'.[22] This is a circumstance that is unlikely to be altered by future discoveries.

No more is it likely that the fundamental concepts of the classical theories will ever become superfluous for the description of physical experience. The recognition of the indivisibility of the quantum of action, and the determination of its magnitude, not only depend on an analysis of measurements based on classical concepts, but it continues to be the application of these concepts alone that makes it possible to relate the symbolism of the quantum theory to the data of experience.[23]

Now it must be remarked here that it does not follow from these statements that Bohr is postulating a continuity between the theoretical structures of classical physics and quantum mechanics. On the contrary, he is concerned vigorously to distinguish the two epistemologies. '(T)here is no question of conceptual transmutation of the quantum scheme as we approach the classical limit. Conceptually, the two theories remain unchanged in the classical limit. They agree about predictions but they derive the predictions in different ways.'[24] This point will be justified and elaborated in the following pages. Nevertheless at the same time Bohr's conclusions do seem to be open to a different objection, which we shall simply mention here in passing. It is not obvious that the concepts of classical mechanics are indispensable for the description of the world of experience, as Bohr claimed in the passage quoted above. On the contrary, it is quite conceivable that a different set of concepts could just as adequately apprehend this experience; it will be suggested below, for example,[25] that in fact the world-view of traditional Chinese society deviates in fundamental respects from the Western 'classical' perspective. What is more, it is not even true that the 'forms of our perception' are necessarily classical, as Bohr also assumed. Rather, phenomenological studies have shown that perception often takes quite different forms.[26] The same can be said about other aspects of our experience: it may be the case, as has been often argued, that the laws of psychology and sociology are essentially of a different kind from those of Newtonian physics. Further arguments are available to support this objection but they will not be adduced here. The point itself is not in fact a crucial one but is merely mentioned here for its interest, revealing as it does a curious prejudice in Bohr's outlook.[27]

The other direction in which Bohr proceeded was quite different. Here, he subjected the classical concepts to the closest scrutiny, questioning many of their deepest assumptions. The problems of knowledge, of ontology, of the relationship between subject and object, were all examined in detail and the classical solutions found wanting. The outcome of Bohr's deliberations constitutes his mature philosophy of complementarity.

Complementarity

It was Bohr's conviction that many of the difficulties encountered by classical thought were attributable to the absence of conceptual tools adequate to the task of explaining the new experimental results. In particular, the commitment to the production of a picture of reality that faithfully represented the latter's internal structure presented a major obstacle to the further development of physics.[28] The problem confronting theory, Bohr considered, was not that of providing a more accurate such picture, but rather the attainment of clarity respecting the language used in physical science. The issue, that is, was not the presumed reconstruction of the physical world in the realm of theory, but rather the recognition of theory itself as a source of truth obeying its own internal exigencies.

The quantum theory starts with the assumption that energy and mass are distributed discontinuously. This means that any exchange of information must involve the transmission of a finite quantity of energy. In the macroscopic domain this quantity is so small as to be without significance. Regarding the observation of atomic phenomena, however, this is not the case: here all such acts of observation will involve an interaction with the agency of observation that cannot be neglected.[29] Accordingly, in quantum theory 'the logical comprehension of hitherto unsuspected fundamental regularities governing atomic phenomena has demanded the recognition that no sharp separation can be made between an independent behaviour of the objects and their interaction with the measuring instruments which define the reference frame.'[30] The quantum of action intrudes into every interchange that we have with the world. Every attempt that we make to determine the behaviour of an object will involve a finite interaction with it. This means that we must give up forever the notion of an objective knowledge, in the classical sense, of an independently subsisting reality. Indeed, an independent reality in the ordinary physical sense can now no longer be ascribed either to the phenomena or to the agencies of observation. After all, 'the concept of observation is in so far arbitrary as it depends upon which objects are included in the system to be observed ... The circumstance ... that in interpreting observations use has always to be made of theoretical notions entails that for every particular case it is a question of convenience at which point the concept of observation involving the quantum postulate ... is brought in.'[31]

The radical implications of these claims are not difficult to recognize; their acceptance must involve not only a renunciation of the classical concept of causality but also a revision of the ontology assumed in classical thought.[32] Furthermore, the respective roles of the apparatus and of the theory are for the first time explicitly brought into question. In Newtonian physics the objects and the instruments had been described in identical ways. In quantum physics however the apparatus and its results are described, as we have seen, in physical terms, whilst the quantum state of the system is described by the symbolic formalism.[33] The location of the partition, therefore, between the objects under study and the observing framework are of extreme importance for the subsequent results. What is more, this partition is variable, changing as different experimental perspectives are applied.

The essence of the notion of complementarity is the recognition of the epistemological role of the processes of investigation. As Bohr put it:

> (t)he apparently incompatible sorts of information about the behaviour of the object under examination which we get by different experimental arrangements can clearly not be brought into connection with each other in the usual way, but may, as equally essential for an exhaustive account of all experience, be regarded as 'complementary' to each other. In particular, the frustration of every attempt to analyse more closely the 'individuality' of single atomic processes, symbolized by the quantum of action, by a subdivision of their course, is explained by the fact that each section in this course definable by a direct observation would demand a measuring arrangement which would be incompatible with the appearance of the uniformities considered.[34]

The individuality, therefore, of the typical quantum effects finds its expression precisely in this circumstance: that

> any attempt of subdividing the phenomena will demand a change in the experimental arrangement introducing new possibilities of interaction between objects and measuring instruments which in principle cannot be controlled. Consequently, evidence obtained under different experimental

conditions cannot be comprehended within a single picture, but must be regarded as *complementary* in the sense that only the totality of the phenomena exhausts the possible information about the objects.[35]

Every experimental arrangement which permits the accurate determination of one particular physical quantity necessarily excludes other arrangements which would allow for the measurement of different quantities. A well-defined description of phenomena therefore, must take into account the whole experimental context,[36] only under this condition can the quantum mechanical formalism be meaningfully applied. It is at this juncture that the classical problem of objectivity enters the theory of complementarity. On the one hand, as has been seen, the object and the context of investigation – which of course contains both theoretical and 'practical' components – cannot be distinguished univocally. On the other, however, is the demand in all science for objective truth. Objectivity furthermore, involves a distinction between subject and object, a distinction which is not only irreducible but is even responsible for defining 'the general limits of man's capacity to create concepts.'[37] The problem therefore is this: '(f)or describing our mental activity, we require, on the one hand, an objectively given content to be placed in opposition to a perceiving subject, while, on the other hand, as is already implied in such an assertion, no sharp separation between object and subject can be maintained, since the perceiving subject also belongs to our mental content.'[38]

To overcome this dilemma Bohr first proposed a change of terminology (which we have already anticipated). He criticized especially the description of the measurement problem as that of 'disturbing the phenomena by observation', since such expressions owe allegiance to the old, classical ontology. Instead, he proposed to apply the word 'phenomenon' exclusively to refer to the observations obtained under specific circumstances, including the account, called for above, of the whole experimental arrangement. 'In such terminology,' he argued, 'the observational problem is free of any special intricacy since, in actual experiments, all observations are expressed by unambiguous statements referring, for instance, to the registration of the point at which an electron arrives at a photographic plate.'[39] A 'phenomenon' then, cannot be subsumed exclusively under either category of subject or object; it is an entity of a different kind. Nor are observations restricted to a single, designated subject or to a putative realm of subject-free 'objectivity'; *they* depend on the totality of the investigative and conceptual apparatus employed. True objectivity will henceforth emerge from the unambiguous and consistent use of language[40] within which the variety of perspectives may be accommodated. Objectivity therefore, refers to the whole, or to formulations interpreted in their theoretical context; the meanings of specific concepts, or indeed of words, are no more than relative. For these meanings '(depend) upon our arbitrary choice of viewpoint,' as a result of which 'we must, in general, be prepared to accept the fact that a complete elucidation of one and the same object may require diverse points of view which defy a unique description.'[41]

Ontology and objectivity in quantum mechanics

It follows from these results that the *objects* with which Bohr's theory deals deviate in fundamental respects from the objects of either classical mechanics or relativity theory. His 'phenomena' are as distinct from the subject-independent objects of objectivism as they are from the intentional subject-object unities of Einstein's theory. In contrast to these other approaches quantum mechanics deals with states of a total system; further, these states are conceived in the strict sense as *relations* between the system and an arrangement of measuring apparatuses. The phenomena – that is, the specific objects of the new theory – naturally vary with the experimental arrangements. Indeed, we may regard the latter as providing the *theoretical perspective* from which the physical system is studied.

An analogy to relativity theory is obvious here. In that theory the 'phenomena' under investigation are described as they present themselves to the enquiring subject, whose perspective is varied in the pursuit of invariant relations. *These* perspectives, of course, are frames of reference which may or may not be inertial according to the circumstances; nonetheless they are characterized in terms of their dynamical properties, as determined by experiments in space-time. In quantum theory we also see the world revealed from a certain perspective; however here the perspective is that of the measuring apparatus – or perhaps more precisely, of an arrangement consisting of an (admittedly hypothetical) infinite array of measuring apparatuses distributed throughout space-time and capable of registering independently the interaction-events. Although the 'perspective' here is of a different kind, the way in which it is employed is possibly not so different: here too the perspective is varied in the search for principles of invariance.

A simple analogy may help to visualize the state of affairs in quantum theory. We may think of the experimental arrangement as performing a physical 'cut' through the system under investigation. The resulting cross-section is examined and inferences are drawn concerning the structure of the system. Different cuts may reveal different properties; furthermore, it may occur that one kind of dissection excludes in principle another particular one contemporaneous with it. The inferences that are drawn, of course, are based on the traces left in the cross-section – or, put in more familiar terms, the phenomena observed which the theory interprets are nothing other than the interactions of the system with the apparatus. The relevance of any analogy can be exaggerated of course. However one final, useful point may still be added. The cross-section in question, unlike in relativity theory, may be independent of the time-course of the system; that is, the devices registering the interactions may be separated in a space-like fashion. This means that, whereas in relativity the theoretical picture is essentially diachronic, the cross-section in quantum theory may be synchronic.

This analogy is meant to be no more than suggestive. However it is substantially consistent with Bohr's theory as we have presented it. The objects of the quantum mechanical world are not substances in the Aristotelian – or Einsteinian – sense.[42] They are *relations between substances*. Hence they can only be understood in terms of their place in relation to a totality. They can no longer be conceived as 'having' specific properties, independently of those of other objects. Instead, their properties emerge from a particular set of relations – those which define the procedures of measurement. Unlike for Einstein, for whom relations are defined by substances, for Bohr, substances are defined by relations. Similarly, whereas for the former a measurement reveals a state existing in itself, for the latter it actually constitutes a reality.[43] This difference was stated quite explicitly by Bohr himself when he wrote: 'in our description of nature the purpose is not to disclose the real essence of the phenomena but only to track down, so far as it is possible, relations between the manifold aspects of our experience.'[44]

Thus both the ontology and the object domains of the two theories are radically different. Against relativity's ontology of substances quantum theory proposes an ontology of *relations*. And in contrast to the noema-noesis intentional objects of the former are the states of the latter. It is important to emphasize here the special character of these objects in the quantum domain. Here the object

271

is taken literally to be a disturbance propagated through the frame of reference. Particles, waves etc. strictly speaking are not substances or conjunctions of substances but *trails of interactions* which are subsequently taken as *signs to be interpreted* accordingly. Our knowledge of nature is determined by the ways in which the latter manifests itself in interactions that can be rendered apprehensible to us. Or to put the same point in more phenomenological terms: in quantum mechanics we know nature just 'as it intervenes in our world'. This mode of expression however must not occlude the peculiar role of the subject in this theory. For here the subject is not privileged as it is in phenomenology. It is not the source and locus of all meaning. The 'trail of interactions' is in fact taken not as a direct representation to a consciousness of the system under investigation but as *a statement to be interpreted* or a *text to be read*. This is why in quantum mechanics the question of language emerges so forcefully.

Here, however, we are anticipating ourselves. Before turning to Bohr's remarks on language let us pause briefly to review what has been seen so far.

According to Bohr, quantum mechanics reveals the world not as it is in itself but as it is revealed by the application of a frame of reference imposed by a given experimental arrangement. This frame of reference is itself made up of 'phenomena' which incorporate immanently what had been regarded in the old philosophy as 'subjective' and 'objective' components. Within it, events, such as the formation of droplets by condensation in a cloud chamber or the exposure of certain regions of a photographic plate, occur and are registered in some way. These events, taken together, insofar as they are themselves relations between the system under investigation and the measuring apparatus, constitute the objects of the theory. Indeed, a more general statement than this can be made: it is implicit in the ontology of quantum mechanics that reality actually consists of relations between substances, in terms of which these substances are in fact defined. These interactions that occur in an act of measurement form a special case of such relations. It is the patterns and the properties of the objects that reveal the structure of the system. However this structure is itself not reached directly; its determination is the outcome of a process of interpretation applied to the results of the measurements, now taken as signs. In the entire operation, embracing both experiment and interpretation, the structuring of the perspective and the conclusions is accomplished by a subject. However, in direct contrast to relativity theory, this subject nowhere appears explicitly: it is present, but only in a 'decentred' form.

* * * * * *

Much is required, of course, to complete this account, the elaboration of which will presently be resumed. Before we do so, however, it will be convenient here to make brief reference to some additional points. In particular, it is important to recognize the great novelty of Bohr's philosophy. His conception of complementarity contains a profound reflection on many of the most fundamental assumptions of science. The radicalness of quantum mechanics, as interpreted in his philosophy, is comparable only to the radicalness of relativity theory. Indeed, at practically every point at which Einstein's theory deviates from classical mechanics so also does quantum theory, albeit in a different way. This lends to the two theories a peculiar similarity, to which we have already adverted and of which Bohr himself frequently made mention.[45] Both theories, for example, examine the appearance of phenomena from different perspectives in order to identify invariant relations. In relativity theory however these perspectives are frames of reference; in quantum mechanics they are experimental arrangements. Both undertake detailed critiques of the problem of observation as a result of which both arrive at conclusive refutations of objectivism.[46] The rejection of objectivism by relativity theory, however, is based on the imperatives of the phenomenological problematic while the conclusion of quantum mechanics is based on quite different considerations. In the latter, objects are understood not in relation to a subject but in relation to a complex theoretical apparatus: collections of phenomena are taken to constitute a text, articulated in a predetermined language, susceptible to subsequent interpretative analysis. Both revise the role of the subject in the theory of nature, although once again in quite different ways. Many further points of similarity and difference could be mentioned – especially regarding epistemology and ontology.[47] However here we shall refer only to one additional source of divergence, which will permit us to return to our presentation of Bohr's philosophy. A major innovation of quantum theory is the role it attributes to the symbolic apparatus in the development of scientific theory: to the mathematical formalism, that is, and to language.

Bohr and language

Bohr regarded the problem of language as a crucial one in the development of science. Formerly it had been assumed that such issues were peripheral to the study of nature – or even lay outside it altogether. Bohr however pointed out forcefully that physics could no longer take this attitude.

As the goal of science is to augment and order our experience, every analysis of the conditions of human knowledge must rest on considerations of the character and scope of our means of communication. Our basis is, of course, the language developed for orientation in our surroundings and for the organization of human communities. However the increase of experience has repeatedly raised questions as to the sufficiency of the concepts and ideas incorporated in daily language. Because of the relative simplicity of physical problems, they are especially suited to investigate the use of our means of communication. Indeed, the development of atomic physics has taught us how, without leaving common language, it is possible to create a framework sufficiently wide for an exhaustive description of new experience.[48]

The first reason for the importance of the study of language, then, is that 'even when the phenomena transcend the scope of classical physical theories, the account of the experimental arrangement and the recording of observations must be given in plain language, suitably supplemented by technical physical terminology'.[49] To be sure, quantum theory had revealed several difficulties concerning the representation of atomic phenomena in ordinary language.[50] However, Bohr maintained, these problems involved substantially no more than misunderstandings regarding the use of language.[51] Indeed, it was even suggested that much philosophical disputation could be attributed to misunderstandings of this kind.[52]

Now these deceptively simple formulations should not be taken to imply that the problems of language arise only with the reportage of results. On the contrary, as we have in fact already seen, they are present at the very outset of the investigation. The ambiguities encountered by the quantum theory, Bohr demonstrated, frequently involve a confusion between two or more conceptual frameworks assumed by the experimenter. If these frameworks are contradictory then so also will be the results. For the meanings of concepts are determined by the viewpoints from which they are articulated. Indeed, more than this is the case, for the conceptual framework actually determines the possibilities of definition. For example, a given perspective allows for the specification of a concept of position and hence also for its determination; another perspective excludes position measurements but admits of those of momentum. The resolution of these apparent ambiguities however is not difficult: in accordance with the notion of complementarity all that is necessary is the careful elaboration of the framework employed during the use of a given concept. Then, the supposedly conflicting statements will be reconciled – or rather, they will be seen to be in fact incomparable, owing to their reference to alternative experimental perspectives.

These considerations are of decisive importance. However, there is a deeper level still at which the problem of language emerges: the level of *interpretation of results*. The application of a particular measuring arrangement to a physical system results in a certain collection of phenomena; these phenomena, if they are to provide insights regarding the structure of the system, subsequently require interpretation. As has just been found, the arrangement itself places limits not merely on the extent of a measuring procedure but also on the meanings of concepts available under its rubric. The question must now be raised of the actual work of producing these concepts; in fact, on examination, this activity proves to constitute a separate event. Furthermore, the interpretation of phenomena – which is, after all, just what we are speaking about here – utilizes resources which are exogenous to the processes so far described. For such interpretation must be able to accomplish both the transformation of the phenomena into signs for underlying properties of the system and the subsequent drawing together of these signs into a condition of sense. Of course, exactly as in the previous chapter, a procedure of this kind is very familiar to us – predominantly, from our everyday use of language. Indeed, it is precisely from language that quantum mechanics draws this particular faculty.

The concepts produced in the act of interpretation may be of two different kinds, the distinctions between which may be more or less profound. On the one hand these concepts may be of the sort utilized in familiar, everyday experience. For example, certain processes may be described in terms of the behaviour of waves or particles as collisions, reflections, diffraction, interference and so on. This is the region within which Bohr was convinced classical ideas were unchallengeable. On the other hand however the concepts may be more abstract, seeking to describe in new or different

275

ways the properties discerned. Here the form of expression may be predominantly technical and mathematical laws might be formulated. That the two kinds of concepts involved are in some way analogous is an underlying hypothesis of the correspondence principle; from the foregoing considerations, which show how both are derived by similar processes of interpretation from identical phenomena, this contention may indeed now appear hardly surprising. There are, however, some difficulties with these notions, as was indicated earlier,[53] and that is why we have remarked that the distinctions may be more or less clear-cut. The earlier comments regarding these difficulties will not be repeated; here we merely add the further point that apparently unproblematic concepts like 'waves' and 'particles' are not always in fact so transparent. Rather, they themselves may depend on complex theoretical formulations bearing simultaneously on the implied philosophical problematic and on their constitutive elements. Consequently, their acceptance in everyday discourse may be due less to their inherent naturalness than to cultural influences or even to mere habituation.

The process of interpretation in quantum mechanics must be distinguished from that of either objectivism or phenomenology. In objectivism, the natural phenomena are taken as constituting a direct representation of reality. In phenomenology, meaning refers either to sense, understood in the context of an evidential giving to a subject, or to reference; accordingly, interpretation here is always associated with the intentional aimings of a subject.[54] In quantum theory on the other hand, as we have repeatedly pointed out, the theoretical perspective determines the meanings, yet in the absence of an explicitly localized subject. Except possibly where attempts are made to establish a continuity with discordant perspectives at use in the macroscopic world, quantum theory approaches phenomena as constituting a *text to be deciphered*. The elementary units of sense of this text are measurements – patterns of interaction marked out in an event space. They are taken as forming a closed system of signs, out of which, immanently, the relations of sense emerge. The job of the physicist is now, strictly, to describe the grammar of this newly recognized 'language of nature'. It should be emphasized that what is at stake here is not what has been called 'readable technologies' – that is, 'technologies that mediate between subject and object and which are modulated by the World in such a way that the modulations can be "read" by the subject as if they constituted the "text" of a "dialogue" between the world and the subject.'[55] On the contrary, from the point of view of quantum theory, the world is itself identical to the phenomena emerging from the application of a technology; it is no arcane collection of substances anterior to it. Nor is the world conceived as standing in opposition to a subject, into relation with which it is subsequently brought by the technological apparatus; the subject too is involved in the world's original formulation. The task of theory, from the perspective of quantum mechanics, is the interpretation of the formal play of differences constituted by the phenomena – that is, of *traces*.[56]

The theoretical grammar that is the outcome of this endeavour we know as the formalism of quantum mechanics. This is the mathematical apparatus that gives expression to the philosophical ideas we have been considering. Quantum theory, as was said at the outset of this discussion, must be understood as a region of discourse embracing both language and a set of mathematical principles. In this association both components retain the capacity to generate new meanings; indeed, both participate in the control of the possibilities of definition in the quantum domain. It is not necessary for the purposes of the present essay to discuss in detail the mathematical aspects of the quantum theory; accordingly, a deliberate emphasis has been placed on the philosophical issues. We will not depart here from this restraint and will satisfy ourselves with only three further comments on the role of the formalism.

In the first place, the special role of this formalism in quantum mechanics is consistent with the ontological precept on which it is based. The issue in quantum physics is not that of obtaining a pictorial representation of an underlying reality but rather the displaying of the logical terms or grammatical relations that unify phenomena. This is precisely what the formalism accomplishes; furthermore, its precise, axiomatic presentation allows particular insight into relations that would not otherwise be conspicuous. Secondly, it must be recognized that in spite of the priority often attributed to the formalism it does not in itself convey meaning – or more precisely, it does not convey meaning independently of a theoretical perspective which would require expression in language. The mathematical apparatus produces only mathematical expressions. These are subsequently complemented with a hypothetical experimental arrangement, thereby permitting the formulation of a statement which may be judged to be true or false. This is an important point: the manipulation of the mathematical symbols is not directly productive of truth; the latter requires the simultaneous application of a definite epistemological perspective.

At the same time, however, the potency of the mathematical domain should not be underestimated. This, in fact, is the final point. Much of the evolution of the quantum theory was due to mathematics rather than to philosophy. Of course, the original formulations of the important equations – the quantum hypothesis, Schrödinger's equation and so on – were precipitated by philosophical deliberations. However following this, many of the important results were generated unambiguously from the mathematics itself; this included even results – like the uncertainty relations and Dirac's equation – which later produced major philosophical consequences. To be sure, it might be said that an axiomatized mathematical formalism is particularly congenial to the overall philosophical disposition of quantum theory. But such a claim would clearly be insufficient, since both objectivism and phenomenology also possess adequate expressions in mathematics. This question of the relationship between philosophy and mathematics will be examined in detail later; here, on the basis of the foregoing considerations, the conclusion is suggested merely that, whatever this relationship may be, at the least, it permits substantial epistemological variation.

*　*　*　*　*　*

The results that we have so far achieved allow us to add to our previous remarks a conclusion regarding the epistemology of quantum mechanics. We have seen that, due to the peculiar way of defining its objects, this theory can adopt neither the objectivist nor the phenomenological conception of truth. Of course, as in those other theories, propositions are judged empirically; however here there are radical differences in the ways in which the empirical questions are posed, and in which the answers are read. The 'evidential givings' on which the empirical propositions recognized by quantum mechanics are based are not identifiable at a particular subjective locus. Rather, as we have seen, the empirical data are read from a kind of text of macroscopic events provided by a (putative) infinite array of measuring instruments. This was, of course, the fundamental assertion of the correspondence principle. To this result the principle of complementarity added that different arrays of experimental apparatuses provide different theorerical perspectives on subatomic phenomena: they produce different texts from which different, but equally valid, conclusions can be read. The quantum formalism is very general and is capable of generating propositions consistent with any of the available empirical perspectives. More precisely, these propositions, when completed by their endowment with an empirical perspective, can be accepted as valid or potentially valid (well-formed) propositions. In other words, at both levels in the quantum theory truth is a textual phenomenon. It is an effect of a determinate symbolic apparatus. This apparatus, of course, is a system of differences, the grammar of which the theory seeks to formulate. The differences themselves are now identified precisely with phenomena – not through a mere interpretation but literally. This may be the most distinctive philosophical innovation of the quantum theory.

Quantum mechanics, structuralism and objectivity

The foregoing discussion has relied heavily on the writings of Neils Bohr. Its conclusions are consistent in all important respects with those at which he himself arrived. Nevertheless it must be stressed that we are not claiming that the view propounded here should be taken to be identical with Bohr's own position as he stated it definitively. The present essay is an interpretation of Bohr's philosophy; it does not pretend to provide a faithful representation of it. This point is being emphasized to avoid the impression that, by means of a tendentious argumentation, views have been attributed to Bohr that he did not hold.[57] Nevertheless, enough has been said to demonstrate the great originality and true depth of his insights, to which in future all those who reflect on science and philosophy must remain indebted. In particular, it should be apparent that his ideas regarding quantum mechanics are too novel and too complex to be subsumed, as is often done, under the rubric of a single conventional philosophical viewpoint such as 'positivism', 'empiricism' or even, 'idealism'.[58]

The result that this chapter set out to prove has now been established. Quantum mechanics realizes the second of the two problematics emerging from Husserl's deliberations. In its metaphysics and ontology, its epistemology and object domain, in its characterization of the role of the subject, this theory can be seen to bear the principal determining features of structuralism. Additionally (and in consequence) quantum theory provides an implicit critique of objectivism which sets it apart radically from classical mechanics.[59] Thus it is possible to say that quantum mechanics completes the critique of objectivism, at least insofar as this critique is considered within the parameters of the contemporary debates.

It is perhaps worth adding one additional note on the question of what we have been calling metaphysics. Quantum mechanics, as much as relativity theory, presupposes a conception of the opposition between subject and object, in relation to which both its ontology and its epistomology are defined. As Bohr emphasized in his discussion of the correspondence principle, there is an inescapable requirement that data concerning empirical studies be communicable – an exigency which was said to lead to the necessity of using classical concepts. Communication as such however, as is immediately evident, itself incorporates the notion of subject – without, furthermore, excluding the formation of this subject along with the process of signification.[60] At the level of the phenomena themselves a similar assumption is implied: the relations that are being claimed for the system under investigation must have an objective existence, in the sense that they must be able to be formulated in an unambiguous and replicable way. Objectivity here also stands in opposition to 'subjectivity', but now the dependence on the structural context is made explicit. Objectivity, and hence also subjectivity, are presupposed in the assignment of tasks to the new theory.

This small conclusion, of course, is hardly surprising. As we have previously argued, science, or the theory of nature, in the familiar sense is necessarily *objective* science. It is possible to conceive of non-objective approaches to the study of nature. The construction of mythologies in tribal societies or various extant notions currently regarded as 'superstitious' or 'religious' provide examples; the view of nature which emerges from ancient Chinese philosophy may also be of this kind. Indeed, recently it has been argued with some sophistication that quantum mechanics can be interpreted as consistent with either Taoism or Buddhism.[61] While these other perspectives are of great interest, however, it seems clear that none would on its own be capable of providing a satisfactory alternative theoretical programme for the study of nature. For each departs – in one way or another – from the most elementary requirements placed on *Western* science. To mention just one example: in the mythological world-view it is impossible to sustain even an idea of nature itself.

On the other hand, between its different versions objective science can vary profoundly in the actual conceptions of objectivity it adopts; these notions, as we have seen, may be radically distinct from objectivism. Western science as we know it works with a conception of nature in relation to which the place of man is charted. Modern physics has produced new and profound reflections on this relationship and in the process has contributed to the debates concerning a number of other issues of abiding philosophical interest. Once again, this aspect of the new role of science was clearly recognized by Bohr, as is exemplified by the following quotation:

> While the theory of relativity reminds us of the subjective character of all physical phenomena, a character which depends essentially on the state of motion of the observer, so does the linkage of the atomic phenomena and their observation, · elucidated by the quantum theory, compel us to exercise a caution in the use of our expression similar to that necessary in psychological problems where we come upon the difficulty of demarcating the objective content. Hoping that I do not expose myself to the misunderstanding that it is my intention to introduce a mysticism which is incompatible with the spirit of modern science, I may perhaps in this connection remind you of the peculiar parallelism between the renewed discussion of the principle of causality and the discussion of a free will which has persisted from earliest times. Just as the freedom of the will is an experiential category of our psychic life, causality may be considered as a mode of perception by which we reduce our sense impressions to order. At the same time, however, we are concerned in both cases with idealizations whose natural limitations are open to investigation and which depend upon one another in the sense that the feeling of volition and the demand for causality are equally indispensable elements in the relation between subject and object which forms the core of the problem of knowledge.[62]

The central issue, however, around which the discoveries of modern science turn is that of the nature and place of the subject. And here the conslusions are very striking: 'the new situation in physics has ... forcibly reminded us of the old truth that we are both onlookers and actors in the great drama of existence.'[63]

Science and philosophy: implications of these ideas

We have been arguing that the problematics of both relativity theory and quantum mechanics can be characterized in terms of concepts developed within modern philosophy. Now this result is not of interest only for purely formal reasons; on the contrary, it seems to us that its consequences may be quite far-reaching. On the one hand the view we are proposing would renew the recognition of the prominent place played by science not only in philosophical discourse but also in the development of culture generally.

On the other hand it would open up not philosophy to science but science to philosophy. If science in fact works with the very ideas that have been extensively developed in contemporary philosophy then it must also be able to utilize the not inconsiderable achievements of the latter. If indeed this is the case then we have available an extensive, hitherto unrecognized, additional resource which might be brought to bear on outstanding dilemmas in the theory of nature. Modern philosophy, social theory and natural science have all produced insights of extraordinary depth and intensity. It is now conceivable that these insights can be mobilized mutually in a systematic way to facilitate further developments in each individual field.

Regarding quantum mechanics and the physics of subatomic phenomena in general it is our conviction that such an approach may be useful in the further consideration of several abiding, perplexing questions. The problems of logic in quantum theory, of the uncertainty relations, of completeness and hidden variables and of the quantum postulate itself can all receive some degree of clarification and perhaps illumination from the application of philosophical and sociological ideas. Further, it appears that the theory of elementary particles, which of all the contemporary scientific theories is perhaps the one most conspicuously in need of a clarification of its conceptual foundations, may also benefit from considerations of this kind; indeed in this last field of study it would be no small advance merely to identify what it is that the theory hoped to achieve.

No direct discussion of these issues will be entered into in the present essay, which has set itself the rather more limited task of demarcating problems and identifying potentially fruitful courses of investigation. Instead, a detailed study of quantum theory and elementary particle theory from the perspective indicated will have to be set aside for the intended extension of this project. In spite of this, two problems are of such importance and suggest themselves so forcefully from the foregoing discussion that it is impossible to avoid making specific reference to them here; these problems concern causality in quantum mechanics (and hence also the completeness of the quantum theory) and the relationship between relativity theory and quantum mechanics. Accordingly, to conclude this chapter a very brief description will be given of some of the issues involved in these two questions.

Quantum mechanics and relativity theory

To consider the latter problem first, it is widely recognized that considerable theoretical obstacles confront the project of reconciling the two great theories of contemporary physics. Certainly, it is not difficult to discern important conceptual differences which separate these theories as they are presently constituted. For example, the space-time geometry of non-relativistic quantum mechanics is Euclidean, in opposition to that of general relativity, which is of course Riemannian. Further, the working logic of general relativity is Boolean, whilst the propositional structure of quantum theory is non-classical. Quantum mechanics is a non-local and non-causal theory, in the sense that any reconstruction of it in terms of hidden variables must display these properties; in contrast, relativity theory is both local and causal. Finally, there is the problem of the observer. In the full theory, psi would be, quite literally, a wave function for the entire universe, embracing all possible observers and hence leaving no outside agency which could reduce this wave function. Yet quantum fluctuations of the space-time metric would occur. A quantum relativity would have to deal with the problem of the 'cosmic' observer.

We are here speaking of the possibility of a general relativistic quantum theory. However it must be understood that for the present, even a special relativistic quantum theory that is fully acceptable mathematically is lacking, owing to the presence of apparently unavoidable divergences in quantum field theory. This of course is in spite of the considerable progress that has been made, not least important of which was the very first step: the formulation of the Dirac equation in 1928.[64] Indeed, the very success of the latter was itself rather perplexing. For here, in consequence of what was essentially a straightforward application of the requirements of special relativity to Schrödinger's equation, there emerged results of extraordinary accuracy. Further, the additional fine structure terms that had been appended by Sommerfeld to account for the spectrum of hydrogen now appeared quite naturally within the theory. The source of the perplexity was just that all this was achieved in the absence of any convincing conceptual account of the unification!

Regarding the development of a quantum theory of gravity, in recent years much productive activity has occurred; this has been the case especially since the discovery in 1974 by S. W. Hawking of the radiative properties of rotating black holes.[65] At present, several major approaches to the problem of quantizing the gravita-

283

tional field are available. However, it appears that each of the programmes so far devised encounters impediments of a fundamental kind.[66] Two of the most important overall such perspectives that have been applied may be generally referred to as 'canonical' and 'covariant' quantizations. The canonical theories seek a Hamiltonian realization of Einstein's gravitational theory. This can be accomplished in several ways. For example, the isometry group of classical theory – the Galilean group – can be replaced by the Einstein group, which expresses the space-time symmetries of general relativity; thereby, with the help of Killing's equations, a preferred set of vector fields can be obtained. From these we may derive canonical position variables and hence also, through the use of Euler's equations, canonical momentum variables; the field and momentum variables are then required to obey certain conditions such as those imposed by the commutation relations. Under this approach there is the possibility of the choice of at least several pairs of variables depending on the particular problem being considered. In all cases however, the calculations become notoriously difficult owing to the non-linearity of the field equations. In addition, the appropriate interpretation of the quantum states derived remains controversial and indeed agreement is lacking regarding even how the observables are chosen; it seems that each of the various canonical approaches contains its own advantages and disadvantages in these respects.

The covariant approach is somewhat more formal than the canonical one: its objective, in fact, is to provide a formalism which is covariant – at least in the sense of Lorentz covariance. A set of calculation rules is devised which maintain unitarity, covariance and the handling of divergences. Such rules have proved helpful in the study of particle production and various other virtual and real processes. A number of techniques is available here, as well as a number of theoretical models to which they are applied. The main difficulties concern the rather intractable mathematical problems, especially those emerging from the persistence of singularities in the solutions of the field equations. Further, in this approach clarity is conspicuously absent regarding the conceptual aspect of these manipulations.

Indeed, it might be said that the main deficiency of all the quantization programmes so far developed is a conceptual one. What is more, this weakness may have contributed significantly to the fact that it has so far proved impossible to complete the unification process. In practically all cases, philosophical, or even merely 'conceptual', issues are given little attention – and where they are, it is often merely to provide a justification for results already established; it would perhaps not be unfair to characterize the 'many-worlds' theory of Everett, Graham, Wheeler and de Witt and the 'consciousness' theory of Wigner in this way.[67] This in fact brings us to the main points we would like to make in this connection. The brief references above to the quantization programme clearly do not provide any semblance of a survey of the field. We have omitted altogether reference to several important techniques and approaches, such as those deriving from Hawking's result referred to above, the theories of spinors and twistors, the 'already unified' theory, claimed to emerge from the geometrodynamics programme, and so on. Instead our comments are intended merely to show three things: that the unification of relativity theory and quantum mechanics involves exceedingly complex technical considerations; that at present the accomplishment of this unification is certainly far from having been completed; and that the conceptual issues at stake await a precise and clear characterization. It is in regard especially to this last point that the conclusions of the present essay may have something to offer.

In the history of science the major innovations have been directed by new philosophical insights rather than merely effective technical manipulations; indeed, it might be said that both Galileo and Einstein were philosophers first and employed mathematics only secondarily to give effect to their philosophical intuitions.[68] The reconciliation of quantum theory and relativity theory may well require an innovation if not of the same magnitude then at least of the same kind as the discoveries of these thinkers. We maintain that a plausible case exists that profound *conceptual* differences separate the two theories and that, accordingly, their unification – if it is at all possible – will presuppose a resolution of these differences.

The results established in this essay substantiate such a contention. Relativity theory represents the realization in the field of natural science of the theoretical problematic of phenomenology; quantum mechanics is the realization of the other problematic uncovered in the critique of objectivism – that of structuralism. The two theories are thus in fact conceptually quite distinct; they might even be said to inhabit different continents of thought.[69] Viewed from this perspective the reconciliation problem can be precisely characterized – at least in its 'conceptual' aspect: it is just the problem of establishing the relationship between two given problematics. Now it must be stated immediately that the solution to the question thus formulated is not yet properly understood; accordingly, the outcome of the problem cannot be anticipated. The two problematics may prove to be closely linked; or else it may emerge that they are in fact irreconcilable. This latter alternative in particular – as undesirable as it would be – cannot be discounted in advance of the close study of the issues at stake. It is possible that – at least in important respects – the propositional contents of the theories simply do not intersect; in this case the theories would be either wholly or partially incommensurable.

Now a result such as this would certainly offend our sense that 'nature' is a unified whole and that science 'represents' a single objective reality. But at the same time it must be conceded that we are familiar with – and accept – the existence in other areas of contiguous structures of thought, each of which is taken to bear a valid reference to reality, but which together do not admit of unification into a single totality. There are many examples of this, perhaps the most obvious of which are the common conceptions of the divisions (to which we have previously referred critically) between the natural and the human sciences, between the study of inanimate objects and the study of life, between the realm of facts and the realm of values. In certain scientific disciplines such oppositions also occur. For example, the various stages in the development of sexuality as described by Freud may be of this kind:[70] each stage may represent a particular disposition to the world which commands its own proper mode of description and which stands in no precisely delimitable relationship to either the preceding or the succeeding stage. Finally, the coexistence in the contemporary world of two opposing economic systems with widely differing and opposing self-conceptions may also be an example of the same phenomenon.

In brief then, to return to relativity theory and quantum mechanics, we are arguing that it is in principle possible that these two theories cannot in fact be completely reconciled. It may be the case that what they achieve is the application to the study of nature of two alternative but equally valid theoretical perspectives, with the outcome that they elucidate two quite different and separable aspects of its structure. If this is so then their overlap will only ever be partial, for truly fundamental reasons. This may be a fact we shall merely have to learn to accept.

But what of the formal programme of unification to which we referred above and which still appears to hold great promise? On this subject we shall make only three remarks. In the first place, if such a unification is conceptually possible then so also is the formal programme practicable. This will be the case whether the theories prove to be fully or - as seems most likely at the present time - only partially reconcilable. Secondly, where the formal unification exceeds the conceptual possibilities - if indeed it is possible to speak of such an event - then the outcome will be only formal; the results will remain without practical effect. There is no evidence to suggest that the two theories are contradictory; hence there is no a priori obstacle to the strictly mathematical project. However the decisive test of this project will lie in the new insights to which it gives rise. Finally, and most importantly, the distinction between the philosophical and the formal programmes is itself incomplete. Rather, conceptual determinations enter from the very beginning in the construction of a formal theory. One of the reasons for providing the description above of the canonical approach to the quantization of general relativity was just to illustrate this point. For the conceptual presuppositions of this apparently formal endeavour are here quite conspicuous: in the assumptions regarding the existence and structure of the isometry groups is contained a profound conception of the constitution of space and time; this conception both gives direction to the mathematical inquiry and contributes to the interpretation of the results. We conclude that even the formal programme has need of the philosophical determinations, which thus cannot be regarded as merely adscititious.

The resolution of the conceptual issues associated with the possible unification of modern physics, and hence the completion of this unification, must await the clarification of the strictly philocophical issues involved. Here, much remains to be accomplished. However as is evident from the discussions of the previous chapter, substantial insights have already been achieved which may well prove useful to the future development of science. Several philosophers - most notably Merleau-Ponty, Paul Ricoeur and their followers - have devoted themselves to profound reflections on the precise problem that is here at issue: the relationship between phenomenology and structuralism, or, equivalently, between speech and language. Some aspects of their provisional conclusions were referred to previously and these will not be recapitulated. Nor will any attempt be made to show how these results might be applied to physics - save for the perhaps suggestive remark that Ricoeur's proposal seems to resemble a hypothesis of a 'complementarity' between the two perspectives. The important point here is twofold: that the relationship between relativity theory and quantum mechanics may well be thinkable as the familiar problem of the relationship between speech and language; and that, while non-negligible philosophical resources have been established to deal with this issue, the problems nevertheless remain open.

To close these brief comments regarding the problem of the unification of the two major theories of modern physics, we should just like to state once more the overall conclusion. The theory of nature cannot be considered in isolation from the great social and philosophical issues of the times. The formal apparatus may well be productive, through its own internal mechanisms, of new results; however even this depends on the conceptual structure of the theory, both for its immediate direction and its interpretation. The development of our understanding of nature may well be facilitated by a reconsideration of some of the dilemmas of science in the light of contemporary social and philosophical thought.

Completeness and causality

Regarding the questions of causality and completeness in quantum mechanics, our comments will be much briefer still, with a full account being postponed for a later essay. This brevity is not suggestive of the lesser importance of these issues; on the contrary it indicates that they are simply too important to leave out altogether.

The debate about completeness derives from an objection to quantum mechanics raised in a celebrated paper by Einstein, Podolsky and Rosen published in 1935.[71] Bohr's personal reply was published soon after,[72] to be joined later still by comments from many other of the most eminent scientists of the day. This debate – which must surely rate as one of the greatest debates in the history of science – was subsequently expanded to cover the problems of causality in physics, hidden variables in quantum mechanics and many other issues that we have already touched upon, concerning ontology, epistemology and the aims of science. These questions and the discussion itself are now the subject of a vast – and still growing – literature. In what follows, this literature will not be described and both the background to the debate and the main contributions of Einstein and Bohr will be assumed; for as we have indicated our purpose is merely to state a few conclusions in order to indicate how these considerations might be regarded from the perspective established in the foregoing chapters.

In the first place, it must be emphasized once more that the views stated personally by Einstein cannot be identified with the philosophical outcomes of relativity theory. Thus the debate cannot be understood, as is sometimes suggested, as a confrontation between the two theories. Rather, it seems to us that Einstein in these discussions was putting a view that was somewhat closer to objectivism than it was to phenomenology. Hence a difference in principle does in fact exist between the two main protagonists – a difference which we have previously attempted to characterize under the rubric of ontology[73] and to which we could add a further difference embracing epistemology. Thus Einstein and Bohr were indeed at cross-purposes and the real problem with the debate is not to decide who is right but rather to determine how the two points of view might be compared at all.

Secondly, the two notions of completeness employed in the discussion should also be carefully distinguished, for they identify two different conceptions of physical reality and of the aims of science. The view put by Einstein was simply that a theory is complete if 'every element of the physical reality (has) a counterpart in the physical theory'.[74] Opposing this, Bohr elaborated once again the viewpoint of complementarity and its associated analysis of the process of measurement. His conclusion, familiar to us, was that from the quantum perspective 'we are not dealing with an incomplete description ... but with a rational discrimination between essentially different experimental arrangements and procedures'.[75] The point to be made here concerns science itself. Einstein was convinced that our knowledge of nature could be subsumed under a single theoretical perspective; science in principle could be unified in the sense that all its propositions could be expressed in terms provided by a single problematic. This is a view with which Bohr disagreed. For him the completeness of science was established at a higher level, which may well accommodate different perspectives; 'we must ... be prepared to accept,' he argued, '... that a complete elucidation of one and the same object may require diverse points of view which defy a unique description.'[76] Thus whereas Einstein sought a unified theory of phenomena Bohr in effect denied its possibility in principle. In his view reality was more heterogeneous, and perhaps more intractable, than Einstein would allow.

The third point here concerns causality. In a previous chapter we have mentioned Einstein's – and relativity theory's – commitment to the classical idea of causality. Bohr repeatedly emphasized that this conception could not be sustained in quantum mechanics. Indeed, he believed that the renunciation of causality was a necessary consequence of the new theory, precipitated principally by the uncertainty relations.[77] Einstein of course disputed the abandonment of causal determinism, once again considering this result to be a symptom of the incompleteness of quantum mechanics.[78] Others took the same view and accordingly, attempted to restore the role of causality by elaborating theories of so-called 'hidden variables'. In 1932, however, hidden variable theories obeying certain apparently natural conditions were excluded by a now famous theorem of Von Neumann,[79] which thus further substantiated Bohr's point of view. Von Neumann himself considered it proven that 'quantum mechanics is in compelling logical contradiction with causality', adding that in any case there was at present 'no occasion and no reason to speak of causality in nature'.[80]

The need to abandon the classical concept of causality in quantum mechanics is now widely, but by no means universally,[81] accepted amongst physicists. Nevertheless the issues raised by Bohr regarding causality do not seem even now to have been properly clarified. In this context, the purpose of the present comments is precisely to suggest that quantum mechanics does indeed have available to it a coherent conception of causality and that this conception, furthermore, is consistent with the problematic of structuralism; in addition, we seek to make plausible the proposal that Bohr's own writings on this subject are once again themselves consistent with these ideas. As previously, results only will be offered here; both theoretical arguments and mathematical formulations will be omitted.

The causality assumed in Newtonian physics was a mechanistic causality. Essentially a transitive relation between phenomena, it presupposed the possibility of an exhaustive and deterministic description of the future course of a system given its initial conditions. According to Bohr this mechanistic causality can no longer be upheld, for 'in the region of atomic physics there appear new uniformities which cannot be fitted into the frame of the ordinary causal description'.[82] This 'renunciation of the ideal of causality' which has been forced upon us 'is founded logically only on our not being any longer in a position to speak of the autonomous behaviour of a physical object, due to the unavoidable interaction between the object and the measuring instruments which in principle cannot be taken into account, if these instruments according to their purpose shall allow the unambiguous use of the concepts necessary for the description of experience.'[83]

In Bohr's view the measuring apparatus and the observed object must be regarded as a single, indivisible system.[84] This indivisibility is to be taken literally: the entire object-apparatus unity is incapable of being analysed, even conceptually, into more elementary parts. Hence individual effects, such as fluctuations in measurements for example, cannot be traced to causal factors occurring in a single part, such as the measuring instrument, since the latter no longer has recognition as a separate entity. In this circumstance it does not follow that phenomena occur only randomly, independently of the whole; the possibilities of pattern and prediction show this. Rather, the determinations are of a new kind; they are, in brief, of the elements of the whole by the structure of the whole.

The problem of causality in quantum mechanics thus is different from that in either objectivism or phenomenology; nevertheless it can be stated precisely: it is just the problem of the mode of presence of the structure in its effects. The divergence from classical causality is now not difficult to explain. In quantum mechanics the effects are not entities bearing an independent reality, external to the structured whole. They are not pre-existing objects on which the structure arrives to imprint its mark. Rather, the phenomena themselves exist only insofar as they obtain a specific location in relation to the whole, while conversely the apparatus-object totality can be said to exist only insofar as it is productive of phenomena.[85] The causal problem in quantum theory is to describe, within the constraints of the uncertainty principle, the complex relationship between a series of phenomena and their constitutive whole.

Expressed thus, the affinity of the problem of causality in quantum theory to that of structuralism is easy to discern. We shall not go so far as to claim that Bohr's solution - the viewpoint of complementarity - can be explained in terms of the structuralist concepts of displacement, condensation and overdetermination. However the problem is the same and is clearly distinguishable from the classical one. What is more, from the formulations above it should be clear that the conception of complementarity provides at least a plausible solution, for it gives an account of the appearance of different sub-classes of phenomena in such a way as to elucidate their mutual dependence on the whole, without compromising their pairwise non-commutativity. Thus, in conclusion, both the problem of causality in quantum mechanics and Bohr's proposed solution are intelligible in structuralist terms. The arguments that he has used to suggest this here have of course been purely qualitative. It seems however that it would not be impossible to express the entire problem mathematically; such an endeavour may help provide a useful assessment of the statistical interpretation of quantum mechanics and the hidden variables problem.[86]

Fourthly and finally, a brief comment on the continuing controversy over Bell's theorem.[87] We shall confine ourselves to a few short remarks. First, it seems to us that there are open questions here and that these questions are of pre-eminent importance. At the present time it is impossible to state definitively just what should be accepted as the outcome of Bell's result. The implications of his assumptions are not altogether clear (and nor, it might be added, are those of Wigner, whose argument is in fact not identical to Bell's). Further, theories can be devised, consistent with the theorem, which preserve the notions of locality, of hidden variables, of Bohr's relational interpretation of quantum mechanics and so on. The debate about the locality assumption is especially interesting in the present context, in view of the above comments regarding causality; it may be that a concept of a structural causality, or perhaps of a quantum potential operating in a space-time characterized by the property of 'unbroken wholeness', obviates the need for such an assumption. Although firm conclusions cannot be drawn it can nevertheless be said that Bell's result appears to be not inconsistent with an anti-objectivist position. If this is the case it will be hardly surprising from the point of view of the present essay; indeed, the somewhat stronger implication claimed for the theorem – that quantum mechanics is actually in contradiction to objectivism – would even be expected from the foregoing considerations. Here however, one last cautionary point must be made. In the discussion of Bell's theorem it has often been assumed that epistemological precepts are susceptible to empirical confirmation or refutation. This assumption however is false. Experiments cannot test epistemologies; they cannot test what will count as true. The value of Bell's result lies not in its exposure of an underlying epistemological disposition to experimental falsification but simply in its statements concerning particular entities whose existence is predicted by a theory which proposes certain specific hypotheses; the empirical results then reflect either on the existence of these entities or on the procedures according to which their properties were calculated.[88]

V
Introduction to the sociology of objectivity

Introduction to the theory of object domains

Science is concerned with the theory of nature. For many years this apparently simple proposition was widely accepted as absolutely straightforward and unproblematic. To be sure, in some quarters doubts lingered on about the real validity of the claims of science. However it was only with the elaboration of the critique of objectivism that the true complexity of the scientific enterprise began to be fully appreciated. For this critique exposed in detail the presuppositions on which the classical study of nature was based. It showed the degree to which the theoretical penetration of natural phenomena was subject to variation. Indeed, it demonstrated that even the most fundamental concepts, 'science', 'theory' and 'nature' itself, could not be limited to unequivocal meanings. Within the theoretical corpus to which the name 'natural science' could legitimately be attached, the intellectual apparatus, the criteria of truth and even the objects themselves were subject to continual modification or on occasions, to radical transformations.

Hitherto in this essay the critique of objectivism and its application to contemporary science have been examined. In the course of this discussion several results have emerged. In the first place, at the beginning, in our early review of the sociology of science, a number of aspects of the relationship between society and science were elucidated, along with the identification of many outstanding issues. In particular, we observed that from its very inception modern science has been inextricably intertwined with social and cultural themes, which circumscribe not only the direction of research but even its meaning and truth. We witnessed some aspects of the early, implicit critiques of objectivism and raised the question of whether a non-objectivist theory of nature could be possible. We considered some issues regarding the structure of science and asked whether a relationship could be defined between this dimension and that of meaning. We suggested that the question should be considered of how a social theory of science might be possible at all.

In subsequent chapters we pursued these problems more or less directly. Our study of Husserl's philosophy revealed some further major features of the structure of science; in addition, it brought to light a curious dichotomy in the attack on objectivism. Subsequent to this, in our discussion and development of the Marxian theory of fetishism, our attention was directed to the question of a possible relationship between objectivism and the social forms of capitalism. This investigation made possible the formulation of some tentative hypotheses regarding the role of social variables within domains of objectivity in general. Furthermore, some conclusions regarding the broad relationship between the study of nature and extant theoretical structures could be drawn. On the basis of these results we were able to analyse two of the major theories of contemporary physics with perhaps surprising results: in opposition to the usual interpretations, we found that these theories lie within contending philosophical frameworks, each of which realized its own distinctive – and efficacious – critique of objectivism.

The fifth part of this essay seeks to make use of these results in order to return to the specifically sociological questions that we introduced at the outset. Here, the overall task can be easily described: we must seek to lay the basis for a theory which might render accessible the problem of the interdependence of the historically contingent variables of a social formation and the contemporaneous forms of scientific knowledge. Now from what has been said previously it will be clear that it is the view taken in this essay that a promising region in which to search for this social mediation of science is that occupied by the theoretical problematics applied in the study of natural phenomena. These problematics, as we have seen at length, incorporate simultaneously metaphysical presuppositions and criteria for the assessment of meaning and validity. They circumscribe broadly the theoretical structures of scientific bodies of knowledge. At the same time, they depend for their acceptance on the processes of social discourse according to which at a given moment the conceptions of truth and sense are fixed. In other words, problematics are intersubjectively variable entities which place definable limits on contemporary scientific thought.

Problematics in general, and the specific problematics of modern science, are certainly susceptible to theoretical investigation. However for many reasons, including some which will be apparent already and others to be explained below, it is both more convenient and more fruitful to concentrate instead on regions of objectivity. Every problematic is associated with a particular object domain, while conversely every domain of objects presupposes in its constitution an epistemology and a metaphysics. Furthermore, it is clear that a given conception of objectivity is explicitly dependent on intersubjective variables and that at the same time any science – self-evidently – is limited by the set of objects it sets out to theorize. Thus all the questions we seek to ask regarding problematics, science and society can be asked still when 'problematics' are replaced by 'object domains'. Indeed, these questions – as we shall see – can be asked both more directly and more concretely.

For the last part of this essay then, we turn to the investigation of some problems which might contribute to the development of what could be called a 'sociology of objectivity'. As we shall argue at length in the following chapter it is our contention that such a theory is the proper locus for a social theory of science. This theory would have to direct itself to the many, perplexing problems that have been raised in the course of our discussions. For example, it must consider the question of the origin of specific object domains. If it is true that the objects of science are contingent, then where do they come from, and how are they formed? Furthermore, what role, if any, have the social and historical variables played in the rich process of development and change that has marked its history? And reciprocally: whence derives the capacity that is asserted for science to make claims in respect of questions of social and philosophical interest? These questions, together with many others, are among the legitimate issues with which a sociology of objectivity would be concerned. Answers to them, however tentative, may advance the search for a clarification of the intimate links binding science and society.

Before passing directly, however, to a consideration of these and related problems it is necessary to engage in some further preliminary reflections. These reflections will concern the nature and structure of object domains and their role in science in general. The results will be required for the sequel. However they will be also in themselves of intrinsic interest; what is more, they will permit us to consider briefly some formal issues regarding science and theory which were raised at an earlier stage.

In summary, then, the concluding part of this essay will seek to lay the basis for a more detailed account of the structure of science, at least in respect of that aspect of science within which the social variables may be active. Subsequently, it will attempt to provide some adumbrations of the direction in which the yet to be realized social theory of science might move. Science and society may interact reciprocally: the social phenomena may penetrate the scientific forms and influence their development, while at the same time, science, by virtue of its capacity to express meanings, may enter social life and predominate there with its own concepts. It is to the clarification of these manifold and complex issues that we seek to address ourselves.

Having said all this however, it is appropriate to add some words of circumspection. In the understanding of science and of its place in society the development of the proposed theory would certainly be of the utmost importance. However, as we have maintained consistently, the present work makes no pretensions for providing such a theory in its entirety. In particular, it is not our objective to elaborate a detailed account of the structure of science. Such an endeavour would pass well beyond the limits we have set for our project; what is more, it refers to a region that has been extensively studied elsewhere. It is not even our aim to provide a complete outline of the projected sociology of objectivity; indeed, it appears that for the present no such outline is possible. Rather, our purpose is no more than to make a preliminary attempt to delimit an object domain on which future work might proceed; in this context it will be possible to establish some first orientations and elementary clarifications and to raise some fruitful, related questions for consideration. This is a point which we have emphasized at some length previously; we mention it once more here because it is important to appreciate that both the substantiation and the detailed explication of the themes of this essay are dependent upon the future development of its principal consequences.

With these issues clear we proceed to clarify more precisely the problems to be addressed. Here, as previously, phenomenology provides a convenient point of departure.

Phenomenology and the problem of a social theory of science

Husserl's theory, as we saw, offered one possible response to the crisis of science. Within it, natural science was no longer understood as merely an elegant collection of techniques or a site of arbitrary theoretical manipulations. Instead, it was now recognized to contain genuine meanings, arising from the social praxis of human subjects – meanings long suppressed, to be sure, but nevertheless still capable of reactivation for the guidance of future investigations. It was in the later works of Husserl that the formulations most fruitful for social theory occurred. Here two of the major problems to be faced by Husserl's philosophy came together. The first, on which we have dwelt at length, concerned the dual character of the theory of nature – its character, that is, as a systematically structured unity subject nevertheless to historical flux. The other was the need to provide through its metatheory an account of the theoretical foundations that would enable it to be realized as authentic science. In our earlier discussions we rejected as not entirely satisfactory Husserl's efforts to solve these problems. We shall not attempt to repeat here our previous arguments. Instead, we shall merely mention again one aspect of Husserl's proposed solution which contains, symptomatically, many of the latter's major problems. One of the principal functions of the concept of the lifeworld in *The Crisis of European Sciences* was just to provide a firm foundation on which reliable, incontestable knowledge could be established; it was to accomplish this, at least partly, by encompassing at once both the structural and the phenomenological moments to which we have adverted. However as we saw previously this concept was from the outset incapable of concealing the heterogeneous origins it was supposed to reconcile. For in the light of the fact of linguistic communication Husserl was compelled to accept the existence in the lifeworld of irreducible cultural accomplishments. But this meant that the most fundamental tenet of phenomenology could no longer be upheld without modification. Phenomenological theory had begun with the concept of individual subjectivity as the ultimate source and centre of all meaning. However, one of its own outcomes was the diminution of the role of subjectivity in the process of knowledge – or, at least, its displacement in favour of intersubjectivity and sociality.

This of course was exactly the result at which we arrived from our examination of the implicit dualism that emerged in Husserl's thought. The opposition between 'historicity' and 'unity' was found to be no less than the abiding index in phenomenology of the unresolved classical dilemma between the contending problematics of subject and system. This problem in Husserl's account asserted itself again and again. As we saw previously in detail, within his work not only the meaning of science but even the notion of objectivity on which this meaning depends were given simultaneously two different formulations: science was either the appropriation and achievement of an individual subject or it was the effect of a determinate theoretical system; objectivity was either a diminished, shared form of subjectivity or it was a precondition for theory built into the structure of linguistic communication.

All this was described above in detail, where we followed also its repercussions and its consequences. The dichotomy in Husserl's thought issues in a dual conception of objectivity, a dual epistemology and a dual critique of objectivism. Whereas Husserl in his work sought specifically to demonstrate the particular efficacy of phenomenology for the dismantling of science's objectivistic selfmisunderstanding, he succeeded instead in producing two distinct – although not necessarily independent – refutations; furthermore this bifurcation is irreducible. Indeed, as we have seen at length each of these critiques has found a realization in a contemporary scientific theory. Here then is an extraordinary result which emerges from the phenomenological theory of science: the reformulation of science as a meaningful unity not only refutes objectivism but at the same time draws out its extreme consequences – a theoretical bifurcation which must henceforth be taken into account not only within the metacontext of scientific interpretation but also immanently within the scientific interpretation of nature itself.

Husserl of course did not explicitly draw these conclusions. On the contrary, it is clear from his work that he regarded objectivism as rooted not in the scientific theories themselves – that is, not in their formal apparatus – but in their philosophical and cultural apprehension instead; we could say, therefore, to use the analogy with language to which we referred earlier, that for him the advent of objectivism occurs in the domain not of syntax but of semantics. In fact, Husserl's admiration for the achievements of science – and even for its methods and objectives – are repeatedly made clear. Thus the crisis of science is paradoxical, precisely because it is contemporaneous with – and perhaps even an effect of – science's most spectacular successes. The plausibility of this view however is undermined by several immediate, severe problems. For in the first place this approach presupposes the isolation within science of disparate dimensions of form and of meaning. Further, since in this account the latter is clearly distinguishable both from its testing procedures and from its potential technical applications, within it there must be assumed a radical separation between form and meaning and the practical context within which the practitioners work. In other words Husserl's theory presupposes a mutual disjunction in science of syntax, semantics and pragmatics. But then the problem arises of the relationships between the three components. Thus we have a series of questions which emerge naturally from this aspect of the phenomenological theory of science. We must ask, for example: whence derive the rules that guide the behaviour of the scientists who, working within a well-defined community, make the decisions not only about formal procedures but also about the truth or falsity of propositions? Are the rules of discourse of the scientific community developed independently of either the formal imperatives of science or its contemporary meaning? Is it conceivable that the objectivistic misunderstanding of science which has so compromised its philosophical and cultural interpretations would leave unscathed the actual technical productions derived within this milieu? Indeed, just what are the sources of objectivism? Do they lie in society, do they lie in a quirk of philosophical reflection, or do they lie elsewhere? In particular, what is the actual role here of science itself: is it the culprit or the victim?

Of course, to a certain extent some of these questions have been pursued already – in particular, in relation to our discussions concerning phenomenology. We noted then that even in the self-conception of phenomenology true science was at once both methodical and founded. This was so in spite of its claims that the methods of natural science and philosophy differed radically and that the foundations of the former could be secured only by way of the latter. For both, scientificity was guaranteed only by the fulfilment of conditions imposed simultaneously in both its syntactical and semantic dimensions. Nevertheless, at the same time, in the attempt to secure the foundation of science phenomenology sought not to justify a continuity between phenomenon and concept but rather to discover the human presuppositions of both. Thus the thing itself became intelligible within phenomenology only insofar as it was constituted – that is to say, only insofar as it acquired a meaning for a subject, and thereby for all subjects. Hence in the objective world was presupposed the intersubjective constitution of nature. In this sense, within the phenomenological purview the thing was understood as just the insertion of matter into the intersubjective matrix, which therefore was to become the proper focus of science in general.

However, even these advanced formulations, which we extracted earlier from the work of the later Husserl, are partial. For in their shift of emphasis to the 'semantic' and 'pragmatic' dimensions they ignore all reference to the characteristic formal structure of science; more precisely, they ignore the inner imperatives to which specific scientific theories are subject anterior to either philosophical interpretation or experimental verification. Of course, Husserl was acutely aware of these formal structures and in fact, as we saw, analysed them closely. Nevertheless in his discussions the question was never raised – or indeed, even considered indirectly – of the inherent expressive potential of such structures. That alternative theoretical perspectives within mathematical science might enforce qualitatively different philosophical contents was not even suggested. What was important was not so much the substance of the continuity between theory and life but the mere recognition of the existence of such a continuity.

However the formal structure of science is *not* innocent, as we concluded at the very beginning of this essay, from our study of *Dialectic of Enlightenment* and other works. Rather, the stigma of scientific thought is universal: it can be traced in the social processes, in the shape of the perceptual world, in philosophy and in culture. In fact, so potent and virulent is its influence that even the context within which the meaning of science is interpreted falls under its sway, seriously compromising the historical search for alternatives. Science today circumscribes its own meaning. By perfusing its metacontext in the way described it closes the circle of critical reflection. This is, of course, the elementary outcome of objectivism. By abolishing the reflexivity immanent in communicative discourse objectivism isolates science from its own insights; the closing of the circle turns science into an ideology.

From phenomenology therefore (together, in this case, with critical theory), there issues a second series of questions regarding the relationship between science and social theory. In addition to the questions formulated previously we must ask: What is the discursive site of science's epistemological biases? Where, within its philosophical and formal apparatus are the social variables efficacious? To what extent are the philosophical and social outcomes an effect of science's characteristic formal structure? Is science committed to certain ontological precepts by virtue alone of its syntactical forms? Indeed: how in principle can a theory address a social project?

It is on the basis of these two series of questions that we intend to proceed in the present and following chapters. As we said above, we are not pretending to offer conclusive solutions to these great problems. Rather, our objective will be satisfied if we succeed in achieving no more than a satisfactory formulation of the issues at stake and an adumbration of some possible fruitful lines of research. To this end, before considering the general problem of objectivity, we pass to a more detailed examination of the concept of object domain, to which we have so often had recourse.

The concept of object domain

The simplest possible interpretation of the expression 'object domain' is in fact strictly correct: an object domain of a theory is just the set of objects that make up the domain of the theory, this theory being considered as a conventional function between two sets. It is immediately evident, however, that this supposed simplicity is only apparent. For as we have repeatedly stressed, it is precisely the objects themselves that are in question. We have been seeking to discover how to characterize the objects with which a given theory is concerned and just how it is that these objects are formed within a given conceptual environment. Thus the domains to which we are referring must be regarded as the loci in which specific classes of objects crystallize and hence the entities towards which further analysis must be directed.

In the course of our discussions we have come across a variety of object domains. We have had occasion to consider, for example, the object domains of classical physics, of relativity theory and of quantum mechanics. In a broader context, we have examined the object domains of objectivism, phenomenology and structuralism. However it must be understood that every coherent body of knowledge has its own characteristic domain of objects. There is an object domain specific to geology, for instance, or to botany or to pure mathematics; similarly with contemporary zoology, physiology or physical geography. On the other hand, where a discipline is subject to theoretical variability at a deep level, no unique object domain can be identified. Thus each of philosophy, psychology and, of course, physics in general has associated with it not one but a number of classes of objects, not all of which are consistent – or even, for that matter, commensurable. This complexity in the formulation and elaboration of object domains implies problems to which we have in fact previously made explicit reference. In addition to the question of the origin of these domains, it is necessary to clarify the relationship between a specific such entity and the epistemology to which its accompanying theory is committed. Furthermore, this process of explication must also provide an understanding of the theoretical transformations associated with variation of object domains and, in particular, of the relationship in which they stand to the social and cultural configuration.

The investigation of object domains however must start with the acceptance of a number of simple propositions. In an important sense a class of objects logically precedes the theory which explicates it. Such objects presuppose an organization of experience that is both a priori and prior to science. In this organization of experience systems of concepts are incorporated which are capable of being formulated into stable, intersubjectively invariant entities. From the very beginning, that is, there are, immanently implied in any object domain, variables which are dependent at least on verification within the mode of intersubjectivity. This is an important point, for it means that, although object domains logically precede the theories that are articulated on them, their advent nevertheless is necessarily posterior to more general processes of concept formation; in particular, they depend upon the shaping of questions and possible answers in relation to socially specific and historically variable discursive practices. It follows therefore that these domains are not themselves problematics.[1] However they do arise within problematics; accordingly, it is not surprising that a given set of objects displays a unified and distinctive style.[2]

Here at once a number of important problems suggest themselves. The first we mention only in passing; it is the question of the method of exposition appropriate to the proposed theory. At first sight it appears that the entire endeavour is embroiled in a fatal circularity. For it would seem that an account of the object domains in science would have to presuppose a general theory of objectivity – and indeed intersubjectivity – while conversely the latter could not advance without the prior development of a theory of object domains. Our only comment on this issue here is that in practice such a circularity does not present a problem, for it is of a familiar type frequently encountered in interpretive contexts. It is now widely recognized that processes of exposition in general are subject to difficulties that can be precisely formulated. In particular, as pointed out by Ast and Schleiermacher, and later emphasized by Dilthey and others, they are subject to a 'hermeneutic circle': the whole acquires its definition from its parts, whereas conversely, the parts cannot be understood except in relation to the whole.[3] In such circumstances the development of a theory itself must proceed hermeneutically, the questions and answers which it addresses unfolding together out of an evolving context. We shall not pursue this issue here; instead we shall merely proceed on the assumption that an effective account will be attained at the conclusion of the argument.

On the other hand a detailed account of the motivating circumstances, and so also, implicitly, the potential efficacy of the approach we are following – which may also be at issue – can be provided. Most generally: our objective, of course, is to contribute to the development of a theory of natural science that would render apprehensible both its philosophical content and its social determinations. To this end we have chosen to apply our focus to the classes of objects with which different sciences deal. The immediate reasons for this are simple. Objects are what scientists actually treat in their practice of science. In fact, in times of qualitative scientific change one of the crucial issues is invariably the question of the proper domain on which the emerging theory should be defined. Further, being entities embracing (as we have said) both material and categorial components, the specification of a class of objects, together with a description of the methodological apparatus, is sufficient to identify a science. Indeed, the isolation of object domains in this way also permits an examination of the relationship between philosophy and scientific method – a major issue, as we shall see.

For the purposes of this essay however object domains are important for an overwhelming reason: within them our two principal concerns come together in a fundamental unity. On the one hand, the forms of objectivity of a science contain its social moment, as is suggested by the mere juxtaposition of the term to its commonly assumed opposite, 'subjectivity'. This is a central question and one on which we shall focus in detail later, where we shall argue that it is exactly on this issue that a sociology of science should focus. Some intimations of this conclusion have already been given: the discussion of Husserl, for example, revealed in his theory of science irreducible presuppositions concerning intersubjectivity and discourse; and the interpretation of the Marxian theory of fetishism explicitly presented objectivism as a social construct. In the next chapter these discussions will be elaborated in detail and some reference will be made also to the theory of truth proposed by Habermas, which is of the utmost interest in this respect. On the other hand, the meaning-content of a science – the philosophical perspective it expresses – is also contained substantially in the domain of objects on which the science operates. For as was noted above, an object domain presupposes a problematic, which defines the theoretical unity within which its key categories are inscribed. It is this problematic, which can in large part be inferred from an examination of the objectivities, that constitutes the philosophical disposition of a body of theory. In fact, it is only in the context of this theoretical field that scientific formulations can acquire an intersubjective validity and so be assessed as propositions.

But if this is the case then why discuss object domains and not the problematics themselves? The first reason for this has already been given: objects are the raw material with which scientists actually work and hence are generally well-characterized; the corresponding problematic, by contrast, is invariably hidden and more often than not its existence is even denied altogether. In fact, to expose the problematic and to elucidate its details is a complex and arduous work of theory. In addition to this reason of accessibility is a reason concerning the fineness of distinctions. The class of objects treated by science can vary both within and between specific disciplines; this variation may or may not involve differences in the elementary philosophical outlook. For example, within the general scope of objectivism are included many, widely differing sciences. Thus the concept of problematic is too crude to characterize a given theory adequately.

In this context it may be mentioned in passing that the approach that is here being adopted of examining the object domains of science in their embeddedness within larger, more comprehensive theoretical formations seems preferable to alternative schemata usually adopted within the theory of science. Certainly, it is consistent with the major insights that have been discussed above – in particular, with the conclusions that the objects of a theory are always already theory-laden and that science itself progresses through sequences of transformations between theoretical unities.[4] Commonly, these phenomena are incorporated into theories employing rather vague and indistinct concepts such as 'framework' or 'paradigm'.[5] In contrast, both 'object domain' and 'problematic' can be rigorously delimited and furthermore, as we have just pointed out, variations between sciences can be recognized without compromising the possibility of an abiding background perspective. For out of these two kinds of unities it cannot be presupposed at any given time which is of greater importance. In addition, the strategy employed here permits useful insights into the social component of scientific thought. In contrast to the notion of 'paradigm', which – as we saw – can proceed no further than an arbitrary, postulated 'consensus' obtaining within a putative 'community of scientists', the examination of object domains draws the focus directly to the intersubjective processes in terms of which science is constituted. As the natural locus of the intersection of the social processes within science, the field of objects subsists in relation to a larger context which is itself not self-evidently social in character. Indeed, different problematics in general appear rather to represent theoretical conditions of possibility which can be mobilized in relation to certain objective formations on the basis of possible social and historical contingencies. Such a conception of science thus admits an immanent relation to social life without denying the existence of a more extensive theoretical ambient that cannot be so characterized.

An additional argument in favour of the proposed strategy takes us immediately to an issue at the very heart of the current perplexity regarding science. It is a consequence of what was said above that an object domain is embedded in the matrix of social meanings from which it is thus strictly inseparable. Indeed it is precisely this conceptual environment that endows objects with a potential place and value. Thus once again a basic distinction must be recognized between objectivity and truth: the latter congeals at the interface of the social relations and discursive media of a society, whereas the former emerges heteronomously, by processes that we will examine later, within the object domains. Nevertheless it remains fundamental that any system of objects always bears an irreducible, immanent relation to that zone within which meanings and truth values are conceivable. This then is the problem. Every object domain carries within it an abiding tension between truth and objectivity which must be recognized in any theory of scientific knowledge. Such a theory must be able to accommodate the variability of the perspectives in the study of nature and thus the accompanying variability of both objects and propositional truths, while preserving the integrity of the concept of truth itself. That is, it must be capable of admitting the prodigious heterogeneity of science without compromising the continuous commitment of the latter to a single, unifying process directed towards the elucidation of truth.[6]

It is our contention that this result can be readily accommodated within the approach we are adopting. Indeed, it has been implicitly assumed in our arguments ever since our first contact with the problem in question in the discussion in Chapter 4 of Husserl's analysis of science in *Formal and Transcendental Logic*. Furthermore, the circumstances leading to the apparent dilemma are, from this perspective, susceptible to further analysis.

Thus we are able to see that within domains of objects there is effected an organization of experience into systematic unities that are capable of obtaining intersubjective validity. These domains are themselves not necessarily justifiable according to some rigorous argument seeking proofs. However they do acquire acceptance and can be utilized to reveal further continuities and discontinuities in the world of facts – that is, in the material world as it is rendered in discourse. Thus these regions of objects incorporate an immanent reference to action, although the details of the form of this action cannot in advance be specified with precision. Furthermore, insofar as objectivities represent stable structures of experience and action, they also represent domains within which the meanings of certain actions or types of action are stabilized. Now the categories that are applied in the determination of the objective forms are not adopted gratuitously: on the contrary, they are, as we have seen, systematically structured within a problematic which prescribes also the forms of legitimate problems and of their solutions, together with what have been referred to as 'conditions of validity'. In fact, this problematic defines the epistemology within which the classes of objects are inserted.

Herein lies a major result. The problematics accessible to science are, as we saw earlier, inscribed within a constant metaphysics. However at the same time they provide for science a substantial epistemological variation. This means that the object domains of a science, and through them the science itself, stand in a relation not just to action and to meaning – as described – but also to truth. This must be accepted; nevertheless it is important to recognize immediately in addition that this does not imply that thereby, either through the object domain or its related epistemology, truth as such is actually determined. Rather, a problematic supplies no more than the conditions according to which a proposition can be judged to be meaningful. This is consistent with what has been said above: the categories associated with a given epistemology contribute to an organization of experience and a concomitant stabilization of meaning structures within which discourse may occur that is directed towards the attainment of truth. Such discourse is subject to processes of argumentation that transcend any particular epistemology – and indeed may well be presupposed as conditions of possibility in *all* epistemologies. This point will be elaborated somewhat in our discussion of Habermas below. Here what is important is a dual result: truth is established according to transcendental conditions underlying exchanges within discourse, while conversely, actual discursive processes depend not merely upon practical but also on theoretical circumstances. There can be no discourse that is absolutely free of presuppositions. All propositions, before their truth-value can be considered, must be subject to criteria of meaningfulness that are embedded within the larger unity of a problematic. In this sense the latter supplies a priori conditions of validity – largely realized through the delimitation of its object domains – yet leaves intact the concept of truth itself.

It may be remarked that this state of affairs applies to differing epistemologies in general. A 'theory of knowledge' can neither extend nor curtail the processes of argumentation on which even its own formulations depend. However it can certainly specify the legitimate conditions under which such processes can be realized. This is precisely the nature of the conditions of validity – rather than criteria of truth in the strict sense – with which a given epistemology is associated. Furthermore, where actual conflicts occur concerning the truth-values of particular propositions it is to sources such as these that they can generally be traced. Thus, for example, a statement that is properly constituted and fully intelligible within a dialectical or phenomenological world-view may be anathema to a logical positivist.

Meaning and truth

To return now specifically to science, it must be said immediately that the one conspicuous exception to the circumstance just described is to be found in mathematics. For both the objects of mathematics and its methods are essentially formal and conventional – subject of course to several abiding, universal (and not always uncontroversial) principles. Certainly, there have been several major philosophical debates in the recent history of mathematics, to which we shall have occasion to refer presently; nevertheless, insofar as that part of mathematics of relevance to natural science is concerned it may be considered to be applicable to a range of object domains consistent with a variety of epistemological perspectives. In other words, the objects of a theory that incorporates mathematical techniques into its syntactical apparatus are not thereby determined univocally (though this does not of course deny that restrictive conditions of some kind might nevertheless be implied).

That this is the case follows from the fact that the productions of mathematics are formal theoretical structures that are in themselves devoid of meaning, which arises only in intersubjective contexts. It is for this reason that the 'truth' of a mathematical statement diverges from, for example, the truth of a statement uttered in a conversation between two people. The latter of course depends for its value on the field of social meanings; by contrast, the mathematical form is judged against criteria of consistency and, if possible, logical proof with respect to a conventional series of base axioms. Thus mathematical theories can be articulated on object domains that already embrace epistemological dispositions independent of any that might be inherent in the mathematical techniques themselves. The elaborate constructions that are produced by the formal apparatus are then susceptible to having assigned an

309

identity within the chosen philosophical ambient and subsequently measured according to its own internal imperatives.

In spite of this fact, that 'meaning' is an intersubjective affair subsisting strictly independently of the techniques of mathematics, it is nevertheless true that the latter does indeed appear to display some genuine endogenous meaning-generative capacity of its own. There is however no anomaly here. Both the 'domain' and the 'range' of mathematical science consist of entities constituted within and subject to the life processes of a society, and it is from these alone that future truths are constructed. The special insights of the theory of relativity for example were philosophical ones. To be sure, the actual calculations produced 'correct' results and it is possible that there are inferences to be drawn from this. It does *not* follow however that mathematics is 'the language' of nature: mathematics is at most a technique applied to objects that are subject to and in some sense the product of linguistic entities.

Nevertheless it is indeed true that an a priori concinnity *of some sort* must exist between the social field within which the objects are formed and the peculiar statements offered by mathematics. In other words, a mathematization of the object domains must indeed precede any possible mathematical theorizing of them – and such a mathematization, furthermore must be a cultural, and philosophical, accomplishment. Now 'mathematization' refers to a praxis of measurement, as described convincingly by Husserl, which certainly presupposes metaphysical ideas that are themselves by no means self-evident. Some of these ideas were discussed in Chapters 2 and 5. They include possibly, assumptions about the idealization or perfectibility of the world, about its infinitude, about the commensurability of its disparate entities and so on; these in turn may have derived from the Christian conception of God, the generalization of the commodity economy[7] or merely from a fortuitous philosophical achievement. Which of these possibilities might be true is not a concern of ours at this point. Here we are only interested in making one emphatic assertion regarding something that is *not* true: it is *not* the case that the mathematization of the world implies an *objectivistic* concept of nature. It is not true that, as has been traditionally assumed, objectivism is the only, the logically necessary or even the most appropriate object domain for science. On the contrary, a range of divergent object domains is possible amongst which objectivism is only one. In particular, as we have of course already demonstrated at length, non-objectivistic object domains are not only conceivable for science, but have actually already been realized – even if within science itself this decisive achievement is not yet fully appreciated.

In the light of our discussion above about the relationship between objectivity and truth it may yet appear that the existence of a dimension within which refined techniques are applied might confute the commitment of a theory of nature to the pursuit of true knowledge, in the sense in which the term might be used elsewhere in social life. To show that this is in fact not the case some further elaboration is needed. Theoretical objects, as we have repeatedly pointed out, come into being within problematics, where they possess a meaning and value in respect of the intersubjective processes. On these objects the technical apparatus of science – for example, the concepts and methods of mathematics – can be brought to bear. The resulting theoretical formations do not in themselves possess more than a merely formal truth-content. It is only when they are inserted once again into the theoretical field that was their provenance that they can be associated with truth in any more comprehensive sense. In this case they are converted once again from theoretical structures into propositions, and can be discursively tested. Thus different sciences, or even different theories within a given science, can apply divergent criteria of validity and yet employ equivalent technical instruments. And indeed – it is worth stressing – it is the theoretical perspective that determines the precise features of the insights of which a particular science is capable within circumscriptions that apply to communicative processes in general. Neither mathematics nor the possibility of future technical applications is sufficient to characterize scientific knowledge: the latter's scope is richer and more varied, and its reference to the world must be understood first of all in terms of social life and not the idiosyncratic constructs of the latter.

Neither absolute truth nor free discourse exists. On the one hand the criteria for truth cannot be separated from the criteria for the settlement of truth claims in argumentative discourse. On the other, such argumentation always presupposes a categorial schema that is not susceptible to conclusive rational justification. Where two such schemata are sufficiently different the truth claims admitted for discursive testing might only partly coincide; in this case we can say that a degree of 'incommensurability' obtains. Here the problem arises of the evaluation of progress within science. For if two bodies of theory can in principle be incommensurable then it is clear that no total order exists for the class of all scientific theories, and hence scientific progress cannot be a monotonic process. Of course some way of choosing between different sciences must be possible and thus some relation on this class must exist. However the precise identity of such a relation is not an issue with which the present essay is concerned; accordingly no suggestions regarding it will be offered here. Instead, we note that the criteria that are applied in practice are rarely of a formal kind but are usually social or cultural in character; typically, for example, these criteria might concern questions of cultural, cognitive or (exceptionally) technical utility.[8] This fact also is consistent with the conceptions we have been outlining. For it means that progress in science is judged not primarily with respect to technical questions, but rather with respect to social variables - at least insofar as the latter intercede in science to provide their own preponderant conditions of validity. Thus what at first sight might seem to be exogenous circumstances with no particular relation to the theory of nature may well bear on reformulations of the objectivity of phenomena or of their places in theoretical discourse. In this way they may not only enter into the content of science but they may also participate in the direction and evaluation of their development.

This is a satisfying result, for it explains the circumstances within which a circularity might occur such as we have discussed earlier between a scientific theory and its predominant metacontextual interpretations.[9] In addition it may suggest a possible approach to a systematic assessment of the place of a theory of nature in relation to a social and economic configuration in general. Some aspects of this problem will be considered below; in relation to the question of progress in science, to which no further discussion will be devoted, we add the following final points. It seems desirable - and certainly not merely 'relativist' - to be able to say that for example within tribal societies the mythological conceptions of the nature-culture relation that are accepted are not only more meaningful, but also *truer* than their modern counterparts would be in an identical context; for otherwise complexity of experience would, at a stroke, be rendered completely inaccessible to us. Indeed, as has been often remarked, Newton's Second Law of Motion could command no truth-content whatsoever in a culture which had not yet accomplished the mathematization of nature. On the other hand, in contemporary capitalist society theories of nature based on mythologies are simply false, whereas the truth of Newton's laws is incontrovertible. Now if such a usage is to be possible then it must follow here also that scientific truth must in some sense be socially contingent. Or, to put this more precisely: the processes according to which a particular series of theoretical formulations is endowed with the property of being true must at some stages be subject to social, historical and perhaps philosophical contingencies. This is exactly the case within the conception of science being proposed. In consequence, changes in science need be considered neither as an exclusively endogenous affair nor as a product of some adventitious whimsy of the scientific community. Rather it is systematically bound to social variables in ways that can be discovered through a close analysis of both the content of science and the social processes.

The questions of change and progress in science, of course, refer to issues of the utmost importance. In spite of this, only the most rudimentary formulations are offered here. For this essay is concerned primarily with other, broader theoretical issues: in particular, it is concerned to render plausible the elementary hypothesis that science in fact conveys a philosophical content which can be understood in the light of the social and historical conjuncture. The problems associated with the details of scientific change represent an important and related, but nevertheless separate, field of endeavour. They will not be pursued further here; instead, they must remain a topic for future study.

Neither free discourse nor absolute truth exists. We have stressed this point in order to emphasize simultaneously that a body of theory depends on an a priori, systematically structured context and that knowledge of the world must always pass through a mediation provided by the intersubjective and linguistic processes. As Habermas showed in his argument against Popper discussed earlier, it is impossible to speak of a simple correspondence between a theory and its real objects.[10] Theories refer to 'facts' which occur only in discursive communication. These facts, of course, embody assertions about objects in the world. However insofar as they are indeed assertions, articulated within a structured theoretical context, the objects are already subject to categorial determinations. Schematization of the categories occurs in social action – especially in that marked by communicative exchanges. This will be discussed presently. What is important here is just that there can be for science no linguistically naked reality – and hence no immediate pretheoretical experience.

Just as we cannot speak, therefore, of a correspondence between truth and the world,. neither can we speak of 'categorial objectivities' standing in opposition to their yet to be supplied 'material cores'. Indeed, our discussion of Husserl's work and, in particular, the identification of the problematic it incorporated, together with its irreducible presuppositions in intersubjectivity, are enough to show this.[11] This point need not be elaborated further. However, it may not be inappropriate to add the trivial observation that to make these claims is not to deny the possibility of different levels of abstraction. Certainly, the object domain of relativity theory is not identical to the object domain of phenomenology, even though it shares its categorial features. Phenomenology exists at a higher level of generality than the specific sciences that occur within it, but this does not imply a difference between material and categorial objectivities. On the contrary, as we have seen, both occur indissolubly: the fact that the objects of phenomenology must be specified in more abstract terms refers only to this generality, and not to any imputation that there it is categories only that are at issue.

* * * * * *

The conclusions of this brief introduction to the theory of object domains in science can be summarized in a number of simple propositions. Science deals with objects and is directed towards truth. The two are related but not identical. A variety of forms of objectivity is possible and in fact actually occurs within science. Truth occurs only in communicative contexts and according to invariant conditions of discourse. Object domains are social constructs in which systems of concepts are applied to impose organizational forms on experience. Sciences in general treat such domains and are thus open to social phenomena. As theoretical structures however sciences are at the same time systematic unities. This unity is derived from the theoretical framework or problematic within which the regions of objectivity are inscribed. Problematics provide conditions of validity in a specific sense, to which all the theoretical structures generated by the technical apparatus of science are subject. Frameworks can differ sufficiently between two bodies of theory to render them incommensurable. Finally then, from this perspective, among a number of sciences each can maintain its own theoretical integrity and can employ similar or different formal techniques without sacrificing a fundamental unity that subsists at the level of social life, where truth is established.

Mathematics and physics

From the point of view of the present perspective a number of more or less important consequences follow and in particular, several hitherto perplexing problems can be elucidated. Before passing on to more substantial issues we shall advert briefly to two such problems: the question of Galileo's mathematization of nature and that of the contemporary relationship between physics and mathematics.

Regarding the former, the approach proposed here allows the accomplishment of Galileo to be more precisely specified. Galileo's innovation was, as Husserl showed, not the simple application of pure mathematics to an intuitively given nature. Rather it was nothing less than *the formulation of an appropriate object domain to which mathematics could be applied.* To the extent that such a domain presupposes simultaneously a problematic and a region of objectivities characterized in relation to corresponding categories, its construction was primarily a work of philosophy rather than physics. Husserl recognizes this and focuses upon it specifically. The process over which Galileo presided was just the identification of a specific region of objects for mathematical science. What was new in this was the particular conception of natural phenomena involved – 'the idea that the infinite totality of what is in general is intrinsically a rational all-encompassing unity that can be mastered, without anything left over, by a corresponding universal science.'[12] The philosophical preconditions for scientific object formation are described in great detail by Husserl. Thus he explains, for example, how 'knowledge, which determines the ... objective being of the world, ... was idealized and thus turned into the purely geometrical way of thinking';[13] he describes how the ideas developed of a 'universal inductivity'[14] and of a 'universal causality which ... precedes and guides all induction of particular causalities',[15] and so on.

The problematic within which these objectivities were formulated was of course that of objectivism, and herein precisely lay Galileo's tragic error. Only one step remains to be completed in the account of the birth of modern science: the description of the actual processes involved in the mathematization of the sensible plena, or equivalently, in the actual constitution of the object domains. As we have just seen, this process is an intersubjective one and so cannot be understood independently of social phenomena. Nevertheless Husserl's sketch – which is presented in Section 9b of the *Crisis* and was described at length above[16] – consistent with his phenomenology in general, makes no reference to such considerations. Accordingly, as we commented at the time the passage in question was somewhat disappointing. To appreciate this however is not to minimize Husserl's achievement, but rather to recognize the extent of the task yet to be accomplished. What remains outstanding is a theory of the relationship between the object domains of a science and the social and discursive variables in relation to which they are constructed. What remains to be developed, that is, is just a sociology of science.

* * * * * *

The second problem we mention here – also briefly – is that of the contemporary transformation in the relationship between mathematics and physics. Admittedly, this issue is not of overwhelming theoretical significance. Nevertheless it has in recent years become an important topic of conversation amongst physicists and mathematicians and it does raise some interesting questions; for these reasons, it is appropriate to mention it here.

Formerly, physics and mathematics were very close. We speak here not of the highly developed abstract geometry of the Pythagoreans which was so important to Galileo, but of its gifted child, the multifaceted mathematics with diverse interests to which his science gave rise. Thus the great mathematicians from the seventeenth century onwards were almost invariably great physicists also and their mathematical innovations almost always came as a result of the contemplation of scientific problems. To prove this it is not necessary to detail specific instances; it is enough merely to list the names of important mathematicians over three centuries: Newton, Leibniz, Huygens, d'Alembert, Euler, Lagrange, Laplace, Cauchy, Gauss, Riemann, Hilbert, Poincaré and so on.[17] All were deeply immersed simultaneously in both physics and mathematics. Consequently, even in their practice of the latter they considered themselves to be concerned not with purely symbolic objects but with problems in the world. Thus the methods of explicating and elaborating problems were the same: the question would be explained, alternative approaches examined and a particular mathematical intuition developed in the hope of establishing a satisfactory solution.

This was the classical situation which no longer exists. Paradoxically, physics and mathematics have once more diverged. Paradoxically, because mathematics, in turning away from science, is retracing the steps of its geometrical progenitor: a rare case perhaps of ontogeny recapitulating phylogeny.[18] Today, physicists are no longer deeply involved in mathematics, which was once the source for them of valuable conceptual material. And reciprocally, mathematicians are increasingly ignorant of or unconcerned with physics, from which the great problems once arose.

It is not an exaggeration to say that this circumstance has caused considerable alarm amongst some scientists, to whom it signifies the impending decay of their disciplines. Certainly, in recent years heated controversies have raged over the issue. In 1947 John Von Neumann, one of the foremost mathematicians of this century, stated his view bluntly:

> As a mathematical discipline travels far from its empirical source, or still more, if it is a second and third generation only indirectly inspired from 'reality' it is beset with very great dangers. It becomes more and more pure aestheticizing, more and more purely *l'art pour l'art* .... (A)t a great distance from its empirical source, or after much abstract inbreeding, a mathematical subject is in danger of degeneration ....
> (W)henever this stage is reached the only remedy seems to me to be the rejuvenating return to the source: the reinjection of more or less directly empirical ideas ...[19]

Many scientists today would accept the same view. In a recently published book Morris Kline, an American mathematician, issues a similar call for a return to practical problems. '(I)ntellectual efforts not tempered by reality,' he writes, 'are almost sure to prove sterile.' He adds: '(d)isregard for applications leads to isolation and possibly to the atrophy of mathematics as a whole.... (M)athematics must take its motivation from concrete specific substance and aim at some layer of reality.'[20]

What are the reasons for the divergence of physics and mathematics? The study of this problem would itself make an interesting sociological project. Indeed the withdrawal from reality and the flight into abstraction has long been emphasized as one of the main symptoms of the malaise of contemporary society.[21] The present predicament of mathematics could in this sense be regarded as an ultimate, extreme case of the modern crisis of science. Alternatively, one could consider the considerable pressures that are now exerted on professional scientists; the need to specialize, for example, and the urgent need to publish may well constitute profound influences for the trivialization – or at least the extreme formalization – of mathematical thinking. At the same time however, and in spite of the suggestiveness of this view, it must be remembered that the discrepancy between the two disciplines is a mutual one and that physicists have lost contact with mathematics to the same extent that mathematicians have withdrawn from practical concerns. This implies that at least part of the problem is that the study of mathematics has changed rather than that its focus has simply shifted.

This does indeed seem to be the case, and it provides an interesting illustration of the variability in the relationship between two bodies of thought whose object domains intersect but do not overlap. An examination of the history of mathematics since the seventeenth century in fact reveals a developing preoccupation with problems that emerged from its own internal material. The discovery of the need for careful definitions of terms (once not so obvious as it is today), the encounter with the problem of establishing criteria for the convergence of series, the need to clarify once again the foundations of geometry and its relation to physical space together with other problems led by an inescapable logic to the familiar axiomatized method of argument. Mathematics became more intensely rigorous than ever before. Definitions and technical terms came to abound where once intuition sufficed. This style in fact was the only one adequate to the requirement – implicit in mathematics from the beginning – of certainty and univocity in theoretical discourse. However at the same time the highly refined style of argumentation rendered the texts themselves accessible to fewer and fewer people. Now only extensively trained technicians were able to decipher their content – and often even then only after the expenditure of considerable effort. At the end of this dramatic, complete and probably inevitable development mathematics was available to professional mathematicians alone.

Of course it was not only the need for precision and rigour that influenced the development of mathematics. Several crucial problems, also exposed as a result of the operation of the internal imperatives of the discipline, were also of significance. Amongst these, of overwhelming importance were the problems of consistency and completeness. These two issues probably more than any other have affected the direction in which the subject has moved. The development of set theory by Dedekind, Cantor, Zermelo, Fraenkel and others, the formalist approach of Hilbert and Bernays, the logicist school of Russell and Whitehead and the seminal discoveries of Gödel, and Löwenheim and Skolem all owe a debt to the problems of completeness and consistency. The innovations that they produced however bore little or no relevance to natural science.

Physics, then, benefited less and less from the direction mathematics was taking. Indeed it can be said that for it the axiomatic method in particular was never even possible. For the domain inhabited by physics is not autonomously conceptual and its criterion of truth is thus not primarily absence of contradiction in the internal discourse. Indeed, from the strictly formal point of view there need be no a priori limitation on the number of available theories consistent with any given empirical point of departure. Thus, while with the maturation of mathematics from mere technique to a body of thought with its own ontology and epistemology its object domain was transformed, that of physics has remained constant. But physics of course is still mathematical, and this fact is exactly what has imposed the ambiguity both on the professions and on the disciplines themselves. For mathematics now has to play a dual role. On the one hand it is still a method for physics. Here, both its domain and its image refer to classes of objects generated exogenously in the socially constituted field of meanings of the natural sciences. Thus its propositions are subject to epistemological dispositions conceived independently of its internal structure. In this function mathematics is no more than a collection of technical operations. On the other hand however it is at the same time a theory articulated reflexively on the object domain of this method itself. Here, it is subject exclusively to internal criteria of consistency, completeness, precision of expression, and so on. In this function mathematics is a body of knowledge with its own theoretical integrity, its own object domain and its own criteria of meaning and truth. Thus in consequence, mathematicians and physicists have parted company to the extent that today it is not uncommon to find treatises written by each on what should be closely related topics that make little or no reference to the achievements of their colleagues in the other discipline.[22]

This modern version of the 'Two Cultures' clearly has dire possibilities for the future development of science – perhaps almost as great as does the isolation of scientists from the most vibrant trends of contemporary philosophical thought. Unlike the latter however there seems no obvious solution to the perplexity, since the discrepancy between mathematics and physics may well be fundamental. That is, it may be rooted in the internal constitution of each discipline, a circumstance, of course, which would render vacuous any exhortation to mathematicians to become more worldly. This would be an interesting result, which would of necessity bear heavily on any future interpretations of either physics or mathematics.

Such a conclusion would also be of particular interest for the present essay, for it would tend to substantiate some of the conclusions that were reached from a more theoretical perspective at an earlier stage. In the first place this result is consistent with our arguments in favour of the epistemological variability of science under the continuing mathematical rubric. For it suggests that the techniques of mathematics can be applied to domains of objects subject to different philosophical perspectives. This is of course a point that we have stressed repeatedly. On the other hand, this conclusion elucidates the character of mathematics itself, independently of its role in natural science. Specifically, it emphasizes that mathematics embraces theoretical imperatives of its own; furthermore, these may be relatively autonomous with respect to – though obviously not in contradiction with – the basic philosophical claims of science as a whole. This double role of mathematics, which at first sight seems so perplexing, arises, very simply, because mathematics operates on two different object domains (or, more precisely, it operates on one object domain which contains two different sub-domains). One of these domains contains the objects of physics; here mathematics functions as technique alone and the philosophical disposition of the science is undisturbed. The other consists exclusively of strictly mathematical objects; in this case the relevant epistemological criteria are just those of the pure theory.

The form of science and the form of truth

It may seem with these last considerations that we have deviated somewhat from the main purpose of this chapter, which was to provide an introduction to the systematic study of object domains in science. This is however not the case, for the question of the potential expressive power of the technical apparatus of science is of major importance for the development of a coherent theory. What is more, the problems we have been considering are ones that have suggested themselves on numerous occasions in the course of this essay. In fact several of these issues are still outstanding and now require resolution.

In our discussion of the relationship between mathematics and physics – and in particular, of their contemporary divergence – we have shown that the conceptual content of science cannot be derived from its formal apparatus alone. Indeed, each must be examined separately and analysed for its own idiosyncratic philosophical commitments. This is of course by now a familiar, even obvious, result, the effect of which is seen rather dramatically in modern physics. In addition, we argued previously that the conceptual content of science cannot be exhausted in the putative possibility of technical applications of its results. Taken together these two conclusions imply simply that the meaning of science is not reducible either to its formal structure or to the practical circumstances surrounding its construction or effect. Now while this seems a straightforward outcome it in fact fails to answer some obvious and substantial questions. For to prohibit a conflation of the various dimensions of science is not also to deny any possible relation between them. In fact, of course, we discovered at an early stage from critical theory and phenomenology that an interpenetration occurs between society and science and that accordingly, processes occurring at the pragmatic level contribute to the production of scientific meaning and truth. The outstanding question concerns the relationship between the syntax of science and its epistemological content; in particular, we are interested in whether the dependence on mathematics places substantive limitations on the kinds of insights of which the modern theory of nature is capable.

In the remainder of this chapter we turn at last to a direct consideration of this issue. As we have stressed previously, our results so far are here only tentative and partial. Nevertheless the question is of great importance, and indeed has perplexed philosophers for many years; for this reason the mere proposal of suggestive hypotheses in this area may be of use.

* * * * * *

One of the best-known contemporary attempts to clarify this problem is that proposed by the American analytical philosopher W. V. O. Quine. It is therefore to this work that we should first turn in search of preliminary help and guidance. The part of Quine's philosophy relevant in the present context is that which was developed in response to the enquiry about the possibility of an 'ontological commitment' of a given theory. Now it must be stated at the outset that this problem is not identical to the ones with which we are concerned. Quine is primarily interested, for example, in the mere existence of entities, whereas we are seeking to examine also both the claims the theory makes about their structure and the relationships presupposed within it between the discursive apparatus and the theorized entities. Nevertheless, as we have said, his theory does have some relevance for our purposes, even if that relevance is largely restricted to the identification of issues and problems requiring more detailed scrutiny. With this in mind the following brief comments are offered.

In his answer to the question about ontological commitment Quine proposes a 'criterion', in which he asserts that existential claims are embodied in language which effectively represents the implicit truth claims of formal propositions involving bound variables. Two famous formulations express essentially the same idea:

321

> The variables of quantification, 'something', 'nothing', 'everything', range over our whole ontology, whatever it may be; and we are convicted of a particular ontological presupposition if, and only if, the alleged presuppositum has to be reckoned among the entities over which our variables range in order to render one of our affirmations true.[23]

> In general, entities of a given sort are assumed by a theory if and only if some of them must be counted among the values of the variables in order that the statements affirmed in the theory be true.[24]

In an alternative formulation Quine asserts that a theory assumes a given object if the non-existence of the object would render the theory false.[25]

Now two relevant points can be noted immediately from these sentences. In the first place the 'criterion' is explicitly intended to be 'semantic' rather than 'pragmatic', that is, it is supposed deliberately to apply 'in the first instance to discourse and not to men'.[26] Thus Quine from the outset places an emphasis on language and meaning rather than speech acts or communication. Secondly, it is clear that for Quine the theory in question must be able to be assumed to constitute a coherent logical unity. It must be considered to be 'a deductively closed set, ... (including) all its own logical consequences insofar as they are couched in the same notation'.[27] In the case of science, of course, such a situation never appertains exactly; nevertheless for the purposes of argument little is lost by assuming it.

The importance of Quine's theory for this essay can be stated immediately, even from these brief formulations. It lies essentially in a fundamental dual contention. On the one hand the theory asserts that access to the world occurs through language alone. It is only through discursive formulations that its properties become available to us. This of course is an underlying assumption of Quine's entire philosophy. On the other hand, the theory claims that a natural intersection of language with the formal structures of a theory occurs specifically in the bound variables of the latter. This contention, which is certainly far from obvious, is the major innovation, in relation to the question at issue, which Quine is proposing. For the application to science these two results could be generalized; it would then appear, according to the view being discussed, that a theory could make metaphysical claims by virtue alone of its formal structure. These claims could be communicated through a linguistic interpretation of the formal sentences. Such an interpretation, furthermore, would not be arbitrary in the sense of model theory; it would evolve unambiguously out of the syntactical structure of the theory.

Of course it must be emphasized once more that the actual claims made by Quine himself are more limited than these ones. Nevertheless it is our contention that the case we have stated is strictly consistent with his position. What is more, to the extent that his theory is in fact a special case of that which we have described both its abiding insights and its defects will appear in the generalization. Certainly, if the theory stated proves to be true major consequences will follow for the understanding of science. In particular, it would follow that the major philosophical implications of a scientific theory could be delineated by means of a rigorous analysis of its formal structure. Thus major dilemmas in the interpretation of science could be resolvable through the application alone of the techniques of formal logic and algebra. Quine himself does not refer to these possibilities; however it is of interest that a remarkably similar view has been proposed, quite independently, by the philosopher of science Clifford Hooker in his work on the foundations of the quantum theory.[28]

These are the implications of Quine's position. Regarding the theory of ontological commitment specifically, it seems to us that contained therein are several major problems of which a discussion may be instructive. We shall therefore proceed to mention a number of these deficiencies, albeit in extremely abbreviated form.

In the first place, it is easy to see that the theory in question incorporates implicit assumptions about the nature of language, not all of which are self-evident. Assumed, for instance, is that categories of language can be identified unambiguously. This is of course a defensible view; nonetheless it is surely clear, in the light of the work of many authors,[29] that at the least, it needs to be substantiated. Or to take another example, Quine's theory assumes that the interpretation of a language occurs - again unproblematically - in a context-independent environment. Like the previous claim this one has been subject to considerable and continuing dispute; consequently, it must be accepted that in the present circumstances the question of its validity remains undecided.[30]

These are general problems of linguistic theory which intersect with Quine's work. Other assumptions are to be found at other levels of his theory. Here, more detailed observations can often be made which apply regardless of how the above disputes might be resolved. It seems clear, for example, that the single relationship that he allows between language and objects - that of naming - is not the only one possible. Indeed, 'ideal objects' (Husserl) or even 'facts'[31] may stand in a quite different relation to language; furthermore, these relations may be mediated in a number of possible ways, such as 'expression',[32] 'assertion'[33] and so on. Again, it may be observed that in Quine's 'criterion', even in relation to the formal theory, the means by which metaphysical claims arise is very rudimentary. For example, the 'criterion' depends explicitly on the logic of quantification. However, it is readily conceivable that formal theories could be developed from which quantifiers would be omitted.[34] In such a case, on the one hand, it would follow that the 'criterion' is not exhaustive, while on the other, the question would be raised as to whether the alternative guarantees operated in favour of an identical category. Certainly, within Quine's work the opportunity for alternative modes of existence, even such as those examined by Hooker, seems to be rather limited.

We have emphasized that we are not presuming here to be offering, on the basis of a few elementary objections, a refutation of Quine's whole theory of ontological commitment. Rather, we are merely adverting to a number of problems the theory seems to encounter; we hope thereby to demonstrate the complexity of the issues as well as to emphasize some fundamental points. Nevertheless it is possible to draw together some of our comments regarding Quine's approach into a few simple conclusions. It appears to us, in brief, that Quine's theory is compromised by a presupposed conception of objectivity – a deficiency that reflects not just on the ontological problem but also, equally, on the structure of science and its interpretation. More specifically, Quine insists on one particular language-object relation and employs one particular, contingent formal device. Thereby the possibility arises that any commitment that emerges might be valid for certain classes of entities only; thus these entities would have to be introduced into the theory in advance. But if this is the case then the 'criterion' does not in fact derive a theory from certain mathematical structures, as it claims to do. Rather the reverse happens: a presupposed theory is projected into the mathematical relations, which are subsequently obliged to accommodate it.

That such a circumstance often obtains certainly seems plausible. Indeed a projection such as that referred to is exactly what occurs when, as we are accustomed to do, we render the existential quantifier in English as 'there exists'. However, we shall not pause here to make our claims more than merely plausible, by attempting to construct a rigorous proof. For the results that we have obtained so far will suffice for the conclusions we wish to draw here regarding the theory of science in general. In fact, simply to raise the question of such a rigorous proof and to reflect on the conditions for an answer reveals some fundamental truths regarding the problem which we set out to address. For if our contentions can indeed be proved then such proof can be realized only in a determinate linguistic context. An examination would have to be undertaken of possible different modes of existence and of alternative syntactical systems. Such an investigation obviously could not be purely formal, for it could not escape a dependence on the peculiar, self-reflective character of language on the one hand and on forms of validity established and sustained within contexts of intersubjective communication on the other. A scrutiny of the syntactical properties of language, that is to say, must of necessity raise wider questions of meaning which can be decided only in the social field within which linguistic formulations are both articulated and evaluated. To put this another way: it is a consequence of our analysis of Quine's theory that the theory itself can be assessed only if an irreducible interdependence involving syntax, semantics and pragmatics actually pre-exists this investigation!

Husserl found science to be both methodical and intersubjectively founded. Horkheimer and Adorno showed that the formal system, suffusing the social institutions, indeed conveyed cultural effects. In addition to these results, our reflections on Quine further reinforce other conclusions we articulated earlier: there is a danger, within the metadiscourse of science, of simply reproducing the philosophical positions of its object and thus of failing to achieve any theoretical penetration whatsoever. And, more specifically, the formal structure of a theory cannot be dissociated either from its interpretations or from the specific intersubjective context within which it is realized.

This last point has in fact emerged repeatedly in the analyses undertaken in this essay. It has become apparent on a number of occasions that the syntax of a science is from the outset implicated both in its semantics (wherein its characteristic form of objectivity is established) and in its pragmatics (which define the locus of truth). Charles Morris, from whom we adopted the tripartite schema, himself arrived at a similar conclusion when he observed that on the one hand 'semantics presupposes syntactics',[35] while on the other 'when a language as a whole is considered, its syntactical structure is a function of both pragmatic and empirical considerations and is not a bare mirroring of nature considered in abstraction from the users of language'.[36] The claim that we make is specifically in respect of science, although it may well be of more general application. We are arguing that the object domains to which formal operations are applied are at once both the product of and subject to the social processes – understood in the broadest sense. Furthermore, the processes of the formation of these object domains must obviously presuppose the technical language that will be employed to theorize them; if an argument therefore is to be made for the existence of philosophical imperatives emerging from the syntactical apparatus then it cannot neglect either the cultural issues or the questions of social meaning.

Within this important circumscription however, on the basis both of our previous results and of arguments to be presented shortly, we are prepared to propose an answer to the question of the relationship between syntax and epistemology. In the first place, the use of mathematics in science, we shall claim, imposes conditions on the possible object domains but does not determine them. Thus alternative epistemological options remain available within the broad project of Western science. Now in contemporary science the objectivist programme is of course the most familiar one, for, originally introduced into the theory of nature through the object domain of classical mechanics, it still enjoys hegemony in all other branches as well. As this essay has been seeking constantly to argue, however, anti-objectivist programmes are also possible. Indeed, we have even identified problematics and object domains of the two most prominent candidates. What is more, we have shown that each of these strategies – and thereby each component of Husserl's dual critique of objectivism – is actually realized within contemporary science. Thus relativity theory recapitulates the phenomenological attack on objectivism, while implicit in quantum mechanics is a critique rather close to that realized within the structuralist problematic. The details of these contentions were argued in Chapters 7 and 9 respectively; there we suggested also that if they are true they may bear potentially profound consequences not just for the metatheory of science but even for science itself.

In respect of the converse implication raised by our question we can also be specific. However here it is necessary to speak not of syntactical systems but rather of logical structures obtaining within systems of theoretical statements in science. Precisely, we claim the following: while no direct conclusion can be drawn from the object domain of a science regarding the logical structure it employs it is nevertheless possible to identify object domains, and hence bodies of theory, that are susceptible to adequate theorization only within, respectively, classical and non-classical logics.

On this last point we add, before passing on, an observation that is relevant in the present context. It frequently goes unnoticed that the relationship of classical logic to nature is anything but self-evident. On the contrary this relationship in fact represents a problem of considerable proportions. In spite of this, and in spite of the fact that the notion of a 'dialectics of nature' (whether articulated by a Hegel or by an Engels) has been rigorously and justly criticized,[37] the notion of a 'classical logic of nature' has nevertheless been generally accepted without question. This has been the case even for the most rigorous and careful critics of science. For Bertrand Russell, for example, the inherently mathematical character of nature was 'one of the greatest discoveries of modern times',[38] while for Rudolf Carnap it was just a great 'stroke of luck'.[39] Without wishing to overstate the case, it might not be too extravagant to suggest that, philosophically, the doctrine of a classical logic of nature may have proved no less pernicious than its reviled 'dialectical' counterpart.

Our overall claim, then, in respect of the question we are addressing, is twofold. The use of mathematics, and thus classical logic, does not rigorously determine the epistemological project to which a science is committed. On the other hand, however, conversely, it is not true that all epistemologies are compatible with all logics: indeed, an object domain can be found for which classical logic is needed and another exists for which only a non-classical logic can apply.

It is only the latter – that is, the converse – implication for which a proof remains to be supplied. In what follows a sketch only of part of such a proof will be offered. We propose that an example of an object domain requiring a non-classical logic is that of intuitionism,[40] while one demanding a classical logic – not surprisingly – is that of objectivism. No attempt will be made here to provide an argument in respect of the case of intuitionism. Such an excursus would take us too far from our main themes and besides, sufficient discussion of this issue is available in the literature; in particular, the inapplicability of the law of the excluded middle can be readily obtained.[41] Instead, it is only the latter case that will occupy us here. However, regarding even this problem no pretence will be made to supply a conclusive proof. Here, the arguments offered constitute a suggestion only regarding the direction in which a rigorous proof might move. Furthermore, a number of assumptions are made. For example, the 'Platonist' version of mathematics, with which we are associating a classical logic, is assumed to presuppose the logical laws of identity, non-contradiction and the excluded middle and to incorporate the rule of inference, *modus ponens*. In addition, we are assuming the applicability of the phenomenological method of argument; this is justified merely by the existence within it of an extra-logical apparatus which may possibly permit the theoretical invariants associated with the object domain to be formulated. With these provisos manifest we proceed to outline our proof.

* * * * * *

We are interested in the consequences of the selection of a given object domain. Thus let us suppose that the object domain with which we wish to deal is that of natural phenomena, objectivistically conceived; that is, suppose that it consists of objects which perdure absolutely independently of any conscious, cognizing subject. Our problem is then: what conditions are thereby imposed on the statements which we may employ to formulate properties either of these objects or of their possible interrelations? Or alternatively: if such objects can be revealed to us then what can we say about the theoretical apparatus by means of which this occurs? To attempt to answer these questions it is convenient, as we said, to utilize the phenomenological method of argument.[42] In particular, it will be helpful to employ some concepts and conclusions from the logical works of both the founder of phenomenology and one of his most important and influential interlocutors: Edmund Husserl – of course – and Gottlob Frege, who considered in some detail a number of related issues.[43]

Frege distinguishes what he calls the 'meaning' and 'sense' of a sign from its 'associated idea'.[44] This last entity is an internal image, arising from memories of sense impressions and past acts; it is completely subjective and often imbued with feeling. Meaning and sense on the other hand – which, of course, constituted the origin of Husserl's distinction between expression and indication in the first *Logical Investigation* – are of a rather different character. For a proper name (that is, a word, a sign, a sign combination or an expression) the sense is just what is expressed and the meaning what is designated.[45] For an assertoric statement, by contrast, the meaning is the truth-value – that is, the circumstance according to which the statement is true or false.[46] Thus the truth-value is taken to be a variety of object, a claim that is justified by Frege in his discussion of concept and object.[47] As for the sense of such a statement, its specification requires the introduction of a new term. Frege defines a 'thought' as the 'objective content' of thinking, 'which is capable of being the common property of several think-ers'[48] - that is, as distinguished from its subjective performance. Then the thought is exactly the 'sense' of the statement; it is related to the 'meaning' by a 'judgement', which is in general the process according to which a truth-value is assigned to a thought.[49] Else-where, Frege defined these distinctions in slightly different terms - and indeed not always identically.[50] Nevertheless, what is impor-tant is that a 'thought' is the 'sense' of a statement and that it therefore - by virtue of the possibility of judgement - is essentially something for which the questions of truth and falsity can arise.[51] (In passing, it will be noticed at once that Frege thus discards any notion of a correspondence theory of truth, restricting the notion of truth instead to the 'truth of statements'.)

A statement, then, has both an 'ideal' and a 'thought-meaning' component. Formulated according to this terminology, the ques-tions in which we are interested here concern (a) the conditions imposed on a 'thought' associated with a statement about the ob-jectivistic world of things and (b) whether a 'thought' of such a character would in fact be knowable. In his attack on idealism Frege examined the nature of the 'thought' in detail; for this reason, where they are of relevance for our purposes we shall refer directly to these arguments of his.

Frege first of all begins an analysis of 'ideas' - that is, as we said, of the inner world of sense impressions, feelings, moods and so on. Our question will be: is this the world to which *thoughts* belong? An answer however, requires some preliminary investigation; in particular, the characteristics of ideas must be described. Four such characteristics can be easily established.[52] Ideas cannot be seen, or touched, or smelled. Ideas are something we have; they belong to the contents of our consciousness. Ideas need an owner; unlike things of the outside world they are dependent on the thinker. Finally, every idea has exactly *one* owner; no two men can have the same idea, for otherwise the latter would enjoy an independent existence. Frege now goes on to consider the (idealist) question of whether 'all my knowledge and perception is limited to the range of my ideas, to the stage of my consciousness',[53] pointing out that in this case I would have only an inner world and could know nothing of other people.[54] He concludes however that such is not the case, and adduces several arguments to support his position. Amongst these arguments is the following (simplified) one: if every-thing were an idea then the same would apply precisely to myself; but I am the owner of the ideas and thus necessarily something essentially different.[55] From this result Frege deduces further that

the thesis that only what belongs to the content of my consciousness can be the object of my awareness is false.[56]

To return to 'thoughts': if any statement can be made regarding
objectivistic entities – that is, regarding objects which are independent of any consciousness – then the 'sense' of such a statement –
that is, its 'thought' – must be similarly independent. For otherwise
its truth-value, and hence its 'meaning', would be dependent on
events occurring within the consciousness of specific individuals.
But then the properties of the objects to which the statement ad-
verts would either exist or not exist depending on subjective processes – contradicting the hypothesis regarding the object domain.
This point can be expressed conversely: to the extent that 'thoughts'
are dependent on the immanent conditions of the stream of experience of a subject, to that extent is the world of objects revealed
by these 'thoughts' also, dependent on the subject; that is, to that
extent this world cannot endure independently of such experiences.
Thus, since the object domain in question is the objectivist one of
subject-independent phenomena, the result must be a general one:
the 'thoughts' associated with statements made about such a domain must be strictly independent of conscious processes (and
hence, in a sense, 'timeless'[57]). But are such 'thoughts' knowable?
This is the question that must now be asked. For it is one thing to
demand that statements about the objective world must have an
independent 'sense'; it is another to show that these conditions are
not purely formal ones and that such statements are in fact possible
in practice.[58]

The 'refutation of idealism' presented by Frege shows that entities other than those belonging to my consciousness can be the
object of my awareness. In particular, the owners of ideas are such
entities. Thus we are now free to make the supposition that several
such owners exist, who may then enter into communication regarding common objects of thought.[59] Such objects may include things,
ideas and so on which, by virtue of their communicability are such
that they are not owned by any one individual. Specifically, we can
now acknowledge 'thoughts' as similarly independent of us. Thus
in fact a 'thought' can be the object of consciousness of which it is
nevertheless not a member. This result is a condition of the possibility of communicable statements about the external world; Frege
points out in addition that it is necessary if I am to be able to have
an 'environment' rather than an inner world[60] only and that
furthermore only in such circumstances could there be constructed
a science 'common to many, on which many could work'.[61]

The actual status of a 'thought' is nevertheless not quite settled.

330

We know that it is not an inner object of my consciousness. But certainly nor can it belong to the world of perceptible things. Thus it must have a special kind of existence which while irreducible to either consciousness or things nevertheless stands inextricably in relation to both of them. Frege himself recognizes this special character of 'thoughts' and in fact refers to it emphatically; indeed he designates the peculiar region to which they belong a 'third realm'.[62]

Let us quickly review the argument so far. We have assumed the existence of a domain of objects characterized by a strict independence from any consciousness and are seeking the conditions that must be satisfied by statements which purport to refer coherently to them. For this purpose we have adopted an anatomy of assertoric statements proposed by Frege which has enabled us to conclude that the 'thoughts' embraced by such statements are of a particular kind. More precisely, we have been able to conclude that if we are to be able to speak about such an object domain then there must exist entities of which truth and falsity can be predicated which are both apprehensible to us and yet perdure independently of us. Our task is now to use this insight in turn to effect a more exhaustive characterization of the statements themselves. For example, it is obvious that the mere requirement that such statements be sentences (which is in fact how Frege himself refers to them when formulating the distinctions quoted above) is not enough, for the sense of a sentence may certainly depend on the contingent knowledge of a speaker. Rather, they must be particular kinds of sentences obeying special rules.

Let us now try to identify these entities and the rules governing them. For this purpose it is appropriate to turn from the work of Frege to that of Husserl. The latter contains in great detail exactly what we now require: a consideration of the acts of judgement involved in statements about objects. We use the term 'judgement' here, it should be noted at once, already as Husserl used it and not in the Fregean sense. For Frege, as we said, a judgement is just 'the advance from a thought to its truth-value'.[63] For Husserl, by contrast, a judgement is specifically dissociated from 'an assent or acceptance, or a denial or rejection, of some presented state of affairs'.[64] In a judgement, to be sure, a 'state of affairs' appears before us,[65] though through neither a presetation[66] nor a reference.[67] A judgement is rather an act of consciousness that 'sets before our eyes'[68] an attribution, making it 'intentionally objective to us'.[69] It may well be *preceded* by a presentation of a particular kind; it becomes however accepting or assertive of it only in a context of fulfilment.[70]

It is apparent at once that such judgements are involved when we theorize the objects of an objectivistic domain. Nevertheless we must ask how precisely the entities we are seeking stand in relation to judgements. Clearly these entities (constituted as they are in sentences) are no fleeting moments of meaning in the thought acts and indeed refer to no individual feature of our thought experience. For the sense of such sentences must remain identical, regardless of the multiplicity of speakers and acts associated with them. When we propound such sentences then certainly we *judge*. However the sentences themselves must be regarded as rather the ideal contents of judgements. Furthermore they must be capable of sustaining the predicates 'true' and 'false', and these can be applied not to judgements themselves but only to their ideal meanings.

This description of the sentences we are seeking to characterize is in fact exactly a recapitulation of Husserl's characterization of propositions.[71] For as he argued at length, the propositions to which he referred constitute the ideal meaning or content of judgements, are independent of individual acts of consciousness and are precisely that of which truth and falsity can be predicated.[72] He himself was indeed acutely aware that such propositions are the essence and object of (objectivistic) science: '(M)eaning, rather than the act of meaning, concept and proposition, rather than idea and judgement, are what is essential and germane in science....'[73] However, as he also realized, propositions are not unrelated to judgements: in fact, the latter are the a priori conditions of possibility of the former.[74] Propositions are 'objective unities of meaning' corresponding to particular structures of intentionality, that is, they are ones 'adequate to the objectivity' which is thus 'self-evidently "given", thereby correspond(ing) to (the) subjective thought-connections'.[75]

But what are the rules that the propositions must obey? It is now possible to determine these by means of an examination of the judgements associated with the object domain in question; to the extent that the ideal contents of such judgements will be thereby characterized, the results will be applicable also to the corresponding propositions. Once again, phenomenology is well-suited to the task of such an examination. In fact we already have at our disposal an example of exactly the kind of analysis we need: that appearing in Chapter 3 of the second part of *Formal and Transcendental Logic*, to which we had occasion to refer, in another context, in an earlier chapter. To conclude the present argument, therefore, we shall make extensive use of these formulations of Husserl.

In the first place, we can say at once that, since the objects are independent of the acts of judgement, if a judgement about them is true then it is true (that is, it can be brought to a positive adequation) once and for all. In other words, 'if it is evident at one time, if it is legitimated at one time in the evidence of a fulfilling adequation then it cannot be shown at some other time ... to be false.'[76] In other words, for the propositions describing the object domain in question the *principle of identity* is valid.

Secondly, it can also be seen that it must be the case that, in the circumstances we have established, 'of two judgements that (immediately or mediately) contradict one another, only one can be accepted by any judger whatever in a proper or distinct unitary judging'.[77] This is the case because the 'general evidence of the analytic consequence, united with the attempting and starting of its negation, shows ... the general impossibility of this unity (sc. the unity that would be produced by conjoining a judicial meaning and the negative of any analytic consequence of that meaning in "distinct evidence").'[78] When this statement is translated into its propositional content it says no more than that a second law, the *law of non-contradiction* must also hold in respect of the object domain in question. If a judgement can be brought to an adequation in a positive material evidence then, a priori, its contradictory opposite is not only excluded as a judgement but also cannot be brought to such an adequation; and vice versa.[79]

It is worth noting here that phenomenology is useful in the present context precisely because it is capable of providing an analysis of the subjective contents corresponding to objective laws. In our previous discussion we attempted to fix the relationship between the objects we are considering and subjectivity. What we are in the process of doing now is making manifest the regularities within the subjective side of this relationship, for these are the ones which specify the logical laws. This entire endeavour, of course, assumes a basic premise of phenomenology, that there does in fact stand 'on the subjective side ... the a priori structure of the evidence and of the other effective subjective performances pertaining to it – a structure, the uncovering of which actually brings out the essential subjective situations corresponding to their objective sense.'[80]

By the same procedure, to the two laws we have derived we can add a third. With respect to the world of objects in question any judgement we make, if it can be brought to an adequation – that is, to a synthesis with an evidential giving – then it can be brought to either a positive or a negative adequation.[81] Furthermore, an adequation of either kind is always possible – at least in principle.

For otherwise there would exist an object in respect of which a proposition could be formulated that was neither true nor false. But this would mean that the object in question would not belong to the object domain we are considering. This is so, briefly, because in such a case the quality referred to in the proposition, which implies a particular kind of categorial objectivity, would in principle be incapable of adequation on the basis of potential evidential givings. However then the object would be open to determinations contingent upon any subjectivity. The alternative possibility, that the proposition might be universally neither true nor false, can be dismissed; for that would entail the existence of a higher order proposition, asserting the absence of either the quality in question or *its* absence – and this proposition would itself be subject to adequation. But that would be absurd, for any such result would necessarily require the existence of evidence directly bearing on the original quality, a possibility which has already been excluded. Thus we can conclude that in the object domain we are considering, the *law of the excluded middle* can be assumed to hold, in addition to those derived above.[82]

Finally, it is clear that if one judgement is the analytic consequence of another then we can say at once that 'the possibility of distinct evidence of the analytic antecedent judgement necessarily entails the possibility of such evidence of the consequent judgement'.[83] Indeed, this is almost a tautology, for this affirmation merely restates the meaning of 'consequence' in the phenomenological view. Hence we have also the *rule of inference, modus ponens*.

We have now reached the conclusion of the argument. Let us state once again what we have found. We assumed at the outset the existence of a domain of objects satisfying the criteria of objectivism. We then set about inquiring into the conditions thereby placed on any theoretical formulations regarding these objects. With the help of results derived by Frege and Husserl we were able to characterize these statements and subsequently to identify some logical laws to which they must conform. We found, in brief, that the theorization of these objects requires a system of propositions obeying the laws of identity, non-contradiction and excluded middle and subject to the rule of inference, *modus ponens*. In this sense, therefore, we are prepared to conclude that the claim that we made regarding objectivism is true: that objectivism and classical logic (in the sense in which we are using the term) stand in a natural and necessary relationship, to the extent that the adequate theorization of an objectivistic object domain commands the employment of classical logic.

The sociology of objectivity

Ever since the elements of a critique of objectivism first became available philosophers and social scientists have either derided science for its enduring philosophical crudity[1] or else expended great effort in constructing special places in their theories to accommodate it.[2] Yet curiously, little thought was given to applying within science the insights gained outside it. On the other hand, the attack on objectivism was indeed pressed relentlessly and produced sometimes surprising results: two coexistent critiques emerged, interdependent but nevertheless distinct. It is only in retrospect that it becomes apparent that the three object domains thus produced are in fact just those most prominent in the natural sciences: objectivism, of course, for classical mechanics and for most of the rest of contemporary science, and phenomenology and structuralism (whose relationship is presently unclear) respectively for relativity theory and quantum mechanics. The sciences of nature therefore, contrary to what was hitherto thought, express an authentic conceptual content independently of the question of their potential technical applicability; furthermore the continuity between philosophy and science thereby established renders them mutually susceptible. Substantial consequences may follow from this both for science and for its interpretations. In particular, in respect of the sociology of science new questions are raised.

More precisely, we are now faced not so much with the problem of the sociology of *science* as with that of the sociology of *objectivity*. Indeed it seems to us that this is exactly the locus of any proper sociology of science: the generation of an account of the evolution of object domains within the conceptual environment of a given social configuration. There are several reasons why such an account is necessary. In the first place clearly, objectivity is immanently social and thus, at least in principle, subject to the confluence of social forces. An adequate social theory of objectivity could therefore potentially yield insights that would render intelligible competing objective styles and hence alternative natural theoretical perspectives. In particular, as suggested previously, the process of scientific change, which has so far resisted attempts at a systematic theorization,[3] may also be susceptible to interpretation within such a theory – at least to the extent that such processes are indeed apprehensible under the rubric of social and cultural transformations. Further, such an account could contribute to more general projects of social self-clarification. We have seen that science is indeed productive of qualitatively new meanings – that is, of social significations that exceed the strict requirements of potential technical utility. Consequently, no comprehensive characterization of practical social life – including of course, the dimensions of communicative action and freedom – is possible which ignores the mediations through science. To claim this is not merely to repeat that science can be mobilized for positive or for malign purposes, either to enhance the technical possibilities open to us or to intensify domination; it is to emphasize rather that science itself plays a part in the formation of the cultural structures and indeed even in the theoretical means available to reflect upon them.

This point has however already been elaborated at length. In addition, we have seen that object domains in themselves already presuppose elaborate social and conceptual environments which, accordingly, must be explicated if even the intricate claims implicit within scientific theories are to be accessible. Thus a sociology of science could contribute also to the project of the self-clarification of science itself. Finally, the existence already of a powerful *social* critique of objectivism, some indications of which we have considered on the basis of a development of the Marxian theory of fetishism, additionally contributes to the need for a more general theory.

Despite the conclusions, from the very outset the development of such a theory is confronted with the most profound difficulties. In particular, for the very reasons mentioned above, no independent characterization of objectivity is possible: rather, such a characterization must at once both precede and be preceded by other cultural phenomena. But this raises the questions of the kind of account that must be sought and of the criteria according to which its adequacy might effectively be judged. Indeed, to the extent that any such theory must itself claim some objective validity beyond that of the regulative unities it is studying, the status of the investigation itself becomes a critical question. In fact these problems multiply upon inspection. Accordingly, we do not claim here to offer solutions – much less, even the rudiments of a coherent theory. Instead we are seeking merely to achieve two things: a description both of the range of issues that such a theory must address and of the kinds of difficulties with which it will find itself faced; and an identification of some continuities between the present project and investigations already well advanced elsewhere in philosophy and social theory.

There is a trivial sense in which objectivity certainly depends on social factors. According to the very nature of the concept, an entity to be 'objective' must display an invariance across factors dependent either directly or indirectly on the productions of a given subject; this is as true for structuralism, in which as we have seen, the subject is present as a negative absence, as it is for phenomenology, in which it is given explicitly. Thus all objectivity must carry some sense of intersubjective stability. Nevertheless within the terms of this requirement, as we have also seen, alternative conceptions of objectivity remain possible such that entities that are 'objective' within one conception may well not be within another. Now any science – to the extent that it can be called a science at all – must aspire to some degree of systematic unity and for this a minimum requirement is that its objects be unambiguously identifiable. Only in these circumstances could the propositions of the science be rendered communicable; indeed only then would it be possible to meet the stronger condition – essential also to science – that such propositions can be formulated in a way that, as defined within the scientific apparatus itself, their meanings can in principle be reproduced indefinitely.[4] Accordingly, it is necessary that just one conception from amongst those available is chosen, establishing a series of unities of entities exhibiting stable relations with respect to consciousness, to the cultural apparatus or to some other specific system of social phenomena. These unities are of course the object domains. From the argument just formulated it can be seen that the question therefore arises quite naturally of the conditions of evolution of these domains within a given conceptual environment – that is, within a given culture. Finally, in circumstances in which a proliferation of object domains exists an explanation for this fact must also be sought – and here again the cultural variables are the most natural ones to consider.

337

Certainly the dependence of object domains on immediately contiguous, more comprehensive social phenomena is not difficult to distinguish. For implied in the choice of a given conception of objectivity is an extensive partitioning of the social field in respect of ontological and epistemological issues. This observation was made above, where it was pointed out that on the one hand a proposition can have meaning only insofar as it bears an immanent relation to a stable region of discourse within which both objectivity and truth come into being, while on the other, an object can assume a place and value also only in relation to some problematic. Thus immediately our problem of the evolution of object domains is seen to be embedded in a larger problem: how can we give an account of the emergence of the stable discursive unities within which objectivity is formed?

In what follows we shall consider in detail some aspects of the issues we have been outlining. It is important however to state at the outset once again that no attempt will be made here to provide definitive answers to the questions outstanding. Instead, we shall be seeking no more than to establish plausible possibilities and fruitful orientations for the future understanding of these problems. This point is so important that it is worth repeating it deliberately: in what follows it will not be our intention to propose a developed sociology of objectivity that would claim to answer all - or even most - of the outstanding questions. In fact, it seems to us that such a theory may be neither possible nor even desirable. Instead, the aim of this discussion will be somewhat more modest. On the one hand, we will seek to establish the mere possibility of a social theory of objectivity; that is, we will aim to show that a sociology of objectivity can indeed be developed. On the other, we shall attempt to elaborate in some detail the complexity of the problems at stake and to demonstrate their continuity with the issues dealt with by other, already well-established, theories. This last claim will not be merely incidental; on the contrary, it will be claimed as a major result. We shall argue explicitly that the sociology of objectivity cannot be conceived as a self-contained field of study, considering well-defined problems with the aid of a determinate theoretical apparatus. Rather, we shall maintain, it can be understood only in relation to the vast body of theory which treats the problems of knowledge and society in general. If this claim can be upheld then, as we shall see, it will convey important consequences - both positive and negative - for the future development of a social theory of science: for such a theory will thus have available to it a rich and extensive complement of insights and hypotheses, while, at the same time, the very fecundity of the field will limit the conclusiveness of its results.

In the discussion of the sociology of objectivity which follows therefore, we shall abstain from any attempt to formulate a fully coherent theory. Instead we shall merely consider a number of possible approaches arising naturally from the foregoing investigations. These will include, not surprisingly, perspectives we have already considered at length; in particular, both Marxism and phenomenology, as we shall see, remain richly suggestive in the present context. In addition, we shall describe the rudiments of a perspective which seems to us to emerge from an appreciation of both the insights and the deficiencies of these two viewpoints. This approach will draw on results established in Wittgenstein's works and show a broad consistency with some aspects of the thought of Habermas. Finally, we shall propose several, so far unresolved, objections to this last approach, and close with some general conclusions.

Approaches to the sociology of objectivity

We commence, as usual, with phenomenology. Throughout his work, Husserl grappled with the problem of objectivity, which he sought to understand in terms of the conscious acts of essentially isolated subjects. Of course, for him truth also is dependent on the evidential giving of objects to an ego; more specifically, it is an accomplishment that is characterized by the fulfilment of an intentional thought act by an experience of evidence within which an object is intuitively given.[5] We have already discussed in detail this aspect of Husserl's thought. We have seen how for him things are, therefore, things of experience and that it is the latter which alone endows them with their unity.[6] And we have seen how for things to be *objective* they must also be in principle conceivable at once by *every* ego.[7] For even though nothing exists for me except by virtue of the performance of my own consciousness there is nevertheless only one identical world to which all of us must have experiential access.[8] For Husserl, then, the problem of objectivity was coterminous with the 'problem of others': the problem of how my transcendental ego could constitute within itself another transcendental ego, and then too an open plurality of such egos.[9] In his thought objectivity was possible only if the world was constituted in this way, showing itself to be as it is in an intersubjective

339

cognitive community.[10] Two immediate consequences follow from these results, to which we have already made extensive reference. In the first place, in Husserl's philosophy, exactly as for truth itself[11] the category of objectivity and the category of evidence are perfect correlates; that is, to every fundamental species of objectivity there corresponds a fundamental species of evidence.[12] Hence within Husserl's theory objectivity and truth necessarily appear together. Secondly, phenomenology must at the same time face the task of showing how a sense of 'everyone' – as community rather than as isolated individuals – is already constituted in the transcendental ego.

With respect to the latter problem, of course, we have referred previously to some of the arguments of the fifth *Cartesian Meditation* and we have considered some of the difficulties associated with them.[13] Indeed we have noted that problems associated with intersubjective processes recur throughout the theory. For example, as early as the *Logical Investigations* an elaborate apparatus had to be constructed for the concept of categorial intuition,[14] which after all is only the form that communicative constitution must take in a theory based on consciousness and evidence. Notwithstanding this, the difficulties with the concepts of intersubjectivity and objectivity were only brought to a central focus in Husserl's last work. For only there, at last, did the explicit theme become the natural sciences and their historically produced crisis. We have discussed the consequences of this investigation at length; here we shall only mention once again one of the substantive results regarding the theory of objectivity. It was found that the notion described above of object domains partitioned according to the correlative categories of meaning, evidence and truth, which had at the outset seemed so promising, ultimately proved inadequate to the task of providing a comprehensive account either of the characteristic methodical aspect of science or of its dependence on the historical and intersubjective variables. Accordingly, as we also saw in detail, Husserl was driven to the use, instead, of an ambiguous concept of objectivity, which fluctuated according to the context: at one moment objectivity was to be constituted by a transcendental ego; at another it was a sedimented accomplishment of a method.[15]

As a direct consequence of these inherent difficulties, when Husserl came to study his central problem the solution that was to emerge was also ambiguous. Not merely coincidentally, this problem was rather similar (at least on the surface) to the one we are posing. In brief, it was the question of how to establish a foundation for the discursive unities of science in such a way that their historical and cultural variation would also be rendered intelligible. Unfortunately, for our purposes Husserl's answer was unsatisfactory. His concept of the lifeworld – which was intended to embrace much of the solution – was an unstable one, attempting as it did to reconcile incommensurable problematics (from the point of view of one of them); like the concept of truth itself it was forced to oscillate between an immediately intuited, actually experienced and experienceable world and a site of social and cultural sedimentations.[16]

We shall not discuss in any more detail at this juncture the implications of Husserl's theory for the suggested sociology of objectivity. Many of the major points have already been covered at length. Furthermore, additional possibilities emerging from his work will be elaborated and developed as we proceed. The purpose of the foregoing remarks was merely to restate a few elementary conclusions and to re-emphasize the importance of Husserl for our present deliberations. Here as always Husserl's works contain powerful insights and pregnant possibilities. Indeed it should be clear that the problem itself which we are considering owes its formulation largely to the conclusions we have gleaned from his philosophy. However here as previously the limitations of phenomenology are palpable: through its own techniques is revealed an incapacity to resolve the very problems it brings into view.

If phenomenology, then, is incapable alone of supplying a satisfactory programme for the elaboration of a sociology of objectivity, is such a resource to be found instead within Marxism? For after all, much of Marx's work was directed specifically towards an explication of the relationship between the social structures and the dominant epistemological forms. As is already apparent from our discussion of the theory of fetishism it is our view that there is indeed much to be gained in this regard from a study of the writings of the Marxian tradition. Accordingly, we shall offer some brief remarks on the relevance of these results for the particular project at hand. Before doing so, however, we would like to take the present opportunity to make some critical comments on an alternative approach, which also claims to be derived from Marx's thought but which seems to us to be without efficacy regarding the development of a theory of objectivity.

The approach referred to is, briefly, the attempt to locate social origins for the theoretical structures – deep causes within the social system, from which the various forms of science are to be derived. In the context of Marxism, of course, it is often claimed that the 'origin' lies in the economic structure of the society – and indeed

Marxists from time to time have even attempted such pro-grammes.[17]

It seems to us that a characterization of object domains in this way, that is, in terms of social origins, would not be appropriate. Our principal objection concerns specifically the limitations imposed on the outcomes of the theory by the assumption a priori of a particular causal style. Now the specific standpoint which appeals to final causation as the ultimately determining order did not of course begin with Marx; on the contrary, it can be traced at least to Aristotle, in whose writings the metaphysical consequences of this presupposition were already worked out.[18] It would not be useful to enter into a detailed discussion of Aristotle here. However it should be stated that the fact that for him finality was an ethical goal immanent in the ethical subject, whereas in the modern version it is in the economy that final determination is vested is in our context not decisive. For the structure of the theory remains undisturbed by such a transition to social theory. Whether finality is replaced by the World Spirit, by all of humanity or by the unfolding of an economic essence, theoretically the outcome is the same: there is a potentiality and what the theory seeks to apprehend is no more than the paths to its necessary actualization.[19]

It has been argued that a social theory based on such a presupposition would necessarily incorporate a seriously circumscribed political practice. In particular, it is claimed that since socio-historical activity could no longer be seen as existing for itself a natural continuity follows with Stalinist bureaucratic politics.[20] For our purposes however it is the specific *epistemological* consequences of this approach that are of most interest. In fact, it seems to us its adoption would impose such limitations as to compromise the task we are trying to accomplish.

Certainly, at the least, it is not difficult to see that the very posing of the questions in terms of origins would designate in advance the forms of the potential relationship between the various phenomena. In particular, it would impose on them what might be called a 'causal style', according to which the theory's adequacy might be determined by the extent to which it could identify entities that were logically prior to those it is studying. When such a perspective is applied to social theory, of course, the logical categories are converted into social ones. In consequence, forms of both experience and communication which threatened to exceed the narrow determinations imposed by the principle of causality must be automatically excluded. In the search for origins nothing can be admitted which cannot be explained within the universal causal scheme. However, as we have seen previously,[21] it is now known that the field of social phenomena is not exhausted by the theoretical schema associated with causal explanation, for other methodologies exist which belong to distinct conceptual frameworks.

In particular, we have had occasion to refer in this regard to the theoretical schema of 'understanding', which encompasses aims, motives, reasons, practical considerations and communicative processes, together with the interpretations of actions that utilize them; each of these phenomena is simply not apprehensible under the causal schema.

The point here – that the universality of causal explanation cannot be taken for granted – may today seem so simple and obvious as to be hardly worth stating. However in the context of the search in which we are engaged for a theory that would render apprehensible the relationship between objectivity and society the temptation is great to adopt the perspective of causality. What we have shown is that such an approach to the sociology of objectivity would necessarily impose in advance profound restrictions, not justified by argument, on the kinds of relationships that would be conceivable between the social entities, or between the social and the theoretical ones. That is, in short, the choice a priori of a theory of origins would, by excluding certain theoretical possibilities, potentially limit the kinds of explanations that could be considered – thus throwing into question the entire investigation.

We noted above that the approach under criticism is often attributed to Marxism. Now we would not like to enter the discussion as to whether legitimate sources for such an interpretation are in fact to be found in Marx's writings. However we do claim, on the basis of arguments adduced in a previous chapter, that whatever the result of such a discussion might be, Marx himself also demonstrated[22] that such a way of posing the problem places unconscionable restraints on the theoretical medium and so must be discarded. He achieved this, moreover, by doing exactly that for the omission of which he has been criticized:[23] by raising the question of the radical historicity of theory,[24] as we saw previously, he showed the mutual interdependence of social facts and of their means of conceptualization.[25] According to this view, any description of social phenomena which claims to isolate as logically prior some particular aspect of the social whole implicitly denies this relationship[26] and in consequence falls victim to 'fetishism'. In the specific context which we have been considering this can be put more simply: the adoption a priori of a partial viewpoint (such as the logic of origins) necessarily condemns the resulting description to objectivism.

Marxism, at least as we are interpreting it here, provides some valuable indications for a social theory of objectivity. It demonstrates the contingency of the contemporary form of objectivity and shows how this is systematically related to the capitalist social forms. It provides a useful mode of theorizing the relationship between objectivity and society which has efficacy – at least in capitalist society. This use of theory can be described variously: it is often called, for example, 'dialectical'; for our purposes however it may be more effectively described by means of the metaphor of psychoanalysis. According to this view (which was also referred to earlier) the general procedure of Marx's analysis of fetishism is formally that of a 'psychoanalysis of society'.[27] For the purpose of a psychoanalyst is not principally to solve problems but rather to allow them to be *symbolized*, and this is exactly what Marx achieves in his account of fetishism. By rendering both the social phenomena and the conceptual ones at the same level of symbolization he ensures that these disparate entities are commensurable; hence their interconnection can be elucidated.

The Marxian theory suggests some of the features that would be required of a sociology of objectivity. It shows that such a theory would have to provide a dynamics of the modes of givenness of objects with respect to the social and historical variables. In fact, it would have to accomplish more than this, for it would have to render intelligible also the *reciprocal* dependence of the structures of objectivity and the social matrix. In this sense (we note in passing) it may emerge from the analysis that it is indeed legitimate to speak of Western science as a 'capitalist science' – that is, not as a causal outcome of the capitalist infrastructure but as the realization of a regulative principle that is common to both.

Finally, from Marxism it is possible to infer some general hypotheses regarding the relationship between objectivity and society. In our discussion in Chapter 6 we formulated a basic thesis which proposed a relation between socially formed problematics and the object domains of possible theories of nature. In addition, we suggested that one of the means by which the unity of a scientific body of thought could be typified was in terms of what we referred to there as the specific fetishism – that is, the underlying conception of objectivity – of a society. In the ensuing chapters we have clarified many of the problems implicit in these hypotheses. We have elaborated, for example, the concepts of object domain and problematic; we have discussed the relationship between phenomenology and structuralism; and we have attempted to characterize the perspectives of the three outstanding scientific theories in terms of objectivity and truth. Many of the results we have achieved have been both interesting and suggestive; what is more, they have been consistent with, and in large part even the fulfilment of, the hypotheses we articulated on the basis of our study of the Marxian theory. Nevertheless, substantial outstanding problems remain. The theory of fetishism, like Husserl's phenomenology, gives no indication regarding the precise mechanisms by which, in general, object domains come into being. Like phenomenology, it lacks a comprehensive description of the objective forms, from the point of view of their dependence on social and historical variables. And, like the other theory, it lacks a detailed account of the structures of communication and discourse in general.

Both Marxism and phenomenology, therefore, offer rich resources for the future development of a sociology of objectivity. However, at least from the point of view of the interpretations offered here, neither is entirely adequate for this task. For this reason we would like to turn to a discussion of another possible strategy – a strategy which would bring together major themes of both bodies of thought. This third approach would take as its point of departure the reference to discourse in the formulation of the problem of the lifeworld. Subsequently it would set itself the task of developing a conceptual framework that would make possible the apprehension of the specific discursive unities of science as stable regions within a flux of communication. Thereby the forms of objectivity typical of a scientific theory could be characterized in terms of historically contingent intersubjective variables. In its contemporary elaboration this kind of approach is associated most notably with the names of J. Habermas and Karl-Otto Apel, who have worked on the formulation of a communication theory of society based on a programme for developing a universal pragmatics of language. It seems to us that this work is particularly relevant in our context, even though both authors – holding to the view of science as constrained within the cognitive interest of technical control, which we criticized earlier[28] – explicitly deny the possibility of such an application. In accordance with this last circumstance, it is necessary to add that the construction which follows has been devised by us and does not pretend to provide a faithful representation of either Habermas's or Apel's thought. Nonetheless it is intended to be, at least, consistent with that thought, from which, as we have said, an explicitly formulated account is in any case lacking.

345

Pragmatics and objectivity

In respect of Husserl, Habermas starts implicitly from the arguments of C. S. Peirce that no ultimate recourse is possible to an unshakeable underlying foundation of intuitive givenness.[29] In consequence, for Habermas as for Peirce, *reality* can be determined no longer by the constitutive activities of a transcendental consciousness but instead only by the collective efforts of all those who participate in the processes of inference and interpretation that make up an inquiry.[30] Indeed, he says: 'The predicate "real" has no explicable meaning apart from states of fact about which we can make true statements.'[31] More precisely, in relation to specific validity claims, if truth can no longer be derived from evidence then such claims can be justified only through arguments in the process of discourse.

It would not of course be appropriate for us to try to outline the main features of Habermas's theories of communication and truth. Rather we shall attempt only to describe the critique of Husserl that seems to be implicit in such a theory and to suggest where this might be relevant for our present purposes.

For the theory proposed by Habermas[32] the only meaning of which we can intelligibly speak is linguistic meaning – that is, meaning which can be formulated and thus belongs a priori to the matrix of communication of a society. No meaning therefore can exist for an isolated monadic subject because meaning constitution is now necessarily a communicative process in which validity is established – either potentially or in fact – only in relation to a number of different subjects. Thus Habermas both utilizes and extends some of the familiar insights of Wittgenstein. In *Philosophical Investigations* the latter had pointed out that 'It is what human beings say that is true and false; and they agree in the language they use. That is not agreement in opinions but in forms of life.'[33] Thus 'the meaning of a phrase is characterized by the use we make of it', so that it is not a mere 'mental accompaniment to the expression'.[34] For the purpose of social analysis Habermas develops these arguments, employing also Wittgenstein's concept of 'following a rule'. Indeed, this is particularly appropriate, for 'obeying a rule' implies at once both an interpretation[35] and a practice.[36] Hence 'it is not possible to obey a rule "privately": otherwise thinking one was obeying a rule would be the same thing as obeying it'.[37] It follows therefore at once from Wittgenstein's own arguments that the identity of meanings depends upon the application of intersubjectively valid rules and that validity claims can be vindicated only in the process of linguistic communication involving at least one other subject.[38] Furthermore, as we shall see, it is these rules – which presuppose on the part of participating subjects a 'competence' in rule-governed behaviour – which will provide the systematic unities into which meaning is partitioned.

As for the validity claims themselves however, for Habermas, reflecting on their conditions of possibility, it now becomes apparent that implicit in any instance of discourse are four different types of claims: claims to comprehensibility, to truthfulness, to appropriateness and to truth.[39] Thus that which has formerly been stressed to the exclusion of all others emerges as in fact only one type of validity claim – albeit of course a rather privileged one. Nevertheless, even propositionally differentiated truth must be viewed in a pragmatic context as a particular kind of claim that we connect with statements by asserting them; that is, there can be no separation of the criteria for truth from the criteria for the argumentative settlement of truth claims.[40]

We have here only in the most rudimentary way alluded to some of the basic themes of Habermas' 'consensus theory of truth' and his theory of communication in general. Even so, the potential advantages of this approach in relation to phenomenology are apparent. For example, the starting point is now taken not as the monadic subject but rather intersubjectivity itself, thus obviating the need for elaborate – and perhaps rather implausible – secondary mechanisms such as 'empathetic understanding'[41] to explain its advent. Further, not only does linguistic communication no longer present a major obstacle for the theory but rather it becomes an explanatory tool in its own right, without the possibility of a deep study of its own structures being prejudiced; indeed we have already seen how the most elementary initial considerations lead to the exposure of the multi-dimensionality of the claims implicit in discourse. Other difficulties produced by Husserl's system can also be easily overcome. Thus 'categorial intuition', which too caused difficulty above, now appears naturally as the forms themselves of the rules that govern communicative behaviour. For those 'forms of connection of matter' – such as conjunction, disjunction, etc. – which, from the phenomenological perspective, must be regarded as intuitable categorial objects,[42] from the viewpoint of the present theory are merely the rules of syntax that control the construction and use of symbols in communication. And again, to the extent that all meaning now derives from intersubjective sources in a linguistic form, neither does the disjunction between subjective meaning and intersubjectively communalized experience appear as a problem within the theory.[43] Finally, in relation to the concept of a 'lifeworld': as the quotation above from Wittgenstein suggests, such a notion could still be preserved. However it would refer no longer to an 'immediately intuited ground of all theoretical and practical life', replete with its inherent perplexities and paradoxes.[44] Instead it would encompass the systematic forms – in principle socially and historically variable – which characterize the structure of intersubjectivity in a given epoch and which thus provide the cultural and institutional context within which meaning and truth congeal. In such a theory then the crucial link between *knowledge* and social life would still be maintained at the core, as also would the social constitution of *objects*: for as might be expected, like truth, the 'objectivity of the individual's experience is structurally entwined with the intersubjectivity of understanding among individuals'.[45]

This last issue is of course exactly the problem with which we are concerned. Further, since the objectivity of experience consists precisely in its being intersubjectively shared, the conditions of possibility of meaning apply equally to both objectivity and truth. But while these conditions may indeed be necessary ones they are by no means sufficient. For, as we have repeatedly emphasized, the two concepts are in fact distinct. Certainly, every object domain has associated with it what Karl-Otto Apel has called a 'categorial meaning'[46] a propositional claim in respect of the characteristic categorial environment of its particular species of objectivity. However, while the truth claims are indeed connected with these meanings, to the extent that they share as conditions of possibility the same structures of linguistic intersubjectivity, their specific reference is nevertheless rather to the argumentative corroboration in discourse – according to procedures and principles that can be universally justified – of potentially falsifiable hypothetical claims.[47] This is not a minor point, for it is just this unity of reasoning that allows for the differential meaning-constitution of object domains. The continuity of argumentation ensures that in all sciences the same conditions govern the discursive redemption of validity claims.[48] This means that, to the extent that the propositions of science can be converted into discursively testable truth claims, a continuous reference can be maintained between the variable epistemological contents of different sciences and the abiding underlying intersubjective structures; thus the proliferation of object domains need be seen neither as purely gratuitous nor as *meaningless* from the point of view of social life.[49]

On the other hand however the problem must now be faced

directly of the systematic differences between the various realms of objects. One possibility at least is excluded by the conclusions just described: we cannot conceive of the constitution of scientific object domains as a mere continuation of the objectivations that occur in practical life.[50] For a commitment to everyday experience would vitiate the possibility of the corroborative vindication of hypothetical claims which must certainly form a part of any true science; indeed the conceptual operations of science generally would thereby be undermined. In addition, we ourselves have rejected previously Habermas's constant claim that all theories of nature are subject to the technical knowledge-constitutive interest. Nevertheless we believe that this claim is not altogether fundamental to his theory and that indeed other concepts he has introduced in a broader context are potentially helpful also for the understanding of science. We refer in particular to yet another major theme from the work of Ludwig Wittgenstein which has been taken up and developed by Habermas and also at length notably by Apel, a philosopher (to whom we referred above) whose project intersects substantially with Habermas's own. The concept is that of the 'language-game'.

* * * * * *

In the *Tractatus* the younger Wittgenstein had sought to construct a universal language that would mirror the facts. It was intended that all those sentences in this language that were meaningful would be exactly those which were generated in accordance with its syntactical rules.[51] Conversely, the only meaning that could be considered was linguistic; for meaning itself was thought of as just the information content of linguistic propositions.[52] Truth similarly was dependent on the linguistic form: a fact, if true, necessarily corresponded with some sentence in the language.[53] Nevertheless truth and meaning were to be sharply distinguished, for a sentence could certainly be meaningful without being true.[54] Truth required a correspondence with the facts – either directly, for elementary propositions, or indirectly, through the reduction of a proposition to its elementary constituents by the application of the logic of truth-functions.[55] Thus we have the famous opening lines of the *Tractatus*:

1   The world is all that is the case.
1.1 The world is the totality of facts, not of things.[56]

But even if truth and meaning were distinct the preconditions for

349

the establishment of the former and for the understanding of the latter were of course closely related. Precisely: '(t)o understand a proposition means to know what is the case if it is true'.[57] That is, to understand a proposition is to be acquainted with the procedures according to which its validity could be established. That is, meaning is coterminous with the logico-linguistic processes of verification.

The *Tractatus* sought to circumscribe the object domain of the natural sciences by characterizing all the possible propositions that may occur within them.[58] Of course it claimed for itself much more than this, maintaining that such propositions were in fact the only meaningful ones. Indeed this work was probably the first thoroughly rigorous attempt to generalize the objectivistically formulated conception of knowledge associated with natural science to encompass explicitly the human sciences also. The difficulties associated with this project have of course been studied in detail. For example, the difficulties with belief sentences which Wittgenstein treated in 5.54 and with his solution, in which he proposed a radical reduction of the psychological understanding of intentional meanings to the semantic understanding of meanings of propositions;[59] the problems with possible mystical thinking in 6.0 to 7, and so on – these issues and others have attracted a vast literature. For the present argument however it is necessary to focus only on a single deficiency of the *Tractatus*: the profoundly monological conception of knowledge on which the whole work depends. This may seem somewhat paradoxical, since the existence of just one universal language would appear to guarantee a priori the possibility of communication and indeed that even the most private experience would be inherently intersubjective. Certainly this is how Wittgenstein himself seems to argue in 5.64 and elsewhere. But in fact the reverse is true. In the *Tractatus* it is up to every individual language user to extract for himself the rules according to which meaning and truth can be identified. The possibility of a communal development of meaning is excluded. The very universality and univocity of the language protects it from the variable impacts of history and culture. The possibilities therefore of both the historical development of the forms of speech and the proliferation of languages are abolished in principle. The unyielding precision of the language prevents the expression of nuances of meaning that occur only in specific contexts of interaction. Indeed, in general, the unfolding of a complex and multifaceted meaning out of the continuum of human communication is denied at the very heart of the theory.

It was precisely the encounter with communication that produced the latter Wittgenstein's own idiosyncratic critique of objectivism: the critique that was embodied in the concept of the 'language-game' – perhaps the pivotal notion of *Philosophical Investigations*. The development of this concept emerged from a reconsideration from the perspective of communication of a theme that provides an underlying continuity between the early and the late Wittgenstein; this theme, to which we have in fact already adverted in both contexts is just that of 'the rule'. We have seen how in the *Tractatus* the syntactical rules, which subsist absolutely independently of the behaviour of particular subjects, constitute the a priori conditions of all meaning. And we have seen also how later the concept was expanded precisely to encompass the behaviour of communicating subjects. In the latter case rules certainly still regulated the production of meaning, but now only insofar as they appeared in conventions of behaviour and patterns of language use that were accepted in communication and from which departures could be identified and criticized. But the essence of a rule is to endow with a systematic unity the range of entities to which it applies. How are the corresponding unities of communicative behaviour to be understood?

It is here precisely that the concept of language-game enters. The idea of a language-game is developed from examples of different sorts of games. Just as universal properties cannot be found which characterize every possible game,[60] so is the same true for different uses of language.[61] Nevertheless against the diffuse background of everyday speech and action coherent, reproducible patterns can be identified; these patterns Wittgenstein calls 'language-games'. The regularities to which the concept refers are not restricted exclusively to the linguistic realm. Indeed, from the very first use of the term it is made clear that it is to refer to 'the whole, consisting of language and the actions into which it is woven'.[62] As might therefore be expected there is a multiplicity of such language-games – and furthermore new language-games come into existence and old ones become obsolete.[63] Language-games may include: giving orders and obeying them, reporting an event, play-acting, forming and testing a hypothesis, singing catches, making a joke and so on.[64] Thought and action are interwoven in a language-game, which may apply to any aspect of communicative behaviour.

But a language-game does not just 'apply' to an instance of behaviour: it is at the same time constitutive of it. Under the sign of the language-game new categories of modes of behaviour actually come into existence. The rules of the corresponding language-games constitute the depth grammar[65] of language which contains the criteria of sense and nonsense and, at the same time, prescribes the a priori ontological structure of the situational world that belongs to those language-games.[66] Here it is important to stress one more time that the rules referred to are not exclusively linguistic. Instead, what is now fundamental is communication. Rather than the generation of sequences of symbols what is constantly at issue are patterns of interaction and 'forms of life',[67] and these only become accessible to us as meaningful and intelligible behaviour on the presupposition of the public 'institution' and 'customs' of the language-games.

Thus the conception of language in the *Philosophical Investigations* is both narrower and wider than that of the earlier work. It is narrower, because universal themes are no longer sought; there is no attempt any more to identify the 'general form of propositions'.[68] However it is also wider, because it now takes into account the manifold complexity of human communication and the interweaving of language and action on which the latter depends. The 'use-theory' of meaning described above, according to which the meaning of a word or sentences derives from the role it plays in the system of language, emerges directly out of the theory of language-games. But from the same theory has been added also the insight that 'the axis of reference' of the study of meaning must be rotated 'about the fixed point of our real need'.[69] The two come together in the extreme differentiation of language-games which can thus be understood only as a partitioning into stable regions of meaning of the variable flux of social activity. Two further consequences can be noted: the theory of language-games implies the relinquishing of the priority, upheld in the *Tractatus*, of (a caricatured) natural science. And furthermore the theory itself is profoundly anti-objectivist, rendering as it does all meaning explicitly dependent on the processes of social life.

The potential then within the language-game conception for the development of a general theory of objectivity is evident. But at the same time, compared to Wittgenstein's earlier work, its omission is startling. For whereas the *Tractatus* has been concerned almost exclusively with the cognitive use of language, in the *Investigations* it is the communicative aspect of language that is stressed above all else and a discussion of truth is almost completely absent. This was of course no accident for, although the abstention from theory is not made explicit in the later as it is in the earlier work, it is nevertheless clear that Wittgenstein consciously resists the temptation to develop a general theory of language-games. 'We must do away with all explanation,' he says, 'and description alone mus take its place.' Philosophical problems 'are solved ... by looking into the workings of our language ... in such a way as to make us recognize those workings ... The problems are solved, not by giving new information, but by arranging what we have always known.'[70] For Wittgenstein the language-game was strictly a device for the explication of ordinary communication. By the study of everyday instances of language he believed that patterns of interaction otherwise inaccessible could be rendered intelligible. But clearly this is not enough. The cognitive and communicative uses of language are inextricably intertwined. If it is possible in principle to develop an understanding of the emergence of characteristic patterns of objectivity against the background of the 'forms of life' of a society then so also must a theory be conceivable of the intromission of sets of objects into the epistemological field. A mere descriptive theory of language-games, on the other hand, that denies the possibility of a more general level of abstraction will remain incapable of apprehending the conditions according to which reality is made the object of experience.

* * * * * *

Here of course we have returned to Habermas, who takes up the challenge precisely of developing a depth grammar of language-games.[71] For him this requires the realization of an extensive theoretical programme that would seek to reconstruct the underlying systems of rules according to which utterances capable of consensus can be formed. Some elements of this universal pragmatics have been adverted to already in our description of the four kinds of validity claim implicit in any utterance. Habermas describes in detail also the correlations that obtain with several other fundamental variables of discourse: with – to use the technical language that he employs – the domains of reality to which every speech action takes up relation, with the attitudes of the speaker prevailing in particular modes of communication and with general functions that grammatical sentences assume in their relations to reality.[72] The programme of a universal pragmatics is developed at length in Habermas's works. The precise details of the full theory however are not of relevance here, for Habermas's concern is of course not with the theory of science but primarily with the development of a theory of communicative competence; accordingly, many of his formulations bear on unrelated themes. What is important for the former project – at least from the particular perspective under examination – is rather, on the one hand, the existence of the latter and, on the other, of the possibility of its application to the problem of the description of the evolution of the social forms. Such an application has in fact also been the subject at length of Habermas's work, as we shall see shortly.

The approach of the point of view of 'pragmatics' to a social theory of objectivity is therefore as follows. The starting point is taken to be intersubjectivity, which is the substratum presupposed by both objectivity and truth. In this theory, objectivity and truth must be carefully distinguished from the very beginning. Truth is an invariant, both within a society and across cultural boundaries. It emerges only in relation to discourse, its constancy deriving from the existence of imperatives immanent in the processes of human communication and cognition; thus a proposition is true if it can be corroborated, either in principle or in fact, in argumentative discourse. Objectivity on the other hand is subject to extensive differentiation so that even within a given society a range of domains is possible, each exhibiting its own principle of objectivity. It is precisely the formation of these various object domains that the theory seeks to describe.

In the flux of communication certain repetitive and stereotypical patterns of language use and behaviour can be observed. These language-games represent regions of intersubjective agreement and are thus constitutive of meaning; they are the source of criteria of sense and non-sense and also designate a priori the ontological structure of a situational context. But while they thereby define systems of objects their elements are not objects. Furthermore they are by no means coextensive with object domains: one object domain would require many language-games to specify it. Nor are they mutually exclusive: two language-games may have a non-empty intersection or – expressed somewhat differently – be 'intertwined'.[73] Finally, the boundaries of the language-games are infrequently precisely defined; indeed the diffuseness of their outlines is often taken as a distinguishing characteristic.[74] Therefore although the eventual specification of an object domain of language-game is exact, the process is certainly not an unambiguous one. If a mathematical analogy were appropriate, one could say that the language-games supply an 'open cover' for the object domain.

In a previous chapter we elaborated the comparative characteristics of the problematics referred to as phenomenology and structuralism. Elsewhere, we examined in detail the structures of the theories of relativity, quantum mechanics and objectivism. To clarify the present discussion we may now bring together some of these results, showing how the various theories can be associated with sets of language-games. As before, it may be useful to present this material in the form of a table setting out the specific features of each problematic. If this is done, the following schema is obtained:

Problematic:	Objectivism	Phenomenology	Structuralism
Object domain:	Objects and objectivities defined to exist independently of all subject-related variables	Intentional subject-object unities	States of systems; interactions
Language-game:	Description of the properties and behaviour of entities according to pre-assigned criteria	Determination of qualities and quantities defined with respect to operational criteria	Textual interpretations of classes of data – especially those distributed discretely
Scientific perspective:	Classical mechanics	Relativity theory	Quantum mechanics

Thus described, a language-game forms a language-action unity. It incorporates elements both of an object domain and of the problematic within which that domain is embedded. Such a formulation however is a prolepsis: the problem is exactly how it occurs that the primitive units coalesce into object domain and problematic, which subsist at a higher level of abstraction. Here, two possibilities seem to present themselves. The language-games could be regarded merely as problematics in embryo – that is as substructures of the larger unit, to which they were structurally isomorphic. This is an implausible solution, given the rudimentary character of some language-games and the possibility that one must belong to a number of problematics. Alternatively, a more elaborate theory must be sought, which would provide a second order account of language-games: a general theory that could itself appeal to a conception of truth rooted in the preconditions for both.[75] It would not be required of the theory that it provide at this stage an understanding of the formation of particular object domains, much less, problematics: it would be necessary only that the possibility in principle of such processes be justified. It seems to us that such a step may well be able to be accomplished by a programme – if it

355

could be sustained – of a universal pragmatics. For such a theory would reinterpret the language-action units of language-games as units of discourse and action. Thus it would find in them systems of rules underlying and presupposing the use of sentences in utterances that could be brought to consensus.[76] That is, language-games would be interpreted as providing the intersubjective frameworks against which particular kinds of claims would be made that would be susceptible to vindication in discourse. Consequently, against the background of the imperatives inherent a priori in the latter, the transition from communication to cognition could be theorized.

If it can be demonstrated that out of the structures of intersubjective life consistent unities defining problematics – and, consequently, object domains – can indeed congeal, then one further task would have to be accomplished. The development of an adequate sociology of object domains requires also a theory of the historical determinations to which the structures of objectivity are subject. More precisely, it has to be shown that systematic variations in the cognitive and communicative potential of a society occur which may privilege the emergence of certain problematics over others. Thereby the emphasis in a given epoch on a particular object domain (or object domains) could perhaps be rendered intelligible to social theory, as also could the well-established process of a transformation öf problematics. For then an explanation may well be accessible as to why from the manifold possibilities always available at the level of practical life – which thus define an ever-present *de facto* 'proliferation' – a few problematics only are systematically identified. In addition, hopefully, such a theory would elucidate the interrelation of such variations with developmental processes occurring at the level of the productive forces. However it is unlikely that the relationship between the two would be – as is occasionally supposed – one of causal determination;[77] for indeed as Marx recognized it is impossible to grasp the development of the productive forces independently of the forms of social integration and their corresponding world-views. The absence of such a causal relation would however have no bearing on the success or failure of the project, for it is clear that what is needed is independent of such requirements. What is needed rather amounts to an expanded theory of historical materialism which could encompass the processes of social evolution simultaneously at the material and at the practical levels.

Exactly the development of such a theory has of course been the precise focus of a substantial part of Habermas's work. In *Legiti-*

mation Crisis and in his essays on 'the reconstruction of historical materialism' he has elaborated a proposal for the development of a general theory of social evolution capable of explaining particular evolutionary transformations in terms of both production and social life. Since our purpose in this sketch has been merely to show that the formulation of a social theory of the emergence of object domains is in principle possible from the point of view of a communication theory of society, historically mediated, it would not be appropriate to attempt here to describe in detail this aspect of Habermas's work. Instead, to conclude the discussion we shall merely, with the help of a few quotations, illustrate some of its important themes.

In *Legitimation Crisis* Habermas describes 'three universal properties of social systems':

(a) The exchange between social systems and their environments takes place in production (appropriation of outer nature) and socialization (appropriation of inner nature) through the medium of utterances that admit of truth (*wahrheitsfahiger Ausserungen*) and norms that have need of justification (*rechtfertigungsbedurftiger Normen*) – that is, through discursive validity claims (*Geltungsanspruche*). In both dimensions, development follows rationally reconstructible patterns.

(b) Change in the goal values of social systems is a function of the state of the forces of production and of the degree of system autonomy; but the variation of goal values is limited by a logic of development of world-views (*Weltbilder*) on which the imperatives of system integration have no influence. The socially related (*vergesellschafteten*) individuals form an inner environment that is paradoxical from the point of view of steering.

(c) The level of development of a society is determined by the institutionally permitted learning capacity, in particular by whether theoretical-technical and practical questions are differentiated, and whether discursive learning processes can take place.[78]

He proceeds to expand some of the points further. Social behaviour, he maintains, is subject to the imperatives of validity claims, the influence of which is mediated through the structures of linguistically produced intersubjectivity. Here, however, a specific feature of the human interchange must be recognized. Linguistic communication, by its very nature, entails at once not only a particular propositional content but also an inner reflection on the interpersonal relations thereby established; that is, both cognitive and normative behaviour occur together in any intersubjective process based on language.[79] Accordingly, he argues, '(l)anguage functions as a kind of transformer; because psychic processes such as sensations, needs and feelings are fitted into structures of linguistic intersubjectivity, inner episodes or experiences are transformed into intentional contents – that is, cognitions into statements, needs and feelings into normative expectations (precepts and values)'.[80] This transformation, which is of crucial significance for social life, is especially important here because it illustrates a fundamental point. It is only on the level described above as the level of utterances and norms that the contingency associated with single individuals can be transcended and generality attained. The generality of norms is what we usually call 'legitimacy'; that of utterances is equivalent to that which we regard as the 'objectivity of knowledge'. The achievement of both is required if we are to be able to speak of meaning in anything other than a purely private sense.[81] Indeed, rather more even than this can be said, for it is only on the basis of such validity claims that the possibility of social life could arise at all. It is only through linguistically mediated intersubjective processes of the kind described that it is possible to ensure the existence of 'the *community* or *shared meaning* ... that is constitutive for the socio-cultural life-world'.[82]

In relation to learning processes Habermas's radical thesis is that the species learns simultaneously in the dimension of technically useful knowledge and the dimension of moral-practical consciousness; furthermore each developmental process 'follows its own logic'.[83] Evolution in both dimensions 'takes place in the form of directional learning processes that work through discursively redeemable validity claims'.[84]

The development of productive forces and the alteration of normative structures follow, respectively, logics of growing theoretical and practical insight. Of course, the rationally reconstructible patterns that collective learning processes follow – that is, the history of secular knowledge and technology on the one hand and of the structural alteration of identity-securing interpretive systems on the other – explain only the logically necessary sequence of *possible* developments. The *actual* developments, innovations and stagnations, occurrence of crises, productive or unproductive working out of crises, and so on can be explained only with the aid of empirical mechanisms.[85]

In sum, Habermas argues that there are indeed systematic processes of development exhibited by the cognitive and communicative structures and that these issue in systematic unities of meaning
and truth which in turn become institutionalized in world views
and 'principles of social organization'.[86] Thereby the range of possibilities for the material and conceptual structures is determined.
It is 'possibilities' also that define the nature of the interdependence
between the two levels: in a vague sense each can be considered to
supply the limits of the other; but nevertheless the precise forms
can only be discovered empirically.

$$* \quad * \quad * \quad * \quad * \quad *$$

Now it can readily be seen that these results are just those that
were required for the completion of the theory constructed from
the proposed perspective. It is our contention that this theory, if it
will prove capable of being sustained by rigorous argument, could
provide the rudiments of an account of the emergence of particular
theories of nature in the contexts of particular societies and cultures. In so doing it could also contribute to an understanding of
the profound relationship between science and knowledge. It must
be emphasized however that such rigorous argumentation is
presently lacking and for this reason the proposed strategy can for
the moment be regarded as no more than provisional. Indeed,
Habermas himself presents his works only as a preliminary deli-
neation of a theoretical programme which awaits a full elaboration.
This is not the only circumscription however to which the foregoing
account is subject. If the development of this programme is to be
taken up then attention must also be given to a number of objections to which the theory in its present form would seem to be
susceptible. Such objections are not difficult to construct; this in
itself is a substantial indication of the provisional character of these
arguments. In what follows, to close the present section, we shall
sketch - with extreme brevity - just three of the major problems
which the pragmatic theory must confront. While these objections
are not being explicitly presented as constituting by themselves an
additional possible coherent approach to the sociology of objectivity, it seems to us that they do nevertheless display a unity in their
joint concern for the problem of intersubjectivity. Accordingly, it
is conceivable that, if it were desired, their implicit contentions
could be developed into a coherent programme in its own right.

The *first objection* we mention refers directly to the problem of
foundations. The attempt to secure for objectivity a grounding in

intersubjectivity[87] rather than in either consciousness or the material structures of production does not altogether overcome the objections first raised in relation to the logic of origins. This is so for two reasons. First, if a starting point for the theory is to be considered at all, its extent must certainly exceed the boundaries of intersubjectivity. In particular, since objectivity is what is to be explained it cannot be presupposed in the origin – and neither therefore can the differentiation between subject and object. But certainly neither is it true that subjectivity and objectivity are exhausted in intersubjectivity. Furthermore, both language and the interaction with things are presupposed in both communication and the constitution of material nature. Indeed, as Habermas himself puts it: '(l)abour and language are older than man and society'.[88] Thus if we are able to sanction any foundation for the theory of objectivity, then it would have to include all these things: that is, it would have to include a world in itself about us and the possibility of our relations with it, a mind capable of knowing the universe, and the primordial possibilities of language and of intersubjective communication. If the theory is to start anywhere then, it must be with what Merleau-Ponty has called 'brute being',[89] towards which 'we are already thrown'.[90] For we cannot choose either 'a philosophy that takes our experience from within (or) a philosophy ... that would judge it from without, in the name of logical criteria'. Instead we must 'situate ourselves in ourselves *and* in the things, in ourselves *and* in the other, at the point where, by a sort of *chiasm*, we become others and we become world'.[91] Such a foundation would be entirely possible, as Merleau-Ponty has demonstrated, but it would of course lead to quite a different programme from that which was sought above.

Even an empirically derived, quasi-transcendental foundation that seeks to provide the conditions for the possibility of discourse[92] does not overcome this problem. On the other hand neither can it resolve a problem of circularity that both Habermas and Apel explicitly recognize. This problem – a version for the present special context of the hermeneutic circle – concerns the reciprocal dependence between intersubjectivity and culture on the one hand and between culture and objectivity on the other.[93] The fact that these entities are reciprocally constitutive of each other frustrates the attempt to proceed from any beginning that could be analytically circumscribed. For the outcome of any such account would thereby be prejudiced in advance: it would effectively present a description of objectivity in terms of variables which themselves presuppose it.

It may be worth adding in this context that the reference to Merleau-Ponty above was not merely coincidental. In fact, a problem similar to the present one provided the explicit focus for many of the deliberations of his last work (published posthumously), *The Visible and the Invisible*. There, from his analysis of Husserl's philosophy, Merleau-Ponty identified a fundamental, abiding dilemma of traditional thought. Whether the primary emphasis was placed on objects, on consciousness or on intersubjectivity it seemed that an irreducible bifurcation had to be assumed between '"the consciousness-of" and the object'.[94] Husserl demonstrates this difficulty with great clarity. In spite of the radicalism of his insights, '(t)he whole Husserlian analysis is blocked by the framework of acts which imposes on it the philosophy of *consciousness*'.[95] Accordingly, his approach, 'in order to constitute the world', must presuppose 'a notion of the world as preconstituted';[96] what is more, it is left incapable of apprehending the complexity of the relationship between being and the world.[97] Instead, argues Merleau-Ponty, we must refuse to admit 'a preconstituted world, a logic, except for having seen them arise from our experience of brute being, which is as it were the umbilical cord of our knowledge and the source of meaning for us'. Moreover, we must avoid assuming in advance 'concepts issued from reflection' since these are 'more often than not only correlatives or counterparts of the objective world'.[98] At the beginning, we must

> eschew notions such as 'acts of consciousness', 'states of consciousness', 'matter', 'form' and even 'image' and 'perception'. We must exclude the term perception to the whole extent that it already implies a cutting up of what is lived into discontinuous acts, or a reference to 'things' whose status is not specified ... Not that these distinctions are definitely meaningless, but because if we were to admit them from the start we would re-enter the impasses we are trying to avoid.[99]

Merleau-Ponty's solution, to which we have adverted above, is the whole theory adumbrated in *The Visible and the Invisible*, but never properly elaborated. It consists of the pursuit of an underlying ontological stratum based on the intertwining of flesh and the world; of the chiasm, mentioned above; of intercorporeity;[100] and of the priority of language.[101] Here, it would be inappropriate to attempt to explain these ideas in detail. Rather, what is important for our present purposes is no more than that which is implied by their mere existence – that the objection we are proposing potentially has extensive consequences and that, furthermore, at least one alternative perspective exists within which a plausible solution is embodied.

The *second objection* appears initially to be just the opposite of the first. It is the criticism that a pragmatic account of objectivity tied to a theory of language-game is incapable of providing an appreciation of the full complexity of object domains because of its implicit reductionism: because it effectively collapses these domains into the a priori functional circles of instrumentality and communicative action. Accordingly, such a theory could convey no explanatory power since, in the absence of any such inner structure, its exposition can merely be offered descriptively *ex post facto*. To be sure, from the argument constructed the false conclusion is no longer inevitable that the conceptual content of science is fully determined by its experimental procedures. Nevertheless objectivity remains parasitic on behavioural regularities of practical life. Thus in particular, the fact cannot be accommodated by this approach that forms of objectivity may emerge as systematic effects of a given conceptual apparatus; that is, that conceptual systems, which may or may not be explicable as outcomes of social processes, may produce through endogenous mechanisms their own characteristic objective structures, and that further, these 'conceptual systems' may be languages themselves or substructures of them.[102]

Of course, from the point of view of this essay such a circumstance would be unconscionable. For it would vitiate many of our most important results. If the objection in question can be sustained then the pragmatic approach, by the very strategy of its argument, must elide the two critiques of objectivism that have emerged in modern physics; hence it must sacrifice the undoubted profound insights that have developed from this bifurcation. Furthermore, it would render unavailable the results of many of our reflections on the epistemological consequences of the formal constitution of science, that is, regarding the existence of inner imperatives not only within discourse but also within theory itself. It would, in other words, obscure the limited but important truth contained in the following affirmation:

(S)cience ... may well arise from ideology, detach itself from its field in order to constitute itself as a science, but precisely this detachment, this 'break' inaugurates a new form of historical existence and temporality which altogether saves science (at least in certain historical conditions that ensure the real continuity of its own object ...) from the common fate of a single history ...[103]

362

These two objections, which seem at first to be directly opposed, come together in a *third objection*. It is clear that the adoption of the category of intersubjectivity presupposes the priority of subjectivity, even if the latter is no longer intended to be understood as a strictly autarkic entity. Similarly, a pragmatic approach, by its very conception, assigns a privileged place to the patterns of language use and to other regularities of communicative behaviour. Thus some conception of a 'language-game' will always appear naturally within such a theory.[104] But a 'language-game' also presupposes the operation of a conscious subjectivity which is capable of acknowledging or even identifying rules and of recognizing mistakes when they occur. The mere conception of a language-game, that is, assumes the existence of a subject which pre-exists its own symbolic engagements, and such a presupposition can therefore be attributed also to any pragmatics. Further, it can be seen immediately that essentially the same conclusion can be drawn regarding the concept of constitution, which is also central to the argument above. Indeed, the concept – and even the term itself – comes directly from Husserl's phenomenology – in which, of course, it is from the beginning indissolubly linked to the concept of subject.[105]

Thus the argument elaborated above incorporates extensive assumptions regarding the subject of both discourse and action. However societies are themselves symbolic systems which both embody and give rise to the exchange processes identified as communication. But this is not all, for the subject itself is also in an important sense the *outcome* of these processes. This has been shown in detail by Jacques Lacan who has analysed the structure of the subject from the point of view of the supremacy of the signifier in discourse. Thus, in opposition to the 'ego' – which is merely the reified product of successive imaginary identifications – the subject appears as a 'resonance in the communicating networks of discourse'.[106] In fact, it is in no more than this that the subject consists: 'What constitutes me as subject is my question. In order to be recognized by the other, I utter what was only in view of what will be. In order to find him, I call him by a name that he must assume or refuse in order to reply to me.'[107] Thus discourse is a continuous process, out of the pregnant systems of presences and absences of which emerge subjects, as patterns of tensions and mutations. 'Man speaks, because the symbol has made him man';[108] and indeed we can even add: 'the world of words creates the world of things'.[109]

The subject therefore, according to these conceptions, is no pure consciousness apprehensible in advance of its putative 'constitution' of others and of things. Rather, it is a series of stable points in the network of symbolic exchanges that can be taken to characterize a culture. Such a conception seems to achieve more fundamental insights regarding the nature of both subjectivity and inter-subjectivity than are available under the approaches hitherto considered – that is, it makes available definite insights from which the pragmatic theory is excluded. This is in fact precisely the point of this last objection, which can now be summarized as follows: the argument under consideration presupposes a particular conception of the subject. This conception however is deficient, for not only does it incorporate dubious claims of its own but, in addition, it prevents other, more fundamental, insights from being made. Finally, the assumptions on which this concept of subjectivity is based are themselves very deeply situated within the pragmatic approach.

As was said, no attempt will be made to elaborate in detail the possible objections to the pragmatic approach to the sociology of objectivity. Nor will we attempt to provide a formulation which would display these objections as constituting in their own right an independent, alternative strategy to that theory. Nevertheless it is likely that such a formulation could be developed: the three objections we have listed – the problem of the relationship between man and world, the problem of the conceptual autonomy of science and the problem of the subject – do indeed appear to be susceptible to development into an additional, coherent programme. The demonstration of this would certainly constitute a worthwhile endeavour. Alternatively, it would be worthwhile to attempt to construct in detail answers to these questions from within the perspective being criticized; at the present time it appears that this too is a plausible possibility. For our present purposes however it is enough merely to establish the existence of alternatives. What is more, the lack of definitive solutions helps to emphasize an important point we have been repeating – that the questions being considered here, for the moment at least, remain open, no conclusive answers being ready to hand.

The prospect for a sociology of objectivity

Science, at its deepest conceptual core, embodies social meanings that can be identified and elaborated. More specifically, within the structured symbolic field of social discourse, a science is associated with a system of categories displaying a number of overall structural regularities. These categories are themselves to a degree socially contingent – within limits imposed by the internal requirements of the theoretical system. Accordingly, the proper locus of a social theory of science does not lie in a mere description of the behaviour of scientists; nor even does it lie in an elaboration of science's social consequences. On the contrary, such a discipline should concentrate on the actual shaping of science as a theoretical system with respect to the social and historical variables and on its specific role in relation to other structures of discourse. That is, in brief, what is needed is an account of the process by means of which differentiated object domains emerge in the contexts of specific social configurations.

From the theory of object domains developed above it is clear that the account to be provided could be of either of two types. In the first place, it could refer to particular conditions appertaining to a given empirical context – as, for example, in Marx's analysis of capitalist society and the historical form of objectivity that there prevails. On the other hand, the account of the development of object domains could be *general* in character, referring to the social conditions of possibility for the formation of such domains and to their systematic variation; here, arguments from a variety of perspectives are available, all of which seek to explain the development of forms of objectivity in relation to social processes, independently of cultural and historical contingencies; examples of such an approach have been suggested on the basis of the work of Marx, Husserl, Habermas and Wittgenstein.

Whatever the strategy that might be chosen, it will be subject to substantial, often perplexing, objections. In the present circumstances irrefragable conclusions are simply not available. In fact, there is reason to consider that they should not even be sought. The most fecund approach at present would take care to preserve the openness of the available possibilities, stressing the range of potentially fruitful orientations rather than the strengths of any particular one. This point is so important that it may be stated explicitly as a principle: that within the fields encompassing not only the theory of science but even science itself it is undesirable, and in fact would most likely be unproductive, to attempt to insist on the priority of a single set of epistemological or methodological precepts.

Of course, from the point of view of this essay the circumstances in which such a principle could be put forward are clear. Not only have we observed that a variety of perspectives is capable of producing substantial insights but also we have pointed out that the requirements of any social theory of science are manifold. For example, such a theory must be capable of engaging at once not only scientific thought but social theory and philosophy as well. This point – also simple – in itself carries non-trivial implications. It is an outcome of this essay that the social reflection on science cannot evade an engagement with the major issues of contemporary social and philosophical investigation. What is more, we have seen that at least some of the great, abiding problems, both of the theory of nature and its metatheory, in fact at the same time constitute fundamental perplexities in modern philosophy and social theory. The sociology of science in the form that we have given to it – the sociology of objectivity – will be called on to reflect upon and to interpret this far-reaching circumstance. It will be one of its tasks to explain that the interests of science are continuous with the great themes of culture and language, history and society, meaning and truth.

From these elementary reflections emerge some simple points that are worth stating – or restating – explicitly. There is no unique path that is to be taken by a 'proper' sociology of science. Rather, the underlying concerns of such a theory are continuous with those of the multiplicity of disciplines with which its object intersects. Insofar as these fields of study are committed to a proliferation of methods and perspectives then so also must be theory of sciences. Furthermore, to the extent that in the former might be contained dilemmas currently unresolved – and perhaps even in principle irresolvable – the possibility cannot be excluded that likewise similar dilemmas may occur within the latter. It is probably unnecessary to add that in spite of the fact that we are speaking here specifically of the social theory of science exactly the same conclusions apply to science itself.

Coming at the end of such laborious argumentation such a conclusion may seem disappointing. In fact, it is at once both constricting and liberating. It is constricting because henceforth neither science nor its metatheory can be considered as an autonomous discipline with its own precisely delimitable theoretical apparatus. Instead, both must render themselves open to the vast field of social and philosophical thought as it has been developed, meticulously though inconclusively, over the centuries. It is liberating for exactly the same reasons. Although the theory of science, at least, is a young discipline it nevertheless is thereby granted access to this vast wealth of accumulated insight. Accordingly, even where the answers to pressing problems are not immediately to hand it is unlikely that resources will be lacking with which to begin to deal

366

with them; once again, this last affirmation applies as much to the theory of nature as to that of objectivity. For all these reasons therefore the theory that we are proposing is not impoverished by the discovery of its proper place in the vast fabric of human inquiry; quite the contrary, it is incalculably strengthened and enriched by it. Philosophy, social theory and the study of science in both senses can now be recognized as standing in continuity with each other. It is our hope that this openness may eventually make mutually available to each discipline the special 'treasures of insight' of all. If so, perhaps the result will be a new fecundity which will prove of not inconsiderable benefit to all.

VI
Conclusions

Epilogue: Paths to be explored

This essay has been concerned with the understanding of science – with the elucidation both of its substantive hypotheses and its social and historical contingency. Our starting point was the contemporary crisis of science: the perception that science no longer answers the important questions of the times, that it serves the interests of domination, oppression and destruction at least as much as it does those of liberation and creation and that fundamental dilemmas perdure within its specific disciplines. Our objective was to contribute to the development of a social theory of science. It was anticipated that such a theory would in turn contribute to the process of social reconstruction in a twofold way: by clarifying the extent to which the social structures, and hence their transformation, are, or will be, constrained by the preponderance of specific intellectual structures and reciprocally, by explicating the degree to which scientific innovation is compromised by its subjection to the conditions of a rigorously circumscribed social environment.

We have spoken repeatedly of the 'treasures of insight' at the core of modern science and have sought, in a humble way, to contribute to their elucidation. We have tried to justify the contention that the relationship between a social configuration and an interpretation of natural phenomena is accessible to theory. We have attempted to show that science and philosophy have much to offer each other. At the same time – and not just in passing – we have stressed that the present work is to be regarded as no more than a prolegomenon – that is, as a means of establishing theoretical preliminaries for a wider project yet to be elaborated.

We began with the crisis of science. It immediately became apparent that this crisis was in fact a multiple crisis: at once, it involved perplexities bearing on the internal structure of science, on its interpretation and on its social institutions. Accordingly, we came to recognize that in the contemporary reflection on science there are at stake two broad constellations of problems. On the one hand, there are those dealing specifically with the relationship between society and science and on the other, there are the problems concerned directly with meaning and truth in the theory of nature itself.

In our attempt to address these great questions we found it appropriate to call on far-reaching resources – on the results of studies within not only social theory but also philosophy and physics. Indeed, one of our elementary premises at the very outset of this essay was the necessarily catholic nature of the modern metatheory of science, an assumption from which we drew the specific implication that such investigations can no longer renounce concern – as they so often did in the past – with the actual contents of the extant theory of nature. Concerning our endeavours regarding the problems we have mentioned, these were not altogether without consequence. We found, for example, that science has a philosophical content, or more precisely, that it depends upon a set of philosophical presuppositions, and that furthermore these presuppositions can be both identified and criticized. Specifically, we were able to characterize the theoretical outlook of classical science; this we determined to be the viewpoint of objectivism. Now of objectivism two things in particular can be said. In the first place, much available material demonstrates that, at least in respect of its application to natural phenomena, it is susceptible to arguments disputing the actual truth-content of its claims; this is in spite of the fact that objectivism is the viewpoint which has predominated in science at least since the time of Galileo – and indeed, which is still widely considered to be the only conceivable viewpoint for *any* theory of nature. Secondly, by pervading the metatheoretical context it has exerted malign effects on the attempts to understand the meaning of science – and indeed has possibly even obstructed the development of the latter.

For the sake of pursuing these themes further we turned to a consideration of some aspects of the works of Husserl and Marx. In the case of Husserl we examined in some detail the analysis he presents of the structure of science and, in particular, his refutation of objectivism. It emerged, somewhat unexpectedly, that in the process of the development of the phenomenological project not one but two distinct critiques of objectivism had been elaborated. Later we were to discover that the differences separating these two critiques were fundamental, for they were in fact the outcomes of irresolubly distinct problematics. These problematics were susceptible to a rigorous characterization: subsequently it became apparent that they embodied the two perspectives that have been extensively investigated under the familiar rubrics of phenomenology and structuralism. At the same time it became clear that the relationship between them could not be the one that is familiarly accepted. The two outlooks do not stand intractably in opposition to each other; their hypotheses are not irreducibly in contradiction. Rather, they represent complementary theoretical alternatives, each with its own special insights, its own epistemology and its own effective refutation of objectivism. Indeed, even more than this was found to be the case: we discovered – again rather unexpectedly – that each of the two problematics already actually possesses a realization in the contemporary theory of nature.

These elementary conclusions cast light on a great theoretical achievement which, remarkably, has over many years gone largely unrecognized. Fully developed, it could potentially embody substantial consequences for science itself. For example, if it is true that the contemporary theory of nature must now be understood in terms of a variety of contending problematics then it may also occur that at least some of its outstanding dilemmas are not merely formal in character, but rather philosophical or conceptual. If in turn this is true then it will be at such a level – that is, at the level of concepts rather than of the formalism – that clarification must first be sought. Notwithstanding this, in the light of these results a further, possibly unattractive, alternative must also be considered: it may be that not all of the dilemmas of science are resoluble by any means whatsoever. It may emerge for instance that some of these dilemmas are no less than manifestations of underlying incommensurable problematics, hence representing inexorable and irreducible subterranean theoretical distinctions.

Regarding Marx, we attempted, with the help both of his work and that of some of his major commentators and critics, to pursue directly the problem of the dependence of science on social variables. Taking as our main theme the critique of the fetishism of commodities as it has been developed in this tradition, we considered the general question of the process of formation of various regions of objectivity within different social configurations. In addition, more specifically, we examined the possibility of a relationship between objectivism and the cultural environment associated

373

with capitalism. In this context we proposed some general hypotheses regarding society and science. We suggested that there is indeed a constitutive process that occurs at the level of social relations – understood in the broad sense to encompass both relations of production and the symbolic relations established in symbolic interchange. This is the process according to which there congeal within social life domains of objectivity; these domains subsequently provide the substrata for theories which are developed with a view to rendering intelligible the complex, fluid and always perplexing distinction between nature and culture. The theories which emerge thus comprise representations of natural phenomena insofar as these phenomena are established in accordance with a given historically-produced conception of objectivity. In other words, it is proper to speak of forms of objectivity 'natural' to particular social and cultural contexts; furthermore, these forms can be employed to characterize the deep structure of the contemporaneous theory of nature.

Still following these themes we were able, on the basis of our study of contemporary physics to show that science in general displays both an object structure and a meaning structure which while certainly not unrelated are by no means identical. In addition, we identified within these structures a number of specific features of science which were subject to variation between theories; these included the set of objects addressed, the criteria employed, according to which it is determined whether a given theoretical or empirical proposition is well-formed, and the conception of truth adopted by a particular theory. It emerged that the existence of these features was characteristic of all science as the latter is presently conceived. In fact, all the dimensions of science – its formal structures, its communicative structures and its structures of meaning – were seen to depend on the particular ways in which these fundamental variables were fixed.

At this point it became clear once again that the bifurcation in the systematic study of science – that is, the distinction between the meaning of science and its social components – must be respected. On the one hand it is necessary to turn to a detailed study of science's internal structure: an anatomy must be undertaken of the formal procedures employed in science, of the objects with which different theories operate, of the theoretical implications of the choice of a particular logical structure or indeed of mathematics, of the processes by means of which both qualitative and quantitative changes occur in an established body of knowledge and so on. In the course of our discussion all these issues were addressed to a greater or lesser extent. In some cases substantive conclusions were proposed. In others we were content to suspend the analysis while it still remained inconclusive. In all, our primary purpose was to raise issues and to provoke problems, to offer hypotheses and alternative perspectives, the pursuit of which might in the future prove fruitful.

On the other hand, we found that it is also necessary to attempt to specify in detail the substructure of the relationship between society and science. Here again our previous considerations were helpful; they showed that what needs to be examined is the question concerning the means by which particular object domains are generated within a social field characterized by certain forms of productive, conceptual and communicative behaviour. To state the same problem more generally: what must be explicated is the evolution of structures of objectivity and meaning out of, or in relation to, the social processes. Turning to this problem – which we referred to as the task of elaborating a 'sociology of objectivity' – we considered a number of possibilities available from the existing body of social and philosophical thought, including phenomenological, Marxist and structuralist conceptual strategies. Of these the approach which seemed to us to be potentially the most fruitful was one which we fashioned from some aspects of the works of Jürgen Habermas and the late Wittgenstein. Utilizing themes from a number of theoretical traditions, this approach focussed particularly on communication, discourse and the intersubjective conditions of truth; furthermore, it emphasized both the pre-eminent importance of rules in the constitution of social language-games and the fundamental role of these language-games in the constitution of different conceptions of objectivity. This strategy does indeed appear to us to be the best presently available; however it remains the case that like the others it is subject to deep problems and contains substantial lacunae.

In the discussion of the sociology of objectivity many of the results of our previous investigations came together. Nevertheless no definitive conclusions were proposed. Indeed, one of the few conclusive results we proclaimed was precisely the need to accept for the present the impossibility of closing any of the major issues we had raised. On the contrary, in almost every case our studies have revealed ever widening and deepening implications attached to what invariably had at first seemed to be rather modest questions. Subsequently we even proposed this conclusion as an important outcome of the whole essay: we claimed that the social study of the theory of nature, formerly taken largely to be self-subsistent, raises precisely the same fundamental issues of knowledge, truth and society that have long perplexed social and philosophical thinkers. This simple but crucial result has a dual consequence. It prevents the theory of science from proceeding too far alone – that is, from isolating itself from the insights that have been won elsewhere in philosophical and sociological thought. And at the same time it opens up to science itself vast, rich resources from the benefit of which it has hitherto been excluded.

This essay is offered as a prolegomenon. We have stressed this point so vigorously that at times a suspicion of tergiversation may almost have been raised. However our purpose in insisting on the preliminary character of our present deliberations was not to evade responsibility for our own arguments, nor even to avoid indiscreet overstatements of our results. Rather, our concern was with an issue that has arisen repeatedly in the course of the discussion: the problem of truth, insofar as it bears on the subject matter of this essay itself. Here the question at stake is just how the conclusions of an enterprise such as the present one could be verified or corroborated. Now it is immediately clear that in respect of this issue empirical tests are automatically excluded – for after all, one of the major problems under consideration is precisely that concerning the basis of *all* empirical verification. But it is equally clear that nor is it sufficient to rely upon the substantiation of conclusions by argumentation alone, no matter how artful or compelling this argumentation might be. Indeed, the acceptance of such a procedure is exactly what was exposed by Husserl as constituting the 'crisis of science'! In sympathy with this view, throughout this essay we have stressed that the realm of concepts is not self-subsistent: rather, ideas always bear an immanent, ineradicable reference to the domain of practical life – the domain within which not only are things encountered but also theoretical and practical needs are formed. Thus we find ourselves apparently caught in a dilemma: the results we have obtained undoubtedly contain some force; however their own content prevents their acceptance as conclusive arguments.

This is a problem, of course, which has emerged repeatedly, either explicitly or implicitly, in the course of this essay. It arose at the very outset, when we first considered the question of the methodological precepts on which, without compromising itself, such a study might rely. It arose in our discussions of phenomenology and of science; and it arose again during our examination of the problem of the social determinations of the theory of nature. In order to meet the most conspicuous difficulties we chose a procedure directed towards the mutual interrogation of varying perspectives – an endeavour which would be guided by problems, dilemmas and hypotheses emerging from the existing theory. Subsequently, we proposed a number of hypotheses of our own; these we substantiated, to a greater or lesser degree, by arguments drawn from a variety of sources which we were prepared to subject to assessment on the basis of criteria of plausibility, coherence, consistency and so on. However no more than this has been claimed. We have not asserted that our arguments provide conclusive evidence in respect of their particular contents. On the contrary, we have insisted strenuously that they alone cannot be regarded as self-subsistent. Our intellectual presumptions regarding natural phenomena are incapable of establishing conclusively their own proof – or, for that matter, their disproof. This of course is only a repetition of an old Galilean precept; nevertheless, it is a precept which has been disregarded all too often in the practice of the philosophy of science. The adequate corroboration of the theses we have proposed cannot be provided exclusively through the purely theoretical media of this essay. A work such as the present one can aspire to no more than the objectives which we have declared; its legitimate purpose is to provoke ideas and reflections, to challenge the established ways of looking at the natural world and its interpretations, to open up new perspectives, to hazard new concepts and hypotheses. The question of actual proof is, and should be, unanswerable within the boundaries of such a project. If corroboration is to be obtained it will be in the form of consequences of its main hypotheses. In this sense the vindication of our claims still rests with experience. Fecundity is the empirical criterion on which these claims must be judged.

It is with this circumspect, but still positive, affirmation that we draw this essay to a close. A few ideas have been proposed; the task now is to elaborate their consequences in relation to specific domains of natural objects. Physics, biology, medicine, psychology – these fields and many others today face deep, abiding dilemmas, dilemmas which we must now recognize compel us to take a second look. Herein lies the real task in the defeat of objectivism and the overcoming of the crisis of science; and herein resides the means for transforming social conditions imprisoned by an unyielding, uncompromising conception of the natural world.

The ancient dream of a philosophy which would transcend the purely contemplative, which would overcome the disunity between knowledge of nature and human activity, is not dead. Yet we are still grappling to establish its foundations. The ageing Faust, in a mixture of hope and despair, cried out:

What a drama! But alas a drama only!
Boundless Nature, where shall I grasp thee?[1]

For us the dream is still a potent one, but the question remains unanswered. It is conceivable that the new insights into objectivity and its historical vicissitudes will lead to a broadening of the possibilities available not only to science but also to culture; thus, they may contribute to the establishment of the intellectual conditions for the liberation of both society and nature. That, of course, is the hope. For the moment, however, the fulfilment of this hope remains a great task for the future.

Notes

Chapter 1

1 Cf. Max Weber, 'Science as a vocation', in H. Gerth and C.W. Mills, eds, *From Max Weber*, London, Routledge & Kegan Paul, 1964, pp. 129–59.

2 J.W. Goethe, *Faust*, pt. 1, tr. L. MacNeice, London, Faber & Faber, 1948, p. 22.

3 E.g. H. Marcuse, *One Dimensional Man*, London, Routledge & Kegan Paul, 1968.

4 Cf. ibid., Chapters 2, 9 and T. Adorno, 'Cultural criticism and society', in *Prisms*, London, N. Spearman, 1967, pp. 17–35.

5 J. Ravetz, *Scientific Knowledge and its Social Problems*, Melbourne, Penguin, 1973.

6 See below, Chapter 2 (pp. 45ff.), Chapter 4 (pp. 106ff.), Chapter 5, etc.

7 It is perhaps appropriate at this point to affirm explicitly that this study, in seeking to adumbrate the elements of a social theory of science, will be concerned primarily with the interchange between the structures of society and those of epistemology; it is not an essay in either the philosophy or the sociology of technology. This is not to suggest, of course, that technology does not play a fundamental role in the process of the social adaptation to nature; however it *is* an assumption of this work that an adequate understanding of this process will in fact require the clarification of the underlying theoretical forms on which the very conception of technology depends. There are many rich and evocative studies of the multifarious aspects of the social mediation of technology; amongst the authors of these works of particular note, and indeed, of particular importance for the formulation of many of the ideas contained in this essay, are the following: H. Marcuse, M. Heidegger, E. Husserl, H. Jonas, J. Ellul, D. Ihde.

8 See Chapter 10.

9 W.B. Macomber, *The Anatomy of Disillusion: Martin Heidegger's Notion of Truth*, Evanston, Northwestern University Press, 1967, pp. 185-6, 20-7.

10 Cf. also M. Heidegger, *Hegel's Concept of Experience*, New York, Harper & Row, 1970; 'On the essence of truth', in *Existence and Being*, Chicago, Gateway, 1970; and *The Question Concerning Technology*, New York, Harper & Row, 1977.

11 Or perhaps, indication rather than expression. Cf. E. Husserl, *Logical Investigations*, tr. J. N. Findlay, London, Routlege & Kegan Paul, 1970, Investigation 1, Chapter 1, pp. 269 ff.
12 Cf. T. Adorno, *Negative Dialectics*, London, Routledge & Kegan Paul, 1973, pp. 162–6.
13 See also Chapter 11.
14 It should be noted that of all these thinkers the affinity of the last to 'critical theory' was by far the loosest; this remains the case in spite of his readiness in more recent works to refer to his own programme as a 'new version' of critical theory.
15 The only members who published material directly on the nature of science were Franz Borkenau and Edgar Zilsel. The former was largely concerned with the role of technology in the transition from feudal to bourgeois society and will not be considered here; the work of the latter, which is of more direct relevance for sociology, will be discussed in the following chapter.
16 M. Horkheimer and T. W. Adorno, *Dialectic of Enlightenment*, tr. J. Cumming, London, Allen Lane, 1976, p. 3.
17 See ibid., pp. 168–70, 179 ff., 189–90, 201–2, 204, 207–8.
18 M. Horkheimer, *Eclipse of Reason*, New York, Seabury Press, 1976, p. 93.
19 M. Horkheimer and T. Adorno, op. cit., p. 26.
20 Ibid., p. 7.
21 Ibid., p. 6.
22 Ibid., p. 7.
23 Ibid., p. 28.
24 Ibid., p. 27.
25 M. Horkheimer, *Eclipse of Reason*, p. 101.
26 M. Horkheimer and T. Adorno, op. cit., p. 32.
27 Ibid., p. 14.
28 Ibid., p. 21.
29 Ibid., p. 35.
30 Ibid., p. 28.
31 Ibid., pp. 17–18.
32 Ibid., p. 104.
33 Ibid., p. 106.
34 Ibid., p. 36.
35 M. Horkheimer, *Eclipse of Reason*, op cit., p. 23.
36 M. Weber, 'Science as a vocation', op. cit.; and *The Protestant Ethic and the Spirit of Capitalism*, New York, Charles Scribner's Sons, 1958.
37 Of course Weber too regarded them as only one aspect of the process of social rationalization; also involved – and at least as important – was the cultural dynamic. Cf. J. Arnason, 'Rationalization and modernity: towards a culturalist reading of Max Weber', *La Trobe Sociology Papers*, La Trobe University, Number 9, 1980.
38 Cf. M. Horkheimer and T. Adorno, op. cit., p. 5.
39 Ibid., pp. 17–18.
40 Ibid., p. 25.
41 Ibid., p. 10.
42 Ibid., p. 84.
43 Ibid., p. xii.
44 Ibid., p. 26.
45 Ibid., p. 25.
46 Ibid., pp. 25, 37.

47 Ibid., pp. 84–5.
48 Ibid., p. 25.
49 Ibid.
50 Ibid., p. 26.
51 Ibid.
52 Ibid., p. 27.
53 See M. Horkheimer, 'On the problem of truth', in A. Arato et al., eds, *The Essential Frankfurt School Reader*, Oxford, Blackwell, 1978, pp. 407 ff. Of course, the sense in which truth was intersubjective for Horkheimer was rather different from that for which Habermas was later to argue. Cf. below, Chapter 11.
54 M. Horkheimer and T. Adorno, op. cit., p. 85.
55 Ibid., p. 27.
56 Ibid., p. 84.
57 As we shall see below (Chapter 3) Habermas also failed to challenge the truth-claims of science. In *his* work however this result emerges as a consequence of the adoption not of an Hegelian conception of truth but of an instrumental conception of science.
58 M. Horkheimer and T. Adorno, op. cit., pp. 24–5.
59 See below, Chapter 9.
60 M. Horkheimer and T. Adorno, op. cit., p. 34.
61 Ibid., p. 32.
62 It is appropriate to remark that, accordingly, such a critique would be less a 'theory' in the classical sense than what might perhaps better be called a 'permanently self-questioning process of thought'.
63 M. Horkheimer, *Critical Theory*, New York, Seabury Press, 1972, p. 208.
64 Ibid., p. 211.
65 Ibid., p. 240.
66 It is important to emphasize that the conception of truth implied in this view, which contains an undoubted ontological residue, must be sharply distinguished from Habermas's discursive conception of truth. This is the case in spite of an apparent similarity, attributable to the fact that Habermas concedes the truth-content of science in the strict sense.
67 M. Horkheimer and T. Adorno, op. cit., pp. 11, 15.
68 Ibid., pp. 6–7.
69 Ibid., p. xiii.
70 Cf. ibid., pp. 61–2, 104, 106. Of course for Horkheimer and Adorno the negative moment of exchange is largely restricted to the special case of the contrast between feudalism and the market economy. In general, exchange itself is deeply implicated in the logic of domination: this is emphasized in *Dialectic of Enlightenment* in the context of their rather unusual view that exchange is a secularization of sacrifice, having been elaborated in the imaginary relation between man and gods prior to its application in society. See the 'excursus' on Odysseus, pp. 43 ff.
71 Cf. ibid., p. xv. This theme, which pervades the text of *Dialectic of Enlightenment*, is also one of the main concerns of *Negative Dialectics*. See S. Buck-Morss, *The Origin of Negative Dialectics*, New York, Free Press, 1977, pp. 60–1. For Adorno, some degree of transcendence was retained also in art, which incorporated a rather special transformation of the spontaneity of the concept. See especially T. Adorno, *Prisms*, op. cit.
72 Cf. also S. Buck-Morss, op. cit., pp. 66–9 regarding the differences between the two authors.

381

73 Cf. for example, L. Colletti, 'From Hegel to Marcuse', in *From Rousseau to Lenin*, New York, Monthly Review Press, 1972, pp. 111–42; and G. Therborn, 'The Frankfurt School', *New Left Review* 63, 1970, pp. 65–96.

74 Regarding the forms of the social mediation of nature admitted by critical theory, cf. M. Horkheimer and T. Adorno, op. cit., pp. 31, 84 f., and M. Horkheimer, *Critical Theory*, p. 259.

75 Cf. M. Horkheimer, *Critical Theory*, op. cit., pp. 210–11.

76 Cf. M. Horkheimer and T. Adorno, op. cit., pp. 81–6.

77 T. Adorno, *Prisms*, op. cit., pp. 236.

78 Cf. J. Derrida, *Edmund Husserl's 'Origin of Geometry': An Introduction*, New York, Nicolas Hayes, 1978, *passim*.

79 R. Descartes, *Discourse on Method*, London, Penguin, 1968, pp. 53–60.

80 I. Kant, *Critique of Pure Reason*, tr. N. K. Smith, London, Macmillan, 1970, p. 22.

81 Cf. M. Heidegger, *What Is a Thing?*, Chicago, Henry Regnery, 1967, pp. 98–9.

82 R. Descartes, *Rules for the Direction of Mind*, tr. F. P. Lafleur, New York, Liberal Arts, 1961, p. 8.

83 R. Descartes, *Selected Works of Descartes*, tr. N. K. Smith, vol. 12, London, Macmillan, 1953, pp. 8–9.

84 R. Descartes, *Discourse on Method*, op. cit., pp. 35–44.

85 A. Koyré, *From the Closed World to the Infinite Universe*, Baltimore, Johns Hopkins University Press, 1968.

86 Ibid., p. 106.

87 Ibid.

88 Cf. Aristotle, *Physica*, in *The Basic Works of Aristotle*, ed. R. McKeown, New York, Random House, 1941, pp. 218–398.

89 R. Descartes, *Meditations*, London, Penguin, 1968, pp. 102–12.

90 R. Descartes, *Discourse on Method*, op. cit., pp. 53–4.

91 I. Kant, op. cit., p. 378.

Chapter 2

1 Cf. R. K. Merton, *The Sociology of Science: Theoretical and Empirical Investigations*, ed. N. Storer, Chicago, University of Chicago Press, 1974, pp. 174–6; and *Science, Technology and Society in Seventeenth-century England*, New Jersey, Humanities Press, 1970, p. 224.

2 R. K. Merton, *The Sociology of Science*, op. cit., p. 183.

3 M Weber, *From Max Weber*, op. cit., p. 155.

4 Ibid., p. 143.

5 Cf. ibid., p. 355.

6 Ibid., p. 144.

7 Ibid., p. 142.

8 Ibid., p. 357.

9 R. K. Merton, *Science, Technology and Society*, op. cit., pp. 59, xvii.

10 Ibid., p. 56.

11 Ibid., p. 60.

12 Ibid., pp. 61–2.

13 Ibid., p. 63.

14 Ibid., pp. 66 ff.

15 Ibid., p. 83.

16 Ibid., p. 80.

17 Ibid., p. 72.

18 Ibid.

19 Ibid., p. 90.
20 Ibid., p. 95.
21 Ibid., p. 96.
22 Ibid., p. 75. This question will be considered at some length in Chapters 10 and 11 below.
23 Ibid.
24 Ibid., p. 79.
25 Ibid., p. 81.
26 Ibid., p. xviii. (This is the '1970 Preface' to the book.)
27 Ibid., p. xx.
28 Ibid., p. xix.
29 Ibid., pp. 107-9.
30 R. K. Merton, *The Sociology of Science*, op. cit., p. 136.
31 R. K. Merton, *Science, Technology and Society*, op. cit., p. xix.
32 R. K. Merton, *The Sociology of Science*, p. 209.
33 Cf. ibid., p. 260.
34 E.g. ibid., pp. 21, 37 (in Merton's famous essay on the sociology of knowledge). In addition, an extensive debate has occurred regarding both the nature and the consequences of Puritanism; the dimensions of this debate are apparent from, e.g. C. Hill, *Puritanism and Reduction: Studies in the Interpretation of the English Revolution in the Seventeenth Century*, New York, Schocken Books, 1964.
35 Ibid., p. 134.
36 R. K. Merton, *Science, Technology and Society*, op. cit., p. 225.
37 Ibid.
38 E. Zilsel, 'The sociological roots of science', *American Journal of Sociology* 47, pp. 544-62, 1942; 'The genesis of the concept of physical law', *Phil. Rev.* 51, pp. 245-79, 1942; 'The genesis of the concept of scientific progress', *Journal of the History of Ideas* 6, pp. 325-49, 1949; 'Copernicus and mechanics', *Journal of the History of Ideas* 1, pp. 113-18, 1940.
39 E. Zilsel, 'The sociological roots of science', op. cit.
40 M. Jay, *The Dialectical Imagination*, London, Heinemann, 1974, p. 115.
41 A. Kojève, 'L'origine Chrétienne de la science moderne', *Mélange A. Koyré 11: l'aventure de l'esprit*, Paris, Hermann, 1964, pp. 295-306.
42 E.g. S. L. Goldmann, 'A Kojève on the origins of modern science: Sociological modelling gone awry', *Stud. Hist. Phil. Sci.* 6 (2), 113-24, 1975.
43 A. Kojève, op. cit., p. 297.
44 Ibid., p. 298.
45 Ibid.
46 Ibid., p. 303.
47 S. L. Goldmann, op. cit., p. 118.
48 Ibid.
49 B. Hessen, *The Social and Economic Roots of Newton's 'Principia'*, New York, Howard Fertig, 1971, p. 21.
50 Ibid., p. 20.
51 Ibid., p. 33.
52 Ibid., p. 34.
53 Ibid., p. 37.
54 Ibid., p. 40.
55 P. Forman, 'Weimar Culture, causality and quantum theory 1918-1927: adaptation by German physicists and mathematicians to a hostile intellectual environment', in R. McCormack, ed., *Historical Studies in the Physical Sciences*, vol. 3, Philadelphia University of Pennsylvania Press, 1971, pp. 26 ff.

56 Ibid., p. 4.
57 Ibid., p. 16.
58 Cf. ibid., pp. 30 ff.
59 Ibid., p. 72.
60 Ibid., p. 8 ff.
61 Ibid., p. 63 ff.
62 Ibid., pp. 80–1.
63 Ibid., pp. 98–9.
64 Ibid., p. 110.
65 Cf. ibid., p. 109.
66 Ibid., p. 110.
67 Outstanding examples are contained in the following: H. Rose and S. Rose, 'The radicalisation of science', in *The Radicalisation of Science*, London, Macmillan, 1976, pp. 1–31; M. Mulkay, *Science and the Sociology of Knowledge*, London, George Allen & Unwin, 1979; B. Barnes, *Scientific Knowledge and Sociological Theory*, London, Routledge & Kegan Paul, 1974; E. Mendelson, 'The social construction of scientific knowledge', in E. Mendelson, P. Weingart and R. Whitley, eds, *The Social Production of Scientific Knowledge*, Dordrecht, D. Reidel, 1977, pp. 3–26; K. Hübner, 'The concept of truth in an historical theory of science', *Struct. Hist. Phil. Sci.* 11 (2), pp. 145–51, 1980; J-P. Vernant, *Mythe et pensée chez les grecs: études de psychologie historique*, Paris, Maspero, 1966.
68 R. K. Merton, *Science, Technology and Society*, op. cit., p. (xiii).
69 Ibid., pp. 137 and xiii–xiv.
70 R. K. Merton, *The Sociology of Science*, op. cit., p. 270.
71 R. K. Merton, *Science, Technology and Society*, op. cit., p. 83.
71 R. K. Merton, *Science, Technology and Society*, op. cit., p. 83.
72 R. K. Merton, *The Sociology of Science*, op. cit., p. 323.
74 'The normative structure of science', first published as 'Science and technology in a domestic order' in *J. Leg. Pol. Soc.* 1, pp. 115–26, 1942; reprinted in *The Sociology of Science*, op. cit., pp. 266–78.
75 R. K. Merton, *The Sociology of Science*, op. cit., p. 270.
76 E.g. originality, humility, independence, emotional neutrality and impartiality. See B Barber, *Science and the Social Order*, New York, The Free Press, 1972; N. Storer, *The Social System of Science*, New York, Rinehart & Winston, 1966; R. K. Merton, *The Sociology of Science*, op. cit.; 1. I. Mitroff, *The Subjective Side of Science*, Amsterdam, Elsevier, 1974.
77 B. Barnes and R. G. Dolby, 'The scientific ethos: a deviant viewpoint', *Eur. J. Soc.* 2, pp. 3–25, 1970; W. O. Hagstrom, *The Scientific Community*, New York, Basic Books, 1965; M. Mulkay, 'Some aspects of cultural growth in the natural sciences', *Soc. Res.* 36 (1), pp. 22–52, 1969.
78 R. K. Merton, *The Sociology of Science*, op. cit., p. 264.
79 Ibid., pp. 254–60.
80 Ibid., p. 266.
81 Ibid., p. 270.
82 M. Mulkay, *Science and the Sociology of Knowledge*, op. cit., pp. 19–20. (See also pp. 22–5).
83 R. K. Merton, *The Sociology of Science*, op. cit., p. 268.
84 R. K. Merton, 'Paradigm of the sociology of knowledge', first published in G. Gurevitch and W. E. Moore, eds, *Twentieth-century Sociology*, New York, Philosophical Library, 1945; reprinted in *The Sociology of Science*, op. cit., pp. 7–60.

85 Y. Elkana, 'Review essay on Merton', *A. J. S.* 81, 1976, p. 908.
86 R. K. Merton, *The Sociology of Science*, op. cit., pp. 475, 541 ff.
87 Ibid., pp. 470, 448.
88 Ibid., pp. 447, 479.
89 Ibid., p. 462. Note that this is exactly what Merton refers to as the 'communication system' of science.
90 H. Rose and S. Rose, op. cit., p. 4.
91 J. D. Bernal, *The Social Function of Science*, Cambridge, Mass. MIT Press, 1939, p. 221.
92 Ibid, p. 290.
93 It is appropriate to add here, however, that, in view of their common attitude to the Soviet Union at this time, not all writers are so sanguine about the integrity of the British radical scientists. Cf., for example, D. Caute, *The Fellow Travellers: A Postscript to the Enlightenment*, London, Weidenfeld & Nicolson, 1973.

Chapter 3

1 The following discussion of Popper will concentrate almost entirely on the two works cited and on the issues which emerge from them; it is, after all, through the means of these two texts that Popper has influenced most heavily the development of the modern philosophy of science. Limitations of space prevent the development of a discussion of the subsequent modifications of Popper's ideas such as, for example, those contained in the interesting collection of essays, *Objective Knowledge*, Oxford University Press, 1972.
2 K. Popper, *The Logic of Scientific Discovery*, London, Hutchinson, 1977, p. 27.
3 Ibid., p. 34.
4 L. Wittgenstein, *Tractatus Logico-Philosophicus*, London, Routledge & Kegan Paul, 1972, Propositions 6:53, 6:54.
5 Cf. ibid., 4.11.
6 K. Popper, *Conjectures and Refutations*, London, Routledge & Kegan Paul, 1972, p. 39.
7 Cf. R. Carnap, *The Logical Structure of the World*, tr. R. A. George, London, Routledge & Kegan Paul, 1967, pp. 290-98.
8 K. Popper, *Conjectures*, op. cit., pp. 268-70.
9 Ibid., p. 40.
10 K. Popper, *Logic*, op. cit., p. 40.
11 Ibid., p. 41.
12 K. Popper, *Conjectures*, op. cit., p. 240.
13 Ibid., pp. 233-5.
14 Ibid., p. 233.
15 Ibid., p. 215.
16 Ibid., p. 46.
17 Ibid., p. 222.
18 K. Popper, *Logic*, op. cit., pp. 100-5.
19 K. Popper, *Conjectures*, op. cit., p. 246.
20 See, for example, K. Popper, *The Poverty of Historicism*, London, Routledge & Kegan Paul, 1967.
21 I. Lakatos and K. Musgrave, eds., *Criticism and the Growth of Knowledge*, Cambridge University Press, 1974, p. 1 n.
22 Ibid., pp. 1-2.
23 T. Kuhn, *The Structure of Scientific Revolutions*, University of Chicago Press, 1970, Chapter 3.

24 Ibid., Chapter 4.
25 Cf. I. Lakatos and A. Musgrave, eds, op. cit., p. 8; T. Kuhn, op. cit., Chapter 6 and pp. 37, 39; B. Barnes, ed., *Sociology of Science*, London, Penguin, 1972, p. 314.
26 T. Kuhn, op. cit., p. 146. Cf. p. 77.
27 I Lakatos and A. Musgrave, eds. op. cit., p. 250.
28 T. Kuhn, op. cit., p. 85. See also Chapter 8 and p. 69.
29 P. Feyerabend, *Against Method*, London, New Left Books, 1975, p. 223.
30 Ibid., p. 271.
31 Ibid., p. 274.
32 B. L. Whorff, *Language, Thought and Reality*, Cambridge, Mass. MIT Press, 1956, p. 121, quoted in P. Feyerabend, op. cit., p. 223 n. 1.
33 P. Feyerabend, op. cit., pp. 230, 236–8, 245 etc.
34 Ibid., p. 252.
35 Ibid., p. 274.
36 Ibid., p. 275.
37 Ibid., pp. 275–7.
38 E.g. ibid., pp. 165–9.
39 Ibid., pp. 145–52.
40 Ibid., pp. 51–2, 298–300.
41 I. Lakatos and A. Musgrave, eds, op. cit., p. 198.
42 Ibid., pp. 52–3.
43 Cf. J. Ravetz, op. cit., p. 31.
44 Cf. the discussion above, pp. 18–19, and also that below, pp. 342, 395 ff., etc.
45 See, for example, M. Masterman, 'The nature of a paradigm', in I. Lakatos and A. Musgrave, eds, op. cit., pp. 59–90; and T. Kuhn, 'Second thoughts on paradigms', in *The Essential Tension*, University of Chicago Press, 1977, pp. 293–319.
46 M. Masterman, op. cit., p. 61.
47 Ibid., p. 65.
48 K. Popper, *The Open Society and its Enemies*, London, Routledge & Kegan Paul, 1951, p. 380.
49 I. Lakatos and A. Musgrave, eds., op. cit., p. 55.
50 Ibid., pp. 56–7.
51 Ibid., p. 55.
52 Ibid., p. 57.
53 K. Popper, 'The bucket and the searchlight: two theories of knowledge' (the text of a lecture delivered in 1948), *Objective Knowledge*, Oxford, Clarendon Press, 1972, p. 345. See also pp. 346–7.
54 Cf. M. Hesse, *The Structure of Scientific Inference*, London, Macmillan, 1974.
55 The term appears to have arisen with G. Ryle, *The Concept of Mind*. London, Hutchinson, 1949.
56 T. Kuhn, *The Essential Tension*, op. cit., pp. 294–5.
57 Ibid., p. 297.
58 Ibid., p. 298.
59 N. Campbell, *What is Science?*, New York, Dover, 1952; A. Child, 'The problem of truth in the sociology of knowledge', *Ethics* 58, pp. 18–34, 1947–8.
60 T. Kuhn, *The Structure of Scientific Revolutions*, op. cit., p. 18.
61 Ibid., p. 37.
62 B. Barnes, Preface to part 2 of B. Barnes, ed., *Sociology of Science*, London, Penguin, 1972, p. 62.
63 E.g. T. Kuhn, *The Structure of Scientific Revolutions*, op. cit., pp. 168–9.

64 T. Kuhn, *The Essential Tension*, op. cit., p. 118.

65 Ibid., p. 119.

66 I. Lakatos and A. Musgrave, eds, op. cit., p. 238.

67 T. Kuhn, *The Structure of Scientific Revolutions*, op. cit., p. 154.

68 Ibid., p. 152.

69 Ibid., p. 153.

70 Ibid., p. 155.

71 I. Lakatos and A. Musgrave, eds, op. cit., p. 21.

72 E.g. T. Kuhn, *The Structure of Scientific Revolutions*, op. cit., pp. 153, 185; *The Essential Tension*, op cit., p. 7, 269.

73 I. Lakatos, 'Methodology of scientific research programs', in I. Lakatos and A. Musgrave, op. cit., p. 178.

74 Nor will a discussion be pursued of other contributions to the contemporary philosophy of science; in particular, we shall, unfortunately, have to omit any consideration of the subtle and profound ideas of I. Lakatos and R. Harré.

75 Indeed, when he mentions this issue it is often only to announce his execration of it – for example, as in the following passage from *Criticism and the Growth of Knowledge*:

> I cannot conclude without pointing out that to me the idea of turning for enlightenment concerning the aims of science, and its possible progress, to sociology or to psychology ... is surprising and disappointing. In fact, compared with physics, sociology and psychology are riddled with fashions and with uncontrolled dogmas. The suggestion that we can find anything here like 'objective, pure description' is clearly mistaken (op. cit., pp. 57–8).

See also the remainder of this paragraph.

76 English translations of some contributions to this debate are collected in T. Adorno, H. Albert, R. Dahrendorf, J. Habermas, H. Pilot and K. Popper, *The Positivist Dispute in German Sociology*, tr. G. Adey and D. Frisby, London, Heinemann, 1976.

77 J. Habermas, *Knowledge and Human Interests*, London, Heinemann, 1972, p. 67.

78 R. Carnap, *Erkenntnis*, 2, 1932, p. 438, quoted in K. Popper, *Logic*, op. cit., p. 96.

79 Ibid., p. 102.

80 Ibid., p. 103.

81 Ibid., p. 106.

82 Ibid., p. 104.

83 T. Adorno et al., *The Positivist Dispute*, op. cit., pp. 151–2.

84 Ibid., p. 152.

85 Cf. ibid., p. 204.

86 Ibid., pp. 202–3.

87 Ibid., pp. 147–8.

88 See, for example, T. Kuhn, *The Structure of Scientific Revolutions*, op. cit., pp. 126 ff.

89 See, for example, I. Lakatos and A. Musgrave, eds, op. cit., pp. 259 ff.

90 Ibid., p. 261 etc..

91 J. Habermas in T. Adorno et al., *The Positivist Dispute*, op. cit., p. 152.

92 Ibid., pp. 152–3, 201.

93 Ibid., p. 206.

94 Ibid., pp. 135, 140.

95 Ibid., p. 152.

96 K. Popper, *Logic*, op. cit., pp. 193 ff.

97 J. Habermas, in T. Adorno et al., *The Positivist Dispute*, op cit., p. 215.

98 Ibid., p. 203.

99 Ibid., p. 199.

100 Cf. ibid., p. 208.

101 T. Kuhn, *The Structure of Scientific Revolutions*, op. cit., Chapter 10.

102 See T. Adorno in T. Adorno et al., *The Positivist Dispute*, op. cit., especially, pp. 69, 107; Adorno's entire contribution, 'Sociology and empirical research', ibid., p. 68–86, is relevant in this context.

103 I. Lakatos and A. Musgrave, eds, op. cit., p. 238.

104 T. Kuhn, *The Structure of Scientific Revolutions*, op. cit., p. 167.

105 T Adorno et al., *The Positivist Dispute*, op. cit., p. 135.

106 Ibid., p. 139.

107 Ibid.

108 Ibid., p. 135.

109 Perhaps closely following in his account those of Zilsel and Borkenau.

110 Ibid., p. 156.

111 Ibid., p. 154.

112 Ibid., p. 220 and also p. 132.

113 Ibid., p. 220.

114 In recent years an attempt has been made from a perspective not inconsistent with that of Habermas to formulate a theory of scientific change. According to this approach scientific theories describe a tripartite course of development, culminating in a mature phase of 'finalization': a condition in which a hitherto autonomous body of knowledge emerges as susceptible to direction in relation to externally-conceived goals. (See, for example, G. Bohme, W. van den Daele, W. Krohn, 'Finalisation in science', *Soc. Sci. Inform.* 15 (2–3), 1976, pp. 307–30; W. Schafer, 'Finalisation in perspective: toward a revolution in the social paradigm of science', *Soc. Sci. Inform.* 18 (6), 1979, pp. 915–43; G. Bohme, 'On the possibility of the closed theories', *Stud. Hist. Phil. Sci.* 11 (2), 1980, pp. 163–72; W. Schafer, 'A note on the social natural science project (SNSP): science, politics and nature', *Soc. Sci. Inform.* 19 (3), 1980, pp. 663–70.)

It would not be appropriate here to discuss in detail these ideas or their interesting implications. Accordingly, we restrict ourselves to the following brief remarks.

Firstly, it is not the case that the 'finalization' programme can be identified with that of Habermas; the success or failure of one would not have bearing on the other. Secondly, there is a number of obvious, though unresolved problems associated with the approach; in particular, there are historical discrepancies in the account of scientific development; furthermore, the task of formulating a rigorous conception of the 'closure' of a scientific theory – and consequently, of finalization itself – appears to have proved intractable. Thirdly, in spite of this, the perspective seems, at least potentially, to be a useful one: it poses the problem of applied science in a new way and revives the discussion of the role of a public science policy in directing the future development of specific disciplines. Fourthly, while these questions are certainly interesting, in the present essay the concern is with a rather different set of issues: we are interested less in the question of technical control than in scientific knowledge itself. Thus the problem being posed here is that of the trajectory of natural scientific knowledge within a structured field of social discourse; in this context, the possibility must be considered that finalization occurs *at the very beginning* – not in the mechanistic sense sometimes proposed but through a process of the joint constitution of society and nature. Associated with this problem is one concerning the epistemological diversity within modern science itself and the implications of this diversity for social life; any adequate social theory of science must be able to provide an account of – for example – the disparity between relativity theory and quantum mechanics, both at the level of social forms and at that of meaning. The finalization perspective does not exclude such considerations in principle; however it provides no further apparatus for their further development. Finally, the formulation of a satisfactory policy requires an understanding – presently lacking – of the deep structure of the relationship between society and its epistemological forms. Here the question of the technical direction of scientific endeavour will certainly be relevant; but so also will be the communicative dimension inhabited by the scientific discourse – that is, the very dimension left unconsidered by the finalization programme.

Notwithstanding its deficiencies, the approach of finalization is likely to prove both interesting and fruitful. However, its realization will not affect the need for the development of a true social theory of natural scientific knowledge.

115 J. Habermas, *Knowledge and Human Interests*, op. cit., Appendix.
116 Ibid.
117 Ibid.
118 J. Habermas, *Theory and Practice*, London, Heinemann, 1974, p. 8.
119 J. Habermas, *Knowledge and Human Interests*, op. cit., p. 312.
120 Ibid. Cf. T. McCarthy, *The Critical Theory of Jürgen Habermas*, Cambridge, Mass. MIT Press, 1979, p. 65.
121 Ibid., pp. 156–7.
122 Cf. J. Habermas, *Towards a Rational Society*, London, Heinemann, 1971, pp. 88–90.
123 J. Habermas, *Knowledge and Human Interests*, op. cit., pp. 307 and 67–8.
124 J. Habermas, *Theory and Practice*, op. cit., pp. 8, 19–20.
125 J. Habermas, 'A postscript to *Knowledge and Human Interests*', *Phil. Soc. Sci.* 3, 1973, p. 175.
126 Cf. J. Habermas, *Knowledge and Human Interests*, op. cit., pp. 130–9.
127 J. Habermas, *Theory and Practice*, op. cit., p. 87.
128 Ibid., p. 88.
129 J. Habermas, *Knowledge and Human Interests*, op. cit., p. 308 (emphasis added).
130 Ibid.
131 Cf. W. Leiss, *The Domination of Nature*, New York, George Braziller, 1972.
132 T. Adorno et al., *The Positivist Dispute*, op. cit., p. 209.
133 As, for example, is argued by Merleau-Ponty. M. Merleau-Ponty, *The Phenomenology of Perception*, London, Routledge & Kegan Paul, 1962; *The Visible and the Invisible*, Evanston, Northwestern University Press, 1968, *passim*.
134 See C. Lévi-Strauss, *The Savage Mind*, Chicago, University of Chicago Press, 1973.
135 See below, Chapters 7, 9.
136 J. Arnason, 'Marx and Habermas', in *Habermas Symposium*, Melbourne, Department of Sociology, La Trobe University, 1977 (La Trobe Sociology Papers, no. 42), pp. 13 ff.
137 These terms were employed in the sense introduced by Morris: C. Morris, *Foundations of the Theory of Signs*, Chicago, University of Chicago Press, 1938. See also below, Chapters 10 and 11.
138 Cf. D. Joravsky, *The Lysenko Affair*, Boston, Harvard University Press, 1970.

Chapter 4

1 See below, pp. 129 ff.
2 E. Husserl, *Phenomenology and the Crisis of Philosophy. Philosophy as Rigorous Science and Philosophy and the Crisis of European Man*, tr. Q. Lauer, New York, Harper & Row, 1965, p. 76.
3 Ibid., p. 136.
4 Loc. cit.
5 Ibid., p. 140.
6 Ibid., pp. 141-2.
7 Ibid., p. 130. See also below.
8 E. Husserl, *Formal and Transcendental Logic*, tr. D. Cairns, The Hague, Martinus Nijhoff, 1969, p. 278.
9 E. Husserl, *The Crisis of European Science and Transcendental Phenomenology*, tr. D. Carr, Evanston, Northwestern University Press, 1970, p. 15.
10 Ibid., p. 6.
11 Ibid., p. 17.
12 For an illuminating discussion of the intellectual ambience during this period see F. K. Ringer, *The Decline of the German Mandarins: the German Academic Community, 1890-1933*, Cambridge, Mass. Harvard University Press, 1969.
13 *Crisis*, pp. 194-5.
14 *Philosophy as a Rigorous Science*, p. 136.
15 Ibid.
16 Ibid.
17 E. Husserl, *Logical Investigations*, op. cit., p. 66.
18 Ibid., p. 67.
19 Ibid., p. 66.
20 Ibid., p. 63.
21 E. Husserl, *Ideas, General Introduction to Pure Phenomenology*, W. R. Boyce Gibson, London, George Allen & Unwin, 1969, §1.
22 *Logical Investigations*, p. 562.
23 *Ideas*, §24.
24 *Philosophy as a Rigorous Science*, p. 90.
25 *Ideas*, §24.
26 *Philosophy as a Rigorous Science*, p. 90.
27 *Formal and Transcendental Logic*, p. 248.
28 *Ideas*, §59.
29 Ibid.
30 *Philosophy as a Rigorous Science*, p. 102.
31 *Ideas*, §77-8.
32 *Ibid.*, §59.
33 *Crisis*, p. 265.
34 Ibid., p. 5.
35 Ibid., p. 12.
36 E. Husserl, 'The Vienna Lecture', in *Crisis*, p. 270.
37 E. Husserl, 'The method of clarification', *Southwestern J. Phil.* 5 (3), 1974, p. 59-60.
38 T. Adorno, 'Husserl and the problem of realism', *J. Phil.* 37 (1), 1940, p. 18.
39 *Formal and Transcendental Logic*, p. 161.
40 *Crisis*, p. 13.
41 *Formal and Transcendental Logic*, p. 130.
42 Ibid., §39.
43 Ibid., p. 125.

44 Ibid., §23, §24. S. Bachelard, *A Study of Husserl's 'Formal and Transcendental Logic'*, Evanston, Northwestern University Press, 1968, pp. 38-9.
45 *Formal and Transcendental Logic*, pp. 71, 86.
46 *Ideas*, §10, p. 67.
47 *Formal and Transcendental Logic*, p. 78.
48 Ibid., §27b, pp. 24-5. R. Sokolowski, *Husserlian Meditations*, Evanston, Northwestern University, 1974, p. 275.
49 Ibid., §27b. R. Sokolowski, op. cit., p. 274.
50 *Logical Investigations*, pp. 525-6.
51 *Formal and Transcendental Logic*. p. 50.
52 Ibid., §16.
53 Ibid., §14.
54 Ibid., §18.
55 Ibid., p. 61.
56 Ibid., §19.
57 Ibid.
58 Ibid.
59 Ibid., pp. 108, 124.
60 See, for example, E. Husserl, *Experience and Judgement: Investigations in a Genealogy of Logic*, tr. J. Churchill and K. Ameriks, Evanston, Northwestern University Press, 1973, §12.
61 *Formal and Transcendental Logic*, p. 116.
62 Ibid., p. 146.
63 Ibid.
64 Ibid., pp. 77-8.
65 Ibid., §35.
66 Ibid., p. 103.
67 Ibid., pp. 103-4.
68 Ibid., p. 145.
69 E. Husserl, 'Prolegomena to pure logic', §70, in *Logical Investigations*, p. 241.
70 Ibid.
71 *Formal and Transcendental Logic*, p. 185.
72 Ibid., §45.
73 For what follows cf. *Experience and Judgement*, §47.
74 *Formal and Transcendental Logic*, §38.
75 Ibid., p. 118.
76 Ibid., p. 113.
77 Ibid., §42.
78 Ibid., pp. 102-3.
79 Ibid., p. 103.
80 Cf. *Experience and Judgement*, p. 11.
81 *Formal and Transcendental Logic*, p. 103.
82 Ibid., §28, §29.
83 Ibid., p. 98.
84 Ibid., p. 124.
85 S. Bachelard, op. cit., p. 68.
86 The remarks about the convergence between formal ontology and formal apophantics do not, of course, pretend to provide a full account of Husserl's argument of this point; we have, for example omitted any reference to the role of mathematics in relation thereto.
87 *Experience and Judgement*, p. 12.
88 S. Bachelard, op. cit., p. 12.

89 *Formal and Transcendental Logic*, p. 111.
90 Ibid., p. 150.
91 Ibid.
92 *Ideas*, §73.
93 *Formal and Transcendental Logic*, p. 127.
94 Ibid.
95 *Experience and Judgement*, p. 17.
96 *Logical Investigations*, pp. 765–7.
97 *Formal and Transcendental Logic*, p. 129.
98 *Experience and Judgement*, p. 283.
99 Cf. ibid., §4.
100 E. Husserl, *Cartesian Meditations*, tr. D. Cairns, The Hague, M. Nijhoff, 1960, p. 57.
101 Ibid.
102 'Prolegomena' in *Logical Investigations*, p. 194.
103 *Cartesian Meditations*, p. 58.
104 *Formal and Transcendental Logic*, p. 146.
105 *Experience and Judgement*, p. 21.
106 *Formal and Transcendental Logic*, p. 196.
107 Ibid., p. 197.
108 Ibid., p. 198.
109 Ibid., p. 246. See also Chapter 6, below.
110 Ibid., p. 161.
111 Ibid.
112 Ibid., p. 271.
113 *Ideas*, §72.
114 Ibid., §138.
115 Ibid., §153.
116 *Formal and Transcendental Logic*, p. 165.
117 Ibid., pp. 146, 251.
118 Ibid., p. 279.
119 *Cartesian Meditations*, p. 48.
120 See pp. 122 ff.
121 *Ideas*, p. 395.
122 'Prolegomena', in *Logical Investigations*, p. 140.
123 Cf. *Crisis*, pp. 372–4.
124 *Formal and Transcendental Logic*, p. 225.
125 Cf. ibid., pp. 157, 250.
126 Ibid., p. 234.
127 Ibid.
128 Ibid., p. 238.
129 Ibid., p. 251.
130 Ibid.
131 Ibid., p. 263.
132 *Experience and Judgement*, p. 11.
133 Ibid., pp. 48–9.
134 Ibid., pp. 49–50.
135 Cf. below, Chapter 11.
136 Ibid., p. 165.
137 Ibid., p. 168.
138 Ibid., p. 203.
139 Ibid., p. 204.

140 Ibid., p. 236.
141 Ibid., p. 242.
142 Ibid., p. 274.
143 *Cartesian Meditations*, p. 115.
144 Ibid., p. 126.
145 *Formal and Transcendental Logic*, p. 272.
146 Ibid.
147 Ibid., p. 268.
148 Ibid., p. 273.
149 Ibid., p. 274.
150 Ibid., p. 273.
151 Ibid., p. 278.
152 Ibid.
153 Ibid., p. 279.
154 J. Cavaillès, 'On logic and the theory of science', in J. Kocklemans and T. Kisiel, eds, *Phenomenology and the Natural Sciences*, Evanston, Northwestern University Press, 1974, p. 400.
155 Ibid.
156 S. Bachelard, op. cit., p. 222.
157 Ibid., pp. 223-4.
158 For the following see R. Ingarden, *On the Motives which Led Husserl to Transcendental Idealism*, The Hague, Martinus Nijhoff, 1975.
159 Ibid., p. 31.
160 Ibid., p. 32.
161 *Formal and Transcendental Logic*, pp. 291-3; cf. also p. 243.

Chapter 5

1 Cf. *Crisis*, p. 356.
2 E. Husserl, *The Phenomenology of Internal Time-consciousness*, tr. J. S. Churchill, Bloomington, Indiana University Press, 1964.
3 *Crisis*, p. 48.
4 Ibid., p. 49.
5 Ibid., p. 24.
6 Ibid., p. 26.
7 Ibid.
8 Ibid., p. 27.
9 Ibid.
10 Ibid., p. 33.
11 Ibid., p. 38.
12 Ibid., p. 66.
13 Ibid., p. 38.
14 Ibid., p. 111.
15 Ibid., p. 23.
16 Ibid., p. 135.
17 Ibid., p. 148.
18 Ibid., p. 138n.
19 Ibid., p. 138.
20 Ibid., p. 50, §9d.
21 Ibid.
22 Ibid., p. 50.
23 Ibid., p. 49.
24 Ibid., p. 50.

25 Ibid. Cf. ibid., p.106.
26 Ibid. Cf. ibid., p. 121.
27 Ibid., p. 347.
28 Ibid., p. 94.
29 Ibid., p. 43.
30 Ibid., p. 22.
31 Ibid., p. 29.
32 Ibid., p. 34.
33 Ibid., p. 139.
34 Ibid.
35 Ibid., pp. 139–40.
36 Ibid., p. 30.
37 Ibid., p. 31.
38 Ibid.
39 Ibid., p. 31. Cf. p. 345.
40 Ibid., p. 35.
41 Ibid.
42 Ibid., pp. 36–7. In *Logical Investigations* Husserl refers to this as an 'indicative sign'.
43 Ibid., p. 37.
44 Ibid., p. 121.
45 Ibid., p. 51.
46 Ibid., p. 347.
47 E.g. ibid., pp. 26, 29, 51, 348, etc.
48 Ibid., p. 130.
49 Ibid., pp. 48–50.
50 Ibid., p. 51.
51 Ibid.
52 Ibid., p. 56.
53 Ibid., p. 48.
54 Ibid., p. 60.
55 Ibid., p. 52.
56 Ibid., p. 57.
57 Ibid., p. 72.
58 Ibid., p. 131.
59 Ibid., pp. 71–2.
60 Ibid., p. 59.
61 Ibid., p. 12.
62 Cf. ibid., pp. 53–4, 123–4, 133 etc.
63 Ibid., p. 133.
64 Ibid., p. 53.
65 Ibid.
66 Ibid., p. 348.
67 Ibid., p. 121.
68 Ibid., p. 132.
69 Ibid.
70 Ibid., p. 124 (emphasis added).
71 Ibid., p. 125 (emphasis added).
72 Ibid., p. 53.
73 Ibid., p. 98.
74 Ibid., p. 127.
75 Ibid., p. 128.

76 Ibid., p. 69.
77 Ibid., p. 92.
78 Ibid., p. 130.
79 Ibid., p. 131.
80 Ibid., p. 124.
81 Ibid., p. 132.
82 Ibid., p. 113.
83 Ibid., p. 121.
84 Ibid., p. 113.
85 Ibid., p. 99.
86 Ibid., pp. 178-81.
87 Ibid., p. 27.
88 Ibid., p. 133.
89 Ibid., p. 349.
90 E.g. ibid., pp. 130, 175.
91 Ibid., p. 69.
92 Ibid., p. 113.
93 Ibid., p. 100.
94 Ibid., p. 128.
95 Ibid., p. 366.
96 Ibid., p. 128.
97 Ibid.
98 Ibid., p. 131.
99 Ibid., p. 139. Cf. the passage in *Formal and Transcendental Logic* referred to above.
100 Ibid., p. 166.
101 Ibid., pp. 163, 166.
102 Ibid., p. 133.
103 Ibid., p. 44.
104 Ibid.
105 Ibid., p. 46.
106 Ibid., p. 52.
107 Ibid., p. 56.
108 Ibid., p. 46.
109 Ibid., p. 189.
110 Ibid., p. 130.
111 Ibid.
112 Ibid., p. 131.
113 Ibid.
114 Ibid.
115 Ibid., p. 175.
116 Ibid., p. 348.
117 Ibid., pp. 209-10.
118 Ibid., p. 49.
119 *Experience and Judgement*, p. 42.
120 *Crisis*, p. 140.
121 Ibid., p. 131.
122 E.g. ibid., p. 104.
123 See also below, Chapter 10.
124 *Experience and Judgement*, p. 62.
125 *Crisis*, pp. 360-1, 368-9.
126 Ibid., p. 361.
127 Ibid., pp. 367-8.

128 Cf. *Cartesian Meditations*, p. 133, where Husserl declares that 'nature is fashioned into a cultural world'.
129 *Crisis*, pp. 368-9.
130 See below, Chapter 10.
131 Ibid., p. 369.
132 Ibid., p. 51.
133 *Logical Investigation*, number VI, Chapter 8.
134 These, unresolved, problems in Husserl's thought have given rise to a vigorous debate and to widely varying interpretations. See, for example, D. Carr, 'The "Fifth meditation" and Husserl's Cartesianism', *Phil. and Phen. Res.* 34, 1974, pp. 14-35; P. Hutcheson, 'Husserl's problem of intersubjectivity', *J. Brit. Soc. Phen.* 11 (2), 1980, pp. 144-62; P. Ricœur, *Husserl: An Analysis of his Phenomenology*, Evanston, Northwestern University Press, 1967, Chapter 5; L. Landgrebe, 'Husserl's departure from Cartesianism', in R. O. Elveton, ed., *The Phenomenology of Husserl: Selected Critical Readings*, Chicago, Quandrangle Books, 1970, pp. 259-309.
135 Cf. *Formal and Transcendental Logic*, p. 243n., where Husserl refers to this version as a 'short exposition', to be amplified later in detail (a task that was never executed).
136 *Cartesian Meditations*, p. 91.
137 Ibid., p. 92.
138 Ibid., §44.
139 Ibid., p. 96.
140 Ibid., p. 97.
141 Ibid.
142 Ibid., §47.
143 Ibid., p. 104.
144 Ibid., p. 109.
145 Ibid., p. 105.
146 Ibid., p. 110.
147 Ibid., p. 111.
148 Ibid., pp. 112-13.
149 Ibid., p. 114.
150 Ibid., p. 115.
151 Ibid., p. 129.
152 Ibid., p. 116.
153 Ibid., p. 118.
154 Ibid., p. 123.
155 The question of intersubjectivity and its vicissitudes in Husserl's work is developed with particular insight and suggestiveness by M. Merleau-Ponty. See, for example, 'On the phenomenology of language', in *Signs*, Evanston, Northwestern University Press, 1964, pp. 84-97; and *The Visible and the Invisible*, op. cit., esp. pp. 28-49.

Chapter 6

1 It might be added that, insofar as Marx's original formulation implied that under certain conditions cultural objects appear in the guise of natural objects, the *generalization* of the theory proposed here is also in a sense simultaneously an *inversion*. (See below.)
2 K. Marx, *Capital*, vol. 1, tr. S. Moore and E. Aveling, London, Lawrence & Wishart, 1970, Chapter 1, Section IV.
3 G. Lukács, *History and Class Consciousness*, London, Merlin Press, 1971, p. 84.

4 Ibid., pp. 86-7.
5 G. Marcus, 'Alienation and reification in Marx and Lukács', *Thesis Eleven*, 5-6, 1982, pp. 144 ff.
6 Ibid., pp. 154-6. Cf. G. Lukács, op. cit., pp. 86, 100.
7 Cf. ibid. pp. 124-5, and 160-3.
8 Cf. ibid., pp. 163 ff.
9 E.g. ibid., pp. 159 ff. (and see also below). Cf. G. Markus, op. cit., pp. 142-3.
10 G. Markus, op. cit., pp. 154-5. Cf. G. Lukács, op. cit., pp. (xxii)-(xxiv).
11 G. Lukács, op. cit., p. 105.
12 Ibid., pp. 97-8.
13 G. Markus, op. cit., p. 158.
14 Ibid.
15 G. Lukács, op. cit., pp. 130, 234.
16 Although admittedly, the actual processes of mediation vary substantially between capitalist and non-capitalist societies. (See below, pp. 185 ff.)
17 Ibid., pp. 223 ff.
18 Ibid., p. 234. (Cf. p. 136.)
19 Cf. ibid., pp. 92, 176.
20 Ibid., pp. 228, 231.
21 Ibid., pp. 84, 93, 86-7, 165, 100, 156 etc.
22 See ibid. pp. 176, 230, 166, 132, 135 etc.
23 Ibid., pp. 84, 166, 87, 229, 232.
24 Ibid., p. 232.
25 Ibid.
26 E.g. ibid., pp. 83 ff., 92 ff., 98 ff.
27 Ibid., pp. 230, 233, 237.
28 Ibid., pp. 234-5.
29 Ibid., p. 233.
30 Ibid., pp. 220-1, 237-8.
31 Ibid., p. 235.
32 Ibid.
33 Cf., for example, ibid., pp. 92 ff.
34 Also cf. J. Arnason, 'Rationality and modernity', op. cit.
35 Cf. G Lukács, op. cit., p. 237.
36 Cf. ibid., pp. 128-31.
37 Cf. ibid., pp. 237, 235.
38 Ibid., p. 237.
39 Especially in, for example, the essay 'Reification and the consciousness of the proletariat'.
40 K. Marx, op. cit., p. 72.
41 Ibid., p. 75.
42 Cf. S. Avineri, *The Social and Political Thought of Karl Marx*, Cambridge University Press, 1968, Chapter 4; and N. Geras, 'Essence and appearance: aspects of fetishism in Marx's *Capital*', *New Left Review* 65, 1971, pp. 69-85.
43 E. Balibar, 'The basic concepts of historical materialism', in L. Althusser and E. Balibar, *Reading Capital*, London, New Left Books, 1968, p. 217 n.
44 L. Althusser, 'From *Capital* to Marx's philosophy', in ibid., p. 17.
45 L. Althusser, 'The object of *Capital*', in ibid., p. 179.
46 J. Rancière, 'The concept of "critique" and the "critique of political economy" (from the *1844 Manuscripts* to *Capital*)', *Economy and Society* 5 (2), 1976, p. 368.
47 See Chapter 8, note 45.

48 E. Balibar, 'Self-criticism: an answer to questions from *Theoretical Practice*', *Theoretical Practice* 7-8, 1973, pp. 56-72. See also E. Balibar, 'Sur la dialectique historique (quelque remarques critiques à propos de *Lire le Capital*)', in *Cinq études du materialism historique*, Paris, Maspero, 1974.

49 E. Balibar, *Cinq études*, op. cit., p. 222.

50 Ibid., p. 223.

51 Ibid.

52 Ibid., p. 224.

53 H. Lefebvre, *Hegel, Marx, Nietzsche,* Mexico, Siglo Veintiuno, 1976, p. 128. It is worth noting that it is Lefebvre's own view that the theoretical status of the concept of alienation is actually *lacking* (ibid.); however this seems a difficult position to maintain in view of the extensive and rigorous theoretical writings of, on the one hand, J.-P. Sartre and, on the other, those of the members of the Budapest School. See J.-P. Sartre, *Critique of Dialectical Reason*, London, New Left Books, 1976, pp. 153 ff.; I. Meszaros, *Marx's Theory of Alienation*, London, Merlin Press, 1970.

54 H. Lefebvre, op. cit., p. 131.

55 C. van Peursen, *Phenomenology and Reality*, Pittsburg, Duquesne University Press, 1972, Chapter 4.

56 E.G. M. Merleau-Ponty, *Phenomenology of Perception*, op. cit., part 2; 'Eye and mind', in J. O'Neill, ed., *Phenomenology, Language and Sociology*, London, Heinemann, 1974, pp. 280-312.

57 M. Merleau-Ponty, *The Visible and the Invisible*, op. cit., p. 137; *Phenomenology, Language and Sociology*, op. cit., p. 285.

58 K. Marx, *Capital*, vol. 3, Moscow, Progress Publishers, 1956, p. 819.

59 *Capital*, vol. 1, p. 72.

60 Ibid. p. 91.

61 *Capital*, vol. 3, p. 830.

62 I. I. Rubin, *Essays on Marx's Theory of Value*, Detroit, Black and Red, 1972, p. 39.

63 *Capital*, vol. 1, p. 74.

64 *Capital*, vol. 3, p. 814.

65 K. Marx, *Theories of Surplus Value*, vol. 3, Moscow, Progress Publishers, 1968, p. 483.

66 *Capital*, vol. 1., p. 74.

67 Cf. *Theories of Surplus Value*, vol. 3, pp. 129, 181.

68 K. Marx, *Grundrisse*, tr. M. Nicolaus, London, Penguin, 1973, p. 157.

69 P. A. Rovatti, 'Fetishism and economic categories', *Telos* 14, 1972, p. 98.

70 *Capital*, vol. 3, p. 830.

71 *Capital*, vol. 1, p. 72.

72 It is of interest to observe at this point, as a consequence of these results, both a harmony and a divergence between Marx's theory of the fetishism of commodities and the text of Horkheimer and Adorno considered earlier. On the one hand, we saw previously how the authors of *Dialectic of Enlightenment* developed a theory of history which sought to establish an inexorable continuity between domination and exchange; it can now be recognized that in so doing they were remaining faithful to Marx's writings; for the relationship between domination and exchange is one of the core constituents of the theory of fetishism. On the other hand, however, regarding the relation between man and nature there is a fundamental divergence. For Marx, this latter relation cannot be understood independently of the dimension of intersubjectivity; indeed, to the extent that it has become a relation of domination, for him this is

no more than an exposition of the underlying distortions of the capitalist social field. By contrast, in *Dialectic of Enlightenment* domination is the primary category in the establishment of the man-nature relationship, and hence is independent of the social variables; accordingly, here, intersubjectivity is more an outcome of domination than conversely. Thus, in spite of the important convergences between Horkheimer and Adorno and Marx's thought, in relation to the questions of nature and sociality major discrepancies are to be found.

73 *Capital*, vol. 3, p. 880.
74 Ibid., p. 830.
75 See, for example, *Grundrisse*, pp. 471–514, 459–71; K. Marx, *The German Ideology*, in L. Easton and K. Guddat, eds, *Writings of the Young Marx on Philosophy and Society*, New York, Anchor, 1967, pp. 455 ff., *Capital*, vol. 1, part VII.
76 *Capital*, vol. 1, pp. 91 ff.
77 *Grundrisse*, pp. 156–7.
78 M. Merleau-Ponty, *Phenomenology, Language and Sociology*, op. cit., p. 178. Cf. J.-P Sartre, 'Materialism and revolution', in *Literary and Philosophical Essays*, London, Hutchinson, 1955.
79 *Grundrisse*, p. 157. Cf C. Lévi-Strauss, *Structural Anthropology*, vol. 1, London, Penguin, 1978, pp. 60–1.
80 J. Baudrillard, *For a Critique of the Political Economy of the Sign*, St Louis, Telos Press, 1981, pp. 91–2.
81 J. Baudrillard, *The Mirror of Production*, St Louis, Telos Press, 1975.
82 Ibid., pp. 18–20, 42–5.
83 Ibid., p. 33.
84 Ibid., p. 32.
85 Ibid., p. 29.
86 Ibid., p. 45.
87 Ibid., p. 23.
88 Ibid., p. 25.
89 Ibid., p. 18.
90 J. Baudrillard, 'Fetishism and ideology: the semiotic of reduction', in *For a Critique*, op. cit., p. 92.
91 Ibid., p. 93.
92 Ibid.
93 One important instance of this difference is to be found in the theories propounded in the two works regarding the nature of money. In the *Grundrisse* the symbolic aspects of money are emphasized; in *Capital* money is once again reduced to the objectification of abstract labour.
94 See Chapters 10 and 11.
95 Regarding these 'convergences and divergences' we can add the following two points. In the first place, it is apparent once again from this discussion that for Marx our knowledge could not be established in a 'lifeworld' fashioned and experienced independently of the social and historical reality together with its theoretical and cultural effects. On the contrary, the 'foundation' Marx reveals is fundamentally an intersubjective and discursive one, crucially dependent both on the structures of sociality and on those of natural science itself. Such a foundation however cannot consist in a postulated 'praxis' rather it is the material structure of intersubjectivity of which praxis itself is a 'making sense'.

Secondly (and on the other hand), it seems possible to identify a convergence between the fetishism of commodities as we have here represented it and Husserl's theory of the 'crisis'. For Husserl, as we have seen, a situation of crisis obtains when the relationship is occluded between a categorial framework and the lifeworld for the fulfillment of the *telos* of which this framework was developed; this is precisely the case in capitalist society, where objects are stripped of their social texture and instead appear to be derived from a series of categories given a priori. For both Husserl and Marx what is demanded by this circumstance is a re-examination of the relationship between categories and things – though of course a deep discrepancy remains between the two respective programmes for the overcoming of objectivism. To put this another way: Husserl's 'crisis of science' is just its *fetishistic representation* – that is, for him, science is in crisis when it is subject to processes of representation that are dominated by objectivism. This is an unexpected result, especially given that a notion of 'crisis' in the Marxian sense – that is, as a discontinuity in a temporally articulated social manifold – is entirely lacking from Husserl's work.

96 Of course, regarding Marx himself, even in respect of this particular issue he is concerned to achieve rather more than this. For example, he is especially interested in the conditions according to which in a given society the dominant form of objectivity is rendered problematical. (This issue cannot be discussed in detail here, in spite of its considerable interest for the theory of science.)

Chapter 7

1 We have spoken here of the 'forms of life' of capitalist society. It is possible that a case could be made to the effect that the mediation between a social formation and its predominant conceptual forms occur not just in the *symbolic* but also in the *political* realms. Cf. R. Mandrou, *L'Europe 'absolutiste': raison et raison d'état, 1649–1775*, Paris, Fayard, 1977.

2 E.g. A. Einstein, 'Autobiographical notes', in P. A. Schilpp, ed., *Albert Einstein: Philosopher-Scientist*, London, Cambridge University Press, 1949, pp. 11-13; *Ideas and Opinions*, London, Souvenir Press, 1973, pp. 290-3.

3 See Chapter 9.

4 M. Polanyi, *Personal Knowledge*, London, Routledge & Kegan Paul, 1962, pp. 9-15. Einstein himself explicitly affirms that the Michelson – Morley experiment had no role in the foundation of the theory of relativity. Polanyi comments:

The usual textbook account of relativity as a theoretical response to the Michelson-Morley experiment is an invention. It is the product of a philosophical prejudice. When Einstein discovered rationality in nature, unaided by any observation that had not been available for at least fifty years before, our positivistic textbooks promptly covered up the scandal by an appropriately embellished account of his discovery (p. 11).

5 Cf. I. Kant, *Critique of Pure Reason*, op. cit., pp. 19-22.

6 E. Cassirer, *Einstein's Theory of Relativity*, New York, Dover, 1953, p. 394.

7 I. Kant, op. cit., p. 135.

8 Ibid., pp. 134 ff., 156.

9 Ibid., pp. 135-6, 224.

10 Ibid., pp. 65, 368.

11 Cf. ibid., pp. 654-5, 102, 534, etc.

12 Another major parallel between the critical philosophy and the theory of relativity is worth mentioning in passing: the principle of causality. Einstein's theory – and indeed, Einstein himself, explicitly, in his philosophical writings – adopted as a basic presupposition the classical notion of causality which had acquired its first clear formulation in Kant's work.

13 I. Kant, op. cit., pp. 134 ff.

14 Cf. G. Lukács, *History and Class Consciousness*, op. cit., pp. 114 ff., 145.

15 Cf. E. Husserl, *Crisis*, op. cit., §28 and §57.
16 Cf. e.g. I. Lewis, *Mind and the World-order*, New York, Dover, 1956, pp. 265 ff. However, see also H. Reichenbach, *The Theory of Relativity and A Priori Knowledge*, Berkeley, University of California Press, 1966, ch. 6; and E. Cassirer, op. cit., pp. 415 ff., 434 ff.
17 See also H. Reichenbach, 'The philosophical significance of the theory of relativity', in P. A. Schilpp, ed., op. cit., pp. 287-312 and *The Theory of Relativity and A Priori Knowledge*, op. cit., 1966. We disagree with Reichenbach's contention that theory of relativity disproves in principle the possibility of synthetic a priori knowledge (see P. A. Schilpp, op. cit., pp. 307 ff.).
18 G. Martin, *Kant's Metaphysics and the Theory of Science*, England, Manchester University Press, 1961, pp. 23-4, 29, 40 etc.
19 I. Kant, op. cit., p. 398 note b. Cf. the following remarkable passage from ibid., pp. 235-6, the rich suggestiveness of which regarding relativity theory can hardly be denied!

> The word community is in the German language ambiguous. It may mean either *communio* or *commercium*. We here employ it in the latter sense, as signifying a dynamic community, without which even local community (*communio spatii*) could never be empirically known. We may easily recognize from our experiences that only the continuous influences in all parts of space can lead our senses from one object to another. The light, which plays between our eyes and the celestial bodies, produces a mediate community between us and them, and thereby shows us that they co-exist. We cannot empirically change our position, and perceive the change, unless matter in all parts of space makes perception of our position possible to us. For only thus by means of their reciprocal influence can the parts of matter establish their simultaneous existence, and thereby, though only mediately, their co-existence, even to the most remote objects. Without community each perception of an appearance in space is broken off from every other, and the chain of empirical representations, that is, experience, would have to begin entirely anew with each new object, without the least connection with the preceding representation, and without standing to it in any relation of time ...

20 Ibid., p. 76.
21 Ibid., p. 78.
22 A. Einstein, 'The foundations of the general theory of relativity', in A. Einstein, H. Lorentz, H. Minkowski and H. Weyl, *The Principle of Relativity*, London, Dover, 1952, p. 117.
23 Ibid.
24 I. Kant, op. cit., p. 194.
25 An attempt is made to discuss these questions in some detail in P. Komesaroff, 'A study of the socio-political significance of the philosophy of science with respect to Kant's *Critique of Pure Reason*. A phenomenological point of view.' Unpublished MA (prelim.) thesis, Monash University, 1975.
26 H. Reichenbach, in P.A. Schilpp, op. cit., p. 294.
27 E. Cassirer, *Einstein's Theory of Relativity*, op. cit., p. 381.
28 J. Habermas, *Knowledge and Human Interests*, op. cit., Chapter 1.
29 Cf. G. W. F. Hegel, *The Phenomenology of Mind*, tr. J. Baillie, London, Allen & Unwin 1971, pp. 136 ff.; *Logic*, tr. W. Wallace, Oxford, Clarendon Press, 1975, vol. 1, p. 197.
30 Cf. G. W. F. Hegel, *Phenomenology*, op. cit., pp. 142 ff.; *Logic*, op. cit., vol. 1, pp. 218-30.
31 I. Kant, op. cit., p. 601.

32 Ibid., pp. 134 ff.
33 J. Habermas, *Knowledge and Human Interests*, op. cit., p. 16.
34 Cf. H. Reichenbach, *The Theory of Relativity and A Priori Knowledge*, op. cit., pp. 69–73.
35 A. Gurwitsch, *Phenomenology and the Theory of Science*, Evanston, Northwestern University Press, 1974.
36 O. Becker, 'Contributions toward the phenomenological foundation of geometry and its physical applications', in J. Kocklemans and T. Kisiel, *Phenomenology and the Natural Sciences*, op. cit., pp. 119–46.
37 H. Weyl, *Philosophy of Mathematics and Natural Science*, Princeton, Princeton University Press, 1949; *Space, Time, Matter*, New York, Dover, 1952.
38 S. Bachelard, op. cit.; 'Phenomenology and mathematical physics', in J. Kocklemans and T. Kisiel, op. cit., pp. 413–25.
39 J. Kocklemans, 'The mathematization of nature in Husserl's last publication', in J. Kocklemans and T. Kisiel, eds, op. cit., pp. 44–67.
40 This is also in spite of his purely logical, though instructive discussions in *Formal and Transcendental Logic*, op. cit., pp. 90–104.
41 As it was later called.
42 Note that this result follows, as stated, from the special theory of relativity and the principle of equivalence alone and does not require the field equations as is sometimes claimed. In fact, it appears that Einstein himself followed the chain of thought described. See A. Einstein, 'Foundations', op. cit., pp. 97 ff.
43 H. Weyl, *Space, Time, Matter*, op. cit., p. 147 points out the similarities here with Husserl. Note also that Einstein specifically endorsed Weyl's book. See A. Einstein, *Relativity*, New York, Crown Publishers, 1961, Preface; cf. also the preface to *Space, Time, Matter*.
44 Ibid., pp. 283–4.
45 An excellent philosophical account of Wheeler's programme appears in J. Graves, *The Conceptual Foundations of Contemporary Relativity Theory*, Cambridge, Mass. MIT Press, 1971.
46 Conversion quoted by M. Jammer, *The Philosophy of Quantum Mechanics*, New York, John Wiley & Sons, 1974, p. 57.
47 Cf. also M. Heidegger, 'The principle of ground', *Man and World* 7 (3), 1974, pp. 207–22 and Husserl's discussion of the crisis of science (considered above). This conclusion also constituted one of the major, implicit, insights of the *Critique of Pure Reason*.
48 K. Marx, 'Towards the Critique of Hegel's philosophy of law; Introduction', in L. Easton and K. Guddat, eds, op. cit., p. 250.
49 Cf. H. Laborit, *Decoding the Human Message*, London, Allison & Busby, 1977, p. 10.

Chapter 8

1 Especially in the essay 'The origin of geometry'. See E. Husserl, *Crisis*, op. cit., pp. 361, 365–6, 367, 368–9, 371 etc.
2 Ibid., p. 361.
3 Ibid.
4 Ibid.
5 Husserl's brackets.
6 Ibid., p. 366.
7 Ibid., p. 365.
8 Ibid., p. 364.
9 Ibid., p. 365.

10 Ibid., p. 371.
11 Ibid., p. 366.
12 Cf. ibid., pp. 361, 365.
13 Ibid., p. 366.
14 Ibid, pp. 361-2.
15 Note that we are taking Ricœur as our *guide*; we are not simply recapitulating his arguments. Nevertheless, the course of our discussion is consistent with the development of his programme, especially as it is developed in the following works: *The Conflict of Interpretations*, tr. D. Ihde, Evanston, Northwestern University Press, 1974; *Interpretation Theory: Discourse and the Surplus of Meaning*, Texas, Texas Christian University Press, 1976; *The Philosophy of Paul Ricœur: An Anthology of his Work*, ed. C. Reagan and D. Stewart, New York, Beacon Press, 1976; 'New developments in phenomenology in France: the phenomenology of language', *Soc. Res.* 34, 1967, pp. 1-30.
16 P. Ricœur, *Conflict*, op. cit., p. 247.
17 M. Merleau-Ponty, *Phenomenology of Perception*, op. cit., Ch. 6.
18 Cf. P. Ricœur, *Conflict*, op. cit., p. 249.
19 M. Merleau-Ponty, *Signs*, op. cit., p. 96 (quoted in ibid., p. 249).
20 P. Ricœur, *Conflict*, op. cit., p. 248.
21 M. Merleau-Ponty, *Signs*, op. cit., p. 85.
22 Ibid., pp. 86-8.
23 P. Ricœur, 'New developments in phenomenology', op. cit., p. 12.
24 Ibid., p. 12n.
25 Ibid., p. 16.
26 P. Ricœur, *Conflict*, op. cit., p. 250.
27 F. de Saussure, *Course in General Linguistics*, London. Fontana, 1974, p. 14.
28 M. Merleau-Ponty, *The Prose of the World*, London, Heinemann, 1976, pp. 22-3.
29 Ibid.
30 This is not to say, of course, that substantial parallels do not exist between the projects generated by the two problematics. In this respect see, for example, J. M. Edie, 'Husserl's conception of "the grammatical" and contemporary linguistics', in L. Embree, ed., *Lifeworld and Consciousness*, Evanston, Northwestern University Press, 1972, pp. 233-62; and K-O. Apel, 'Noam Chomsky's theory of language and contemporary philosophy: a case study in the philosophy of science', in *Towards a Transformation in Philosophy*, London, Routledge & Kegan Paul, 1980, pp. 180-224.
31 P. Ricœur, *Conflict*, op. cit., p. 251.
32 Ibid., p. 252.
33 Ibid.
34 Ibid., p. 260.
35 Ibid., p. 261. In this connection it may be useful to append a note on a subject that has attracted some attention in relation to Husserl's philosophy. J. Derrida has argued (*Speech and Phenomena*, Evanston, Northwestern University Press, 1973, pp. 92-9) that in respect of the question of the meaning of the personal pronoun 'I' Husserl's arguments in the first *Logical Investigation* issue in a contradiction. Husserl had maintained that in the intertwining of expression and indication, meaning is realized precisely for the one who is speaking. 'In solitary speech the meaning of the "I" is essentially realized in the immediate idea of one's personality' (E. Husserl, *Logical Investigations*, op. cit., §26, quoted in J. Derrida, op. cit., p. 95). Against this, Derrida claims that the meaning of the word 'I' is ideal, emerging from the significative system in such

a way that it perdures even in the absence of – or perhaps *necessarily* in the absence of – the speaking subject. 'Whether or not I have a present intuition of myself, "I" expresses something; whether or not I am alive, "I am" means something' (J. Derrida, loc. cit.). 'The anonymity of the written *I*, the impropriety of the *I am writing* is ... the normal situation' (ibid. p. 97).

From the preceding discussion we might conclude that Derrida is right – but that so also is Husserl. The *I* is a creation of language insofar as its meaning cannot be abstracted from the semiotic system in which it occurs. Further, to this extent the privilege of subjectivity must give way to an acknowledgement of the irreducible communicative presupposition for all discourse. Here, in the realm of the sign and its significations the *hic et nunc* of the phenomenologist vanish – reappearing only subsequently, as an artifice of the semiotic apparatus. On the other hand however, it cannot be denied that the existence of subjectivity – or at least, of intersubjectivity – is in some sense a presupposition for the system of signs: it is the extralinguistic condition of discourse. Prior to its 'realization' in a communicative exchange the personal pronoun represents merely an empty potential. In discourse the expression 'I' as a location in a system of differences is irreducible; however at the same time 'I' as the subject of either utterance or recognition is an inescapable condition for both the realization of discourse and the designation of its present occurrence. (See also B. P. Dauenhauer, 'On speech and temporality', *Phil. Today*, Fall 1974, pp. 1–10; P. Ricœur, *Conflict*, op. cit., pp. 254 ff.; and P. Ricœur, *Interpretation Theory,* op. cit., ch 1.)

36 In, for example, G. Bachelard, *Le Rationalisme appliqúe*, Paris, 1970, p. 51.
37 L. Althusser, *For Marx*, London, Allen Lane, 1969, p. 46.
38 Ibid., pp. 67 n; 80 n.
39 L. Althusser, in L. Althusser and E. Balibar, *Reading Capital*, op cit., p. 25.
40 Ibid., pp. 25–6.
41 Cf. C. Lévi-Strauss, *Structural Anthropology* I, Great Britain, Penguin, 1978, pp. 33, 56–7.
42 L. Althusser, *Politics and History*, London, New Left Books, 1972, pp. 182 ff.
43 Cf. also Piaget's emphasis on not the individual subject but 'the *epistemic subject*, that cognitive nucleus which is common to all subjects at the same level' (J. Piaget, *Structuralism*, London, Routledge & Kegan Paul, 1971, p. 119).
44 Çf. F. de Saussure, op. cit., pp. 106 f., 114 f., 117 f., 120 f., etc.
45 Cf. for example, F. George, 'Reading Althusser', *Telos* 7, 1971, pp. 73–98; J. Rancière, 'On the theory of ideology', op. cit.; M. Plaut, 'The problem of positivism in the work of Nicos Poulantzas', *Telos* 36, 1978, pp. 159–166. Such arguments have also been advanced by J. Arnason.
46 M. Foucault, *Power, Truth, Strategy*, Sydney, Feral, 1979, p. 47.
47 Also, perhaps even Derrida. See *Speech and Phenomena*, op. cit., Ch. 1.
48 M. Merleau-Ponty, *The Prose of the World*, op. cit., pp. 38–9.
49 It is perhaps appropriate to add that we are here attempting to identify some abiding themes of structuralism; we are not seeking to minimize the variation within the school as a whole. Indeed, structuralism is by no means an homogeneous body of thought: within its compass are to be found substantial ruptures, transformations and changes of emphasis. For example, whereas Lévi-Strauss concentrates on the problem of meaning Althusser focuses on the problem of knowledge and Foucault on that of truth. This does not however contradict the substantive claims we have made in respect of the existence of a coherent structuralist problematic.

50 For this notion of value cf. F. de Saussure, op. cit., pp. 110 ff.
51 See the preface to the Italian edition of *Reading Capital* (L. Althusser and E. Balibar, op. cit.); also see L. Althusser, *Essays in Self-criticism*, London, New Left Books, 1976.
52 See J. Rancière, *La Leçon d'Althusser*, Paris, Editions Gallimard, 1974; and 'On the theory of ideology', op. cit.
53 It has been claimed (J. Arnason) that in Lévi-Strauss's work the positivism is distributed temporally rather than spatially, with the earlier writings being the worst offenders and the later ones showing some signs of a movement away from positivism. This suggestion seems to have merit; however it will not be further discussed here.
54 C. Lévi-Strauss, *The Scope of Anthropology*, London, Jonathan Cape, 1967, p. 16.
55 Cf. P. Ricœur, 'Structure, word, event', in *The Philosophy of Paul Ricœur*, op. cit., pp. 109-119. Cf. also J. Derrida, 'Structure, sign and play in the discourse of the human sciences', in *Writing and Difference*, Chicago, University of Chicago Press, 1978, Ch. 10.
56 Cf. R. Barthes, *Elements of Semiology*, London, Jonathan Cape, 1972, pp. 35 ff.
57 C. Lévi-Strauss, *The Savage Mind*, Chicago, University of Chicago Press, 1973, p. 131.
58 C. Lévi-Strauss, 'Confrontation over myths' (with P. Ricœur), *New Left Review* 62, 1970, p. 82.
59 See, for example, M. Dufrenne, *Language and Philosophy*, Bloomington, Indiana University Press, 1963.
60 C. Lévi-Strauss, *Tristes Tropiques*, Great Britain, Penguin, 1976, p. 70.
61 C. Lévi-Strauss, *The Savage Mind*, op. cit., pp. 268-9; *Structural Anthropology*, 2 Great Britain, Penguin, 1978, pp. 55-65.
62 Cf. C. Lévi-Strauss, *The Savage Mind*, op. cit., Ch. 9, esp. pp. 247-8; *Structural Anthropology*, 1, op. cit., pp. 65, 296-302.
63 C. Lévi-Strauss, *The Savage Mind*, op. cit., p. 247 and note.
64 Cf. P. Ricœur, *The Conflict of Interpretations*, op. cit.; J-P. Sartre, 'Replies to structuralism: an interview', *Telos* 9, 1971, pp. 110-15; B. Scholte, 'Lévi-Strauss's Penelopean effort: the analysis of myth', *Semiotica* 1, 1969, pp. 99-124.
65 This suggestion has been made by J. Arnason.
66 Foucault is, in the context of this chapter, of considerable interest since in his early work he, like Lévi-Strauss, was also committed, paradoxically, to what we might call a 'super-objectivism'. At the same time, however, there are to be found in his writings themes which genuinely transcend the metaphysics of the subject. Unfortunately, Foucault's thought cannot be discussed at length here.
67 This is a point that has been emphasized in particular by P. Ricœur and M. Merleau-Ponty.

Chapter 9

1 See below. Also see M. Jammer, *The Philosophy of Quantum Mechanics*, New York, John Wiley & Sons, 1974, Chapter 1.
2 Ibid., p. 11.
3 Ibid.
4 W. Heisenberg, *Physics and Philosophy,* London, Allen & Unwin, 1958, Chapter 2; N. Bohr, *Atomic Theory and the Description of Nature*, Cambridge University Press, 1934, pp. 26-9.

5 See W. Heisenberg, 'The development of the interpretation of the quantum theory', in W. Pauli, ed., *Neils Bohr and the Development of Physics*, London, Pergamon, 1955, pp. 12–29.

6 E. Schrödinger, in E. Schrödinger, M. Planck, A. Einstein and H. Lorentz, *Letters on Wave Mechanics*, New York, Philosophical Library, 1967, pp. 10–11.

7 Cf. M. Jammer, op. cit., pp. 32–3 and n. 22.

8 See M. Born, *Experiment and Theory in Physics*, Cambridge University Press, 1943.

9 N. Bohr, *Atomic Theory*, op. cit., p. 4.

10 Ibid.

11 Ibid., p. 16.

12 For early formulations see N. Bohr, *Collected works*, ed. L. Rosenfeld, Amsterdam, North-Holland, 1972, vol. 3, pp. 249 ff, 351, 377 f., 478 ff. etc.; and *Atomic Theory*, op. cit., Chapter 1.

13 See also W. Heisenberg, *The Physical Principles of the Quantum Theory*, New York, Dover, 1949, pp. 82, 105–7.

14 *Collected Works*, vol. 3, p. 249.

15 Ibid., p. 250.

16 *Atomic Theory*, p. 37.

17 Ibid., p. 37.

18 Ibid.

19 Cf. ibid, pp. 1, 8, 22 etc.

20 N. Bohr, quoted in A. Petersen, *Quantum Physics and the Philosophical Tradition*, Cambridge, Mass., MIT Press, 1968, p. 121.

21 *Atomic Theory*, p. 17.

22 Ibid., p. 94.

23 Ibid., p. 16.

24 A. Petersen, op. cit., p. 118; see also N. Bohr, *Atomic Theory*, op. cit., pp. 85–7.

25 See below, p. 289.

26 See P. Heelan, *Space-Perception and the Philosophy of Science*. Berkeley, University of California Press, 1983.

27 N. Bohr, *Atomic Physics and Human Knowledge*, New York, John Wiley & Sons, 1958, p. 89; 'Discussion with Einstein on epistemological problems in atomic physics', in P.A. Schilpp, ed. op. cit., p. 209. See also A. Petersen, op. cit., p. 179 and P. Feyerabend, 'Complementarity', *Proc. Arist. Soc.*, Suppl. 32, 1958, pp. 81–6.

28 Cf. *Atomic Physics*, p. 90.

29 *Atomic Theory*, pp. 53–4.

30 'Discussion with Einstein', p. 224 (cf. also p. 234).

31 *Atomic Theory*, p. 54.

32 N. Bohr, 'Can quantum mechanical description of physical reality be considered complete?', *Phys. Rev.* 48, 1935, p. 697.

33 A. Petersen, op. cit., p. 158.

34 N. Bohr, 'Causality and complementarity', *Phil. Sci.* 4, 1937, p. 291.

35 'Discussion with Einstein', p. 210.

36 Ibid., p. 230; *Atomic Physics*, p. 90.

37 *Atomic Theory*, p. 96.

38 Ibid.

39 'Discussion with Einstein', p. 238.

40 Cf. A. Petersen, op. cit., p. 180.

41 *Atomic Theory*, p. 96.

42 Cf. Heisenberg's discussion of this issue, op. cit., Chapter 5. Heisenberg argues

that the great philosophical innovation of quantum mechanics lay in its discovery that the fundamental ontological conceptions of classical physics could not be upheld. The conceptions included Descartes' doctrine of the extended and thinking substance, which conveyed the epistemological consequence of 'dogmatic realism': the view that statements about the material world are strictly independent of their conditions of verification (ibid., p. 74). Heisenberg concludes that '(i)t is only through quantum theory that we have learnt that exact science is possible without the basis of dogmatic realism' (ibid.,

43 K. Hübner, 'The philosophical background of hidden variables in quantum mechanics', *Man and World* 6, 1973, p. 423. See also P. Feyerabend, 'Neils Bohr's interpretation of the quantum theory', in H. Feigl and G. Maxwell, eds, *Current Issues in the Philosophy of Science*, New York, Holt, Rinehart, Winston, 1961, pp. 383-4.

44 *Atomic Theory*, p. 18.

45 E.g. 'Causality and complementarity', p. 291.

46 Cf. *Atomic Theory*, p. 97 (and 'Discussion with Einstein', p. 211).

47 Cf. 'Discussion with Einstein', p. 238.

48 *Atomic Physics*, p. 88.

49 Ibid., p. 72.

50 *Atomic Theory*, p. 19; W. Heisenberg, *Physics and Philosophy*, op. cit., pp. 153 ff.

51 Cf. A. Petersen, op. cit., p. 172.

52 'Discussion with Einstein', p. 240.

53 See above, p. 266.

54 Cf. E. Husserl, *Ideas*, op. cit., p. 319.

55 P. Heelan, 'Hermeneutics and the humanities', unpublished paper, Department of Philosophy, State University of New York at Stony Brook, 1980, p. 3.

56 Cf. J. Derrida, *Positions*, London, Athlone, 1981, pp. 24-9.

57 There has, of course, been considerable debate over the question of the most appropriate characterization of Bohr's philosophy. Cf., for example, R. N. Hanson, 'Five cautions for the Copenhagen interpretation's critics', *Phil. Sci.* 26, 1959, pp. 325-37; P. Feyerabend, 'Neils Bohr's interpretation of the quantum theory', op. cit.; C. A. Hooker, 'The nature of quantum mechanical reality', in R. Colodney, ed., *Paradigms and Paradoxes*, Pittsburgh, University of Pittsburgh Press, 1972, pp. 67-301. It is not appropriate for us to enter this debate here.

58 For examples of such differing viewpoints see P. Heelan, *Quantum Mechanics and Objectivity*, The Hague, Martinus Nijhoff, 1965; and D. I. Blochinzev, *The Philosophy of Quantum Mechanics*, Dordrecht, D. Reidel, 1968.

59 Cf. W. Heisenberg, *Physics and Philosophy*, op. cit., Chapter 5.

60 J. Derrida, *Positions*, op. cit., p. 23 contradicts this last assertion.

61 F. Capra, *The Tao of Physics*, London, Wildwood House, 1975; G. Zukav, *The Dancing Wu-li Masters*, Suffolk, Fontana, 1979.

62 *Atomic Theory*, pp. 116-17.

63 Ibid., p. 119.

64 We are speaking of elementary electron theory; Schrödinger in 1926 proposed a relativistic spin O equation that applies to pi mesons. See P. Dirac, *Principles of Quantum Mechanics*, Oxford, Clarendon Press, 1958 (4th edition), Chapter 9; 'The quantum theory of the electron', *Proc. Royal Soc.* A117, 1928, p. 610.

65 S. W. Hawking, 'Particle creation by black holes' *Comm. Math. Phys.* 43, 1975, p. 199.

66 For what follows see for example, R. Arnowitt, S. Deser and C. Misner, 'The

dynamics of general relativity', in L. Witten, ed., *Gravitation: An Introduction to Current Research*, New York, John Wiley & Sons, 1962, pp. 227-65; J. Anderson, 'Quantization of general relativity', in H-Y. Chiu and W. Hoffman, eds, *Gravitation and Relativity*, New York, Benjamin, 1964, pp. 279-302; C. J. Isham, R. Penrose and D. W. Sciama, *Quantum Gravity 2: A Second Oxford Symposium*, Oxford University Press, 1981.

67 Cf. M. Jammer, op. cit., pp. 502 ff., 438 ff.

68 Although, at least in the case of Einstein – who affirmed that his thinking was deeply mathematical – this is probably an exaggeration.

69 Cf. L. Althusser, *For Marx*, op. cit., Chapter 3.

70 Cf. S. Freud, *Three Contributions to the Theory of Sex*, 'Contribution III: The transformations of puberty' in A. A. Brill, ed., *The Basic Writings of Sigmund Freud*, New York, Random House, 1938, pp. 604-29. The same point applies of course with particular force to Piaget.

71 A. Einstein, B. Podolsky, W. Rosen, 'Can quantum mechanical description of physical reality be considered complete?', *Phys. Rev.* 47, 1935, pp. 777-80.

72 N. Bohr, 'Can quantum mechanical description of reality be considered complete?', *Phys. Rev.* 48, 1935 pp. 696-702.

73 See above, pp. 271 ff.

74 A. Einstein, P. Podolsky, N. Rosen. op. cit., p. 777.

75 N. Bohr, 'Can quantum mechanical description of reality be considered complete?' op. cit., p. 699.

76 N. Bohr, *Atomic Theory*, op. cit., p. 96.

77 See, for example, ibid., pp. 4-5, 116-17; 'Causality and complementarity', p. 293; 'Discussion with Einstein', p. 211.

78 Cf. 'Discussion with Einstein', p. 671-2.

79 J. Von Neumann, *Mathematical Foundations of Quantum Mechanics*, Princeton, Princeton University Press, 1955, Chapter 4.

80 Ibid, pp. 327-8.

81 Cf. J. Bub, 'Hidden variables and the Copenhagen interpretation – a reconciliation', *Brit. J. Phil. Sci.* 19, 1968, pp. 185-210; D. Bohm, *Causality and Chance in Modern Physics*, Philadelphia, University Press, 1957 and *Wholeness and the Implicate Order*, London, Routledge & Kegan Paul, 1980. Other important contributions to the debate have been made by J. M. Jauch, C. Piron, A. M. Gleason and others.

82 N. Bohr, 'Causality and complementarity', op. cit., p. 290.

83 Ibid., p. 293; cf. 'Discussion with Einstein', op. cit., p. 211.

84 N. Bohr, 'Can quantum mechanical description of reality be considered complete?', op. cit., p. 696.

85 Cf. L. Althusser, *Reading Capital*, op. cit., pp. 186-9; M.Foucault, *The Archaeology of Knowledge*, London, Tavistock, 1972, pp. 162-4.

86 Cf. a related, but not identical, approach taken by D. Bohm in 'Space, time and quantum theory – understood in terms of discrete structural process', *Proceedings of International Conference on Elementary Particles*, Kyoto, 1965. See also J. Bub, op. cit.

87 Bell's original results were published in J. S. Bell, 'On the problem of hidden variables in quantum mechanics', *Rev. Mod. Phys.* 38, 1966, pp. 447-52. We shall not enter into the now extensive literature on Bell's theorem here.

88 On this point cf. J. Bub, 'On the completeness of quantum mechanics', in C. A. Hooker, ed., *Contemporary Research in the Foundations and Philosophy of Quantum Mechanics*, op. cit., p. 44.

Chapter 10

1 Cf. the discussion in Chapter 8, above and pp. 305 ff., below.

2 Cf. E. Husserl, *Crisis*, op. cit., p. 31.

3 Cf. R. E. Palmer, *Hermeneutics*, Evanston, Northwestern University Press, 1969, pp. 77 f., 118 f., 87 f.

4 Cf. Chapter 3, above.

5 As also was seen in Chapter 3.

6 See also below, Chapter 11 pp. 353 ff.

7 Regarding the generalization of the commodity economy see A. Sohn-Rethel, *Intellectual and Manual Labour*, London, Macmillan, 1978.

8 See Chapters 2 and 3; also P. Feyerabend, *Against Method*, op cit.

9 Cf. the discussion of *Dialectic of Enlightenment* in Chapter 1; also see Chapter 3, pp. 84 ff.

10 See Chapter 3.

11 See Chapter 4.

12 E. Husserl, Crisis, op. cit., p. 22 (cf. also p. 38).

13 Ibid., p. 28.

14 Ibid, pp. 38, 51.

15 Ibid, p. 39.

16 See esp. pp. 162 ff.

17 See, e.g. E. T. Bell, *Men of Mathematics*, London, Penguin, 1953; D. Struik, *The Land of Stevin and Huygens*, Dordrecht, D. Reidel, 1981; D. Struik, *A Concise History of Mathematics*, New York, Dover, 1967; M. Kline, *Mathematical Thought from Ancient to Modern Times*, London, Oxford University Press, 1972.

18 It is the view of some authors that abstract geometry was developed largely in response to practical problems. See M. Kline, *Mathematics: The Loss of Certainty*, New York, Oxford University Press, 1980, p. 292.

19 J. Von Neumann, 'The mathematician', in *Collected Works*, Oxford, Pergamon Press, 1961-2, vol. 1, pp. 1-9.

20 M. Kline, *Mathematics*, op. cit., pp. 296, 298, 299.

21 See, for example, Adorno's argument in *Prisms*, op. cit., pp. 23-4.

22 A good current example of this is elementary particle theory and gauge theory.

23 W. V. O. Quine, 'On what there is' (1948), in *From Logical Point of View*, New York, Harper Torchbooks, 1963, p. 13.

24 W. V. O. Quine, 'Logic and reification of universals' (1961), ibid., p. 103.

25 W. V. O. Quine, *Ontological Relativity and Other Essays*, New York, Cambridge University Press, 1969, p. 93.

26 W. V. O. Quine, *From a Logical Point of View*, op. cit., pp. 130-1.

27 W. V. O. Quine, *Ontological Relativity*, op. cit., p. 51.

28 It is not appropriate to discuss Hooker's project in detail here. It is sufficient merely to mention that, as he himself puts it, his aim has been 'to develop a characterization of the *spirit* or *essence* of the ontologising of classical physics'. (C. A. Hooker, 'Metaphysics and modern physics', in C. A. Hooker, ed., *Contemporary Research in the Foundations of Quantum Theory*, Dordrecht, D. Reidel, 1979, p. 182). He has sought to achieve this by attempting to argue that there is 'a profound and intimate connection between the mathematical structure of a theory, its conceptual structure for physical description and its basic ontology' (ibid., p. 208). On the basis of these claims he has proceeded to seek a characterization of the conceptual structure of quantum mechanics. In respect of this problem he has concluded that 'quantum mechanics shares with both classical particle mechanics and classical field theory the general Lagrangian -

Hamiltonian dynamical structure and it shares with classical field theory the general formulation of the dynamical structure characteristic of a field theory, but with respect to its specific dynamics, quantum mechanics retains as closely as possible the fundamental form of the dynamics of classical particle mechanics' (ibid, p. 252). More briefly, this amounts to the conclusion that 'a review of the propositional structure of quantum mechanics' shows that 'quantum mechanics has the form of an analysis of the structure of classical field theory and classical particles mechanics, but that classical field theory dominates the structure' (ibid. p. 259). From this result Hooker draws the inference that '(t)here is no strictly coherent conceptual structure for quantum mechanics couched in terms of the traditional conceptual structures for particle and field theories, neither is there any coherent ontology for quantum mechanics specifiable in terms of the classical particle and field ontologies' (ibid. p. 210).

Hooker's programme, it must be stated at once, has not yet been fully elaborated; nevertheless, its early formulations are certainly both interesting and suggestive. The attempt to deduce ontological claims from the formal structure of a theory and subsequently to apply this approach to outstanding problems in the interpretation of contemporary physics may well produce new and fertile consequences. However for the present it must be accepted that the programme faces substantial difficulties. For example, in the absence of a more precise theory it is compelled to rely upon vague and inadequately elaborated expressions, such as 'mixture' (ibid. p. 252), 'fusion' (ibid., p. 209) or 'amalgam' (ibid., p. 259) of structures. But also, and more importantly, it must confront the general issues with which any such linguistically-oriented programme is inevitably faced. Just to mention two of these issues: it must be able to provide an account of the transition between a formal theory and the language within which the philosophical assertions are formulated; and similarly, it must be able to explicate the process of the interpretation of the linguistic hypothesis itself. These problems – which advert to matters of principle and could conceivably threaten the whole of Hooker's enterprise – are just the problems that are raised in their generality by Quine's theory. See also C. A. Hooker, ed., *The Logico-algebraic Approach to Quantum Mechanics*, Dordrecht, D. Reidel, 1979 (2 volumes).

29 E.g. B. L. Whorff, E. Benveniste.
30 Cf., for example, J. R. Searle and the 'pragmatist' theorists of language.
31 E. Hall, *What is Value?*, London, Routledge & Kegan Paul, 1952, Chapter 4.
32 E. Husserl. Cf. 'indication': see *Logical Investigations*, op. cit., pp. 269 ff.
33 E. Hall, loc. cit.
34 As Quine himself suggests.
35 G. Morris, *Foundations of the Theory of Signs*, Chicago, University of Chicago Press, 1938, p. 23.
36 Ibid.
37 Cf. A. Schmidt, *The Concept of Nature in Marx*, London, New Left Books, 1971.
38 B. Russell, *Introduction to Mathematical Philosophy*, London, Muirhead Library of Philosophy, 1979, p. 5. It is interesting that Russell's position in fact changed substantially over the years. Whereas in 1901 he was claiming that the edifice of mathematical truth – logical and physical – was unshakeable, by the second edition of the *Principia* in 1926 he had conceded that logic and mathematics, like Maxwell's equations of electromagnetic theory, are believed 'merely because of the observed truth of certain of their logical consequences'.

39 Quoted by T. Adorno, in T. Adorno et al., *The Positivist Dispute*, op. cit., pp. 21-2.

40 It is not nowadays difficult to think of other examples. Quantum mechanics is a controversial possibility.

41 E.g.: L. E. Brouwer, 'Intuitionism and formalism', *Amer. Math. Soc. Bulletin* 20, 1913-14, pp. 81-96; H. Weyl, *Philosophy of Mathematics and Natural Science*, op. cit.; P. Bernays, 'Platonism and mathematics', in P. Benacerraf and H. Putnam, eds, *Philosophy of Mathematics*, N. J. Prentice Hall, 1964.

42 Cf. G-C. Rota, 'Edmund Husserl and the reform of logic', in D. Carr and E. Casey, eds., *Explorations in Phenomenology*, The Hague, M. Nijhoff, 1973, pp. 299-305. Rota in fact claims that the whole of Husserl's *Crisis* can be understood from the point of view of a revision of classical logic. According to him, it is an outcome of this work that one must penetrate traditional thought; in particular, 'one must first come to a vital, actual realization that the physical object is no longer to be taken as the standard of reality' (p. 301); instead, phenomenology has been developed to bring out the 'experiential reality of ideal phenomena ...' (p. 302).

Now Rota's assessment of the *Crisis* is certainly not the same as our own; furthermore, he does not even advert to the main questions with which we are concerned. Nevertheless, regarded as a general programme, his approach is largely consistent with the one sketched in the following pages.

Cf. also R. Tragesser, 'On the phenomenological foundations of mathematics', in ibid., pp. 285-98.

43 It is beginning to be appreciated that the relationship between Frege and Husserl is closer than has hitherto generally been accepted - especially in the case of the logical writings of the latter. See D. Follesdal, 'Husserl's notion of noema', *J. Phil.* 66 (20), 1969, pp. 680-7; also W Mays and B. Jones, 'Was Husserl a Fregean?', *J. Brit. Soc. Phen.* 12 (1), 1981, pp. 76-80.

44 G. Frege, *Translations from the Philosophical Writings of Gottlob Frege*, ed. P. Geach and M. Black, Oxford, Basil Blackwell, 1977, p. 59. In what follows, where appropriate, terms used in Frege's own technical sense will be indicated by their inclusion within single quotation marks ('...').

45 Ibid., pp. 60-1.

46 Ibid., p. 63.

47 Ibid., pp. 64, 42 ff.

48 Ibid., p. 62 n.

49 Ibid., pp. 64, 1 ff.

50 Cf. ibid., pp. 121-2.

51 G. Frege, *Logical Investigations*, tr. P. T. Geach and R. H. Stoothoff, Oxford, Basil Blackwell, 1977, p. 4.

52 Ibid., pp. 14-15.

53 Ibid., p. 19.

54 Ibid.

55 Ibid., pp. 21-2.

56 Ibid., pp. 18-19, 22.

57 Ibid., pp. 27-9.

58 Cf. G. Frege, *Philosophical Writings*, op. cit., pp. 79, 172.

59 G. Frege, *Logical Investigations*, op. cit., pp. 22-3.

60 Ibid., p. 23.

61 Ibid., p. 17.

62 Ibid., pp. 17, 26.

63 G. Frege, *Philosophical Writings*, op. cit., p. 78.

64 E. Husserl, *Logical Investigations*, op. cit., p. 615. (Cf. *Formal and Transcendental Logic*, op. cit., p. 196.)

65 Ibid., p. 611.

66 Ibid., p. 612.

67 Ibid., pp. 632–3.

68 Ibid., p. 629.

69 Ibid., p. 611.

70 Ibid., p. 615. Cf. p. 259.

71 See ibid., pp. 332, 329, 324, 184, 184 n.

72 Ibid. See also E. Husserl, *Formal and Transcendental Logic*, op. cit., p. 195.

73 Ibid., p. 325.

74 Ibid., p. 190.

75 Ibid., p. 325.

76 E. Husserl, *Formal and Transcendental Logic*, op. cit., p. 194.

77 Ibid., §75, p. 190.

78 Ibid.

79 Ibid., p. 193.

80 Ibid., p. 190.

81 Cf. ibid., §77. Also cf. *Prolegomena* in *Logical Investigations*, op. cit., §50.

82 Cf. Aristotle's argument, *Metaphysics*, IV, 7, in R. McKeon, ed., *The Basic Works of Aristotle*, op. cit., pp. 749–755. Aristotle adds: 'while the doctrine of Heraclitus, that all things are and are not, seems to make everything true, that of Anaxagoras, that there is an intermediate between the terms of a contradiction, seems to make everything false; for when things are mixed, the mixture is neither good nor not-good, so that one cannot say anything that is true' (ibid.).

83 E. Husserl, *Formal and Transcendental Logic,* op. cit., p. 195.

Chapter 11

1 Cf. M. Merleau-Ponty, *Phenomenology of Perception*, op. cit., p. (viii).

2 Cf. J. Habermas, *Knowledge and Human Interests*, op. cit.

3 Cf. T. Kuhn; this is the case, notwithstanding the efforts of P. Feyerabend, G. Radnitzky, etc. See also T. Nickles, ed., *Scientific Discovery, Logic and Rationality*, Dordrecht, D. Reidel, 1980.

4 In *Cartesian Meditations* (§8), *Crisis* and 'The origin of geometry' Husserl introduces the notion of repeatability as a condition of objectivity. J. Derrida has shown that repeatability presupposes the possibility of a meaning present to a consciousness – and thus the 'metaphysics of presence'. For him there is no absolute identity of meaning: there are only likenesses established across constantly changing patterns of language use. Nevertheless, it is clear that no science of nature would be possible that did not meet the condition of repeatability. This does not however compromise Derrida's insight because within a science, which has a methodical aspect, laws of identity can if necessary be defined conventionally. See especially J. Derrida, *Edmund Husserl's 'Origin of geometry': An Introduction*, New York, Nicolas Hays Ltd., 1978, pp. 72 ff. and *Speech and Phenomena*, Evanston, Northwestern University Press, 1973, pp. 52, 115, 128 etc.

5 See above, Chapter 4. (Also cf. E. Husserl, *Ideas*, op. cit., §138 etc.)

6 E. Husserl, *Ideas*, op. cit., §47, §38.

7 See above (and ibid., §48).

8 See above (and *Formal and Transcendental Logic*, §95).

9 See above (and ibid.).

10 Cf. above (and ibid.).

11 E. Husserl, *Ideas*, op. cit., §47.

12 Cf. above, pp. 107 ff. (and *Formal and Transcendental Logic*, §60).

13 See above, pp. 164 ff.

14 Cf. above, pp. 129 ff.

15 See Chapter 5.

16 See above (and E. Husserl, *Crisis*, op. cit., pp. 49–50, 71–2).

17 Cf. for example, A. Sohn-Rethel, op. cit., and J. D. Bernal, 'Frederick Engels and science', *Science and Nature* 2, 1979, pp. 39–54 (to choose merely two obvious examples).

18 See Aristotle, op. cit., pp. 691 ff., 240 ff.

19 Cf. C. Castoriadis, *L'Institution imaginaire de la société*, Paris, Editions du Seuil, 1974, part 1; 'On the history of the workers' movement', *Telos* 30, 1976–7, pp. 3–43; cf. also 'From Marx to Aristotle, from Aristotle to us', *Social Research* 45(4), 1978, pp. 667–739.

20 C. Castoriadis, *L'Institution imaginaire*, loc. cit.

21 See Chapter 8, pp. 237 ff.

22 I.e. in his more critical writings, such as the *Grundrisse*, the *German Ideology* and so on.

23 D. Howard, *The Marxian Legacy*, London, Macmillan, 1977, pp. 283–4.

24 K. Korsch, *Marxism and Philosophy*, London, New Left Books, 1972.

25 See above and also cf. G. Lukács, 'The changing function of historical materialism', in *History and Class Consciousness*, op. cit., pp. 223–55.

26 Cf. K. Kosik, *Dialectics of the Concrete*, Dordrecht, D. Reidel, 1976, pp. 61 ff.

27 Cf. M. Merleau-Ponty, 'Working note, November 1960', in *The Visible and the Invisible*, op. cit., p. 267.

28 See Chapter 3.

29 C. S. Peirce, 'Questions concerning faculties claimed for man', in *Selected Writings*, ed. P. P. Wiener, New York, Davis Publications, 1966, pp. 15–38.

30 J. Habermas, *Knowledge and Human Interests*, op. cit., Chapter 5.

31 Ibid., p. 100.

32 See in this context especially: J. Habermas, *Communication and the Evolution of Society*, Boston, Beacon, 1979; *Knowledge and Human Interests*, op. cit.; *Legitimation Crisis*, Boston, Beacon, 1973; and 'Thoughts on the foundation of sociology in the philosophy of language: six lectures', presented as the Christian Gauss lectures at Princeton University, Spring, 1971 (unpublished).

33 L. Wittgenstein, *Philosophical Investigations*, Oxford, Basil Blackwell, 1974 §241.

34 L. Wittgenstein, *The Blue and Brown books*, Oxford, Basil Blackwell, 1975, p. 65.

35 L. Wittgenstein, *Philosophical Investigations*, op. cit., §20.

36 Ibid., §202.

37 Ibid.

38 J. Habermas, 'Gauss lectures', op. cit., no. 3.

39 J. Habermas, *Communication and the Evolution of Society*, op. cit., pp. 2–5, p. 55 etc.

40 J. Habermas, 'Gauss lectures', op. cit.

41 E. Husserl, *Cartesian Meditations*, op. cit. V; *Crisis*, op. cit., p. 231.

42 E. Husserl, *Logical Investigations*, op. cit., pp. 817–24.

43 See below, pp. 351 ff.

44 Cf. J. Habermas, *Legitimation Crisis*, op. cit, p. 8.
45 J. Habermas, *Communication and the Evolution of Society*, op. cit., p. 173.
46 J. Habermas, 'A postscript to *Knowledge and Human Interests*', op. cit., p. 170.
47 See J. Habermas, *Communication and the Evolution of Society*, op. cit., pp. 1–5; 'Postscript', op. cit., pp. 170–4.
48 J. Habermas, 'Postscript', loc. cit.
49 Such an assumption may even underlie the possibility of any study such as the present one; this is of particular relevance for works which seek to deal with divergent meanings.
50 J. Habermas, 'Postscript', op. cit., p. 174.
51 L. Wittgenstein, *Tractatus Logico-Philosophicus*, op. cit., 3.314, 4 ff., 4.5.
52 Ibid., 3.3, 3.314.
53 Cf. ibid., 4.06–4.063, 4.25.
54 Ibid., 4.061, 4.466.
55 Ibid., 4.26 ff., 4.06, 5–5.2.
56 Ibid., 1, 1.1.
57 Ibid., 4.024.
58 Ibid., 4.11.
59 See K-O. Apel, *Towards a Transformation in Philosophy*, London, Routledge & Kegan Paul, 1979, Chapter 1; and *Analytical Philosophy of Language and the Geisteswissenshaften*, Dordrecht, D. Reidel, 1967, *passim*.
60 L. Wittgenstein, *Philosophical Investigations*, op. cit., §66.
61 Ibid., §82–4.
62 Ibid., §7.
63 Ibid., §23.
64 Ibid.
65 Cf. ibid., §664, §111, §89.
66 K-O. Apel, *Towards a Transformation in Philosophy*, op. cit., p. 22.
67 L. Wittgenstein, *Philosophical Investigations*, op. cit., §19, §23, §241.
68 Cf. ibid., §65.
69 Ibid., §108.
70 Ibid., §109, §654–6.
71 See J. Habermas, *Knowledge and Human Interests*, op. cit., p. 168.
72 J. Habermas, *Communication and the Evolution of Society*, op. cit., p. 68.
73 K-O. Apel, 'Causal explanation, motivational explanation, and hermeneutical understanding. (Remarks on the recent stage of the explanation-understanding controversy.)', in G. Ryle, ed., *Contemporary Aspects of Philosophy*, London, Oriel, 1976, pp. 161–176.
74 E.g. L. Wittgenstein, *Philosophical Investigations*, op. cit., §76.
75 I.e. for both theory and language games.
76 See J. Habermas, 'Gauss lectures', op. cit., 4 and 5.
77 Cf. *Communication and the Evolution of Society*, pp. 132–8.
78 *Legitimation Crisis*, p. 8.
79 Cf. *Communication and the Evolution of Society*, pp. 98 ff.
80 *Legitimation Crisis*, p. 10.
81 Cf. *Communication and the Evolution of Society*, pp. 116 ff.
82 *Legitimation Crisis*, p. 10.
83 *Communication and the Evolution of Society*, p. 148.
84 *Legitimation Crisis*, p. 14.
85 Ibid., pp. 14–15.
86 *Communication and the Evolution of Society*, p. 153.
87 See J. Habermas, 'Gauss lectures', op. cit., 4.

88 *Communication and the Evolution of Society*, p. 137.
89 M. Merleau-Ponty, *The Visible and the Invisible*, op. cit., pp. 157, 101.
90 Ibid., p. 101.
91 Ibid., p. 160.
92 Cf. *Communication and the Evolution of Society*, pp. 8 ff.
93 Cf. *Knowledge and Human Interest*, pp. 171, 173; cf. K-O. Apel, 'The problem of philosophical-fundamental grounding in the light of a transcendental pragmatic of language', *Man and World* 8, 1975, esp. pp. 250-1.
94 M. Merleau-Ponty, *The Visible and the Invisible*, op. cit., p. 141.
95 'Working note, April 1960', ibid., p. 244.
96 Ibid., p. 34.
97 Ibid., pp. 35, 43 etc.
98 Ibid., p. 157.
99 Ibid., p. 158.
100 Ibid., p. 141.
101 Cf. ibid., pp. 48, 153-5, 161-2.
102 Cf. E. Benveniste, op. cit.; B. L. Whorff, op. cit, *passim*.
103 L. Althusser, in L. Althusser and E. Balibar, *Reading Capital*, op. cit., p. 62.
104 For example, in the works of C. S. Peirce, W. James etc. See C. Morris, op. cit., p. 31.
105 See above. Also, see: G. Lukács, *Existentialisme ou Marxisme*, Paris, Nagel, 1948; H. Lefebvre, *L'existentialisme*, Paris, Editions du Sagittaire, 1946; T. Adorno, 'Husserl and the problem of idealism', op. cit. Adorno in particular claims that the concept is consistent with the activity of the subject in earlier German idealism.
106 J. Lacan, *Ecrits; A Selection*, London, Tavistock Publications, 1977, p. 55.
107 See ibid., pp. 65-71, 1-7. Cf. also A. Wilden, 'Lacan and the discourse of the other', in J. Lacan, *The Language of the Self*, ed. A. Wilden, New York, Delta Publishing Co., 1968, pp. 262 ff.
108 J. Lacan, *Ecrits*, op. cit., p. 65.
109 Ibid.

Chapter 12

1 J. W. Goethe, *Faust: eine Tragödie*, part 1, Stuttgart, J. G. Cotta, 1856.

Bibliography

Note: the following bibliography comprises only works which either were referred to in the text or were of particular importance for the formulation of its main ideas.

Abel, L. 'Jacques Derrida: his *"difference"* with metaphysics'. *Salmagundi* 25: 3–21, 1973.

Adler, R., Bazin, M. and Schiffer, M. *Introduction to General Relativity*. New York, McGraw-Hill, 1965.

Adorno, T. W. 'Husserl and the problem of idealism'. *J. Phil.* 37 (1):5–18, 1940.

Adorno, T. W. 'Introduction'. In Adorno, T. *et al. The Positivist Dispute in German Sociology*, pp. 1–67.

Adorno, T. W. 'Metacritique of epistemology'. *Telos* 38:77–103, 1978–9.

Adorno, T. W. *Minima Moralia*. London, New Left Books, 1974.

Adorno, T. W. *Negative Dialectics*. London, Routledge & Kegan Paul, 1973.

Adorno, T. W. 'On the logic of the social sciences'. In Adorno, T. *et al. The Positivist Dispute in German Sociology*, pp. 105–22.

Adorno, T. W. 'On the social situation of music'. *Telos* 35:129–65, 1978.

Adorno, T. W. *Prisms*. London, Neville Spearman, 1967.

Adorno, T. W. 'Sociology and empirical research'. In Adorno, T., *et al. The Positivist Dispute in German Sociology*, pp. 68–86.

Adorno, T. W. 'Sociology and psychology'. *New Left Review* 46:67–80, 1967.

Adorno, T. W. Albert, H., Dahrendorf, R., Habermas, J., Pilot, H. and Popper, K. *The Positivist Dispute in German Sociology*, tr. Adey, G. and Frisby, D. London, Heinemann, 1976.

Adorno, T. W. *Against Epistemology*, tr. Dominy, W., Oxford, Blackwell, 1982.

Agassi, J. *Science and Society*. Dordrecht, D. Reidel Publishing Co., 1981. (Boston Studies in the Philosophy of Science, Vol. 65.)

Albert, H. 'The myth of total reason'. In Adorno, T. *et al. The Positivist Dispute in German Sociology*, pp. 163–197.

Alexander, G., Bell, T., Foss, P., Gross, E. *et al., eds. Working Papers, Studies in the Discourses of Sex, Subjectivity and Power*, no. 3. Sydney, Tea Pot Press, 1977.

Allison, D. 'Structuralism revisited. Lévi-Strauss and diachrony'. In Bruzina, R. and Wilshire, B., eds *Crosscurrents in Phenomenology*, pp. 51–65.

Alston, W. P. 'Ontological commitments'. In Benacerraf, P. and Putnam, H., eds *The Philosophy of Mathematics*, pp. 249-57.

Althusser, L. *Essays in Self-Criticism*. London, New Left Books, 1976.

Althusser, L. *For Marx*. London, Allen Lane, 1969.

Althusser, L. *Lenin and Philosophy and Other Essays*. London, New Left Books, 1971.

Althusser, L. *Politics and History*. London, New Left Books, 1972.

Althusser, L. and Balibar, E. *Reading Capital*. London, New Left Books, 1970.

Anderson, A. R. 'Mathematics and the "language-game"'. In Benacerraf, P. and Putnam, H., eds *The Philosophy of Mathematics*, pp. 481-90.

Anderson, J. J. 'Quantisation of general relativity'. In Chiu, H. Y. and Hoffman, W., eds. *Gravitation and Relativity*. New York, Benjamin, 1964, pp. 279-302.

Apel, K.-O. *Analytic Philosophy of Language and the Geisteswissenschaften*, Dordrecht, D. Reidel, 1967.

Apel, K.-O. 'Causal explanation, motivational explanation, and hermeneutical understanding. (Remarks on the recent stage of the explanation-understanding controversy.)' In Ryle, G., ed. *Contemporary Aspects of Philosophy*. London, Oriel, 1976, pp. 161-76.

Apel, K.-O. 'C. S. Peirce and the post-Tarskian problem of an adequate explication of the meaning of truth: towards a transcendental-pragmatic theory of truth, part 1'. *Monist* 63 (3): 386-407, 1980.

Apel, K.-O. 'The a priori of communication and the foundation of the humanities'. *Man and World* 5:3-37, 1972.

Apel, K.-O. 'The common presuppositions of hermeneutics and ethics: types of rationality beyond science and technology'. In Barmark, J., ed. *Perspectives in Metascience*, pp. 39-56.

Apel, K.-O. 'The problem of philosophical fundamental-grounding in the light of a transcendental pragmatic of language'. *Man and World* 8:239-275, 1975.

Apel, K.-O. *Towards a Transformation in Philosophy*. London, Routledge & Kegan Paul, 1979.

Apel, K.-O. 'Types of social science in the light of human interests of knowledge', *Social Research* 44:425-470, 1977.

Arato, A. and Gebhardt, E., eds *The Essential Frankfurt School Reader*. Oxford, Basil Blackwell, 1978.

Arditti, R., Brennan, P., Cavrak, S., eds. *Science and Liberation*. Boston, South End Press, 1980.

Aristotle, *The Basic Works of Aristotle*, ed. McKeon, R., New York, Random House, 1941.

Arnason, J. P. 'Marx and Habermas'. In *Habermas Symposium*, Melbourne, Department of Sociology, La Trobe University, 1977, pp. 1-60. (La Trobe Sociology Papers, no. 42.)

Arnason, J. P. 'Marx and Weber – contrasts and convergences'. Paper presented to SAANZ conference, Brisbane, May 1978.

Arnason, J. P. *Rationality and Modernity: Towards a Culturalist Reading of Max Weber*. La Trobe University, Department of Sociology, 1980. (La Trobe University Sociology Papers, no. 9.)

Arnason, J. P. 'Universal pragmatics and historical materialism'. Unpublished paper.

Arnowitt, R., Deser, S. and Misner, G. 'The dynamics of general relativity'. In Witton, L. ed. *Gravitation: An Introduction to Current Research*. New York, John Wiley & Sons, 1962, pp. 227-65.

Asquith, P D. and Kyburg, H. E., eds *Current Research in the Philosophy of Science*. Michigan, Philosophy of Science Association, 1979.

Attig, T. and Spiegelberg, H. 'New light on Edmund Husserl's "Cartesian meditations"'. *J. Brit. Soc. Phen.* 7 (1): 3–11, 1976.

Austin, J. L. *How to do Things with Words*. Oxford University Press, 1976.

Avineri, S. *The Social and Political Thought of Karl Marx*. Cambridge University Press, 1968.

Ayer, A. J. 'Can there be a private language?' In Pitcher, G., ed. *Wittgenstein: The 'Philosophical Investigations'*, pp. 251–66.

Ayer, A. J. *Logical positivism*. New York, Macmillan, 1959.

Bachelard, G. *Le rationalisme appliqué*. Paris, Maspero, 1970.

Bachelard, G. 'The philosophical dialectic of the concepts of relativity'. In Schilpp, P. A., ed. *Albert Einstein: Philosopher-Scientist*, pp. 563–80.

Bachelard, S. *A Study of Husserl's 'Formal and Transcendental Logic'*. Evanston, Northwestern University Press, 1968.

Bachelard, S. 'Phenomenology and mathematical physics'. In Kocklemans, J. and Kisiel, T., eds *Phenomenology and the Natural Sciences*, pp. 413–25.

Bachelard, S. 'The specificity of mathematical physics'. In Kocklemans, J. and Kisiel, T., eds *Phenomenology and the Natural Sciences*, pp. 426–42.

Balibar, E. 'Self criticism: an answer to questions from '*Theoretical Practice*'. *Theoretical Practice* 7–8:55–72, 1973.

Balibar, E. 'Sur la dialectique historique (quelques remarques critiques à propos de *Lire le "Capital"*)'. In *Cinq études du materialisme historique*. Paris, Maspero, 1974.

Barber, B. *Science and the Social Order*. New York, The Free Press, 1972.

Barmark, J., ed. *Perspectives in Metascience*. Goteborg, Kungl, 1979.

Barnes, B. *Scientific Knowledge and Sociological Theory*. London, Routledge & Kegan Paul, 1974.

Barnes, B. ed. *Sociology of Science*. London, Penguin, 1972.

Barnes B. and Dolby, R. G. 'The scientific ethos: a deviant viewpoint'. *European Journal of Sociology* 2:3–25, 1970.

Barthes, R. *Elements of Semiology*. London, Jonathan Cape, 1972.

Barthes, R. *Mythologies*. London, Paladin, 1973.

Barthes, R. 'The structuralist activity'. *Partisan Review* 34 (1): 82–88, 1967.

Bastin, T., ed. *Quantum Theory and Beyond*. Cambridge University Press, 1971.

Bateson, G. *Steps to an Ecology of Mind*. London, Paladin, 1973.

Baudrillard, J. *For a Critique of the Political Economy of the Sign*. St Louis, Mo., Telos Press, 1981.

Baudrillard, J. *The Mirror of Production*. St Louis, Telos Press, 1975.

Beatty, J. 'Communicative competence and the skeptic'. *Phil. Soc. Crit.* 6 (3): 269–287, 1979.

Becker, O. 'Contributions toward the phenomenological foundation of geometry and its physical applications'. In Kocklemans, J. and Kisiel, T., eds *Phenomenology and the Natural Sciences*, pp. 119–46.

Becker, O. 'The philosophy of Edmund Husserl', in Elveton, R. O. ed. *The Phenomenology of Husserl: Selected Critical Readings*, pp. 40–72.

Bell, E. T. *Men of Mathematics*. London, Penguin, 1953. (vols. 1 and 2.)

Bell, J. S. 'On the problem of hidden variables in quantum mechanics'. *Rev. Mod. Phys.* 38: 447–452, 1966.

Benacerraf, P. and Putnam, H., eds *The Philosophy of Mathematics*. New Jersey, Prentice-Hall, 1964.

Ben-David, Joseph. 'Emergence of national traditions in the sociology of science. The United States and Great Britain'. *Soc. Inq.* 48 (3–4): 197–217, 1978.

Benjamin, W. *Illuminations*, ed. Arendt, H., New York, Schocken Books, 1969.

418

Benton, T. 'Winch, Wittgenstein and Marxism'. *Radical Phil.* 13:1-6, 1976.

Benveniste, E. *Problems in General Linguistics*, tr. M. E. Meek. Florida, University of Miami Press, 1971.

Bergman, H. 'The controversy concerning the law of causality in contemporary physics'. In Cohen, R. and Wartofsky, M., eds *Boston Studies in the Philosophy of Science*, vol. 13. Dordrecht, D. Riedel, 1975, pp. 395-462.

Bergmann, P. G. 'General relativity and our view of the physical universe'. In Yourgrau, W. and Breck, A. D., eds *Cosmology, History and Theology*, pp. 23-8.

Berlin, I. 'The divorce between the sciences and the humanities'. *Salmagundi* 28:9-39, 1974.

Bernal, J. D. 'Frederick Engels and science'. *Science and Nature* 2:39-54, 1979.

Bernal, J. D. *Science in History*. London, Pelican, 1965. (4 vols.)

Bernal, J. D. *The Extension of Man*. London, Paladin, 1972.

Bernal, J. D. *The Social Function of Science*. Cambridge, Mass., M.I.T. Press, 1939.

Bernays, P. 'On Platonism and mathematics'. In Benacerraf, P. and Putnam, H. eds *The Philosophy of Mathematics*, pp. 274-288.

Bernow, S. S. and Raskin, P. D. 'Ecology of scientific consciousness'. *Telos* 28:125-44, 1976.

Bernstein, J. *Einstein*. London, Fontana, 1973.

Bernstein, R. J. *Praxis and Action*. University of Pennsylvania Press, 1971.

Bernstein, R. J. 'The Frankfurt School'. *Midstream* Sept. 1973, pp. 55-66.

Bernstein, R. J. *The Restructuring of Social and Political Theory*. New York, Harcourt Brace, Jovanovich, 1976.

Bernstein, R. J. *Beyond Objectivism and Relativism: Science, Hermeneutics and Praxis*. University of Pennsylvania Press, 1983.

Bhaskar, R. *A Realist Theory of Science*. Leeds, Leeds Books, 1975.

Biemel, W. *Martin Heidegger: An Illustrated Study*. London, Routledge & Kegan Paul, 1977.

Biemel, W. 'The decisive phases in the development of Husserl's philosophy'. In Elveton, R. O., ed. *The Phenomenology of Husserl: Selected Critical Readings*, pp. 148-73.

Bien, J. 'Merleau-Ponty's conception of history'. In Gillan, G., ed. *The Horizons of the Flesh*. pp. 127-42.

Birchall, B. C. 'Radicalisation of the critique of knowledge: epistemology overcome or restatement of an error?'. *Man and World* 10 (4): 367-381, 1977.

Birkhoff, G. and Von Neumann, J. 'The logic of quantum mechanics'. *Annals of Mathematics* 37 (4): 823-843, 1936.

Blackburn, R., ed. *Ideology in Social Science*. London, Fontana, 1972.

Blackburn, R. and Jones, G. S. 'Louis Althusser and the struggle for Marxism'. In Howard, D. and Klare, K., eds *The Unknown Dimension*, pp. 365-87.

Blakely, T. J. 'The logic of *Capital*: some recent analyses'. *Studies in Soviet Thought* 16:281-88, 1976.

Blanchette, O. 'Language the primordial labor of history: a critique of critical social theory in Habermas'. *Cultural Hermeneutics* 1:325-382, 1974.

Bloch, E. 'Causality and finality as active, objectifying categories (categories of transmission).' *Telos* 21:96-107, 1974.

Blochinzev, D. I. *The Philosophy of Quantum Mechanics*. Dordrecht, D. Riedel, 1968.

Blumenberg, H. 'The lifeworld and the concept of reality'. In Embree, L., ed. *Lifeworld and Consciousness*, pp. 425-44.

Bodington, S. *Science and Social Action*. London, Allison & Busby, 1978.

Boehm, R. 'Basic reflections on Husserl's phenomenological reduction'. *Int. Phil. Q.* 5 (2): 183–202, 1965.

Boehm, R. 'Husserl's concept of the "absolute"'. In Elveton, R.O., ed. *The Phenomenology of Husserl: Selected Critical Readings*, pp. 174–203.

Bohm, D. *Causality and Chance in Modern Physics*. Philadelphia University Press, 1957.

Bohm, D. 'On Bohr's views concerning the quantum theory'. In Bastin, T. ed., *Quantum Theory and Beyond*, pp. 33–40.

Bohm, D. 'Space, time and quantum theory – understood in terms of discrete structural process'. *Proceedings of the International Conference on Elementary Particles* (Kyoto, 1965).

Bohm, D. *Wholeness and the Implicate Order*. London, Routledge & Kegan Paul, 1980.

Bohm, D. and Hiley, B. J. 'On the intuitive understanding of nonlocality as implied by quantum theory'. *Foundations of Physics* 5 (1): 93–109, 1975.

Bohme, G. 'Alternatives in science – alternatives to science'. In Nowotny, H. and Rose, H., eds *Counter-movements in the Sciences*, pp. 105–26.

Bohme, G. 'Cognitive norms, knowledge-interests and the constitution of the scientific object'. In Mendelsohn, E., Weingart, P. and Whitley, R., eds *The Social Production of Scientific Knowledge*, pp. 129–42.

Bohme, G. 'On the possibility of "closed theories"'. *Studies in History and Philosophy of Science* 11 (2): 163–172, 1980.

Bohme, G., Van den Daele, W. and Krohn, W. 'Finalization in science'. *Social Science Information* 15 (2/3): 207–330, 1976.

Bohme, G., Van den Daele, W. and Krohn, W. 'The "scientification" of technology'. In Krohn, W., Layton, E. and Weingart, P., eds *The Dynamics of Science and Technology*, pp. 219–50.

Bohr, N. *Atomic Physics and Human Knowledge*. New York, John Wiley & Sons, 1958.

Bohr, N. *Atomic Theory and the Description of Nature*. Cambridge University Press, 1934.

Bohr, N. 'Can quantum mechanical description of physical reality be considered complete?' *Physical Review* 48:696–702, 1935.

Bohr, N. 'Causality and complementarity'. *Philosophy of Science* 4:289–298, 1937.

Bohr, N. *Collected Works*. Ed Rosenfeld, L. Amsterdam, North-Holland, 1972. (Vols. 1–4.)

Bohr, N. 'Discussion with Einstein on epistemological problems in atomic physics'. In Schilpp, P. A., ed. *Albert Einstein: Philosopher-Scientist*, pp. 199–242.

Born, M. *Einstein's Theory of Relativity*. New York, Dover, 1965.

Born, M. *Experiment and Theory in Physics*. Cambridge University Press, 1943.

Bourdieu, P. 'Campo intelectual y proyecto creador'. In Poullon, S., ed. *Problemas del estructuralismo*, pp. 135–182.

Bourgeois, P. L. 'Phenomenology and the sciences of language'. *Research in Phenomenology* 1:118–136, 1971.

Brand, G. 'Intentionality, reduction and intentional analysis in Husserl's later manuscripts'. In Kocklemans, J., ed. *Phenomenology*, pp. 197–220.

Brewster, Ben. 'Fetishism in *Capital* and *Reading Capital*'. *Economy and Society* 5 (3): 344–351, 1976.

Bridgman, P. W. 'Einstein's theories and the operational point of view'. In Schlipp, P. A., ed. *Albert Einstein: Philosopher-Scientist*, pp. 333–54.

Brody, B. A., ed. *Readings in the Philosophy of Science*. New Jersey, Prentice-Hall, 1970.

420

Brough, J. B. 'The emergence of an absolute consciousness in Husserl's early writings on time-consciousness'. In Elliston, F. and McCormack, P., eds *Husserl: Expositions and Appraisals*, pp. 83–100.

Brouwer, L. E. J. 'Consciousness, philosophy and mathematics'. In Benacerraf, P. and Putnam, H., eds *The Philosophy of Mathematics*, pp. 78–84.

Brouwer, L. E. J. 'Intuition and formalism'. *Amer. Soc. Bulletin* 20:81–96, 1913–14.

Brown, H. *Science and the Human Comedy: Natural Philosophy in French Literature from Rabelais to Maupertuis.* Toronto, University of Toronto Press, 1976.

Bruzina, R., 'Merleau-Ponty and Husserl: the idea of science'. In Gillan, G. ed. *The Horizons of the Flesh*, pp. 160–76.

Bruzina, R. and Wilshire, B., eds *Crosscurrents in Phenomenology*. The Hague, Martinus Nihoff, 1978.

Bub, J. 'Hidden variables and the Copenhagen Interpretation – a reconciliation'. *Brit. J. Phil. Sci.* 19:185–210, 1968.

Bub, J. 'On the completeness of quantum mechanics'. In Hooker, C. A., ed. *Contemporary Research in the Foundations and Philosophy of Quantum Theory*, pp. 1–65.

Buchdahl, G. *Metaphysics and the Philosophy of Science: The Classical Origins, Descartes to Kant.* Oxford, Basil Blackwell, 1969.

Buck-Morss, S. F. 'T. W. Adorno and the dilemma of bourgeois philosophy'. *Salmagundi* 36:76–98, 1977.

Buck-Morss, S. F. 'The dialectic of T. W. Adorno.' *Telos* 14:137–144, 1972.

Buck-Morss, S. F. *The Origin of Negative Dialectics.* New York, Free Press, 1977.

Bunge, M. 'Relativity and philosophy'. In Barmark, J., ed. *Perspectives in Metascience*, 75–88.

Bunge, M. *Scientific Materialism.* Dordrecht, D. Reidel, 1981.

Burtt, E. A. *The Metaphysical Foundations of Modern Science.* London, Routledge & Kegan Paul, 1932.

Campbell, N. R. *What is Science.* New York, Dover, 1952.

Čapek, M., ed. *The Concepts of Space and Time: Their Structure and their Development.* Dordrecht, D. Reidel, 1976. (Boston Studies in the Philosophy of Science, vol. 55.)

Capra, F. *The Tao of Physics.* London, Wildwood House, 1975.

Carnap, R. 'Empiricism, semantics, and ontology'. In Linsky, L., ed. *Semantics and the Philosophy of Language*, pp. 208–30.

Carnap, R. *The Logical Structure of the World.* London, Routledge & Kegan Paul, 1967.

Carnap, R. 'The logicist foundations of mathematics'. In Benacerraf, P. and Putnam, H., eds *The Philosophy of Mathematics*, pp. 31–41.

Carr, D. 'History, phenomenology and reflection'. In Ihde, D. and Zaner, R., eds *Dialogues in Phenomenology*. The Hague, Martinus Nijhoff, 1975, pp. 156–75.

Carr, D. 'Husserl's *Crisis* and the problem of history'. *Southwestern Journal of Philosophy* 5 (3): 127–148, 1974.

Carr, D. 'Husserl's problematic concept of the lifeworld'. *A. Phil. Q.* 7 (4): 331–339, 1970.

Carr, D. 'Intentionality'. In Pivcevic, E., ed. *Phenomenology and Philosophical Understanding*, pp. 17–36.

Carr, D. 'On history and the lifeworld'. In Tymieniecka, A.-T., ed. *Analecta Husserliana*, vol. 5. Dordrecht, D. Reidel, 1976, pp. 71–82.

Carr, D. *Phenomenology and the Problem of History.* Evanston, Northwestern University Press, 1973.

Carr, D. 'The "Fifth meditation" and Husserl's Cartesianism'. *Phil. and Phen. Res.* 34:14–35, 1974.

421

Carr, D. and Casey, E. eds *Explorations in Phenomenology*. The Hague, Martinus Nijhoff, 1973.

Cassirer, E. *Substance and Function* and *Einstein's Theory of Relativity*. New York, Dover, 1953.

Cassirer, E. *The Problem of Knowledge*. Yale University Press, 1950.

Castoriadis, C. 'From Marx to Aristotle, from Aristotle to us'. *Soc. Res.* 45 (4): 667–738, 1978.

Castoriadis, C. *L'Institution imaginaire de le société*. Paris, Editions du Seuil, 1974.

Castoriadis, C. 'On the history of the workers' movement'. *Telos* 30: 3–43, 1976–7.

Castoriadis, C. 'Science moderne et interrogation philosophique'. *Encyclopaedia Universalis* 17:43–73, 1968.

Caute, D. *The Fellow Travellers: A Postcript to the Enlightenment*. London, Weidenfeld & Nicolson, 1973.

Cavaillès, J. 'On logic and the theory of science'. In Kocklemans, J. and Kisiel, T., eds *Phenomenology and the Natural Sciences*, pp. 353–412.

Charbonnier, G. *Conversations with Claude Lévi-Strauss*. London, Jonathan Cape, 1970.

Chihara, C. 'On criteria of ontological commitment'. In Severens, R., ed. *Ontological Commitment*, 69–86.

Child, A. 'The problem of truth in the sociology of knowledge'. *Ethics* 58:18–34, 1947–8.

Clauser, J. F. and Shimony, A. 'Bell's Theorem: experimental tests and implications'. *J. Phys.* 43: 1882–1927, 1978.

Colletti, L. *From Rousseau to Lenin*. London, New Left Books, 1973.

Colletti, L. 'Marxism and the dialectic'. *New Left Review* 93:3–30, 1975.

Colodny, R. G. ed. *Beyond the Edge of Certainty*. New Jersey, Prentice-Hall, 1965.

Colodny, R. G., ed. *Frontiers of Science and Philosophy*. University of Pittsburgh Press, 1962.

Colodny, R. G., ed. *Paradigms and Paradoxes*. University of Pittsburgh Press, 1972.

Colodny, R. G., ed. *The Nature and Function of Scientific Theory*. University of Pittsburgh Press, 1970.

Compton, J. J. 'Reinventing the philosophy of nature'. *Review of Metaphysics* 33 (1): 4–28, September 1979.

Connerton, P. *The Tragedy of Enlightenment: An Essay on the Frankfurt School*. Cambridge University Press, 1980.

Cranston, M. *The Mask of Politics and Other Essays*. London, Allen Lane, 1973.

Crocker, L. G., ed. *The Age of Enlightenment*. London, Harper & Row, 1969.

Culler, J. 'Jacques Derrida'. In Sturrock, J. ed. *Structuralism and Since*, pp. 154–79.

Cunningham, F. 'In defence of objectivity'. *Phil. Soc. Sci.* 10:417–426, 1980.

Dallmayr, F. R. 'Between theory and practice'. *Human Studies* 3:175–184, 1980. (Review of McCarthy, T. *The Critical Theory of Jürgen Habermas*.)

Dallmayr, F. R. 'Critical theory criticized: Habermas's *Knowledge and Human Interests* and its Aftermath'. *Phil. Soc. Sci.* 2:211–229, 1972.

Dallmayr, F. R. 'Marxism and truth'. *Telos* 29:130–159, 1976.

Dallmayr, F. R. 'On critical theory'. *Phil. Soc. Sci.* 10:93–109, 1980.

Dallmayr, F. R. 'Phenomenology and critical theory: Adorno'. *Cultural Hermeneutics* 3:367–405, 1976.

Dallmayr, F. R. 'Phenomenology and Marxism: a salute to Enzo Paci'. In Psathas, R. ed. *Phenomenological Sociology: Issues and Applications*. New York, John Wiley & Sons, 1973, pp. 305–56.

Dallmayr, F. R. 'Reason and emancipation: notes on Habermas'. *Man and World* 5:79–109, 1972.

Dallmayr. F. R. and McCarthy, T. A., eds *Understanding and Social Inquiry*. Notre Dame, University of Notre Dame Press. 1977.

D'Amico, R. 'Husserl on the foundational structures of natural and cultural sciences'. *Phil. & Phen. Res.* 42 (1): 4–22, 1981.

D'Amico, R. 'The contours and coupures of structuralist theory'. *Telos* 17:70–97, 1973.

Dauenhauer, B. P. 'On speech and temporality'. *Phil. Today*, 18:2–9, 1974.

Department of Philosophy, Australian National University. *Proceedings of Phenomenology Conference, 1976.* Canberra, Department of Philosophy, ANU.

Derrida, J. *Edmund Husserl's 'Origin of Geometry': an Introduction.* New York, Nicolas Hays, 1978.

Derrida, J. *Of Grammatology.* Baltimore, Johns Hopkins University Press, 1978.

Derrida, J. *Positions,* Alan Bass, tr. London, Athlone, 1981.

Derrida, J. *Speech and Phenomena.* Evanston, Northwestern University Press, 1973.

Derrida, J. 'The copula supplement', tr. D. B. Allison. In Ihde, D. and Zaner, R., eds. *Dialogues in Phenomenology.* The Hague, Martinus Nijhoff, 1975, pp. 7–48.

Derrida, J. 'The ends of man'. *Phil. & Phen. Res.* 29:31–37, 1969.

Derrida, J. *Writing and Difference.* University of Chicago Press, 1978.

Descartes, R. *Discourse on Method* and *The Meditations.* London, Penguin, 1968.

Descartes, R. *Philosophical Writings,* tr. and ed., Anscombe, E. and Geach, P. T. London, Thomas Nelson, 1971.

Descartes, R. *Rules for the Direction of Mind,* tr. Lafleur, F. P. New York, Liberal Arts, 1961.

Descartes, R. *Selected Works of Descartes,* tr. Kemp-Smith, N. London, Macmillan, 1952.

d'Espagnat, B. 'The quantum theory and reality'. *Scientific American* 241:158–80, Nov. 1979.

DeWitt, B. 'Quantum theories of gravity'. *General Relativity and Gravitation* 1 (2): 181–189, 1970.

DeWitt, B. 'The quantization of geometry'. In Witten, L., ed. *Gravitation: An Introduction to Current Research.* New York, John Wiley & Sons, 1962, pp. 266–381.

Diderot, D. *Diderot; Interpreter of Nature: Selected Writings,* ed. Kemp, J. New York, International Publishers, 1963.

Dillon, M. C. 'A phenomenological conception of truth'. *Man and World* 10 (4): 382–392, 1977.

Dillon, M. C. ' "Eye and mind": the intertwinings of vision and thought'. *Man and World* 13:155–171, 1980.

Dilthey, W. *Pattern and Meaning in History.* New York, Harper & Row, 1962.

Dingle, H. 'Scientific and philosophical implications of the special theory of relativity'. In Schilpp, P. A. ed., *Albert Einstein: Philosopher-Scientist,* pp. 535–54.

Dirac, P. A. M. *Principles of Quantum Mechanics.* Oxford, Clarendon Press, 1958. (4th edition.)

Dirac, P. A. M. 'The quantum theory of the electron'. *Proc. Royal Soc.* A117: 610–24, 1928; 118: 351–61, 1928.

Disco, C. 'Ludwig Wittgenstein and the end of wild conjectures'. *Theory and Society* 3:265–287, 1976.

Dolby, R. G. A. 'The sociology of knowledge in natural science'. In Barnes, B., ed. *Sociology of Science,* pp. 209–320.

Dostoyevsky, F. *Notes from Underground.* London, Penguin, 1972.

Drake, S. *Galileo at work: His Scientific Biography.* University of Chicago Press, 1981.

Drake, S. 'Galileo's language: mathematics and poetry in a new science'. *Yale French Studies* 49:13-27, 1973.

Dreyfus, H. L. 'The priority of *the* world to *my* world: Heidegger's answer to Husserl (and Sartre)'. *Man and World* 8:121-29, 1975.

Dufrenne, M. *Language and Philosophy*. Bloomington, Indiana University Press, 1963.

Easlea, B. *Liberation and the Aims of Science*. Sussex University Press, 1973.

Eddington, A. *The Nature of the Physical World*. Cambridge University Press, 1930.

Eddington, A. *The Philosophy of Physical Science*. Ann Arbor, 1974.

Edie, J. M. 'Husserl's conception of "the grammatical" and contemporary linguistics'. In Embree, L., ed. *Lifeworld and Consciousness*, pp. 233-62.

Edie, J. M. 'Phenomenology as a rigorous science'. *Int. Phil. Q.* 7: 21-30, 1967.

Edie, J. M., ed. *Phenomenology in America*. Chicago, Quadrangle books, 1967.

Edie, J. M. 'Was Merleau-Ponty a structuralist?' *Semiotica* 2:297-323, 1970.

Edwards, W. F. 'Averroism and the development of the modern concept of science'. *Telos* 1:41-47, 1968.

Ehrmann, J., ed. *Structuralism*. New York, Doubleday & Co., 1970.

Einstein, A. 'Autobiographical notes'. In Schilpp, P. A., ed. *Albert Einstein: Philosopher-Scientist*, pp. 1-96.

Einstein, A. *Ideas and opinions*. London, Souvenir Press, 1973.

Einstein, A. *Relativity*. New York, Crown Publishers, 1961.

Einstein, A. 'Remarks to the essays appearing in this collective volume'. In Schilpp, P. A., ed. *Albert Einstein: Philosopher-Scientist*, pp. 663-88.

Einstein, A. and Infeld, L. *The Evolution of Physics*. Cambridge University Press, 1961.

Einstein, A., Lorentz, H. A., Minkowski, H. and Weyl, H. *The Principle of Relativity*. London, Dover Publications, 1952.

Einstein, A., Podolsky, B. and Rosen, N. N. 'Can quantum mechanical description of physical reality be considered complete?' *Physical Review* 47:777-780, 1935.

Elkana, Yehuda. 'Review essay on Merton'. *A.J.S.* 81 (4): 906-910, 1976.

Elliston, F. and McCormick, P., eds. *Husserl: Expositions and Appraisals*. University of Notre Dame Press, 1977.

Elveton, R. O., ed. and tr. *The Phenomenology of Husserl: Selected Critical Writings*. Chicago, Quadrangle Books, 1970.

Embree, L. 'Gurwitsch's theory of logic'. *Social Research* 42:129-37, 1975.

Embree, L., ed. *Lifeworld and Consciousness: Essays for Aron Gurwitsch*. Evanston, Northwestern University Press, 1972.

Engel, S. M. 'Wittgenstein and Kant'. *Phil. and Phen. Res.* 29:483-513, 1969.

Engels, F. *Dialectics of Nature*. Moscow, Progress Publishers, 1954.

Engels, F. *Selected Writings*, ed. Henderson, W. O. London, Penguin, 1967.

Enzensberger, H. 'A critique of political ecology'. *New Left Review* 84:3-32, 1974.

Euclid *Elements*. New York, Everyman, 1979.

Farber, M. *Phenomenology and Existence. Towards a Philosophy Within Nature*. New York, Harper & Row, 1967.

Farber, M., ed. *Philosophical Essays in Memory of Edmund Husserl*. Harvard University Press, 1940.

Farber, M. 'The ideal of a presuppositionless philosophy'. In Farber, M., ed., *Philosophical Essays in Memory of Edmund Husserl*, pp. 44-64.

Farganis, J. 'Critical theory and praxis'. *Theory and Society* 5:435-440, 1978.

Federici, S. 'Notes on Lukács's aesthetics'. *Telos* 11:141-151, 1972.

Federici, S. 'Viet Cong philosophy: Tran Duc Thao'. *Telos* 6:104-117, 1970.

Feher, F. 'The dictatorship over needs'. *Telos* 35:31-42, 1978.

Feher, F., Heller, A., Markus, G., Vajde, M. 'Notes on Lukács's *Ontology*', *Telos* 29:160-80, 1976.

Ferguson, T. 'The political economy of knowledge and the changing politics of philsophy of science'. *Telos* 15:124-137, 1973.

Feyerabend, P. *Against Method*. London, New Left Books, 1975.

Feyerabend, P. 'Changing patterns of reconstruction'. *Brit. J. Phil. Sci.* 28:351-382, 1977.

Feyerabend, P. 'Complementarity'. *Proc. Arist. Soc.*, Suppl. vol. 32:75-104, 1958.

Feyerabend, P. 'Consolations for the specialist'. In Lakatos, I. and Musgrave, A., eds *Criticism and the Growth of Knowledge*, pp. 197-230.

Feyerabend, P. 'Dialectical materialism and the quantum theory'. *Slavic review* 25:414-417, 1966.

Feyerabend, P. 'Niels Bohr's interpretation of the quantum theory'. In Feigel, H. and Maxwell, G., eds *Current Issues in the Philosophy of Science*. New York, Holt, Rinehart, Winston, 1961, pp. 371-90, 398-400.

Feyerabend, P. 'Problems of empiricism'. In Colodny, R. G., ed. *Beyond the Edge of Certainty*, pp. 145-260.

Feyerabend, P. 'Problems of empiricism, Part 2'. In Colodny, ed. *The Nature and Function of Scientific Theory*, pp. 275-353.

Feyerabend, P. 'Problems of microphysics'. In Colodny, R. G., ed. *Frontiers of Science and Philosophy*, pp. 189-283.

Feyerabend, P. 'Wittgenstein's *Philosophical Investigations*'. In Pitcher, G., ed. *Wittgenstein: The 'Philosophical Investigations'*, pp. 104-50.

Feyerabend, P. and Maxwell, G., eds. *Mind, Matter and Method*. University of Minneapolis Press, 1966.

Finch, P. D. 'On the structure of quantum logic'. In Hooker, C. A., ed. *The Logico-Algebraic Approach to Quantum Mechanics*, vol. 1, pp. 415-26.

Findlay, J. N. 'Hegel and the philosophy of physics'. In O'Malley, ed. *The Legacy of Hegel*, pp. 72-89.

Findlay, J. N. 'Husserl's analysis of the inner time-consciousness'. *Monist* 59 (1): 3-20, 1975.

Fink, G. 'The phenomenological philosophy of Edmund Husserl and contemporary criticism'. In Elveton, R. O., ed. and tr. *The Phenomenology of Husserl: Selected Critical Readings*, pp. 73-147.

Finkelstein, D. 'The physics of logic'. In Colodney, R., ed. *Paradigms and Paradoxes*, pp. 47-66.

Finkelstein, D., Jauch, J. M. and Speiser, D. 'Notes on quaternian quantum mechanics'. In Hooker, C. A., ed. *The Logico-Algebraic Approach to Quantum Mechanics*, vol. 2, pp. 367-422.

Floistad, G. 'Notes on Habermas's proposal for a social theory of knowledge'. *Inquiry* 13:175-198, 1970.

Follesdal, D. 'Husserl's notion of noema'. *J. Phil.* 66 (20): 680-687, 1969.

Folse, H. J. 'Quantum theory and atomism: a possible ontological resolution of the quantum paradox'. *Southern J. of Phil.* 16 (1): 629-640, 1978.

Forman, Paul. 'Weimar culture, causality, and quantum theory 1918-1927: adaptation by German physicists and mathematicians to a hostile intellectual environment'. In R. McCormach, ed. *Historical Studies in the Physical Sciences*, vol. 3. University of Pennsylvania Press, 1971, pp. 1-115.

Foucault, M. 'Cuvier's position in the history of biology'. *Critique of Anthropology* 4(13-14):125-130, 1979.

Foucault, M. 'History, discourse and discontinuity'. *Salmagundi* 20:225-248, 1972.

Foucault, M. *Language, Counter-memory, Practice*. Cornell University Press, 1980.

Foucault, M. 'Orders of discourse'. *Soc. Sci. Inform.* 10 (2): 7–30, 1971.

Foucault, M. *Power/Knowledge: Selected Interviews and Other Writings 1972–1977*. New York, Pantheon Books, 1980.

Foucault, M. *Power, Truth, Strategy*. ed. by Morris, M. and Patton, P. Sydney, Feral, 1979.

Foucault, M. *The Archaeology of Knowledge*. London, Tavistock, 1972.

Foucault, M. 'Truth and power: an interview with Michel Foucault'. *Critique of Anthropology* 4 (13–14): 131–138, 1979.

Fraassen, Bas C. van 'A re-examination of Aristotle's philosophy of science'. *Canadian Phil. Rev: Dialogue* 19 (1): 20–45, 1980.

Fraassen, Bas C. van 'The labyrinth of quantum logics'. In Cohen, R. and Wartofsky, M. W., eds *Methodological and Historical Essays in the Natural and Social Sciences*. Dordrecht, D. Reidel, 1974, pp. 224–254. (Boston Studies in the Philosophy of Science, vol. 13.)

Frege, G. *Logical Investigations*, tr. Geach, P. T. and Stoothoff, R. H. Oxford, Basil Blackwell, 1977.

Frege, G. 'Review of Dr. E. Husserl's *Philosophy of Arithmetic*'. In Mohanty, J. N., ed. *Readings on Edmund Husserl's 'Logical Investigations'*, pp. 6–21.

Frege, G. *Translations from the Philosophical Writings of Gottlob Frege*, ed. Geach, P. and Black, M. Oxford, Basil Blackwell, 1977.

Freud, Sigmund. *The Basic Writings of Sigmund Freud*, ed. and tr. Brill, A. A. New York, Random House, 1938.

Frings, M. 'Husserl and Scheler'. *J. Brit. Soc. Phen.* 9 (3): 143–149, 1978.

Frisby, David. 'The Popper-Adorno controversy: the methodological dispute in German sociology'. *Phil. Soc. Sci.* 2:105–119, 1972.

Fuchs, W. W. *Phenomenology and the Metaphysics of Presence: An Essay in the Philosophy of Edmund Husserl*. The Hague, Martinus Nijhoff, 1976.

Fulton, J. S. 'The Cartesianism of phenomenology'. In Natanson, M., ed. *Essays in Phenomenology*. The Hague, Martinus Nijhoff, 1966.

Funke, G. 'Husserl's phenomenology as the foundational science'. *Southwestern Journal of Philosophy* 5 (3): 187–202, 1974.

Gadamer, H.-G. *Hegel's Dialectic: Five Hermeneutical Studies*. Yale University Press, 1976.

Gadamer, H.-G. *Philosophical Hermeneutics*. Berkeley, University of California Press, 1977.

Gadamer, H.-G. 'The science of the Lifeworld'. In Tymieniecka, A. T., ed. *Analecta Husserliana*, vol. 2, 1972, pp. 173–185.

Galileo, Gallei 'Against the Aristotelians'. *Telos* 4:67–79, 1969.

Galileo, Galilei *Dialogue Concerning the Two Chief World Systems*, tr. Drake, Stillman. University of California Press, 1967, 2nd edn.

Galileo Galilei *Dialogues Concerning Two New Sciences*. New York, Dover, 1954.

Galileo, Galilei *Discoveries and Opinions of Galileo*, tr. Drake, Stillman. New York, Doubleday, Anchor Books, 1957.

Gallagher, S. 'Suggestions towards a revision of Husserl's phenomenology of time-consciousness'. *Man and World* 12 (4): 445–464, 1979.

Gardner, H. *The Quest for Mind*. New York, Vintage Books, 1974.

Gaukroger, Stephen W. 'Bachelard and the problem of epistemological analysis'. *Studies in the History and Philosophy of Science* 7 (3): 189–244, 1976.

Gay, W. C. 'Merleau-Ponty on language and social science: the dialectic of phenomenology and structuralism'. *Man and World* 12 (3): 322–338, 1979.

George, F. 'Reading Althusser'. *Telos* 7:73–98, 1971.

Geras, N. 'Althusser's Marxism: an account and assessment'. *New Left Review* 71:57–88, 1972.

Geras, N. 'Essence and appearance: aspects of fetishism in Marx's *Capital*'. *New Left Review* 65:69–85, 1971.

Giddens, A., ed. *Positivism and Sociology*. London, Heinemann, 1974.

Gier, N. F. 'Wittgenstein and forms of life'. *Phil. Soc. Sci.* 10:241–258, 1980.

Gierulanka, D. 'The philosophic work of R. Ingarden'. *Dialectics and Humanism* 4:117–28, 1977.

Gillan, G. 'In the folds of the flesh: philosophy and language'. In Gillan, G., ed. *The Horizons of the Flesh*, pp. 1–60.

Gillan, G. ed. *The Horizons of the Flesh*. Carbondale, Southern Illinois University Press, 1973.

Glucksmann, A. 'A ventriloquist structuralism'. *New Left Review* 72:68–92, 1972.

Glymour, C. 'The epistemology of geometry'. *Nous* 11:227–251, 1977.

Gödel, K. 'What is Cantor's continuum problem?'. In Benacerraf, P. and Putnam, H., eds *The Philosophy of Mathematics*, pp. 258–73.

Godelier, M. 'Anthropology and ecology'. *Intervention* 5:38–58, 1975.

Godelier, M. 'The appropriation of nature'. *Critique of Anthropology* 4(13–14):17–28, 1979.

Goethe, J. W. *Faust*, tr. Macneiece, L. London, Faber & Faber, 1948.

Goethe, J. W. *Faust: eine Tragödie*. Stuttgart, J. G. Cotta, 1956. [German]

Goldman, S. L. 'Alexander Kojève on the origin of modern science: sociological modelling gone awry'. *Stud. Hist. Phil. Sci.* 6 (2): 113–22, 1975.

Goldmann, L. *Lukàcs and Heidegger*. London, Routledge & Kegan Paul, 1977.

Goldmann, L. *The Human Sciences and Philosophy*. London, Jonathan Cape, 1969.

Goldmann, L. *The Philosophy of the Enlightenment*. London, Routledge & Kegan Paul, 1973.

Gorz, A. *Ecology and Politics*. Boston, South End Press, 1980.

Gorz, A. 'On the class character of science and scientists'. In Rose, H. and Rose, G. eds. *The Political Economy of Science*, pp. 59–71.

Gould, S. J. 'Episodic change versus gradualist dogma'. *Science and Nature* 2:5–12, 1979.

Graham, L. *Philosophy and Science in the USSR*. London, Allen Lane, 1971.

Grahl, B. and Piccone, P., eds. *Towards a New Marxism*. St Louis, Telos Press, 1973.

Gramsci, A. *History, Philosophy and Culture in the Young Gramsci*, ed. Cavalcanti, P. and Piccone, P. St Louis, Telos Press, 1975.

Graves, J. C. *The Conceptual Foundations of Contemporary Relativity Theory*. Cambridge, Mass., M.I.T. press, 1971.

Greechie, R. J. and Gudder, S. P. 'Quantum logics'. In Hooker, C. A., ed. *The Logico-Algebraic Approach to Quantum Mechanics*, vol. 1, 545–76.

Greimas, A. J. 'Estructura y historia'. In Pouillon, J., ed. *Problemas del estructuralismo*, pp. 120–34.

Gribanov, D. P. 'The philosophical views of Albert Einstein'. *Soviet Studies in Philosophy*. Fall 1979:72–94.

Grieder, A. 'Geometry and the life-world in Husserl's later philosophy'. *J. Brit. Soc. Phen.* 8 (2):119–22, 1977.

Groh, Dieter and Sieferle, Rolf-Peter. 'Experiences of nature in bourgeois society and economic theory: outlines of an interdisciplinary research project'. *Social Research* 47:557–581, 1980.

Grünbaum, A. *Philosophical Problems of Space and Time*. Dordrecht, D. Reidel, 1973. (Boston Studies in the Philosophy of Science, vol. 12).

Grünbaum, A. 'Popper vs. inductivism'. In Radnitzky, G. and Andersson, G., eds. *Progress and Rationality in Science*, pp. 117-42.

Gudder, S. P. 'A survey of axiomatic quantum mechanics'. In Hooker, C. A. ed. *The Logico-Algebraic Approach to Quantum Mechanics*, vol. 2, pp. 323-66.

Gurwitsch, A. *Phenomenology and the Theory of Science*. Evanston, Northwestern University Press, 1974.

Gurwitsch, A. 'Review of "The Cartesianism of phenomenology"'. *Phil. & Phen. Res.* 2 (4): 55-58, 1942.

Gurwitsch, A. 'The last work of Edmund Husserl'. *Phil. & Phen. Res.* 16:380-399, 1955, part 1; and 17:370-398, 1956, part 2.

Gurwitsch, A. 'Towards a theory of intentionality'. *Phil. & Phen. Res.* 30:354-367, 1969.

Gutting, G. 'Husserl and scientific realism'. *Phil. & Phen. Res.* 39 (1): 42-56, 1978.

Gutting, G. ed. *Paradigms and Revolutions*. Indiana, University of Notre Dame Press, 1980.

Habermas, J. 'A positivistically bisected rationalism'. In Adorno, T. *et al. The Positivist Dispute in German Society*, pp. 198-225.

Habermas, J. 'A postscript to *Knowledge and Human Interests*'. *Phil. Soc. Sci.* 3:157-189, 1973.

Habermas, J. 'A review of Gadamer's *Truth and Method*'. In Dallmayr, F. R. and McCarthy, T. A. eds *Understanding and Social Inquiry*, pp. 335-63.

Habermas, J. *Communication and the Evolution of Society*. Boston, Beacon, 1979.

Habermas, J. 'History and evolution'. *Telos* 39:5-44, 1979.

Habermas, J. *Knowledge and Human Interests*. London, Heinemann, 1972.

Habermas, J. *Legitimation Crisis*. Boston, Beacon, 1973.

Habermas, J. *Legitimation Crisis*. [Reviewed by James Miller in *Telos* 25:210-220, 1975.]

Habermas, J. 'On social identity'. *Telos* 19:91-103, 1974.

Habermas, J. 'On systematically distorted communication'. *Inquiry* 13:205-218, 1970.

Habermas, J. 'Some distinctions in universal pragmatics'. *Theory and Society* 3(2):155-167, 1976.

Habermas, J. 'The analytical theory of science and dialectics'. In Adorno, T. *et al The Positivist Dispute in German Sociology*, pp. 131-62.

Habermas, J. 'The place of philosophy in Marxism'. *Insurgent Sociologist* 5 (2): 41-48, 1975.

Habermas, J. 'The public sphere'. *New German Critique* 3:49-55, 1974.

Habermas, J. *Theory and Practice*. London, Heinemann, 1974.

Habermas, J. 'Thoughts on the foundation of sociology in the philosophy of language: six lectures'. Presented as the Christian Gauss lectures at Princeton University, spring 1971. Unpublished.

Habermas, J. *Towards a Rational Society*. London, Heinemann, 1971.

Habermas, J. 'Towards a reconstruction of historical materialism'. *Theory and Society* 2:287-300, 1975.

Habermas, J. 'Towards a theory of communicative competence'. *Inquiry* 13:360-375, 1970.

Habermas, J. 'Wahrheitstheorien'. In *Wirklichkeit und Reflexion*. Pfulligen, Neske, 1973, pp. 211-65.

Habermas, J. 'Zur rekonstruktion des historischen materialismus'. [Review by Johann P. Aranason in *Telos* 39:201-217, 1979.]

Habermas, J. *The Theory of Communicative Action. Vol. 1: Reason and the Rationalization of Society*, tr. McCarthy, T. Boston, Beacon Press, 1984.

Hagstrom, W. O. *The Scientific Community*. New York, Basic Books, 1965.

Haldane, J. B. S. *Science and Human Life*. New York, Harper & Row, 1933.

Hall, E. *What is Value?* London, Routledge & Kegan Paul, 1952.

Hall, H. 'Intersubjective phenomenology and Husserl's Cartesianism'. *Man and World* 12 (1): 13–20, 1979.

Hans, James S. 'Hermeneutics, play, deconstruction'. *Phil. Today* 24:299–317, 1980.

Hanson, R. N. 'Five cautions for the Copenhagen interpretation's critics'. *Phil. Sci.* 26:325–37, 1959.

Harré, R. *The Philosophies of Science: An Introductory Survey*. Oxford University Press, 1972.

Harré, R. *The Principles of Scientific Thinking*. University of Chicago Press, 1970.

Harris, E. E. 'Hegel and the natural sciences'. In Weiss, F. G., ed. *Beyond Epistemology*, pp. 129–153.

Hartmann, K. 'Abstraction and existence in Husserl's phenomenological reduction'. *J. Brit. Soc. Phen.* 2 (1): 10–18, 1971.

Hawkes, T. *Structuralism and Semiotics*. London, Methuen, 1977 (New Accents).

Hawking, S. W. 'Black holes and thermodynamics'. *Physical Review D* 13 (2): 191–197, 1976.

Hawking, S. W. 'Particle creation by black holes'. *Comm. Math. Phys.* 43:199–220, 1975.

Hawking, S. W. and Ellis, G. F. R. *The Large Scale Structure of Space-time*. Cambridge University Press, 1973.

Hazard, P. *The European Mind*. London, Hollis & Carter, 1953.

Heelan, P. 'Comment on Alex Comfort's "Demonic and historical models in biology".' *J. Social Biol. Struct.* 3:217–18, 1980.

Heelan, P. 'Complementarity, context dependence, and quantum logic'. In Hooker, C., ed. *Logico-Algebraic Approach to Quantum Mechanics*, vol 2, pp. 161–80.

Heelan, P. 'Hermeneutics and the humanities', Unpublished paper. State University of New York at Stony Brook, 1980.

Heelan, P. 'Interpretation and the natural sciences'. Unpublished paper. State University of New York at Stony Brook, 1980.

Heelan, P. Space-perception and the Philosophy of Science. Berkeley, University of California Press, 1983.

Heelan, P. 'Quantum logic and classical logic: their respective roles'. *Synthèse* 21:3–33, 1970.

Heelan, P. *Quantum Mechanics and Objectivity*. The Hague, Martinus Nijhoff, 1965.

Heelan, P. 'Quantum relativity and the cosmic observer'. In Yourgrau, W. and Breck, A. D. eds. *Cosmology, History and Theology*, pp. 29–38.

Hegel, G. W. F. *Logic*, tr. Wallace, W. Oxford, Clarendon Press, 1975.

Hegel, G. W. F. *Philosophy of Nature*, tr. Miller, A. V., Oxford, Clarendon Press, 1970.

Hegel, G. W. F. *Science of Logic*, tr. Johnson, W. H. and Struthers, L. G. London, Allen & Unwin, 1966.

Hegel, G. W. F. *The Phenomenology of Mind*, tr. Baillie, J. London, Allen & Unwin, 1971.

Hegel, G. W. F. *The Philosophy of History*, tr. Friedrich, C. J. New York, Dover, 1956.

Heidegger, M. *Basic Writings*, ed. by Krell, D. F. London, Routledge & Kegan Paul, 1978.

Heidegger, M. *Being and Time*. Oxford, Basil Blackwell, 1978.

Heidegger, M. *Existence and Being*. Chicago, Gateway, 1970.

Heidegger, M. *Hegel's Concept of Experience*. New York, Harper & Row, 1970.

Heidegger, M. 'The principle of ground'. *Man and World* 7 (3): 207–222, 1974.

Heidegger, M. *The Question Concerning Technology and Other Essays*. New York, Harper & Row, 1977.

Heidegger, M. *What is a Thing?* Chicago, Henry Regnery, 1967.

Heidelberger, M. 'Towards a logical reconstruction of revolutionary change: the case of Ohm as an example'. *Stud. Hist. Phil. Sci.* 11 (2): 103–21, 1980.

Heisenberg, W. *Natural Law and the Structure of Matter*. England, Rebel Press, 1981.

Heisenberg, W. *Physics and Philosophy*, London, Allen & Unwin, 1958.

Heisenberg, W. 'The development of the interpretation of the quantum theory'. In Paull, W., ed., *Niels Bohr and the Development of Physics*. Oxford, Pergamon, 1955, pp. 12–29.

Heisenberg, W. *The Physical Principles of the Quantum Theory*. New York, Dover, 1949.

Heitler, W. 'The departure from classical thought in modern physics'. In Schilpp, P. A. ed. *Albert Einstein: Philosopher-Scientist*, pp. 179–98.

Held, D. *Introduction to Critical Theory. Horkheimer to Habermas*. Berkeley, University of California Press, 1980.

Heller, A. 'The positivism dispute as a turning point in German post-war theory'. *New German Critique* 15:49–56, 1978.

Heller, A. *The Theory of Need in Marx*. London, Allison & Busby, 1976.

Heller, A. 'Towards a Marxist theory of value'. *Kinesis* 5 (1): 4–76, 1972.

Hemmendinger, D. 'Husserl's concepts of evidence and science'. *Monist* 59 (1): 81–97, 1975.

Hempel, C. G. 'A logical appraisal of operationalism'. In Brody, B. A., ed. *Readings in the Philosophy of Science*, pp. 200–10.

Hempel, C. G. 'On the nature of mathematical truth'. In Benacerraf, P. and Putnam, H., eds *The Philosophy of Mathematics*, pp. 366–81.

Hempel, C. G. *Philosophy of Natural Science*. New Jersey, Prentice-Hall, 1966.

Hesse, M. *The Structure of Scientific Inference*. London, Macmillan, 1974.

Hessen, B. *The Social and Economic Roots of Newton's 'Principia'*. New York, Howard Fertig, 1971.

Heyting, A. 'The intuitionist foundations of mathematics'. In Benacerraf, P. and Putnam, H., eds *The Philosophy of Mathematics*, pp. 42–9.

Hiley, B. 'Ghostly interactions in physics'. *New Scientist*. 6 March, 1980, pp. 746–52.

Hill, C. *Puritanism and Reduction: Studies in Interpretation of the English Revolution of the Seventeenth Century*. New York, Schocken Books, 1964.

Hill, E. L. 'Classical mechanics as a limiting form of quantum mechanics'. In Feyerabend, P. K. and Maxwell, G., eds *Mind, Matter and Method*. pp. 430–48.

Hindess, B. 'Transcendentalism and history: the problem of the history of philosophy and the sciences in the later philosophy of Husserl'. *Economy and Society*, 2:9–42, 1973.

Hirst, P. 'Althusser and philosophy'. *Theoretical Practice*, 2:16–29, 1972.

Holmes, R. H. 'Is transcendental phenomenology committed to idealism?' *Monist* 59 (1): 98–118, 1975.

Holton, G. 'Einstein, Michelson, and the "crucial" experiment'. *Isis* 60 (2): 133–197, 1969.

Holton, G. and Blanpied, W., eds *Science and its Public: the Changing Relationship*.

Dordrecht, D. Reidel, 1976. (Boston Studies in the Philosophy of Science, vol. 33.)

Hongimann, J., ed. *Handbook of Social and Cultural Anthropology*. Chicago, Rand McNally, 1973.

Hooker, C. A., ed. *Contemporary Research in the Foundations and Philosophy of Quantum Theory*. Dordrecht, D. Reidel, 1973.

Hooker, C. A. 'Metaphysics and modern physics: a prolegomenon to the understanding of quantum theory'. In Hooker, C. A., ed. *Contemporary Research in the Foundations and Philosophy of Quantum Theory*, pp. 174–304.

Hooker, C. A. ed. *The Logico-Algebraic Approach to Quantum Mechanics*. Dordrecht, D. Reidel, 1979. (2 vols.)

Hooker, C. A. 'The nature of quantum mechanical reality'. In Colodny, R., ed. *Paradigms and Paradoxes*, pp. 67–301.

Horkheimer, M. *Critical Theory*. New York, Seabury press, 1972.

Horkheimer, M. *Eclipse of Reason*. New York, Seabury press, 1974.

Horkheimer, M. 'On the problem of truth'. In Arato, A. and Gebhardt, E., eds *The Essential Frankfurt School Reader*, pp. 407–443.

Horkheimer, M. and Adorno, T. W. *Dialectic of Enlightenment*, tr. Cumming, J. London, Allen Lane, 1976.

Hottois, G. 'L'instance du language dans la phenomenologie post-Husserlienne'. *Rev. phil. de Louvain* 77:50–70, 1979.

How, A. 'Debate, language and incommensurability: the Popper-Adorno controversy'. *J. Brit. Soc. Phen.* 11 (1): 3–15, 1980.

Howard, D. 'Ambiguous radicalism: Merleau-Ponty's interrogation of political thought'. In Gillan, G., ed. *The Horizons of the Flesh*, pp. 143–59.

Howard, D. 'On Marx's critical theory'. *Telos* 6:224–333, 1970.

Howard, D. 'On the transformation of critique into dialectic: Marx's dilemma'. *Dialectical Anthropology* 5:75–110, 1980.

Howard, D. *The Development of the Marxian Dialectic*. Carbondale, Southern Illinois University Press, 1972.

Howard, D. *The Marxian Legacy*. London, Macmillan, 1977.

Howard, D. and Klare, K. eds *The Unknown Dimension*. New York, Basic Books, 1972.

Hübner, K. 'Some critical comments on current Popperianism on the basis of a theory of system sets'. In Radnitzky, G. and Andersson, G., eds *Progress and Rationality in Science*, pp. 279–290.

Hübner, K. 'The concept of truth in a historistic theory of science'. *Struct. Hist. Phil. Sci.* 11 (2): 145–151, 1980.

Hübner, K. 'The philosophical background of hidden variables in quantum mechanics'. *Man and World* 6:420–440, 1973.

Hübner, K. *Critique of Scientific Reason*, tr. Dixon, P. R. and Dixon, H. M. University of Chicago Press, 1983.

Hunter, J. F. M. ' "Forms of life" in Wittgenstein's *Philosophical Investigations*'. In Klemke, E. D., ed. *Essays on Wittgenstein*, pp. 273–97.

Husserl, E. 'A reply to a critic of my refutation of logical psychologism'. In Mohanty, J. N., ed. *Readings in Edmund Husserl's 'Logical Investigations'*, pp. 33–42.

Husserl, E. *Cartesian Meditations*, tr. Cairns, D. The Hague, Nijhoff, 1960.

Husserl, E. *Experience and Judgement: Investigations in a Genealogy of Logic*, tr. Churchill, J. and Ameriks, K., Evanston, Northwestern University Press, 1973.

Husserl, E. *Formal and Transcendental Logic*, tr. Cairns, D. The Hague, Martinus Nijhoff, 1969.

431

Husserl, E. *Ideas: General Introduction to Pure Phenomenology*, tr. Boyce Gibson, W. R. London, Allen & Unwin, 1969.

Husserl, E. 'Kant and the idea of transcendental philosophy', tr. Klein, T. E. and Pohl, W. E. *Southwestern Journal of Philosophy* 5:9–56, 1974.

Husserl, E. 'Letter to Aron Gurwitsch, April 15, 1932'. In Embree, L., ed. *Lifeworld and Consciousness*, pp. xv–xx.

Husserl, E. 'Letter to Frege: July 18, 1891', tr. J. N. Mohanty. In 'Frege–Husserl correspondence'. *Southwestern J. Phil.* 5 (3): 83–96, 1974.

Husserl, E. 'Letter to Roman Ingarden: November 19, 1927', tr. Kisiel, T. In Kisiel, T. 'On the dimensions of a phenomenology of science in Husserl and the young Dr Heidegger'. *J. Brit. Soc. Phen.* 4:228, 1973.

Husserl, E. *Logical Investigations*, tr. Findley, J. N. London, Routledge & Kegan Paul, 1970 (2 vols).

Husserl, E. *Phenomenology and the Crisis of Philosophy: 'Philosophy as rigorous science' and 'Philosophy and the crisis of European man'*, tr. Lauer, Q. New York, Harper & Row, 1965.

Husserl, E. ' "Phenomenology": Edmund Husserl's article for the Encyclopaedia Britannica (1927): new complete translation', tr. Palmer, R. E., *J. Brit. Soc. Phen.* 2:77–90, 1971.

Husserl, E. 'Pure phenomenology, its method and its field of investigation', tr. Jordan, R. W. In Embree, L., ed. *Lifeworld and Consciousness*, pp. 4–15.

Husserl, E. *The Crisis of European Sciences and Transcendental Phenomenology*, tr. Carr, D. Evanston, Northwestern University Press, 1970.

Husserl, E. *The Idea of Phenomenology*, tr. Alson, W. P. and Nakhnikian, G. The Hague, Martinus Nijhoff, 1964.

Husserl, E. 'The method of clarification'. *Southwestern J. Phil.* 5 (3): 57–68, 1974.

Husserl, E. *The Paris Lectures*, tr. Koestenbaum, P. The Hague, Martinus Nijhoff, 1964.

Husserl, E. *The Phenomenology of Internal Time-consciousness*, tr. Churchill, J. S. Bloomington, Indiana University Press, 1964.

Husserl, E. 'The task and the significance of the *Logical Investigations*'. In Mohanty, J. M. *Readings in Edmund Husserl's 'Logical Investigations'*, pp. 197–215.

Husserl, E. 'Universal teleology', tr. Schurger, S. *Telos* 4:176–180, 1969.

Hutcheson, P. 'Husserl's problem of intersubjectivity'. *J. Brit. Soc. Phen.* 11 (2): 144–162, 1980.

Hyppolite, J. *Genesis and Structure of Hegel's 'Phenomenology of spirit'*. Evanston, Northwestern University Press, 1974.

Hyppolite, J. *Studies on Marx and Hegel*, ed. and tr. O'Neill, J. London, Heinemann, 1969.

Ihde, D. *Experimental Phenomenology*. Canada, Putnam, 1977.

Ihde, D. *Hermeneutic Phenomenology: The Philosophy of Paul Ricœur*. Evanston, Northwestern University Press, 1971.

Ihde, D. 'Interpreting hermeneutics: origins, developments and prospects'. *Man and World* 13 (3–4): 325–344, 1980.

Ihde, D. *Sense and Significance*. Pittsburg, Duquesne University Press 1973.

Ihde, D. *Technics and Praxis*. Dordrecht, D. Reidel Publishing Company, 1979. (Boston Studies in the Philosophy of Science, vol. 24.)

Ingarden, R. *On the Motives which led Husserl to Transcendental Idealism*. The Hague, Martinus Nijhoff, 1975.

Ingarden, R. 'On the ontology of relations'. *J. Brit. Soc. Phen.* 6 (2): 75–80, 1975.

Ingarden, R. 'The letter to Husserl about the 6th *Investigation* and "idealism" ', In Tymieniecka, A. T. ed. *Analecta Husserliana*. Dordrecht, D. Reidel, 1976, vol. 4, pp. 419–38.

Ingarden, R. 'What is new in Husserl's *Crisis*'. In Tymieniecka, A-T., ed. *Analecta Husserliana*, Vol. 2. Dordrecht, D. Reidel, 1972, pp. 23-47.

Isham, C. J. 'Quantum field theory in curved space-time: an overview'. *Annals of the New York Academy of Sciences* 302:114-57, 1976.

Jakobson, R. *Six Lectures on Sound and Meaning*. Cambridge, Mass, M.I.T. Press, 1978.

Jameson, F. *Marxism and Form*. New Jersey, Princeton University Press, 1971.

Jammer, M. *The Conceptual Development of Quantum Mechanics*. New York, McGraw Hill, 1966.

Jammer, M. *The Philosophy of Quantum Mechanics*. New York, John Wiley & Sons, 1974.

Jay, M. 'The concept of totality in Lukàcs and Adorno'. *Telos* 32:117-138, 1977.

Jay, M. *The Dialectical Imagination*. London, Heinemann, 1974.

Jensen, K. M. *Beyond Marx and Mach. Aleksandar Bogdanov's Philosophy of Living Experience*. Dordrecht, D. Reidel publishing co., 1978. (Sovietica, vol. 41.)

Johnson, G. A. 'Husserl and history'. *J. Brit. Soc. Phen.* 11 (1): 77-91, 1980.

Johnston, R. 'Finalization: a new start for science policy?' *Soc. Sci. Inform.* 15 (2/ 3): 331-336, 1976.

Jonas, H. *Philosophical Essays*. New York, Prentice Hall, 1974.

Jonas, H. 'Towards a philosophy of technology'. *Hastings Centre Rep.* 9:34-43, 1979

Joravsky, D. *The Lysenko Affair*. Harvard University Press, 1970.

Kant, I. *Critique of Pure Reason*, transl. Smith, Norman Kemp. London, Macmillan, 1970.

Kant, I. *Prolegomena to any Future Metaphysics that will be able to Present itself as a Science*, tr. Lucas, P. G. Manchester University Press, 1953.

Kattsoff, L. O. 'The relation of science to philosophy in the light of Husserl's thought'. In Farber, M., ed. *Philosophical Essays in Memory of Edmund Husserl*, pp. 202-218.

Kaufmann, J. N. 'Husserl et la project d'une semiotique phenomenologique'. *Dialogue (Can. Phil. Rev.)* 17 (1): 20-34, 1978.

Keane, J. 'On turning theory against itself'. *Theory and Society* 4:561-572, 1977.

Keane, K., 'On tools and language: Habermas on work and interaction'. *New German Critique* 6:82-100, 1975.

Kersten, F. and Zaner, R., eds. *Phenomenology: Continuation and Criticism. Essays in Memory of Dorian Cairns*. The Hague, Martinus Nijhoff, 1973.

Kisiel, T. 'Hegel and hermeneutics'. In F. G. Weiss, ed. *Beyond Epistomology*. The Hague, Martinus Nijhoff, 1976, pp. 197-220.

Kisiel, T. 'Husserl on the history of science'. In Kocklemans, J. and Kisiel, T., eds *Phenomenology and the Natural Sciences*, pp. 68-92.

Kisiel, T. 'Phenomenology as the science of science'. In Kocklemans, J. and Kisiel, T., eds. *Phenomenology and the Natural Sciences*, pp. 5-44.

Kisiel, T. 'Scientific discovery: logical, psychological, or hermeneutical?' in Carr, D. and Casey, E., eds. *Explorations in Phenomenology*, pp. 263-284.

Kisiel, T. 'Science, phenomenology, and the thinking of being'. In Kocklemans, J. and Kisiel, T., eds *Phenomenology and the Natural Sciences*, pp. 167-83.

Klemke, E. D. ed. *Essays on Wittgenstein*. University of Illinois Press, 1971.

Kline, M. *Mathematical Thought from Ancient to Modern Times*. Oxford University Press, 1972.

Kline, M. *Mathematics in Western Culture*. Melbourne, Penguin, 1972.

Kline, M. *Mathematics. The Loss of Certainty*. New York, Oxford University Press, 1980.

Kocklemans, J. *A First Introduction to Husserl's Phenomenology.* Pittsburgh, Duquesne University Press, 1967.

Kocklemans, J. ed. *Phenomenology.* New York, Doubleday, 1967.

Kocklemans, J. *Phenomenology and Physical Science.* Pittsburgh, Duquesne University Press, 1966.

Kocklemans, J. ed. *Philosophy of Science.* New York, The Free Press, 1968.

Kocklemans, J. 'The mathematization of nature in Husserl's last publication'. In Kocklemans, J. and Kisiel, T., eds *Phenomenology and the Natural Sciences,* pp. 44-67.

Kocklemans, J. and Kisiel, T. eds *Phenomenology and the Natural Sciences.* Evanston, Northwestern University Press, 1970.

Kojève, A. *Introduction to the Reading of Hegel.* Cornell University Press, 1969. (Agora Paperback Editions).

Kojève, A. 'L'origine Chretienne de la science moderne'. In *Melange A. Koyré II: l'aventure de l'esprit.* Paris, Hermann, 1964, pp. 295-306.

Kolman, E. 'The philosophical interpretation of contemporary physics.' *Studies in Soviet Thought* 21:1-14, 1980.

Komar, A. 'The general relativistic quantization program.' In Hooker, C. A., ed. *Contemporary Research in the Foundations and Philosophy of Quantum Theory,* pp. 305-27.

Komesaroff, P. 'A study of the socio-political significance of the philosophy of science with respect to Kant's *Critique of Pure Reason.* A phenomenological point of view.' M.A. (prelim.) thesis, Monash University, 1975.

Korner, S. *The Philosophy of Mathematics.* London, Hutchinson, 1971.

Korsch, K. *Marxism and Philosophy.* London, New Left Books, 1972.

Korsch, K. 'The crisis of Marxism'. *New German Critique* 3:7-11, 1974.

Korsch, K. *Three Essays on Marxism.* London, Pluto Press, 1971.

Kosik, K. *Dialectics of the Concrete.* Dordrecht, D. Reidel, 1976.

Kosok, M. 'The dialectical matrix: phenomenology as a science', *Telos* 5:115-59, 1970.

Kosok, M. 'The formalization of Hegel's dialectical logic'. *Int. Phil. Q.* 6: 596-631, 1966.

Koyré, A. *From the Closed World to the Infinite Universe.* Baltimore, Johns Hopkins University Press, 1968.

Krohn, W., Layton, E., Weingart, P. eds. *The Dynamics of Science and Technology.* Boston, D. Reidel, 1978.

Kuderowicz, Z. 'The problem of the relation of philosophy to special sciences as discussed in Cracow in the period 1944-1974'. *Dialectics and Humanism* 2 (2): 147-55, 1975.

Kuhn, T. S. 'Logic of discovery or psychology of research?' In Lakatos, I. and Musgrave, A. eds *Criticism and the Growth of Knowledge,* pp. 1-24.

Kuhn, T. S. 'Reflections on my critics'. In Lakatos, I. and Musgrave, A., eds *Criticism and the Growth of Knowledge,* pp. 231-78.

Kuhn, J. S. *The Copernican Revolution.* Cambridge, Mass., Harvard University Press, 1957.

Kuhn, T. S. *The Essential Tension.* University of Chicago Press, 1977.

Kuhn, T. S. *The Structure of Scientific Revolutions.* University of Chicago Press, 1970.

Kurzweil, E. 'Michel Foucault. Ending the era of man'. *Theory and Society* 4:395-420, 1977.

Kutschera, F. van *Philosophy of Language.* Dordrecht, D. Reidel, 1975.

Laborit, H. *Decoding the Human Message.* London, Allison & Busby, 1977.

434

Lacan, J. *Écrits: A Selection*. London, Tavistock, 1977.

Lacan, J. *The Four Fundamental Concepts of Psychoanalysis*. London, Penguin, 1979.

Lacan, J. 'The insistence of the letter in the unconscious'. In Ehrmann, J., ed. *Structuralism*, pp. 101-36.

Lacan, J. *The Language of the Self*, tr. Wilden, A. New York, Delta Publishing Co. 1968.

Ladrière, J. 'Mathematics in a philosophy of the sciences'. In Kocklemans, J. and Kisiel, T. eds *Phenomenology and the Natural Sciences*, pp. 443-65.

Lakatos, I. 'Falsification and the methodology of scientific research programmes'. In Lakatos, I. and Musgrave, A., eds *Criticism and the Growth of Knowledge*, pp. 91-196.

Lakatos, I. *Proofs and Refutations*. Cambridge University Press, 1976.

Lakatos, I. and Musgrave, A. eds. *Criticism and the Growth of Knowledge*. Cambridge University Press, 1974.

Lampert, L. 'Heidegger's Nietzsche interpretation'. *Man and World* 7:353-378, 1974.

Landé, A. *New Foundations of Quantum Mechanics*. Cambridge University Press, 1965.

Landé, A. *Quantum Mechanics in a New Key*. New York, Exposition Press, 1973.

Landé, A. 'Why the world is a quantum world'. In Suppes, P. ed. *Logic and Probability in Quantum Mechanics*. Dordrecht, D. Reidel, 1976, pp. 433-44.

Landgrebe, L. 'Husserl's departure from Cartesianism'. In Elveton, R. O., ed. *The Phenomenology of Husserl: Selected Critical Readings*, pp. 259-306.

Lane, M. 'The structuralist method'. In Lane, M. ed. *Structuralism: A Reader*. London, Jonathan Cape, 1970, pp. 11-39.

Laskey, D. 'Ingarden's criticism of Husserl'. In Tymieniecka, A.-T. ed. *Analecta Husserliana*, vol. 2, Dordrecht, D. Reidel, 1972, pp. 48-54.

Lauer, Q. 'Phenomenology: Hegel and Husserl'. In Weiss, F. G., ed. *Beyond Epistemology*, pp. 174-96.

Leach, E. *Culture and Communication*. Cambridge University Press, 1976.

Lecourt, D. 'Biology and the crisis of the human sciences'. *New Left Review* 125:90-96, 1981.

Lecourt, D. *Marxism and Epistemology*, tr. Brewster, B. London, New Left Books, 1975.

Lefebvre, H. *Dialectical Materialism*. London, Jonathan Cape, 1968.

Lefebvre, H. *Everyday Life in the Modern World*. London, Allen Lane, 1971.

Lefebvre, H. *Hegel, Marx, Nietzsche*. Mexico, Siglo Veintiuno, 1976.

Lefebvre, H. *L'existentialisme*. Paris, Editions du Sagittaire, 1946.

Lefebvre, H. *Logica formal, logica dialectica*. Mexico, Siglo Veintiuno editores, 1970.

Lefebvre, H. *The Sociology of Marx*. London, Allen Lane, 1969.

Lefort, G. 'Marx: from one vision of history to another'. *Soc. Res.* 45 (4): 615-666, 1978.

Lefort, C. 'Presenting Merleau-Ponty'. *Telos* 29:39-42, 1976.

Leibniz, G. W. *Philosophical Writings*, tr. Morris, M. London, Dent, 1934.

Leiss, W. 'Husserl's *Crisis*'. *Telos* 8:109-120, 1971.

Leiss, W. *The Domination of Nature*. New York, George Braziller, 1972.

Leiss, W. 'The problem of man and nature in the work of the Frankfurt School'. *Phil. Soc. Sci.* 5:163-72, 1974.

Lemaire, A. *Jacques Lacan*, tr. D. Macey. London, Routledge & Kegan Paul, 1970.

Lenin, V. I. *Collected Works*. Moscow, Progress Publishers, 1972.

Levinas, E. *Existence and Existents*. The Hague, Martinus Nijhoff, 1978.

Levinas, E. *Totality and Infinity*. Pittsburgh, Dusquesne University Press, 1979.

Lévi-Strauss, C. 'Confrontation over myths' (with P. Ricœur). *New Left Review* 62:57–74, 1970.

Lévi-Strauss, C. *From Honey to Ashes. Introduction to a Science of Mythology: 2.* New York, Harper Torchbooks, 1974.

Lévi-Strauss, C. *Myth and Meaning.* London, Routledge & Kegan Paul, 1978.

Lévi-Strauss, C. *Structural Anthropology.* 2 vols. London, Penguin, 1968 and 1978.

Lévi-Strauss, C. 'Structuralism and ecology'. *Graduate Faculty Phil. J.* 7 (2): 153–78, 1978.

Lévi-Strauss, C. *The Raw and the Cooked: Introduction to a Science of Mythology: 1.* New York, Harper Torchbooks, 1969.

Lévi-Strauss, C. *The Savage Mind.* Chicago, University of Chicago Press, 1973.

Lévi-Strauss, C. *The Scope of Anthropology.* London, Jonathan Cape, 1967.

Lévi-Strauss, C. *Totemism.* Melbourne, Penguin, 1969.

Lévi-Strauss, C. *Tristes Tropiques.* London, Penguin, 1976.

Levy-Leblond, J. 'Ideology of/in contemporary physics'. In Rose, H. and Rose, S., eds *The Radicalisation of Science*, pp. 136–75.

Lewis, C. I. *Mind and the World-Order.* New York, Dover, 1956.

Lewontin, R. and Levins, R. 'The problem of Lysenkoism'. In Rose, H. and Rose, S., eds *The Radicalisation of Science*, pp. 32–64.

Lilienfeld, R. 'Systems theory as an ideology'. *Social Research* 42: 637–60, 1975.

Lingis, A., 'Being in the interrogative mood'. In Gillan, G., ed. *The Horizons of the Flesh*, pp. 78–91.

Lingis, A. 'Sense and nonsense in the sexed body'. *Cultural Hermeneutics* 4:345–65, 1977.

Lingis, A. 'The difficulties of a phenomenological investigation of language'. *Modern Schoolman* 57:56–64, 1979.

Linsky, L. ed. *Semantics and the Philosophy of Language.* 2nd ed. University of Illinois Press, 1972.

Lowethal, R. 'Social transformation and democratic legitimacy'. *Soc. Res.* 43 (2): 246–75, 1976.

Lozinski, J. 'On the relation between Marxism and phenomenology: truth and revolution – Husserl and Lenin'. *Dialectics and Humanism* 3 (1):120–31, 1976.

Luhmann, N. 'The future cannot begin: temporal stuctures in modern society'. *Soc. Res.* 43:130–152, 1976.

Lukács, G. *Existentialisme ou Marxisme.* Paris, Negel, 1948.

Lukács, G. *History and Class Consciousness.* London, Merlin Press, 1971.

Lukács, G. *Marxism and Human Liberation.* New York, Delta books, 1973.

Lukács, G. 'Max Weber and German Sociology'. *Economy and Society* 1:386–398, 1972.

Lukács, G. *The Young Hegel.* London, Merlin Press, 1975.

Luke, T. 'Radical economy and the crisis of political economy'. *Telos* 46:97–101, 1980–81.

Lyons, S. J. *Semantics.* Cambridge University Press. 2 vols. 1977.

Lyons, T. *Introduction to Theoretical Linguistics.* Cambridge University Press, 1968.

Macomber, W. B. *The Anatomy of Disillusion. Martin Heidegger's Notion of Truth.* Evanston, Northwestern University Press, 1967.

Malcolm, N. 'Wittgenstein's *Philosophical Investigations.*' In Pitcher, G., ed. *Wittgenstein. The 'Philosophical Investigations'*, pp. 65–103.

Mandrou, R. *L'Europe 'absolutiste': raison et raison d'État, 1649–1775.* Paris, Fayard, 1977.

Marcuse, H. 'Contributions to a phenomenology of historical materialism'. *Telos* 4:3–34, 1969.

Marcuse, H. *Counterrevolution and Revolt*. Boston, Beacon Press, 1972.

Marcuse, H. *Five Lectures*. Boston, Beacon, 1970.

Marcuse, H. *Negations*. London, Allen Lane, 1968.

Marcuse, H. 'On science and phenomenology'. In Giddens, A., ed. *Positivism and Sociology*. London, Heinemann, 1974, pp. 225-38.

Marcuse, H. *One-dimensional Man*. London, Sphere Books, 1964.

Marcuse, H. *Reason and Revolution*. London, Routledge & Kegan Paul, 1967.

Marcuse, H. *Studies in Critical Philosophy*. London, New Left Books, 1972.

Margolis, J. *Persons and Minds*. Dordrecht, D. Reidel, 1978. (Boston Studies in the Philosophy of Science, vol. 57.)

Markus, G. 'Alienation and reification in Marx and Lukács'. *Thesis Eleven* 5/6:139-161, 1982.

Markus, G. 'Natural science, world view and philosophy'. *Budapest, Tudomanyegyetem annales sectio philosophica* 4:159-175, 1965.

Markus, G. 'The soul and life: the young Lukács and the problem of culture'. *Telos* 32:95-116, 1977.

Marsh, J. L. 'The triumph of ambiguity: Merleau-Ponty and Wittgenstein'. *Phil. Today* 19:243-55, 1975.

Martin, B. *The Bias of Science*. Canberra, Society of Social Responsibility in Science, 1979.

Martin, G. *Kant's Metaphysics and the Theory of Science*. Manchester University Press, 1961.

Marx, K. *Capital*, tr. Moore, S. and Aveling, E. London, Lawrence & Wishart, 1970, vol. 1.

Marx, K. *Capital*. Moscow, Progress Publishers, 1956, vols 2 and 3.

Marx, K. *Grundrisse*, tr. Nicolaus, M. London, Penguin, 1973.

Marx, K. *The Economic and Philosophical Manuscripts of 1844*, tr. Milligan, M. New York, International Publishers, 1964.

Marx, K. *The Poverty of Philosophy*. New York, International Publishers, 1963.

Marx, K. *Theories of Surplus Value*. Moscow, Progress Publishers, 1968, 3 vols.

Marx, K. *Writings of the Young Marx on Philosophy and Society*, edited and translated by Easton, L. D. and Guddat, K. H. New York, Anchor, 1967.

Marx, K. and Engels, F. *Selected Works*. New York, International Publishers, 1969.

Marx, W. 'Habermas's philosophical conception of history'. *Cultural Hermeneutics* 3:335-347, 1976.

Masterman, M. 'The nature of a paradigm'. In Lakatos, I. and Musgrave, A., eds *Criticism and the Growth of Knowledge*, pp. 59-90.

Mauss, M. *The Gift*. London, Routledge & Kegan Paul, 1969.

Mays, W. 'Editorial'. *J. Brit. Soc. Phen.* 6 (2): 72-74, 1975. [On R. Ingarden.]

Mays, W. 'Phenomenology and Marxism'. In Pivcevic, E., ed. *Phenomenology and Philosophical Understanding*, pp. 231-50.

Mays, W. 'The later Husserl'. *Inquiry* 17:113-25, 1974.

Mays, W. and Jones, B. 'Was Husserl a Fregean?' *Journal of the British Society for Phenomenology* 12 (1): 76-80, 1981.

McBride, W. 'Marxism and phenomenology'. *J. Brit. Soc. Phen.* 6 (1): 13-21, 1975.

McCarthy, T. A. 'A theory of communicative competence'. *Phil. Soc. Sci.* 3:127-56, 1973.

McCarthy, T. A. *The Critical Theory of Jürgen Habermas*. Cambridge, Mass., M.I.T. Press, 1979.

McGill, V. J. 'Evidence in Husserl's phenomenology'. In Kerston, F. and Zaner, R., eds. *Phenomenology: Continuation and Critique*, pp. 145-66.

McMullin, E. 'Compton on philosophy of nature'. *Review of Metaphysics* 33 (1): 30-58, 1979.

Mehlberg, H. *Time, Causality and the Quantum Theory*. Dordrecht, D. Reidel, 1980.

Mendelsohn, E. *Introduction to Mathematical Logic*. Toronto, D. Van Nostrand, 1963.

Mendelsohn, E. 'The continuous and the discrete in the history of science'. *Journal of Social Reconstruction* 1 (2): 1-31, 1980.

Mendelsohn, E. 'The social construction of scientific knowledge'. In Mendelsohn, E., Weingart, P. and Whitley, R., eds *The Social Production of Scientific Knowledge*, pp. 3-26.

Mendelsohn, E. and Elkana, Y. *Sciences and Cultures*. Dordrecht, D. Reidel, 1981.

Mendelsohn, E., Weingart, P. and Whitley, R., eds *The Social Production of Scientific Knowledge*. Dordrecht, D. Reidel, 1977.

Mendelson, J. 'The Habermas-Gadamer debate'. *New German Critique* 18:74-106, 1979.

Mepham, J. 'The structuralist sciences and philosophy'. In Robey, D., ed. *Structuralism: An Introduction*. Oxford, Clarendon Press, 1973, pp. 104-37.

Mepham, J. and Ruben, D-H., eds *Issues in Marxist Philosophy*. Brighton, Harvester, 1976. Volume 3: *Epistemology, Science. Ideology*.

Mercier, A. 'Conjectures'. *General Relativity and Gravitation*. 8 (8): 673-77, 1977.

Mercier, A. 'Does science coincide with our knowledge about nature?' *Dialectics and Humanism* 3 (1): 43-50, 1976.

Mercier, A. 'Speculative remarks on physics in general and relativity in particular'. *Dialectics and Humanism* 2 (3): 125-131, 1975.

Merleau-Ponty, M. *Adventures of the Dialectic*. Evanston, Northwestern University, Press, 1973.

Merleau-Ponty, M. *Phenomenology, Language and Sociology*, ed. O'Neill, J. London, Heinemann, 1974.

Merleau-Ponty, M. *Phenomenology of Perception*. London, Routledge & Kegan Paul, 1962.

Merleau-Ponty, M. 'Philosophy and non-philosophy since Hegel'. *Telos* 20:43-105, 1976.

Merleau-Ponty, M. *Sense and Non-sense*. Evanston, Northwestern University Press, 1964.

Merleau-Ponty, M. *Signs*. Evanston, Northwestern University Press, 1964.

Merleau-Ponty, M. *The Prose of the World*. London, Heinemann, 1976.

Merleau-Ponty, M. *The Structure of Behaviour*. Boston, Beacon Press, 1963.

Merleau-Ponty, M. *The Visible and the Invisible*. Evanston, Northwestern University Press, 1968.

Merleau-Ponty, M. *Themes from the Lectures*. Evanston, Northwestern University Press, 1970.

Merton, R. K. *Science, Technology and Society in Seventeenth-century England*. New Jersey, Humanities Press, 1970.

Merton, R. K. *Social Theory and Social Structure*. Illinois, Free Press, 1957.

Merton, R. K. *The Sociology of Science. Theoretical and Empirical Investigations*, ed. Storer, N. W. University of Chicago Press, 1974.

Merzbacher, E. *Quantum Mechanics*. London, John Wiley & Sons, 1974.

Messiah, A. *Quantum Mechanics*. 2 volumes. Amsterdam, North-Holland, 1961.

Meszaros, I. *Lukacs's Concept of Dialectic*. London, Merlin Press, 1972.

Meszaros, I. *Marx's Theory of Alienation*. London, Merlin Press, 1970.

Minkowski, C. 'Prose and poetry'. In Kocklemans, J. and Kisiel, J., eds *Phenomenology and the Natural Sciences*, pp. 239-50.

Misgeld, D. 'Discourse and conversation: the theory of communicative competence and hermeneutics in the light of the debate between Habermas and Gadamer'. *Cultural Hermeneutics* 4:321-44, 1977.

Misner, C. 'Feynman quantization of general relativity'. *Rev. Mod. Phys.* 29:497-509, 1957.

Mitroff, I. I. *The Subjective Side of Science*. Amsterdam, Elsevier, 1974.

Mohanty, J. N. 'Consciousness and lifeworld'. *Social Research* 42:147-166, 1975.

Mohanty, J. N. 'On Husserl's theory of meaning'. *Southeastern Journal of Philosophy* 5 (3): 229-244, 1974.

Mohanty, J. N. ed. *Readings in Edmund Husserl's 'Logical Investigations'*. The Hague, Martinus Nijhoff, 1977.

Mohanty, J. N. *Husserl and Frege*. Bloomington, Indiana University Press, 1982.

Morris, C. *Foundations of the Theory of Signs*. University of Chicago Press, 1938.

Morrison, J. C. 'Husserl's *Crisis*: reflections on the relationship of philosophy and history'. *Phil. and Phen. Res.* 37 (3): 312-330, 1977.

Morrison, R. P. 'Kant, Husserl, and Heidegger on time and the unity of "consciousness"'. *Phil. and Phen. Res.* 39:182-198, 1978.

Morriston, W. 'Experience and causality in the philosophy of Merleau-Ponty'. *Phil. and Phen. Res.* 39 (4): 561-74, 1979.

Moszkowski, A. *Conversations with Einstein*. London, Sidgwick & Jackson, 1972.

Mulkay, M. 'Cultural growth in science'. In Barnes, B. ed. *Sociology of Science*, pp. 126-43.

Mulkay, M. *Science and the Sociology of Knowledge*. London, Allen & Unwin, 1979.

Mulkay, M. 'Some aspects of cultural growth in the natural sciences'. *Social Research* 36 (1): 22-52, 1969.

Mure, G. R. G. *A Study of Hegel's 'Logic'*. Oxford University Press, 1950.

Murphy, R. T. 'The transcendental "a priori"; in Husserl and Kant.' In Tymieniecka, A. T., ed. *Analecta Husserliana*, vol. 3. Dordrecht, D. Reidel, 1974, pp. 66-79.

Murray, J. P. 'Enlightenment roots of Habermas's critique of Marx'. *The Modern Schoolman* 57:1-24, 1979.

Nagel, E. 'Logic without ontology'. In Benacerraf, P. and Putnam, H., eds *The Philosophy of Mathematics*, pp. 302-21.

Nagel, E. 'Mechanistic explanation and organism biology'. In Brody, B. A. ed. *Readings in the Philosophy of Science*, pp. 296-306.

Natanson, M. *Edmund Husserl: Philosopher of Infinite Tasks*. Evanston, Northwestern University Press, 1973.

Natanson, M. ed. *Essays in Phenomenology*. The Hague, Martinus Nijhoff, 1966.

Natanson, M. 'Phenomenology as a rigorous science'. *Int. Phil. Q.* 7:5-20, 1967.

Natanson, M. 'The empirical and transcendental ego'. In Tymieniecka, A. T., ed. *For Roman Ingarden; Nine Essays in Phenomenology*. The Hague, M. Nijhoff, 1959, pp. 42-53.

Needham, J. 'History and human values: a Chinese perspective for world science'. In Rose, H. and Rose, S., eds. *The Radicalisation of Science*, pp. 90-117.

Needham, J. *Moulds of Understanding*. London, Allen & Unwin, 1976.

Needham, J. *Science and Civilization in China*. Cambridge University Press, 1975. (Vols 2 and 3.)

Needham, J. *The Grand Titration*. London, Allen & Unwin, 1969.

Nelson, B. 'Science, technology and society in Seventeenth-Century England, by Robert K. Merton'. [Review.] *Amer. J. S.* 78:223-231, 1972.

Nemeth, T. '*Capital* and phenomenology'. *Studies in Soviet Thought* 16:239-249, 1976.

439

Nemeth, T. 'Husserl and Soviet Marxism'. *Studies in Soviet Thought* 15:183–96, 1975.

Newton, I. *Newton's Philosophy of Nature: Selections from his Writings*, ed. Thayer, H. S. New York, Hafner Press, 1974.

Newton, I. *Principia*. Berkeley, University of California Press, 1962. (Vols. 1 and 2.)

Nickles, T., ed. *Scientific Discovery, Logic and Rationality*. Dordrecht, Reidel, 1980.

Nicolaus, M. 'The unknown Marx'. In Blackburn, R., ed. *Ideology in Social Science*. Suffolk, Fontana, 1972, pp. 306–32.

Nietzsche, F. *The Gay Science*. New York, Vintage, 1974.

Nietzsche, F. *The Philosophy of Nietzsche*. New York, Random House, 1937.

Norcia, V. di, 'Ordinary language and radical philosophy'. *Radical Philosophy* 12:25–9, 1975.

Northrop, F. S. C. 'Einstein's conception of science'. In Schilpp, P. A., ed. *Albert Einstein: Philosopher-Scientist*, pp. 385–408.

Nowotny, H. and Rose, H., eds., *Counter-Movements in the Sciences*. Dordrecht, D. Reidel, 1979.

Null, G. T. 'The role of the perceptual world in the Husserlian theory of the sciences'. *J. Brit. Soc. Phen.* 7 (1): 56–59, 1976.

O'Connor, R. 'Ortega's reformulation of Husserlian phenomenology'. *Phil. and Phen. Res.* 40 (1): 53–63, 1979.

Oliver, J. F. 'Ontic Content and Commitment'. In Severans, R., ed. *Ontological Commitment*, pp. 91–104.

O'Malley, J. J., ed. *The Legacy of Hegel*. The Hague, M. Nijhoff, 1973.

O'Neill, J. 'Perception, expression and history in the philosophy of Merleau-Ponty'. *Social Research* 34:47–66, 1967.

Ortega y Gasset. *Man and Crisis*. New York, W. W. Norton and Co., 1962.

Overend, T. 'Enquiry and ideology: Habermas's trichotomous conception of science'. *Phil. Soc. Sci.* 8:1–13, 1978.

Overend, T. 'Habermas's *Knowledge and Human Interests*'. Melbourne, La Trobe University Sociology Department, 1976.

Paci, E. 'Lifeworld, time and liberty in Husserl'. In Embree, L., ed. *Lifeworld and Consciousness*, pp. 461–467.

Paci, E. *The Function of the Sciences and the Meaning of Man*, tr. Piccone, P. and Hansen, J. E. Evanston, Northwestern University Press, 1972.

Paci, E. 'The phenomenological encyclopaedia and the *telos* of humanity'. *Telos* 2:5–18, 1968.

Palmer, R. E. *Hermeneutics*. Evanston, Northwestern University Press, 1969.

Passmore, J. *Man's Responsibility for Nature*. London, Duckworth, 1974.

Pauli, W. 'Einstein's contribution to quantum theory'. In Schilpp, P. A., ed. *Albert Einstein: Philosopher-Scientist*, pp. 147–160.

Paztig. G. 'Husserl on truth and evidence'. In Mohanty, J. N., ed. *Readings on Edmund Husserl's 'Logical Investigations'*, pp. 179–96.

Peat, F. D. 'Quantum physics and general relativity; the search for a deeper theory'. In Hooker, C. A., ed. *Contemporary Research in the Foundations and Philosophy of Quantum Theory*, pp. 328–345.

Peirce, C. S. *Charles Peirce: The Essential Writings*, ed. Moore, E. C. New York, Harper & Row, 1972.

Peirce, C. S. *Selected Writings*, ed. Weiner, P. P. New York, Davis Publications Inc., 1966.

Peritore, N. P. 'On formal, transcendental and dialectic logic'. *Cultural Hermeneutics* 4:217–233, 1977.

Petersen, A. *Ludwig Wittgenstein*. Pittsburg, Duquesne University Press, 1974.
Petersen, A. 'On the philosophical significance of the correspondence argument'. In Cohen, R. and Wartofsky, M., ed. *Boston Studies in the Philosophy of Science*, Vol. 5. Dordrecht, D. Reidel, 1969, pp. 242–52.
Petersen, A. *Phenomenology and Reality*. Pittsburg, Duquesne University Press, 1972.
Petersen, A. *Quantum Physics and the Philosophical Tradition*. Cambridge, Mass. M.I.T. Press, 1968.
Petersen, A. 'Some remarks on the Ego in the phenomenology of Husserl'. In Tymienlecka, A-T., ed. *For Roman Ingarden*. The Hague, M. Nijhoff, 1959, pp. 29–41.
Piaget, J. *Biology and Knowledge*. University of Chicago Press, 1971.
Piaget, J. *Structuralism*. London, Routledge & Kegan Paul, 1971.
Piana, G. 'History and existence in Husserl's manuscripts'. *Telos* 13:86–124, 1972.
Piccone, P. 'Dialectic and materialism in Lukács'. *Telos*. 11:105–134, 1972.
Piccone, P. 'Dialectical logic today'. *Telos*. 2:38–83, 1968.
Piccone, P. 'From tragedy to farce: the return of critical theory'. *New German Critique* 7:91–104, 1976.
Piccone, P. 'Phenomenological Marxism'. In Grahl, B. and Piccone, P., eds. *Towards a New Marxism*. St. Louis, Telos Press, 1973, pp. 133–159.
Piccone, P. 'Reading the *Crisis*'. *Telos*. 8:121–129, 1971.
Piccone, P. 'Reading the *Grundrisse*: beyond "orthodox" Marxism'. *Theory and Society* 2:235–255, 1975.
Piccone, P. 'Science, art and revolution: Introduction to Galileo as a poet'. *Telos*. 4:55–61, 1969.
Piccone, P. 'The changing function of critical theory'. *New German Critique* 12:29–38, 1977.
Piccone, P. 'Towards a socio-historical interpretation of the scientific revolution'. *Telos* 1:16–26, 1968.
Pierce, D. C. 'Lévi-Strauss – the problematic self and myth'. *Int. Phil. Q.* 19 (4): 380–406, 1979.
Pietersma, H. 'The concept of horizon'. In Tymieniecka, A-T., ed. *Analecta Husserliana*, vol. 2. Dordrecht, D. Reidel, 1972, pp. 278–282.
Pietersma, H. 'Intuition and horizon in the philosophy of Husserl'. *Phil. and Phen. Res.* 34:95–10, 1973-4.
Pitcher, G., ed. *Wittgenstein. The 'Philosophical Investigations'*. London, Macmillan, 1966.
Pivcevic, E. '*Logical Investigations* by Edmund Hussserl' [review]. *Mind* 80:462–72, 1971.
Pivcevic, E. ed. *Phenomenology and Philosophical Understanding*. Cambridge University Press, 1975.
Plaut, M. 'Positivism in Poulantzas'. *Telos* 36:159–166, 1978.
Poggeler, O. 'Metaphysics and topology of being in Heidegger'. *Man and World* 8:3–27, 1975.
Poincaré, H. *Science and Hypothesis*. New York, Dover, 1952.
Polanyi, M. *Personal Knowledge*. London, Routledge & Kegan Paul, 1962.
Poncelet, G. *Considérations épistemologiques sur la théorie de la relativité*. Bologna, Centro superiore di logica e scienze comparate, 1980.
Popper, K. R. *Conjectures and Refutations*. London, Routledge & Kegan Paul, 1972.
Popper, K. R. 'Normal science and its dangers'. In Lakatos, I. and Musgrave, A., eds. *Criticism and the Growth of Knowledge*, pp. 51–58.
Popper, K. R. *Objective Knowledge*. Oxford, Clarendon Press, 1972.

Popper, K. R. 'Reason or revolution?' in Adorno, T. et al. *The Positivist Dispute in German Sociology*, pp. 288–300.

Popper, K. R. *The Logic of Scientific Discovery*. London, Hutchinson, 1977.

Popper, K. R. 'The logic of the social sciences'. In Adorno, T. *et al. The Positivist Dispute in German Sociology*, pp. 87–104.

Popper, K. R. *The Open Society and its Enemies*. London, Routledge & Kegan Paul, 1951. (Vols 1 and 2).

Popper, K. R. *The Poverty of Historicism*. London, Routledge & Kegan Paul, 1957.

Post, H. R. 'The incompleteness of quantum mechanics or the emperor's missing clothes'. In Bastin, T., ed. *Quantum Theory and Beyond*, pp. 275–82.

Pouillon, J. ed. *Problems del structuralismo*. 6th ed. Mexico, Siglo Veintiuno Editores, 1975.

Putnam, H. 'Is logic empirical?' In Cohen, R. and Wartofsky, M., eds. *Boston Studies in the Philosophy of Science*, vol. 5. Dordrecht, D. Reidel, 1969, pp. 216–41.

Quine, W. *From a Logical Point of View*. 2nd ed. New York, Harper Torchbooks, 1963.

Quine, W. 'Notes on existence and necessity'. In Linsky, L., ed. *Semantics and the Philosophy of Language*, pp. 77–94.

Quine, W. 'On what there is'. In Linsky, L., ed. *Semantics and the Philosophy of Language*, pp. 189–207.

Quine, W. *Ontological Relativity and Other Essays*. New York, Cambridge University Press, 1969.

Quine, W., *Philosophy of Logic*. New Jersey, Prentice-Hall Inc., 1970. (Foundations of Philosophy Series.)

Quine, W. 'Truth by convention' in Benacerraf, P. and Putnam, H., eds *The Philosophy of Mathematics*, pp. 322–345.

Quine, W. *Word and Object*. Cambridge Mass., M.I.T. Press, 1978.

Radnitszky, G. *Contemporary Schools of Metascience*. Goteborg, Akaddemiforlaget, 1968.

Radnitszky, G. and Andersson, G., eds *Progress and Rationality in Science*. Dordrecht, D. Reidel, 1978.

Radulet, R. 'Creativity and revolution in science and technology'. *Science of Science* 1 (3): 197–208, 1980.

Rancière, J. *La leçon d'Althusser*. Paris, Editions Gallimard, 1974.

Rancière, J. *La leçon d'Althusser*. [Reviewed by Brian Singer in *Telos* 25:224–232, 1975.]

Rancière, J. 'On the theory of ideology'. *Rad. Phil.* 7:2–14, spring 1974.

Rancière, J. 'The concept of "critique" and the "critique of political economy" (from the *1844 Manuscripts* to *Capital*)'. *Economy and Society* 5 (3): 352–384, 1976.

Rasmussen, D. M. 'Advanced capitalism and social theory: Habermas on the problem of legitimation'. *Cultural Hermeneutics* 3:349–366, 1976.

Rasmussen, D. M. 'Issues in phenomenology and critical theory'. In Bruzina, R. and Wiltshire, B., eds *Crosscurrents in Phenomenology*, pp. 13–29.

Rasmussen, D. M. 'Marx: on labor, praxis and instrumental reason'. *Studies in Soviet Thought* 20:271–289, 1979.

Rasmussen, D. M. 'The Marxist critique of phenomenology'. *Dialectics and Humanism* 2 (4): 59–70, 1976.

Rassmussen, D. M. 'The symbolism of Marx: from alienation to fetishism'. *Cultural Hermeneutics* 3:41–55, 1975.

Rasmussen, D. M. 'The quest for knowledge in the context of society'. In Tymieniecka, A. T., ed. *Analecta Husserliana*, vol. 5. Dordrecht, D. Reidel, 1976, pp. 259–68.

442

Ravetz, J. R. *Scientific Knowledge and its Social Problems*. Melbourne, Penguin, 1973.

R'egnier, M. 'Hegelianism and Marxism'. *Soc. Res.* 34:31–46, 1967.

Reichenbach, H. *Space and Time*. New York, Dover, 1958.

Reichenbach, H. 'The philosophical significance of the theory of relativity'. In Schilpp, P. A., ed. *Albert Einstein: Philosopher-Scientist*, pp. 287–312.

Reichenbach, H. *The Rise of Scientific Philosophy*. Berkeley, University of California Press, 1968.

Reichenbach, H. *The Theory of Relativity and A Priori Knowledge*. Berkeley, University of California Press, 1966.

Renault, G. 'From bureaucracy to *l'imaginaire*: Cornelius Castoriadis's immanent critique of Marxism'. *Catalyst* 13:72–110, 1979.

Ricœur, P. 'A critique of B. F. Skinner's *Beyond Freedom and Dignity*'. *Philosophy Today* 19:166–175, 1975.

Ricœur, P. *Hermeneutics and the Human Sciences*. Cambridge University Press, 1981.

Ricœur, P. *Husserl: An Analysis of his Phenomenology*. Evanston, Northwestern University Press, 1967.

Ricœur, P. *Interpretation Theory: Discourse and the Surplus of Meaning*. Texas Christian University Press, 1976.

Ricœur, P. 'New developments in phenomenology in France: the phenomenology of language'. *Social Research* 34:1–30, 1967.

Ricœur, P. 'Phenomenology'. *Southwestern J. Phil.* 5 (3): 149–68, 1974.

Ricœur, P. *The Conflict of Interpretations*, tr. Ihde, D. Evanston, Northwestern University Press, 1974.

Ricœur, P. 'The model of the text'. In Dallmayr, F. R. and McCarthy, T. A., eds *Understanding and Social Inquiry*. University of Notre Dame Press, 1977, pp. 316–34.

Ricœur, P. *The Philosophy of Paul Ricœur: An Anthology of his Work*, ed. Reagan, G. and Stewart, D. New York, Beacon Press, 1976.

Ringer, F. K. *The Decline of German Mandarins: The German Academic Community, 1890–1933*. Cambridge, Mass., Harvard University Press, 1969.

Ronchi, V. *Optics, the Science of Vision*, tr. Rosen, E. New York University Press, 1957.

Rorty, R. *Philosophy and the Mirror of Nature*. Oxford, Basil Blackwell, 1980.

Rosdolsky, R. 'Comments on the method of Marx's *Capital*'. *New German Critique* 3:62–72, 1974.

Rose, H. and Rose, S. 'Radical science and its enemies'. In Milband, R. and Saville, J., eds *Socialist Register*. London, Merlin Press, 1979, pp. 317–335.

Rose, H. and Rose, S. *Science and Society*. London, Penguin, 1969.

Rose, H. and Rose, S. 'The incorporation of science'. In Rose, H. and Rose, S. eds *The Political Economy of Science*, pp. 14–31.

Rose, H. and Rose, S. eds *The Political Economy of Science*. London, Macmillan, 1976.

Rose, H. and Rose, S. 'The problematic inheritance: Marx and Engels'. In Rose, H. and Rose, S., eds *The Political Economy of Science*, pp. 1–13.

Rose, H. and Rose, S., eds *The Radicalisation of Science*. London, Macmillan Press, 1976.

Rose, H. and Rose, S. 'The radicalisation of science'. In Rose, H. and Rose, S., eds *The Radicalisation of Science*, 1976, pp. 1–31.

Rose, S., Hambley, J. and Haywood, J. 'Science, racism and ideology'. In Miliband, R. and Saville, J., ed. *Socialist Register*. London, Merlin Press, 1973, pp. 235–60.

Rosenberg, E. 'Scientific theories and American social thought'. In Van Tassel, D. and Hall, M. E., eds *Science and Society in the U.S.* Illinois, Dorsey Press, 1966.

Ross, D. *Aristotle.* London, Methuen, 1974.

Rota, G-C. 'Edmund Husserl and the reform of logic'. In Carr, D. and Casey, E. eds *Explorations in Phenomeology*, pp. 299-305.

Rotenstreich, N. 'An analysis of Piaget's concept of structure'. *Phil. and Phen. Res.* 37 (3): 368-380, 1977.

Roth, M. S. 'Foucault's "history of the present" '. *History and Theory* 20 (1): 32-46, 1981.

Routley, R. and Meyer, K. 'Dialectical logic, classical logic and the consistency of the world'. *Studies in Soviet Thought* 16:1-25, 1976.

Rovatti, P. A. 'A phenomenological analysis of Marxism'. *Telos* 5:160-173, 1970.

Rovatti, P. A. 'Critical theory and phenomelogy'. *Telos* 15:25-40, 1973.

Rovatti, P. A. 'Fetishism and economic categories'. *Telos* 14:87-105, 1972.

Rovatti, P. A. 'Marcuse and the *Crisis of European Science*'. *Telos* 2:113-115, 1968.

Rovatti, P. A. 'The critique of fetishism in Marx's *Grundrisse*'. *Telos* 17:56-69, 1973.

Rubin, I. I. *Essays on Marx's Theory of Value.* Detroit, Black and Red, 1972.

Russell, B. *Introduction to Mathematical Philosophy.* London, Muirhead Library of Philosophy, 1979.

Russell, B. and Whitehead, A. N. *Principia Mathematica.* Cambridge University Press, 1910-13 (edition 1) and 1927 (edition 2).

Ryle, G. *The Concept of Mind.* London, Hutchinson, 1949.

Sachs, M. 'On the elementarity of measurement in general relativity: toward a general theory'. In Cohen, R. S. and Wartofsky, M. W., eds *In Memory of Norward Russel Hanson.* Dordrecht, D. Reidel, 1967, pp. 56-80. (*Boston Studies in the Philosophy of Science*, vol. 3.)

Sahlins, M. *Culture and Practical Reason.* University of Chicago Press, 1976.

Said, Edward W. 'Abecedarium culturae: structuralism, absence, writing'. *TriQuarterly* 33-45, Spring 1970.

Said, Edward W. 'The problem of textuality: two exemplary positions'. *Critical Inquiry* 4:673-714, 1977-8.

Sallis, J. *Phenomenology and the Return to Beginnings.* Pittsburgh, Duquesne U. P., 1973.

Salomon, J. J. *Science and Politics.* London, Macmillan, 1973.

Santillana, G. de, *The Crime of Galileo.* University of California Press, 1955.

Sartre, J-P. *Between Existentialism and Marxism.* London, New Left Books, 1974.

Sartre, J-P. *Critique of Dialectical Reason.* London, New Left Books, 1976.

Sartre, J-P. 'Intentionality: a fundamental idea of Husserl's phenomenology'. *J. Brit. Soc. Phen.* 1 (2): 4-5, 1970.

Sartre, J-P. *Literary and Philosophical Essays*, tr. Michelson, A. London, Hutchinson, 1955.

Sartre, J-P. 'Replies to structuralism: an interview'. *Telos* 9:110-115, 1971.

Sartre, J-P. *The Transcendence of the Ego.* New York, The Noonday Press, 1957.

Saussure, F. de. *Course in General Linguistics.* London, Fontana/Collins, 1974.

Schafer, W. 'A note on the social natural science project (SNSP): science, politics and nature'. *Soc. Sci. Inform.* 19): 663-670, 1980.

Schafer, W. 'Finalization in perspective: toward a revolution in the social paradigm of science'. *Soc. Sci. Inform.* 18 (6): 915-943, 1979.

Schäfer, W., ed. *Finalization in Science: The Social Orientation of Scientific Progress.* Dordrecht, D. Reidel, 19?.

Scheler, M. *Ressentiment*, ed. Coser, L., A. New York, Schocken Books, 1972.

Scheler, M. *Selected Philosophical Essays*, tr. Lachterman, D. R. Evanston, Northwestern University Press, 1973.

Schiff, L. I. *Quantum Mechanics*. New York, McGraw Hill, 1955.

Schilpp, P. A., ed. *Albert Einstein: Philosopher-Scientist*. Cambridge University Press, 1949.

Schmidt, A. *The Concept of Nature in Marx*. London, New Left Books, 1971.

Schmitt, R. 'Husserl's transcendental-phenomenological reduction'. *Phil. and Phen. Res.* 20 (2): 238–245, 1959.

Scholte, B. 'Lévi-Strauss's, Penelopean effort: the analysis of myth.' *Semiotica* 1:99–124, 1969.

Scholte, B. 'The structural anthropology of Claude Lévi-Strauss'. In Honigmann, J. ed. *Handbook of Social and Cultural Anthropology*. Chicago, Rand McNally, 1973, pp. 637–716.

Schrag, C. O. 'The crisis of the human sciences'. *Man and World* 8:131–140, 1975.

Schrödinger, E., Planck, M., Einstein, A. and Lorentz, H. *Letters on Wave Mechanics*, ed. Prizibram, K. New York, Philosophical Library, 1967.

Schrödinger, E. *What is Life?* and *Mind and Matter*. Cambridge University Press, 1967.

Schroyer, T. 'Marx's theory of the crisis'. *Telos* 14:106–125, 1972.

Sciama, D. 'Black holes and their thermodynamics'. *Vistas in Astronomy* 19:385–401, 1976.

Searle, J. R. *Speech Acts*. Cambridge University Press, 1969.

Sedgwick, P. 'Natural science and human theory: a critique of Herbert Marcuse'. In Miliband, R. and Saville, J., ed. *Socialist Register*. London, Merlin Press, 1966, pp. 163–192.

Seeburger, F. F. 'The conversion of nature and technology'. In Tymieniecka, A-T., ed. *Analecta Husserliana*, Vol. 5. Dordrecht, D. Reidel, 1976, pp. 281–90.

Severens, R. 'Channeling commitments'. In Severens, R., ed. *Ontological Commitment*, pp. 1–17.

Severens, R., ed. *Ontological Commitment*. Athens, University of Georgia Press, 1974.

Shalvey, T. *Claude Lévi-Strauss. Social Psychotherapy and the Collective Unconscious*. Amherst, The University of Massachusetts Press, 1979.

Shapere, D. *Galileo: A Philosophical Study*. University of Chicago Press, 1974.

Shaw, William H. 'The handmill gives you the feudal lord': Marx's technological determinism'. *Hist. and Th.* 18 (2): 155–176, 1979.

Sheehan, T. J. 'Heidegger, Aristotle and phenomenology'. *Phil. Today* 19:12–20, 1975.

Shenkman, M. H. 'Commodities and value: categorial production in Marx'. *Cultural Hermeneutics* 4:107–122, 1977.

Shiner, L. E. 'Husserl and historical science'. *Soc. Res.* 37:511–532, 1970.

Shmueli, E. 'Can phenomenology accomodate Marxism?' *Telos* 17:169–181, 1973.

Shmueli, E. 'Consciousness and action: Husserl and Marx on theory and praxis'. In Tymieniecka, A. T., ed. *Analecta Husserliana*, vol. 5. Dordrecht, D. Reidel, 1976, pp. 343–382.

Shmueli, E. 'Critical reflections on Husserl's philosophy of history'. *J. Brit. Soc. Phen.* 2 (1): 35–51, 1971.

Shmueli, E. 'Pragmatic, existentialist and phenomenological interpretations of Marxism'. *J. Brit. Soc. Phen.* 4 (2): 139–152, 1973.

Short, T. L. 'Peirce and the incommensurability of theories'. *Monist* 63 (3): 316–326, July 1980.

Siemek, M. J. 'Marxism and the hermeneutic tradition'. *Dialectics and Humanism* 2 (4): 87–103, 1975.

445

Silver, P. W. *Ortega as Phenomenologist.* New York, Columbia University Press, 1978.

Simons, P. M. '*Experience and Judgement: Investigations in a Genealogy of Logic,* by Edmund Husserl' [review]. *J. Brit. Soc. Phen.* 7 (1): 61–65, 1976.

Sinha, D. *Studies in Phenomenology.* The Hague, Martinus Nijhoff, 1969.

Sloman, A. 'What are the aims of science?' *Rad. Phil.* 13:7–17, 1976.

Smart, J. J. C. *Problems of Space and Time.* New York, Macmillan, 1976.

Smith, N. 'Symptomatic silence in Althusser: the concept of nature and the unity of science'. *Science and Society* 44 (1): 58–81, 1980.

Smith, P. *The Enlightenment, 1687–1776.* New York, Collier books, 1962. (A History of Modern Culture, vol. 2.)

Sohn-Rethel, A. *Intellectual and Manual Labour* London, Macmillan, 1978.

Sohn-Rethel, A. 'Science as alienated consciousness'. *Rad. Sci. J.* 2–3:65–101, 1975.

Sokolowski, R. *Husserlian Meditations.* Evanston, Northwestern University Press, 1974.

Sokolowski, R. *The Formation of Husserl's Concept of Constitution.* The Hague, Martinus Nijhoff, 1964.

Solomon, R. C., ed. *Phenomenology and Existentialism.* New York, Harper & Row, 1972.

Spiegelberg, H. *The Phenomenological Movement.* The Hague, Martinus Nijhoff, 1982.

Stegmüller, M. *Main Currents in Contemporary German, British and American Philosophy.* Bloomington, Indiana U.P., 1970.

Stegmüller, W. *The Structuralist View of Theories.* Berlin, Springer-Verlag, 1979.

Storer, N. *The Social System of Science.* New York, Rinehart & Winston, 1966.

Strasser, S. 'The "Introduction" to *Husserliana* volume 1', tr. Attig. T. *J. Brit. Soc. Phen.* 7 (1): 12–17, 1976.

Strawson, P. F. *Logico-Linguistic Papers.* London, Methuen, 1974.

Strawson, P. F. 'Review of Wittgenstein's *Philosophical Investigations*'. In Pitcher, G., ed. *Wittgenstein. The 'Philosophical Investigations'*, pp. 22–64.

Stroker, E. 'Edmund Husserl's phenomenology as foundation of natural science'. In Tymieniecka, A-T., ed. *Analecta Husserliana,* Vol. 2. Dordrecht, D. Reidel, 1972, pp. 245–257.

Strozewski, W. 'Phenomenology and dialectics'. *Dialectics and Humanism* 4:129–136, 1977.

Struik, D. J. *A Concise History of Mathematics.* New York, Dover, 1967.

Struik, D. J. *The Land of Stevin and Huygens.* Dordrecht, D. Reidel, 1981.

Sturrock, J., ed. *Structuralism and Since.* Oxford University Press, 1979.

Suppes, P., ed. *Space, Time and Geometry.* Dordrecht, D. Reidel, 1973.

Swiderski, E. 'Some salient features of Ingarden's ontology'. *J. Brit. Soc. Phen.* 6 (2): 81–90, 1975.

Symes, J. M. D. 'Policy and maturity in science'. *Soc. Sci. Inform.* 15(2/3):337–347, 1976.

Synowiecki, A. 'Hegel's logic in the light of graph theory'. *Dialectics and Humanism* 1:87–96, 1973.

Szomilewicz, I. 'Incommensurability and the rationality of the development of science'. *Brit. J. Phil. Sci.* 28:345–350, 1977.

Tarnowski, K. 'Roman Ingarden's critique of transcendental constitution'. *Dialectics and Humanism* 3:111–120, 1976.

Taylor, C. *Hegel.* Cambridge University Press, 1975.

Therborn, G. 'Jürgen Habermas: a new eclecticism'. *New Left Review* 67:69–83, 1971.

Therborn, G. 'The Frankfurt School'. *New Left Review* 63:65–96, 1970.

Tibbetts, P. 'Feyerabend's *Against Method:* The case for methodological pluralism'. *Phil. Soc. Sci.* 7:265-275, 1977.

Toulmin, S. 'Conceptual revolutions in science'. In Cohen, R. S. and Wartofsky, M. W., eds *In Memory of Norwood Russell Hanson.* Dordrecht, D. Reidel, 1967, pp. 331-347. (Boston Studies in the Philosophy of Science, vol. 3.)

Toulmin, S. 'Does the distinction between normal and revolutionary science hold water?' In Lakatos, I. and Musgrave, A., eds *Criticism and the Growth of Knowledge*, pp. 39-48.

Toulmin, S. *Foresight and Understanding.* New York, Harper & Row, 1961.

Tragesser, R. S. 'On the phenomenological foundations of mathematics'. In Carr, D. and Casey, E., eds *Explorations in Phenomenology*, pp. 285-298.

Tragesser, R. S. 'Some observations concerning logics and concepts of existence'. *J. Phil.* 69:375-383, 1972.

Tran Duc Thao 'Marxisme et phenomenologie'. *La Revue internationale* 2:168-174, 1946.

Tran Duc Thao 'The phenomenology of mind and its real content'. *Telos* 8:91-108, 1971.

Tran Duc Thao 'The rational kernel in the Hegelian dialectic'. *Telos* 6:118-139, 1970.

Tran Duc Thao, *Phenomenology and Dialectical Materialism.* Dordrecht, D. Reidel, 1985.

Trogu, G. 'Vasco Ronchi's revolution in optics'. *Telos* 8:3-20, 1971.

Tymieniecka, A. T. 'Beyond Ingarden's idealism/realism controversy with Husserl - the new contextual phase of phenomenology'. In Tymieniecka, A. T., ed. *Analecta Husserliana.* Dordrecht, D. Reidel, 1976, vol. 4, pp. 241-418.

Tymieniecka, A. T. *Phenomenology and Science in Contemporary European Thought.* New York, Farrer, Strauss and Cudahy, 1961.

Ureña, E. M. 'Teoria y praxis en la phenomenologica trascendental (E. Husserl) y en la teoria critica (J. Habermas)'. *Pensamiento* 31:231-44, 1975.

Vajda, M. 'Lukács's and Husserl's critiques of science'. *Telos* 38:104-118, 1978-79.

Vajda, M. 'Marxism, existentialism, phenomenology'. *Telos* 7:3-29, 1971.

Van Der Pitte, M. M. 'Husserl's solipsism'. *J. Brit. Soc. Phen.* 8 (2): 123-125, 1977.

Van Der Pitte, M. M. 'Husserl, the idealist *malgre lui*'. *Phil. and Phen. Res.* 37:70-78, 1976.

Van Fraasen, B. C. 'The labyrinth of quantum logics'. In Hooker, C. A., ed. *The Logico-Algebraic Approach to Quantum Mechanics*, vol. 1, pp. 577-607.

Van Hooft, S. 'Merleau-Ponty and the problem of intentional explanation'. *Phil. and Phen. Res.* 40 (1): 33-52, 1980.

Van Parijs, P. 'Karl Popper, le cercle de Vienne et l'ecole de Francfort'. *Rev. Phil. de Louvain* 76:359-370, 1978.

Vernant, J. P. 'Commentary'. In Crombie, A. C., ed. *Scientific Change.* London, Heinemann, 1963, pp. 102-7.

Vernant, J. P. *Mythe et pensée chez les grecs: études de psychologie historique.* Paris, F. Maspero, 1966.

Vico, G. *The New Science of Giambattista Vico*, tr. Bergin, T. G. and Fisch, M. H. Cornell University Press, 1970.

Von Neumann, J. *Mathematical Foundations of Quantum Mechanics.* Princeton University Press, 1955.

Von Neumann, J. 'The mathematician'. In *Collected Works.* Oxford, Pergamon Press, 1961-2 vol. 1, pp. 1-9.

Waerden, B. L. van der, ed. *Sources of Quantum Mechanics.* Amsterdam, North-Holland, 1967.

Wagner, Hans. 'Husserl's ambiguous philosophy of science'. *Southwestern J. Phil.* 5 (3): 169–186, 1974.

Wartofsky, M. W. 'Conciousness, praxis and reality: Marxism vs. phenomenology'. In Elliston, F. and McCormack, P., eds *Husserl. Expositions and Appraisals*, pp. 304–13.

Waterhouse, R. 'Husserl and phenomenology'. *Rad. Phil.* 16:27–38, 1977.

Watson, J. *The Double Helix.* London, Weidenfeld & Nicolson, 1968.

Weber, M. *From Max Weber*, ed. Gerth, H. H. and Mills, C. W. London, Routledge & Kegan Paul, 1964.

Weber, M. *The Protestant Ethic and the Spirit of Capitalism*, tr. Parsons, T. New York, Charles Scribner's Sons, 1958.

Weinberg, S. *Gravitation and Cosmology: Principles and Applications of the General Theory of Relativity.* New York, John Wiley & Sons, 1972.

Weingart, P. 'The relation between science and technology'. In Krohn, W., Layton, E. and Weingert, P. eds *The Dynamics of Science and Technology*, pp. 251–86.

Weiss, F. G., ed. *Beyond Epistemology.* The Hague, Martinus Nijhoff, 1976.

Weizsacker, C. F. von. 'The Copenhagen interpretation'. In Basten, T. ed. *Quantum Theory and Beyond*, pp. 25–32.

Weizsacker, C. F. 'The unity of physics'. In Bastin, T., ed. *Quantum Theory and Beyond*, pp. 229–62.

Welch, E. P. *The Philosophy of Edmund Husserl: The Origin and Development of his Phenomenology.* New York, Octagon Books Inc., 1965.

Wellmer, A. *Critical Theory.* New York, Seabury Press, 1974.

Werskey, P. G. 'British scientists and "outsider" politics 1931–1945'. In Barnes, B., ed. *Sociology of Science*, pp. 231–50.

Weyl, H. *Philosophy of Mathematics and Natural Science.* Princeton University Press, 1949.

Weyl, H. *Space, Time, Matter.* New York, Dover, 1952.

Weyl, H. 'Subject and object (the scientific implications of epistemology)'. In Kocklemans, J. and Kisiel, T., eds *Phenomenology and the Natural Sciences*, pp. 100–18.

White, D. 'A science of liberation'. *Arena*29:19–26, 1972.

White, D. 'No way out'. *Arena* 42:30–35, 1976.

White, H. 'Michel Foucault'. In Sturrock, S. ed. *Structuralism and Since.* Oxford University Press, 1979, pp. 81–115.

White, H. 'Foucault decoded: notes from underground'. *History and Theory* 12:23–54, 1973.

Whitehead, A. N. *Science and the Modern World.* Cambridge University Press, 1945.

Whorf, B. L. *Language, Thought and Reality*, ed. Caroll, J. B. Cambridge, Mass. M.I.T. Press, 1956.

Widmer, H. 'Conocimiento y interés en Jürgen Habermas'. *Pensamiento* 32:281–301, 1976.

Wigner, E. 'Epistemological perspective on quantum theory'. In Hooker, C. A., ed. *Contemporary Research in the Foundations and Philosophy of Quantum Theory*, pp. 369–85.

Winch, P. *The Idea of a Social Science and Its Relation to Philosophy.* London, Routledge & Kegan Paul, 1958.

Wittgenstein, L. *Lectures and Conversations on Aesthetics, Psychology and Religious Belief.* Oxford, Basil Blackwell, 1970.

Wittgenstein, L. *On Certainty*, tr. Anscombe, G. E. M. and von Wright, G. H. London, Basil Blackwell, 1977.

Wittgenstein, L. *Philosophical Investigations*, tr. Anscombe, G. E. M. Oxford. Basil Blackwell, 1974.

Wittgenstein, L. *The Blue and Brown Books*. Oxford, Basil Blackwell, 1975.

Wittgenstein, L. *Tractatus Logico-Philosophicus*, tr. Pears, D. F. and McGuinness, B. F. London, Routledge & Kegan Paul, 1972.

Wittgenstein, L. *Zettel*. Oxford, Basil Blackwell, 1967.

Wolniewicz, B. 'A parallelism between Wittgensteinian and Aristotelian ontologies'. In Cohen, R. and Wartofsky, M., eds. *Boston Studies in the Philosophy of Science*, vol. 4. Dordrecht, D. Reidel, 1969, pp. 208-17.

Woodiwiss, T. 'Critical theory and the capitalist state'. *Economy and Society* 7 (2): 175-193, 1978. [Review of Habermas, J. *Legitimation Crisis*.]

Young, B. 'Science *is* social relations'. *Radical Science Journal* 5:65-131, 1977.

Yourgrau, W. and Breck, A. D., eds *Cosmoogy, History and Theology*. New York, Plenum, 1977.

Zabeeh, F. 'On language games and forms and life'. In Klemke, E. D., ed. *Essays on Wittgenstein*, pp. 338-73.

Zeldovich, Ia. B. and Novikov, I. D. 'Contemporary trends in cosmology'. *Soviet Studies in Philosophy*, Spring 1976:28-49.

Zilsel, Edgar 'Copernicus and mechanics'. *Journal of the History of Ideas* 1:113-118, 1940.

Zilsel, Edgar 'The genesis of the concept of physical law'. *Phil. Rev.* 51:245-279, 1942.

Zilsel, Edgar 'The genesis of the concept of scientific progress'. *Journal of the History of Ideas* 6:325-349, 1945.

Zilsel, Edgar 'The sociological roots of science'. *American Journal of Sociology* 47: 544-561, 1942.

Zukav, G. *The Dancing Wu Li Masters*. London, Fontana, 1979.

Index

450